Dedication

To all my children, grandchildren, and their children.
May you appreciate your roots - from whence you came! To all
who read this, the hope is that you will be inspired to
reach for the prize of the high calling of the Master!

Hope you enjoy my book
Sincerely
Kenny Shenk

GO AHEAD ON 'ER!

By Kenneth M. Shenk

ISBN #0-9664557-0-3

Cover and Book Design by Dal Farias
Printed by Northwest Graphics, Mount Vernon, Washington

For information and comments regarding this book
Please call Donna Cross @ 425-743-1236

Go Ahead On 'er!

Acknowledgements

Let me say that much midnight oil was burned in the production of this book, and like the fellow said, "Ya gotta do what you gotta do!" Without our daughter, Donna's help, and sacrifice of time which she didn't have, it would never have seen the light of day! My grandson, Kent Fowler, Donna's son, also did proofreading and his help was invaluable. They were willing helpers and I appreciate it very much!

For quite some time I have been urged by family and friends to write a book telling of some of my life's experiences and events. I have been reluctant to do so, but the pressure was relentless! As I began writing, however, so many memories flooded my mind that I was amazed! I can remember the first time I tasted ice cream. It was homemade, just delicious and served at a cousins' wedding. I surely thought it was terrific and for awhile, I was all for people getting married!

My Dad signed a note, or promise to pay a debt for a relative and when the note came due, the relatives did not fulfill the obligation, so my family was forced to pay this debt! My Mother wept hysterically and carried on, for they had no great resources! Thus, my parents, as well as Lloyd and I, were forced to work extremely hard to take care of this debt! The lengths to which my parents scrimped, sacrificed, and saved in order to make this payment would not be believed today. Nowadays people just file for bankruptcy, but not MY parents! Every egg, every quart of cream, anything, Lord, anything, just so Dad doesn't go to jail! This was, of course, many years before the O.J. Simpson saga and the "Dream Team"! It seemed that back then, if something had to be done, well, you just got it done! Leisure time had not been invented and there were no coffee breaks; in fact, there was very little coffee!

Go Ahead On 'er!

I never recall my parents drinking coffee, except on special occasions, until later in their lives. My Father always had a herd of dairy cattle and we farmed, mostly with horses. Since these animals were our main source of income, we worked very diligently to keep them healthy and profitable! Never did my Dad own a milking machine and all these cows were milked by hand, morning and night!

Through all the ups and downs of my life, my good wife, Frances, labored faithfully at home and never complained about lack of modern facilities. For example, we were not able to get electricity until our oldest son was in high school. Those of us who lived up Mill Creek Road had to pay a proportionate fee in order for the power company to agree to bring service to us. I know there were times I might have given up had I not been so fortunate to have such a wonderful, devoted wife as Frances. I used to hear the fellows talk about fixing their lunch, breakfast, and sometimes their own dinner, but I didn't have to deal with such matters. Frances went about her tasks without complaint and usually she sang as she worked! It is said that children learn by example. Needless to say, I am so grateful that our kids proved to be assets and a joy to be around!

As I now view the changing world, the demise of America and the freedom as we have known it and the One Worlder's getting control, I can see that the free enterprise system and opportunities are rapidly eroding. Oh, this may not be readily visible to some, but the fact is, Big Brother wants to feed you, tell you what to do, and when to do it! Many private industries, including the timber industry, are dying a slow death. The truth of the old poem which states: "Life is real and life is earnest, and the grave is not the goal. Dust thou art, to dust returneth, was not spokin' of the soul", is pointing in the right direction. It should serve as a reminder that we are just traveling through on our journey.

In this book, if there are mistakes, they are not intentional as I merely tried to convey some of the details and experiences in my life. Of course, I have omitted many things which were not kosher to put in a book. I trust you will enjoy reading this and it will help you to appreciate your life - whether in the Far West - or wherever! These accounts are just a glimpse into the vast experiences which marked my life! My immovable faith in God and the loving support of Frances steadied us through thick and thin! There is a verse in the Bible which states, "Be not deceived, God is not mocked. For whatsoever a man soweth, that shall he also reap!" This goes for each person and for America, also, and the reaping time is here! This is an immutable law which never changes, nor ever will! You reap what you sow. If you give of yourself and are generous, you will get it back! Friends are priceless and precious, so strive for the prize which the Good Lord has promised to those who run the race!

Sincerely,

Kenny Shenk

About the Author - My Father

Often as we'd listen to many of Dad's unique stories, many of us felt that it would be a wonderful privilege to have some written form of part of this history and we encouraged him to write some things down. I always knew his encyclopedia of knowledge would fill many, many pages! Little did I dream that I would devote a chapter of my own life to assist him in this task! It is with deep gratitude, love, and humor that this book has come about! To comprehend the struggle, sacrifice, diligence, and perseverance which both my Father and Mother displayed is humbling, indeed! Additionally, they have done this with honesty, dignity and a zest for life.

Kenneth is an individual who, had he been given the opportunity of a formal education, could have been a college professor! He is one of the most intelligent, well-read and unstoppable individuals I've ever known! His range of reading materials had no limitations, just as his interests knew no boundaries. To have him share with you is much like being carried away in the pages of a book! The care he took in details let you feel that you can live the experience with him. I like what Emily Dickinson wrote: A Book - There is no frigate like a book, to take us lands away, nor coursers like a page, of prancing poetry. This traverse may the poorest take, without oppress of toll; how frugal is the chariot, that bears a human soul!

Undoubtedly, there were few people whom Dad considered strangers, for he always readily engaged people in conversation and was interested in others. His association with people never depended upon their rank or status, for he had friends in high places, as well as in the lowly and their friendship was never measured by what they owned or who they knew! Rather, his choice of friends was based upon whether they were honorable and truthful. Two characteristics which mark this man are his incredible memory and penchant for detail! He also possesses an innate ability of prediction and assessment! Often he would tell us something was going to happen, and sure enough, it did! It seemed that whatever he set his mind to do, well, he just did it! Indisputably, among his greatest gifts are his wit and humor! Even today, a phone call or conversation with him can put a lasting smile on my face because of a humorous comment, an astute observation, or some sage advice!

Another one of Dad's loves was music and when he was young, he taught himself to play a violin, harmonica, and the accordion. Never was he privileged to have formal lessons, but through perseverance, he taught himself! This just illustrates his determination and also, his range of interests.

As we were growing up, he "tagged" nicknames on all of us – no one escaped and at times, we could have more than one! I came to realize through the years that he did this with deliberation and it was one way in which he expressed his affection for us. To the many grandchildren who have been privileged to grow up with Grandpa, there is an enrichment and enjoyment which can never be duplicated! My own sons have gained much inspiration from him - his knowledge and information on so many subjects, was always readily shared with them! If they were privileged to correspond with him, the letters received are to be treasured, for they could never be duplicated! I'm certain that each grandchild in this entire family could share something special about him!

Clearly, a most devastating blow to my Dad was that after he and Mother moved to Canada, an individual whom they had considered a "friend", managed to extract the home place from the family, without one cent ever being received in remuneration! Beyond that, the total lack of consideration, respect, and conscience, was just about more than my parents could bear! To consider all the years both he and Mother labored so honorably, honestly and with such integrity, and then to be treated with such utter disrespect, is incomprehensible! Like Dad said, "God always has payday! You reap what you sow!

In each of his children he instilled determination and attitude - that we can do what we set our minds to do! Never were we spared from hard work and accountability! We always had to account for our deeds and it was not acceptable to place the blame on others! Additionally, we were taught that you can judge a person's character on whether or not they are willing to admit their mistakes, and we lived by that rule. Thankfully, we had wonderful role models!

Without my Mother, Kenneth could not have accomplished all he did in his lifetime. She was an unselfish, utterly devoted wife, and lived sacrificially so that Kenneth could live out his dream! She is to be recognized and commended for her dedication to him and to her family throughout all these years! She truly helped and allowed him to become a "Living Legend" in his own time!

Fondly,
Donna Cross
(Billie Jo)

TABLE OF CONTENTS

What you are about to read may be better for your well-being if you are in a relaxed state of mind and in a good chair. This is the amazing story of one man's journey through life, a few events which occurred, some giants which had to be slain, and significant observations along the way.

EARLY LIFE IN THE FAR WEST

The rooster crowed, dawn cracked, and so was ushered in another day, which turned out to be eventful for me. I was born at an early age into a very poor and humble home in the state of Oregon, and this special day was December 30, 1912. At that time our home had no phone, radio, newspaper or running water, or perhaps, I should say, ALL the water was running - you just had to catch it! One brother, Lloyd, had arrived ahead of me and we were later joined by another brother, Ronald, and then a sister, Mildred. Our parents were Daniel and Fannie Shenk. Some tragic events in my Mothers' life (the loss of two sisters and her Father passing away within about a month's time), took their toll on my Mother. As a result of these events and subsequent circumstances, Mother became a chronic worrier and she retained this characteristic throughout much of her life. She believed in Murphy's law - that if anything bad can happen, it will, so she really was an optimist and didn't know it!

At this time, we lived near Hubbard, a little town southeast of Salem. At a very young age, I learned to milk cows and used to accompany my Dad on his regular routine of milking, doing chores, feeding calves and caring for the horses. Those horses were our only means of transportation, at that time. I made the fatal mistake of learning to milk Swiss Fashion; that is, thumbs down! So I had to milk the younger heifers and some cows which did not have the proper handles!

My Mother had a twin sister, Lilly, who lived close by and this helped my Mother immensely. Dad was active in a local church, and before long, was appointed Deacon, a task which he took very seriously. The Bible says Moses was the meekest man that ever lived, and I shall take that for what it's worth, but I am sure Dad was pressing very hard on his record! He deplored violence of any kind, and even when we were kids, he forbid us to wrestle. He told us that when he was younger, while traveling to Oregon, he was staying in Idaho, and stopped two men who were fighting, as he was sure they were trying to kill each other.

One morning, just as it was getting daylight, Dad and I were going into the house with the milk. Suddenly, we heard the town bell in Hubbard, and as it began ringing, my Dad burst out crying, so I asked him what was wrong. He said, "I think they have stopped the war." This was World War I, and sure enough, soon the news was announced that the war was over, indeed! So life continued on and Dad did many things to provide for our family. He drove a team of horses and hauled milk to the Creamery, painted churches and other buildings, raised onion sets and did whatever he could to stave off the wolves, which were never far away, or so it seemed!

We had an Uncle Jim Mishler, who was married to my Mothers' sister, Carrie. Uncle Jim was a Master of the first degree in teasing. Uncle Jim and Aunt Carrie had Ray, Florence, Mel, Orval, and Lucille. When Lloyd and I were little kids, we had a small dog named, Snip, of the Terrier family. Now it is noteworthy to state that Snip was endowed with a nice, long tail. Our dog was an important part of our family and of my childhood. Uncle Jim had a large butcher shop in Woodburn, and every time Uncle Jim and Aunt Carrie came to our place, Uncle would call Snip. Obediently, Snip would go to him, wag his tail and conduct himself with some reservations, for he always acted as if he, too, had some real misgivings regarding Uncle. Uncle told us he made wieners (weenies) out of dogs tails - just like Snips' nice tail! He always admonished us, "Keep feeding him real good and I will take him off your hands on my next visit!" Shortly after this episode, I saw Uncle come driving into our yard, so quickly I ran, got Snip and beat it out to our barn! I hurriedly dug a hole in the hay, held Snip in my arms and saved his life! If we boys accompanied my parents into Uncles' butcher shop, he'd quickly grab a tray of shiny wieners and tauntingly say, "Here boys, have some weenies!" To us, this was undoubtedly, absolute heresy, as we were positive they represented someone's beloved dog, just like our Snip. It was a number of years before I could eat a hot dog without a guilty conscience.

One November my entire family caught smallpox and as Thanksgiving Day arrived, my Mother lay in bed, giving me instructions on how to mop the kitchen floor. Feeling the awesome responsibility of the entire family on my shoulders, I was fretting that here it was Thanksgiving and what did we have to be thankful for? After all, everyone except me was too ill to be up and around. As I was struggling with the task of mopping, there was a knock on the door. Upon opening it, I was so happy to see Aunt Lilly, Mom's twin sister, for she brought us a stuffed chicken and all the fixings for a Thanksgiving meal. She just handed it to me through the opened door, but could not come in as our entire family was quarantined. Receiving that food was such a bit of cheer to me and my Mother heard me say, "I guess we do have something to be thankful for after all!"

Sadly, my Aunt Lilly became ill and died when she was just a young mother, leaving a number of children. This also added to my Mother's sad state of affairs. As a child, I didn't understand how devastating this must have been for my Mother to lose her twin sister. Looking back, and after having twins, and knowing the close relationship which they have, it truly was a blow to my Mother to lose Lilly. When Aunt Lilly died, she left behind five young children, Cliff, Clayton, Blanche, Helen and Luella for her husband, Hugh, to care for. The responsibility thrown upon Cliff and his brother and sisters was immense, however. Cliff was only eight years old, when his Mother called him to her bedside, and knowing that she was not going to make it, she made him promise to take care of his brother and sisters! They experienced heartache at a very early age.

The neighbors used to fill silos with corn and since they did not have mechanical devices to cut it, we cut it by hand with a machete. It was placed in bunches, then loaded on sleds, pulled by horses and taken to the insilage cutter. This cutter chopped up the corn and then blew it into the silo. They had two men in the silo to tramp down the silage, which helped compress it real well and aided in preservation. Of course, at the very bottom, a lot of liquid formed and many of the neighbors used to place jugs there in the silo to collect the corn liquor. I never heard of anyone meeting his maker over this liquor, but some sure talked about it!

One fall I worked on Bill Brandt's hay bailer and then came the grain threshing. Bill had lots of calls for baled straw, so he got a brilliant idea! Bill's brother, Otto, worked with him occasionally, as did his brother, Ed. My job was to poke wire through the blocks which separated the bales and Art Matuesch hooked these wires. Bill sat up on the threshing machine and was running the blower right into the baler. You cannot imagine the noise! The threshing machine had huge fans on it which could blow that straw fifty feet or more in the air and that's how they made a straw stack!

One bright morning they were threshing springs oats, which were full of smut and that meant those oats were black! They were also full of a weed called dog fennel, and since no roads were paved, these oats were very dusty from the dirt roads. The spot where I stood was right where that blower blew that stuff, so I was practically covered! Otto came and uncovered me once. This, of course, was a fast way to go as they did not have to table, or pitch the straw out of the stack to bale it. The third time I was completely covered, I called to Art, "Let's go, I can't stand it!" He said, "Me neither. We have to run clear to the county road." Bill saw us take off, came running and said, "Come back boys, and we'll pitch the straw in!" I said, "Not me," and Art wouldn't go either. As a result of that job, I broke out in sores all over my body and spit up dirt and foul stuff for more than a month! This experience did not treat me kindly at all!

A Mr. Hood owned some acreage which joined my Dad's farm, so Dad rented it and his lease was to expire on October 1st that fall. Mr. Hood had moved somewhere back East. My Father and I were in the barn one morning milking our twelve cows, when here came Jim Lee, a neighbor. He was a big man and always had a large, curved stem pipe in his mouth. Here is what took place: Mr. Lee began to curse and scream at my Dad, saying, "You know darn well I wanted that big log! Besides, I am renting the Hood place come October 1st!" During high water, a big, fir peeler log had come down the Yamhill River and lodged on a gravel bar on the Hood place, so that was the log he was referring to. Dad had Blind Rube cut this log into sixteen-inch wood, ready for the wood stove. After being screamed and cursed at, my Dad set his milk pail down and as he did so, I thought he was going to cry. He said, "No, Mr. Lee, I was not aware that you wanted that log and I want to pay you! How much do you think I owe you?" I was about eight feet away, right by a good pitch fork, ready to grab it in order to defend my Dad, for I was positive Mr. Lee was going to strike him. Jim clutched his pipe and kinda blubbered, cussed awhile, and finally left. I felt sorry for my Dad as he would never cheat <u>anyone</u> out of <u>anything</u>!

Many years later, Jim Lee called and asked my Dad to come to his bedside, which Dad gladly did. Mr. Lee said to him, "Mr. Shenk, I have lived with that log ever since that day I went to see you and talked like I did. I don't have peace with my Maker and I'm asking if you will please pray for me?" This is one lesson I never forgot, for the good book says, "A soft answer turneth away wrath!"

When I was around twelve years old, my family moved to a farm in Whiteson, near McMinnville and we lived there one year, after which time my folks bought the old Frank Chapman place near Sheridan. After I completed eighth grade, high school began and I attended the first semester. When first semester was over, I dropped out of school, not by my choice, but of necessity. Mr. Roe, the high school principal, called and asked me if I had a knowledge of the Bible, and I told him I had a fair amount, so he said, "Please come down to Linfield College in McMinnville on May Day. I will give you a test and if you score well, I will promote you to your second year in High School." The test was very easy for me, so I received a good grade, and that fall, I began my second year of high school. My Mother's health was not good and neither was my Dad's, so they decided I should drop out of school in order to help them out financially. Against my wishes, I was forced to drop out of school and began my labors in the cruel, wicked world!

PICKLES PERISHES

Shortly after my folks bought the Chapman place, a friend gave our family a snow-white, collie dog named Pickles. Now I know there are various kinds of pickles, just as there are various kinds of dogs. This Pickles had evidently, at some time or another, gotten some bird shot in his butt, because even the sight of a gun would send him under the house! When Pickles saw a gun, this poor dog would shake and shiver violently. A neighbor, George Gutbroad had a nice band of fine sheep, and one day, here comes George! Forget the nice, neighborly small talk! He says, "That white dog of yours helped kill eight of my nice ewes!" My Dad was really sad about it and said, "Well, if he did that, it'll be the LAST sheep he will kill and we'll have to dispose of him!" Then Dad asked ME to shoot the dog. Now how you gonna' do that? My sister, Millie, as we called her, volunteered to help. At least I think she did.

Millie got one of our Mothers' black stockings and away we go down towards the river. We proceeded to pull the stocking over Pickles' head so I could put a rope on him and then get the gun. Millie *held* the stocking so it wouldn't come off, and I shot the dog! Later on, I learned this was standard practice when hanging a man - they placed a black shroud over his face. Nothin' like going first class! While we were taking care of Pickles, my Mother was gone, but when she came back ....well, that's another story! Sometimes you just can't win! She wanted her stocking! Watch your back, look ahead, you never know when you might be dead!

An incident happened in Sheridan when I was around fifteen and I always rated this as being my most embarrassing moment! I went into a barber shop which had two barbers working there, and I knew both of them quite well. One barber was exceptionally good and the other one was a real, fine fellow, but he missed his calling, and was a first class butcher! He just had an awful time trying to cut hair! While I was waiting my turn, I began to figure out how to engineer my way over to the corner so I could get the good barber. There were four other fellows ahead of me, waiting for a turn, so I went over to the corner and sat down. I picked up a big, Life magazine and put it up in front of my face. Big, Sig Weiss was sitting in there and after a time, the less desirable barber said, "Okay, Kenny, you're next!" I said, "Go ahead, Sig, I'll wait for this fellow here (motioning to the barber in the corner)." Sig sat there with his mouth full of Copenhagen. He never cracked a smile and said loudly, "Oh, I don't like this barber, either! I was waiting for Emery, too!" Talk about embarrassment! I was SO embarrassed I didn't know what to do, so I just sat there! Sid finally got up and got in the chair. I thought that was about the worst situation I had gotten into out in the big, wild world, up to this point! That really made an impact on me! About a week later, I saw Sig on the street in Sheridan and he said, "Hello," and immediately began to chuckle! I said, "Hello, Sig!" He just laughed and never discussed it with me, but he was tickled!

MANUAL LABOR/SLAVE LABOR

My first job was in a sawmill cutting planks and ties for Henry Scholl, of Hubbard. His mill was on Mill Creek Road, out of Sheridan, and I helped load the plank. My next job was at the Willamina Brick Plant, another small town just West of Sheridan, for which I was paid $1.59 per day, with $.01 being withheld for worker's compensation. They had a five minute starting whistle, which blew at five minutes before 8:00 o'clock and then another five minute whistle at 1:00 o'clock. Believe you me, you had to be in gear and leaning towards your work, or you would be terminated. There was no union here, nor safety inspectors, or anything like that. It was called manual labor and bordered on slave labor!

On the job one day, I witnessed a brutal fight between two men, which I never forgot. A younger fellow was cursing one of the older wheelers and calling him terrible names. Suddenly, Irv Yokum threw a brick at his tormentor and the fight was on! Irvin was back in a corner, behind his big buggy they wheeled bricks on, and couldn't get out. The younger man beat him to a pulp and didn't have brains enough to stop. I helped clean the blood off Irv's face and bathe his bruises. The younger man didn't have a friend in that plant, and at that time, there were approximately ninety employees working there.

I was built very lean and small and was given the job of cleaning the kilns, restoring the grates, and cleaning out the refuse. One boss took an unholy delight in picking on me in front of a group of men, generally while we ate our lunch. Charley Snow was one of my friends and one day I told him, "If Carl Holt picks on me today, I am going to take him down and sit on him, or I am going to quit!" Charley laughed and asked, "Do you mean that, Kid?" "I sure do," I said. Sure enough, here came the boss and he started in, so being a man of my word, I threw him down so hard he was totally and utterly astonished! He rolled, tossed, cussed, and pounded on me, shouting, "Let me up!" I said, "Carl, you've been picking on me for a long time! When I let you up, you never will pick on me again!" I held him down for a good, long spell with the whole bunch of men looking on. Sure enough, Carl never touched me again, and I think that very day, I grew up somewhat! Carl never canned me either!

DOWN THE HILL

Right after this, I bought a Model T Ford truck which had a two-speed, rear axle and a big transmission out of another truck. I was fixing it up and had a new set of brakes to put on, along with a number of things. Then two different friend's of my Dad said the livestock market is up and asked if I would haul livestock for them. I told them the truck was not yet ready to haul, but they said that it would be just fine, so after being pressured, I loaded the truck with livestock! One bull weighed around 1,300 pounds and there were eight hogs, each weighing around 200 pounds. My Uncle, Hugh Wolfer, rode with me as we began the trek to the stockyards in Portland. At the top of Terwilliger Boulevard and starting down Sloevin Hill, I tried to shift the truck down, to no avail, and the truck started to gain speed rapidly. My Uncle had a big topcoat in his lap and he just jumped out and hit the ground rolling. He bruised his hand and got shook up quite badly. Down the hill we went – me and my truck, and at the bottom was a large crew of men, and a sharp curve. I knew I'd better get out of that truck, but couldn't get out on the driver's side, so I shot out on the right side. I lit on my left hip and burned a hole through my clothes and also burned some skin. The truck sailed out in space and the bull landed in a clump of maples about six feet off the ground. Three hogs died and the rest were dazed! Here came the crew of men to find where I had landed, and soon, my Uncle came running, too! He tore through the circle of men and said, "My nephew was in that truck!" One man said, "Yeah, I saw the little devil - he didn't make it!" All at once, my Uncle saw me and he said, "Here he is and he is ALIVE!" All were amazed that I even survived! Let me assure you, I was a sore lad for some time! I believe that when I left that truck, it was going at least seventy-five miles per hour, or more. I have gone eighty-five and ninety, but nothing seemed to compare with the speed of my truck that day! Without my family being aware, the Alpenrose Dairy sent a truck down and the livestock was taken to the stockyards. All the livestock was stolen right out from under us and my Dad did not receive one dime for those animals.

Later I bought another truck and took a contract to cut and haul one hundred cords of fir firewood to the McMinnville Laundry. Another young man, Stacy Kilmer, hired out to cut wood, so the two of us camped in a cabin on Mill Creek and cut wood on the

Hugh Walker place. Rube Rhinebold came to cut wood for me after I had this contract with the McMinnville Laundry. Rube was completely blind and a very interesting person. At one time he was at the Michigan State School For The Blind, along with 1,500 students. There was a ring leader there who Rube said was the smartest man he ever knew, and this is what he did: Nobody liked the school superintendent very well, so the ring leader said, "Just give me time, boys! I'll get rid of him!" Immediately he put out the word that the food was not good. One day the governor of the state, many of the state officials, plus other important leaders, came to visit the school. The ring leader said to his friends, "Okay, fellows, eat your bread dry today - no butter, no jam, no nothin' - eat 'er dry!" Everyone was gathered at noon in the big dining hall. Suddenly, the governor of the state noticed all the students eating dry bread. "Here's the butter and jam," he offered. "No," the boys said, "We can't have any!" No amount of encouragement by anyone could make the blind boys butter their bread. The governor asked the superintendent, "What's going on here, anyway?" The superintendent tried to convince the state officials he had not forbidden them to have butter and jam, but to no avail! The state officials said, "No way are these blind boys lying," and sure enough, the superintendent lost his job!

Blind Rube (as we fondly called him) could stroke a horse and tell what color it was. He could do so many things, it was simply amazing, one of which was that he could play the violin. Since I had taught myself to play and owned a violin, you can be sure we had some real fine music in that cabin. Rube used to cord, or play two strings, and he was sure good at it!

The next spring I got a job falling and bucking timber right close to where Stacy and I had cut the 100 cord of firewood for the laundry. There was an old camp saw filer, Calvin Harrington, who also lived on Mill Creek. One Saturday I went to pick up our saws and Cal said, "Boy, why don't you learn to file saws? My eyes are shot and are so bad, that after the first one, I just guess at it." I told Cal that I really would like to learn, but no one would show me how. He said, "I'll show you all I know about it!" So he did, and that is how it all came about that I began to learn the saw filing business. All of a sudden, saws from all over the area were appearing for me to file! For seventeen years, I filed saws, and lots of them!

THE NEW GIRL IN TOWN

The saying goes that in the spring a young man's fancy turns to love and at about this time, I began to think it might be proper and fitting for me to think about such things. In about 1926, a family named Kilmer, moved into the Sheridan area and they began to attend the same church my folks did. They had a number of girls and one boy, and were related to Stacy Kilmer. There was Emily, Frances, Elnor, Ruth, Irene, Arlene, and Paul. Mr. Kilmer's first name was Odessa and he was called "Dessie", for short, and Orva was his wife. Dessie was a friendly fellow, who drove a milk truck, and then later on, had a body shop. He was well thought of in the community, as he was a fine fellow. I began to concentrate on his one daughter in particular and of course, with all the manual labor we had in those days, it seemed like there was little opportunity to take off on a cruise to the Caribbean seas, as people do now. So, back then, we had to settle for the occasional date, whenever time would permit. Frances was the daughter I had my eye on and she, too, began to work out at an early age, as she helped care for elderly ladies, doing housework, and various other tasks. I began to date Frances as frequently as time would allow.

TO KILL A DEER - OR WILL I GET KILLED?

Early in life, I had an interest in hunting and so, when I was about sixteen years of age, I wanted to kill a deer in the worst way! My Father thought it was the most foolish thing anyone could do. In 1931, Dad traded an older Chev car in for a new one. His old car was a 1926 Chev with over 86,000 miles on it. The new car he bought was a brand new 1931 Chev Sedan and he was having a Kari Keen trunk installed on the back, which I was to pick up and drive home. Down at Houser's Garage in Sheridan, is his 1926 car by the new 1931 model, when a rather coarse-looking fellow walks up to me and says, "Say, Boy, do you know anything about this 1926 car?" "I sure do! I put many a mile on it," I informed him. He asked, "Is that the actual mileage on it - only 36,000 miles?" I said, "Yes, that is the actual miles on it, plus 50,000 more!" He put his hand out and said, "Thanks, Kid! My name's Ed Gray." I asked him where he lived and he said, "Up East Creek, out of Blaine" (towards the Oregon Coast). I asked, "Is there any place out there where I could hunt?" "Oh, do you want to hunt?" he asked. I replied, "I sure would like to kill a buck!" "Well," he said, "Come on out this fall!"

In 1931, my folks took a trip East to Lima, Ohio, to visit my Dad's relatives. At the time, my brother, Lloyd, was working at the brick plant, and I drove my Dad's team of horses twelve hours a day to a stationary hay baler for George Finney. Because I had to feed, water, and harness the horses, this made it necessary for me to be there three quarters of an hour early. At night, I'd again stay the additional time required to care for the horses before I went home. Once home, there were ten cows to milk and after milking, we had to separate it, and then feed the chickens and hogs. Once this was all finished, we'd eat our supper and then go to WORK! We went round a binder with three horses. One would run the binder, the other one would shuck until about eleven o'clock at night! Four o'clock in the morning came very early! Lloyd and I both loved fried potatoes, so we'd have fried potatoes in the morning and fried potatoes at night! I don't even remember what we took for our lunches, but do recall that at that time, neither of us drank coffee. I can tell you, our menus weren't full of the snacks and fancy gourmet items people can get for their lunches nowadays!

This was in the spring and now comes hunting season in the fall, so I head my Ford Roadster up to Blaine, inquired as to how to get to East Creek, and go driving up.

Soon the road was rough and narrow and as I carefully drove along, I soon saw an old Dodge Touring car coming towards me! I stopped, pulled off a little, and prepared to let him pass. As he began to pass me, I suddenly called out, "Hey, are you Ed Gray?" He stopped, backed up to talk to me and answered, "Yes, who are you?" I said, "You remember that 1926 Chev you looked at in Sheridan at Houser's Garage?" "Oh, yes, I do. Now I remember you! You want to go hunting don't you!" I said, "Yes." He replied, "Well, one of my wife's relatives passed away in Corvallis and we are on our way to the funeral. You go up to the mail boxes at the end of the road and about 11:00 o'clock, an old man will come down the hill, and his name is Maxfield. You tell him you are my friend and he will take you hunting."

Talk about drama! Hold on! Here comes Maxfield, just like Ed told me. Maxfield said, "I don't hunt, but there's a new fellow here and I'll talk to him and see if he'll take you out." We ate a little lunch and right close by was Ed Gray's modest cabin, so Maxfield goes over and talks to this man. The fellow who came out was a very tall man, with piercing eyes, and at first glance, you could see, here was a man who could cut a wide swath! He came up to me and makes this speech: "I don't know you, Kid. You may be from the city, but I'll take you out. I'll warn you that if you take a shot at me and don't kill me, I'll put a bullet through your heart, so help me, God!" I didn't take long to assure him, I was NOT a city-slicker! However, I was uneasy as to just what a character this fellow was. He told me his name was Lindsay Moore, commonly called, "Happy." He was up here in the wilds of Oregon hiding out from the law! So we planned our hunt, packed our "grub" and began hiking. We went back a long ways to a place where there was a rough barn, or sort of a shack, called McGuff's cabin. Around the cabin was some meadow grass, which someone had cut with an old scythe and we spent the night there, way back on the Nestucca River Watershed.

In the morning, Hap says, "We are out of meat here and I will try to kill meat for us and the neighbors. If you see a deer, you are to shoot it! Do you understand that, Kid?" I said, "Yes!" We started out and about an hour later, he had me go ahead. Here on a huge windfall stands this deer, looking back to where Happy was. He was behind me about eight hundred feet away, and as the deer continued watching him, I up and shot it. The bullet clipped his neck, and he fell off this huge windfall, which was a good eight feet on the butt.

All of a sudden, Happy screams out, "You s.o.b.! I am coming up there and kill you! You don't deserve to live! Okay, I'll give you one more chance to live," he said as he came charging my way. I just didn't know what to do! I didn't want him to shoot me and I didn't want to shoot him! When he was about twenty feet from me, he stopped and said, "Any d— fool that can't tell the difference between a deer and a snag doesn't deserve to live! What did you shoot at?" I said, "A deer!" "Where was the deer?" he asked. "Standing right on this big windfall," I said, trying to sound convincing! He looked at me and said, "Okay, I'll go around and look and if there's no deer, when I come back, I'm gonna kill you!" So Happy goes around the base of this huge windfall, makes his way through the brush and there lays a deer! He then came back, embraced me, lit his pipe, and I can tell you, with ALL honesty, my vibrations started to calm down!

We dressed the deer out, began to pack it back to Ed Gray's cabin and things were looking up! In the meantime, I learned the real reason why Happy got so mad at me! I had a 25/35 Carbine gun and there was a huge snag across this canyon. After I fired, Happy said he saw the bullet after it had passed through the deer's neck - that it hit in this big snag. The next morning we went down a ways and I killed a nicer buck, so Happy says, "I'll help you pack it down to your Ford." As we were going along with this deer, Happy says, "I got a bear trap set up ahead." Pretty soon he stopped, lit his pipe and said, "Praise the Lord, Kid. I caught a bear!" I asked, "How do you know you caught a bear?" He just said again, "Praise the Lord, I caught a bear!" We went a little ways further and heard a real commotion. Here was a big, black bear in the trap. Happy had the trap toggled to a Chittum tree, which he had peeled. (The word, "Chittum" is a nickname for Cascara bark.) I asked, "Happy, can I shoot the bear?" He said, "No, your gun's too big! I have a 25.20, but your gun's too big!" "Let me use your gun," I pleaded. He said, "No! I've got the hide sold for $5 and I only want one hole, right in the forehead." I said, "I'll just shoot once!" Finally, he said, "Okay, you walk right up here real close and just shoot once!" So as I walked up to within six feet from this big bear, she sat up and raged something awful! She frothed at the mouth and roared ferociously, constantly moving her head back and forth! So I got to "swinging with her", my aim was good, and down she went! Upon examination of the trap, there was only ONE toenail that was holding this bear in that trap and she had nearly escaped! We also discovered she had two, big cubs and they were part of the noise we heard!

Happy said, "There's a family about a mile from here that would sure like to have some of this bear to eat. Let's pack it to them." We dressed the bear out and started walking. Now it is completely dark and we didn't have a light, except for a little moonlight. Finally we got to this cabin and Happy calls out, "Hello! Anybody home?" A call comes back, "Who are you?" Happy says, "Lindsay Moore, the new fellow at Ed Gray's." He asked, "What do you want?" Happy says, "We've got a present for you!" A man came to the door with a coal oil light and his name was Dan Poole. Right behind him was Mrs. Poole, and when she saw we had some meat, she began to cry. She said, "Oh, Dan, now I can render some of that bear fat and I will make some pies!" These folks were the poorest people I ever saw! They made their living peeling the bark from the cascara trees and would put up salmon when they were running in East Creek. If someone in the area killed a deer, they would share it. They also had the best gardens I ever saw and it's for sure, there wasn't any welfare here!

Happy and I went on back to the cabin and I stayed another night. Happy then told me his life story. He said he and his cousin were making moonshine for a prominent lady named, Madame Queen, down South. On one side of the street, it was Kentucky, and on the other side, it was Tennessee. Happy had a long, handle-bar mustache and he and his cousin were walking into town one evening, packing a six gun, which they always had with them! They came upon a couple making out and the woman said, "That young s.o.b. with that mustache sure is a smart alec!" Happy said his cousin just whipped out his 45 Colt and plugged this guy, so his cousin was caught and prosecuted. Happy quickly made his way out to Oregon to avoid any further problems. He showed me a picture of himself with his mustache, and I'll admit, it was a dandy! This hunting trip was just the beginning of many, many hunting trips.

RUMBLING WITH THE RUMBLE SEAT

After I bought my Model T Ford Roadster, I made a rumble seat in the back, and we used to double-date with my cousin, Cliff Wolfer, and his girlfriend. Now Cliff was courting another cousin of mine, Mildred Shenk; however, they were not closely related to each other - just both related to me, so I was a contributing factor to delinquent minors. Cliff and Mildred later married and are still together, so I don't think I should be charged with any crime!

A number of times I have said I could forgive Adam and Eve for putting out the bad apples, but the life sentence to hard work was truly grim! Frances worked for some people, who, even though they were friendly and all, the one man in particular, possessed an insane, or violent temper when he was drinking, and would become very angry and mean! So I could see that the proper thing to do was to rescue this young lady from this questionable environment.

My sister Millie, brother Lloyd with his 1923 car, and Ken with 1927 Model T Roadster.

HORSE SENSE

Willamette William Harris was born near Oregon City, where his Father had a sawmill. Bill, as he was known, said that as a young lad, he drove a team of oxen. He began thinking that if one could teach oxen to work by command, surely a good, smart horse could also be taught, so he secured a fine pair of horses, whom he named, Dick and Nell. They were a beautiful pair - about 1,200 pounds each. He bought a 1000 shot Daisy repeating rifle and enrolled them in his school! He spoke to them and would say, "Come back here, Dick." The horse would then start up, and turn to the left. He'd say to Nell, "Get up, Gee Nell," and she would swing to the right. If he wanted them to go straight ahead, he would simply say, "Get up!" Dick and Nell were the leaders and behind them walked two other horses, which Bill called the "wheelers". Bill ran a log chain back to the double trees and usually skidded logs with a big skidding tong. Sometimes he would have a man ride Dick and maneuver the horses, when the going was rough.

When Dick and Nell were skidding logs to the landing, Bill would have a man there who would position the logs on the rollway, unhook the tongs, or sometimes skidding dogs, and merely say, "Get up!" They would go up the hill to where the swamper (the man who cut limbs off the logs) was and he would hook them up, and away they would go! If they had a log hang up on a root, they knew exactly which way to turn to release that log. It was amazing how incredibly smart those horses were! Bill had a terribly bad habit of swearing at the horses and they could tell by the tone of his voice just what their chances of survival were. He would scream at them and threaten them with murder, but they knew *exactly* what degree of punishment was to be their lot!

Out on Salmon River one Saturday, we worked up behind the Amacher place, where Ellis and Roy Breeden had a yarder rigged up to a tall, Spar tree, yarding the logs up this canyon. I helped Bill put in a skid road down to the rollway and then we loaded the logs on trucks. On this particular Saturday, we were skidding these big, fir logs and I was sniping them and barking the ride, especially on the big logs. Sniping is a sharp rounding of the log so it would not tear out the cross skids. Well, something went terribly wrong! Bill screamed and cussed 'till I thought he'd never quit! All of a sudden, he came back to where I was, put his head down, and just sat there. Then he said, "Ain't it a d— shame for me to lose my temper like that!" I said, "Yes, Bill, it's a shame and also a sin!" He said, "I'm gonna cut it out! That's just all there is to it - no more of that!" Then he went up between Dick and Nell, put a hand on each ones' head, stroked them, and just kinda loved them. After about two minutes, we had to get the logs rolling, so he spoke real reverent-like and said, "All right, get up!" Dick just turned his head and looked Bill right in the face, opened up his mouth and wiggled his lips at Bill. Bill screamed at him and said, "Why, you sorrel b————, are you laughing at me? I'll kill you for that!" He ran at Dick with a sharp, double-bited axe and said, "I'll cut your guts out!" Just as Bill brought that axe down on Dick, he turned the axe so that it came down flat on him and it sounded like a 30/06 rifle! I have never seen a horse actually laugh like Dick did, and the same thought went through my mind when Bill said to that horse, "Are you laughing at me?" Bill's repentance lasted less than ten minutes!

Bill had another team he called Nig and Ted. Nig was a big, black horse and Ted was a sorrel. These horses weighed about 1,350 pounds each and they really knew how to pull! Bill hated Ted something fierce! One day they were running in a little meadow and in recent days, it had been raining almost constantly. The mud was up to the horse's collars and soon after this, they got mud fever. To try and heal them up, we used to wash them in the creek.

Bill said to me one day, "I wish you would try and catch those horses and put the harness on them so that maybe you could help me skid these logs." I had a terrible time with Ted! He tried to crush me when I got him in his stall and I could easily see how Bill could engender hatred towards him. Anyway, I got them going and skidded a couple of rather large logs. As I did this, I noticed Bill watching me very closely. Soon he came over and said, "Kenny, I believe you can drive those horses if you don't lose your temper and beat the h— out of them like I do." I said, "No, I won't have that problem!" I could see that the one, single tree we were trying to skid was nearly in two pieces, so I said, "Bill, we have to change that!" He said, "Oh, that's the toughest piece of wood you ever saw - it won't break!" On the second day, while we were making a good, hard pull, the tree broke! I went to find Bill and told him, "The single tree met

Go Ahead On 'er!

her Maker today!" He screamed, cussed, and dammed like you can't believe, so we put on another one.

The next day I was skidding a log, which was short, but had a big circumference and down the hill it was going - in a sea of mud! Right in front of the log, this mud was about two feet high! That log just kept rolling along, but Ted suddenly tripped, and went down he went until he was completely covered with mud! First thing I noticed was that the log was resting on his one hind leg and I thought, "Now what?" I ran up a steep hill and said, "Bring Dick and Nell and the skidding chain - Ted is drowning!" Bill asked, "He is?" I said, "Yes, he is!" "Well, let him drown," was Bill's response. Quickly, I got Dick and Nell loose, took them down and all I could see of poor Ted was one hind leg! I hooked onto his leg and pulled him out. When I unhooked him, his head was downhill and he was covered all over with mud. Bill just stood there and laughed and told me he never liked Ted and all that stuff! Here is a horse which is practically dead and Bill isn't mad; yet two days ago I broke a single tree, and he cussed a blue streak. The next morning at the barn, here stood this poor, decrepit horse! Mud was oozing out his nostrils, his head was down, his eyes barely opened, and he was a cake of mud, the likes of which you have never seen! Bill looked at him in utter astonishment and said, "Why, you old so and so! If you haven't got sense enough to know when you're dead, we'll work you 'til you ARE dead!" So Bill said, "Put his harness on him and get going!" Ted got pneumonia and was very sick for about a week, but work he did!

SALMON RIVER SAGA

When I started falling timber for Bill, I cut with Delbert Glass, known as "Deb", who had worked for Bill a long time. Deb was a very nice guy, but also quite bashful! One day Bill said, "I've got a little job for you boys. Bring all your tools into the landing tonight." We took our springboards, saws, axes, wedges, and oil bottles in and Bill put them in the pickup. Next morning he drove us out towards the Oregon Coast, to an area known as Boyer Station. There was a big, fir tree and Bill told Mervin Boyer he would have us fall it. Not far away was a creek and Mervin told Bill he didn't want the tree to fall into the creek. Deb and I started to work, put in an extra big undercut, and away she went - right where Mervin had told me to put it! Merv's wife came out, looked it over, and all of a sudden, she said, "Oh, Mervin, they have fell that tree right on top of that nice crabapple tree." Merv said, "Well, they sure did!" The air was quickly charged and now turned from gloating to mayhem! Bill began to scream, "To h— with you and your d— crabapples!" So we rode back up the tram road and went to work. Deb and I never got a nickel for falling that big tree!

Bill had asked Deb, Roy Hubbard, and myself to come to his place and go out to Salmon River one Saturday to repair the plank road. We piled into his vehicle and started out. Bill stopped at the Valley Junction Cafe and Service Station to get gas for his pickup. There they had a bunch of monkies and all kinds of animals, which were interesting to watch and it was sort of a little tourist attraction. Just as Bill stopped, a big, black Cadillac with California license plates stopped also. Five people got out to take a look at the sights. Three of the five were young girls, very good looking, and their dresses were extremely short, for that era, as this was 1933. Bill had the gas nozzle in this 1929 Model A Ford and the tank was on the cowl, just ahead of the windshield. He had his head turned to look at the girls and said, "Look at those blankety-blank dames from Hollywood!" The gas was running all over the pavement while Bill was just a cussin' those young ladies out real good. Finally, he turned and looked and saw all this gas on the pavement! He shouted to us, "Did you fellows see my gas spilling?" Roy Hubbard said, "Yes, of course, we saw that!" "Well, why in h— didn't you tell me?" Roy said, "We would have, but we didn't want to spoil your fun!" Bill never spoke to us the rest of the day!

I worked on and off for Bill both before and after I was married. We worked wherever work was available and for whoever needed us. Winston Churchill used to talk about blood, sweat, toil, and tears, but he didn't have anything on me! I was still living at my parents' home, and naturally helped with the chores; milk cows, turn the separator, do this and that - all in addition to cutting timber. Throughout this entire time, Lloyd and I both gave nearly all of our money to our folks to help out all we could, and did so right up to the last pay check before getting married.

THE LOGGER TAKES A WIFE

In the fall of 1933, Frances and I decided to get married, and set the date for November 19! I would turn twenty-one on December 30th and the following June 18th, Frances would be eighteen. The couple who served as Best Man and Matron Of Honor was Cliff and Mildred Wolfer, whom I mentioned earlier, as we used to double date. At this time, I was working up Gopher Valley (out of Sheridan), cutting logs. It was cold and raining like everything on this Sunday, our wedding day! Come Monday morning, I had to be on the job, as usual. No extended honeymoon allowed and with the ceremony, we began our voyage on the sea of life! I think we had about $75 and this Ford Model T Roadster, which was our car and it served us very well.

In the fall of 1934, we bought 103 acres up Gooseneck Creek Road, out in the country, about eight miles from the small town of Sheridan. That became our home for several years. Years before, there had been quite a sawmill there and the cook house was still standing. We moved into that and began working to make it livable. Later on, we put water in the house, a shower and toilet, and to us, it was going "First Class!"

Soon I got a job on Salmon River on the Walt Hayden Plank Road, cutting timber for Elmer Weaver. This job was not without a great deal of discomfort! I had my trusty Model T Roadster and of course, it was totally air conditioned; in other words, *all* fresh air! It had no heating system and the distance to work was twenty-one miles each way! Bear in mind, we're not talking about freeway traveling, either, but rather, the typical curvy, winding, narrow, old-fashioned roads!

At one time, there were four outfits operating down this big, plank road which Walt Hayden had built with a couple other fellows. It took several years to build this road, but it was a real, fine one, going through some great timber! On this particular job, we were working nine hours a day, six days a week and were paid $.60 an hour! It was quite a long drive from Gooseneck and Deb lived in Willamina, so we decided to build a cabin in which to live during the week and not have to commute each day. We worked on the cabin until it was complete and livable. Frances would drive us out on Sunday afternoon and we would take up our domain there for the work week. Then she'd faithfully drive back out again on Saturday evening to pick us up.

In the fall, we gave the cabin up and my brother, Ron, moved in for awhile. To keep him company, he had a jet-black, hound he called, Black Sam. Ronnie worked on the rigging there and helped load. One day I was filing saws and Deb was falling with his brother, Floyd. The timber was very tall and there were a bunch of beetle-kill trees, which were extremely dangerous! Just below us, Bill Harris had John Breeden rig a Spar Tree for him. It was two hundred twenty feet to the top and I assure you, that is one tall tree! After some time, Ronnie quit staying in the cabin, and the company hired a different hooker. "Hooker" is the term for one who managed the end hooks which were used to pick up the logs.

Mike Michaelson worked for Bill and had married a young gal, who was expecting their first child. Mike planned to live in the cabin we built, so he asked, "You guys don't care if I bring my wife here to the cabin, do you? That way, if she goes into labor, I can take her to the hospital." So everybody said that would be fine! He had brought her out and she was in the cabin reading a magazine. Deb and Floyd fell a nice, green fir and as it went down, it brushed against one of these beetle-kill trees and knocked that tree right through that cabin! The impact threw Mike's wife clear outside on the ground and she lay there crying. Ron's dog, Black Sam, was pinned down, could hardly get his breath, and was yelping like everything! Mike and I both saw all this happen, as we were bucking right close by. Mike came running up there, tears streaming down his cheeks and he uttered a prayer. I can tell you, no pastor ever uttered a more appropriate one than Mike did, and this is what he said: "Oh, Lord, I know I'm a wayward old b———, but what did I do to ever deserve a thing like this?" With tears streaming down his face unashamedly, he grabbed his wife, put her in his car, and away they went! She turned black and blue and a day or two later gave birth to a fine baby, which was perfectly all right!

The plank road went right through the timber and we left what was called a "rub" tree, si-wash and they would butt the line around the tree, thus leading the logs away from the plank road so they wouldn't tear it out. They logged so much timber along this plank road, the haul-backs would go up in the air about seventy-five feet high and it sawed into the tree underneath a big knot. It went in about a foot deep and they couldn't pull the eye through. Mike was too lazy to cut it out, so he spliced a new one! Then Ronnie said, "I'll get Ken's springboard and go up there and chop that out!" That crazy kid did exactly that! He springboarded up there with one springboard and chopped that haul-back out. Then he got back down without getting killed and I'll tell you, I wish you could only imagine how dangerous and foolish that was! You wouldn't believe what all is involved! Mike laid on the ground, and again prayed, saying, "Oh Lord, don't let the little devil fall! PLEASE, Lord, don't let the little devil fall!"

Not long after Mike's wife had the baby, Mike quit working for Elmer and went to work for Ray and Adams. Elmer Weaver then hired another fellow, Roy Hurst, who was a good logger. The Yarding Engineer, Red Bales, from Philomath, was a good engineer, and he knew Roy Hurst, as well as a lot of other fellows. Roy asked, "Mind if I move in your cabin?" We had left the little stove, bedding and everything, so we said, "No, go ahead!" A day or two later, here was a nice-looking gal sweeping out the cabin when we walked by and I wondered what was going on.

There at our cabin, about a week later, here sits a big, tall husky fellow with his mouth full of Copenhagen. He said, "Good morning Boys!" We said, "Good morning." So I went to Red Bales, the Engineer and asked, "What the world is going on around here, anyway?" "Oh, you don't know?" I said, "No!" "Well, that's Curly, Jack's wife. Jack was doing high climbing in Valsetz and he and Curly got into a scrap. She just up and asked where Roy was and when she found out he was down on Salmon River, she ended up in your cabin. They're the best of friends, don't worry," he quickly added. As it turned out, the three of them lived there for quite some time!

Back in those days, there really were no rain clothes designed to wear while running a falling saw! We wore a minimum of clothing as we worked! One time, it rained for ninety days straight and during that period, at times, it POURED BUCKETS! Also, it was VERY foggy! We would face four big trees in the afternoon, prior to quitting, and mark in the bark as to how much wood we wanted to hold. We'd also figure out where we wanted to lay them when they fell. In this manner, we prepared for the next morning, because we were unable to see the treetops until about ten o'clock, due to the fog! Here we were, out in the elements in that pouring down rain, and the damp fog, day after day! We had in our heads that black, wool underwear was to be worn by sissies and we didn't want that classification! Later in life, we found out that what the old, Jewish clothier in Portland said, was true, indeed! He told the loggers, "Ven you is vet and cold, den vil you be varm and dry in my undervear!" How we ever lived through this experience for three winters, I'll never know! We were logging over the coast summit and many times, it was raining there, but absolutely not a drop was falling in the valley! Wool clothing simply cannot be beat for rain clothing!

Deb and I had worked there for some time and one day I told him, "Deb, I'm going to hit Elmer up for a raise!" He said, "Oh, don't do that! We've got a good job and he'll get mad!" I said, "Well, I don't care if he gets mad or not, I'm going to jump him!" The entire time we worked there, I think Elmer only came out to see us no more than two or three times. Soon after I made my comments to Deb, here comes Elmer. We were putting a face in a big tree, so I stopped and said, "Hello." "Hi, fellas," Elmer responded. "Elmer, I happen to be married and have no intention of marrying either one of your daughters, but I think we deserve a raise," I said. Deb just started chopping like crazy and Elmer walked up to him and said, "Give me your darned axe!" Deb looked at him kinda funny, gave him his axe, and Elmer started chopping. "When you're facing big trees, you take turns," he commented. He chopped about a dozen strokes, then turned to us and said, "You know, fellas, that's awful hard work! I'd be happy to give you a raise!" Away he went and when he got out of sight, I stopped chopping, looked at Deb and said, "Deb, you Rascal, you! You mean to tell me you couldn't stop chopping while I hit the boss up for a raise? Don't you ever do that again!" He said, "I'm sorry,

Kenny, I'm really sorry!" He was so bashful that many times he wasn't even good company! I worked with him for over two years before he'd even talk to me and here we lived at the ends of a cross-cut saw!

President Roosevelt was on the "throne" when Deb and I were working above Willamina one time. A fellow came out to the woods and said, "Hey, Deb, I hear Roosevelt's going to close the banks down!" Bill Harris had owed Deb a bunch of money and hadn't paid it for years, then suddenly paid him around $3,000, which was an enormous sum of money in those days! This fellow knew Deb real well and was aware that he had put his money in the Willamina City Bank. "Go down and get your money out, quick, Deb," he warned! "Roosevelt's going to close the bank tomorrow!" Deb said, "Thanks a lot, but Kenny won't have a partner if I go!" Quickly I said, "Go on down, Deb, I'll chop undercuts!" "Yeah, well, thanks a lot," was his response. I kept begging him to go, but he wouldn't. That evening a fellow named Frank Baird, who had quite a logging operation, put a big payroll check in the Willamina bank and the next morning, on the door of the bank was a big sign, "Closed by order of State Bank, signed by A.A. Schram." It was a very impressive looking closure sign. Frank went down to that bank, began banging on the door and it sounded like he was going to break down the door. The banker came to the door and said, "Frank, I can't let you in here! Don't you see that sign?" Frank said, "You dirty so and so! You get that check and give it back to me or you'll never look at another sign; I'm gonna kill you! Last night you knew this was going to happen and should have told me!" The banker went and got his check, gave it back to him and Roosevelt never knew the difference! Many years later, Deb got back ten cents on the dollar for the money he had in there and I well remember that, because for years, Deb used to cuss Roosevelt for doing that to him!

President Roosevelt instituted a number of things; Works Progress Administration, being one of them. I heard of an incident which happened over by Carlton. There was a big slide in the road and they had two hundred men lined up with wheelbarrows and shovels; supposedly to move this dirt out of there. About three o'clock one afternoon a call went into Sheriff Manning of Yamhill County, "Come quick! One of the workers just had a heart attack!" Manning takes a deputy with him, drives out to Carlton, took a look around and told the deputy, "I'm sorry! We're just out of luck. We'll have to wait until quitting time. I can't tell which one had the heart attack!" That's how ambitious they were.

Working out on Salmon River, there was a fellow they called Fat Maxfield, the Whistle Punk. He was a simple sort of a fellow. Roy Hurst and Jack Wooley pulled a really dirty trick on him. All three of them had gone to a big dance around Pee Dee one time and afterwards, they told Fat he was in big trouble – that he had gotten a girl pregnant. They then offered to take care of the situation if Fat would give them so much money each month. Let me assure you, it was a BIG sum of money they came up with! Every month those guys used to take Fat's paycheck, giving him just a little for tobacco and a few groceries, with barely enough to live on. What a rotten thing to do, but that's just some of the jokes those guys used to pull and I thought that was pretty grim when I found out what was going on. The funny part was, Fat thought he was really lucky these boys were taking care of him like this. He just didn't know the truth of it and when you're drunk, you're drunk! So what?

PARENTHOOD

In 1935, on January 16, our first son, Wilbert, came to our house, and he proved to be a keeper! We enjoyed him very much. As with most new parents, we thought he was the greatest and were very proud of him!

My brother, Ron was quite a bit younger than I and he bought a bicycle and got hold of a 25-20 carbine (gun). He started from my parents' home in Sheridan one day to come out and spend some time at our place on Gooseneck. The whole mountain back of our acreage was solid timber, and there were still plenty of trees on our place as well, and he liked to go out into the woods. Riding his bicycle out from Sheridan, a black mink crossed the road in front of him, so Ron bailed off his bike and chased it. It ran up a tree and he shot it, then he rode on to our house, skinned that mink out, and made a stretcher to put it on. Soon he sold it and got a good price for it.

Another day Ron went hunting on our place, up on the hill. He saw a nice deer and so just ups and shoots! Down goes the deer! He dressed it out and cut off one ear to bring to the house to show Frances. He also cut a notch in a tree and made a "Gambel stick" and somehow got that deer up and off the ground! It was dark when I got home from work, and here was my Mother to see her grandkids! This posed a very grave problem! Mother is going to find out about Ron's deer! Okay, then, in the darkness, up the hill Ron and I go with the coal oil lantern. The young timber was very thick and we almost gave up, when at last we found Ron's deer! It was his FIRST deer and by now, was already quite stiff, but I saddled it up and down to the wood shed we go! Ron finally HAD to tell Mother, so he said, "Mom, I shot a deer!" She started to cry and carry on, putting her imagination, which was quite considerable, in gear! We had quite a time, to say the least!

The reason Mother was so upset was that deer season was closed (minor detail). She said, "Well, I'll have Dad go and talk to Sheriff Manning!" I quickly pointed out that she was now in Polk County and Dad didn't know this Sheriff. Sheriff Manning was from Yamhill County, where they lived. This fact brought another outburst of tears! Throughout this scene, Ron looked as if he were prepared to make his last statement, prior to being hung! Finally, I had enough of this nonsense and I asked, "Mom, do you know who made these deer?" I continued, "God did, and He made them for poor people to eat, and we are poor! We raised this deer on our place, for which we pay taxes! We have a right to eat this deer!" She said, "Oh, they will find out!" I asked, "How will they?" She said, "I don't know, but they will!" I said, "No, they won't!" She then called Ron to her chair and gave him the eleventh commandment, which is, "Thou shalt not get caught!" Of course, her words to him were, "Now YOU promise me that you will NEVER, NEVER kill another deer!" Ron bowed his head, crossed himself, I think, and gave his solemn word! Sad to say, that's one he never intended to keep!

The next evening I instructed Frances to cut, and cut deep, and fry up a big skillet of steak off that deer and let's give Mom some good eatin'! It was very good meat and my Mother ate a generous portion and this calmed her down greatly! The neighbors in those days used to hunt and it was not unusual to have someone drop off buck meat from time to time. Thus was life in the "Far West"!

GOOSENECK GAB

When we moved up Gooseneck, there were two ex-convicts and then later on, another one joined the ranks, so there were some very colorful characters living there! I want to tell you about just a few events which took place during our years in Gooseneck and the various people we came to know. First, let me tell you about Halsey Rogers. Halsey was our closest neighbor, and a better one could not be found! One day he was doing some harrowing in the field with his horses. That field bordered on our place, and along the field was a path which went through the timber to Charlie Allen's place. Charlie was another neighbor whom we really enjoyed. Wilbert was a small boy and had found some cow bells, which he dearly loved. One day this little kid was down on his hands and knees playing out in this field with a bell around his neck. Halsey had lost a bell off one of his cows and every time he came close to the edge of this field, he'd hear that bell ring! Halsey couldn't see this small kid down on his hands and knees since the tall grass hid him! Halsey naturally thought his cow was over there. After some time, he jumped over the fence and here he found Wilbert! Halsey just laughed his head off as he told us about that! Here was one man I could visit with, discuss various subjects, and feel a common bond!

A McNess Products man used to visit in our community and he always sent out a postcard a day or two prior to his coming. McNess products were sold door-to-door because back in those days, many folks didn't have cars, or couldn't get to town often to do their shopping. Halsey said this fellow always wanted to leave things for him to try - shaving soap, or whatever. Halsey told him, "No thanks, don't leave things! I'll buy what I want and pay for it, and that's that." There was no way this fellow named Dasheill, would listen to Halsey! Being a salesman, he always insisted on leaving something for Halsey to try, which he no doubt figured was good "bait." Halsey told his wife, "Next time he comes, I'm going to break him of this habit," and he did just that. In the mailbox, as usual, came the announcement of his impending arrival, "Your McNess man will call tomorrow!" Sure enough, next day he stopped in front of their house. Halsey beat it out in back, behind his house and told his wife to send the guy out there. Halsey was in his woodshed with a big, double-bit axe raised above his head, his hair pulled over his eyes, and he assumed a strange look in his eyes. Mr. Dasheill went out and greeted him, "Hello, Mr. Rogers." Halsey shouted at him, "Roosts!" The McNess man said, "Oh, you want that lice oil for your chicken roosts, don't you?" Halsey screamed again, "Roosts," and came closer to the salesman, with that axe still raised in the air. To every question, Halsey just said, "Roosts," and soon he was close enough to chop that fellow in two! The McNess man became frightened and beat a hasty retreat! He told the neighbors, "Mr. Rogers just lost his mind!" The McNess man never bothered the Rogers again!

If Halsey went to a public auction and people would crowd him, he'd open his shirt and begin making a popping noise with his fingernails. Then he'd ask anyone near him, "Are the cooties bothering you? They're just driving me crazy!" So the people around him would back off and give him a wide berth.

Out hunting one time, Halsey had just stepped out of the timber onto the county road, when he was nearly hit by a Game Warden driving by in his car. The Warden clamped on his brakes, and thinking he had a "victim", asked, "How's hunting?" Halsey asked, "Did you just see a yellow dog?" The warden said, "No, I didn't!" "When I see that yellow dog, hunting's going to be real good," Halsey told him and with that, he vanished into the brush. The Warden just sat there awhile and finally left. I'm sure he didn't know what "hit him"!

WHITMAN THE WHIZ

Bernie Whitman, another neighbor, moved into a cabin close by our place and was a very likable fellow in many respects. He had a story or comment to make for any and all occasions! A few illustrations will suffice as explanation. One day he wrote Sears Roebuck a letter and ordered a compass. He told me that he wrote in the letter that he was a Surveyor of great repute. As a matter of fact, all his great deeds took place in Michigan when he supposedly was a Superintendent for Lobdell & Emery Lumber Company. So Sears sent him, not one, but two compasses. He gave me one, which was made for use on a transit. Bernie informed me he could set it on 75 - 90 degrees and run a line any place in the U.S.! Talk about talent!

Two neighbors boys were handling a rifle one day and the gun accidentally discharged. An ambulance was called and I rode in the ambulance to take Frankie Abderhallen and Tommy Mishler to the hospital in McMinnville. The news of the accident quickly spread throughout our small community. The next day Bernie hastened over with this question, "Was the lad bleeding at all?" I said, "Yes, he bled some." Bernie got very angry and upset! He said, "I took great pains to stop any and all bleeding just before he was placed in the ambulance!" This was Bernie's story: "He said that one day at Lobdell and Emery, the superintendent came out and called, Bernie Whitman, are you around? One of the other fellows told the boss that Bernie was forty feet high on the cold deck of logs. The fellow called out and said, 'You come down right away'! Bernie said he could tell something dreadful must have happened and asked the superintendent what was wrong? The superintendent said, 'Frank Greene just got shot and you must come at once.' Bernie said he looked around and picked out a husky, young fellow and told him to come with him. Frank Greene was one of Bernie's best friends and so they took him to where Frank lay. Bernie said, Sure enough, it was awful! Someone had shot Frank in the stomach with a 38-55 rifle, which had a 265 grain bullet. Bernie said Frank's intestines were out and he said, 'I could see, I had no time to waste. I looked in his eyes and said, Frank, do you want to live?' Frank answered, 'Bernie, you know I do!' 'Okay, Frank no hollerin,' Bernie told him and then took sulphur and carbolic acid, which he mixed up, put his insides back and clamped on this poultice. He said Frank just let out one scream and that was it! They took him on into the hospital and a doctor came in. The doctor pulled back the covers and asked, 'Who's been doctoring you?' Frank answered, 'Bernie Whitman.' The doctor said, 'He's in the best of hands then! There's nothing further that I need to do'!" After Bernie told me this story, I waited a modest amount of time and then asked, "And did he recover?" Bernie gave me a look I will never forget! It was a mixture of disgust and pathos, and he replied softly, "Of course he did!" After Frankie and Tommy's accident, for days Bernie told stories relating to his powers as a healer and his skill in restoring the wounded and dying!

A couple of ministers visited Bernie and they asked him about his faith and so on. One minister asked him if he had ever been baptized. Bernie's answer was the following story: "I surely was baptized! One Sunday morning, rather than going to Sunday School, I went down to the sawmill where they had a big pond with a large raft of logs. I got to playing around on the logs, slipped and fell into the pond. When I came up, my head bumped a log and I couldn't get any air. I went down into the water three times and finally came up and was able to get out. Then it hit me! I had been baptized three times - Father, Son, and Holy Spirit!" This at least silenced the ministers because one of them wanted to laugh and could hardly restrain himself from doing so!

Bernie's biggest hang-up was his music! He imagined that he was a great concert violinist and he did have a very fine violin, which he kept wrapped in a velvet cloth. One time he was playing a hymn and I could scarcely recognize part of it. I said, "Bernie, you have two hymns mixed up." He looked at me with a look which practically implied that I was pathetic, and he said, "Kenny, you don't understand! The greater the artist, the greater his liberty for embellishment!" In other words, Bernie could create anything he wanted to and had no problem. Matter of fact, you shouldn't either, was the implication!

During World War II, we had to go by Bernie's cabin to our logging show, so he came out and stopped us one morning and it was obvious, he was very upset. His question was, "Did you see the Big Battle last night?" "No, I didn't," I said, to which he quickly said, "Oh, it was awful! The whole sky was lit up by the bombs and shrapnel, and I could even hear the screams and crying of the wounded and dying men!" We went on to work. No work for Bernie that day. There were a bunch of mail boxes right by his cabin and around noon, Halsey Rogers went to get his mail. Bernie met him there and asked him, "Did you see the Great Battle in the sky last night?" Halsey said, "I sure did, but I was a keepin' it to myself because I was afraid if I told anyone, they would think I was crazy!" Halsey said Bernie brightened up and said, "Halsey, I saw it, too, and I know you're not crazy!"

Bernie was trying to cut some wood once and his old saw just wouldn't go, so here he came with this wreck of a saw, saying, "Kenny, I myself am a great saw filer and I want you to know, I don't let just anyone file my saw, but I will let you!" What a task! I straightened it out, jointed it, cleaned off some rust, and filed it. When he came to pick it up, he asked, "Kenny, where in the world did you learn that Tuttle Tooth? I didn't know anyone West of the Mississippi knew about it!" I thought I was on to something, so I asked, "Bernie, how many kinds of points or tooth designs are there?" He promptly said, "Sailor, Half Sailor, and Diamond Tuttle Tooth." I told the fellows on my cutting crew this story and I got a lot of flack from it! They would usually ask, "And did you give this one the Sailor or Tuttle Tooth?" Somehow Bernie seemed to realize that his elevator never went to the top floor!

On a Saturday evening, I went over to visit Bernie and as always, he gladly welcomed me. We visited at length, making small talk on various subjects and events in the community. It was a humid evening and so very warm, that the air seemed oppressive! I said, "Well, Bernie, I must be going!" He said, "Oh, no, Kenny, we are going to have some violin music!" He got up, went into his bedroom and brought out his violin case. As usual, it was resting in its' beautiful, soft, red velvet cloth. Tenderly he began to unravel this wrapping and took the violin out. Just as he was doing this, I said, "Bernie, I heard that the Voice Of The Prairies, in Calgary, Alberta, was going to broadcast some lovely violin music on the radio tonight." He looked quite hurt (as if I had implied his music wasn't good enough for me), and then said, "Well, all right! I'll turn my radio on." Here came the strains of the most wonderful violin music! All of a sudden, his radio cracked, made terrible sounds of static, and was very noisy. Bernie started to laugh and motioned with his hand towards the radio, "That's the D.M.!" I asked, "The what?" He said, "The D.M., The Director of Music! You know, Kenny, it's against the law to boot-leg the radio stations across the International Border, but I've been doing it for a long time and haven't been caught yet! Didn't you know that?" "No, I didn't," I said. The music finished on the radio broadcast, and an announcer said very clearly, "This is Radio Station KOAC, Corvallis, Oregon." I said, "Oh, Bernie, that came from Corvallis!" Bernie looked at me once again, as if I were pretty pathetic, and said, "I'm sorry, Kenny, you just don't understand! I brought that from Calgary!" Sometimes it just wasn't worth trying to confuse him with the facts!

OVER THE PATH AND

THROUGH THE WOODS

Another neighbor, Charlie Allen, was truly a character! There was a path through the woods from our place to Charlie's cabin. Tom Otis and Guy Coon owned 160 acres up Gooseneck, and they gave me this account: Tom and Guy had a barber shop, pool hall and restaurant in downtown Portland. Charlie would come in and buy a cup of coffee or something, but he was always dead broke. One day Tom said, "Charlie, we have a place out in the country and it has an old house on it. Why don't you build a little cabin, cut some wood and perhaps you can make it." Charlie came out to this acreage, did just like Tom said, building a cabin right by the lovely, little stream and began to cut a little wood.

One day Frank Aikman went up the creek to go hunting, stopped by to talk to Charlie, and they discovered they hit it off pretty good. Consequently, Frank used to stay there quite a bit. Charlie's cabin was on Rowell Creek, right close to where there was a Y in the road and to the left, a road went up Frazier Creek. Up Frazier there were some cabins that people would live in now and then, as water and wood was always available. Charlie had a friend, Barkey Broom, and Barkey took up with a woman named Inez. Inez had fine clothes and had been a beautiful lady in her time. She came from an aristocratic family in Kansas, her uncle having served as governor for many years, however, she could not leave booze alone! Inez and Barkey moved up Frazier Creek and I gave Barkey a job bucking timber at Erickson's on Salmon River. He owned a 25-20 rifle and asked me to put a front sight on it and line it up, which I did. Once I finished it, I dropped it off at Charlie's and out at work that day, I informed him I had left his gun at Charlie's cabin. Martin Caswell Broom, a brother to Barkey, was released from the Oregon State Penitentiary in Salem, and upon his release, he bought a new Plymouth Coupe. He knew that Barkey was down on Salmon River, so Mart began to spend time up Gooseneck with Inez. On a Friday evening, Barkey came home from Salmon River, picked up his rifle at Charlie's, and drove up to see his lovely. At once, he could see that someone had spent much time there! He drove back to Charlie's and said, "My brother, Mart, has been with my woman, hasn't he?" "Oh no, he hasn't," Charlie said. Barkey said, "Don't lie to me! I'm going over and shoot the b———!"

I was at home filing saws and here comes Charlie, just screaming and cussin' a blue streak. He was so angry, I could hardly understand him. "Throw that d— file down and get your car keys - we have to avert a murder," he shouted, so we took off. I knew where Martin had a house on the Greenwood road, towards Salem and we drove in to his place. Charlie ran up on the porch and yelled, "Get out, get going! Barkey's coming to kill you!" Mart asked, "Did Barkey say he was going to kill me?" Charlie said, "He sure as heck did!" "Thanks fellows, I'll be leaving," Mart replied, as he jumped in his car and took off towards Independence. I turned my car around to start for home and here came Barkey! We were about 400 feet from Mart's driveway when we met him, but he didn't even seem to notice us!

On Monday out at Erickson's Camp where I was the Bullbuck and saw filer, here was Barkey on deck, as usual. I just could not let it rest and made up my mind I would confront Barkey and get it over with! These Broom boys came out West from Georgia. There were three brothers, Martin, Barkey, and John, and all of them were real hot-heads and could get riled easily. Barkey had a nice dog he called Brownie, who was always with him and on this Monday morning, Barkey was bucking a big log. As I approached him, I said, "I need to talk to you, Barkey, and I want you to promise me you will bear no ill will towards me." He paused quite a spell and then said, "Okay, Kenny, I won't hold anything against you." I told him the story of how Charlie came over and what we did. He was silent for a long time and finally said, "Well, the minute he came to the door, I would have shot him for messin' with Inez, but I guess I shouldn't kill my brother over a woman!" Barkey then told me that the evening before he had driven into Dallas to buy a bottle of whiskey and that's what gave Charlie and I time to get to Mart's place. Had he not driven into Dallas, goodness only knows what might have happened!

Charlie always read detective magazines and I noticed from time to time how he would get all steamed up - especially about murders and at the time, the Bowes murder was a great sensation throughout most of the United States, generating a lot of publicity. One Saturday at his house, he said to us, "You know, I went to McNeil Island one time to visit a friend. When that big gate clanged shut, it gave me a strange feeling!" Barkey laughed like crazy for a while and then the subject changed. Out at the logging show on Monday, Barkey asked, "Say, Kenny, did you know Charlie did time at McNeil?" I said, "No, I didn't know that!" He said, "Well, I do, and I'll tell you how I know! My brother, John, ran a big still up on the McKenzie River and made whiskey for a prominent family in Portland. One day John told me he had to go to Eugene and asked me to watch his still, as he was running off a big batch of liquor. I agreed to do this for him and about midnight, someone said, 'Stick 'em up, John, we got you this time!' Barkey said, 'I just laughed and said, You didn't catch John, you caught Barkey'!" So it was that Barkey knew what he was talking about, as he had done one year in the slammer for his brother, John. Later, I found out that Charlie did his year for counterfeit money. Barkey said if you visit someone at McNeil, they would take the convicts out across the water to a meeting place. McNeil Federal Prison is in Washington on an island. When that gate clangs shut, you sure can get the feeling Charlie said he got!

Charlie's right eye was out and his left foot was severed in the instep. He told us he was a railroad engineer, had lost his eye when a water glass broke and that his foot had been injured in a train wreck. He smoked Velvet and was always a rolling another one! One bright morning I was fishing up Frazier Creek and Charlie was cutting some wood up there. He was sitting on a stump with his back to me, just a talkin' away, but had turned his head, and I thought he saw me. Evidently, it was his blind side. Just as he started to lick his paper on his cigarette, I took my steel rod and drew a line down his back with the tip. He literally exploded, screaming and cussing, and I thought he was going to fight me. I apologized profusely and after some time, he let it go!

One time he asked me to take him to town for groceries. I asked, "Where will I find you, Charlie?" He said, "Oh, I'll be around!" I did my shopping and about an hour later, I went into the White Circle Cafe and Tavern and here was Charlie. He had a tall beer in his hand and said, "Boys, I'm about to propose the most famous toast in Portland!" Just then, Charlie dropped his glass of beer, looked my way and asked quite loudly, "Where have you been? I've been looking all over for you!" I said, "Well, Charlie, I've been looking for you!" He had five pounds of rice and five pounds of beans with him; that's what constituted his grocery shopping!

On the way home he kept cussing the gutter sows, so finally I said, "Charlie, I don't follow you! What is a gutter sow?" "Oh," he said, "that's people who take a drink and can't hold their liquor and end up in the gutter!" I drove into Charlie's yard, went around and opened the car door for him. He had the bag of rice in one arm and the beans in the other. I said, "Here ya go, Charlie, let me give you a hand," as I began to offer him help. He said, "Stand back! I don't need a hand!" The poor rascal fell face down and spilled his groceries. He actually hurt himself when he fell and began to cuss the uneven ground and I let him go at that.

There was another ex-con by the name of Friendly Lamb, living in our community, up the Finn Road. This man had to be the most misnamed person in the whole world! He had a look on his face that would make Satan shiver! He also had just one eye and was always watching his back track. He liked to visit with Halsey Rogers and Halsey would tell me about his visits with him. One day I asked Halsey, "Can you arrange a visit with Friendly to include yourself and me?" He said, "I'll ask him." So Halsey asked Friendly if I could visit too. Friendly wasn't too sure at first, but finally asked Halsey what kind of a car I drove and what color, and so on, and a date was set for the three of us to get together. On the evening of our scheduled visit, I drove up with Halsey, fairly close to Friendly's cabin. Halsey went to the door and called out, "Open up, it's Halsey!" No answer. Again he called out, "Open up!" The door did not open. At last, Halsey called, "Friendly, you old bum, open the door!" Just then Halsey heard something inside he didn't like, so came to my car and said, "He won't let me in, let's go." We left and the next day at the mailbox, our puzzle was solved! Halsey talked to Friendly and discovered what the problem was. I had traded cars and my new one was a different color! Old Friendly was mad that the car's color did not match the description Halsey had given him. He told Halsey, "I had a double-barreled shotgun right in the middle of that door!" So it's a good thing Halsey backed off.

Frank Aikman had an old, cut down bug - an old Ford, and on the door he had painted the title, "Lady Damfino." He didn't have a license on it, nor a drivers license. One evening Charlie just had to have some beer, so into Sheridan they went. Charlie took on quite a snootful, but Frank never drank a drop, which was quite unusual. On the way home, below Buell, a fellow ran into Frank and demolished Lady Damfino, as well as tearing up his own car. When this guy discovered that Frank didn't have a license, he waxed real bold. A Polk County Sheriff was called and Frank was promptly arrested and ordered to appear in Dallas on such and such a day, before Judge Charles Gregory.

Frank and I were falling timber and when the day came for the hearing, he asked me to take him in. He was quite despondent and told me he would get a year in the slammer. Once we got into town, he said, "I'm going to go into the tavern and drink up." I said, "Please Frank, don't drink! It will go against you!" He said, "No, it won't! I'm gonna drink!" I raised such a fuss and finally talked him out of that. Now it's the appointed hour for him to go before the Judge! We went to the stairs and a Deputy Sheriff appeared to escort Frank up the stairs to the courtroom, while I followed. Judge Gregory had a cud of tobacco in his mouth. He aimed a mouthful at the spittoon and his aim was good! He said, "Mornin', Frank." "Mornin', Judge," replied Frank. Judge Gregory asked, "How do you plead, Frank?" Frank said, "I'll plead guilty even though I ain't guilty, 'cause this other fellow ran into me!" The Judge said, "I'm sorry, Frank, but I'm going to fine you $5!" Frank looked at me and said, "Aw, h—, Kenny, give him $5," which I did.

We went downstairs and right outside, here was the fellow who ran into Frank's car, just waiting for him. He said to Frank, "You got the money to fix my car up? I want it and I want it RIGHT NOW!" Frank said, "No, I ain't got the money, but I have asked my brother-in-law, who has a shop, to fix it for you!" Just then, this fellow said, "I sure hate like heck to take it out of your hide!" Frank was smoking a cigarette, which he forcefully threw on the ground, then he made a dash towards that fellow, shouting, "Oh, it's excitement you crave, is it! I'll sure as h— accommodate you!" You never saw a man leave so fast in your life! Then it was my turn to light into Frank!

I said, "And what do you think now? If you had gone up to the Judge smelling like a brewery, do you think you would have gotten off so easy?" The Deputy who had escorted Frank up the stairs was livid at the Judge because Frank had been before him several times in the past and the deputy wanted the Judge to "throw the book" at him!

MY BROTHER'S KEEPER?

Ron and I decided one day to go hunting, so we walked from Gooseneck up over the mountain and down to Cedar Creek Camp, in Mill Creek, on the other side. There were a bunch of fellows up there hunting; Frank Aikman, Allen Raines, Kenny Barnum, Stub Mortz and Tom Syron. There were quite a few cabins still standing and this was close to the old Locy shed. These fellows just chopped a hole through the floor in their cabin and made a fire right there. They'd tear some wood right off the ceiling to put in the fire, had gathered some limbs from outside, and weren't too terribly consumed with life's problems! They had enough whiskey there so that they weren't suffering any, although it was bitterly cold outside and the ground was frozen. Frank went outside and cut some fir boughs to lay on the floor for cushion. The second night, the pitch began oozing out from these branches and were quite close to the fire. Stub had just gotten a piece of ceiling lumber and set Frank's bed on fire! The minute this fire hit Frank's fir boughs with all that pitch, his entire "bed" was aflame! Frank suddenly jumped up, grabbed Stub and tried to shake him into this bed of red-hot, glowing coals there in the fire! That bed of coals was at least two and a half feet in circumference and about a foot high. Stub nearly lost his balance and fell into those coals and he must have gotten his back-side burned as he fought with Frank! Stub screamed for dear life and said, "No, no, no!" Frank shouted, "If you want excitement, I'll accommodate you!" (That seemed to be one of his favorite phrases!) Believe me, there was no sleep the rest of the night! We sat in silence, for we all knew that we had nearly witnessed a murder! That scene made an indelible impression on us and Ron was still just a kid then!

Ron did something very foolish on that trip. The following night, Tom Syron went to sleep with a cigarette in his mouth. It had burned down to about one inch from his lips, and Tom was just snoring away for all he was worth! Ron took a sliver of wood, lit Tom's cigarette, and it burned right up to his lips! Everybody was laughing and thought that at any moment, he might inhale this cigarette. He woke up and must have suspected Ron had done it, as he started picking on him. Tom was Frank's Uncle, so Frank called him some names (not printable) and told him to knock it off! That hunting trip was so many years ago, but a memorable one! Ron was getting an education he'd never receive any other way!

HINTS FOR HUNTING

A book I purchased early on is entitled, <u>The Still Hunter</u>, and I have that book yet! This great author had some good points, although sometimes the reading was a little tiresome. I tried to glean any good tips on hunting, as I knew hunting was something I enjoyed! One bright, frosty morning I hiked up into and above Foster's logging show, heading for Doran's Peak. I suddenly jumped a big buck, but rather than tearing directly after him, I made a circle, and sure enough, the book was right! The author said many times, upon jumping a deer, they'll run hard for a short distance, then turn around and watch their backtrack. Well, this is what this big buck was doing! I had a 99 Savage 30/30 and had just learned to load my own shells. As I aimed and shot, he went to the ground. Then I saddled him up and packed him home.

One day Frank, Ron, and I decided to go hunting over the Gooseneck ridge and down into the center of the Wild Cherry Thicket. In those days, it was all big, Old Growth timber and no logging for miles. It started to rain quite hard and was very foggy, so Frank built a dinner fire and we ate our cans of sardines in silence. The fire was dying down, with only a little smoke left, when I decided to tell Frank that I had bought a cheap compass for $.50. Frank looked at me and said, "Why, any darn fool knows you can't buy a compass for four bits! Now just where does that thing say North is?" So I got it out and Frank couldn't believe it! After he finished with his smokes, he said, "Let's get going," and started out, so we followed. In the meantime, the fog had gotten even worse and it was nearly impossible to see, but we were able to use my compass and followed it. Eventually, we got up on the main ridge and finally made it home! Frank didn't have too much more to say about my compass!

I could always tell when buck season was getting close, for it seemed as if my neck would begin to swell and I couldn't enjoy my food or anything - the only cure was to go hunting! I'm not sure if Frances ever "bought" my diagnosis or not! Ron and I decided to walk over the mountain from Gooseneck, down into Mill Creek. At this time, there were no roads up Mill Creek whatsoever. The Sheridan Timber Company at one time had a big logging camp at Cedar Creek. They had taken a big locomotive up there and built a railroad up Camp Creek. Dams were constructed, one at Cedar Creek, one in Bear Creek, and one at South Branch. They would bring logs into these various "ponds" and then float them down to the mill, which was below Bridge One. The engine bases are still evident there at Bridge One and this was quite a large operation. I believe Sheridan Timber Company began operation about 1900 and operated until about 1924. At one time, there was even a post office in the Herber homestead. There is some very interesting history about the Mill Creek area!

COPING WITH THE COPS

Along Mill Creek, between Wind Creek and the Gorge Bridge, there was a cabin called, Jack Brown's Fire Cabin! We were out on another hunting trip, so Ron and I followed the trail over the hill and went down to this cabin to "hunker down" for the night! There were no beds in this cabin, so we cut some fir boughs and laid them on the floor for cushion! We had each taken a blanket and some food; which was a couple cans of sardines and a sandwich apiece. About midnight, we heard a terrible commotion, woke up, and saw a couple of burly fellows coming through the door of the cabin. Immediately, I knew they were feeling no pain! They were carrying on with great frivolity and I asked, "Who are you fellows?" The one said, "My name is L.L. Morton. I am of the Portland Police Force! I do the mugging and fingerprinting and my friend here is Travors. He has charge of the Record Bureau and everything that goes through the Police Department, we know all about it!" I said to him, "In view of your drunken condition, I think my brother and I ought to get up and put you out of the cabin!" He laughed and said, "Well, I don't doubt but what you could!" When they stumbled into our cabin, one of them had a flashlight and had shined it around the place, looking all around and then asked, "You mean to tell me there are no other beds in this shack?" We said, "No," to which he said, "It sure beats h— how Jesus loves me! I'm gonna have to sleep on the floor!"

They regaled us the rest of the night with yarns and telling stories of how the police force operated and I found their information to be utterly true! For the third time that year, I had read in the Portland Oregonian (Oregon's leading newspaper) reports on this subject: "The Vice Squad Promises Clean Up Of City - Chinese Lottery Raided - Two Suspects Taken!" When I said this to Morton, he cut loose! He was immediately agitated and asked, "Do you want to know what REALLY happened?" "I sure do," I said. "Okay," he said, "there's a lottery going down there and they have some really big jackpots. One day a fellow told one of the most well-known Reverend's in Portland that there was open gambling in Portland and the Reverend was just aghast! He doubted it, but the officer said, 'Oh, yes, they do!' The Reverend said, 'Well, I am going to do something about it,' so he phoned the Chief of Police and the chief registered alarm! The Police Chief said, 'Well, I will take action at once!' In the meantime, the Chief had called this Chinese fellow up and said, 'I'm gonna have to make a raid to calm things down! I want you to get two Burnside bums (street alcoholic boys) and have them stand behind the door. Of course, you'll have to pay them $5 apiece, then we'll come make the raid! We'll take 'em in, mug them and fingerprint them, then turn them loose. This will take the pressure off us regarding gambling and it will look good to the public!' So the Chinese fellow agreed, and down through Portland at 12:00 o'clock we went, with the sirens blazing, two squad cars, and two machine guns! We charged the joint, taking these two suspects in. What the people didn't know was that we bought tickets to this big lottery while we were in there," and then he just laughed uproariously! Immediately he made a comment which I never forgot, "Do you know what happened Sunday morning?" "No, I don't," I answered. Morton said, "Righteousness flowed like a river! This Reverend got up and told a big audience, 'See friends, what happens when citizens get involved in government! You CAN CHANGE the world'!" The officer said, "We found out long ago you can't change human nature by passing a few laws!"

Another story he told us was this: "One time I was a city cop with several blocks to patrol, and while out on my beat, I heard a woman screaming. I was sure she was being killed, so I hurried towards this fine house, walked up on the porch, and through the window I could see that a guy was beating on a woman. It was a terrible scene, so I broke the door down, charged in, and grabbed that fellow, pulling him away from the woman. She got up off the floor and about that time, somebody turned my lights out! SHE had crashed me over the head with a chair and knocked me unconscious! When

I came to, she told me, 'I'll have you know, this is our own little ritual we're going through and we don't need any interference from you!' That's the principle I've operated on ever since: I leave people alone if they are not bothering me!"

The stories went on and on and it was quite an educational time! Morton said one time the Police Department hired a real fine, young, red-blooded American boy, gave him a beat, a few instructions and told him to go to work. The instructions, however, were not complete! Slot machines were illegal then and as this young cop was making his rounds, he went into this one place of business, and here were fellows running these "one-arm bandits"! He hurriedly went over to a phone and was going to call the Chief. The owner asked him, "What are you doing?" The young cop said, "You know this is illegal!" The fellow said, "Hey, knock it off! I'm paid up!" The cop went ahead with the phone call and said, "Send out a squad car. I have a guy here operating slot machines!" The Chief said to the young cop, "When the squad car gets there, will you please get in the car and come to the office at once!" So, the young cop went in to headquarters and the Chief asked, "Don't you know how this system operates?" The kid said, "No, I don't!" So the Police Chief began to enlighten him and the young officer was flabberghasted! He said, "If that's the way you run this Police Department, I don't want anything to do with you!" Morton said the young cop didn't last the day out! It was amazing the things those fellows told us. Guess human nature hasn't changed all that much, has it!

GLEANING GREAT GUNS

Ron and I went into Salem one day to the Star Exchange, which was owned and operated by a man named Volchock. I had a 32 Winchester Special Carbine with a brand new barrel and it kicked something terrible. At this time, these guns were very popular, and yet, Mr. Volchock tried to tell me I couldn't buy shells for this 32 Special, plus he told us a whole bunch of nonsense! Ron and I promptly left there and went to the Parker Sporting Good's Store. The gentleman there had two, long-barreled, twenty-six inch Octagon Barrel 30/30's. He readily traded with me and Ron also bought one, so we took them home. Then I cut the magazines back so that each held six shots, instead of eleven. They both shot just superbly and were terrific guns!

Shortly after this, Frank, Ron and I went hunting again, and way down the Gorge Canyon, I killed a big, four-point buck. Frank came over a ways and called out, "Is it a big one?" I answered, "Yes," and he asked, "Are you going to pack it up?" I said, "No," so he came down to me, sat down and began to roll a cigarette. He looked at my buck and said, "Why, you little devil, why did you kill such a big one? You have to pack him out!" He sat there awhile and suddenly he said, "Aw, h—, you can pack him! Here, I'll help you up!" So he did, and by alternating his cussin' and then encouraging me, he conned me into packing that buck by myself up that terribly steep hill! Once we got on top, he then took his turn helping pack. He told us that one time one of his friends killed a buck close to the size I had just killed, and that he and Kink Porter were the only two fellows who could pack it. That, of course, made me feel real good! What a con artist!

FIGHTING FOR FUN

I had a contract to fall and buck timber up Gooseneck on what was known as the Olmstead Place. We had three buckers, while Frank and I were doing the falling. In the evenings, at home, I would file saws. One day Lou Kramer came up where Frank and I were falling a forked tree. We were two springboards high and just a sawing like blue blazes, when Kramer said, "You boys watch out for dat Kramer, he's a mean old cuss! Jack Dempsey ain't so dumb, he stays on the other side of this island 'cause he knows if he comes over here, Kramer will beat the h— out of him!" Frank said, "Hold her!" He stepped straight off that springboard, about an eight or nine foot drop, and nearly landed right on Kramer's shoulders! He said, "Here's one man that ain't afraid of you, and I'll fight you right here for nothin'!" Kramer took one look at Frank and said, "I ain't had anybody talk like that to me for a long time! How would you like some whiskey and some money?" Frank said, "Sure, I'll drink your d— whiskey and take your money, too!" So at 10:00 o'clock in the morning, away they went in Kramer's new Chevy sedan. Kramer managed to hit a stump with his new car, but he could still drive it, so he just kept going, and into Sheridan they went! It was payday and I owed the buckers, plus my wages were due as well! Frank had only cut with me for four or five days, so I didn't owe him very much. I didn't know exactly what to do because I was supposed to pay the men, so in the evening, I went into Sheridan and found Frank. He was quite loaded with booze, as well as the company check!

Kramer had given Frank a check for $300, which he had cashed! Then I discovered that the $300 was being tightly clenched in his fist, so I followed him into Mrs. Barker's restaurant. Mrs. Barker didn't serve liquor and Frank said very loudly to her, "Three beers for three steers, set 'em up, d— you!" She said, "Frank, you know I don't sell beer!" Frank then said, "What a h— of a joint - no beer!" Then he walked across the street to Fraker and Neely's Tavern and shouted the same command. The bartender said, "No, Frank, I think you have had enough!" There were two other fellows in there that I knew, as well as a town Marshal, so I asked the Marshal, "Would you please help me get Frank in my car?" He said, "You'd better stay away from him, 'cause somebody's going to get hurt!" I went over to Frank, got hold of his arm, and said, "Frank, come out to my car, somebody wants to talk with you." He said, "Oh h—, yes, but what's your hurry?" I kept at him until he finally went out with me to my car. After I got him in, I took him up to Charlie's cabin. During this time, I was able to get some of the money from him. When I let him out, he told me, "I'll be in the State of Washington by morning, 'cause they're going to get me on the habitual criminal charge!" We knew that he had lots of brushes with the law.

Next morning, to my utter astonishment, here was Frank - lunch bucket, caulk shoes and all, so I said, "Morning, Frank." He seemed rather subdued, but answered, "Morning." We fell one nice, big tree and I saw that Frank was really bothered! He rolled a cigarette and looked very grim. Then I asked him if he had any recollection of what had happened the evening before. He confessed, "No, I don't!" I told him about what I saw and heard him do and say and he seemed amazed! He just couldn't believe how he cussed and swore in front of Mrs. Barker, and that seemed to really bother him! Frank looked at me and said, "Kenny, you know what I'm going to do the next time someone offers me a drink?" I said, "Yes, Frank I know! You're going to reach out and grab a friend by the neck!" He gave me a sour look and said, "The h— of it is, all my friends drink!" I said, "Frank, you need to get new friends!"

TOUGH TIMES

Right about this time, the economy turned really poor, so Tom Otis, his wife, and Guy Coon came out from Portland to reside on their property. Tom told me the property taxes in Portland were just too high and they had no money to pay them, so they came out to Gooseneck. Also, Tom had just had a serious cancer operation and his doctor told him to get out in the country, eat buck meat, and drink goats' milk to try and regain his health. He was really not in good shape at all and work had been hard to get. Even though he wasn't well, he had taken a job painting a tower six hundred feet high! What was really amazing was that in spite of the fact that he was terribly afraid of height, he had taken the job to try and make ends meet! The pay was good and he did whatever he could to make keep the wolves away from the door! They had built a nice dam in Rowell Creek and it was deep enough that one could swim a short distance. Once again, Frank had some of my payroll, so I went over on Saturday afternoon. Here was Frank, Tom's wife, and Charlie, and all of them are really drunk! All of a sudden Frank said, "Let's go swimming," and just like that, Tom's wife shucked her clothes off, and walked out a little ways in the water. Being drunk, Frank made a very lewd remark about what a luscious piece of flesh Tom's wife was! Tom had an .25 automatic pistol, which he held up, and was just ready to shoot Frank! Then, for some reason, he suddenly turned around and came back to where I was. Was I ever relieved! That was TOO close for comfort and I had no intentions of being an eyewitness to a murder! Tom began to talk and told me many things regarding his efforts to rescue his wife, who was Spanish. Her first husband had been a pilot and was killed in the war. After this happened, she took her vows to become a nun, but soon after this, she decided that wasn't for her and wanted out. Tom did get her out, but it was at great risk to himself. It was a very fascinating story!

Across from Charlie's cabin, I had some traps set out for mink and skunk. One morning while checking my traps, I spied a nice big buck! I shot him, dressed him out, propped him up, and went to their cabin. Things were real gloomy there, I can tell you for sure! No money, no nothing! I said, "Tom, I see where a buck's been hanging out across the creek and if you'll come with me, I know we can get him!" He asked, "Are you sure?" I said, "Yes, I'm pretty sure," so away we went! I sneaked up close to where I had propped that buck and then I said, "I see him! I see him," and raised my gun, as if to shoot. Tom looked at me, then at the deer, and began to catch on. He began to smile and asked, "Kenny, did you kill that deer?" I confessed that I had killed it about an hour earlier, so I saddled him up and packed it to their woodshed. Once there, I took the hide off, and cut him right down the middle. When I presented them half that deer, Tom and Guy were so moved and thankful that tears came to their eyes! That Christmas they gave us a gift, which we still have! There was one Remington steak knife, a village blacksmith cleaver, a large steel (to sharpen knives), and a straight edge razor. Tom was one of the nicest fellows you could ever meet, but not too long after this, he died.

When Wilbert was a little fellow, he loved to walk over to Charlie's place. I needed to go over to see Charlie about something and Wilbert went with me. We were out some distance from his cabin when little Wilbert needed to drain his plumbing system, so he walked back about ten feet behind me, turned his back and proceeded to relieve himself. Charlie was standing outside his cabin and he just started to cuss and carry on! I couldn't make out what was wrong! Wilbert finished and walked up closer and then Charlie asked, "Do you know what happened to me the other day?" Even before I could respond, he continued, "Russell Johnson's little boy peed on my knee and it ran down on my shoe, and Russell just laughed!" Charlie didn't think it was funny, nor did I think so either! Never had I told Wilbert that what he did was proper in any circumstance.

SON NUMBER TWO

Our family was increasing with the arrival of another son, whom we chose to name Russell. He joined us October 24, 1936, so Frances now had two little boys to occupy her time. Since she did not have an automatic washer and dryer and all the modern conveniences young mothers have today, she was kept plenty busy!

One day when work was just not to be found, I decided to cut wood and deliver it. I had a little Ford truck to haul it on, so went to work! I put a big face (undercut) in a large tree and a neighbor, Johnnie Johnson, helped me fall it. In return, I helped him fall a tree. When we fell this tree, it went into a deep canyon. No problem! I went down there, cut it into 16-inch lengths, merely carried it up the steep bank and placed it on the truck! Wilbert was just a little shaver and I had bought him a pair of gum boots which had a red band around the tops. Those boots were his pride and joy! He spent much time tucking his pant legs inside so the red tops were showing. I asked him why he did this, and he said, "So people can see the red tops!" That's pretty good thinking when something is that important to a little boy! Anyway, that little kid helped me carry wood and worked like a beaver!

That wood was beautiful and I sold seventeen cords! There was no pitch or rot, and I always made sure it was honest measure, delivered for $3 a cord! The Buell store owner, Joseph Supry, said he would buy three cord from me if I would take it out in trade, which I said I'd be glad to do. Joe was a great fellow, and as I delivered the last cord, he said, "Kenny, I'm sure you folks could use some cash! You now have $1.54 coming, and I will just give you this cash!" I said, "We surely could use some cash, Joe, but that wasn't the original deal. If you want to do that, however, I'd be very grateful!"

He went to the cash register, cranked her up, and out came the drawer with the money. He gave me the $1.54 and to Wilbert he gave a nice sack of hard candy. Eureka! What a transaction! Wilbert was really impressed!

As I milked our cows the next morning, Wilbert was on deck as usual, and he said, "Daddy, I'm gonna buy Mom a new dress and you some new overalls, and I'm gonna get me some shoes." I said, "Hold it, Sonny, where are you going to get the money?" He said, "Down at Joe's - that's where the money is!"

PULLING POLITICAL RANK

Since employment was hard to get during this time, I continued to cut wood, and look for opportunities to do whatever I could to earn income. The wood cutting was going well, and I took good care of my truck, greasing and servicing it so that it was ready to go. When I went down the road one day, there was a sign at the highway which said, "NOTICE: This road is closed to hauling of all wood products, lumber, logs, poles, piling, shakes, wood: all forest products!" This called for some action, so I put on my old "tin pants" and an old "tin coat" which looked pretty grim! My younger brother, Ron, agreed to go with me, so we went over to the court house in Dallas. Once there, I didn't waste any time in finding where the county judge's office was, and we went in! The judge was sitting there chewing on about six bits' worth of plug tobacco, and as if for our entertainment, hit the spittoon a crack and said, "Good morning, boys, what can I do for you?" "There's a sign up there at the Gooseneck Road that says I can't haul wood. I wanted to haul wood to earn some money," I told him. He asked, "Do you read English?" I said, "Some!" "What does the sign say?" he asked. "The sign says I can't haul wood!" "That's right," he said, "so what's your question?" "My question is, where do I go around here to get on welfare, the Red Cross, or something? I'm willing and able to work and now I can't work," I explained. After my comment, he became very exasperated and said, "Oh, I don't know! Sit down, sit down," and he motioned us to some chairs, "the Commissioners will be here in a minute!"

Not even five minutes had gone by, when here came three Commissioners. They nodded to us, went over and took their respective chairs and the Judge said, "These boys came in here and said they want to haul wood down the Gooseneck Road. What'd you think?" One of them shook his head quite vigorously and asked, "What kind of wood do you have?" I said, "Sixteen inch, Old Growth fir." "What kind of drag saw do you have?" I said, "Seven-foot, Royal Chinook, bucking saw!" He laughed and commented, "Nobody cuts wood with a bucking saw!" "Well," I said, "I do!" "Why?" he asked. "Because I don't have money to buy a drag saw," I explained. Another one spoke up and said, "Well, Judge, everybody up Gooseneck is on welfare, except for two families. I move that we let him haul wood, under certain restrictions!" The third one nodded his head, they looked at me and asked, "Do you promise you won't haul wood when it rains?" I replied, "I don't have to promise you that! I couldn't begin to haul wood out of that place if it's raining! It has to be a dry land show!" "Well, all right, then," they said, "we'll give you a permit, but don't you dare tell a soul!" They promptly issued me a permit and told me to come in at the first of the year and they'd renew it. I said, "Well, thanks, fellows! If I hadn't paid up those back taxes, I wouldn't be in this jam!" One of the Commissioners said, "Great Scott! You mean to tell me you're a taxpayer, Kid?" I said, "Yes, I am!" "Oh, well, go to 'er!" Ron and I left: Mission Accomplished!

Back in Gooseneck, Ed Schultz came up to my place and asked, "Are you going to haul wood?" I had already loaded the truck up and it was parked there. I said to him, "I'll tell you what, if you promise to ride on top of that load of wood, I'll go down the road at 8:00 o'clock in the morning!" He agreed. That night it froze and was cold, but that old boy sat up there on top of the load and down the road we go! The Commissioners and Judge had asked me not to advertise the fact I had a permit, so I never told him I had a permit. When I came back for the second trip, a fellow came running out to stop me! He was very angry and said some very unkind words to me. I said, "Well, why don't you go do something about it!" He said, "Don't worry! I'm on my way!" He was about halfway back to his house and started screaming, "Stop! Stop!" Again he began running towards me and said, "I didn't get your license number!" "Oh, well, go ahead! I ought to run over you, but I won't," I admonished! He had to get down, wipe the mud off the license plate, and finally I went on my way, while he went to fulfill his calling!

Later on, I learned what happened and it's very funny! That fellow went over to the court house in Dallas and was going to swear out a warrant for me. He had just started to try and do business when they said, "Oh, you have to go up to see the District Attorney." So he had to walk out, go across the street, and up the stairs to that office. The Sheriff phoned up the DA's office and said, "When this fellow gets there to your office, send him back to the County Clerk!" They ran him back and forth between several offices and just gave him the royal run-around! When he left the courthouse, he was the maddest fellow they'd ever seen! They didn't want to tell him what happened and that's how they got rid of him! That little chapter added immensely to my insight as to how the "system" works and it was very amusing! A couple years later, the fellow became very friendly to me and we got along just fine! Just goes to show you that life isn't always easy and it pays to get on the inside track!

K-JUNCTION LOG CAMP

In the dead of winter, 1936, with a heavy snowfall, Deb Glass and myself got a job falling timber up above Black Rock for the Willamette Valley Lumber Company. The man catcher for Willamette Valley was Jack Hayes. By way of explanation, a man catcher was sort of like an unemployment office of today. The various business people would let him know if they needed workers for certain tasks and anyone looking for work could contact this person to see what was available. Jack Hayes later became County Judge for Polk County. Deb and I knew nothing of the conflict that was going on and were issued a "pass," to get to this job. We were put on a speeder - no railing around it -just a flat top and completely open, and they pulled a little trailer-like contraption behind it. Most of the supplies going out to that camp consisted of beer and a little mail. The kid who ran that conveyance was half drunk, so he opened her up and let her go! The extreme height of the trestle at one place was one hundred thirty-five feet and this goofy contraption would lurch from side to side, and blame near leave the tracks on the level. You talk about a nightmare, well, Friend, you couldn't beat that! They had big steam shays and locomotives and pulled thousands of cars of logs down that awful railroad! We had been told that when we got up to camp, we should find Dan Valley, the Bullbuck. Dan was a very colorful man; ex-wrestler, bar room brawler, faller, saw filer, and additionally, he had no scruples, to say the least! We walked into his office and I spoke to him, saying, "We were sent up to fall timber." He curtly said, "Is that right?" I said, "That's right!" "Who hired you?" he asked. "Jack Hayes did," I answered. "Does Jack Hayes hire my cutters?" he asked and I said, "It looks like it!" He laughed rather sarcastically and said, "It sure does!"

Dan said we should pick out some tools, so we got springboards, falling handles for the saw, axes, and then went to our bunk house. When we got up very early the next morning, we discovered the snow was three feet deep on the level, with much higher drifts. We ate breakfast, and just before the locomotive whistle blew, a scaler rushed up and said, "Dan changed his mind! You boys go bucking today!" I just couldn't figure it out, so I asked, "Well, where are the bucking tools?" He said, "D——, if I know! Just grab an axe and a saw!" "Where's the saw handle," I wanted to know. Again, he didn't have a clue - same response! Out we went to the flat railroad car and climbed on, along with about fifty men; cutters, rigging crew, and all!

We went out on the Central line and there the ground was straight up and down! The scaler said, "Follow that trail to the bottom and then work up on that ridge. The two buckers that had been cutting up there said they left the saw handles on the stumps." Now how were we supposed to find them out there? Here was a fresh snowfall, quite deep, and that meant those handles were now under that snow, so we had no choice but to begin our search for saw handles out there in the woods! Deb found his after looking about an hour, but I continued looking. Over an acre of ground I searched, cleaning off every stump, and at last, found the saw handle! To my chagrin, "my" saw was a beat up thing! It had three teeth knocked out, was kinked and wouldn't cut! If anyone on the crew would have bitched about how his saw cut, he would have been fired immediately! The reason for this was that generally, in the big camps, the filer and the Bullbuck worked as a team.

That night, after supper, our education began in earnest! Here was the most motley group of men you could ever have assembled! Right next to my bunk was a powerful looking fellow who had muscles like Dolly Parton. Next morning when he got up, I noticed he could hardly walk. So I commented, "I notice you have some problems, how did you get crippled up?" He said, "Yes, I am crippled," and with that comment, he sat down, pulled up a trouser leg and pointing to his leg, asked, "Do you see that?" I said, "Yes, what happened?" "Did you ever hear of Pancho Villa?" he asked. "Yes, I have," I said. "Well, I thought I wanted some excitement, so I hired out as a mercenary fighter for him and I got machine gunned in both knees," he said. "I used to be a high-powered, rigging man, but after being at Pancho, I now work as a bucker." His name was Victor Lame, and he was lame! How that man ever got up and down those steep slopes, I could never understand. It took one and a half hours to get down to the ridge where we were bucking, and another hour and a half to get back up to the railroad for the long, cold ride back to the camp. If one was late getting there? Forget it! You only had to walk back to camp!

There were fellows there from all over the USA. One afternoon I turned an old grindstone the entire afternoon for a fellow named Gene Ahern, who was from Vermont. There was a little Finlander bucker, Little Benny, who sat next to me at the supper table. I got a really big bang out of Little Benny, for he had the greatest ceremonial breakfast of anyone I ever knew! His ritual began with a big bowl of rolled oats. They had butter in cubes on the table, as margarine was not yet born! He would dig a hole in the rolled oats, insert one fourth cube of butter, cover it up, and then he'd sprinkle sugar on, at least one-half inch thick, all over it. Next, he'd take a can of condensed milk in his hand and as the butter began to melt, he started eating. He never spilled a drop - but just poured on the milk, and ate his cereal. Now this was just for starters! Following that ceremonial conquering of the rolled oats, he'd then generally eat four to six eggs, plus a huge stack of hot cakes, just swimming in syrup! That little fellow could certainly put away the grub!

We soon found out there was real unrest in that camp! Dan Valley was hiring fellows "off the board", as they used to say. In Portland you could pay the labor agency $50, or the stated amount, and then you had a job - or so you thought! Dan Valley got half the hiring fee, so he started to discharge cutters. In January and February, he went through one hundred twenty-five men, so I was told. Now we understood what made Dan so mad when we were sent up by Jack Hayes! The Logging Superintendent for this crew was Johnny Livingstone. Sure enough, on the fourth day, the scaler said, "Dan is laying off all the cutters on this side!" There was an old bucker named Bud Daugherty, who wanted to buck after Deb and I, as he had done so for some time and he certainly didn't want to be laid off.

All the fellows were just getting fed up with Dan, so Tom Scott, a faller had agreed to fight him! The fight was scheduled for a certain date and all the cutters agreed to help Tom, as he knew he was no match for Dan. Each bunk house had a variety of axes, some long handles, some short; mostly clubs of axes. However, at close range, they could prove to be formidable! Bud witnessed the fight shortly after we left and told me all about it. Dan was by the car, which the fellows were just about to board. Words were exchanged, and Dan made a dive for Tom Scott, but he didn't reckon with Tom's helpers! He barely escaped with his life and began running down a trail which led to Falls City. Dan left behind his caulk shoes, filing tools, and all personal items, and never went back because he loved life, booze, and lewd wimmin!

Guess what! In 1941 when I was working at Sweet Home, running the cutting crew, I heard that Dan Valley was filing saws for Archie Hessman. Archie had a big, side logging show about four miles away. I decided to pay Dan a visit, so I drove the crummy up one afternoon and walked into his filing house. I said, "Hello, Dan. Do you remember me?" He said, "No, I don't!" "Well, let me refresh your memory, I'll tell you who I am! I am one of those unlucky fellows you canned up at K-Junction Camp in February of 1936," I told him. "Oh," he said, and laughed. "Well, they was a comin' and a goin' so fast, I never did get to know them!" The Bullbuck there at

Archie's camp was a fellow named Henry Dick and I was acquainted with him. Henry and his partner fell timber at Murphy's camp one time when Deb and I fell there. I learned that not long after my visit to Dan, a bucker named Jack McClean took his saw into the filing house and told Dan he couldn't get it to cut through the bark. Dan said, "Why, you griping so and so, I'll choke you to death!" Jack was about six feet tall, but rather slender, and Dan seized Jack by the throat and held him. Jack was almost dead when Henry Dick burst in on the scene! He promptly made Dan release Jack and gave Dan his walking papers! Jack came down to see me and I gave him a job. He was a fine bucker and had bucked for years out of Carlton, for Joe Flora Camp.

The reason Deb and I were so mad at Dan Valley was that this was the only time in our lives we were ever "canned," if you call it that! A man's life at that K-Junction Camp wasn't worth six bits! Two days after we rode that "speeder" down to Dallas, they put an empty box car ahead of the Locy and some fellows were riding in it when she jumped the track and at least two men lost their lives. Tough luck? Maybe we weren't so unlucky, after all, not being there!

HOBOS AT HEPPNER

In 1938, Bill Harris told me he had a promise of a thirteen year logging job above Heppner, which is in Eastern Oregon. Reportedly, there was years worth of work cutting big, Yellow Pine peeler timber, so quite a few of us went there to work for Bill. There was John Breeden, Roy Hubbard, Fred Rhodes, Bill's nephews, Tom and Jay Davies, my brother, Ron, and myself. It was below the Arbuckle Ranger Station, which was about 6,800 feet elevation and twenty-one miles southeast of Heppner. Bill wanted to raise, or had to raise, a skyline or, as the loggers called it, a "Crotch-line" to load logs on the railroad siding. He got an old hay baler, which we buried to use for a tail hold, as there were no stumps down there. One morning about 8:00 o'clock, Bill had not fully decided just where he wanted that hay baler buried and we walked up and down the railroad track several times trying to find a good spot. Along the railroad tracks, we came upon three hobos preparing to boil water in a tin can so they could make some coffee. We didn't bother them, but when we passed them for the third time, this one fellow said, "Just a minute, Pardner, and you can use our can!" The hobos were a tough looking bunch! Bill stopped, looked at them, and then at us, and asked very loudly, "Do I look THAT tough?" Roy Hubbard said, "Yes, darn near!" Bill said, "Well, I'll go to the barber shop and get a haircut and shave!" He left, went downtown and waited until 9:00 o'clock when the shop opened. In the meantime, we waited until Bill came back. He came back all right, but he was mad all day over Roy's comment!

I fell three miles of right-of-way with Fred Rhodes and then we started falling the big, pine peelers. One day an old cowboy rancher named Percy Hughes, rode up on his saddle horse and watched Fred and myself fall a big pine which leaned off center very badly. I put an undercut past the heart, started the back cut good and high, cornered her sharp, and away she went! Percy said he had never seen a double-bitted axe before. He said, "Boys, that looks like hard work. I think I'll just raise cattle!" Bill was also watching us and admitted that he was afraid I would "barber chair" the tree. That was not a problem for me as I knew how to handle that!

What a summer we fellows spent together - first out of Heppner, then on the Little Fork of the North Fork on the Santiam River, closer to the Oregon Coast, not far from Lyons. John Breeden's first wife had left him and he told me he believed that had he remained in the Willamina area, which was his home, he would have gone nuts! In spite of primitive living conditions and a lot of hard work, we did manage to have some good times and being together with all of us kept John's mind off the terrible dilemma he found himself in. Throughout the years, John remained a good friend to me and my family.

DOUBLE THE PLEASURE,

DOUBLE THE FUN

On November 1, 1938, Frances gave birth to twin sons, Myron and Byron - handsome little fellows, they were! Our little clan now boasted four little boys! Their arrival created quite a lot of excitement and since they were identical, hardly anyone (including me), could tell them apart. Frances had three younger sisters and they took great delight in visiting and helping care for the babies, as did my sister, Millie.

Just west of Sheridan, I had worked at a mill for about five months one time and got to know the Timekeeper, Ray Powers. At one point in working for Bill Harris, the entire crew, Deb and I included, worked ninety days without a drop of money! The more I thought about it, the madder I became! The logs were going to the F.S. York's Lumber Company Mill and I had worked there at one time, so I told Deb, "The next time Bill comes around, I'm going to jump him for my money, or I'm going to quit!" Deb said, "Don't do that! Bill will get madder than the devil!" I told Deb, "I don't care how mad he gets, I'm mad too." The next day, here he comes and normally would say, "Morning, fellows." So he did this and I replied, "Morning, Bill." I continued, "Bill, you know I'm married and I have a family. I need some money and need it now!" He began to cuss and scream and said, "If you don't trust me, I'll write you a requisition (which was an order to pay)." "Bill," I said, "It isn't a matter of trust, it's a matter of money!" So he wrote me a requisition, and with that in hand, I went down to the mill to see Ray Powers. He gave me a cordial greeting and I handed him this paper. "How much money do you want," Ray asked. I said, "All that is due Deb and I." "I see no problem," he said, and gave me a check for the entire amount owed both of us. Then he asked, "What's the matter with Bill? He hasn't been here for over three months to pick up his checks!" I never could figure that one out and was glad I had asked for what was due us!!

SNOWBALL DOES SOME SNOWING!

Bill had some real characters working for him, but one that stands out, and who was in a class by himself, was Walter Schuerch, who was nicknamed, "Snowball". In the early days, state compensation was not mandatory and many agents would come around to sell insurance, which usually wasn't worth the paper the policy was written on! One day an agent came out to the woods during lunch hour and asked if any were interested. The agent spoke to Snowball and asked, "How about you?" Snowball replied, "Sure!" The agent gets out his official form and begins to fill it out, asking Snowball all the questions; except one. As he was handing the form to Snowball for his signature, he added, "By the way, you wouldn't happen to have syphilis, would you?" Walt said, "I sure do!" The agent got very angry! "Why, you dumb fool! Why didn't you tell me that in the first place?" Walt said, "Why you dumb fool, you didn't ASK me that in the first place!"

Instead of just telling these agents, "No", Walt always had to have some fun. Another time, an agent approached Snowball while he was working on a springboard, getting ready to fall a tree with his brother, Elmon. The agent is all dressed up and polished! He says, "Hi, Fellows, how ya doin?" "Good," was their reply. "Any chance either of you is interested in a good insurance policy?" Walt looked down at him from his lofty perch and asked, "Do you have any idea who you are talking to?" The agent said, "No." Walt said, "That's just what I thought! What company do you represent?" The agent told him and Walt started in again, "Do you know why I am out here falling timber?" The agent replied, "Well, I suppose you're trying to earn a living!" "Now that's just what I thought you would say! Let me enlighten you! I have enough money to buy your company out and pay cash! I am only out here to regain my health," Snowball stated and he was really "on a roll"! That Walt could talk so real and believable that he soon had this agent convinced that what he said was true. This was just one of the ways he had fun.

A friend of mine operated a tire shop and at one time, Snowball worked for him and my friend told me this story: He did not know Walt at all, and one morning he began to laugh, and he could really laugh! After listening to him, my friend asked him what was so funny. He said, "Oh, my Old Lady! Last night I got to tickling her and I had a lot of fun!" The next day Walt again relayed stories of tormenting his wife, saying he tickled her until she fell on the floor and started to cry, but he just kept on! He could go into great detail about his teasing and my friend told me that as he listened to him, he was just getting downright mad! He was SO mad, he was thinking of firing him, even though Walt was a good worker. Then my friend said he found out Snowball didn't even have a wife! He had a wonderful sense of humor and life was never dull working around him!

Bill Harris told me that one evening he went to the Schuerch residence, knocked on the door, and Walt opened it. Bill asked, "Is your brother, Elmon, here?" "No he isn't, what do you want to know? I know everything that Elmon does," Snowball declared. Bill said that made him really mad as he didn't know them very well, but he didn't like to talk to Walt. Finally, Bill said, "Well, I want you fellows to hire a couple extra cutters so I can put out more logs on that side of the mountain." Walt said, "That's sure funny! Elmon just made the remark before he left that he alone could cut more logs in a week than you could log in a month!" Bill told me, "I was so mad that I could have shot him and felt good about it!" When Bill learned to know Snowball, he said he felt ashamed of how mad he had gotten at him.

One time Bill was going to hire a new bucker, so he asked this fellow, "Are you an experienced cutter?" "Oh, yes, I am," he assured Bill and was given the job. Come noon time, a group of cutters were eating lunch and Bill drives up. As he walked up to the group, this new cutter asked, "By the way, Mr. Harris, I forgot to ask you, do you undercut them first or last?" That question opened Pandora's Box, pronto!

Bob Patty was one of the fellows working for Bill Harris, and as I'll illustrate later on, he and his family became a very important part of my life, as well as my family's. Bob and I fell about three miles of right of way up on the North fork of the Santiam River. Another fellow, Russell Dorn, worked with us and he used to prime the stumps prior to loading them with the major charge to lift them out. He would prime them while Bob and I were sawing on the back kerf, or falling the tree. They would make a terribly loud bang and it was very hard on the ear drums.

There was a very bad hill down the road a little ways off and Bill decided to build a road around this point. There were a good number of trees to cut, some green and then a patch of tall, "beetle-kill" trees. The ground was straight off a big bluff in places and we had to springboard around the trees to put in the undercut. One day we fell a big, green tree and just in front was a large rock, perhaps thirty feet high. As that tree left the stump, it went right over this rock and everything just worked perfectly. It was about five hundred feet to the bottom of that bluff and with the tremendous force of the fall, what happened next was simply spectacular! This tall, green fir CHANGED ENDS while in the air and lit with the butt down! There was so much force from the fall that the tree stood upright for a short while and then fell clear across Santiam River. I told Bill the Game Commission would sue him as the salmon would bruise their backs and hinder their journey upstream to spawn.

The next tree we fell was quite a different story! It was a beetle-kill fir, as well, and about four feet on the stump. As she left the stump, about seventy feet of it snapped back and came right back across the stump on which Bob and I both were still standing. There we were on our springboards, holding our saw. This top was about twenty inches across and she crashed right across this stump. The amazing thing is that not one limb hit either one of us, but you talk about a close call! Please, don't get any closer! If we had attempted to leave our springboards, the chances are, one or both of us, would have been killed. In the evening we went to this little spot where a bunch of us were "batching", while Bob went on to where his wife, Rosena, was. He told her about our close call, so she came over to our camp that evening and told me that her husband wasn't falling any timber with me or anybody else, and they were leaving. So I said, "Well, I will leave, too." It really was too much for me to be gone from home and Frances had all those little boys to patrol, so the next morning we told Bill of our plans. He carried on and was quite unhappy about us leaving, but quit we did!

When Bill Harris took this job, he was elated as he thought he had a long-term, logging job. Originally, he told us he would build a camp, cook house and facilities, so in the meantime, we just camped "elk hunter style", along a little creek. I would go home for the weekends and then commute out to work on Monday mornings. Each time I returned on Monday morning, I would bring extra food back to camp. The company Bill was logging for was Hallein Lumber Company and the three Principals were: Byron Wolfe, Henry Holland and Hugo Hallein. One evening my brother, Ron made a sign on a nice piece of planed lumber and posted it in a conspicuous place on the bridge, right by our place of abode. He wrote in nice, big lettering, "Lank Gut Creek." In very small letters it said, "Closed To All Angling."

Bill was scheduled to meet with the three company officials and here they came. The company fellows were just ahead of Bill when he turned and saw Ron's sign on the bridge. He stopped and said real loudly, "Darn that bum with the blue chalk! It was a black day in history when he was born!" All of a sudden, he calls out to Roy Hubbard, "Say, Roy, how's your grub holding out?" Roy said, rather quietly to us, "Your sign worked, Ron!" To Bill, Roy said, "Grub? We would have starved to death if Kenny hadn't brought grub with him!" So after the company men left, Bill went to Salem and brought back a big load of groceries. He had five pounds of butter, hotcake flour, syrup, and other miscellaneous items. For conveniences, we had an old orange crate in which to stash our goods and all this was right in the open air, next to this little creek. In two days, there was about three pounds of butter still unused, and since we had no refrigeration, it had become rancid. Bill stopped, saw the butter in the sun and he cursed us, saying we were the most wasteful s.o.b.'s he'd ever seen. Poor rascal, he didn't realize that sometimes you just have to shape up!

FIRE ON THE MOUNTAIN

THE TILLAMOOK FIRE

It was getting close to fall of 1938, and we began to smell smoke, and soon word circulated that the Tillamook region towards the Oregon coast, up the Nestucca River and the Trask Company, was on fire. Officials put out a call for firefighters and I was sent to a camp where Fitzgerald and Holman were logging big timber. This fire covered acres and acres of timber and was so big, there were about seven hundred fifty loggers from the various logging camps now assigned to fight fire. Don Crome, a really nice fellow, was in charge of the crews and he was a no-nonsense sort of a fellow - far too good to work for the government! Five of us were filing saws and my bench was close to Ernie Hill, a filer from Tillamook. The timber ran five to eight feet on the stump and a nine-foot falling saw did not provide enough stroke to fall a big tree, so Don had some twelve-foot falling saws brought in. They were called Pacific Redwood pattern and were Atkins silver steel. I filed some of them, and being brand-new, it took quite a bit of extra work to shape them up properly. They were so long, it took two men to take them out to the woods. One morning Ernie asked me, "How many saws a day do you file, Kid?" I said, "I don't like to do more than three long saws an hour!" (This would be equivalent of about seven, regular length falling saws.) Laughing he said, "H—, I wouldn't get out of bed if I couldn't file forty or forty-five a day!" I said, "Ernie, you've got your reputation made, I'm just working on mine!" There was a very famous filer from Weyerhauser Lumber Company named Benny Matson who was there also. About the second evening, while it was still daylight, some fool said, "Let's have a bucking contest!" "Whoopee," someone yelled! "I get Ernie's saw!" Another one chose Ben's saw, and so on, and my saw was the last one chosen. At last, a fellow said, "I'll run the Kid's saw!"

There was a big windfall right close by and they promptly went at it! There were also some big cedar trees and since I didn't know any of these fellows, I got behind the big cedar trees, as I thought perhaps their magic would come forth! They sawed for about ten minutes, and all of a sudden the other fellows stopped sawing, while the guy who was running my saw, just kept going. He was so far ahead that the others fellows saw it was hopeless for them to try and catch up with him! Then Ben Matson came to me and said, "Say, Boy, are you using the Baker system?" I said, "No, I never heard of the Baker system." Then Ernie came over and said, "Some Rascal has fooled with my raker gauge! My saws cut better than that!" Ben Matson said he knew the longer the raker the thicker the shavings, but I spoke up, "No, that isn't the way it is. The teeth have to penetrate so deep and the raker then lifts out the wood that is marked to the depth of the penetration." Ernie's saw had a very blunt tooth and very little swage on his rakers and on a big log, she was "no go"! The next day, Ernie borrowed my check gauge and was very quiet.

In the Commissary, I noticed a sign which stated wages as $4.00 for Head Faller, $3.80 for Second Faller, and $3.80 for Saw Filer. I made a remark to Ernie as to what I saw, but he said, "Oh, heck, no! Filers always draw top money, I wouldn't stand for that!" "Well, if Mr. Crome comes by, I am going to jump him," I commented. About 10:00 o'clock, here he came, so when he was about forty feet away, I stepped out and greeted him, "Good morning, Mr. Crome." He grinned and said, "Good morning to you!" "Mr. Crome," I said, "we are all up here to get this fire out, but I see that Head Faller gets $4.00 per day. Now I have fell LOTS of big timber and I thought maybe you have an opening for a Head Faller." He said, "No, I haven't an opening. I'll tell you what, though, I have just run all the saws out on the fire line, and your saws are the only ones cutting really good. You see that humped-back fellow over there, (pointing to Ernie)? He couldn't file a shovel! I will be glad to pay you $4.00 per day and only ask that do NOT tell him anything about this! If he wants to talk to me, let him come and talk to me like a man, just like you did!" When I resumed filing, Ernie said, "What did I tell you Kid?" I didn't say much and we just kept filing saws until we were burned out and forced to move to another location.

One evening Don Crome came by and said, "She looks real good tonight (reporting on the fire). We have a road forty feet wide on top of that ridge and right down to mineral earth!" However, that night the wind came up and jumped the fire lines. In some places, it reportedly jumped almost a quarter of mile, so the forty foot road didn't mean much. After we burned out in that area, they took about one hundred of us up on the end of the Flora's Camp log railroad. Here were two big steam donkeys, big Spar tree, heel boom and new track, with logs stacked forty feet high. They were swinging logs up from a big yarder down in a long canyon where the fire had swept through. Here were these once useful, big steam pots (as they were called), with their sleds burned out from beneath them. What a very sad sight to see, for it looked as if six or seven good men could push them over! The Spar tree had about forty feet burned out and was leaning at a goofy angle. The smoke got so bad they made us lay down on the railroad. There was a doctor in the crowd who came along and gave each of us a wet cloth to put over our faces so we could breathe. While down on that railroad, I thought I felt something give, or make a strange noise, and sure enough, I did. In the aftermath, the wind came up and cleared the smoke and here came the Forest Service Department personnel with a new D7 and they were pushing out the new tracks followed by a new, Chevy panel truck. In the truck was a hind quarter of prime beef, and we certainly had a fine feed that night. The fire died down and it began raining. All of us were REALLY TIRED and glad to leave and be able to return to our normal work. This was the second time I fought on this fire. The first time was in 1933, I believe.

After Bob and I left Bill Harris, we soon found a job again down on Salmon River. This time we were falling timber for Erickson's and Schmidt. We hired out to fall timber for $.28 per bushel, or per thousand board feet. We worked the first day with the tools they gave us. The second day, I took my springboards and we each took our own axes. At lunch the second day, a set of fallers, the Harper boys, ate lunch with us. After we were through with lunch, each of us sharpened our axes. I saw Oliver Harper wink at his partner, then he cleared his throat and asked, "Will she shave hair?" Bob said, "Oh sure, I think she will!" He was wearing a Hickory shirt and just rolled up a sleeve, licked down some hair on his forearm, and made a pass with his axe! You should have seen the look on their faces! "What kind of a stone have you got?" they asked. "Oh, it's an old Arkansas Oil Stone," Bob replied, so they wanted to borrow his stone right away. Einar Hill was filing saws at that time and was a good filer, as well as a fine gentleman!

THE FANTASTIC PHILLIPS'

My first introduction to Rollie Phillips and his brother, Ed, was in 1931 and I would see them only occasionally. The more I was around Ed, the more I liked him! A more honest fellow was hard to find and he was great to be around and I worked with him for a total of about sixteen years. He was on my cutting crew for many years when I worked for others, and then when I was logging, he also worked for me. Ed and I were falling timber together on a particular job during the era when prohibition was still in effect. One Friday night he said to me, "Well, Kenny, I have another job and will be working down on the river, so I'll be leaving you." I just couldn't quite figure this out and didn't know what had happened, but thought perhaps it was because of the big balm trees that were being sent down to the John's Furniture Company in Portland, but nevertheless, I was puzzled.

About four months later, I went to see Ed's folks, and when I got there, I quickly found out he was staying there. He looked terrible and said, "Let's walk up the creek," so we walked a ways, then sat down. Ed asked, "Kenny, did you hear what happened?" I said, "No, I didn't, Ed," so he said, "Well, this is my story: I agreed to make some liquor for some businessmen from Corvallis and Eugene and they set up a big distillery in an old hop dryer. They guaranteed me $12 per day, in jail or out of jail! Something went wrong and I was caught with a big batch of liquor, so they took me to Rocky Butte Jail in Portland." (In the meantime, I had heard that Ed made the finest booze that anybody ever made in this country. In fact, one Fire Warden told me Ed's liquor was better than any you could buy from the government!) Ed continued his story and said he was coached and told how to plead when it was time for the hearing. At the trial, the judge asked the plaintiffs for evidence and they had none, so the judge turned him loose! He told me he liked to work in the woods and always looked for a job there, but if he couldn't find one, he'd make moonshine, as he was constantly offered jobs doing that!

Ed had many stories and continued telling me more of them! He said that about once a year, all the bootleggers would get together and bring a sample of their brew. In attendance at this event was the Polk County Sheriff, along with the Sheriff's Father-in-law, who was a great moonshiner! The honorable sheriff always managed to get hopelessly drunk! That always tickled Ed and I'll admit, it's pretty funny! Ed was a great worker and the most scientific bucker I ever saw! He was neat, took good care of the equipment and if he told me something, I could always count on his word! He was a perfect gentleman and I never saw him in any situation in which he wasn't in total command.

Visiting another day at the Phillip's with Ed, I noticed a young fellow and discovered he was staying there. This young man looked like a skeleton and gave the impression he just didn't plan on living too long. Ed told me that his name was Webb and he had been in the Army of Occupation in the Philippines, along with one of Ed's nephews. One night a bunch of thugs jumped Webb and nearly beat him to death. He was then discharged from the Army, but he didn't have family to go live with. Ed's nephew said to Webb, "I'll bet Grandma Phillips could help you out!" So Webb moved to the Phillips' and stayed there until he regained his health. It was the most amazing thing for Mrs. Phillips, being the dear that she was, just loved him and looked after him until he regained his health. The Phillips family had virtually nothing, they were so poor. I know there were several years when not more than $250 passed through their hands, as there was little to no work. They had a garden, and occasionally some buck meat and lived a very frugal life! That made a big impression on me and I thought how wonderful it was that they cared for someone they really didn't know and shared what little they had! That was just the Phillip's family and they were good people to know.

EASTERN OREGON WITH EMMERTS

It was 1935 and I well remember the first time I went hunting in Eastern Oregon! Floyd and Ralph Emmert, my first cousins, asked me to go along with them. Ralph had a little trailer he pulled behind his car, so we all shared in the costs of the groceries, gas, and whatever expenses we incurred. There were a couple other fellows from Molalla, Alex Cuttings and Sid Credell, who also went along. Alex told me that his family fought the last pitch battle in Oregon, with the Nez Perce Indian Tribe, out of Joseph, Oregon. Both Sid and Alex were great, old-time hunters and good companions. We drove into the Murder's Creek Area to a place called the Texe Creek Corrals. This camp had been closed for many years and the country was just alive with deer! Twice we saw bands of deer with over one hundred

1935- Hunting in Eastern Oregon with Floyd & Ralph Emmert, cousins; also Alex Cuttings and Sid Credell. Hunt was in Murder's Creek area and we camped at Texe Creek Corral.

deer! Usually we'd see just spikes and forked-horns with the does and fawns, as the big bucks generally were up higher in the mountains.

There was a big sign up across the road which read, "Belshaw & Eddie Guide Camp - All Hunters Stop Here!" It was Forest Service Land in this area and we knew there was not a fee for hunting, but Floyd felt that we should stop. Bill Eddy came out and said, "You can hunt here, but it'll cost you! I'll take you back and show you a place to hunt." He got in our rig, we drove back a ways, and all of a sudden, a doe came out in the road. Bill called out, "Stop! I'll just drop that piece of meat for you right here, boys. Looks like a good piece of meat to me!" Bill had a 250-3000 Savage rifle and I'm sure he was anxious to use it! Floyd said, "No, no, don't do that! We don't want that deer!" We went on driving and close by, there was another camp where we saw a doe hanging up in a tree and a fellow was cutting meat off of it. Besides knowing we didn't have to pay a fee for hunting, we also knew we did NOT have to pay for a guide, so in order to gracefully extricate ourselves from this delicate situation with Bill, we told him we were going to another area to hunt, which we did! We went East, to an area called Field's Peak. Alex and I were going along the next day and as I looked up on the ridge, here were three big bucks; one was a six-point, and the other two were four-point bucks, just slightly different in size from each other! They were lined up, according to size, and it was a beautiful sight! We shot all three and just then we heard four or five shots off in the distance. Ralph had downed a big buck, so we got the limit of deer right off the bat. We headed for home and had enjoyed a wonderful trip! That trip started something rolling!

Before Floyd, Ralph and I left on that hunting trip, my old Uncle, Jim Mishler, and Dewey Wolfer had been at a family gathering. Upon hearing that I was going hunting with the Emmert boys, they teased and razzed me about going deer hunting. Dewey was married to Uncle's daughter, Florence. Uncle asked, "You know why they call it deer meat?" I said, "No!" "Well, you'll know when you get back," he replied and just laughed and carried on. I didn't know what was going to happen, or what to expect, from his exposition on the subject. We came back and those fellows saw the horns from our bucks, and they WERE impressed! Then Uncle decided HE wanted to go hunting and Dewey begged us to tell them exactly where we had gone. They thought they'd go right over there and kill the first ones that showed up! I asked Uncle Jim, "Did you ever kill a deer?" He said, "Yes. Yes, I killed one, I'm pretty sure I killed one!" "Uncle, what do you mean, pretty sure?" I asked. "Well, we lived out of Lane County one time, by the Long Tom River, and about midnight, I went home one night with the horse and buggy. I had to stop and open the gate and just as I did that, this big buck snorted and jumped. I know if he was half as scared as I was, he died!" That was one of Uncle's stories, and he just laughed and laughed when he told me this!

HORNS AT HERMISTON

Walt Wideman had a 1938 Chevy Car and a trailer, so he, Ron and I planned a trip to Eastern Oregon, out of Ukiah. The three of us were driving to our camp close to 11:30 at night, in extremely cold weather, which was well below zero. The road we were driving on had so many ruts, we were just bouncing along! I was sitting over the battery in Walt's car, and suddenly, I felt it come up! I said, "Oh, oh, fellows, I just felt the battery come up!" Ron said, "Forget it, it ain't gonna happen here!" After traveling only about another hundred yards, everything went dead because that battery came up and tore one cable completely off. There we were, in the middle of the road at 11:30 at night, and it was colder than a step-mother's embrace! What we gonna do? Walt got out to check what tools he had along and found some haywire and a crank. Talk about ingenuity! Ron braided and twisted that haywire around the broken, ground cable wire and attached it to the battery, after which we spun that engine and somehow got that car going!

Just before we got the car going, however, a fellow pulled up behind us, laid on his horn, and then finally got out of his car! Walking towards us, he cursed and screamed, "Get out of the road! What the blankety, blank are you doing blocking my road?" We explained, of course, we weren't purposely blocking HIS road and we were working on our problem! He went back, got in his car, went around us, and away he went! That guy had gone only a short distance when he came to an icy place in the road, his car broke through the ice, and he was stuck! He got out, cut limbs to lay in front of the tires, and was trying to get out! In the meantime, we had gotten Walt's car going and went up to where he was now stopped! I got out and was still quite ups‹ he had treated us, so I said, "Fellow, because you were so rude and c‹… there, it now becomes our time just to pass by on the other side!" We just pulled around him and left him there in the middle of the road!

We finally arrived at our destination, and had to park Walt's car on a steep hillside because we knew that battery had broken along the bottom and all the acid had run out! We were determined that nothing would keep us from hunting. The elk season there allowed us to kill cows and bulls, with the stipulation that horns must be visible on the bulls. Right along the road, we saw that someone had killed a very large elk, and we thought it was awfully big to not have horns! It was, in fact, a bull calf, but no one was claiming it, and there it lay! It was obvious that whoever shot it was afraid to claim him because he didn't have horns! When our hunt was over, we were required to check our animals with the Game Commission near Hermiston, so we found the office, and this Game Warden began questioning us: "How many days did you hunt? How many coyotes did you see? Did you see anything of unusual interest?" I foolishly made a remark about this nice bull I would like to have had. He looked at me and said, "Well, I've got news for you! You're going back up there and get that bull and bring it in here!" I said, "I've got news for you! We're not going back up there and get that bull!" He said, "Oh, yes, you are!" "No, we're not going back up there as we have other problems to attend to and can't possibly go back to pick up that elk," I insisted! He asked, "Why aren't you going back?" "Because I didn't kill that bull elk and I know what you'll do! Even though I didn't kill it and had nothing to do with it, you'll try and arrest me, and I don't have time for all this," I reassured him. Finally, he calmed down and then begged us, "Would you PLEASE go back and bring it in?" We said, "NO!" We had problems with Walt's car, plus that Warden had been rather obnoxious to us and thought he'd coerce us to go bring in that animal! I'm sure others had also reported seeing it, as everyone had to check out!

COMPETE TO BEAT

When Bob Patty was just a young farm boy, he saw an ad saying, "Peter McClarin, World Champion Axe Man from Australia, will be chopping in McMinnville", on such a such a day. Any and all who wanted to compete against him were welcome! Now if there was anything Bob loved, it was competition! The appointed day arrived and here was Peter, who was sponsored by the Plumb Tool Company. Peter beat all competitors who showed up, many of them fallers, as well as Patty. Bob was second highest finalist, however, and Peter told him, "Say, if you knew how to sharpen your axe, you would be a hard man to beat!" Bob was dumbfounded! Peter then showed Bob the secret of how to file and shape an axe in the proper manner, and this is one of the reasons Bob and I were high set at Erickson's in the second month. We fell 1,079,283 board feet of timber in twenty days! I never met any other fallers who knew this secret filing and shaping method. One day a limb came down, hit Bob a glancing blow on the head, and knocked his hat off. Bob picked his hat up just as one of our buckers, Ed Hyman, was moving over to a tree we had just fell. Bob said, "You know, I came real close to getting hurt; I just about got hit on my ear," and as he said that, he took his hat off! Ed looked at Bob and said, "Bob, I didn't know you had such big ears! Are you half Jackass?" Bob said, "Probably so!" Bob might not have been half mule, but he was one of the toughest men there ever was! He never backed down from anything!

There was a huge fellow named Arthur Petersen, who was a bucker there and he was something else! He had been all over the world, was a boatswain on a big ship in the war, could read and speak four languages and was a devout Communist! He subscribed to the paper, "The Pravada, The Voice of Moscow," and he used to talk at lunch-time about his consuming passion; Russia. The Communist paper always had a joke on religion and Peterson would always share them with us. One rainy day, Patty and I had just fell a tree, which was five foot on the stump, and then it was lunch time. I shaved some bark loose, squirted oil on it, lit it, and in no time, we had a fine dinner fire. Other cutters came and joined us and we shared our fire with them, as well. Our Giant Orator gets up on this stump and what an orator he was! He would put one hand behind him, get close to the edge of the stump, and I suppose, in his mind he felt as if he was addressing at least 1,000 people! In a booming voice, with great, dramatic style, he animatedly said, "The viciousness of the Capitalistic System is more apparent everyday!" Just then, off about fifty feet, was Charlie Jensen, one of the owners of the New Grand Ronde Lumber Company, known as the "Swede Mill", and he was making his way towards us. All the principals of the mill were of Scandinavian descent, so the nickname was a result of that fact. Charlie heard every word Art had said and this was just too much for Charlie! He bellowed up at Petersen, "You call me a Capitalist? I AM a Swede, and I own just as many bolts in that mill as any other Swede! I work EVERY day, and you call me a Capitalist?" Petersen paused, looked down at Charlie and said, "Charlie, you is one of them little fellows, what we call a Cockroach Capitalist!" Charlie's anger was promptly kindled, and he WAS fighting mad!

After that incident, Art Scott, who was cutting there, used to call out very loudly, "Watch her, fellows, here comes that Cockroach Capitalist," and Charlie would just go nuts! This was just hilarious! Charlie acted like a Super Bullbuck; came out to visit us nearly every day, would look about, and then scale the logs the steam donkeys were using for wood. One day he was really upset, so he went up to Tony Reed and his partner, Gus Lobst, and asked, "Tony, where are you going to fall that big fir?" "Right over here," Tony replied. Charlie said, "No way! She's gonna break!" "No, she won't," says Tony. They went ahead, fell the tree, and as it fell, she broke, so Charlie later made Erickson discharge them. He then came up to Bob and me, and I wasn't aware of what had just happened, but I did notice that Charlie was really a cussin'! He asked, "Where you gonna fall this big fir?" I had a good lay picked out for the tree and it would have saved her full length. Noting his anger, rather than reply with my explanation, I said, "Charlie, you're an old, Timber Beast, where would you fall 'er, or where do you want me to lay her?" Charlie said, "Put her right up the hill, between those two trees." There was a sharp bluff about twenty feet high and I knew the tree would break short. Rather than argue, I asked, "Is that where you want it?" He said,

"Put 'er there," as he went over a short ways and sat down while we "put her there". It broke at about thirty-six feet and was as fine a peeler as you ever saw! He cried out, "That was a good shot, Kenny!" So he goes down to the office and told Erickson that I was the only faller who could hit his shot!

Not long after this, the bullbuck, Ed Binford, told Ed Hyman to bring his saw and tools to the landing after lunch as they needed another bucker down on the Widow Creek side. During the lunch break, Peterson again lashed out at the capitalistic system, making Hyman REALLY mad! He said, "Shut up, you Communist B——, I can't take it anymore," but Petersen kept right on. All of a sudden, Ed jumped up, grabbed his tools, and started for the landing. Art Scott spoke up and said to Petersen, "See there, you have just run off one of Erickson's best buckers! I am going to get the Union to can YOU!" Now Petersen was a strong union man and upon hearing this, he jumped up and ran after Ed, saying, "Please come back, I apologize! PLEASE come back!" Ed said, "I'll cut your d— head off," and as he said that, he made a pass at Petersen's head, just barely missing him! Then Ed went on walking, and Petersen kept begging Ed to come back. All this time, Ed was cursing Art and calling him names, which are not printable! It was some sight! We all knew Ed was supposed to go in, but the funny part was that Petersen didn't know this, and he was quite upset because of what Art Scott had said to him. This incident could have ended in tragedy, as Ed really tried to cut his head off. Not long after this excitement, things got real nasty!

There was a strong union movement about this time and one morning word came to us that the entire crew was supposed to meet to discuss joining the IWA Local 92. This cutting crew was a big one and we all got together. The talk went this way, and that way; back and forth, for some time. All of a sudden, someone said, "How about Kenny Shenk, can he join the Union?" One asked, "Why not? Then he looked at me and asked, "Is your religion against joining the Union?" They all knew I went to church, but I said, "No, it isn't the church, I was looking for a job when I found this one!" Petersen started to laugh! You cannot imagine what his laugh sounded like, as it was so deep, evil-sounding, and raucous. After laughing, he said, "Oh, that's more of that damnable folklore religion!" All of a sudden, Walt Schmidt, who was one of our buckers, walked up to Petersen and said, "Why you Swede s.o.b., don't you know if it wasn't for some good people, we would all be in hell!" Just like that you could have heard a pin drop and Petersen shut his big mouth!

UP, OVER AND OUT!

Shortly after this, the bullbuck went on a big weekend drunk and as we cut, there were three sets of fallers working right behind us, and instinctively, I knew they were working too close together, and it was not safe. Everett Stout, who was falling with Russell Jones, came over to where Patty and I were just starting to fall a big tree one morning. This huge tree had a big drag off center, so we faced it past the heart. I was two spring boards high, perched right over a fork of Salmon River. Stout said, "Well,

Kenny, I am going to drive a tree that leans backwards, so when I holler, you guys watch out, but you will be all right!" Everett failed to put a good, deep undercut, or face, in and so when the tree he was cutting, hit the tree he was going to knock over, here she came! It was the same size as our tree and it hit right in the limbs of our tree and down the back she came, along with the limbs off our tree and limbs off of Stout's tree. I heard this rushing noise and shouted out, "Oh Bob, she's on top of us!" I swung my springboard to the center of the tree and gripped the bark. Then all went black! A limb struck me, knocked me clear out and into the water, tore my clothes on my left side, broke my jaw and collarbone, and knocked me out! Bob grabbed me by the leg to pull me out of the water, and then I came to.

Just then, Ed Hyman was moving in to buck a tree we had fell. The first thing I remember hearing was, "Don't let Kenny move, but I'm sure he's dead!" All the cutters gathered around and I remember hearing them say, "Let's go home," which they did! I felt rather dazed, but after some time, hobbled to my car and went into Sheridan to see Dr. Murch Russell. Doc's wife had just left him and he was hurtin' a bit, although I still don't think he was hurting quite as much as I was at that moment! He said, "Hello, Kenny. What's your problem?" I said, "I just got struck by a tree!" Doc chewed Beechnut tobacco, and he let drive a good stream of the brown juice, and said, "You know, Kenny, you have been working hard for a long time. You should go home and rest!" He never moved from his easy chair, never examined me, or nothing! He just kept nursing his cud, so I went home.

Bob Patty lived about fifteen miles from us and we didn't have a phone, so I said to Frances the next morning, "I don't know what to do" (about going to work). Finally, I said, "Okay, fix my lunch and I'll go on to work and talk to Bob," so off I went! Upon arrival, there was Bob, caulk shoes, lunch bucket and all, just raring to go! I said, "Bob, I can't move my left arm at all!" He said, "Well, you can surely help me back them up! I'll chop the undercuts!" No workman's compensation here, and right back to work I went!

On the second day back on the job after the accident, I had to chop a springboard hole. I'd always had the ability to chop from both sides, under normal conditions, and Bob just sort of expected me to get right back into high gear, so I didn't feel I had any options. I just had to grin and bear it - mostly it was "bear it", too, for it was painful and I didn't much feel like grinning! My left shoulder would make a popping, or a crunching sound, and did so for a long time. Shortly after my accident, Einar Hill, the saw filer, wanted to take six months off to take out his citizenship papers. He came to see me and said, "I see you and Patty are high set and someone told me you are also a filer." I said, "Yes, I am a filer, but I want to fall timber!" Right after that, Matt Erickson came and asked me to file, so I agreed to do that.

For some reason, Ed Binford didn't like me, and I was well aware of this. One day Ed was in my filing house figuring scale and he said, "I feel sorry for you!" "Why?" I asked. He said, "Art Scott is just raising h— in the woods 'cause your rakers are too long for him. He runs a monkey-motion to his saw." On the next saw I filed for Art, I shortened the rakers a little. Art had never said one word to me and everyone else seemed very pleased with my saws, but shortly after Binford told me this, I noticed Art acted as if he was mad. At that moment, I thought I saw the light! After I filed Art's saw, I stopped a logging truck which was headed out for the woods, and stood on the back of the truck to ride right up to the woods. Once there, I located Art at once and he had just sawed down the middle of a fine log. I said, "Hold 'er, Art, let me put this saw in the kerf!" In she went, and he made a couple strokes, pulled the saw back and asked, "Kenny, who filed that saw?" "Well, I did," I answered. He said, "Can you do it again?" I said, "I sure can, but let me tell you what Binford said!" I then told him what Binford had told me and you better believe, Art sure did cuss! He said, "Wait till I see that two-faced bum! I'll tell him off!" That's exactly what he did, so Binford kept his distance from me for quite some time!

SEEING VENISON IN VINE MAPLE

A really funny thing happened one time when Ron, Frank Aikman, Alex Syron and I were hunting up Mill Creek. All day we hunted one day without having any luck! We decided to "tough it out", spend the night and hunt the next day. Ronnie hiked back over the hill to Gooseneck, got a skillet, pancake flour, eggs, and other supplies from Frances. Then he hiked back up to where we were, making it there before dark! Suddenly, it started to rain, soon followed by lightning and thunder! It just poured down and since we didn't have any shelter, we got soaked! Alex had taken a bad fall and the back side of his trousers was completely gone! An ordinary dinner plate would have been the size needed for a good patch to fix him up! He always wore black, wool underwear and was as hairy as a bear! You couldn't tell where the underwear stopped and the hair started!

The next morning, Frank who was always neat and clean, began making hotcakes for us. He said, "Let's see, what could we put these hotcakes on?" Alex said, "Here," as he grabbed that hotcake, bent over and put it on the back side of his lap, asking, "Does she fit, boys? Sew 'er up!" This big hotcake just barely covered! Then he takes this hotcake, lays it on a log, and as he did this, I noticed Frank scowling profusely. Pretty soon, Frank said, "We've got to get something clean to put the hotcakes on." Alex took off his dirty, old hat, laid it down and said, "Put 'er in there, boys!" Someone came up with a nice piece of bark, which the rain had cleaned spotlessly, for Frank to put them on! Alex couldn't see anything wrong with the first hotcake he plastered on his britches, so he got to eat it! Ronnie and I thought it really was funny the way he plopped that hotcake on his back side! Alex was always "seeing big bucks", but he never killed one! On this trip, he had been out by himself, but reported to us that he watched a big, three-point buck eating on vine maple leaves. He told us, "I said to myself, you just step five feet ahead and I'll get you!" That was the end of his story: the buck never stepped ahead and Frank never shot! Ronnie got quite a charge out of that and I did, too! Ronnie and I would laugh like everything at his stories and Frank would get burned up, but Alex didn't see anything wrong with his stories!

Ron and I did quite a bit of hunting and were up Mill Creek in a steep canyon called Cold Water. We had hunted quite awhile when we came across a couple young lads.

They told us they had shot at a really big, five-point buck, but hadn't been able to find it! It wasn't too long before Ron and I came upon the animal and I finished him off. We gave the boys the horns and half of the deer, and they were really tickled! Ron and I then packed the remainder of the meat up the mountain and over the hill to Gooseneck, which was at least nine miles! I told Ron that I was going to go into Sheridan to see how Frances was doing.

TWINS IN TWOSOME'S

We were expecting again, so Frances had gone into town to stay at her parents' house. Back in those days, many babies were delivered at home, as doctors were happy to make house calls! When I got to my in-law's, here is Doc Barendrecht and his nurse, just ready to leave. He said, "Hello, young man!" I said, "Hello!" Then he said, "I told Frances she wasn't going to have twins, but she insisted she was, so I told her if she did, I would deliver them free!" "That isn't what's bothering me,"

1940 - Two sets of twins; David and Donna in basinette, Myron and Byron in back row.

I told him. "Oh, what's bothering you?" he asked. "I'm just wondering if you're a man of your word," I replied. Doc got real red and was rather at a loss as to how to answer me, but finally he said, "Yes, I'm a man of my word!" As I extended my hand to shake his, I said, "That's the kind of man I like to meet!" Frances had given birth to twins, AGAIN! This time we welcomed a boy, David and a girl, Donna and the date was November 16, 1939! The older boys said they were glad for a sister since they figured she could help do the dishes! Yes, another set of twins! You can imagine the sensation this created, for now we had two sets of twins within a year and sixteen days! Someone contacted the Portland Oregonian, Oregon's leading newspaper and a photographer was sent out to photograph Frances with our two sets of twins. Their photo ended up in the Oregonian!

Now Ron, who was still single, took great delight in teasing me about having all these kids, and his joy knew no bounds! I took so much flack and razzing, that it was just plain obnoxious! Karl Dorsing, a fellow from Sweet Home who had just gotten married to a cousin of mine, also never let a chance go by to ridicule me! Later, when this guy's seventh child arrived, my joy, also, knew no bounds! To really even things up, Ron and his wife, Barb, ended up with a total of nine births in their family. What Frances and I discovered later was that we were living close to Doran's Peak Lookout, which was the high point in the coast range there and the storks had to double up to get over the pass! After we moved up Mill Creek, the storks no longer had to double up and there were no more multiples delivered to our family!

THE HOUSE OF LORDS

Most every family in the community in those days did not have inside plumbing and our place was no exception. We had an outhouse up on the hill a modest distance from the house and it was very faithful. Up in Canada, they are often referred to as, "The House of Lords"! At any rate, every household had them. Irene, one of Frances' younger sisters, came out from town to stay with us and help Frances with all the little ones. She was around fourteen years of age and could attend the country school, which was close by. Being given to having a little fun now and then, I had told Irene that I did a lot of target practice and in fact, had a target tacked up on the side of The House of Lords. I told her that I never knew when the urge to target practice might overtake me. She retorted, "Well, just make sure you never decide to shoot when I am visiting the outhouse!" One night, about 9:00 o'clock, Irene went up to visit "The House" prior to retiring for the night. The moon was full, the stars were out and suddenly, I was seized with the idea, "Why not shoot at the moon!" I took my 30-30 and shot! The moon did not flinch, but kept on shining, but what <u>did</u> happen was something else! You have never heard such screaming and wailing in all your life! Irene was convinced that Ken tried to shoot her, however, nothing could have been further from the truth! Irene gave me a wide berth for some time! She later recovered, nevertheless, and lived a normal and useful life!

RESCUE FROM THE WELL

AND WELLNESS

When Wilbert was about two years old he fell into a well out in yard. The well had been boxed up about two feet high above the ground and had about 2 feet of water in it. On this particular day, Frances thought she heard Wilbert cry and when she went out, she discovered the cry was coming from inside the well. Yes, that's where she found him! She was, of course, unable to call 911, so she pulled him out and tried to help the lad as best she knew how. Then she thought of a neighbor lady who was an RN, so drove over to get some help. The neighbor lady kindly assisted her and told Frances that Wilbert would be all right. Thankfully, Frances heard his cries in time to pull him out, and he was just fine!

After our second set of twins arrived, from time to time, different family members came to stay to help Frances out. Sometimes one of her younger sisters, or my sister, would volunteer, as she had four little ones in diapers, and really had her hands full. One time, my sister, Millie, and first cousin, Blanche, came out to give her a hand. They decided to count how many diapers they washed and reported the total to be sixty-four! That was interesting for them to keep track because Frances said she never had time to count them!

One time Wilbert became very ill with pneumonia, had a high temperature, and became delirious. We had a very strange neighbor who stole things, and he had, in fact, stolen the windows out of our house after we bought it, and then later, brought them back! In his feverish state, Wilbert would cry out, "Daddy, don't let that Schultz man git me!" I would reassure him that Schultz wouldn't get him by saying, "I have hold of your hand, he can't get you!" Pretty soon, he'd say again, "Daddy, don't let Schultz git me!" Frances continuously bathed him, at last his fever broke, and he recovered. We had never said anything in front of Wilbert about this neighbor being strange, but he obviously was a keen observer.

As the kids got a little older, one day when I came home from work, I noticed they were playing on the little hillside behind the barn, and this seemed to be happening on a frequent basis. So I took a hand saw, got a nice, straight mountain maple limb and off of that, I cut little rounds of wood! This made great, little wheels, and presto, the kids saw the light. We nailed these little wheels onto little limbs to make logging trucks, logging cats, and all sorts of vehicles! Then the kids made little roads all over that hillside. When I see all these fancy toys now, my heart goes out for these poor, little Pepsi Cola kids! Even Donna had a truck and all the kids spent hours out there on the hillsides playing. Another favorite and imaginative game they played was "cows". Knowing how Wilbert loved cows as a little boy, he was, of course, the farmer and "rode herd" on all the others, building make-believe stanchions out of branches which he laid on the ground. This kept the children busy and generally very happy. They really got along well, given the fact that there were now six children and they were all quite close in age.

Frances always was very industrious and one day took the kids and our two dogs up the hill on our place. There was on an old logging road where lots of wild blackberries grew. That evening I came home from my work and she was cleaning berries, so I asked, "Where are Wilbert and Russell?" She told me they had gone back up the road to pick some more berries, so as I started up the road to find the boys, Jack, our dog, came along with me. The road made a turn to the left, and just then I heard the boys coming, just talking to one another, like kids often do. I quickly jumped up the bank and into some young jack firs and told my dog to go back and peddle his papers. Jack obediently went back down into the road, and then he saw the boys coming! He joyfully wagged his tail, like any good dog, and ran to meet them. I heard one of the boys greet Jack and they just kept coming on down the road. Just as they were below me in the road, and I was about twenty-five feet from them, Jack started to look up my way. Wilbert said to Russell, "Jack acts like there's something up there." This was my moment! I shook a young fir and roared in my best fashion. One of the boys said, "It's a bear!" There was a big snag right there with a root sticking out quite high, which one of the boys stumbled over, and fell rolling, but he did not stop going! I called out to the boys to stop - that it was me! Later, both of them said they never heard me. As they ran, nearly all the berries they had picked were lost along the way! I always smile when I hear someone ran 100 yards in 10 seconds. That day a new world's record was set, which has never been equaled. What I didn't know until later was, that morning when Frances and the kids were picking berries, they ran into a black, mother bear with her cubs, also picking berries. The two dogs put the bears to flight, but that's why, when Wilbert and Russell heard my roar, they instantly believed it was a bear!

We decided to get some milk goats, which the kids really enjoyed! They milked them and all seemed to be going along real well. We soon had more goats, as they multiplied rapidly. This one Billy goat grew really fast, seemed to be getting quite ornery, and then one day, he butted one of the kids quite hard. I told them that if Billy ever did that again, I'd send him back to Siberia. Shortly after my statement, I came home from work and the news was bad! "Daddy, the Billy goat butted Myron really bad today!" Being a man of my word, I took Billy up in the canyon and sent him on his way to his native land! Just a day or two later, our church had a Thanksgiving service, which we attended and when we came home, the dogs were barking treed. The kids ran up the woods to where the dogs were and came back to the house, very excited! One said, "Daddy, the dogs have a cougar up the tree." Another one said, "No, it's a coyote," but still another one thought it was a bobcat, so I took my 32-20 and went up to have a look. Here was a big bobcat with his gut so full of meat from Billy Goat Gruff, he could hardly stay up that tree! He had just had his last Thanksgiving feast and had dined in style, so I shot him. The bounty which I collected from the county was $10 and also we received a fee from the state, so all in all, we got a good price for that fat cat!

As the kids were growing up, I heard a story which, even though I cannot vouch for its' voracity, it still made me appreciate the fact that we were very fortunate in so many ways. The story goes like this: A family had several kids, but their one little boy had some problems. He didn't want to eat, and never spoke, or even tried to! His parents took him to several doctors, but to no avail, and nothing seemed to help! One day a doctor said, "I don't believe his teeth are properly formed, so I suggest you have them removed and get false teeth for him. Maybe that will help him." So the parents took his advice, as they were very concerned for their son. Now in those days, there did not exist all the specialty services we have nowadays, nor the expertise! If you needed false teeth, Sears Roebuck had them, and they were numbered Plates 1, 2, 3, and 4. They had sets for men and for ladies, same system. This concerned family ordered the set which they thought would prove to be compatible for their little Junior. The idea of a proper fit did not exist, it was the gum line which had to adjust to the plates and that was it!

The new store teeth arrived and in they go! Immediately, the parents saw a tremendous change! The little fellow started to eat everything in sight, he began to grow, and he talked! In fact, he talked a blue streak and they couldn't stop him. Finally, in desperation they took him back to the doctor. After a complete examination, it was determined that he had a set of ladies' teeth in his mouth. Again, here our family lucked out and did not have to deal with such consternation!

STATE PATROL - FRIEND OR FOE?

My brother, Lloyd had a 1936 Chev truck with a canopy over it, designed like a "covered wagon". There were seven of us who used to hunt together a lot! One of our favorite spots was Half Moon Springs in Eastern Oregon and often we had very good luck there! Ron had a big Army tent, 16' X 32' and it weighed three hundred fifty pounds! Talk about heavy! We'd take this along and Ron would "coon" up a tree and "tail hold" the ropes! Once it was up, we'd get a stove going in there and it would get just as warm and cozy as could be, even though it was often very, very cold outside!

On this particular trip, I killed a big, five-point bull with an unusual rack of horns! On one side was the usual five points; on the other, a big spike came up and part of the horn was diverted downward, and had grown around his jawbone! It was such a strange looking sight, but when this bull was much younger, he had obviously been hit by a limb, was in a fight, or something, and it affected the manner in which his horns grew.

When our hunt was complete, each of us had a bull elk to take home! Talk about excitement! Everyone was required to report to a Game Commission Office in Pendleton to have the game tagged (or slugged) before we left the area. All of our sleeping gear, a fifty-five gallon of gas (what was left), our grub boxes, tarps and meat was on the back of the truck. Lloyd drove into Pendleton to the State Police Headquarters and the Sergeant who came out seemed rather upset. He said, "Get out of here, fellows! If the Game Commission wants this meat tagged, let them tag it! Go on home! I just got a report that the Umatilla Indians are on the warpath and I have to go take care of that!" We took his advice and headed out to Pendleton, and as we were going up the Old Rice Ridge Hill, which was about seven miles long, a new challenge arose! Lloyd had a separate clearance switch for the lights on his truck and if there were no other vehicles coming, he would switch the lights off to conserve on the battery! Just as we got to the top of the hill, a State Patrolman sat there, so he flagged Lloyd down. We pulled over, and the cop asked, "What's going on here, anyway?" Lloyd told him about his truck problems and the cop became very sarcastic, asking, "What have you got in here?" "Elk meat," Lloyd replied. "Do you have it tagged," he asked. Lloyd said, "Yes, we have our tags on it!" He said, "That's not what I mean! Is it properly tagged and slugged?" Lloyd said, "No, we tried to get them to do it back in Pendleton, but they wouldn't do it!" "Don't you know you're subject to arrest?" the cop asked, to which Lloyd replied, "No!" Finally the officer said, "Well, I guess I'll tag it!"

The meat was frozen and completely tarped and there was no place to pile the meat in order for him to get down to the bottom piece. Since it was frozen stiff, it was difficult to hold it up for him to get down to the next layer. Lloyd was trying to hold back the brisket piece of this one, big bull elk for the cop to tag it, but it was beginning to slip. This cop, who had been rather curt and unfriendly to us, was down on his hands and knees trying to get a slug on it and Lloyd motioned to us, "Shall I let it go?" We nodded in unison, "Please do!" This piece of meat was slipping out of his hands the entire time the cop was trying to get the slug in and he let go! That piece of meat caught the cop right in the neck and pinned him to the bottom of that truck. We could hardly restrain ourselves from laughing loudly. As soon as he left, we laughed quite vigorously! Without a doubt, we ended his career of tagging meat! Ed Phillips laughed and said, "Any fool with a nickel's worth of brains would have sent us to a Game Commission Office where they had a platform to unload the meat and facilities to tag and slug the meat!"

We continued our journey home and as we got to the top of Cabbage Hill, out of Pendleton, the going became most treacherous! Here the road was a solid sheet of ice! Vehicles were in the ditch, trucks were turned over and the state patrol was telling travelers they would not be allowed to go down the hill. Lloyd said, "We HAVE to go down that hill!" "Beppo," as we used to call him, put his old truck in compound and drove it in the ditch with chains on, clear down to the bottom of the hill and once we were on the flat, everything was fine and we made it on home! What an ordeal, but what a successful and fun trip we had!

BIFOCALS OR TRIFOCALS?

On another trip to Half Moon Springs area, we took a fellow named Rheam Daniels, who was an acquaintance of Ed Phillips. Besides Ed and Rheam, there was Reinold Werth, Bob Patty, Lloyd, Ron and myself. Our group varied from time to time, but this was most of our "usual" gang! Rheam was a neighbor of Ed's in Salem and he worked for Pomeroy and Keene, the largest optical store in Salem, at that time. Rheam was a great fellow and his life-long dream was to kill a bear, although he had never done much hunting at all! We were out in the thicket when I heard four shots in rapid succession and then I heard someone holler, "Hey, Fellows, I need help! Someone come here, I need help!" I was about a thousand feet from Rheam, so I went over and when I found him, he was shaking like a leaf! At once, I saw that he had two, big bear down and talk about excited! He could hardly talk, then blurted out, "Kenny, all my life I wanted to kill a bear! Now here are two!"

Soon the other fellows came through the thicket to find us! This thicket was one of our favorite places to hunt, for usually we had good luck there. As they gathered around, I walked up to Rheam, lifted his glasses off and looked at them. Then I asked him, "Do you just have bifocals?" He said, "Yes! The trouble of it is, three big bear went by and I only got two of them!" I said, "Rheam, here is your problem! If you'd get trifocals, you'd have gotten all three!" He laughed and said, "Well, fellas, I'll buy you all the biggest feed Pendleton can put out, I'll do the dishes, I'll do anything! I've just fulfilled a life-long ambition!"

Lloyd and his wife, Lizzie, and children, Beatrice, Ernie, and Carol had moved out towards the Oregon coast by this time and had a dairy, so he'd always say, "I'll furnish the cheese!" He'd go to the cheese factory and buy a wheel of cheese, which was just barely born! This meant the cheese hadn't aged or anything, and I just didn't care for it in this stage of its' life! On this particular trip, I decided I would take my own supply, and one of my favorites was Limburger. I bought a couple jars of Dutch-made Limburger and a loaf of Bohemian rye bread and put my stash into my pack-sack! The one jar of Limburger, I put clear in the bottom of my sack and the other one near the top, with the loaf of bread. It was noon one day and we came into camp for lunch. Each of us had our jobs to do and mine was running the gas stove and keeping the lanterns filled. Lloyd was the official Cook and he said to me, "We're going to have some coffee and a quick sandwich and then we're going back out to run that Pete Creek Thicket! Ken, get those stoves going," which I did. Then, seeing that he was busy making sandwiches, I said, "Just a minute, Lloyd, I'll make my own sandwich. Esau traded his birthright for a mess of pottage, I'm going to trade mine for a Limburger cheese sandwich!" I got my rye bread and cheese out in front of all the fellows, spread the cheese on about as thick as the slice of bread, and began munching it down. You should have seen the look on Lloyd's face! One glance at his face undoubtedly told me that evil was determined against me!

The next morning we got up and I went outside to get some kindling. Just as I was outside the tent, I heard Lloyd say, "Somebody, quick! Get Ken's Limburger Cheese!" Looking towards the tent, I could see some wrestling over where my sleeping bag was and figured something was going on, but I never said a word. At noon we came to camp for lunch and I saw Lloyd walk out a little distance from camp. At one time, some logging had been done in this area and there were quite a few stumps. As I watched, Lloyd put my jar of Limburger on this one stump and then he announced with a flourish, "Okay, boys, this is it! We're going to have some REALLY fine fun! Everybody start shooting!" I pleaded with them, to not shoot my jar of Limburger, but they ignored my pleas! Soon, somebody hit it and a pile of blue smoke went up from that cheese! I'll admit it was strong, but I couldn't believe that smoke! They were all laughing like crazy as I went out there, scrounged around, and found a little piece of the cheese about the size of a dime, which I hooked on the instep of my shoe!

Inside the tent, Lloyd's spot to sleep was on a cot, right close to the big stove! In other words, he was going "first-class"! He would have none of this sleeping on the ground in a sleeping bag! When no one else was in the tent, I rubbed a little piece of Limburger on the side of his little, iron cot, not more than ten inches from where he laid his dear, little head. That night, everything was all "battened down" and hunkered down for the night when Bob Patty raised up and said, "Good Lord, I can smell that rotten cheese clear in here!" Just then, Lloyd yelled out, "Yes, and I can, too!" I said, "Boys, help yourself! I wasn't bothering anybody, I wasn't any problem, and now this! Help yourself, if you can. If neither one of you can smell it, I'll come over and help you!" Reinold Werth and Ed Phillips started laughing and couldn't stop! Reinold said the next day he was sore from laughing so hard! They promptly tied a title on me and always called me, "The Limburger Kid"! Of course, when Lloyd took the first jar of cheese, he didn't know that I had another one! So I had the last laugh! You know that old saying, "Don't get mad, get even!"

The following year, we went hunting again and stopped in Pendleton to buy groceries at a big Safeway Store, and Reinold went in with me to shop. I looked over the cheese, and then asked the clerk, "Do you have any Dutch-made Limburger Cheese?" He said, "No, I don't. I don't handle that as I had a lot of trouble with that brand." I said, "Well, I've had a lot of trouble with it, too!" Reinold started laughing again and said to the clerk, "You don't know this fellow here, he's had trouble with that cheese like you wouldn't believe!" Anyhow, we had quite a time with the Limburger Cheese on more than one outing!

KILLING THE BULLS AND

SHOOTING THE BREEZE

Camped once again at our favorite spot, it was snowing very hard! It was snowing so much, in fact, that Bob declared the snow flakes were as big as a saddle blanket and of course, we never detracted from Patty's analysis! Truth was, you could hardly see to walk, because of the snow flakes! We had killed three bulls at this point; Bob had gotten one, and Lloyd, and Ron had each killed one. Two fellows came walking up to our camp, dressed in the latest and best hunting garb, carrying fine, scoped rifles! They had tried to tuck their scopes under their arms to shield them from the snowflakes, as scope covers were not available then. We had a fire going on the outside of the tent and had built a little shelter for the elk meat which we had hung up in the trees. By taking the hides and building a little framework, we'd stretch them out and sort of protect our meat. Back then, we used to hide the heads from our elk so the horns wouldn't get stolen. The horns were still under our meat at this point and the guys stopped to greet us, saying, "Hello, fellows!" We said, "Hello," and one of them observed, "You've had some luck, we see. Who killed this bull (and he pointed to the first one)?" I said, "Lloyd did." "What kind of gun you got?" he asked, turning to Lloyd. Lloyd said, "30-30." He exclaimed, "30-30? I'll be darned, I didn't know a 30-30 would kill an elk! Who killed this bull (pointing to the next elk)?" Someone said, "Bob did." "What kind of gun you got?" he again inquired. Bob said, "Oh, a 30-30!" They just shook their heads. Of course, then they asked Ron what kind of gun he had and Ron said, "30-30!" They said, "We never knew a 30-30 could kill an elk!" Just as they started to walk away, I said, "By the way, you see that fellow there (and I pointed to Lloyd)? That's all Lloyd has ever used and he's never missed a shot! He just fires one shot and that's it!" "Is that right?" they wanted to know, and I answered, "Yes." Lloyd got a little red in the face and as they walked out of sight, Lloyd lit into me! He said, "You crazy fool, you!" That was the first bull elk Lloyd had ever killed and it was a beautiful five-pointer!

When Lloyd shot his first elk, I had heard him shoot, and I knew there were some fellows making a drive in the thicket, about a thousand feet from where he was. A Mr. Porter owned a ranch down towards Pilot Rock and he'd bring guys up to this area and turn them loose to hunt. We always called these fellows the "Porter Gang" and they killed a lot of elk, too. They'd go for about five hundred feet and then call out, "Where are you, Jack?" and an answer would come, "Over here!" Then we'd hear two shots from their Colt High Standard 22 Automatic Pistols, and away they'd go. Using this system, they kept track of each other. This bull came out of the brush and Lloyd saw him standing by a tree, so he put a bullet through his neck. Lloyd and Bob dressed it out and then came into camp. We asked Lloyd what he killed and he said, "Oh, a spike!" After lunch, all of us went in Lloyd's truck to drive as close as possible to where his elk was and bring it back to camp. Here was this big bull; yet Lloyd told us the one he killed was a spike! This bull did have a strange set of horns! It looked as if it had huge spikes, and yet they curled downward, but it was a true five-point on each side. The gut pile was already bloating up as it had turned a little warm around noon. Ronnie goes over to this gut pile, reached down and grabbed the end of a gut and yelled at Lloyd, "I'm going to teach you to lie to me, Lloyd! I'm going to wrap this around your neck and choke you to death!" They started through that thicket, with Ron chasing Lloyd, and went at least half a mile, but Ron never could catch Lloyd! Rheam started laughing and laughed until he cried! We all got a big bang out of it! That's the story on Lloyd's first elk!

While out hunting and camping, lots of times different fellows pulled pranks. A friend of mine went hunting with some fellows from Tillamook and one guy who went along and always insisted on doing the cooking, was called Big Bob. He had a big griddle and his mouth was constantly full of Copenhagen. Big Bob would spit on the griddle and if it popped just right, it was time to put the hotcakes on. That was his test! Different cooks have their secrets and methods.

A group of us were at Half Moon Springs again and Lloyd always declared himself to be the Head Chef and liked to do the cooking. He had a tall chef's hat on which the slogan was written: "What'll it be?" On more than one occasion, we wondered what it WAS going to be. On this particular outing, Ron had killed a big, five-point bull, so he took the testicles off him, cleaned and diced them up and stashed them away. Lloyd had gotten a big mulligan stew going on the stove and Ron slipped these "delicacies" in his concoction when he wasn't looking! Ron told everybody in the tent about it, except Lloyd! While we were eating that evening, one of the guys said, "You sure have a good mulligan here, Lloyd. What have you got in it?" Lloyd put his finger over his lips and said, "Shhh! Never ask the cook what he put in the mulligan - never! That's secret!" Of course, everybody laughed and pretty soon Frank Larrew said, "Lloyd, I come from Colorado and in the spring when we'd trim the calves, we used to fry the testicles and always called them 'Rocky Mountain Oysters'. It just seems like I'm tasting Rocky Mountain Oysters." Once again, Lloyd put his fingers against his lips and said, "Shhh! Never ask the cook what's in the stew!" Reinold Werth started laughing, then Ed Phillips, and finally we all laughed until we were sick! Lloyd never did know why we were REALLY laughing!

FEASTING ON THE FATTED COW

On another annual elk hunting pilgrimage to Eastern Oregon, we were up above Starky, right up the Grand Ronde River, and decided to set up camp, just below the Indiana Mines. While we were hoisting Ron's big tent, Bob Patty said he heard a bull bugle and he kept insisting he heard it, so we told him to go look for this bull elk. Right at dusk, Bob came back with the heart and liver, and at once, he prevailed on us, saying we must all go with him and pack it in. We asked, "How far is it? Can you find it in the dark?" "Oh, sure I can," he said. We had a good gas lantern, but Ed Phillips asked, "What's the big hurry, Bob? Why can't we pack it in, come morning?" No way would

Bob let us rest and he prevailed, so out we go. On and on we walked! Nearly always Bob had a good sense of direction, but once in awhile he failed, and this time he failed miserably! Anyway, we finally found the bull and returned to camp about 11:00 o'clock at night - and everyone was bushed!

Our cook, Beppo, and his Chef's gear; "What'll it be?'. We sometimes wondered, too!

About 3:00 o'clock in the morning, Bob gets up, goes outside the tent, and comes back in to wake everybody up. He said, "Fellows, she's a snowin' like you can't believe, and I know where a big herd of elk are right now! They are up on Anthony Butte, feeding on the South hillside." Ed says, "Who the heck cares?" "Well," Bob said, "If we go up there now, as it gets daylight, we can kill some!" I had a cow tag and for some reason, which I never figured out, I asked, "Do you really want to go, Patty?" He says, "Yer dern tootin'!" I said, "You're on!" I got up, dressed, got my rifle and away we went! We walked up a road in the dark for about two and a half miles. Just as streaks of dawn began appearing, we started a very steep climb in a foot of snow! Sure enough, up at the edge of this long glade, was a fringe of timber and a herd of elk just starting to go to their bedding grounds. In this herd, there were, perhaps, forty head of elk! There was a big, black cow, the darkest elk I have ever seen, about one hundred yards ahead. I said out loud, "Watch me bust her, Bob," as I shot her right behind the left shoulder! The bullet went through her lungs and lodged in the right shoulder. She gave a big lunge, hit a tree head on, and then collapsed. Bob came unglued! I had a 99 Model Savage 30/30 and never knew I was "underground". Bob also carried a 30/30 Winchester, and he said, "I'll take care of this elk, you just bring the guns and look out for yourself." He pulled this big cow sideways a bit, and down the hill she went, for at least five hundred feet, then she piled up against a couple of windfalls. Then I helped Bob get her freed and away she went again. Only two times did she hang up, as we yarded that cow in the snow a good half mile. We soon had her right next to this old road, which Lloyd could drive his truck on. As we dressed her out, then headed to camp with the heart and liver, we arrived there just as the rest were getting up and preparing breakfast. Lloyd asked, "You mean you got one?" Bob says, "Yes, Ken got one! It's the poorest and skinniest elk I ever saw! I don't know why Ken shot it!" They lit into me and asked, "You poor fool, couldn't you wait for a better one?" I just let them rave!

After finishing breakfast, we left to go get this "creature" I had killed. Once there, Bob and Ron started skinning her out, but I was being held back as an outcast for exercising such poor judgment! All of a sudden, as Ron started to peel the hide back, he said, "Bob, I thought you said this cow was poor! Look here, her whole carcass is white with fat!" Bob just kinda growled and said, "Well, she looked a little funny!" I'll admit she did, but that was the fattest elk I ever saw. The fat on her hams was one and a half inches thick and that meat was delicious!

Another year a gang of us went hunting and camped at Half Moon Springs. It was the same bunch of fellows, including Frank Larew, a neighbor of Lloyd's. Bob, Ron, Ed Phillips and I made a long drive in a deep canyon one day. The State Game Commission had constructed a seven-strand, barbed wire fence for several miles, and in my humble opinion, this fence should not have been in elk country! As we went along, we jumped a big herd of elk. One was a six-point, bull elk, with massive horns, and as he took off running, he hit this fence head on, like a politician! Immediately, the woods resounded with rifle shots - and plenty of them. The elk were, of course, way ahead of us drivers. We all came walking up, meeting in a clearing, and here are Lloyd and Frank,

What a mass of meat! Pictured left to right: Bob Patty, Ken, Lloyd, Ed Phillips, Ron, and Frank Larrew.

just as excited as June brides! They said, "I know we hit him," and the funny part was that both of them declared they hit him, saying they saw hair and blood.

This took place close to Ron's big tent and our camp, so we hastily grabbed a sandwich and as usual, our Commander-In-Chief took over! Bob said, "Ron, Kenny and I will trail him and finish him off," so the three of us take off! The elk had gotten into some timber and lined out in a rather straight course. We never found where he fell and the blood trail eventually stopped, so we knew he was not wounded. For some reason, we went clear down to the Mt. Emily Lumber Company's railroad track looking for that bull, but finally, Bob says, "Let's go back!" We had been walking steady for two and a half hours. Just before we got back to camp, Bob suddenly said to Ronnie and I, "You fellows keep your mouths shut and let me carry the ball!" I had no idea what Bob had in mind, but soon found out! Out comes Frank and Lloyd, with Lloyd asking, "You find him, Bob?" Bob said, "You bet your life we found him!" Frank said, "I told you I hit him," and Lloyd backed him up on this. Here is what Bob told them: He said, "Just as we came in sight of the railroad track, some section workers came along on a speeder and finished this bull right in front of our eyes. The fellow who shot this bull had a Japanese rifle converted over to shoot a 300 Savage shell, and it was a big, six-point bull." Not once did anyone ask Ron or myself one question; all queries were directed to Bob, and he did a thorough job on them!

About two weeks after we came home from that hunting trip, I was in the Ivie

Hardware Store in Sheridan and Walt Ivie asked, "And how was elk hunting?" I said, "It wasn't too good; could have been better!" Walt always smoked a pipe, and as he listened, he puffed a bit, took his pipe out of his mouth, and said, "Next time take a speeder!" It didn't take me long to figure out Lloyd had been there! They never asked, we never told, sort of like the new Army policy, "Don't ask, don't tell!"

RETREATING, REVERENT REVEREND

Before we moved to Mill Creek, we rented a yarder from Willamina Lumber Company and Ron rigged a nice Spar tree. Bob Patty and Ed Phillips were falling; I was bucking, filing, and helping on the rigging, as needed. On this rainy and foggy morning, there on a sharp knoll, I was bucking a big tree which the fallers had just fell. Bob and Ed put in a big undercut and as the tree had a big lean, I knew it was going to be a short while and it would be down. Before they started the back kerf, Bob said, "Say, Kenny, when I holler, just kinda watch it! You'll be all right, but it will probably hit your tree." I assured him, "I'll watch it! Let her go!" Just after Bob called out to me, and they were now sawing away, here came a Rev. Marcus Lind, in his good, Sunday-go-meetin' clothes, and he wanted to talk to me. From Bob's vantage point, he could faintly see someone close to me, but had no idea who it was. Bob stopped sawing and called out in a loud voice, "Down the hill! Down the hill! If you can hear me, you're too d— close!" Just then, the tree starts to leave the stump and made a great, kinda squeaky noise, and here she came! Marcus cried out, "Oh, what shall we do, what shall we do?" I said, "Fall on your face, man, NOW!" I went down right beside my saw and watched Marcus fall on the other side. The falling tree made a terrific, crashing noise and the earth shook violently! As it went down, it also bumped my tree. You should have heard that Preacher thank God for sparing his life. He was convinced that the Almighty still had work for him to do. I probably should have had my butt kicked for this bit of acting, but it was really funny and may quite possibly have made him more cautious later in life! Without a doubt, Bob could come up with more entertainment than most who are paid to do it!

LET KEN FIX IT!

The rain had been coming down pretty steady at our logging show, which consequently caused a bad mud hole to develop under the Spar tree where the trucks loaded. I told my brother, Ron, "I'll fix that!" Lloyd and Ron were there with me, so Lloyd asked, "How are you going to fix it?" "I'll go down to Burch Gravel Company and get a load of crushed rock and fill it," was my simple explanation. Lloyd quickly informed me, "You can't do that. You don't have a license on your truck." I said, "No problem! It's just a short distance and I can make it!"

Down to Buell I went, put air in the tires and filled my truck with gas, after which I went to Burch Gravel, which was close to the Buell store. I got a big load of gravel, started for home, and just as I started to turn off the main highway to go up Gooseneck

Creek, what should I see, but a State Cop. I waved my most friendly wave at him, and turned up the creek. Here that guy came, pulled right in front of me, and came walking back like he was going to join a lodge or something. His first remark was, "Let me see your driver's license." I said, "I don't have any." He said, "You don't?" I said, "No, when you don't have a license on your vehicle, you don't need a license to drive her!" "Is that right?" he asked. "I didn't know that." I said, "Oh sure, that's the way it is." As we were talking, he was writing things down like crazy and he says, "Fella, how do you get gas to drive this thing?" This was during the war and we had a generous quota of gas for the Yarding Donkey. He said, "I'd like to do some extra 'Tom Catin' around and I can't even get enough gas for that!" "You come up to our landing and I promise you that you'll get all the gas you need," I said and then I told him exactly what I was doing. After I told him, he shook my hand and said, "Nice to have met you. My name is Russell Strawn from Lebanon." Lebanon was his usual territory to patrol, so evidently he was "Tom Catin" then to have been up in our area. What made me sore was, it seemed like every neighbor went by while this was taking place, one of which was Hank Abderhallen. I could see him just laughing himself silly as he S-L-O-W-L-Y passed by, as he seemed to be savoring the moment!

I went on to where we were logging and told Lloyd and Ron about my visit with the State Trooper and of my offer to give gas to the cop! Well, Lloyd really let me have it, screaming and raving! "You just wait, he'll come," Lloyd fumed. I said, "No, Lloyd he won't!" We argued a bit over that one, but in the end, he NEVER CAME! I fixed the mud hole and all was well in the "Far West"!

KIDDING KOLY

In case you haven't figured it out yet I loved to go hunting, as did my brothers. As my sons grew, I taught them to hunt and fish also. An incident which took place in Eastern Oregon on an elk hunt goes like this: Roy Lambert, a neighbor, had a Chevrolet, flat-bed truck and so when elk season came, Roy was in business! He loved to hunt and he loved to help people. Roy went driving around to visit various neighbors and asked, "Would you like to go elk hunting?" The net result was that he got plenty of takers! Those who wanted to go were Koly Kosack, Halsey Rogers, and a number of Roy's kids, and come time for opening day, off they go to an area where Koly had never been before. Once there, Roy said, "Koly, why don't you go down that draw about 1,000 feet because there's a pretty good stand there," so Koly did that. Along towards evening, they heard five shots ring out, so Roy and his group went down to find Koly and upon seeing him, asked, "What did you shoot at?" Koly was so excited he could hardly tell what happened, but this is what he said: "I don't know for sure what the heck it was! It was too big for a deer, but it was as big as an elk and had an enormous rack of horns!" There was a big tree which had an injury on it, with a long, white scar. It was just off in the distance far enough away for good, off-hand shooting. Sure enough, there were five empty shells scattered around in this area. Now things start to get rough! One asked, "Did you hit it, Koly?" He says, "Yer darn right I did!" "Where did you hit it?"

"Well," Koly says, "I got one or two shots in the lungs, I am sure of that." One of the fellows started to look for blood, and even though he looked for quite some time, couldn't find a trace! Matter of fact, he could not find any animal tracks, either, so everybody told Koly that he was dreaming. Here were five cigarette butts and five empty brass, and no meat!

The fellows started back to camp, still razzing Koly. Enter now, Halsey Rogers, who was a past Noble Grand Master in the Art of Deception, as well as in the art of pulling pranks. Halsey asked, "What's going on here?" They said, "Oh, Koly claims he shot at a Monster Animal. He says he doesn't know for sure what it was, as it was too big for a deer, but it didn't look like an elk. Koly is having a nightmare!" Halsey said, "You fellows are nuts! I know Koly better than you fellows do, and if Koly says he shot and wounded this animal, why that's exactly what he did!" "Now," Halsey continued, "I want all you fellows to stay back! Don't anybody dare follow me and I'll soon find out what the score is!" Halsey told me he then went down about 100 yards, got behind a big tree and gave birth to a terrific story! He simply waited until it was dark and being close to camp, he could see that the lantern at the big tent was fired up. A little after dark, he returned to camp with a dramatic entrance, just huffin' and puffin' for all he was worth. They all rushed Halsey and asked, "What did you find?" Halsey said, "I found just what I expected to find! I went about half a mile and here was blood like you never saw. I knew right then and there that Koly had scored and scored big! I only followed the blood trail a little over 100 yards and what a sight I saw! Here were three fellows who had just skinned and already quartered this monster animal and believe it or not, one had an old Stillyard scales and they weighed the meat at 650 pounds. I never saw such a critter in all my life! To tell you the truth, I don't know either if it was an elk or a deer!"

Upon hearing this, Koly went into a rage. He cussed the others out, called them all kinds of terrible names, and said to the guys, "Ya see what I told you, and you thought I was full of bull!" When Roy Lambert brought the trip to a close and came home, Halsey came and told me the whole story. Two days later, here comes Koly's sons, Ed and Jack Kosack, over to our place. Ed asked, "Did you hear about the Old Man's bad luck?" I said, "I don't follow you, what are you talking about?" "Oh," they said, "Dad wounded a monster; Halsey trailed it down and found out what happened. Three fellows were there and just happened to see it fall and never even had to put a finishing shot in it. Halsey said these three fellows were really mean and weren't about to give any of this meat away!" Koly loved to tell this story and he believed it with all his heart!

HARRASSMENT BY HALSEY

Just to show you that, in spite of the fact we were not living in the best part of town, we had people which were capable of making it anywhere! Here is another one of Halsey's pranks: As a young fellow in Minnesota, he said they lived close to an old German fellow, who had a farm which was a sight to behold! His farm was surrounded, with well-maintained, painted fences, a large barn, big Holstein cows, and this farmer could raise wonderful corn! His place was just picturesque, and so charming. Halsey said the cows were loafing in a large barnyard and at dusk each evening, the old fellow always put them inside a corral. This one, big Holstein cow had a huge cow bell around her neck. Well, Halsey and a friend decided to take that bell off of her, which they did, and proceeded to run up and around through the cornfield carrying it. So here they were in this field of corn, running around and since the corn was eight feet tall, they couldn't be seen! The old man hears the bell ringing, and began to investigate! He bailed over the fence and gave chase, stopping every now and then, to call out, "Come, bossy, come bossy!" Then he'd make a run for the bell, which he thought was on this cow. Halsey said he never knew an old man could run so fast and that he blame near caught them! Finally, the old man "lost his religion" and cussed a blue streak! Now what?

One day Halsey and his faithful "Partner in Crime" were going past this inviting farm and the very same cow had just given birth to a big, heifer calf. The county road ran by this old man's farm, with a culvert under the road. Halsey and his friend got this cow bell and hid it in the culvert. What a golden opportunity! When no one was in sight, they got the bell, put it on the calf, and left in a hurry! When the old fellow discovered that bell on the calf, it was almost too much for the old farmer. He told the neighbors how the cow got into the cornfield, that he chased her, she lost her bell; and now here's her calf with the same bell around its' neck! He couldn't believe that the same cow bell which had been on the Mother cow was now on her offspring! Sure beats all, doesn't it!

FILER'S FABLES

Back at Erickson's, Charlie Jensen used to spend time in my filing house, as we had a lot in common. Charlie had also been a big camp filer and gave me a good raker gauge to use. The more I filed and learned, the better my saw filing skills were becoming! Many kept telling me I was getting real good at it and Charlie loved to tell everyone he was the guy who made me a good filer. I made a long saw jointer, which I used to keep my saws jointed, for many years. Charlie said to me one day, "You are a fool, Kenny, for not getting a patent on that! Someone will steal that idea from you!" After much coaxing, I applied for a patent and was granted one. This happened only after much correspondence, waiting, and patience. I contacted the largest firm that made filing tools and sent them a model. They agreed to make the tool and wanted to know what financial arrangement I would accept. We reached an agreement; however, it was just as World War II began and right about then, power chain saws were coming on the market. The tool firm didn't proceed, so I never made any money off my patent.

Charlie Jones was a faller working at Erickson's and his partner was Carl King. One Friday evening Charlie and Carl swamped out around a big fir tree, just before quitting time, and stacked their tools there. Come Monday morning at the logging show there at Erickson and Schmidt's Camp, they discovered that a big windstorm blew this giant fir down and when they found Charlie's saw, it was in three pieces! My brother, Ron, used two of the pieces to make two, fine topping saws, which he used when he topped the big trees to be rigged and used as Spar trees. Out of the broken saw, I got the center section. Charlie always said that saw stayed sharp longer than any saw he ever pulled. I made holes in each end of the saw, put handles on, and my wood cutting problem was solved!

DO AS I SAY - NOT AS I DO

We had purchased the property in Gooseneck from Mrs. James Lee. The abstract to the place had a tax certificate from the Eakin Abstract Company in Dallas, in which it stated: "All taxes are paid up to, and including, 1932. Mrs. Lee pointed out that we would pay all of the 1933 taxes, which we agreed to do. So the fateful day of our tax notice arrived, and I went in shortly thereafter and paid them. About two weeks later, here came a notice from Thomas B. Hooker, Sheriff of Polk County, stating the Personal and Property taxes for the year of 1932 were delinquent! Additionally, it stated that the Sheriff was going to sell the property at Sheriff s sale very soon! There was a huge stump on our place which had been springboarded up one board high, so it was about five or six feet off the ground. I went into Dallas and told the county clerk that no sheriff ever had a better platform from which to conduct a sale than we had on our place up Gooseneck! Little did I know that the Sheriff was a packin' the keys, when he should have been a lookin' through the bars! The county clerk said I'd have to come back in to take care of things. Since I was falling timber down on Salmon River, my Dad agreed to go into the court house for me so I wouldn't have to take time off from work. Over to Dallas he went, and made a deal with Tommy. "I'll tell you what I will do," Tommy told my Dad, "You have Kenny pay the Personal Taxes and I will forgive the Property Taxes." The taxes were paid and Tommy merely put the money in his pocket!

At a Sheriff's Sale conducted later on, Halsey Rogers bought a piece of property across from Ron's place up Gooseneck. Halsey asked the Sheriff, "How do I make the checks out and who gets them?" In answer to his question, Tommy said, "Just make them out to me, Halsey." Halsey did just that, making the checks out to him, but he also did one other thing, which is noteworthy! At the bottom of each check, in small lettering, he wrote, "Payment on Property". Several years later, here comes a notice, "Your property is subject to immediate sale, by order of Sheriff of Polk County." Halsey had kept each canceled check, so he took them and went into Dallas to the court house. He marched right into the Treasurer's office, and asked Louis Plummer, "Just what is going on here?" Mr. Plummer said, "Well, it's quite clear you have not made one payment since your first down payment!" Halsey said, "You get Tommy up here right now!" So here comes Tommy and Halsey told me he never bothered to say, "Hello, go to grass or nothing!" Tommy immediately said, "Please, Halsey, give me a few days, and I will make that up." Halsey said, "I looked Tommy in the face and said, d— you, Tommy, you are foolin' with the wrong man and if you don't do what you say you will, I'll put you in the Pen!" Rest assured, Tommy did make this good, for he perceived that he definitely was foolin' with the wrong man!

Out on our place were a lot of windfalls up on a big hill just behind our house, and they were just the right size for wood for our wood stove. I helped the kids to cut it up and they rolled the wood right up to the road. All we had to do was load it up and take it to the woodshed. I always believed that kids stayed out of trouble if you gave them something to do. Also, since all of them proved to be hard workers in adult life, it surely didn't harm them to learn how to work as children!

One time Koly Kosack took a contract to furnish wood for the Sheridan High School. Koly had two daughters that were in a class by themselves. Their names were Georgia and Alice and they bucked wood into four foot lengths, while their brothers, Ed and Jack, split it. Those two, fine girls worked SO hard! I felt sorry for them, so I filed their saws all summer for them - free. In return, I was the recipient of a crate of wonderful strawberries, which was ample compensation as I wanted to file their saws just to help them out! I wonder how many young girls would know how to buck wood in today's modern world!

There was a little bridge crossing the creek going back to our house and the bridge went out. So I hired Koly to skid some "stringers" down with his horses. After he brought the stringers, I planked it, and soon we had a new bridge! We didn't have a graveled road, however. There was a gravel bar right down at the creek, below the bridge, so I took a shovel and two buckets and began to carry gravel to the road. Talk about manual labor! John Rogers and I were falling timber for Bill Harris at the time, so I would get up early and get down to the gravel bar ahead of the appointed time for work. Each morning my goal was to make fifteen trips with the gravel buckets for that driveway. As the distance increased going up our driveway towards the house, I had to show up ahead of schedule even more to allow for the distance. Little by little, I accomplished my task of spreading gravel on that entire driveway! Life lacked a long ways of being easy!

ILLS AT ERICKSON'S

A fellow named Charlie Hines was boarding with some of the Erickson cutters, and Ed Phillips said to me one day, "Kenny, will you file a saw for Charlie Hines?" I said I would, so Ed brought this saw up. Murphy's had a big camp going close by and Clarence Heiser was their filer. Charlie was bucking for Anderson Brothers and they had Heiser doing their filing. Soon after this, a faller came to the filing house and asked, "Will you file my saw? That bucker is chopping the undercut for me, as he can buck them faster than I can fall them!" I said, "Okay!" Then one day very shortly thereafter, I had a nice, Royal Chinook saw in my bench with the name in big, acid letters, "Anderson Brothers", written on it. Just then I noticed two strangers approaching and as they got near, one greeted me with, "Who the h— authorized you to file that saw?" I said, "I guess nobody did! I haven't gotten any money yet, so I am going to keep some saws, as they are good saws!" He said, "I am Ken Anderson and this is John Link, my Bullbuck and you have raised h— with our crew! They said if you don't file our saws, the cutters are going to quit!" I told him, "Okay, let me talk to Matt." When I saw Matt, I said, "I'll tell you what I'll do. I'll file these saws; you furnish the files, and I will give you half the money I make." Matt drank a fifth of booze a day and this gave him more than enough money for his tonic, so he went for the deal! No problem with him!

Working there at Erickson's, Bob and I got paid twenty-eight cents a thousand falling timber. The buckers got paid twenty-nine cents a thousand for bucking. The second month that Bob and I were high set, we fell a million, seventy-nine thousand, two hundred eighty-three feet! I still have the scale slip with that record and we cut that amount in twenty-eight days! That proves we were making a lot of stumps and some very good ones, at that! People nowadays cannot realize what work was involved. I look at the salaries of some of these government officials who are doing nothing but warming a seat, basically, and with the unions to back them, as long as they can breathe, nobody has the right to "can" them! They've got it made for life as long as the system lasts! I don't begrudge anyone a good salary if they put forth an honest effort and earn it! However, there are so many leeches anymore that the system is being rapidly drained!

In about 1940, the IWA Union started to get real strong and there seemed to be a lot of unrest. When Bob Patty and I started cutting, the camp was AF of L. Earl Harper, a truck driver went into the union office one evening and signed some papers or something, and we were told the camp was now IWA Local 92. The information going around was that Earl was hauling by the hour, as were all the truckers. Then, we also noted that he was only making a couple loads a day. The good, old Grapevine was alive and well, and we found out he'd been stopping at a local service station and "peddling bull" to the owner, Clay James. Soon Matt Erickson heard about Earl's "unofficial broadcast" and canned Earl, although nothing of his actions were known to the crew. The next morning we all report for another days' work, as usual. What a surprise! I was, of course, filing saws steady and my filing house was right in camp. The distance from my filing house to the plank road, was not more than eight feet! Here is a huge pile of planks, all wrapped with cable and spiked down with railroad spikes. Also there is the logging crew, the truckers, mechanics, and cutters. In other words, the whole gang has gathered and they all try to get into my filing house. I built a fire and soon the other fireworks started also! Earl Harper says, "Fellows, I want you to be very careful how you talk and what you say. There's going to be a heck of a lot of cussin' in here, but I don't want you to cuss back!"

Here comes Matt walking into the filing house, heading directly towards Earl. He walked right up to him and said, "Earl Harper, you don't work for me anymore! You get out of here! I want to talk to the rest of the men that still do work for me!" Earl said, "I am acting in my official capacity as President of the IWA Local 92!" Matt got right up in his face and said, "Earl, you know what you are acting like? A little s.o.b. I don't know who you are, IWA! I don't put money in the City Bank and then try to draw money out of the U.S. Bank!" You could have heard a pin drop. All of a sudden, Orin Harper, Earl's brother, was leaning on my big filing bench and he began to laugh, and sort of sneered. Matt walked up to Orin and said real pious like, "Orin, you shouldn't laugh at anyone, that's not nice!" All of a sudden, everybody burst out laughing. Matt had fortified himself with his usual Snake Bite Medicine and you could smell his breath for ten feet! Then Matt walked up to Art Scott, who was on the Grievance Committee for the Cutting Crew, and asked, "Art, what do you want or what do you have to say?" Art says, "Well, Matt, we as buckers would like to get paid for bucking out the breaks and long butts." "Do you buck them out now?" Matt asked, and Art quickly said, "No, we don't." "Do you want pay for something you're not doing? There's a pile of maybe 50,000 feet by the landing that needs to be long butted and so forth, will you fellows buck them out?" Matt questioned. There was silence!

I rode with Art that day and going home in the evening, Art said, "Kenny, I never felt so darn little in all my life!" Here is Matt, two thirds drunk and still in complete control of his faculties, and me asking for something we haven't been doing." Well, it was settled, and the crew went to work; ALL, that is, except for Earl Harper! He started his reign of terror, just like any other union boss. A couple of years later in the union hall, at re-election time, one fellow gets up and said, "I make a motion we get some new blood in this outfit!" A little bucker named Ed Siders, jumped up and he said, "No, no. Keep him, keep him. He gets new clothes, he gets new car, he gets new woman, all in one year! We keep him!" They all decided to do just that, as Siders pointed out, it was cheaper that way! Several of the other officials made it to the Penitentiary, and Harper nearly did. I observed the various union leaders of that era and decided that the best qualifications for a Union Leader were that he should be at least a two-time loser, and would have spent some time in the Pen, for this shows he's been around! Harper later got a yarder from Willamina Lumber Company. Bud Hampton told me that yarder disappeared and Earl never finished paying his woods' crew. Sorry 'bout that fellows! Just goes to show what a Capitalist really can do when he has a chance!

TERMS OF THE TIMBER TEAMS AND

THE REAL SKILL OF THE OLD-TIMERS

People nowadays do not realize what took place back in those days, nor can they comprehend the skill that many of the people possessed. To rig a huge Spar Tree with six, top guylines and six buckle lines, line up a big yarder, plus all the rigging, was just simply a sight to behold! One curse that used to plague many High Riggers was sloppy guylines. In other words, when these big Steam Yarders went into action, they were awesome! When my brother, Ron, worked at Powers Davis Camp out of Sweet Home, a Superintendent there showed him how to put a lock notch on a stump and it kept the lines just perfect, so Ron never had the problem of sloppy guylines. The State of Oregon Safety Man told me that he was going to try and make it a state law that all Spar Trees were rigged in this manner, but he never did. Now they have the steel spars, big diesel yarders, and all the new equipment has completely changed the picture for logging. So if a logging camp had a good High Climber and Hooker, they were in good shape, and the same went for the cutting crew. If the Camp had a good filer, they could hire cutters. Anyone who is not familiar with a cross-cut saw cannot comprehend the

skill involved in filing a saw properly in order to fall a fir which is six-foot on the stump! First off, it has to be in perfect joint; in other words, the teeth have to be all the same length! If a saw ran crooked on the stump, you'd had it! The filer had to work very fast and it was very hard on nerves. Perry Cahill, a salesman for Simonds Saws told me, "Kenny, when I die, I will fill an alcoholic grave! Promise me you will not drink booze." I never did, but at age thirty-five, I had the shakes so badly, I could not hold a newspaper still enough to read. This was just due to nervous tension. Years later, this problem alleviated itself and I got a different bunch of nerves going - trying to figure out just what some company Knot Clipper was going to ask me to do next!

1973 - I am standing on level ground beside this tree which was 12 feet on the stump. Tree was fell on a fork of Rogers Creek and the road we took was up through Falls City, Black Rock and up the Willamette's Main Line road.

In addition to the skill required back then, often the commute was treacherous. One summer we drove forty-nine miles one way to the job site where we were logging. Bear in mind, driving these roads was an experience in itself! They were often narrow, curvy, rugged, and with many corners. Sometimes you'd meet a driver who felt as if he owned the road and didn't care to share it! This particular site was below Valsetz, in an area called "The Valley of the Giants", which boasted Oregon's largest fir trees, at least at that time. One tree measured fourteen FEET on the stump. We cut Willamette Industries' largest known tree, which was twelve feet on the stump. Upon arrival, after this long drive, we set about the task of conquering nature. To be able to winch a cat up a steep bluff and build a road you can skid logs down, is no small feat in itself!

In addition, keeping a crew happy and efficient is a must. Then the Lumber Companies always have their position and because they wear a larger hat than a Contract Logger, you are at their beck and call!

A very colorful fellow, Pete Olsen, lived in my filing house at Erickson's for quite awhile. Pete had a crippled left arm, due to a hunting accident. His job was to have steam up in the two Steam Donkeys, cool them down for the night, keep water in the tanks, and various tasks. When Pete moved into my filing house, I noticed this big fifteen gallon crock at the foot of his bed. He asked, "Kanet (he couldn't say Kenny), are you a drinking man?" I said, "No, not really, Pete." He said, "That's okay, but if you want a bottle of beer, I should tell you the little secret." So Pete's secret goes like this: He says, "The Old Beer is up towards the head of my bed, but I'll let you in on a little secret, there ain't any Old Beer!" Pete simply had too many friends!

Pete was full of stories and another one he told me goes like this: "An old Scots-man had a terrible drinking habit. Late in life he married, and his wife was also a hard drinker! This was simply too much for the old Scotsman, and he didn't want to have to buy so much booze for this woman, so he told her, "I am going to quit!" He did just that, which made his woman very angry, as she simply had to have her grog. She called a doctor to come and upon his arrival, she told him, 'The Old Man comes home every evening at 5:30, and I want you to be here when he comes home, but plan to leave, just as he arrives.' The doctor said he'd go along with the plan, and this started the old Scotsman going. He asked, 'What did the doctor say?' to which she replied, 'The doctor said I must have whiskey, the best whiskey that money can buy and if I won't take it, make me take it!' Every morning as Pete would open his bottle of beer, he would repeat what the old lady said the doctor prescribed. In so many ways, Pete was a fine man, believed in fair play, and I was never uncomfortable around him.

DANGER AND DEATH

One cold winter day in 1941, at Erickson and Schmidt's logging camp, a strong wind was blowing, the ground was frozen, and the rigging crew was tearing up the plank road in order to move to Alder Brook. They built a good, steep plank road up on top, by a fine stand of big timber. Ron had worked as a bucker, then decided he was going to be a Hook Tender and High Climber. So Matt hired Ronnie to do the logging and I to do the cutting. Henry Schmidt was Matt's partner and he was helping, as usual. Now it was hard to find a finer man than Henry, and he went to start a dinner fire at the cat landing, not far from a bunch of diesel drums there. Henry got a fire going, but then decided he wanted to "gee" it up, and he picked up another barrel. Unfortunately, the second barrel he grabbed was one containing gas, which was used to start the D7 motor each day. The barrel blew up - reportedly one hundred feet high, and Henry was a mass of flames! Herman Kramer and the Kongeiser boys were there and tried to roll Henry in the dirt to get the fire out. He had just put on a new suit of black, wool underwear and was wearing the heavy, duck fabric clothes we called, "Tin Pants". When they finally got the flames out, poor Henry was in awful shape! As the fellows took Henry's gloves off his hands, the flesh came off his fingers, clear to the bone! On his one side, he was burned so badly, they could see into his lung cavity. In those days, they had tannic acid as their best remedy for burns. When they got down to the office, Henry somehow could walk, but he was in such pain, he went in to get a gun to shoot himself! The other fellows had hidden the guns, but Henry grabbed a fifth of Matt's whiskey and downed that. The doctor said later that this booze undoubtedly saved his life.

Henry was taken into McMinnville to the hospital, where it was predicted he would not make it. Every morning I would go to the office, which was close to my filing house, and ask if Henry was still with us. I was told that at the hospital, as a nurse made her rounds one evening, she shined a flashlight in Henry's eyes. He spoke up and said, "Don't do that!" The nurse was utterly astonished and ran to the phone to call the doctor at his home to tell him. Upon hearing this, the doctor said, "Good, I believe Henry will make it!" Henry did make it and I went to visit him soon after this episode. When I saw him, I cheerfully remarked, "Well, Henry, you're gonna make it!" He said, "Yes, I will this time, but I won't the next." I said, "Let's hope there won't be a next time!" Little did I know then what was to happen very soon!

After some time, Henry came back to work, and he drove a big KB-12 International truck. He resumed driving truck before the flesh had completely grown back on his fingers. The loaded trucks used to stop in front of my filing house to check everything out, as just beyond my little shack, they had a very steep hill to go down! Henry's brother, Bob, also had a truck and was loaded and stopped right behind Henry's truck. Henry would come in my filing house and ask me to cut his fingers apart, as they would fester and bleed badly. I always did this for him, then dust Bismuth Powder on them, and sometimes put a bandage on his hand for him. On this particular day, Henry said to Bob, "Bob, I am giving you my home in Sherwood, as I won't be needing it anymore." Bob said, "Oh, for gosh sake, Hank, snap out of it! You know I have a good home." Henry said again, "Bob, I just gave you my home!" Down the hill they both went, with Henry in the lead. The next morning the cutters came in, got their sharp saws and here comes Ed Hyman. Ed says, "Okay, fellas, let's get it over with! Somebody's gonna get killed today!" One of the cutters laughed and said, "Ed are you still chasing that woman in Lincoln City?" Ed responded very sharply, "I SAID somebody's gonna get killed today!" That morning I went up with the crew to the woods, and in about an hour, I heard them tie the whistle down on the big steam yarder, so I took off running. I ran across fifteen hundred feet of fell and bucked timber and saw that the fellows were carrying someone on the stretcher. When I got there, I learned it was Henry, and yes, he was dead. In those days, in the woods, they had only cheese blocks instead of stakes, and they were shifting his load of logs. He just pulled in this block, when the top log rolled off, right on top of him, breaking every bone in his body! I was a pall bearer at the funeral, as I was also, when Henry's wife, Helen, preceded him in death. It was a very sad time.

The day after the funeral, A.V. Wanless, who had the loading donkey, and his son Vernon, the operator, came into my filing house. Their responsibility was firing up the donkeys so they had steam up in the mornings for the crews. Pete was still living in my filing house and so when Wanless came in, this is the story he told us: "When I was quite young, we lived in West Virginia, in very humble circumstances. Dad died and my older sister got a job teaching in the local school. She was very happy with her job and helped out financially with our family. She always got up first, fixed the fire for Mother and maybe checked some school papers. (Wanless told us that he was an agnostic and didn't believe in God. He said several times while telling this story, 'If I am lying, may God strike me dead - IF there is a God!') One morning I went downstairs and Mother said, 'You should call your sister to get up, she hasn't come down yet.' During the night I had heard her sobbing, so when Mother told me she hadn't gotten up, I was going to go upstairs and check on her. Just before I went upstairs, there was a knock on the door, and Mother opened it. Here was an old neighbor lady, in tears, saying, 'Grandad went to the back pasture last night to turn on the windmill and he never came back. Something happened to him.' My sister had come downstairs by this time and she cried out, 'Oh, they killed him and threw his body in the well!' Sure enough, that's what they did! I know it's hard to believe, but my sister gave an exact account of what happened, and a description of the two men. Her information enabled the authorities to promptly catch the men. One of the fellows admitted to the crime and is still serving a life sentence for it. As she slept, my sister saw the entire scene, and when she learned this had actually happened, she became very distraught and would not leave her bedroom for some time."

I asked Ed Hyman why he said what he did the morning of Henry's death; that someone was going to die, and he said he would have bet his soul on that fact! He just knew it was going to happen. Also, the day before Henry's death, one of the rigging men was telling how tough he was. He said he once saw a man get hit and cut in two by the haul-back line, but it didn't faze this tough, rigging man one bit! He was loading the logs, or setting tongs on the log that smacked Henry the day of the accident, and when he saw that Henry was dead, he pulled on his hat and started to run. That guy ran out of sight, screaming, "My God, Hank got killed, my God, Hank got killed!" So much for not being fazed at witnessing the death of a co-worker! It was a time for much reflection and soul searching. Not long after this tragic accident, Erickson closed down.

THE KID AND KINKS

Anderson Brothers needed a filer, so I was hired there and was working there when war was declared. Later I also filed for Jim Groat and Sons until he shut down, just prior to our move to Sweet Home. When I went to work for the Anderson Brothers, it seemed that I had it really easy. I had filed so many saws that word was out and I had more than my share of requests for my services. Several funny things happened there which I must relate! There was a high-powered filer, Les Skeels, and he had a brother, Claude, who lived with him. Claude was bucking at Anderson's and one evening took his saw home with him, which I had filed. The outfit Les had been filing for was shut down at the time and the next evening, Claude said to me, "My brother, Les, would like to talk to you." So I stopped in and this is what Les said: "Well, Claude said you got the best saw he ever ran and I'll admit, it looks good! BUT, I told Claude I bet you can't hammer kinked saws like I can." He pronounced all this very proudly, and then, as if it were an afterthought, he asked, "How are you on kinked saws, Kid?" I said, "You're right, that is my weakness!" He swells up like a poisoned pup, and said, "Okay, I'll tell you what I'll do. The next time you get a bad one, I will show you a trick of the Masters!" Believe it or not, less than a week had gone by and a bucker, Ed Siders, had a huge log pull a slab and roll down the hill. Talk about a kinked saw! This was a masterpiece, so I stopped to see this Great Mentor! Les looked at that saw and said, "Why, you stupid b——! Did you ever wonder why they always build filing houses on, or by a steep canyon? It's so you can throw saws like that one away!" He was really mad, and I just went on home, taking the saw with me. There was a good stump close by my filing house, so I laid that saw over it and kept working with it until I put it back in use. So much for my Great Mentor!

One of the bosses stopped by my filing house one morning, and called out, "Hey, Kid, come out here quick! President Roosevelt is about to declare war!" I rushed out to listen to his radio and the first sound I heard was Rosy saying, "Yesterday Japanese forces attacked American installation at Guam," and on and on. Now this logging operation was set up differently than most in those days. The West Coast Orient Company, a huge Japanese Company, owned this timber and were shipping all the logs straight to Japan. Well, while the President was declaring war, the FBI arrested Kato, the elder Japanese fellow who owned West Coast Orient, and put him in the slammer. The other owner was a younger Japanese fellow, American-born and college educated. He went to downtown Portland, where someone beat him half to death. The Government then seized all their assets, froze their bank account and we never received our pay for about ten months. These Japanese fellows used to walk by the filing house, bow to me and smile and I thought it was sort of cute. A.V. Wanless had the logging contract and Vernon, his son, ran the big yarder. That big yarder sure made a real commotion and the timber was just wonderful!

HOME, SWEET HOME!

One of the most pleasant experiences in my life, which added greatly to my "Fond Memories Repertoire" was going to visit Uncle Ben Emmert's, who lived at Sweet Home. Uncle Ben married my Mother's sister, Annie, and they had a big family. Uncle Ben was such a jolly fellow and so very interesting to be around! He did some carpentry, but his real love was steam engines! He loved to be around them and many times worked as a fireman, or Head Engineer in sawmills. When we'd go to visit, he'd always greet me with a chuckle and say, "WWPC Cutchall!" After he said this one day, I asked him the meaning, and this is the story: Back in Indiana where Uncle grew up, prior to coming to Oregon, there was a trial one time and a young man was called to the witness stand. After he was sworn in, the Judge says, "What is your name?" The young fellow replied, with a stern face, "William Wesley Peter Christian"! Evidently this young man thought if he could impress the judge, he'd have a more likely chance of getting a favorable judgment!

When Uncle Ben and Aunt Annie's sons reached adulthood, several of them were in the logging business, as I was. I always enjoyed these first cousins of mine immensely! Near the end of 1941, George asked me to come to Sweet Home to run their cutting crew. Besides George, there was Jess, Floyd, Bert, Ivan, and Ralph, and finer fellows were hard to find! Sweet Home is located down past Lebanon, and about eighty miles from Sheridan. Three of the brothers were involved in this logging company, and the others worked in various occupations. I took Ed Phillips and Barkey Broom with me and we headed out to Sweet Home. We stayed for a short while at a place called, "Dog Patch," and it was rightly named. Later we stayed at the Junction Cafe. I didn't move my family immediately, as some of the kids were in school and we wanted them to finish out the school year, so Frances and the family stayed behind.

The Bullbuck and filer George had in charge, said he injured himself and so the cutters were not working. The first thing Ed and I did was to build a small filing house. George bought new saws and Ed and I fell two big firs, which were five feet on the stump. With those logs, George had a fellow build a nice yarder sled. Never before had I seen such a sloppy job of cutting in my life; split logs which were not trimmed, Russian Couplings, and so on. When the word got around that we were to begin cutting, various fellows began to show up. George had told me who he thought were the chief, sloppy buckers. One day, here came a small lad up to the filing house and he said, "Hello, are you the new cutting boss?" I said, "Yes, that's what George hired me for." He saw I took a vague view of things, or maybe he read my mind, but at any rate, he asked, "Did you hear I was the guy that split all the logs?" I said, "No, I didn't hear that. However, I did hear you split your fair share of them!" He said, "I'll admit I did, but I don't think I was any worse than the rest of them." Earlier George had told me that this lad had split some nice logs. The young fellow then said, "I'll see you later," and he left. He went down to Clark Lumber in Sweet Home and started working for them, setting end hooks. One day he forgot to take his hand away from the hook, and nearly all the fingers on his one hand were severed. After the accident, he started to keep books for the company, and in less than a year, he was the owner! So I always said, "I am the man that made Billy Bauman." He was a fine gentleman and later built a modern complex mill, which is now owned by Willamette Industries. Many years later, I had an embarrassing moment with Billy. I was logging for Willamette Industries and one Saturday I went into Dallas, which was their head office, at that time. When I arrived, here was Billy Bauman talking to Gene Knudson, Aaron Mercer and Jay Johnson. He called out, "Why, hello, Ron. How nice to see you! How have you been?" and all the usual greetings. You see, many years before, Billy had punked whistle for my brother, Ron, on a logging show out of Astoria. Throughout our short conversation, I never had to lie, nor did I tell him I was not Ron, nor that I was that mean Bullbuck, so we parted good friends. I told Jay shortly after they bought Billy's mill that I was the man who made Billy Bauman. Had I given him a job, he very possibly may have continued as a cutter.

George told me that he thought that the previous Bullbuck was a joke, but his brother thought he was a top notch man. I was soon to find out just what the score was! George told me, "Ken, if you want to can him, go ahead!" I said, "No, I'll try to work with him." When the Bullbuck came to work the next day and I shook hands with him, I could see that trouble was in the works. Here is most of his old crew, and only Ed Phillips and Barkey Broom, the new fellows, who had come with me. Right away I told them all, right up front and in plain English, "I am the new Bullbuck and all the logs are marked. All you have to do is buck them ON the mark and don't split them, and we'll get along just fine!" So we went to it! Porter had some die-hard cronies, and without a doubt, he had missed his calling and should have been a preacher, for he had the Gift of Gab! One bucker had a pair of Atkins Bucking saws, which he worshipped. He came to me with his one saw, on which he had filed a notch on one end. On the other end, he had filed two notches. He asked, "Do those notches mean anything to you?" I said, "No, they don't!" "Well, they do to me. You see, this saw has a bad kink in it and Porter (who was also the filer) told me it won't come out. He says when I put the handle on this end, I twist the saw to the left. When I use the other end, I twist it to the right," the fellow explained. I said, "Oh, so that's the way it is!" This bucker went out to buck, so I took his saw, hammered out the kinks, jointed and filed it. The first day he ran this saw, he came in from the woods that evening and actually cried! Furthermore, he asked me to forgive him, 'cause he had taken a dim view of my presence there! I kid you not! He didn't know that I had filed more saws than Porter ever saw! Some of the original crew retired and word soon got around that I had a good saw!

When I first began running the Emmert's cutting crew, close by our operation, there were two, fine fellows also logging up McDowell Creek. They were Elmer Watters and his brother, Everett. Elmer came over one day and he said, "This timber is so hard, the saws won't cut it!" I said, "I didn't know that!" He asked if I would file a saw for them and I said I would. That's what I did and soon discovered, Mistake Number One! Here came another Gypo Logger, Martin Pickens, asking me, "Will you file my saws?" Elmer was overjoyed and told me his cutters were happy now that the timber wasn't so hard. Of course, Porter heard all this conversation, and right away he engaged what little brain he had and he began to plot my demise.

Shortly thereafter, we moved our logging crew up Wiley Creek and so I took the scaling job away from Porter. Now this really made him mad! I gave him a job marking the logs, but he would only mark for a few of his cronies. I now had some of the best cutters from Powers Davis, and this irked Johnny Powers, not just a little bit! One evening, as I was filing saws, he drove into the yard where we lived. He said to me, "Are you the fellow that hired my best cutters away from me?" I told him I needed some cutters and those fellows wanted jobs and it was working out just fine! "Well, how about coming to work for me?" he asked. I said, "No thanks!"

An incident took place one day which was really comical. Two good cutters I hired were Art Menear and Ruben Simonds and although they were somewhat up in years, they were very good cutters. They were both on springboards one day, falling a real big, Old Yellow fir. I was in plain sight on a sharp bench, about thirty feet below them. All of a sudden, Art says real loudly to Rube because he was nearly deaf, "Hold 'er, Ruben, my garter broke!" He started fussing with this sock holder and said, "I guess I'll have to swipe some elastic out of the Old Lady's bloomers tonight!" Rube lifted the saw handle up and down and he says, "Art, it's been so long since I've been at home when my wife went to bed, I'll be darned if I know whether she has any bloomers!" Art suddenly ran up to Rube, grabbed his springboard and shouted, "Ruben, you are one blankety-blank fool! You have as good a woman as God ever made, and here you go down to that d— tavern every night and drink that slop with your friends! One of these days your old body is going to give out and then what?" Rube looked quite chagrined and then said, "Aw, heck, Art, I just drink a LITTLE beer with the boys!" Art said, "No, you don't, Ruben, you're drinkin' way too much!" While we were living at Sweet Home, Ruben gambled away his old '29 Model A Ford. If he couldn't get a ride all the way home to Foster, many times he would stagger along, across the bridge, and way up the hill to where their house was. Close to the little town of Cascadia, Rube was killed some time later, as the car he was riding in ran out of gas and Rube was in the back seat, just dead drunk. As they sat there, another car came along and smashed into the car Rube was in, and he was killed. I never heard a better lecture in my life when Art gave Rube "what for" and everything Art told Rube was true!

Several of the cutters I had working for me continued to nurture trouble! They also continued splitting logs, so I promptly devised a method to cure them! One fellow, Bill Horne, started bucking and I told him to be sure and buck every cut on the marks - don't split them, and we're in clover! The third day he bucked, I went around to look at his work. This was all big timber and here he had not made the top cut in any tree. He bragged profusely about my saw by saying, "That's the best saw I ever ran! She is a dandy, and so forth!" I asked, "Bill, why won't that saw make the top cuts?" He said, "Oh, heck, since the war broke out, they don't take the top cuts!" "Well," I said, "they do here!" "Oh no, I don't think so, he retorted." I asked, "Would you want to go back and make those top cuts, or shall I have my day man make them?" He said, "No, I don't think I would." I just reached down, grabbed his axe and undercutter, and said, "Bring in the rest of your tools! I heard the boss say they made some money last month, so let's go and find out!" I immediately took him to the office, got his money, and he was sent on his way. That night he bellied up to the bar at Bill's Place and told Clarence Myers that was the best job he ever had, and admitted, "That Bullbuck warned me, but I didn't think he would can me!"

HOUK AND HOOKERS

One wintry day, it began to snow and wouldn't stop, so we were forced to quit working. I drove the crummy and as we started home, I'd stop to let the fellows off at their usual places. Afterwards I went to the office to pick up the payroll and found out where some of the fellows lived. This one fallers' name was George Houk, a tall fellow, heavy drinker, and he had somewhat of a short fuse. I drove to where he lived, knocked on the door and soon a nice looking lady opened it. I said, "I'm looking for George Houk." She said, "I'm Mrs. George Houk. Do you have a check for him?" I said, "Yes, I do," and without hesitation she said, "I'll take that check!" The following Monday morning, George came up to me, just fighting mad and he said, "Darn you, I want my check!" I said, "I gave it to your wife!" He said, "Darn you, you didn't give it to me!" "No, George, you weren't home, but I did give it to your wife," I responded. He said, "You get me another check!" So I told the boss about it and asked him to look into the problem. Come to find out, George's wife cashed the check and went to Seattle to her sisters' place where they both worked as hookers. Since George had not put an ad in the paper stating he was not responsible for her debts, the company did not have to reimburse George, so I felt very badly about this.

School got out and Frances and I then moved our family from Gooseneck to Sweet Home, to the Old Harris place. There was no electricity and no running water, but there was a fine spring there on the property. Very early one morning, I heard a knock on the front door and there stood a tall, rather rugged-looking fellow. He said, "Hello, my name is Virgil Menear and I have a good falling partner. Will you give us a job falling timber?" I said, "Yes, I need a good pair," so they came to cut for me. They had been working at the Clear Lake Ranger Station and this is the story Virgil told me: He said one Sunday he and John Bland decided to hike to Lost Lake. Upon reaching the lake, they discovered it was closed to fishing, so they decided to walk to the back side of the lake, which was out of sight from the highway. Here, to their utter astonishment, were a big bunch of Lincoln Continentals and Cadillacs; and quite a group of guys. He said the fellows were friendly, very involved in partying and enjoying quite a bit of booze, and didn't seem to be upset that they were there. Virgil and his partner caught some real nice fish and went back to the Ranger station. That evening, he casually mentioned about the fine fishing they had at Lost Lake. Upon hearing this, the Ranger said, "Why you darn fools, do you know who those fellows were?" Virgil said, "No, we don't know." He said, "That's reserved for the Governor and other high state officials! I bet I'll get canned for this!" "Well, we can fix that, we are quitting right now," Virgil informed him, and quit, they did! They had each just purchased a new pair of Currins caulk shoes and they started walking about 8:00 o'clock in the evening and walked <u>all</u> <u>night</u>, practically all the way to Foster! That was a long distance and there wasn't a sign of a caulk on most parts of the soles of their boots. They were grateful for the job I gave them, and I never regretted hiring them, for they were good cutters!

A couple of Uncle Ben's boys had invited me to go hunting in Eastern Oregon on different occasions, which I did, and truly enjoyed those times. Once when I was visiting with Uncle Ben, we were talking about guns and decided to do a little shooting. He shot a small rifle and I saw that he was a very good shot, yet he never went hunting for big game. Quite late in his life, several of us went antelope hunting and Uncle Ben came along. After hunting a day or two, he made a beautiful shot and got a fine antelope. I went up to Uncle, hugged him warmly, gave him a slap on the back and offered my enthusiastic congratulations! Then I wasn't prepared for what came next and it almost made me cringe! I asked, "How come you haven't been hunting with your boys before?" Uncle Ben got all choked up, started to cry, and said, "Well, I wanted to, but they didn't invite me, and I don't want to push myself on anyone!" I told George what his Dad had said, and you talk about shock! George said, "Well, I declare! I can't believe that we didn't think about asking him to go along!" One thing you can be sure of, none of Uncle Ben's boys were stingy or cheap and they had the warmest relationship with their folks. To my knowledge, they had no pet peeves with their Dad, so how or why that happened, I'll never know, but they had remedied the situation!

Not long after this antelope hunt, Uncle Ben went buck hunting out of Bend and shot a fine, big Mule Deer buck. We have a picture of Uncle with his buck, and he was one proud man! They came over to Sheridan on a Saturday to visit us, went to church on Sunday morning, and that Sunday evening, my beloved Uncle died of a heart attack! They knew his heart wasn't strong, but it came as a real shock to everyone to have him go so suddenly! The Doctor said, however, the excitement of the hunt had nothing to do with his passing!

1942 - Uncle Ben Emmert with buck he shot.

HILL'S SACRED TREES

Now back to logging at Sweet Home! Another interesting thing worthy of note was that Art Menear and Rube Simmonds helped fall, clear, grade, and assemble a short section of railroad. During this process, a picture was taken and Jim Hill took it to Congress in Washington, D.C., telling them that he had a railroad west of Bend, Oregon, heading to the Oregon Coast. They were impressed and the government granted Hill Timber every other section of land, so I was told. Many times when Art was falling a big tree, just as she was leaving the stump, he'd say very loudly, "There goes another one of Hill's Sacred Trees, Ruben!"

Well, what's Porter up to? One evening he went down to see Jess, George's brother, and he took a faller named Clarence Tooley, with him. Roy said to Jess, "Jess, I can't really talk now, I am just a lowly marker, but that young Bullbuck you got is just having a heck of a time and the crew is just fuming!" Jess asked, "What's wrong?" Tooley says, "Well, for one thing, my scale has dropped about 15,000 feet per day." "Well, how come?" Jess asked. Tooley responded, "I don't know." Roy said, "Things are about to explode!" Indeed, they were! I had a big crew going and we were cutting about 250,000 feet per day. Here comes Jess and George out to see me and Jess was terribly upset! He asked, "What's going on up there, Kenny?" I said, "Plenty! You come up in the morning and be sure and have lead in your pencil, because this world is so big, I don't have to work on the same forty with Porter!" I'll bet poor Jess never slept that night!

The next morning I was up on the cutting when here came Jess, and he asked, "Where's Roy?" I said, "Oh, he is down there shooting the bull with one of his friends." Jess asked, "Can you get him to come up?" I went down the hill quite a ways and called to Roy. I said, "Roy, the boss is here and he wants to talk with you." Roy came to where I was, and on the way back up the hill, he started in. "I know there's a lot of dissatisfaction on this crew. All my life I have run big crews, and I have the ability that when a bad spot came up or something difficult, I could shove the crap down their throats and make 'em like it," he bragged. I said, "Roy, I don't have that ability, but let me tell you one thing! I have worked around lots of men of different nationalities, but I have never worked around a fellow as little as you are! Here you are, going around this crew and trying to get someone to bitch about my saws—or something, and I just want you to know that I resent that!" Roy just glared at me, not saying anymore, and by now, we had approached Jess. He was standing by his car and said, "Morning, Roy," and Roy returned the greeting very cheerfully. Jess said, "I am at a loss as to what to do. Clarence Tooley said last night he is short 15,000 feet. What is the answer?" Roy didn't say a word. I said, "I know the answer. I'll go get the new log scaling calipers and an axe and shave the bark off of six trees Roy has scaled and six trees Clarence Gambel has scaled!"

Immediately I went down and got these items. We had a nice amount of timber ahead, so I started to scale the trees. I had Roy's scale and I had Gambel's scale. Porter would tell Tooley to drop a number and he would make a big snag sometimes 10,000 feet, and he would have them number a little tree, cut away with the saw, and then number that. Gambel's scale was very fair, even on logs exposed. He was always over two or three inches, but no invisible snags and cutaways. Suddenly, Jess says, "Roy, you have given thousands of dollars away on us. How could you do this?" This is why Clarence Tooley was short because Gambel didn't give him 15,000 feet per day. Here is Roy's statement and his defense: "Jess, I ran the big office for Coos Bay Timber Company for many years! You plunk my ass in a soft chair and when night comes, my figures will tally, but you run me over the hills doing a two-man job, and my figures will vary!" Jess pipes up and said, "Roy, I got to go to town, please ride in with me!" Away they went! Roy claimed he was a tremendous fighter and he told Jess, "If I ever catch that little blankety-blank in town, I will beat the holy heck out of him!" Fortunately our paths never crossed!

Here is one of Roy's fighting stories: He said below Coos Bay (down South on the Oregon coast), an Indian fellow lived back in the bush, with his wife and some kids. One of these kids was supposed to go to school, but the Indian refused to let him go. The authorities begged and pleaded with him to let the child go to school, but to no avail. Finally, one said, 'Okay, if you don't let your daughter come to school, we are going to send Roy Porter up!' He said this big, mean Indian whom everybody was afraid of, just threw up his hands and said, "No, no, please don't send Porter up - she can go to school!"

One day Porter said, "My Dad always played first violin at the dances while I was growing up. After I was old enough, I played first violin and the Old Man played second." He told us he ran a Coos County Grader for twelve years. Another incident

Roy "impressed" the crew with was that one day as we ate lunch, we were discussing the fact that the company changed their insurance to Lloyds of London. George had asked me to tell my crew of the insurance change and to answer any of their questions. One of the cutters asked, "Who in the dickens is Lloyds of London? I never heard of them before!" Roy piped up and said, "You haven't heard of them? Well, I sold insurance and real estate for them for ten years!" He also told us he was the office manager of a big lumber company in Coos Bay for fifteen years. Denver Davis was working for me as a marker, so on the bulletin board which hung on one end of the filing house, one day he wrote in very bold lettering: "Wanted: Violin Player, Insurance Salesman, Grader Operator, Boxer, Saw Filer......." In fact, he wrote everything up there that Porter had ever bragged about doing. Roy never said one word, and that was still on the filing house when he left. When Jess canned him, he was at least 120 years old!

AULT'S ACHE

Wally Ault was another bucker I hired to buck timber for me. Wally was a big timber man, having worked out of Aberdeen, Washington, and on the coast for many years. He was a husky fellow and a really nice man, but he had a most difficult problem! While he was employed by Shaeffer Brothers cutting timber for them, his wife was due to have their first child. She gave birth right there in the logging camp, and unfortunately, his wife died in childbirth. The baby girl she delivered, survived and was fine. Wally said a couple of other ladies who lived in camp told him not to worry, they'd take care of the baby for him, which they did. Well, Wally moved around several times and the people who were caring for his daughter moved also and after a while, he lost track of her. He told me he had heard that his daughter grew up and had gotten married, but was unsuccessful in tracing her. He went clear up the coast of British Columbia and down into the redwoods area in California, but wasn't able to locate her! At times he would just break down and cry when he talked about trying to find his daughter and it was heart wrenching! My heart really went out to him!

One day Wally said to me, "Kenny, do you know Mrs. White who has the nice restaurant in Sweet Home?" I said, "Well, I don't really know her, but I know who she is." He hesitated a little, and then said, "She asked me to marry her! I told her I didn't want to marry her, but I'll shack up with her! She said, 'Nothin' doin', Big Boy, we're gonna have a Diploma to hang on our bedroom wall'!" Wally then asked me what I thought he ought to do, but I told him, "Wally, I can't answer that for you." Shortly after this, they did get married, were real happy, and I was glad for them.

PUT THAT IN YOUR PIPE AND SMOKE IT!

Going home one evening, I was driving the crummy and most of the men were smoking and talking away. One fellow, however, had a pipe going and it smelled something awful! All of a sudden, Clarence Gambel said, "My Gosh, Tom, does that darn thing ever go out?" This is what Tom Watson replied to Gambel: "She sure did go out; in fact I lost it for two weeks! I got so hungry for a smoke I sat down and went into deep thinking: Where did I last have it? All of a sudden, I had my answer! I went up the hill in back of my house where I had shot an old doe because I remembered I took my pipe out of my mouth, dressed her out, and took her home. I looked over the gut pile, but no, the pipe wasn't there. Then I rolled the guts over, and here was my pipe! I lit her up, even though the bowl was full of maggots and I've been puffin' on her ever since!" One of the fellows said, "I guess that ought to hold you for awhile, Clarence." All the fellows swore it smelled like he _was_ smoking maggots there in that crummy! I could hardly "stomach" the thought of smoking that blame pipe!

SURVIVAL

One day I heard a faller wedging a tree and saying, "Up the hill, up the hill," and then it sounded like someone hit him in the face, so I took off running! I ran right through Wiley Creek up to where he was falling this tree and to where the poor fellow was. His name was George Buckles and he had been injured and obviously had severe head injuries. What a terrible sight I saw and I quickly took him into the Langmack Hospital in Sweet Home. There I helped the nurse take blood and hair out of his head, right close to his brain. He had fractured his skull in three places. A "Widow Maker" had come straight down on his head and driven him right to the ground. He was off work for quite some time and when he came back, he just couldn't hack it. It really finished his career, as far as working in the woods.

Nick Mesqeet was another fellow who worked for the company and was a Blackfoot Indian, who had attended a government Indian school in Montana. He told me some dandy stories! One winter it was particularly cold and he said his comrades just died like flies. The government agent in charge at the school would hang the corpses by the toes and let them freeze stiff. Then in the spring, just as it started to thaw a little, the government workers got a pile driver and because the corpse was straight, they just drove them into the ground and didn't have to dig a grave. Nick was a good faller, but he also had other abilities like you wouldn't believe! He did the marking, or numbered the trees for his partner. If the tree was good size, and I can tell you, most of them were, he would draw a picture in just a flash. He'd draw a picture of Denver Davis, Gambel, or of me, and you didn't have to guess who it was, as he was a fantastic artist! The day Roosevelt declared war, Nick was in a restaurant eating lunch and a fellow said, "All right, you slant-eyed so and so, come outside! I'm going to beat the h— out of you!" Nick soon went outside where he proceeded to beat that fellow to a pulp and said, "Maybe you'll learn what a slant-eyed fellow looks like!"

When we first moved to Wiley Creek, we were cutting Hill timber. The company known at that time as Hill Timber is now known as Barrenger. A fellow drove up to the filing house one day and introduced himself to me. He said, "My name is Gene Ellis and I am to take Thor Helmsman's place since he has died. I need to tell you that I don't know a darn thing about timber. Would you please help me and work with me?" I told him I would help in any way that I could and we got along really well. Time passed swiftly at Sweet Home and I made many friends. I was also able to get in some good fishing and elk hunting in Eastern Oregon.

BIG BIRD IN CHERRY TREE!

Back at home with Frances and her crew, an incident took place one day which I must relate. The Harris place where we lived while at Sweet Home had a great cherry tree just outside the back door. It was a fairly large cherry tree and as the spring months came, it was obvious there should be a good crop of cherries - that is, if the robins didn't get all of them before they were fully ripe! So I had told the kids, "If you see any birds in the cherry tree, you have permission to shoot them with the B-B gun!" On this nice, spring day, Frances suddenly heard the most horrendous screaming coming from one of the boys! She ran outside to investigate and here was Wilbert just howling for all he was worth, and shouting, "Russell shot me, Russell shot me!" Russell stood there with gun in hand saying, "I just THOUGHT there was a big robin in the cherry tree!" He had taken a shot and little did he know, at such a tender age, what a good shot he was! He had, indeed, hit his brother who was up in the cherry tree eating a few of the delicacies! Fortunately, the skin was not penetrated, but it scared all of them rather soundly, including Frances! Later on, of course, it provided a great topic for teasing! I think that in time, Wilbert was able to forgive his brother for "shooting him"!

CHALLENGING THE COPS

One fellow I hired up at Sweet Home was Cyrus Bush and he told me he grew up on the Quinalt Indian Reservation in Washington. He was a good, big timber man, although he was also a real whiskey imbiber. One evening, as usual, the fellows were at Bill's place, quenching their thirst. After awhile, Cy went home, which was the Junction Cafe, not far from Bill's Tavern, and went directly to bed. Cy's partner needed another one or two or three to relieve that burning on his tonsils, so he stayed on. Before the evening was over, Cy's friend was involved in a fight and finally the cops were called. He ran across the street towards his rooming place, all the while, being hotly pursued by the city cop! With the cops right on his tail, he just managed to burst into his room and shut the door right in the cop's face! With this loud commotion, Cy woke up, got out of bed and could hear the cop trying to bash in through the door. Soon the cop burst into the room, but Cy was ready for him. He wrecked a good wooden chair over the cop's head, knocking him unconscious. Cy and his friend then calmly dragged him down the hall, and out into the street. The cop came to, promptly got help and arrested Cy. At the hearing, the judge questioned Cy as to his actions and he simply said, "All my friends knock before entering! I was the one who had rented the room!" In other words, Cy could have had the cop arrested for unlawful entry. Sweet Home was a real rough town in 1942!

One afternoon when we had been snowed out of the woods, Cy came to the trailer house where Barkey Broom, Ed Phillips, Pete Syron and myself were staying, behind the Junction Cafe (before I had moved Frances and the kids up to Sweet Home). Soon here comes Cy with a bottle of corn whiskey. Some of the loggers called that brand, Amiee Semple McPherson, as the bottle just said, 'ASM Corn Whiskey'. Cy said to Barkey, "Have a drink! You are a funny little devil when you're drunk!" Barkey said, "I don't want any. My head don't feel so funny the next day, and we may be able to work tomorrow." "Aw, come on," and so on and on he goes, pleading with Cy, although he never once asked any of the rest of us to share a drink with him. After the proper amount of pressure, Barkey finally tipped her up! He had just bought a new Ford pickup and was SO proud of it. He reached in his pocket, handed me the keys, and said, "Anyplace you want to go is fine with me, 'cause I trust you, Kenny!" Cy leaves shortly and went home, but the rest of us never left the room, and so here we go! At once I started this Phantom Journey. I made a noise like an engine starting, and away we went! I pretended to be driving and called out, "Marcola coming up!" I would then slam on the brakes, make appropriate sounds, and pretty soon called out, "Brownsville," and then, "Albany," and so on! Barkey lay on the bed in a trance-like state and his dog, Brownie, would lick his face to try and rouse him, but he was feeling no pain, until morning. As we were lined up for breakfast the next morning, I said, "By the way, Barkey, here are your keys and thanks a lot!" Barkey said, "You're more than welcome - anytime! I don't know where all we went, but it sure was a great ride!" Of course, we had never left our room, and this was more than Ed Phillips could take! He was right behind me in line, heard every word, and began laughing so hard he could hardly stop. Every time I relate that incident, it seems just as funny as the day it happened!

We were living out of Foster about one mile and a fellow drove into our yard around 6:00 o'clock one evening and, as usual, I was filing saws! He got out of his pickup, lit a cigarette, and asked, "How do I get you to file my saws?" Quickly I responded, "That's the last thing on earth I need is another saw to file!" "You don't know me, do you?" he observed, and I said, "No, I don't!" "Well, I'm an ornery, old Customer and you don't get rid of me talking to me like that! My name is Louie Wodtli and I want you to file my saws," he informed me. I said, "Look, I don't even have a good filing bench, nor lights. Besides, I'm too busy!" He says, "I'll fix that! My Father-in-law is a good carpenter and he will make you a good bench, and I will get some lights for you!" That sounded rather inviting and as if it might not be such a bad deal after all, so the net result was these things did take place! I liked Louie and began to file his saws. At this time I was filing saws for three gypo outfits, plus all the saws for my big cutting crew.

Louie and I quickly became good friends and it was at a time not long before I knew I needed to make a change in my job. When he found out I was quitting to move back to Gooseneck, he said, "Kenny, if you will stay and run my cutting crew, I will split my paycheck in half with you!" It was a temptation, but I declined. I gave the company one months' notice and when the crew found out, it was worse than going to a funeral. One day prior to my leaving, the fallers fell an old seed tree, which was very soft. There was an Indian fellow, Ollie, who had worked for the company for some time. He was very quiet and you never could discern just where you stood with him. Ed Phillips was bucking with Ollie and just happened to draw this really soft tree. That saw loaded up every gullet with shavings so that they could hardly pull it. I happened by just as they were bucking it, so Ollie saw me and said, "Say, Kid I don't have to cut this darn log off with one stroke. Will you shorten the rakers?" I said, "Ollie, my aim is to please!" I already had his other saw in the filing house, filed and ready to go. He told Ed Phillips that he had given me the devil and now his saws were really perfect! I told Ed I never changed anything on Ollie's saws, but his attitude was better because he thought he had told the Bullbuck off! This, of course, tickled me!

SERIOUS SURVEILLANCE

After we had moved the crew up Wiley Creek, the boss asked me, "Do you know where we can get a good watchman?" This was right after a couple fellows stripped the loading boom, blocks, tongs, and shackles. It was not uncommon in those days to have things stolen from the logging operations, so many companies resorted to hiring a watchman to live on the premises and guard the property. I said, "Yes, I do!" Immediately I went to see Rollie Phillips to see if he wanted the job. Rollie did want the job, so they built a cabin close to my filing house for him to live in, and I moved him up! Rollie was Ed's brother and Ed was already working for me, so Rollie and Ed lived together in the cabin. Believe you me, Rollie really took his job seriously! The boss had told Rollie, "We don't want anybody in here at night. If somebody comes in, shoot them!" One night a Game Warden drove in and he told me later, "Here came this old man out, holding his pants up with one hand, and a shot gun in the other hand! He says, 'You get out of here, or I'll plug you'!" The Warden said Rollie had this shot gun and he had the shakes real bad anyway and the Warden was afraid it might go off accidentally. He tried to talk with Rollie, but to no avail! Finally, he said to Rollie, "Look, I AM the Game Warden!" Rollie said, "I don't give a d— who you are! The boss said I am to shoot anyone who comes in here!" The Warden contacted the boss the next day and told him he had visited all the camps up above Sweet Home and said, "Your watchman is the only one who challenged me or even showed up!"

Rollie had a little Cocker Spaniel dog he called Oscar, and he was some dog! No one fooled with him! Oscar always conducted himself like a gentleman, for that's what he was. One evening the cutters were coming in with dull saws and putting their caulk shoes behind my stove, where Oscar lay. He looked as if he were sound asleep. This one goofy cutter was smoking a cigarette, then winked at us to watch him as he bent over and blew a mouthful of smoke in Oscar's ear! Oscar shot up and snapped at this guy's face, narrowly missing his nose. That dog was almost as fast as Lorena Bobbit! I can tell you, it was close! Nobody, but nobody, bothered Oscar from then on!

The logging trucks went right by the filing house, so one day here comes a trucker, all loaded and headed for town. Rollie goes out, flagged him down and asks the trucker, "Will you do me a favor?" "Sure enough," this trucker says, "what do you want?"

Rollie paused a minute and said, "I need some groceries!" "Well, Rollie, just tell me what you need?" Rollie said, "Get me a roll of Copenhagen and a loaf of bread!" This story went all over logging country, and everybody got a laugh out of it!

I had a very good cutting crew at Sweet Home and Eugene Ellis told the company that their crew was far superior to others. Art Menear was a great fellow and a source of fun, as well as being a very good cutter. He had worked for the U.S. Forest Service and had quite extensive experience in many fields. One time he told me of a prank he pulled, which I thought was rather funny. Art was working for the Forest Service and they had packed into this one destination, which was a considerable distance. At that time, they used mules, as they had to take various supplies and tools into different areas where there were no roads. He said the Head Ranger loved to hunt, and there was some game around, but it was rather scarce. The Ranger would hunt while the crew built trails and did the general work, which was their assignment. One evening this Ranger says, "Fellows, I can't seem to get a deer in the daytime, let's get one tonight!" Carefully he laid out his plan for them. "We'll go up this draw and around such and such a hill," he plotted, and so out they go. Art said he told his partner, "Let's steer him onto one of the Pack Mules," so out there in the dark is this Ranger, along with Art, and his partner. Art helped "guide" the Ranger, as he got turned around easily. They weren't far from camp, and sure enough, here are two, big eyes! The Ranger said, "Hold 'er, boys, while I get it!" He just up and shoots, and to his consternation, here lay a fine U.S. Forest Service pack mule in the throes of death! Art said this, indeed, cured the Ranger of his hunting activities at that camp!

While we were logging up on McDowell Creek, a young fellow came into my filing house one morning, shaking his hand and saying, "Man, that hurts and really stings!" He pulled his glove off and here his index finger was missing! I shook his glove, and his severed finger fell out! There was no blood flowing, but it looked like raw flesh, and a bad bruise. About thirty-two years later, we went to a wedding in McMinnville and in the foyer of the church, I noticed a fellow standing there and felt that he was staring at me. All of a sudden, I walked up to him and said, "Hello, you are Wayne Garber, aren't you?" He then said, "Why, hello, Kenny, long time no see!" This was the young man who came into my filing house with the severed index finger!

As Rollie sat in my filing house one day, he asked, "Do you want to buy my parents' place up Mill Creek?" This was, of course, over the hill from Gooseneck Creek, where we still owned our place. I said, "Yes, I do, Rollie!" He said, "Well, you better go and see Mother because Hawkins and Roberts are foreclosing on the place on Monday." This was Wednesday when Rollie told me this, so on Saturday I went and picked up Mrs. Phillips, took her into Robert Kreason, the District Attorney, and signed the papers to buy the Phillips Place. This house was the last one on the county road up Mill Creek. This purchase was to have a major impact on my life and that of my family's! The place was two hundred fifty acres, with many wonderful features. Besides the acres and acres of beautiful woods and timber, there was a great creek for the kids to swim in, plenty of room to raise a family, and we looked forward to living there! The Phillips' homestead, however, was less than desirable and we knew we would have to build a new house.

HAMPTON HAPPENINGS

We pulled up stakes, left Sweet Home, and moved back to Gooseneck, which was not without some strain and emotions. When we made the move to Sweet Home, we had rented out our house up Gooseneck, so we had a place to move back to. We scarcely got moved in, when I heard that someone was starting to log the timber on the big mountain back of our place. I went up to where they had just started to rig up a cat landing and met a fellow named Conner Harmon, so I decided to ask him for a falling job. He said, "Yes, we need cutters! We don't have enough tools though. Would you have your own tools?" I said, "I sure do!" So I started falling with Ed Phillips and about the second day of work, we were busy backing up a big tree (which means we were sawing and getting ready to lay her on the ground). Now a falling saw, makes a licking, cutting sound that can be heard quite a ways off, especially if the tree is leaning and ready to go! We were over halfway through, when two cutters Harmon had hired came walking up to where we were. They said, "Hold it fellows, who filed your saw?" "Oh, some Kid up the creek," I told them. "Can we finish falling your tree?" they asked. We said, "Go ahead," so they got up there and put her down. "Boy, that saw sure cuts a darn sight better than the ones that fellow in Willamina files for us! If Harmon won't get this kid to file our saws, we're going to quit," they declared. Two days later, Harmon asked a "native" in Gooseneck, "Who is the Kid around here who files saws?" The next evening I was busy filing saws when I saw Harmon drive in our yard. Harmon asked, "Oh, are you the saw filer?" I said, "Yes." "Would you file these other cutters' saws? If you will, the company will pay you $1 per saw and the cutters will pay $1 per saw, as well," he told me. I said, "Okay, I will do it!" I fell timber all day, and in addition, filed five or six saw at home each evening.

FRIEND FOR LIFE

About two weeks went by and one evening a tall, broad-shouldered fellow came driving in to our place. He got out, introduced himself to me and this was my very first acquaintance with Lester Meredith Hampton, also known as Bud. Little did I know how this meeting was going to shape my life! I was very impressed with Bud and got some real good vibrations from our first encounter! After we visited for awhile, he asked me to run a cutting crew for him as he owned Willamina Lumber Company. Knowing he was a good man, I didn't hesitate and told him I'd be glad to work for him! This was Thursday, and on Saturday, I went into Dallas. I had just walked by the Real Estate office of Fuller and King, when a fellow called out, "Hey, come back here, I want to talk to you!" Then I noticed Walter, or "Ole", as he was known to his friends, standing there. Ole had surveyed a large portion of Polk County, which is where we were cutting timber. Porter S. King had been the Assistant Oregon State Forester for many years, so they were men of some stature. Fuller asked, "Where have you been? I haven't seen you around for three years!" I said, "Oh, I've been running a big crew out of Sweet Home and I just moved back to Gooseneck and am now running a cutting crew for Willamina Lumber Company. "Who is Willamina Lumber Company?" he asked. "Bud Hampton, from Tacoma, Washington, is the owner," I told him. "Oh, what kind of a fellow is he?" Ole asked. I said, "He is a fine man and I am very impressed with him!" "How is he fixed for timber," he asked and I said, "That's his problem! He needs timber badly!" "Well, well! We just happen to have a fine stand to sell to him," he informed me. I then told him how to contact Bud, did my shopping in town, and went home.

At home on Sunday night about 10:00 o'clock, I heard someone call out, "Hey, Kenny," so I immediately answered. The voice said, "This is Bud Hampton out here. Are you awake?" I said, "Yes, I'm awake." "Please bring your cruiser axe and compass to the office at 8:00 o'clock tomorrow morning. Don't go up with the crew, as I really need for you to come to the office. Will you?" he asked. "I'll be there, Bud," I reassured him. Next morning I go into Willamina and discovered that Fuller and King had sent a man out to show us this piece of timber, which was up Gold Creek, not more than twelve miles from the mill. The fellow who came out was Mars Slack and he was to show us the timber. We drove up to Gold Creek to the eighty acres we were to see and right through the middle of this fine stand, there was a canyon. Bud said, "Kenny, you go to the right side of the canyon and be sure to check the trees for rot. I'll go to the left side and then we will meet back here around 11:00 o'clock." Away we went, meeting again at 11:00 o'clock. Slack said, "Come over here, Mr. Hampton, and I will fill you in on the details of this sale." Bud said, "We don't have to move; you can tell me and Kenny all about it right here!" This is what he said: "The people who own this property live back East, one of the principals has died and they want to close it at once. Foster Lumber Company had a railroad almost touching this property and they wanted to buy the property for $7,500. We think it's worth $10,000 for eighty acres, timber and all." Bud said, "Fine! Please stop by the mill and pick up your check!"

On the way back to the mill, Bud was in a trance. He looked at me and said, "Well, I'll be dog-goned, I'll be dog-goned! Do you see any horse shoes around my neck?" I leaned over, pretended to give a careful look, and said, "No, Bud I don't!" As we drove, he just kept saying, "Well, I'll be dog-goned!" I let Bud "fry in his own juice," so to speak, for about a year. He contracted with a logging outfit named Miller and Gaynor to come in and log this site. They lost no time and began immediately to take lots of peelers to the big U.S. Plywood mill in Willamina. This was wonderful, for Bud had a real source of ready cash to begin to build his company. Well, one fine day I ran into Bud when I was taking the cutters' scale to the office. It seemed that I rarely saw him anymore and every time I did, he would always bring up this Gold Creek Timber deal. On this day, Bud was sitting in his chair, so I walked up behind him, put my hands on his shoulders, and said, "Bud, you're not stupid, you're just ignorant!" He laughed and said, "Maybe that's right!" I asked, "Do you want me to tell you how that timber deal up Gold Creek came about?" Bud replied, "I surely do!" Then I told him exactly what had happened and how it came about. He got up out of his chair and placed a choke hold on me and said, "Kenny, I'll just pay you off right now!" I said, "Oh no, you won't! That didn't hurt one bit, let's just be friends!" Bud said, "Okay then, but I'll get even with you sometime!" Bud told me more than once how thankful he was that I told him what had happened because he had been awake at night trying to figure out why and how Fuller and King had contacted him!

Bud had taken this logging job up on the Gooseneck range, from Pope and Talbot, who owned a large tract of timber. I cut twenty forties, eighteen of the joining and two forties behind. I told Bud that my brother was a good high climber and logger, so Bud said to go ahead and get him to work for him. Ron gladly came to work, as did Enos Schrock, who was my brother-in-law, married to my sister, Millie, and they did the logging. Enos ran the yarder and was very good at it! Many things happened on the cutting crew which were interesting. A noteworthy character was Donald Strunk, who had just bought a place up above where we lived. He came driving in my yard one evening to ask for a job, so I gave Don a job bucking and he was a source of pleasure from the word go! Don's formal education was, in short, very limited for he never got to go to school. Worldly possessions weren't of any concern, and he was accustomed to living life "in the rough"!

Don came up out of a real steep canyon in the woods on evening, and said, "Fellows, I just had the awfulest tormation I ever had in my life! I had to chop all afternoon because the three, big firs were so close together, I was unable to use my saw!" His distinctive words soon became standard lingo! His Dad was killed in a car wreck, so when Don was ten years old, he began cutting wood to help his poor Mother feed the family and that's why he never had the opportunity to attend school. This word, tormation, is from tormenting, plus other ingredients! In Don's mind, the term, tormation just fit, and we all thought so, too! When Don was talking or was tickled about something, he'd use the words, 'Tis and 'Twas. One time he told me, "Kenny, if one takes a quart of water, 'tis, and one takes a handful of salal leaves, 'tis, and boils it, one has the best remedy for diarrhea one can have, 'twas!" There you have it, Don's best remedy!

Don never griped about anything and never buttoned up his shirt! I am sure that in the summertime, his belly button tanned. He went elk hunting once with Bob Patty and Ron in Eastern Oregon in zero degree weather! There was snow on the ground and it was very windy. Don took it "head on" and never wore out the button holes in his shirt! He had huge muscles on his chest - perhaps all the "weathering" contributed to his muscular appearance!

One day a bucker was sawing away and as I approached him, he suddenly stopped sawing and asked, "Do you want me to buck logs for you?" I immediately sensed there was something more to his question, so in reply I asked, "What's the problem?" He said, "I'll tell you my problem! My daughter got married Saturday night and I'm losing $500 credit off my income tax, so if you don't loosen up on that scale stick, I ain't gonna be around!" This didn't set too well with me, so I got right over his axe and undercutter, and I said, "Herman, I have three things to face; one is you, the other is the company, and the third is my conscience! Now if you think you are going to scare me out, forget it! I have always been more than fair with you! When you got in a bad jackpot, I brought your scale up to your average, and that's the way she's gonna be!"

Herman never spoke one word to me for over a month and then one day, he started talking and had gotten over his mad spell. He was very quiet and rather brooding and you never knew where he was at.

MEMORABLE MEETING

John Breeden was another fellow whom I met and our friendship was most pleasurable and a lifelong one! He bought a 1933 Chevrolet log truck, began hauling logs, and that's how I became acquainted with him. He was a high climber, and so were his two brothers, Roy and Ellis. Roy and Ellis did not know how to spell, pronounce, or understand the word, FEAR! They could be at the top of a Spar Tree and that was nothing! Roy was a tremendous fighter and Ellis was a natural-born athlete. Ellis always wore 16-inch top caulk shoes and the old-fashioned "tin pants" woodsmen used to wear. Years later, I saw him standing on top of a stump one day and he just up and did a flip-flop off that stump and landed on his feet! In case you aren't impressed, guess what? He was sixty-five years old at the time! This was in the winter, so he was wearing all the logging gear, heavy canvas duck coat, tin pants and all! John was a terrific hunter! He had the most wonderful capability of going into strange territory and being able to discern the area where the elk, deer, and moose would cross the ridges. He was, matter of fact, just downright good at it!

About this time Bud Hampton hired a Forester and I was in limbo for some time. Bud introduced me to W.H. Christy, also known as Bill. He had been a BLM (Bureau of Land Management) man and also a Reserve Lieutenant in the Air Force. For some reason, to which I never had a clue, he hated my guts! He never once stopped by, nor suggested anything to me, and I used to wonder about him. One day he came up to the woods and screamed at me, "Get those d— fallers out of there! I just declared a reserve there!" John Breeden had just rigged a nice Spar Tree, and now this! Man, talk about communication!

Herman, the bucker, said to me, "Kenny, last night at the Union meeting, Bert Keck, the presiding, Most Worshipful Grand Master, mentioned your name and he said, 'I am going to bring that Kenny Shenk in on his knees and fine the h— out of him'!" I couldn't join as I was a company man anyway. Herman also said, "I hear we are not cutting for Willamina Lumber, but for you, and furthermore, Bud Hampton is paying you under the table!" All this enlightening information came to me around 8:00 o'clock in the morning and at noon, here comes a truck driver to get a load. The trucker said to me, "I have a message for you, Kenny. You are to go to the office at once!" I couldn't figure this out as we just had payday and I had already turned in the weekly cutting scale.

Down I go and right into Bill's office. Here he sat in a nice, big chair and he had a look like Alexander The Great, just after he won the Battle of Copenhagen! Bill said, "Sit down," so I sat down. He ceremoniously picked up a big pipe, blew air through the stem, put about six bits' worth of Granger Rough Cut in it, built a fire and puffed a couple of times. Then he put the fire out, put more tobacco in, lit her up, and started a rollin' out smoke, as if it were smoke from an incinerator. He looked up at the ceiling, then at the floor. Turning to me, with a vicious look, he said, "Look, did anybody tell you the lumber market is bad?" I said, "Yes, I heard someone say it was rough." "Oh, you heard that, did you?" I said, "Yes, I did!" "Well," he said, "Did it ever enter your head that falling timber with visible three, four, and six-inch knots would automatically constitute a low grade of lumber?" "Yes, I suppose it would," I affirmed. He puffed again and then continued, "Would you plead guilty to falling trees adjacent to the Spar Tree with visible three and four and six inch knots?" Without hesitation, I emphatically said, "Yes, I plead guilty." He rose to his feet and asked, "Just what do you have to say for yourself?" All this time a bookkeeper, Jerry Wade, was about eight feet away. So I said to Bill, His Highness, mind you, "Well, Bill, the State of Oregon has a law that requires us to fall a three hundred foot guyline circle, or any tree that might hit a guy line. The Yarding Engineer has to furnish his own shade!" The poor fool didn't even know this! I was getting quite a rise in blood pressure and I said, "By the way, Bill, did you ever hear that the cutting crew was working for me and not for Willamina Lumber Company?" He said, "Oh, h—, yes! That's common knowledge around here!" I turned to Jerry Wade and said, "You'd better get Bud Hampton out here quick!" He said, "Why, I can't do that; I don't even know where he is!" I said, "Well, start phoning," which he immediately did. After awhile, Jerry handed me the phone, saying, "Okay, Kenny, here's your man!" "Hello," says Bud, "how are things going?" I said, "Bud, I will tell you later, but you come down here at once!" He said, "Well, okay, give me one hour and fifteen minutes!"

Right on schedule, here comes Bud. He came in, greeted us warmly and asked, "Do we need to talk?" I said, "We sure do!" He took us in a small room, closed the door and said, "Go ahead." I told Bud about our deal under the table and so on. He laughed and said, "Well, I'll be dog-goned!" Suddenly, he looks up at Bill and asked, "Bill, did YOU ever tell anyone that?" Bill said, "As a matter of fact, I have." Bud said, "Well, I'll be darned! Do you mean to tell me you went to college for four years and you never learned to keep your d—— mouth shut?" Suddenly, this bull-necked guy came fully erect to his feet and said, "Mr. Hampton!" Bud said, "Yes, Bill?" to which he said very loudly, "I have a suggestion for you!" Bud said, "Let me have it, I'll entertain it!" "You can just let Kenny Shenk solve some more of your darn problems," Bill said, to which Bud replied, "Yes, I'll entertain that suggestion, and now you may sit down!" I was utterly astonished that Bill sat down because he was livid with rage and I honestly thought he was going to fight us, or me, at least. I had made up my mind that since I only have to die once, this might be a good place! I think Bill saw the light when Bud made the remark as to his college education being worthless, since he couldn't keep his mouth shut!

The next day, here comes Bud up to the woods and it so happened, John Breeden was there. John asked, "Bud, where in the dickens did you ever hire a fellow like that?" Bud said, "Well, I tell you fellas, Christy had the longest resume of anyone I have ever hired, but guess what? When he left it was a darn sight longer! I am so glad he's gone! I feel as if I just got out of the pen!"

THE SIMPLE SIMON SNIPER

There was a fellow, Wimpy, around the Sheridan area, who was a rather simple kind of guy and he wanted a bunch of us to go hunting with him. He had a Chevy pickup and invited quite a few to go with him. My brother, Ron, Roy Lambert, John Rogers, some of Roy's kids and one of John's boys, Bobby McHerter, Elmer Bogee and myself decided to go. We went over to French Corrals in Eastern Oregon and set up camp. On the way over there, John was driving while Wimpy was busy tormenting the kids! He was ripping their britches open and acting sort of weird, so they told him to cut it out or they'd take his pants off! He just laughed at them and said they couldn't do that! He got so rough with them and kept on, so they proceeded to do what they threatened to do! Wimpy went into an absolute, insane rage and tried to beat them to death! We got them all calmed down, went about twenty-five miles and Wimpy started right in again!

1943 - a nice buck I killed by Doran's Peak Lookout. Shot with a Savage 30/30 rifle and packed ou8t over three miles.

We arrived at camp and the first thing that happened was John took the rotor out of the distributor from Wimpy's pickup and hid it! Wimpy was always flying off the handle during the day and evening and then he'd threaten, "I'm gonna go home! I'll just leave you guys here!" Of course, he didn't know he wasn't about to leave! One day we had real good luck and had four bulls in camp! I had killed a beautiful, six-point bull (the only six-point I ever killed). Wimpy would go out and pat the hams on the elk hanging there and make some strange remarks. We could hear the coyotes howling and Elmer said, "Well, Wimpy, you'll have to sleep out of the tent for coyote bait tonight!" Wimpy laughed. Bobby had walked about thirty-five or forty feet away from the tent before he went to bed and for some reason, he laid down on the ground, took a stick and broke it in two! Somebody asked, "Did you hear that noise" They'd always try to note where Wimpy's gun was, but he suddenly grabbed it and fired out in the dark. Incredulously,

After Ken's picture was taken, Wilbert and Russell wanted theirs taken with the buck. Frances was just ready to snap the camera when Russ said, "Hold it, Mama, til I get the rifle!". You can see the grin of satisfaction on his face!

the shot he fired hit this poor Bobby and went right through his belt! The bullet went through the spine and came out his belt on the opposite side! If you took a leather punch to that belt, you couldn't have made a more perfect hole on both sides!

Here we are out in the mountains and now, this terrible accident! There were some other fellows there in camp and one was named Bill Wenerd, who had a Ford sedan. In fact, I found out that my Father-in-law worked for him in a saw-mill out towards King's Valley one time. Bill volunteered to drive Bobby into St. Anthony Hospital in Pendleton, arriving there about 2:00 o'clock in the morning. Bobby sent word back to everyone to keep hunting, that he'd be fine. Well, it didn't quite work that way as we had to go into Pendleton to make a report to the police and fill out forms. I'm telling you, we were a pretty sad looking group! The Sergeant asked, "Who's the man who did the shooting?" Wimpy stepped up and said he did, so the Sergeant asked, "How did it happen?" Wimpy said the worst thing in the world he could have! He sort of started to cry and then said, "I don't know if I did it on purpose or not!" That Sergeant gave him a dressing down and told Roy, "See that this man never gets hold of a gun again!"

1944 - Ken Holding
some of the trout taken
from East Lake.

In the meantime, we learned that the bullet severed the nerve which controlled Bobby's bladder and bowels! We went on home, more than disheartened by this whole episode! Bobby began to mend and seemed to be getting along fairly well. Then his folks moved down the Columbia River to work on a dairy. At least a year after the accident, Roy Lambert came to our house and said, "Kenny, Bobby McHerter is dying! We've got to go get him and take him to that surgeon in Salem that you know!" I knew Dr. Herman Gilbert, so went over to Salem to see him. He asked, "What do you want to bring him into me for?" I said, "Because you're his only hope," so he finally agreed to do something for Bobby. Roy and I drove over to get Bobby and took him into Salem. Dr. Gilbert told us he took a quart and a half of pus and decayed matter out of that lad's pelvis. He also said that if he had been able to care for him at the time of the accident, in six weeks' time, he would have been absolutely as good as new! Doc fixed him up the best he could, told Bobby to live a clean life, and said he must take care of himself. He also requested that he return systematically for checkups. At last we felt relieved that Bobby was "on the mend," and John went out and bought him a nice Chevrolet car. Unfortunately, Bobby got himself a girlfriend, never went back to see Doc Gilbert and once again, became badly infected and subsequently died! It was so sad that he didn't take care of himself, but there was nothing in the world anyone else could have done for him!

My whole point to this story is that when you're out hunting, you need to be serious and not goof off with guns! Anybody like Wimpy who doesn't have a full load of bricks shouldn't be handling a gun and shooting out in the woods. That was a sad and severe lesson for all involved!

Go Ahead On 'er!

ROY AND THE RIGHT OF WAY

One day I saw a station wagon parked in the brush and I immediately knew whose it was. There was a government forty coming up for sale, so I went to the office and told Bud, "Elmer Werth of Engle and Werth Lumber Company is going to bid against

A group of us hunting in Eastern Oregon. L to R: Ron, Ed Phillips, John Rogers, Roy Lambert and Ken.

you on that sale." He said, "Oh no, he isn't! I have a gentleman's agreement with Elmer Werth! I don't bid in Mill Creek on the government sale there and he doesn't bid against me." I said, "Bud, I'll bet he will. I want you to go up Gooseneck, talk nice to Roy Lambert, drop some money in his pocket and get a Right Of Way through his property. Even Pope and Talbot Lumber Company doesn't have one, Bud, and you need to get it!" Bud just chuckled and said, "Oh, you think I should, do you?" I said, "Yes, I do." Suddenly,

I thought that Bud wasn't paying good attention, so I got hold of his shoulders and said, "Bud, you listen to me! I want you to go right now!"

Here is what happened. This was on a Friday when I talked to Bud, so he took my advice and made a visit! The following Friday, I ran into Roy Lambert and he said, "Kenny, something funny just happened! Last Friday Bud Hampton came up and I had never met him before, but I really liked him! He wanted a Right Of Way through our property, so I sold him one. The really funny thing is, on Tuesday, an Engle and Werth Superintendent came to see me, and they wanted to buy it!" Roy laughed and he said, "It sure beats all!" Well, Werth did bid against Bud and it cost Bud $43,000, which, at that time, would be comparable to around a million or more now!

1944 - Six-point bull elk taken in Eastern Oregon.

THE PORK DEAL

There were a couple Swiss fellows who lived up Gooseneck, clear at the end of the road - Julius and Victor Gleason. There was some timber on their place and Bud said, "Kenny, I'd like to buy the Gleason's timber. Would you please go up and 'soften them up' for me?" I said, "I'd be glad to do that for you, Bud," so I went up one evening, just as they were about to eat supper. Their main dish for supper was most evident! They had a huge kettle about ten or twelve inches high and had a pork head in there (snout up)! Everything looked clean, but I didn't like the way that hog's eye was glaring at me! Victor said, "You have sup-pur vith us." I said, "Thank you, I have had supper." He said, "You can have some more." I said, "No, I can't," and began asking them about selling their timber. Victor had a very pronounced, but pleasant way of speaking English and said, "Vell, vie shoulds ve sell ve gets money. Vhen we come, ve stills gets money, vi shoulds ve sell, ve don't know 'dis Hampton." I said, "I know you don't, but if you did, you would like him and maybe sometime you might want to sell some timber since you can't cut it all into wood!"

I informed Bud of my visit to the Gleason's and about six months later, Bud says, "What do you think Kenny, shall I go up and try them?" "Yes," I said, so Bud goes up and then he told me exactly what happened. He got there at supper time, and here is another pig's head for supper. Bud told me Victor asked him, "You have supper with us?" Bud said, "Sure I will," and Bud ate his portion of dead pig. Victor said, "Have some moor," and Bud said, "Sure will!" Shortly after Bud's visit, Victor drove in my yard and he says, "Dat Buud Hampton come to veset us an' he eat sup-pur vith us an' he go vor seconds! He es nice man an' ve like him, ve sold him our timbur!" I was so tickled and when Bud and I got together, he agreed with me - the thing that climaxed the deal was his going back for seconds of that pork!

AIR BORNE

Bud had asked me to help on the rigging since we were done cutting and he was undecided as to what he wanted to do. I was working away and here came Bud, with slick shoes, tie and nice suit of clothes. We were logging in a steep canyon which had lots of rotten timber. Ron had a short Spar Tree rigged and the tail blocks on the haul back were perhaps one hundred feet higher than the Spar Tree. Paul Kilmer, Frances' brother, and Ron were setting chokers and as these fellows also loaded the trucks out, the Yarding Engineer ran the loading donkey. These boys would loop the choker into the butt rigging pile and the Engineer would tight-line them clear above the tops of these tall, Old Growth trees. I rode her in once, but didn't like it. So here's Bud and now the whistle, and the trucks are here. I said, "Bud, would you like a ride into the landing where your car is?" He said, "I sure would 'cause my shoes are so slick, I'd never make it trying to walk in!" I said, "You're in clover, Bud. You can ride in with Paul and Ron." He asked, "How do you do it?" I said, "They will loop the choker, you can sit in the middle, and Ron will stand on one side and Paul on the other." Bud had no idea what was about to take place!

Ron turned the signal in and the lines suddenly grew tight and they were airborne, about fifty feet off the ground! Bud called out, "Hold on here, Fellows, what's going on?" I started up that steep hill. These three fellows were suddenly at least three hundred feet high in the air and then the yarder starts taking them to the landing. I got there the same time they did and called out to Ron, "Say, it sounds like the bull block is dry." Ron says, "Okay, Ken, we'll look at it in a minute." Enos, the Yarding Engineer, my brother-in-law, had to pull the rigging right into the bull block and slack it down fast or else they would go out a long way before they hit the ground! When Bud put his feet on a log, he was bathed in sweat and said, "By George, fellows, that is one ride I'll never forget!" And he never did! I suppose I should have had my butt kicked for doing that to Bud, but we used to do some foolish things in those days and that was one of them! Besides, Bud was a great sport about it!

As Bud Hampton gained more and more credibility with his logging operation and more involved with the business community, he began to realize that Willamette Industries would be formidable competitors. Some of their personnel were just top notch, he thought. He asked me one day, "Kenny, where does Bill Swindell hire these competent people?" I said, "Bud I don't know where he hires them, but I can tell you what he does after he hires them." "Oh, what's that?" Bud asked quizzically. "He baptizes them by immersion, but instead of water, Bill uses formaldehyde so they are then totally company-minded and will stay that way until death."

Good men were scarce in those war days and Bud was afraid I would lose some of the cutting crew. A number of times he'd say, "Kenny, I have good reasons to complete this logging job and I will tell you the reason after we are done," which he did. The BLM was going to institute a program for qualified companies called, "The Sustained Yield Program." It was this way: A company which met the standards was to be guaranteed timber forever. Bud had given Pope and Talbot as a reference and thus, he wanted to keep his good name. One day the High Climber, who was also the Hooker, or Log Superintendent, was ordered to appear for induction, so I went with Bud to the draft office. We went right to the top, to the Head of the Draft Board, but this fellow said that he could not defer the Climber. Bud told him that he didn't have anyone to take his place and he talked and pleaded, but to no avail. Then I spoke up and asked, "Did you ever see a High Climber with his beard caught in the Bull block?" He said, "No, I never did!" "You never will either, because when they get that old, they don't climb anymore," I told him. In those days, no one had beards or long hair while working in the woods because it was too dangerous. It has always seemed to me they had more sense. I never heard of a college yet that teaches a course entitled, "Common Sense!"

About 1945, Bud Hampton wrote me a letter, which I still have. He said, "You know very well that Bill Foster of the Foster Lumber Company, has ceased operation and has dismantled his mill. He is still angry at me for buying that eighty acres in Gold Creek, so I want you to write Foster a letter and ask to purchase the lands in the Gooseneck area" (where we had logged), so I did this. In about a week, Bill Foster was tired of living and took his life. About two weeks after his death, I received a letter from Mrs. Foster in which she stated that I was the first person to make a formal request to purchase the property and would I please meet her in Willamina at the City Bank at 2:00 P.M. on such and such a day. I took the letter into Bud's office and he then proceeded to purchase a sizeable portion of land which still had millions of feet of prime timber on it.

FIRE ON THE MOUNTAIN - 1945

It was summertime in 1945 and a terrible fire started up in the Black Rock area, at the head of Mill Creek. We were living in Gooseneck and could easily hear the roar of the fire! Willamette Valley Lumber Company had steam yarding donkeys, and it was their steam locomotives which had started the fires. My brother, Ron, and myself were asked to go help fight fire and to bring our falling tools. Our job was to fall big, Old Growth timber for many, many of the tree tops had caught on fire, and the fire readily spread on the trees to the rotten, konky places. They brought down five hundred black boys from Ft. Lewis, Washington, who, as they told us, was "Bu Wackin!" They had a very large Army camp at Bridge One on Mill Creek Road. The Army furnished big, six-wheel drive trucks in which they transported us up the mountains to the site of the fires. We were asked to fall at the head of Rowell Creek, which came down close to Valley Junction. These black boys were scared to death of the big timber. I shall relate some events which took place.

We had to spring board every tree, and nearly all of the trees leaned downhill. I went up to a tree, hung my oil bottle, stuck my axe in, and noticed it had a funny sound. We always called a pitchy tree a "Bee Tree", as so many times the pitch looked like real honey. I called out pretty loudly, "She's a Bee Tree, boys!" Here comes about ten of these fellows, and as they were not gainfully employed, they stood around and watched us fall this big giant of a tree. Sure enough, into the undercut we hit a big seam, and here comes the pitch, just oozing out, honey-golden and looking very inviting! Finally, a big, strapping, black fellow, whose name on his cap said, "Winston", stepped up and asked me, "Where's the bees at, Suh?" I said, "Never mind the bees, all we want is the honey," and we just kept chopping in a big undercut. At last, he could stand it no more and asked me, "Mind if I samples it?" I said, "No, go ahead!" I quit chopping and he stepped up, stuck his tongue out, plunged his finger into this glorious-looking "honey" and drew it through his mouth. It was smeared all over his face! Suddenly, he started to spit and hack, and said, "Suh, dat ain't honey, dat rosum!" I asked, "No foolin'?" "Sho nuff," he informed me. Then another of his comrades stepped up, asking "Mind if I samples it?" I said, "I don't care if Winston doesn't care!" Winston was a good sport and said, "No, I don't mind, go haid!" So this second fellow plunges in, just like Winston had done. He, too, sputtered, gagged and said, "Dat sho nuff IS rosum!" That was their term for turpentine, as this pitch was full of turpentine. Well anyway, here was this pitch running down on the ground and the boys that hadn't sampled it, just couldn't believe it wasn't honey! I don't remember how many of them had to sample the "honey", but a lot of them did!

One day about twenty-five of them were on a little, flat bench, rolling dice, dancing and just having a good time! Directly in line and over them, I heard a big tree burning and then it made a crunching noise, so I yelled a warning to Captain Rhodes, "Get your boys out of there right now!" He had a megaphone and announced very loudly, "Come out and up at once, boys!" They had no more than left, and sure enough, down goes this big tree, right where they had been five minutes before! Captain Rhodes was visibly shaken, thanked me profusely, and then asked me how I knew that tree was going to fall.

Bear taken up Gooseneck by Ken, 1946. He was a huge bear!

One of the young Ft. Lewis recruits asked, "Is there any bears around here, Suh?" Ron had just killed a nice, young bear which dressed out about eighty to ninety pounds, had ground the meat up and made sausage out of it. Ron answered him, "Yes, there's bears around here, and cougar, too!" The recruit asked, "White Boy, what you mean, Cougar?" Ron said, "They are a big cat, or mountain lion, or panther and they get up on logs and large rocks and jump down on deer - and sometimes on people! I just killed a big, Tom cougar a few months ago!" This young recruit's eyes got real big as he registered disbelief and he said, "Sometimes people? Man dats too darn reg-lar." The next morning when we were in camp and the men were lined up to eat, I heard the black boy say, "Dheys some white boys dat live here and de says dat ders varmint in dese mountains. I ain't a goin' up there for God Almighty his self!" But I think he did! We did not try to scare them at all, I don't think! They never really did one lick of work and threw all the axes, shovels, grubbing hoes and Polaskies away.

The wind came up very strong one day and it was so windy and smokey, we couldn't see, as the fire continued to rage and ravage. We were all ordered to get out at once, as it was really dangerous! So we started up this very steep canyon with our springboards, wedges, fourteen-pound mall, axes, oil bottles, saws, lunch buckets, and a big can of saw oil. We even asked several of our Ft. Lewis "friends" to give us a hand,

but no way would any of them help us out! After about one hour, the wind shifted, the atmosphere cleared, and the Captain boomed out on his megaphone, "All right, boys, break it up! Everybody go back to your stations!" It was burning hot and right by our side were about fifteen Ft. Lewis soldiers, while the Captain was at the truck, approximately eight hundred feet away. First one of these fellows said, "I ain't goin' back down dere for God himself!" "Me neither," seemed to come from all of them, and all of a sudden, one of them fell on the ground. They immediately formed a circle around him and the big fellow screamed up to Captain Rhodes, "Deys a man down ova heah, we cain't leave our buddy heah." The Captain boomed back, "What's the matter with him?" The big fellow jumped down, looked in this kids' face and shouted back, "He's a vomitin, he's everything in the book! We cain't leave our buddy heah." Sho nuff, they didn't! They all sat right there in that hot sun until it was time to go in. The next day, this kid who had "Perry" on his cap and who reportedly was a vomitin' and everything in the book, came down to watch us work. I asked him, "Boy, how you feeling this morning?" He gave me a sheepish look and said, "Jes tollable!" At last the rains came and the fire went out; having covered around 45,000 acres of beautiful timber lands.

AUNTIE INSTIGATES INVESTIGATION

My sister, Millie, came out to visit at various times when the kids were small and commenced to read stories to them. She read stories of the Big Bad Wolf, The Three Little Pigs and so forth and the tears would roll down the cheeks of these little boys and their sister. Their eyes would just be fixed on their Auntie while she was telling these Sob Sister stories and it was really impressive! What happened, however, was that she cultivated an interest in those kids which just wouldn't stop! When Millie went home, they gathered around one night and said, "Tell us some stories, Daddy!" I said, "Oh, come on!" "No, please," they begged, so I told them a few yarns and of course, those yarns lacked a long ways from being the truth, but they were SO entertaining! Every night the kids would beg, "Please tell us another story, Daddy." One evening they started begging again and I said, "Well, I'm fresh out! You tell one!" So, at his very tender age, Russ said, "Hey, I know one!" "That's it," I said, "Go ahead!" So this little lad began, "Once upon a time there was a big, black Papa Sow and he had three little white piggies!" Wilbert shouted out, "Stop him, Daddy! He's lying! Is there Papa Sows?" I said, "Keep quiet, Sonny, let him go on with his story!" "I don't want to hear his story," Wilbert said, "sounds like he's fibbing!" "Well, listen, it was fibbing when I told you some stories," I explained, to which Wilbert replied, "Well, I don't care! It sounded better!" I thought that was sort of debatable, but we had a lot of fun! It got to be old hat for Daddy to tell stories.

With the continual requests for stories, I decided we'd do a "to-be-continued story" style, so I could replenish my imaginative powers and gear up for the next session! Thus, I "invented" the exciting stories of Alibaba and the Forty Thieves, with much mystery, adventure, action, and a fearful imagination! The kids looked forward so eagerly to this saga, that when I was persuaded to produce, there were always six pairs of eyes and ears riveted with much devotion and attention! The kids always said this mystery story was their favorite! Donna told me in later years how very sad she felt when she learned that the stories were fabricated, for she believed every word! I don't think the twin boys ever bugged me so much about telling stories, but the others surely did, and as I look back, I regret that I was always so terribly busy! In the evenings, I'd file saws until dark; even when I was working down on Salmon River, filing steady in the big camps. That's all I did was file saws - from daylight until dark! It was just work, work, but all our kids developed a penchant for working and it showed up later, for they always had jobs!

Mildred, was talented in so many ways! She could paint and did a great job at that! Also, she has written a book regarding family history, which she has had published. Had she been privileged to pursue more formal training, she could have attained any goal which she set her mind to! She definitely has great storytelling ability, which our Mother passed along to us!

DUNCAN AND HINES

When Ed Phillips and I were first working for Hampton, Conner Harmon hired a Woods Superintendent named Guy Duncan. Now Guy was a very colorful character, a rather imposing looking fellow, very husky and additionally, he had the gift of gab! Adding to his character, he possessed a fine head of hair, an impressive array of gold teeth and he chewed plug tobacco! We found out he was an expert sheep shearer, as well as an experienced horseman, and had done a lot of teaming around the mines in Eastern Oregon. An Uncle of Guy's, a Mr. Hines, had a little town in Eastern Oregon named after him; Hines, Oregon. There was a mine named after Guy's first wife, Arealia, in that area, as well, and we found that on one of our Oregon maps. Guy had a big, four-horse team and freighted into the mines with them.

One time I went with Duncan to the mill to turn in the cutting scale and when we got there, Bud was in the office. A Scottish lady, Bertie McFitzhugh, was bookkeeper at that time, and a more dedicated bookkeeper you could not find! She said to me, "Kenny, you write PP on the scaling tickets - what does this stand for?" Before I could explain, Dun had a big mouthful of tobacco juice, just looking for a place to spit when he heard Bertie ask me this, and he started to laugh. When he began to laugh, he got some juice in his lungs, as well as on the floor, and my, what a scene! He finally recovered and said, "I thought everyone knew what Pee Pee stood for!" When order was finally restored, I said, "Well, Bertie, I merely write that as an abbreviation for Patty and Phillips, since Bob Patty and Ed Phillips are falling together." "Well, I have another question," Bertie continued, "because I heard you say a couple weeks ago that they still have two more weeks logging on that tree. Please tell me how big it is and how far out is it that it is going to take that long to log ONE tree!" I then explained to her that this was a term commonly used to designate a Spar Tree and this meant it would take another two weeks to finish logging the entire setting of trees. I am sure that Bertie thought the end of the company was in sight before she asked me for an explanation!

Guy had some great yarns and you can judge for yourself whether they are true or not! One of his stories goes like this: "One time in the Ozarks a fellow was walking along a path in the timber when he heard someone coming up behind him. Whoever was coming, was wheezing and puffing something terrible! He stopped at a fork in the trail and just then, saw a woman jump behind a tree. Carefully she peeked out from behind it and said to him, "If anyone is following me, tell them I went that way," and she pointed in the opposite direction. Pretty soon here came a young, husky lad puffing and running for all he was worth! The young lad saw the fellow and asked, 'Which way did she go?' The first fellow said, 'She went that way,' and pointed. As soon as this kid went running out of sight, the fellow went to find the woman behind the tree. The stranger wondered what in the world was wrong, for the woman had fallen to the ground, just exhausted! He said, 'Lady, may I ask what's going on here?' 'Oh, dear! I'm having a terrible time this spring trying to wean John! After all, he is thirteen years old,' she explained." We got quite a bang out of that story!

At that time, Wing Cigarettes were a popular brand, and another one of Duncan's stories was: "A young fellow, just old enough to buy cigarettes, walked into a tavern and said, 'Give me a pack of Wings.' The bartender said, 'I don't sell them and won't because they are not 100% pure. I have a friend who works for that company and he said they're about one-half cabbage leaves and one-half horse manure!' So the kid crosses the street, goes into the drugstore and says, 'Give me a pack of Wings.' The druggist rolls him a pack, the kid pays for them and immediately lights one up. He took a drag and said to the druggist, 'Something funny just happened.' The druggist asked, 'It did? What happened?' So the kid told him what the bartender had said. The druggist said, 'That's a bald-headed lie! My brother-in-law works there and they do not put ANY cabbage leaves in'!"

WHERE THE BUCKS ARE

After the big, Black Rock fire, Bob Patty was not working with me and one morning about 3:00 o'clock, he came up to our house. First thing I realized as I roused from a deep sleep, Patty was calling, "Get out of bed, quick! I know where the big bucks are!" I got up and said, "What's going on here, anyway, Patty?" "Oh," he said, "I've been every place in the United States, except this one spot, and never saw a deer, so I know where they're at!" I got breakfast for us and away we went up Mill Creek. We drove up to Cedar Creek as we knew they had made a fire trail up there on Pine Creek Ridge. Bob said he was SURE there'd be some bucks up there as we took off walking up through the timber. On the Cedar Creek side, the timber was still green as it hadn't been burned in the big fire, although it had on the other side. Going along, Bob was just talking my leg off, so I said, "Keep quiet, Patty! You're going to scare all the deer out of Polk County!" He said, "No, no! They like that! That way they know where you're at! That won't scare 'em!" Just as we got to the top of the hill to an opening, there was a mass of deer! I just couldn't believe it! Soon I shot a big, three-point but Bob didn't get any and it made him mad. He said, "You wouldn't give a man a chance, would you?" I said, "I guess not!" We packed that deer down to the truck and after that initiation, commenced to do more hunting up in that area. Myron, Byron, Davie, and Bob killed some very fine bucks up there. There were new sprouts coming up after the fire and nearly all wild animals love those new sprouts, so that area was a great place to hunt.

GOOD SAMARITANS

One elk season, I got a cow tag for Eastern Oregon, and since George and Ralph Emmert wanted to go also, we made plans. We threw our equipment together and took off in their late model, Willys 4 X 4. We took my tent, stove, various gear, and bought groceries. Our destination was Half Moon Springs where we set up camp. Upon arrival, I scouted around and found some real heavy pine bark, about five inches through. Gathering up a good supply, I took it into camp for our fires. The next morning when we woke up, somebody had made different arrangements! There were great chunks of ice, four feet long hanging next to the tent, and above our faces where we breathed, there were icicles hanging inside the tent!

As I walked outside the next morning, I noticed someone else had set up a camp not far from where we were. Just before I got all the way down there, a fellow called out, "Hello, Kenny!" I said, "Hello, Frank," as I recognized a fellow from Tillamook! "How cold is it," I asked. He said, "Well, it's warmed up a little bit, but it's still 35 below!" George and Ralph had just put the best heavy-duty battery money could buy in the Willys and it wouldn't even growl! There was just a little clicking sound! We went ahead and got breakfast and then figured out other uses for that stove! We put my gas stove underneath the oil pan, put tarps over the jeep clear to the ground and let that thing "cook" for about an hour and a half! Would you believe, we got that rig started and spent the rest of the day helping people! One fellow had a Jeep 4 X 4, with chains on. The ground was frozen so hard, that even with the chains on, and the Jeep in low range, the engine still would not turn over! The soft plugs on many vehicles didn't come out, but would just burst and that was a real problem!

1945 - Bob Patty and Ed Phillips have just fell a large Old Growth tree, three springboards high! Byron is standing next to Bob Patty. Tree fell with axes and a cross-cut saw.

Down below in Bear Valley, they said it was 45 degrees below and we were on a little bench up above a ways, so it couldn't have been much warmer.

At last we made our foray and began walking up a draw. Just then, here came some elk! George's gun positively wouldn't even snap and Ralph's gun wouldn't fire! My gun finally fired, after a delay but once it fired, it was fine! Ralph and I went around toward Peak Creek Canyon, walking through the timber, while George drove around to meet us and pick us up! When George arrived, he was very excited! "Fellas, I just saw the biggest mule deer buck I've ever seen in my life, right along the road! He didn't act like he was scared of me or anything and he's a monster," George reported. We started driving towards camp and as we drove, here came a band of elk, running right along the road. We stopped and I shot a nice cow elk, put her in the Jeep ("feathers" and all), and took off for camp. Before we got to camp, we met an Oregon State Game Commission vehicle with three guys in it and a huge buck strapped on top. Those fellows were just laughing and talking! All of a sudden, George let out a roar and said, "Hey, that's the big buck I saw!" No doubt they were taking it in to make some exhaustive study on what kind of genes he had to make him grow that big! He was, indeed, a monstrous buck with a huge set of horns! We sure had a great time on that trip, in spite of the cold! Fortunately, nothing froze up completely! Had I not had my stove in that tent, we'd been in bad shape for we hadn't really dressed that well for such intense cold. The normal low over there would have been perhaps 15 - 18 degrees below, but not 45 below!

THE DONALD

Don Strunk, who had worked with me at a logging operation, came one evening to see me and said, "Hey, Ken, my sister-in-law is having her annual, fall increase and I have to build her a shack, so I need some lumber. Could I get you to haul a truck load of lumber for me?" I told him I could do that. Don had a gasoline-powered cement mixer and I knew that before long we'd start work on a foundation for our new house up Mill Creek. I figured that perhaps I could borrow his cement mixer, so perhaps we could work out a deal. "Well, Don, I'll haul your lumber and in return, may I borrow your cement mixer?" He said, "You sure can! I also need my bucking saw filed real bad." Don's hair was nearly down to his shoulders and I said, "Well, Donald, I'll haul you a load of lumber, I'll file your saw and cut your hair for the use of your cement mixer!" "Oh," he said, "no problem!"

I went down to the Willamina Sawmill and was planning to buy about two thousand feet of lumber and they said, "Look, there's twenty-seven hundred feet of lumber in that stack there and if you let us put that on your truck, we'll sell it to you cheaper than we'll sell you the exact amount you want. They put that load on my truck and the front end would hardly stay on the ground! Some of that lumber was twenty feet long and I had quite a time getting it to Don's, but he had a great pile of lumber out of that! Later we borrowed his mixer and that's the way people used to live in the Far West! Sure enough, Ann had her fall increase, as Don said she would, and things returned to normal!

BEARER OF BONES AND BEAR

After we had purchased the Phillips homestead and before we could make our move up there, we rented the old Phillips house to some people named Whitney, who had a bunch of boys in their family. Our carpenters were up there working on our new house and I went up to do some work one day. Mrs. Whitney said to me, "There was a bobcat out in the barn! Also, there is a mean bear around here and I had to get a switch and drive him away from the house!" I sort of smiled and said, "Well, that bear isn't long for this world if he hasn't sense enough to stay away from a woman with a club!" Archie and Elmer sort of laughed, and immediately we heard a dog barking! Mrs. Whitney looked at me and said, "Our dog's got him bayed now, but he can't do anything with it!" I asked, "Do you have a gun?" "Well, yes, it's over at the house and my Old Man is there," she said. We went over to the house and Mr. Whitney said, "It's a 22 Single Shot, but the firing pin fell out and the boys put a nail in there. Part of the time it'll shoot!"

I took the gun, in its' delicate condition, and walked up the hill to an area where the Sheridan Timber Company had done some logging. The stumps were all blackened by fire and fairly tall, mostly eight to nine feet tall. I stood there a moment, looking around. These renters had a nice, Guernsey milk cow who had died, so they had dragged her body up here on the hill with their old 10-20 McCormick Deering Tractor. As I stood close to this cow, I noticed a "stump" move! Here was this huge, black bear standing straight up! I shot him in the brisket with that crazy 22 and he jumped and ran into some brush.

That evening I went back up Mill Creek with my big rifle and two dogs to go up the mountain to where I had shot the bear earlier in the day. Just then the Whitney boys came down the hill and said, "Mr. Shenk, we just chased the bear off the cow!" So I told the boys, "You kids stay down here and I'm going to leave my dogs here with you. IF you hear me shoot, I want you to untie my dogs and let them come up the hill." Up on the mountain, as I expected, the bear was busy with his calling! A buzzard had found the cow and that crazy bear had planned to try and move the critter. He had hold of that cow and pulled so hard that he pulled the one hip bone; leg and all, right from the cow! He was in the act of moving her and had managed to get part of the way to the woods! After he moved her that far, he had even partially covered that carcass with leaves! So I completed the job of shooting that bear, with the proper sized rifle! Next day we went back to get the bear down to the house. After skinning it, I had the hide tanned and it was a very large, black bear! As I'll illustrate later, that bear skin provided us with lots of entertainment!

MYSTIQUE OF THE

MILL CREEK MOUNTAINS

In 1946 we moved from Gooseneck, lived briefly in the old Phillips' home and in the meantime, had begun to build a new house (which is still being lived in). I was busy running Hampton's cutting crew, filing saws, and life went on! Building a new house in those days, however, was nothing like doing it today! Nowadays you go to the lumber yard or huge discount stores, and you can expect to readily order and pick up whatever materials are needed. Since it was just after the war, many items were simply not available, and to name a few, windows, siding, and cement were commodities not found in local stores. This posed a real challenge! I discovered that a neighbor, Mr. Allen, had "stock-piled" some extra bags of cement which he was willing to sell to us so we could get a foundation poured. The only problem was that this cement had hardened in the bags, so we worked like everything, pounding and beating on that to

1948 - 'Coons, 'coons and more 'coons! Front row: Byron, Russ, Myron. Back row: Wilbert and Davie.

make it usable! Two carpenters which I hired to build the house for us were Archie Hostetler and Elmer McTimmonds. Since my job in the woods kept me busy during the weekdays, I knew there was no way I could build the new house by myself. It was my job to go buy the materials, keep a handle on the supplies and progress of the building. I kept checking around for siding and finally discovered that since the war was over, the Army had vacated a large base, Camp Adair, which is between Independence and Albany. I went over there and arranged to get siding for our house. Frances wanted a nice, white farmhouse, and this siding was the typical, Army-green color. No problem, we thought! We'd just paint it and everything would be fine. However, there must have been some lead in that paint, for even though we painted the siding white, in several months, there would be this "bleeding" effect, and it looked as if it needed another coat of paint! Throughout the years, that house had many, many coats of white paint, but it seemed that the "bleeding effect" never was completely gone and generally looked as if it needed a new coat of paint!!

In talking to Bud Hampton one day, I told him of my dilemma in not being able to obtain windows for the new house and he told me he had access to an entire load of them in Tacoma, Washington. Being the wonderful, caring person that Bud was, he arranged to have windows brought down to Oregon for our new house. Kids nowadays just don't realize that things back then weren't always easy to cope with! At last we did get our house complete and it was with a sigh of relief that we moved in! That statement was especially true, for the old Phillips homestead was less than livable and it was immediately dozed and burned as soon as we moved into our new house!

In so many ways, our kids had an idyllic setting in which to grow up! The creek, at that time, still had native trout, so the kids could fish, pick berries, and roam around over this place, totally unhampered! Really, it was just one of the most ideal pieces of real estate one could ever hope for. There were two hundred fifty acres in which to do exploration, so they weren't exactly limited! Once when the boys were out, they saw where a bear was also working on the berries, so they took a New House Bear trap, baited it, and caught a black bear. They had a fine time and our dog thought he'd go right in and finish the bear off! Well, he went in all right, but he didn't finish the bear! The boys learned to milk the cows and took care of the stock. They also became very proficient running the tractor, mowing and raking the hay and enjoyed it very much! At a very early age, they learned to accept responsibility!

When we moved up Mill Creek, the kids finished elementary school at the little country school, known as Buell School. It was just a little over three miles each way and they walked back and forth nearly every day. Soon, Wilbert was ready for high school and at that time, there was no bus service available to take students into Sheridan, which was the nearest high school. The school district had told us they couldn't run a bus up Mill Creek for one student and our house was three miles from the main highway where the bus passed by. We had to do some negotiating in order to get bus service! Then, Russell became high school age, as well as other neighbor kids. By 1953, all our kids were in high school and they spent many hours riding that school bus! Some of the families who had kids riding on this route were the Blair's, Thomas's, McKibben's, Yoder's, Mullis's, Baller's, Herber's, Hampton's, and Peterson's. The kids were all very active in Sheridan High School and served in different capacities: Student Body President, Vice President, Secretary, and several received various honors. They also had so many wonderful friends, among them were the Mendenhall kids, Reeser's, Kunzler's, Carlson's, Hughey's, Blair's, Lux, Crisp, Bayliss, Gould's, Sparks, Cody, and so many more! Mr. Frank Smith was a capable, dedicated leader of Sheridan High School and there were many wonderful teachers among the staff!

Davie, our youngest boy, got into big-time gambling one day! He bet the twin boys $500 on some issue, but unfortunately, he lost! Well, we tried to teach them to be diplomatic, so they worked it out like this: Dave had to do the chores and milking at fifty dollars per day until his slate was clean! He did just that because there was really no other way out! This, of course, taught them the value of money! This method was very satisfactory and no money changed hands! Too bad the Secretary of State doesn't implement this principle! I remember I told Davie, "Always bet your small change first!"

One thing we didn't do was SEND our kids to Sunday School! We took them! We tried to instill in them and teach the basic values for good living as well as to have a good knowledge of the Bible! Furthermore, beyond just the knowledge, we taught them the guidelines for living! "Do justly, love mercy, and walk humbly with your God," are wise words from the good book and still appropriate advice for today!

Donna was also a great help to her Mother and her education proceeded at a rapid rate! She became a good seamstress and had an eye for coordinating colors in clothing and decorating. With five brothers and she being the only girl, things were not always ideal, but she learned to cope with the teasing and I think it helped her greatly as she ventured out into life! When she got into high school, she really took a liking to business classes, worked in the school office, and became very proficient with the typewriter and taking shorthand. One time a suitor brought her home about midnight and one of the twin boys fired a 30-30 rifle, a warning shot, if you will! To this day, they have never confessed as to which one did it and I can't imagine where they ever got the idea! Of course, she was embarrassed and very upset, to say the least! She tried for years to get the "protector" to confess, but without success!

HOME ON THE RANGE

We had acquired some cattle and I had a range permit so they were able to graze well beyond our property lines. Engle and Werth Logging Company was doing some heavy duty logging and hauling right down the road, which ran through our place, without a Right of Way. Their huge logging trucks were going past our house at alarming rates of speed! One Saturday I went into the office of Engle and Werth and I asked to see Elmer Werth, who was "top dog"! I said, "Hello, my name is Kenny Shenk and we just bought the Phillips' place. I'm here to ask you if you'd like to have a Right Of Way to haul your logs through my property?" He was sitting down in a big chair smoking a cigarette and looked at me with a rather sarcastic look. "Well, h— no, I don't want a Right Of Way through that place, I'll just run you out of there," he sort of bragged. I said, "I'm sorry, Mr. Werth, I surely don't want to play ball with you!" This tickled him and he kinda laughed and said, "I'd love to play ball with you!"

This was on a Saturday afternoon and since I drove the crummy, on Monday evening I made the usual stop at the Buell store to let four or five cutters off. Back then, we didn't have these official "Park and Ride" lots, but the store was where people could park their vehicles while they worked during the day. As I stopped, a fellow immediately comes up to the truck and asked, "Are you Kenny Shenk?" to which I said, "I am!" He said, "My name is Herbert Brede, Engle and Werth's Logging Superintendent, and I have a check for you! I understand you approached Mr. Werth regarding a Right Of Way." "Yes, I did, but I didn't get to first base," I said. Brede says, "Oh, Mr. Werth is very hard for a stranger to approach." I said, "He sure is, let's make him easy. I have never in my life been treated so rudely!" He said, "All you have to do is sign this form and you can cash the check." I said, "Oh, I don't have my glasses and I suppose I ought to read the fine print!" "Oh no," he responded, "it's just a standard form!" Like fun it was! It said in their little "standard form" that any forest products on our place had to be sold only to Engle and Werth! Now the plot thickens, so guess what happened next!

That same evening, who should come up, but Bud Hampton, and it had been quite some time since I had last seen him. He came in, made himself at home, remarked about how the kids were growing (which they surely were), and then the fireworks started! Bud said, "Guess what, Kenny! I just bought two hundred forty acres which lie west of your property and we truly are neighbors now!" I said, "Well, that's nice, Bud, but I've got something here which will take that smile right off your face!" "What have you got?" Bud asked. So I got the Eagle and Werth contract and check and said, "Read that!" He glanced at it and said, "Well, I guess it doesn't pertain to me, does it?" I said, "It sure would if I sign it!" "Would you let me take it to my lawyer in McMinnville and let him review it for me?" Bud asked. I said, "Sure you can. Take the check and all the paperwork," which he did. The next evening here comes Bud in his big Chrysler. He gets out rather quickly, came into the house and asked, "Kenny, did you sign any papers today?" "No, I didn't," I answered. "Kenny, I'll give you five times what

Engle and Werth offered you if you will let me have it," Bud stated. Without hesitating, I said, "It's a deal!"

Bud sent Roy Hubbard up to my place one Friday evening and had instructed Roy to lock the gate up, which he did. On Saturday morning, here came two crummies full of Engle and Werth's workers. They were rigging up a Spar tree, which involved a lot of work, and so they decided to rig it on Saturday in order to begin hauling logs on Monday morning. Ray Barkley was the Superintendent then for E and W, and as he came up there, here's this gate across the road. He came to our house, knocked on the door, and I opened it. Immediately I could see he was fighting mad! He asked, "Do you have a key to that gate?" I said, "Yes, I do, Ray! I also have a hack saw! I won't loan you the key, but I'll loan you the hack saw!" He gave me a funny look, and then proceeded to cuss! "Knock it off, Ray, I tried to talk to your boss once and I've never been treated so shamefully in my life, so forget it," I told him. He calmed down right away and asked, "What do you think I ought to do, Kenny?" "I think you ought to contact Bud Hampton," I said. Ray called him and Bud said, "Sure, go ahead and go through the gate, so long as you agree to our conditions!" They agreed and went on up and went to work. This was beneficial to Bud and in this way he was able to recoup some dollars in return for the exorbitant price he had paid for that timber up Gooseneck several years earlier when Elmer Werth bid against him and ran the timber price up so high.

RED THE RASCAL

Now things really started to happen! Willamette Valley (which was the name then) made a deal to buy out Engle and Werth's holdings in Mill Creek area; the only proviso was they could log certain portions and then it was all Willamette's. Engle and Werth had a watchman and a good gate just above our property, as well as a cabin for their man to live in and serve as the gate watchman. Dick DeCamp was Willamette's Forester and he and a company official came down from Black Rock into Mill Creek one day. They arrive at this gate and it is locked! Dick blew his horn for the watchman to come out to unlock the gate for him, and out comes Red Darrow! He was a big, ornery old customer who was, at one time, a policeman in Portland. He had also fallen timber several different times for Engle and Werth. He was a large man and quite overpowering! Red walked up to Dick DeCamp and said, "Just who in h— do you think you are and how did you get in here? You don't look big enough to fight! I'm going to paddle your ass and throw you into the creek!" Dick told me he took an awful lot of verbal abuse and thought Red was going to assault him. Finally Red finished cussing him and asked, "Who ARE you?" Dick told him who he was, after which Red finally unlocked the gate and let him go on through. Dick came to our house and was still shook up. "Who is that character at that gate?" he asked. I told him who he was and Dick said, "We certainly don t want anyone like that at our gate!" Then here comes Red. He didn't know me real well, although we had visited some. Red always called me "Shanks," which I didn't appreciate! He said, "Shanks, I should have put my foot in my d—, BIG mouth!" Then he told me his version of the story of what had happened at the gate! "You've got to help get that gate watchman job for me," Red stated. I said, "No, I don't Red! I have no way to do that!"

Dick DeCamp came out the next day and as we talked, he asked, "Do you know of a good watchman?" I told him that I did, and went up to Sweet Home to move Rollie back to Mill Creek! Remember, this is where Rollie had lived with his family and he was more than thrilled to be moving back! Willamette moved a cabin down and it was placed near our new house. They then moved the gate close to our barn and Rollie was in business! Old Red? Well, that ornery guy told everybody in the company that I had beat him out of his gate watchman's job, which didn't set too well with me!

One day the twin boys were at the barn feeding cattle and I happened to be there with them. We heard a vehicle coming and it was Red in his pickup. The gate is closed and Rollie hadn't heard Red drive up. Red called out to me and I could see he was fighting mad! I walked up to his pickup and just stood there while the profanity flew at a fast pace, turning the air blue! "I'm going to get out of my pickup and beat the h— out of you!" he yelled. I said, "Well, if it has to be done, get on out and we'll proceed!" The boys heard all this and took a rather dim view of the suggestion. I was unaware that the boys were listening and they thought surely the battle was imminent, as did I. They each had a fork; one a pitch fork, the other a six-tined, manure fork, ready for action. I just stood there and I felt sure he was going to fight. Old Rollie came out just then, opened the gate and Red drove off! Red still lived behind the gate, however.

One day after the incident at the gate with Red, he stopped and said, "Shanks, I want to talk with you!" I said, "Go ahead." "I didn't like the way you looked at me the other morning. You were ready to fight me, weren't you?" he noted. I said, "Yes, I was, Red!" "I saw that on your face," he commented. Maybe he figured I wasn't about to let him intimidate me! Let me tell you a story Red told me: A nice looking lady, Hazel, from Eugene was living with him and she had the same problem as Red; they both had to have their booze! He said they went into Sheridan to the tavern and each had several beers. After their glasses were empty, they headed out to Mill Creek. At the bottom of the Harmony Road hill, the road makes a rather sharp curve and there was a big ditch, full of water. Right at the bottom of the hill, Hazel said, "Stop, Red! I gotta get rid of some beer!" Hazel got out, squatted down with her posterior against the ditch full of water, and as she did this, Red said the thought came to him, "Wouldn't Hazel look funny if I pushed her backwards into the water!" Well, that's just what this ornery, old cuss did! Poor Hazel went in backwards and nearly drowned! I can imagine how she told him off! That weekend Hazel said, "I have to go to Eugene today," so Red drove her to downtown Eugene. She said, "Just wait here while I go to the drugstore. I'll be right back." He waited for hours, but she never came back. After Red had told me his story, he said, "Ya know, I got to thinkin', maybe Hazel held that against me!" Could have been, ya know! "Hazel really was a fine woman, but she was too strong in the elbows," Red told me. I asked, "What do you mean, too strong in the elbows?" He said, "Oh, Hazel would hook her elbows over the bar and I couldn't pry her loose to go home!" Red was one of the most unpredictable fellows I ever met. Once he chased Ray Barkley down Mill Creek, pursuing him with his pickup and a 30/

30 rifle, intending to kill him. Ray stopped at our house to phone the Polk County Sheriff for help, but they were not interested! Red was a constant pest and problem for several years and was just impossible!

CATTLE CASUALTY

Earlier I mentioned that I had acquired quite a number of white-faced cattle and had grazing permits for them. The logging trucks continued to drive down the road at speeds which were not safe - for the animals often would walk right across the road and there was no way a truck could stop in time when they were going as fast as we observed them going! This situation caused me great concern and sure enough, it wasn't long before two of the cattle were severely injured and one had to be destroyed. I had bought two, fine Hereford cows from John Breeden and both were due to have their third calves. The one was hit in the shoulder and I had a vet come out to examine her. This proved to be greatly beneficial for my "case", for I had a detailed report of what happened. I went down to see Bud, related the incident and expressed my continuing concern. He said, "That's fine, Kenny, I'll act as your agent and we'll get some insurance money to replace your cows. Don't talk to anybody else about it, just write me a letter telling about the accident, and I'll send the bill to our insurance company."

I did as Bud instructed, wrote the informational letter and before long I received a letter from a company in Portland, the Alfred K. Davis Insurance Company. The request was, "Please give the exact time of day, the license number of the truck, the name of the driver, and all the pertinent details so we can honor your claim." Bud called me and said, "That's okay, Kenny, I'll take care of it!" We went along for about a year and in the meantime, I kept receiving letters every so often from the insurance company, "We want to honor your claim, but we cannot process your claim................" I didn't know the fellow who killed the cow, but had a pretty good idea who it was. If I was correct, the fellow who was driving the vehicle, drove an old International truck, with defective brakes, but he was a family man who had a family to support and needed to work. So I just didn't have the heart to turn his name in, and I wasn't completely positive he was the one! Bud asked me one day, "Did you ever get a check from my insurance company?" "No, I didn't," I said. He said, "Just hold on!" A short while later, this agent representing the company went to see Bud and asked, "Are you ready to renew your insurance policy with me, Bud?" "No, I don't think I will," Bud told him and he asked, "What's wrong?" "Well, I have a claim here that you won't honor and it says in my policy with you that you will honor and pay any and all claims. Now I realize this is a rather unusual claim, but it actually happened and you won't pay it. Therefore, I am not going to renew my insurance with your company," Bud explained. The agent was aghast and said, "Oh, we'll take care of that!" Immediately after this meeting, I received a check for the amount we had agreed upon for the cow and could close the chapter on that one! Bud was really there to go to bat for his employees!

WHOLEHEARTED HALFWAY HUNT

Bob Patty and his wife, Rosena, Frances and I planned a hunting trip one fall to Eastern Oregon. We went out of Joseph, on Beeler Ridge, where we killed a couple deer, and then, seemingly, couldn't find anymore, so Bob said, "Let's go look up a new area and maybe we can get some more meat!" Frances and I were in the lead in our vehicle, as we all started driving towards Baker. Near Halfway, I looked in the rear-view mirror of my pickup and couldn't see Bob following me in his car and little trailer. I pulled over and we sat there awhile, waiting for them to show. After some time, we turned around and began driving back and had gone about five miles, when we spotted their vehicle. Rosena was sitting in the car and she pointed, "He's up the hill!" Up the hill I went, found Bob, and asked, "Patty, what's going on?" "Well, I thought we were looking for a new place to hunt," he replied, and I said, "Well, we are!" "Then this is it," he declared. He had seen a beautiful buck up on this hill, so went up there and shot it!

We set up camp there as it was an ideal spot! Water was close by and we were in an area of nice, little pine trees! Both of us had tents, so we pitched them, ate a bite, and afterwards Bob and I walked up on the hill. We each went our separate ways and in the meantime, it began to snow. It was utterly amazing how quickly the ground was covered with snow. It looked and felt just like tapioca! As I looked up on a ridge, I spotted three, four-point bucks walking right toward me! This was something I hadn't seen for some time! They just paused on the point up there, as if in thought, so I put a bullet in the first buck's heart and down he went! We always had a signal we used to give to each other when we killed something while out hunting. Never did we shout out, because you never knew WHO might come running, but rather, we just gave this logging, "tight-line signal," three and two. For some reason, I didn't do this! At this point, I didn't know where Bob was and hadn't seen him for an hour! All of a sudden, I heard Bob shout, "Shall I shoot?" I answered, "I don't know, Bob!" Again, he called out the same question, "Shall I shoot?" Two bucks had run right up to Bob and were literally blowing their breath in his face. Unfortunately, he didn't know if I had shot any or not, and we wanted to get our limit! We needed one more deer to fill our tags and I felt mortified over that and apologized profusely to Bob for not giving our usual tight-line signal. My error of omission stuck in his craw for several days and he was really mad at me over that! The buck I had gotten was just white with fat and Bob said it was one of the finest pieces of meat he had ever seen, and I concurred with him! We did go home with three nice deer, however, and our wives had really enjoyed this hunting trip and their time together! Frances always considered Rosena to be a very good friend!

TRUTH ON TRIAL

I bought two Minneapolis Molene tractors so that each of the twin boys had their own tractor, and they sure put them to good use. Besides the farming on our home place, they could also do the work down at the other farm I had purchased. This other farm was on lower Mill Creek, about three miles below Buell, and close to the Rosenbaum farm. I farmed it one year, together with the neighbor, Elmer Blanchard. Elmer was getting up in years, as he was seventy-eight, and he liked to putter around the farm. One year the twin boys farmed it, and another year, Russell and Myron farmed it! All the kids were really great workers, although they might insist that this was a prerequisite for living under our roof! However, a lot of kids today would stay out of trouble if they were given some chores to do! We planted a large garden every year, so there was always weeding to be done, and Frances canned hundreds and hundreds of quarts of fruit and vegetables of every kind! The boys did most of the farming, and I logged! There was always much to keep everyone busy!

One day the twins were going down to the other farm to spread fertilizer on the ground, and driving back along the field, they noticed Mr. Blanchard working on the fence. Right where the road made a bend, he had a big roll of barbed wire laying in some brush and was nailing wire to the fence posts. The boys drove their car slowly by, unaware that the end of this roll of barbed wire had accidentally caught in the edge of their car's bumper. As they continued on, the wire tightened until the roll Mr. Blanchard was holding in his hand, catapulted him into the air and he landed on the ground. One of the boys just happened to see what was happening in the rear view mirror! They stopped and ran back to where he lay injured. One of them held him in his arms and the other one went to get help!

Mr. Blanchard was taken into a Portland Hospital for surgery, but he died on the operating table. We all felt so badly about the accident and went down to talk to Mrs. Blanchard and her family. They said there were no hard feelings and assured us, "Dad's time was long overdue, he wasn't in good health, and don't you feel badly about this!" We went to his funeral on a Saturday and the following week, on Wednesday, here came two of the Blanchard fellows and I could tell there was trouble! They asked, "What would you think if we brought suit against you regarding Dad's death?" I said, "What difference does it make what I think? I only have one question: On what grounds are you going to sue?" "Oh," they responded, "negligence on your part!"

Mrs. Blanchard and her sons finally secured a lawyer who would take their case and he tried to build a case on prima-facie evidence. Soon we were notified the boys were to go in for a deposition, and I went in with them to see Blanchard's attorney. He was very soft-spoken and said, "Boys, just describe in your own words exactly what happened! Be free, calm and relaxed - nothing is going to happen!" Then Byron began to describe how they had gone down there to farm that evening, had greeted Mr. Blanchard, and that he had responded, "Hello, boys!" Byron said Mr. Blanchard had a hammer up in the air, pounding wire into the fence post. The attorney asked, "How far did you go past him before you saw him fly through the air?" One of the boys answered, "Oh, about fifty feet," and the attorney is writing this all down, although the other twin thought it was about seventy-five feet.

The day of the trial arrived and this lawyer, Sam Speerstra, was a very dramatic fellow and definitely knew how to put his best foot forward! He paced back and forth in front of the jury, was very theatrical, and tried to play on their sympathy by saying,

"Ladies and Gentlemen, this is a very unique case in that Mr. Blanchard is not here in his own defense, for his lips are stilled in death!" Mrs. Blanchard and her daughter would then weep, dab at their eyes, and this is how it went! Mr. Speerstra then turned to the boys and said, "I don't really think these are bad boys, I don't think their parents taught them to lie, but here Myron told me on such and such a day that they went fifty feet, and now he said they went one hundred twenty-five feet! Now what story are we going to believe?" The most amusing part of this trial experience is that the attorney for the Blanchard's had the twins confused; when he was quoting Byron, he stated he was quoting Myron! All Byron had to do was reply, "Sir, my name is not Myron, my name is Byron!" It just blew the attorney's case!

The day of the accident, the boys had made a mark down at the field where they stopped, before they took the wire off the bumper, and told me they had done this. Once we discovered there was going to be a lawsuit, we had gone down and carefully measured the distance with a steel tape before the day of the trial. That was why we knew the distance was, in fact, one hundred twenty-five feet! Prior to that, they had just been estimating! The outcome was that the boys were acquitted! After it was over, as the jurors shook hands with us and the boys, they told us, "We could tell by the testimony of those boys they are as honest as the day is long! In no way were they negligent! We could do nothing less than acquit them!"

Ironically, our insurance company had offered the Blanchard's a settlement prior to going to trial, and they said, "Oh, no, we're going whole hog or none!" The end result was that they were required to pay for the trial, so had those additional costs, as well as funeral expenses. This entire episode was so sad for our family and we regretted everything that happened.

FULL SACKS OF GRAIN - AND MORE!

That fall the twin boys farmed that place and I bought a bale of sacks, four hundred and fifty sacks in this bale, but I didn't think to check the size of the bags. Once opened, we discovered they weren't regular grain sacks, but a size between grain and a beet pulp sack. The boys combined the crop, loaded the bags onto the truck, and took them over to the warehouse in Dallas. Matt Gillis was in charge of the warehouse and I went over one day to see him. "Are you the Father of those little twins who hauled that grain in here on that big corn binder truck?" he asked. I said, "Yes, I am!" "Well, who in the devil loads those sacks for them? Those little devils sure as h— don't load them! Who do they have load them?" he questioned. I assured him, "I don't know, but I'll find out!" Then I was also told, "You've just completely destroyed our manner of stacking the bags! We can only haul five bags of yours on the little wheeling buggy, but for everyone else, we can always haul six! I just cannot believe those kids load those bags by themselves!"

This truck which I bought, had been an old logging truck and had huge overload springs on it. When I put a bed on the truck, it was quite high up in the air, and was really strong! That evening I asked the boys, "How do you boys load those sacks?"

Myron said, "I don't know what you mean!" I said, "Well, how do you load them?" "Simple, I drive the truck one time and Byron loads them, and the next time Byron drives, and I load them," he explained. Those bags averaged 165 pounds apiece and the boys probably didn't weigh more than 115 - 120 pounds apiece! No wonder Matt was utterly astonished!

OUR WATCHFUL WATCHMAN

Living up Mill Creek with Rollie tending the gate provided a lot of fun experiences. Rollie had some strange ideas and it was practically impossible to convince him otherwise. For example, this was one of his beliefs: I noticed that he always bought MJB coffee in two-pound cans, so I said to him, "Rollie, why don't you just buy a one-pound can because your coffee will stay fresher that way!" "No," he said, "you get lots more for your money on a two-pound can than you do by buying two, one-pound cans!" I asked, "Well, why is that?" His answer: "They just simply fill the cans fuller!" Amazing fact, which I didn't know! I asked Frances if she knew that and we had a great laugh out of Rollie's observation!

On a Friday night, a bunch of burly loggers drove up Mill Creek, knowing that buck season opened the next morning. Rollie planned to open the gate on Saturday morning and not before, although he took a lot of cajoling and pleading! This one hunter said, "Rollie, are you going to open up on fast time or standard time?" Rollie told me, "Some of these smart alecs are going to find out these watches and clocks were made to run on standard time! You get to foolin' with 'em and they won't keep good time! I'm going to open up on standard time!" He firmly believed that if you changed the time on your watch or clock a lot, they didn't work as well! Of course, he opened on standard time! There were 117 pickups, cars, and vehicles which went through the gate from 6:00 o'clock in the morning until 10:00 o'clock in the evening. The Game Commission used to tag out from sixty-five to a hundred bucks every opening day on Mill Creek! Now that the coyotes have taken over (as well as the biologists), we only know of three bucks killed up Mill Creek last season (1996)! The hungry coyotes have taken care of themselves and have cleaned the deer out of the mountains!

While logging for Willamette, Gene Knudsen came up to see Rollie and told him, "It's fire season and we're in a very critical situation just now, so I don't want you to let anybody through the gate! If someone really has legitimate business up there and needs to go through, send them over to the office and I'll write them a pass!" Rollie hadn't been watching gate all that long when a Lincoln Continental drove up and sat at the gate. The fellow in the car honked his horn a time or two before Rollie arrived at the gate. Having someone honk the horn more than once didn't set too well with Rollie, so when he got there, he asked, "And just WHO do you think you are?" The fellow responded, "Get that gate open! I'm Bill Swindell!" Rollie said, "You may be Bill Swindell, but I'm not opening that gate for you!" Bill got very angry and used some rather strong language, but soon realized that Rollie was NOT going to budge!

His only choice was to turn around and go back down the road. That evening Gene Knutsen came up to see Rollie, asking him, "Rollie, don't you know who Bill Swindell is?" Rollie said to Gene, "You told me you'd write a pass for anybody who needed to go through there! I thought maybe you were 'trying him out'!" Gene had to swallow his own medicine, for Rollie was following his instructions to the letter of the law! It was very funny! Gene said Swindell was so mad he nearly canned him!

STEENS MOUNTAINS

SHEEPHERDER'S SHELTER

Throughout the years, I always loved to hunt, so began to do considerably more of it and planned a trip to Eastern Oregon. Two different times I went hunting with Louis Swartzentruber from McMinnville. The first time Louie and I went over, I told him I would pay for the gas and groceries because he was taking his new Ford pickup. We drove down to the Steens Mountains, where he was somewhat acquainted. The very first day there, I killed an antelope. One evening we drove back to the foot of a big mountain and saw lots of deer there. Besides the deer, we also saw a pickup sitting there and sort of a tent-house. We knocked, but no one answered, so we went into this cabin, and glancing around, saw some wood and a few furnishings. Louie said, "Oh, this is an old sheepherders cabin, let's get our supper!" Without even

1945 - Steens Mountains - big buck I killed there.

lighting a lantern, we began to fix our supper. Before long, we heard a groan from over in the corner and were shocked, as we never realized there was anybody there! Here was an old man in bed - he looked to be 150 years old! He weakly pulled the covers back and said, "Plenty of grub there, boys, help yourself!" With this weak utterance, he rolled over and went back to sleep. Soon we heard a man outside cursing very loudly, "What the h— is going on here, anyway?" he said, cussing, as we stood by the door. "Come on in," Louie said. "Who are you?" he asked. Louie answered, "We're just hunters from the Coast!" This fellow had two hams from a yearling draped over the stock of his gun and blood all over himself! He asked, "Is that old devil in there drunk yet?" We said, "Yes!" "You know who that is?" he asked. Louie and I said we didn't, so he continued, "Have you ever heard of Harry's Steak House at Drain, Oregon?" "Yes, we've heard of it!" "Well," the fellow said, "that's old Harry, the owner! He always gets drunk on me! I own the Laundry at Cottage Grove and Harry and I like to hunt." Then he sat down to join us for supper and began to visit. On that trip I killed a couple nice bucks and then we came home.

MUSHROOMS AND MIDNIGHT

The next fall, Louie was making plans to go hunting at Half Moon Springs in Eastern Oregon, and asked me to invite Ron to go along also, so we made preparations! Louie's business was buying furs for a Frenchmen from New York, a Mr. Bernard Douwa. Mr. Douwa had just gotten married and brought his pretty, little bride out to Oregon with him to go hunting. His wife told us she had worked for three different Departments of the United States Government; the Social Security Department, the Census Bureau, and the Internal Revenue Service. They were still newlyweds; holding hands and a bit oblivious as to what the rest of the world was doing! They had a nice, new car and hit a root going into the hunting site in Eastern Oregon, causing the transmission on this new car to lock up in low range! Try as he would, Bernard could not get it out of low gear! We towed them into camp and all of us proceeded to hunt; they went their way, and we went ours. As all of us congregated back in camp that evening, Bernard was relating to us that when they were up on a hillside during the day, a big bull elk came out. He said, "I assumed a shooting stance (which we really didn't know what he meant), bringing myself up to full stature, and shot when I got the bead on his shoulder. Then that bull made sort of a coughing sound!" When Bernard said this, he imitated the elk with a coughing sound. My brother, Ron, said, "Oh, oh, he's gut shot!" I said, "No, he's lung shot!" Bernard's wife said, "No, Honey, he didn't sound like that!" So she got up, bent over and made a coughing sound which she thought more closely imitated that of the elk's! Bernard said, "No, he didn't cough like that! He coughed like this!" He bends over and coughed, so they argued back and forth for awhile! If you can visualize those two adults trying to imitate an elk coughing, it was really quite entertaining, to say the least, and we really laughed!

Ron and I had killed an elk that day and packed it into camp in early evening, before it was dark. Bernard got to telling some ribald stories and his wife said, "Come on, Ronald, I don't think you should be around my husband, let's go out and pick some mushrooms!" Bernard started laughing and said, "Ha! Ha! Here's my new wife - running off with that Kid!" He carried on awhile, but in the meantime, Ron had agreed to go find mushrooms with her, so they left. In just a little bit, Louie said he'd go pick some, too, as he could distinguish edible ones from the poisonous variety. Just before dark, Ron and Bernard's wife came back with a pail full of mushrooms. It got dark shortly thereafter, the stars came out and it was quite cold, with snow on the ground. Still Louie hadn't come back, and I said, "Louie's lost out there in the thicket!" Bernard laughed and said, "You couldn't lose that man in the State of Oregon!" "Well, he's managed now and he's lost," I insisted! "Oh, no, he isn't," was Bernard's sure reply! "Oh, yes, he is," I said, feeling just as certain that he WAS lost!

After about an hour, I threw a rifle up in the air and shot, as Louie still hadn't returned to camp. In the far-off distance, we heard a shot in response! I shot again, and another shot came back. Finally, Louie came into camp and he was really mad! He said, "What's the matter with you birds, anyhow?" We got him calmed down and he began to sort his mushrooms, although, since he was still so angry at us, he didn't take great pains to be careful, and was only working with light from the campfire. Bernard's wife decided to fry up a bunch of mushrooms and all of the guys ate some. For some reason, she didn't eat any! Just as we finished eating them, Ron looked at me and asked, "Do your guts feel all right?" I said, "As a matter of fact, they don't!" Just then, I began to vomit; almost without warning, it was so sudden! Ron said, "Oh, oh, I'm sick, too," and he got up to vomit! Louie followed suit almost immediately and was obviously sick, too. Bernard and his wife had fixed their bed in the back of Louie's pickup and had gone to bed. She heard us carrying on, raised up from her bed and said, "Boys, PLEASE, I'm so allergic to such sounds, please go further away from camp to do that! No sooner had she said that to us when Bernard sat up in bed! Suddenly, he jumped out of the pickup, barely getting off, when he began heaving, too! She got up then, and said, "Oh, fellows, I'm sorry, I didn't realize you guys were so sick!" They had a bottle of whiskey, so she tried to make hot toddies for us with whiskey and lemon juice, but we were all too sick to drink anything! Not only were we heaving our insides out, but diarrhea started also!

Soon it was obvious that we fellows were all terribly ill - so ill, that it was frightening! About midnight, it was decided we should go into LaGrande to get some help. We left Half Moon Springs, got into LaGrande about 1:00 A.M, and immediately found a motel. Bernard's wife got on the phone from their motel room, after which she came over to our room, saying, "Please, let me bring the doctor here to see you! The doctor said they just buried a family of five who had eaten poisonous mushrooms and if you guys are this sick, then there's no reason for you to be alive!" Ron spoke up and said, "Keep him out of here, this feels good enough for me to die in!" She begged, cried and wanted to get the doctor, but we said we'd be okay. The next day we were so sore from everything, we could hardly breathe. We walked downtown past the J.C. Penney store where they always had those double windows and Ron said, "I wonder if I look as peaked as you do!" Just then he saw himself and said, "Huh! I guess I do!"

That evening we went back to our hunting site and broke camp. Bernard got his car fixed and they went back to New York. To let you know what happened to the elk that Bernard said he shot at, some other guys also wounded the same bull and were trailing him, and even though they shot at it after Bernard did, they took it away from him. Bernard was very upset and angry about it as he said he'd gladly give $1,000 for it - he wanted it so badly! That was a lot of money back in those days, but he lost out on that bull and we felt very badly for him!

Louie, Ron, and I pulled out of camp and were driving in towards Starkey when we saw a fellow pulling a tiny trailer house behind a new Buick Sedan. As we drove by, we noticed that he had stopped and was walking out towards a little stand of timber. Going down the hill on the other side, some elk came walking out of the woods! There was a bull and a cow and they ran down across Burnt Coral Creek, so we were able to get both of them! Now each of us had an elk, and went on home with our tags filled! That was a rewarding end to our trip after being so very ill, and all of us were fortunate to be alive! For about twenty-five years, just the thought of mushrooms made me ill and I could not eat them, nor stand the taste of them! Thankfully, I can now eat mushrooms with great enjoyment!

EAST LAKE ESCAPADES

We always enjoyed fishing, so Frances and I decided to pack up the kids, groceries, tent, and supplies and drive over to East Lake, which is in the Newberry Crater, South of Bend, Oregon, to do some fishing. We arrived over there, pitched our tent, and camped at the edge of the lake, towards the High Rock Bluff. This, mind you, was before the Californians discovered Oregon! The resort owners had boats for rent, so we rented one, went out on the lake and just had a wonderful time fishing! Each day we would catch our limit - or the term is, 'limit out'! The fish were from fifteen to twenty-three inches in length, averaging nineteen inches! Never before or since have I experienced fishing like that! One of the kids would say, "Hey, I've got a fish on," when another one would also have one on and so it went! Of course, not all was just fun and games, for occasionally the fish would make a big run and tangle up all the lines, if they hadn't been pulled in. A little procedure, if followed, will prevent a mass of tangled lines! These were Rainbow trout, and how they would run, jump, and sometimes fight and it was just a delightful experience!

More than once, on some of our trips to East Lake, some of the Emmert's would join us with their families, and what fun the kids had back in camp while the adults were enjoying their time out on the lake. If you ask any of our kids, they would say that going to East Lake was another one of their most favorite activities! We spent many, happy hours over there fishing and this was just the beginning of many, many trips to East Lake. The fact that fishing was so good was just an added bonus and we all enjoyed it tremendously! Sad to say, such great fishing is not the case now. The last time we were at East Lake, there were many fifth wheelers and motor homes, with nearly all vehicles bearing California license plates, but such is life in the Far West!

WORKING FOR WAGES

Several different years, Frances and the kids picked prunes down on Salt Creek for Silas Starr and family. One year there was a particularly good crop and they all picked prunes with a vengeance! So I told the boys, "You can emulate the Prodigal Son!" Wilbert, being the oldest, caught on right away! He asked, "You mean we can have our money?" I said, "You can, and you may spend your money any way you like!" Frances took those two young lads to town. Wilbert wanted a typewriter and he got one! Russell wanted a new Winchester 30.30, and he got one! Two happier boys did not exist in Polk County! I mention this to show the diversity which exists in people!

Shortly after Russell purchased his gun, he had an opportunity to try it out! He killed a big buck on the edge of the Wild Cherry Thicket and he was ten feet tall! I'm referring to Russ and not the buck! Russ surely loved to hunt and as he got older, we had some real exciting elk hunts in Eastern Oregon. The twin boys also had some unfinished business with those big bucks. During hunting season, they'd get up before dawn and scale a big bluff across the creek from our house to hunt before the school bus came to take them to school. One morning Myron killed a nice three-point buck and sure enough, shortly after that, Byron killed one also! Yes, it, too, was a three-point buck! It wasn't easy, but it can be done, and so they did it! Those boys were identical, and that means in every sense of the word! Even as they began to grow, many relatives absolutely could not tell them apart! This continued on until they were off to college and then married. Then some people would be able to tell who they were by the accompanying wife! To this day, many people still do not know them apart!

One time when Byron and his family had been in India for four years, they came through International Customs in Seattle on their return flight, around midnight. Byron had gone leopard hunting just a few days before returning home, so brought this raw hide, which he felt obliged to report to the Customs Agent. The first Customs Agent went to summons an Agricultural Inspector, and as the second fellow walked up, he greeted Byron warmly and said, "Well, I can't believe I'm seeing you here in Seattle, and began to ask about the leopard hide, and so on. Byron was puzzled and finally said, "I'm really sorry, I don't know you!" The fellow said, "Sure you do! Don't you remember, we went to Oregon State together!" Byron then realized he was being mistaken for Myron, so he said, "Oh, you must know my brother, Myron!" It took some convincing before the fellow would believe that Byron was not Myron! This just illustrates how much alike they are!

FIGHTING THE FLU AND

BAGGING THE BUCK

It was the first day of buck season one fall morning, and I planned to take the boys hunting up Mill Creek, but Davie was sick and said he didn't want to go. He had never killed a deer, so we said, "Oh, come on! You can go, we're just going up to Shumway!" We talked him into it and when we got up there, I went up above with another friend. The twins went around a draw, sort of leaving Davie to hunt on his own, as he just wasn't too enthusiastic! Poor kid, sure enough he was sick all right! Just as he was answering nature's call, he saw a big four-point buck, and shot it with my little 32-20! I still don't know if it's legal to shoot a buck with your pants down, but that's the way Davie shot his first one! The twins were nearby, heard him, and came to help out! About 11:00 o'clock, I was going back down to the pickup when I heard the twin boys holler, "Hey, Dad, come over here! We need help!" As I started over, just around the bend, there was a huge bluff, which was very steep! Right across the rocks was sort of a game trail to follow. These kids had saddled up that big buck, which weighed at least one hundred and sixty-five pounds with the hide on, and had gotten to the rock slide! I couldn't believe they had carried that big buck as far as they did, because they didn't have caulk shoes on or anything, and there was very little traction! I went over there and carried the buck through the slide, went a ways and the friend with me said, "Let me carry it!" "Okay," I said, as I put it down and helped this fellow get into it. He went about ten feet and the ground suddenly rose up and smote him! We helped him get up, but he just couldn't pack it! After I packed it about a half mile, one of the twins said, "Here, Dad, we'll pack it!" They could pack a huge load for their size! Of course, all the kids never let Davie forget that trip!

It was fall and Russell killed a huge bear before he took off for college, so we drove up the road to look at it! Here it lay in a mud hole where the dogs had bayed it and the head on it was the biggest that I have ever seen on a black bear! Russ brought the head down to the house and the next night we went back up to bring the body home. What a sight we were greeted with! A second bear had gotten the first bear out of that mud hole and eaten most of it! What was left of that huge animal was on a little bench up above the mud hole. How in the world that second bear was able to get the first bear out of there, we will never figure out! We didn't see the second bear, but it must have been a big one! Russell's bear head measured ten inches through the ears - the skull was that big!

FELIX TOM CAT, THE COUGAR

One evening I came home from work and decided to drive up the creek to check on the cattle. Since I had acquired grazing permits, they were allowed to roam all over the ranges up the creek! One cow had not calved the year before and gotten very heavy. This year, however, she was going to be a Mother, so I was concerned that she was doing all right. I drove up above Cedar Creek Camp and saw a cougar run across the road! I stopped, built a little tripod out of some limbs, turned around and went back home. Back at the house, when Rollie learned that I had seen a cougar, he wanted to go back up the creek with me, as did the twin boys. I got Russell's 30-30 rifle and the two dogs and we all went back up the creek. My actions from this point on weren't too responsible, I guess, but I did what I did! It was around 5:30 in the evening when we got back up there and I stopped by my little tripod. I never "barked instructions" to those dogs, they just took that track as if they had been shot out of a boot jack - and up the hill they went, going through some jack firs! I've never seen anything like it! Those dogs took off as hard as they could go, running up through these trees! This cougar was just fooling around on the ground there and the dogs ran right

Cougar I shot up Mill Creek. Shown with me is one of our dogs who was self-appointed Guard!

Davie is just thirteen years old helping me in woods by setting chockers when I was logging up Gooseneck for Willamina Lumber.

into him! The dogs just were frenzied with excitement, barking at a high pitch and with a sound I had never heard from them before! Their sounds were more like screams! That cougar went up the first Old Growth tree he found! The dogs had run ahead of us as fast as they could go, and had gone a long ways up a hill. After a little while, we caught up with them, so I told the boys and Rollie to stand back, as I fired a shot, hitting that cougar right close to his left eye! Down the hill he came, just like a high-climber! He was up in that tree about seventy feet high and I thought he'd fall over backwards. Instead, he arched his tail like a high-diver and down he came, nearly landing on top of the twins! Rollie was so frightened, he was shaking like a leaf! He said, "I knew it was a dead shot before you fired, Kenny!" I said, "No, you didn't, Rollie! I was shaking somewhat myself!" Let me assure you, the adrenalin was not in short supply!

Those dogs were just crazy! One grabbed this cougar by the throat, while the other one grabbed hold behind the front leg. They shut their eyes and shook this cougar vigorously, just delirious with joy! I talked to them, but their eyes had turned a glassy green, and they simply did not hear me and I was unable to pull them off that animal! In my pocket I had a little cord, so I fastened it on the cougar's lower jaw and started down the hill. Those dogs finally let go, but each of them wanted to walk behind my heel and they fought for "position" all the way down to the car. We propped the cougar up in the yard on the old sawhorse and he was a beauty! Duncan, our one dog would not let Rollie get close to that cougar, and "guarded" it day and night! I had heard that the Game Commission wouldn't pay a bounty on a dry hide, so I took that cougar down to Portland to their office, but they took a rather dim view of it. They acted as if they had no intention of paying a bounty, but after quite a length of time, we did receive the fee due us.

A side note on Duncan, our dog, is that he often laid out by this one, big fir tree close to our yard, and years later, some friends were

visiting. My friend said, "Hey, Kenny, do you think Duncan remembers that cougar?" I said, "Let's find out!" As I walked up to him, he got up and wagged his tail. I said, "You haven't seen any cougars up this tree lately, have you Duncan?" He began to whine, go around the tree, put his feet up on the trunk, and look up each tree. Sure enough, there weren't any up there, but he was checking! He was absolutely a wonderful dog!

On the way home from Portland with that cougar, I decided to pay Pelzer a visit and drove into his garage in Sheridan, just as he was closing for the day. The town undertaker, Bill Daley, drove the ambulance, as well as Ade. Upon seeing me, Ade greeted me and asked, "What can I do for you, Kenny?" I said, "Ade, I am in big trouble! Is Bill Daley in?" "No, he's out on a run! What's your trouble?" he inquired. I said, "My neighbor died and to tell you the truth, I even have him in my car!" Now I need to tell you that just as rigor mortis was setting in on this cougar, I pulled him up and propped him so he was quite tall, so to speak. I had him on a tarp in the back seat of my car, his hind legs on the floor and his head was nearly up to the back of my neck when I was driving. As I took Ade out to my car and opened the back door, here's this cougar and he looks alive! Pelzer was so surprised and taken back that he let out a scream! He ran to the front of his garage where Mrs. Ernest Huntley was walking by, and said to her, "Come over here, quick!" Then he got on the phone, called his son, Jim, and told him, "Come down to the garage at once!" He looked at me and said, "Darn you Kenny, you really got the best of me! I really thought your neighbor had died!" "Well," I said, "this IS my neighbor 'cause he's been living in the hills with us!" Pelzer was known all over for his pranks and it was hard to pull one on him, but he said, "Kenny, you surely got me this time!"

Back home, I dressed the cougar out and took the hide off. Shortly after this, as our Pastor was visiting, I asked him, "Would you like a ham off that cougar?" He said, "Oh, my, I never ate any meat from the cat family! When I was a missionary in Africa, we ate lots of monkies and they're delicious!" I said, "You can have the monkies, I'll stick with the cougar." I must admit, however, that Frances still does not consider cougar to be kosher! At this time, the Simonson boys were logging up Mill Creek. I gave Rollie a big roast off the cougar and he did a good job of cooking it! One of the truckers, Don Mendenhall, was hauling for Simonson's and he went by, so Rollie asked him, "Would you like to have some cougar meat?" Don said, "I sure would!" Rollie gave him a good portion of it and up the mountain he goes! Don said, "Hey fellows, I have some real meat here for you! It's good eating!" He passed it around and my brother-in-law, Enos Schrock, was running the yarder up there, so he was privileged to sample it, too! Millie never would have allowed cougar meat in her home, so Enos had to sample it in the woods! Ron used to really give our sister a bad time over bear and cougar meat! None of those fellows in the woods ever had any adverse reactions from eating that meat, and they obviously lived fairly normal lives after that! So it seems we got a lot of "mileage" out of this cougar!

As a young lad, Ade started to work at this Ford agency, which was then known as Clyde Niles Agency. After a number of years and a lot of hard work, Ade became the owner of the garage and agency. One Saturday I went to see him, and in his office was a fine looking salesman. They had been visiting and after awhile, the salesman said, "Pelzer, I want to shake your hand and congratulate you for your accomplishments! You are the epitome of the American Dream!" Here is Ade behind the cash register and this salesman in nice suit and tie, wanting to shake Pelzer's hand. "My hands aren't too clean sometimes, you know," Ade warned, and smiled. This salesman says, "Put 'er there!" Under the counter, Ade kept a five-pound bucket, into which he poured used, rear-end oil, so he sticks his hand in the bucket, after which he extends it to the salesman and begins shaking the fellow's hand! This fellow said, "Why, you dirty so and so," and starts cussing!

One fall I went into the Sheridan Grain Company to talk to the Manager, Leon French. He was a very fine fellow and easy to meet and was called, "Frenchie," by those who knew him. Frenchie said, "Kenny, we have your grain all cleaned and if you want to sell some, come down early in the morning and we will do business!" Early the next morning, I went down to Sheridan Grain, arriving at about the same time as Frenchie. He said, "Good morning, Kenny, come on in," as he unlocked the office door. "Nice morning ain't it!" He snapped on the lights, turned up the heating system, got his cigarette going, and we are about to do business. All of a sudden, Frenchie says, "Do you smell something funny?" "I surely do," I said, for just like that, we were smitten with the most horrible, stinking smell you ever smelled! I only wish that Ralph Nader could have been there! Suddenly, Frenchie jumped up, threw the switch to the big electric tubes and here was the source of all sources! Frenchie looked at me and said, "Oh, I know! That Ade Pelzer was in here last night as I was closing up!" Here were rotten, salmon eggs smeared in behind and all over these big, electric heating tubes! You talk about a foul odor! You can't believe how horrible that nice, little office smelled for some time! Yes, Pelzer had been there! Phooey on Kilroy - Pelzer's good enough for me!

Another thing Ade loved to do was fish and was very good at it. Thing of it was, if you fished with him, you had to be on your toes! One time John Rogers was fishing for steelhead out at the coast with him. John left his pole momentarily and while he was gone, Pelzer pulled John's line in and cut the hook off. Sometimes you just can't win! Over at East Lake one day, I was out in my boat very early one morning, but it was very foggy. In fact, it was so dense, it was almost impossible to identify other boaters who were out there. All of a sudden, someone called out in a loud voice, "Hello, Cougar! How ya doin?" I then knew Pelzer was also at East Lake! What fun!

RESPECTING RIGHTS

Without even asking for permission, the Game Commission had posted signs clear across our property and in some instances, even drove nails right into some of the trees! The signs said, "CLOSED TO ALL HUNTING," and incredulously, some of the signs read, "State Game Refuge"! The State Game Refuge signs were on a few trees off our place. The Oregon State Blue Book Laws clearly states and I quote: "The Commission is hereby empowered to post private property upon the consent of land owner."

Not long after the cougar incident, a Biologist came out to our house, driving an Oregon State Game Commission vehicle and I felt that he had evil determined against me! His opening statement to me was, "I understand you killed a cougar!" I said, "As a matter of fact, I did!" "Why did you take the law into your own hands, don't you know we have men hired to do that?" he asked a bit sarcastically. "No, I didn't know that," I answered. He continued to try and give me a bad time, so I told him, "I just saw a thought go across your mind and I'll tell you what it was, if you want to hear!" He looked a little surprised at my remark and said, "Go ahead!" "The thought that went across your mind was, WHAT WAS THAT MAN DOING UP THERE WITH A GUN IN JULY, IN A CLOSED AREA? You probably thought, what if this guy has a tempta- tion to shoot an old doe?" I willingly informed him. He admitted, "That's exactly what I thought!" I said, "Well, I figured that's what you thought! If I wanted to shoot an old doe, I wouldn't ask your permission anyway!" This biologist tried to exert some pres- sure by saying, "Oh, you don't think we have much authority, do you?" "Not on private property," I said! Needless to say, we had a bit of an interesting exchange!

At last, the biologist threw his cigarette down and said, "Okay, I'll tell you a little story! Not many weeks ago, two retired loggers had a commercial garden plot out at Seaside, at the Oregon coast. They had employees working for them helping tend the gardens and the elk got in there, damaging their crops. This one owner went to the Game Commission and said, 'Keep your elk out of our garden or I'm going to shoot them!' The Game Commission said, 'You just try shooting them and see what hap- pens!' 'Well,' he said, 'I will!' The next day he again went to their office and told them, 'I just shot two, cow elk out there! I gutted them, but you can come take them off my property! Tonight I'm going to shoot any others that come on my property, but I'm not going to gut them!' He had a couple fellows help him, and during one night, they shot seventeen elk who had come for a big feed in their garden! The Game Commission served a warrant on him and had him arrested! They went to court and this private citizen "beat the pants off" the Game Commission! The Commission was ordered by the court to completely fence that area with a steel fence to keep the elk out!" So, after he told me this story, I knew that HE KNEW I was completely within my rights and he also knew that when I drove up the creek to check on my animals, I was NOT carrying my gun!

NEIGHBORLINESS AND

NARROW ESCAPE

We had a family move up Mill Creek, close to the Hugh Walker place, and their last name was Peterson. They hadn't lived there all that long when Mr. Peterson died quite suddenly. There was farming to be done on her place, so we neighbor's agreed to help Mrs. Peterson out by doing the farming for her. I took a tractor down and plowed with Hugh Walker and other neighbors. The kids were coming home from school this one particular day, and saw us working there, so they stopped and Myron said, "Hey, Dad, why don't you let me plow?" He was about fourteen years old then, so I said that would be fine for him to finish plowing and I'd go on home and do some other work. Myron went right to work plowing and finally Hugh Walker went out and said, "Say, Boy, you'd better go home! It's getting dark and you don't have any lights on that tractor!" Myron said, "Okay," and headed for home, with the plow in tow!

Not too far from our place, there was a very bad chuck-hole in the county road and Myron remembered that it was there. In an effort to avoid it, however, he got over too far to the edge of the road with that tractor. The wheel suddenly spun out of his hands and over the embankment he went and into the creek! The distance to the creek was about eighteen feet and this big plow went right over his head. The impact of the fall broke the front axle on the tractor, tore the manifold off, and the tractor turned over in the water. Here is Myron, out in the water and that plow literally landed on top of him! The impact tore his one shoe off, broke his nose, broke a couple of ribs, and put a big gash in his back! Dazed, bruised, and shivering, he somehow got out from underneath the plow. Then he waded out of the creek, climbed up that bank, which was no small feat, and staggered home! When Frances saw him, she was shocked, and asked, "What happened, Myron?" He wasn't completely coherent, but explained that the tractor had gone into the creek. We quickly took him into the Dallas Hospital to have him checked. Myron was given a complete examination and we were told there was nothing wrong with him! The staff told us he was very lucky to be alive and that he'd be all right!

For about a year or more, Myron just didn't grow. He felt ill, his head hurt, and he really wasn't himself. Frances decided to take him into a lowly chiropractor, E.J. Fagan, in McMinnville one day, as we were concerned about his health. During the months after the tractor accident, I had taken Myron to several fine doctors, including one in Salem. Always we were told there was nothing wrong with him and he just needed a good "tonic"! Doc Fagan had a different idea and ran a little instrument down Myron's back, finding some pinched nerves. He treated him and little by little, Myron began to improve, although his entire future was affected by that accident! For years, he wore a supportive belt, much like weight-lifters use. We were so very thankful that he survived that ordeal!

TEASING THE TROOPS

The boys, for some reason, used to like to play a few tricks! I still wonder where they ever got the incentive to do these things! One time there were some people across the creek from our house picking wild strawberries. Earlier our kids had been over there picking berries as there was quite an abundance of them this particular year. Here comes this lady and a bunch of kids into this strawberry patch and they were working at it in earnest! One of the boys called out, "Bears, bears!" Another one shouted, "Get the horses, get out of there!" They said those people cleared out of there so fast it was unbelievable! Those people never ever again returned to pick any more berries either!

One of the favorite memories our kids have is that of having the distinction of being able to play some pretty funny tricks on younger cousins. In our household, it was standard practice to have all sorts of guns and rifles around and our kids were all taught to have a healthy respect for guns. Never did they present a problem with our children! However, among Frances's family, many of them were not accustomed to such things and so when her sisters' families or other relatives were coming to visit, corners of the rooms were inspected to make sure no guns were stashed there! Hunting was like second nature to our kids and in addition to an extensive collection of rifles, we had accumulated quite a variety of tanned hides. The hide from the bear I killed just before we moved up Mill Creek was really a large one and I had it tanned. The boys used to get under it, one at the front end and the other at the back and they'd walk around under it! When they'd walk around under that thing, they could simulate a real, life-like animal! More than once, when we knew of the anticipated arrival of younger cousins, the boys would go out beside our driveway and get under this bear hide. Of course, more than once, there was the profuse flow of tears from terrified little ones. After the kids crawled out from underneath that impressive hide, the hard part was convincing the little kids the animal wasn't real! When many of these nieces and nephews grew up, they related that among their worst fears was the thought there might be wild animals at Uncle Ken's house! To our kids, that was standard fare! We had some neighbors, the Chase family, and they had a son named, Wayne. He was up at our house and the kids were goofing off with that bear hide. Mrs. Chase said that poor boy had nightmares for some time, he was so scared!

We often had company for dinner on Sunday after church and on this particular Sunday, we had invited a family who had a little, "Johnny-Come-Lately", whom they called, Junior. His Mother was in the kitchen talking to Frances and Donna as they prepared the meal, while I was visiting with his Dad. This kid was just being disruptive, jumping up and down, running in and out, and so on. The boys went upstairs, got the bear hide out, and came down the stairs with that thing over their heads. Junior took a brief look and that was the most religious, devout little Rascal you've ever seen! His eyes got wide as he just let out one, BIG scream and shook violently! They all came running and asked, "What's wrong with Junior?" I was so pleased, I couldn't believe those boys were thinking on the same wave length I was! I had several alternative ideas in mind for the exact "cure" for Junior, but this one worked extremely well, for he quieted down for the remainder of the day. All of us had a lot of fun with that bear hide and even could tease our little dog with it. His eyes would go glassy green and he'd tear into it and act as if it were alive!

CHILCOTIN CARIBOU CHRISTENING

In 1952, Ed Phillips and a group of fellows from around Sheridan went to British Columbia on a moose hunting trip and when they returned, reported they'd had a great time. I always had wanted to go to moose hunting in Canada, so the next fall, Reinold Werth, Frank Larrew, Ed and his friend, Bill Engles, and I went to British Columbia. The rest of us were pretty much strangers there, only Ed had been there just once before. He had a brand new, Ford pickup and Reinold had a Plymouth car with a trailer. Going North, I was riding with Reinold and after going through customs at the border, we arrived at Clinton. We discovered that Ed wasn't right behind us, so we waited quite a while for him to join us. After he got into town, we rented cabins at the Aurora Auto Court to spend the night. Ed had learned to know the Bones Brothers, who were Indian guides. It was early evening and Ed said maybe Frank Bones would be out at his mothers' place and since we needed to find him, we drove out there. Sure enough, he was there and Ed asked him, "How's the chance to go hunting?" "Fine, fine! I take you out," he said, "Where you staying?" "Aurora Auto Court," Ed informed him. Frank said, "I'll be down tomorrow morning!"

When we were waiting in Clinton for Ed the prior evening, an Indian fellow sort of struggled up to our car. Noticing our license plates, he realized we were "foreigners", although he couldn't read or write! He asked, "You boys come up to make big hunt on moose?" and we told him, "Yes!" "You know how to hunt moose?" he asked, to which we replied, "No, we don't!" "If you see moose, never talk! That scare moose bad. If you see moose, make a cackling noise (and he made a noise); that don't scare moose!" and he continued to talk for a bit. He seemed like a nice fellow and told us his name was Charlie Fenton. We found out he knew the Bones boys and had been hunting with them. Charlie told us that he broke his leg the year before. Here they were out seventy-five miles from Clinton when he broke his leg and no means of communication out in the bush! Three days later, the Bones boys brought him into the doctor and by then his leg was all swollen up and he was in bad shape! The doc put a cast on it and Charlie went right back out to the bush and he began to hunt again before fully recuperating. The cast slipped down and cut through his Achilles tendon and he had a terrible infection in his foot! Frank Bones' brother, Pete, said Charlie smelled so bad, "we make him sleep outside the tent for coyote bait!" Charlie's foot was crippled for the rest of his life, but it didn't stop him!

Ed explained to me why he had been late in arriving in Clinton the previous day. At that time, it was illegal for the Indians to have liquor, so he left the main highway and went into Ashcroft to the liquor store to buy a case of Canadian Club. The storekeeper was just locking the door and said, "See you back here at 2:00 P.M." Ed said, "No, we can't wait that long!" "Sorry, you're out of luck," and he refused to wait on Ed. Ashcroft was five miles from the main highway, so his side trip into Ashcroft was the reason he was late getting into Clinton!

Frank, who was thirty-five, showed up the next morning at the motel, along with his new, sixteen-year-old bride. "Oh, by the way, fellows, give me some money! I must get Pete's gun out of post office. He has new rifle, shipped C.O.D., so I need to get it and I have to get hay for ponies," Frank informed us. "How much do you need?" we asked. Frank said, "Seventy-five dollars!" The evening before, he told Ed and I that our fees would be $100, per bull moose. As soon as we gave him the seventy-five dollars, he went to get the gun and hay, after which we all drove out of town, following Frank. It wasn't long before we saw a sign which said, "Gang Ranch, sixty-five miles," and we turned off the highway. Frank pulled over, stopped, and got out of his car. As we stopped, he came walking back to our car, asking, "You boys have anything to drink?" Reinold said, "You bet! We've got five pounds of fine, MJB coffee!" "No, no, I don't mean that! Do you have any booze to drink?" Frank wanted to know. Reinold said, "No, we don't!" Just then Ed pulled up and Frank went back to him and asked, "Eddie, do you have anything to drink?" Ed said, "No, they locked the liquor store right in my face and I couldn't buy anything!" "Well, we can't go any further, something might happen! You can never tell!" He sat down on the ground beside his pickup and his wife sat down beside him! They obviously weren't going to budge, so Ed asked me, "What do you think we ought to do?" I said, "I don't really know what to do!" "Well, I'll go back into town," Ed said.

Back into town Ed went and bought two cases of stubbies at the local tavern, as there wasn't a liquor store in Clinton. He came back, took a case of beer up to Frank's vehicle and handed it to him. Frank smiled and immediately opened a bottle, gave it to his wife, and then opened one for himself. He began driving again and we followed. We had gone thirty miles, when Frank stopped again. He headed to the brush on one side of the road, and his wife went to the opposite side of the road, into the brush. They answered nature's call, came back, each opened another bottle, and away we went! By now you must have guessed, we went another thirty miles, and they stopped! The same procedure was followed again! We traveled ninety miles; they stopped three times, so we figured they were getting thirty miles to a stubby!

Arriving at our destination, we made camp at a place called "Sawmill's Cabins Gang Ranch," with an old house there. Pete and Frank Bones and their families lived about half a mile up above, in sort of a tent-house. Pete's woman was Mary, a very pleasant Indian lady from Washington. Next day, the snow was fourteen inches deep, with a crust on the top, as we began hunting. Reinold and I had both been working in the woods and were in pretty good physical shape. That afternoon I noticed that Pete seemed very tired, so I said to him, "Pete, your clutch is slipping, isn't it!" (Interpretation: You're tired!) "Yes, I think it's going to give out," he said. He whispered to me and pointed to Reinold, "What does that big fellow do?" I said, "He works on the rigging for Foster." "What do you do?" he asked me. "Oh, I'm scaling logs and filing in a big logging camp," I explained. He grunted and said, "Huh, plenty tough!"

When we were going into the Gang Ranch to make our hunt, we could see quite a ways off, on a long, dusty stretch of road, a pickup coming towards us, with a set of horns tied onto the front of the truck. At first we thought they were elk horns for they were huge, and I don't believe I've ever seen a larger rack of deer horns in my life! The driver laid on his horn as he was neared us, and we stopped. When he was even with us, he stopped his truck and got out. This fellow had a big cowboy hat on, about thirty days growth of whiskers, and as soon as he stopped, shouted out, "Hello, Kenny!" I said, "Hello!" as I looked at him, but didn't recognize him. He laughed and said, "You don't know me, do you?" I admitted I didn't and he continued, "I'm Ted Rhodes and I overhauled a Cummings Diesel Engine up where you were Bullbuck and saw filer at a logging camp. Then I remembered that the company had a new Cummings Diesel seize up and he overhauled that engine. Ted would come into my filing house and eat his lunch! This just proves that you never know WHO you are going to run into, or WHERE!

The first day out with Pete, he built a nice dinner fire and had brought lots of moose meat along. His woman had made a big sandwich out of moose meat for him and I had some Bohemian Rye bread along and my Dutch-made Limburger Cheese, so I made myself a sandwich. Pete whittled a nice stick for toasting over the fire and then handed me the stick. My cheese was about as thick as a slice of bread and I had never toasted the Limburger Cheese before (and never did after this incident, either). As I began toasting my sandwich, the cheese became soft and melted right into the bread! My, that was so good! I ate half of it and then asked, "Pete, do you ever eat Limburger Cheese?" He said, "I don't know! All my life I don't hear of it!" "Well, you can't learn about it any younger! Here!" After I handed it to him, he took one bite and then smelled it. All of a sudden, he

1953 - Guided hunt in British Columbia with Pete Bones - taken behind Gang Ranch - Ken's first bull moose.

asked, "What you call him?" I said, "Limburger Cheese!" "Oh," he said as he rubbed his stomach, and made an awful, growling noise. Then he declared, "That coyote bait," and he threw it in the fire!

The next morning Pete and Frank came down to our cabin to go on our hunt. The distance between where they lived and our cabin was about three eighths of a mile. During the night, approximately four inches of snow had fallen and a cougar, huge grizzly bear and wolf had walked through the area between their tent-house and our cabin! Pete brought himself up to full stature and said, "White boy bring strong cheese to mountain. All game leave mountains because of strong cheese!" They all laughed and he really got a bang out of that! Pete Bones didn't go for Limburger Cheese and I found that out in a hurry!

Out hunting the following day, we began following the tracks of two bulls and after some time, came across them on a hillside. Reinold had a Winchester Model 86, with 33 Winchester caliber. This was about the size of a 35 Remington and was a good, short-range gun. Pete declared this gun was absolutely no good! I had a 30.06 Enfield and as that bull stood there, Pete asked, "Do those horns look okay to you?" I said, "They sure do!" "You shoot first," he said, so I put a bullet right through his shoulders and that bull just disappeared right into the trees. Just then, a bull is running up the hill and as I pulled up to fire, Pete ran right in front of me and I saw him jerk on his gun! I ran again to the side, took aim to fire, but just as I was ready to pull the trigger, he once again ran right in front of me! By now the moose disappeared and turning to me, he asked, "How you miss that moose?" I said, "I didn't miss that moose!" "I show you, you stay here," he instructed, and turned to Reinold, saying the same thing! Frank walked up the hill to where the moose was standing when I first shot and said, "Oh, oh! Plenty of blood! Oh, here bull moose!" Then he started cussing, "My gun fail two times!" I said, "No, it didn't Pete! You didn't take the safety off!" That made him very angry! He said, "I show you!" He grabbed that gun and up and fired, nearly hitting Reinold in the head. When we got to where Frank was, Pete told him, "Darn gun fail twice; otherwise have two bull moose!" I knew that gun had not failed him at all!

We dressed my bull out and Pete opened up the brisket and literally crawled inside to get hold of the lungs and windpipe to pull them out. Then we heard a story: "There was a Canadian out hunting who had killed a moose up in this area just before dark. He had a terrible time dressing it out and as darkness fell, he realized he'd never find his way back to camp in the dark. So this crazy guy crawled up inside the cavity of the moose because he figured the warmth from that animal would keep him warm for awhile and he'd be able to survive the night. The temperature dipped and it was so cold that the moose froze solid and the fellow couldn't get out! His entire life passed before his

eyes! He thought especially of all the wicked things he had done and asked himself, 'What is the last wicked thing I did here on earth?' The Prime Minister at that time was Pierre Trudeau, and as the hunter pondered this question, the thought came to him, 'The last wicked thing I did was to vote for Pierre Trudeau!' The more he thought about this, he felt so small, and just couldn't quit thinking about this. It seemed to haunt him and he felt smaller and smaller. At last, he got so small, he slipped right out through the pelvic cavity of that moose!" So we thought that was a very good story!

Several days went by without any further success and one evening Pete said, "Tomorrow if we don't shoot bull moose, we shoot Game Warden Moose!" Pete and Frank both laughed and I heard them make the remark a couple more times. So I asked, "What you fellows talking about, Game Warden Moose?" They said, "You don't hear? We tell you." So the story went like this: "About two years earlier, a couple Indians were up on a hillside cowboying for the Gang Ranch. Their big herd was down by a lake and as they watched some steers down by a lake, a Game Warden

My brother, Ron, is standing 40 feet up on this tree. Barely visible in lower left corner is my Allis Chalmers HD5. Ron couldn't cut through this tree with power saw, so I springboarded around it and fell these two trees with cross-cut saw and axes! These trees are what we used to call "School Mom" and had to be removed because Ron rigged a landing close by.

drove up. He didn't notice the cowboys up on the hill and just stopped and shot a nice steer standing right by the water! After taking the hams off the steer, the Warden got some rocks and wire and attached those to what was left of the body, rolled the remains of that steer into the lake, and drove off. These cowboys went out and shot a cow moose (out of season, of course) and the Game Warden arrested them! The cowboys said, 'You'd better knock it off or you'll be in trouble!' He just laughed at them and said, 'I'm not in trouble - you're in trouble!' After their arrest, a date was set for a trial. The Indians got a good swimmer to dive down in the lake with a rope, attach it to the carcass, and they hauled it up. They took pictures to present evidence and come time for the trial, it cost the Game Warden around $3,000 and ultimately, his job!" So that was the story on the Game Warden Moose!

The next day Frank Larrew and Bill Engles were hunting together and they spotted a nice bull. Frank killed the moose, but Bill claimed it! We knew Frank had actually killed it because the bull had a different caliber bullet in it than what Bill's gun shot. Bill had come along with Ed, although Ed said he didn't really know him all that well. Ed did know that Bill was quite a connoisseur of fine food and liquor because we sat in Portland for two hours waiting for him! This delay was due to the fact that Bill ran all over Portland trying to find an old German butcher so he could buy some fancy bacon! I'll be the first, however, to tell you, that bacon was tops! Frank Larrew was such a gentleman, he didn't make a big fuss over Bill claiming this moose! After laying claim to that moose, Bill never left the cabin! He purportedly didn't feel all that well and the beer wasn't even a good mouth-wash for him! The beer was gone and all he had was cases of juices which he had planned to use for sobering-up, after his drunken binge! Because the liquor store in Ashcroft wasn't open, he didn't get his stash of Canadian Club and wasn't exactly a happy camper!

These Indians had an old Ford pickup, which they parked on a real steep hillside at night to be assured it would get going the next morning. I rode with them this one morning and the fumes came up so badly from that motor, it was unreal! As I inhaled, this junk went into my lungs and I could hardly breathe, plus it was nearly impossible to see inside the cab, due to the thick, blue fumes! I asked, "Did you ever change plugs in this rig?" They said, "No." "Did you ever drain the oil?" I asked and Pete answered, "No." Looking a short distance ahead, there was a wash-out about six feet wide and four feet deep, right in the road, and they stopped on a little hill just before we got there. Pete asked, "What do you think? If we give him plenty of juice, will he go through?" Frank said, "I don't know. We give him try!" They opened that old thing up and just went ker-thug, down in that pothole! We spent about four hours trying to get that thing out, but without a power winch or anything, what a job it was! We dug and dug, got poles to form a bridge-like platform to get it out, and finally did succeed! Ed's new Ford pickup was one of the first with automatic transmission and they asked Ed if he'd go through the wash-out in his truck, but his quick reply was, "I'm not quite that stupid!"

The Bones boys really liked Frank Larrew and they told him they had a place called, "The Sink-Hole" and that if he wanted to come back and go out with them again, they'd get him a bull moose and a big, buck deer. Once they had made a drive there and saw hundreds of does, but no bucks. Those does were so tame, they would come right up to their old truck. Frank went home from our Canadian trip and lost no time in buying a new Chevy pickup in Tillamook. Taking his wife with him, they went right back up to Canada to hunt with the Bones boys. These fellows kept their word and got the bull moose and buck for Frank. Later when visiting with the Larrew's, we saw the horns from those animals.

Hunting was pretty grim with that crusted snow and Bill was out of sorts, complaining constantly to Ed. "I don't know what to do about Bill! He's on this wild terror, won't go hunting and he claims he's sick, I guess we might as well go home," Ed told me. I said, "Well, okay!" We all got together to close off the hunt and were visiting back and forth. Even the Indian ladies came down and I have a picture of the group standing by Ed's pickup! Then it was down to business! Ed said to the Bones boys, "How much do we owe you fellows, anyway?" Frank turned his back and began looking over towards the land of his ancestors, or towards Sodom, or wherever, and he couldn't talk! Strange thing! He had lost his ability to speak! Pete said, "You owe us three hundred fifty dollars!" Ed asked, "How do you figure that? We've killed two bulls and you said one hundred dollars per bull, didn't you, Frank?" Frank never answered, so Ed reasoned, "We gave you seventy-five dollars in town, didn't we, Frank?" Again, Frank never answered. "You didn't give me seventy-five dollars," Pete said. "Of course not, we gave Frank the money," was Ed's answer. Here we had just given them over ninety dollars worth of fine groceries which we had left over, and we weren't exactly happy with their deal. Bill said, "Oh, poor devils, give it to them, Ed. Give it to them!" Ed said, "No way, it's a matter of principle! I don't like to be treated like this. A deal is a deal and I'll probably never come back here (which he never did)." Bill just wanted to get on the road, so we finally gave them the three hundred fifty dollars. The sad thing was, Ed accidentally left his Dad's Huntington Style, Gold Watch hanging on a nail in that cabin and we were nearly back into Clinton when he realized it had been left there. We just simply couldn't go back to retrieve it! Ed really felt badly about that watch and I truly felt sorry for him at his loss!

Back in Clinton, Bill bought some beer to begin quenching his thirst before we headed South to Cache Creek. All hunters were required to stop to be checked by the Mounties. Right off the bat, Bill and Ed walked up to the Mounties and were asked, "You have any meat?" Ed said, "Yes, we have one bull moose." Next question was, "Are you a natural-born U.S. citizen?" Bill said, "I'll have you know, I was born in a foreign country, but my Dad was in the military and I'm a royal-blooded American!" He immediately got feisty and acted as if he was going to fight the Mountie! Because of Bill, his big mouth and bad behavior, those Mounties made Ed unload everything in his pickup! They came over and talked to us, okayed everything, and were as pleasant as all get out! When Ed got home with that Bill, he was fit to be tied! He said, "I'll never take that character on anymore of my hunting trips!" That was my first hunting trip into Canada and all in all, it was a lot of fun!

On the way home, going down the highway along the Fraser River, we had a most horrifying experience! Reinold made a remark, "When I bought this new car and drove it home the very first evening, the lights went out!" I said, "Well, let's hope that doesn't happen here!" He said, "I took it into the garage and they told me there's nothing wrong with it!" We were getting close to the bluffs between Litton and Boston Bar and let me assure you, there were no city or street lights, and no railing along the sides of the very narrow roads. On the side of the road were canyons going down, sometimes hundreds of feet, and all of a sudden, Reinold's car lights went out - point blank, pitch black! We hadn't gone more than three miles after Reinold had told me of the initial problem with the lights on his new car! There we were, on a sharp bend in the road with no lights, so I grabbed a flashlight, jumped out, and ran ahead to warn any potential on-coming cars, and Frank ran to the back of the car to catch any traffic from that direction! We sat there awhile, but nobody showed up and Reinold said, "I just don't know what to do!" He had, of course, turned the switch off, but in desperation, after sitting there, he turned the car on and lo and behold, the lights came on again! So we drove on down to Boston Bar, found a garage, and a fellow there checked the lights. "There's nothing wrong, I don't think," he informed Reinold, so we had no recourse but to keep driving further South. Reinold said, "Kenny, I want you to drive!" A big truck had passed through as we were sitting at that garage, so I determined to get behind him, just in case the lights went out again! It was snowy and the highway department had put sand on the road to make it passable. That sand from the big truck's tires, landed on our windshield, however, and cluttered it up something horrible, making it nearly impossible to see during most of that drive! The truck driver tried to get away from us, but I wouldn't let him get out of sight and followed him all the way down to the border. At times, the trucker was going upwards to sixty-five miles an hour! Now we're not talking freeway traveling here, either, my friend, for it was dark, and narrow, curvy, treacherous road! I wasn't about to let that trucker get away from us! Reinold's new car was just covered with mud, sand, and dirt and was a horrible sight. That trip was one of the most harrowing experiences I've ever had to endure and I didn't want to go through that again!

RETURN RENDEZVOUS

The second year we went to Canada, our group consisted of Floyd Emmert, his son-in-law, Karl Dorsing, Reinold Werth and yours truly. We booked a hunt with Augustine Rosette, who had two sons, Alex and Raymond. Arriving in Clinton, we immediately went to buy hunting licenses and tags, and the Game Warden told us where to go. We drove out to find Augustine and found where they made their "abode" in a little cabin, or tent-house, along a creek there. When we arrived, however, none of them were there, so we figured they were out hunting. As we were waiting for our guide to show up, we heard five shots, not too far away. In a short time, here came a tall, gangly Canadian fellow carrying a bottle of Canadian Club. He greeted us with, "Hi, fellas. You come up to hunt?" "Yes," we told him. "Something funny happened here last year. I killed a bull in the same place, fired five shots last year, and it was about the same time of day. I brought a bottle of booze over here and need to get a horse from Augustine to pack that bull in." He paused and then asked, "Did you hear about the murder here last year?" We said, "No, we aren't familiar with that." "I'll tell you, then," he volunteered. In the meantime, Augustine and his sons arrived on the scene and went to their tent-house.

1954 hunt hehind Gang Ranch with Indian Guides, ALex and Raymond Rosette. On left, Alex is towing moose I shot, Raymond is towing Reinold's.

The Canadian fellow continued, "When I came in here last year, the women-folk were sitting out in the yard and I tried to talk to them, but they wouldn't talk! I heard a noise, as if someone was in terrible pain, so I walked over to the cabin and here lay a man on the floor with blood all over and he was unconscious. The ladies wouldn't tell me anything, so I took him down to the Gang Ranch (which was about a thirty-five mile drive) and they put this fellow in their airplane. He was flown into the hospital, given several transfusions, and the hospital staff revived him. The fellow came back out to the cabin, but the next time, the Rosette's finished killing him," and he gave details of what supposedly took place in this death. I took this story with a grain of salt.

Two days later, Alex and I were out hunting together and as we were eating lunch, I asked him, "Do you have any sisters?" He said, "Yes, I have one. I was really glad when her man died! He was mean to my sister. He hit her!" "What did he die from?" I asked. Alex looked at me sort of funny and responded, "I think he died from blood poisoning!" Well, the Canadian fellow who had originally told me about the incident, said those fellows had hacked his body with hundreds of knife holes to make darn sure that he didn't hurt their sister anymore! What he had told us, we discovered, was the absolute truth! Alex and Raymond proved to be fine guides and were very nice to be around, as well as Augustine, their Father.

Hunt in British Columbia with Floyd Emmert, Reinold Werth, Karl Dorsing and Ken.

The third day out hunting, Augustine made a remark, "If I had a white snowshoe rabbit, I could make it snow," and they desperately wanted it to snow. "How do you make it snow?" I asked. "You don't know?" he said to me. "No, I don't know," I admitted unashamedly! "Oh, my Dad told me when I was a little boy how to make it snow. You just take the hide off a white, snowshoe rabbit, build a fire, burn the hide, and as the smoke goes up from the snowshoe rabbit, the white snowflakes will come down!" "Well, I didn't know that," I answered. "Oh, sure!" he said. Sounds pretty logical to me! The funny part of this story is that the snowshoe rabbit doesn't turn white until it gets cold and generally there is snow on the ground when these rabbits get their white coat!

A week later, we were camping in a tent, having moved up to Williams Meadow to hunt. Alex and Raymond were in my tent one evening and I said to Alex, "The Old Man told me an interesting story about burning the snowshoe rabbit hide. Will that really make it snow?" Alex gave me a rather wicked look and said, "That what the Old Man say!" That was a very good answer for such a stupid question, I thought! Reinold and I each killed a cow moose, (cows were legal at this time) and Karl Dorsing killed a big buck. Those animals were just delicious and very fine eating! We had a wonderful time on that trip in that vast Canadian country.

KING OF THE HILL

John Breeden moved some logging equipment up Mill Creek one day, across Bridge Two and built a road up into the property which Hampton had bought. After John completed that, he then took his cat to the main Mill Creek haul road, turned around, and bladed a nice road into the landing. He had a donkey and crotch-line rigged up, and was skidding timber down the hill. Gene Knudsen and Aaron Mercer came down Mill Creek and noticed these fresh cat tracks. Being new to the company, they were driving around getting acquainted with the country and were not aware of any logging activity there. Upon seeing these cat tracks, they drove into the landing and saw John, so asked, "Who are you?" John's response was a question to them, "And who are you?" They said, "We're Willamette Valley's Company officials and we want to know what you're doing in here!" John said, "I'm John Breeden and I'm a logger for Willamina Lumber Company." "Who's Willamina Lumber Company?" they wanted to know. "They have an office in Willamina at the mill there," John informed them. So Gene and Aaron left shortly thereafter, driving directly to Willamina, and they just happened to catch Bud in the office.

The Willamette officials "glad-handed" Bud, told him how nice it was to meet him, wanted to be good neighbors, and all the proper pleasantries! "Look, Mr. Hampton, let's make a reciprocal agreement with you on that Right of Way deal," they said. Bud said, "Sure, I want to get along with everybody," and they drafted some sort of agreement. Bud came out to my house a couple nights later and he was just sick! He said, "You know what I just did, Kenny?" and I said, "No." Bud continued, "Do I look that darn stupid to you?" "No, but you look as if you're awfully busy," I told him. "Well, Gene Knudsen and Aaron Mercer came into the office and brought a contract back the next day. In that contract, it said, 'For permission to use Willamette Valley's road, Willamina Lumber Company gives permission to Willamette Valley to use Willamina Lumber Company roads to take timber within this two hundred forty acre stand'." Essentially, Willamette "nailed" Hampton down to only that portion of timber and now he would be unable to buy another timber sale and use Willamette's roads; yet, they had worded this contract so that Willamette had complete use and access to all of Hampton's roads and various right of ways. Bud felt so badly about it, but that just shows how busy he really was with all the matters he was trying to attend to! He obviously needed a good resident Forester and at that point in time, did not have such a person. He also lacked a good Mill Superintendent, as well as other valuable personnel which could have assisted him! It's difficult to be King of the Hill if you don't have enough "Court Jesters"!

I was still running Hampton's cutting crew and the Union was beginning to flex their muscles. They decided they were going to outlaw all cutting by the thousand, so I told Bud I felt the handwriting was on the wall and I might as well quit. Bud said he agreed, as he had lots of little patches of timber he could hire day workers for. We had logged for Bud for two years and were now at the close of another season. An additional reason to shut down was that we didn't have a rock road and it was impossible to work on this site. Then Bud brought Lloyd Lewis for us to meet and his introduction went something like this: "Lloyd is my new Superintendent and I think you fellows will find Lloyd to be fair and a fine fellow!" When I shook hands with Lloyd, it felt good and he proved to be a great guy and certainly was an asset to Hampton's. It was with much pride that I could reflect on my association with Bud! He was one of the most important men in my life and was a super person - one of the finest I have ever known!

BIG HEARTED BUD

An incident which took place at Hampton's Sawmill will substantiate my affirmation of the depth of character Bud possessed. Since he had many other interests, only occasionally did Bud have time to get down to Willamina. One Monday morning as he made a stop in Willamina, he noticed a fellow standing on a street corner. Bud recognized him as one of the fellows who had worked for the company for many years, so called out to him, "Hi, how ya doing?" The fellow just snarled at him and walked off. Bud told me he beat it right down to the mill and asked the superintendent, "How come so and so doesn't work here anymore?" The answer was, "Oh, he came to work drunk last Monday morning, so I canned him!" Bud said he didn't know where this fellow lived, but soon found out, drove there and knocked on the door. This fellow opened the door about three inches and glared at him! Bud said, "Hold it! I want to talk to you! I understand that you were told not to come back to work. How many times did you go to work drunk?" The guy said, "Once." Bud said, "You know, I'm not perfect, either! I always thought you were one of our better workers and what I want is for you to come back to work! I will show on the books you never quit, or was fired, and your retirement program will be back on track!" Bud said the man was overcome with emotion and couldn't choke back the tears. The fellow did, of course, gladly go back to work and a more dedicated worker you never saw. I tell this just to illustrate how great a fellow and how caring Bud really was! It's difficult to find employers like that in this age of "dog eat dog"!

LABORING FOR WILLAMETTE

INDUSTRIES

About 1954 Willamette Industries wanted to begin logging in Mill Creek, so I went into Dallas to talk with Gene Knudsen, as he had just become the General Superintendent. Gene sat on the throne which had previously been occupied by Jack Brandis. Before he came to work for Willamette, I knew him casually and knew he was a very capable man. We talked briefly about this and that, after which Gene asked, "So you want to try it?" I said, "Yes! I have a little HD-5 cat which I've had overhauled and it's ready to go!" As I signed on the dotted line to begin logging at the mouth of Bear Creek Road, Gene said, "Kenny, we've been friends for a couple of years, but when that ink dries, we are no longer friends! It is now root hog, or die! We don't give one d— whether you sink or swim. Furthermore, if you ever write a check to us that bounces, God help you!" So that is the opening scenario of a beginning which lasted nineteen

years! I was in for a very rough ride for most of those nineteen years, because much of the Mill Creek terrain is mighty, steep ground!

Bob Patty began to work for me again and in later years, when he quit, he had worked a total of thirty-five years. Also, he had worked on my cutting crew many times prior to working up Mill Creek! Part of the

Bob Patty cut log, 7'6" on stump, with very thick bark. With my little Allis Chalmers cat, I'm rolling it onto Uel Lambert's log truck.

time, Ed Phillips worked for me, also. Indeed, it was real tough going. I was to log the Old Growth and not take any Second Growth, no matter how big and nice they were. Gordon Olsen, the scaler at Dallas, was a Bureau Scaler. Each scale sheet had an impression of a seal which certified that these logs were scaled in a fair and impartial manner. The seal bore the signature of Vincent I. Kelly. Somehow, by hard work and persistence, I managed to survive. The logs got so bad that Willamette told me to sell them to mills in the area, which I did, so Willamette got their stumpage money and things were better. One day I remarked to someone that my scale was better from the low-grade logs than from the good logs, which went to the Dallas mill. I only sold to the local mills, the logs which showed defect. The first scale they used was on a "Water Scale Basis" and anyone who does not know what that is, doesn't know much about logging! In brief, it's horrible and I was paid only about 50% net scale! Fortunately, they did away with that system and went to scaling the trucks.

One Friday night the phone rang and it was a request from Willamette for me to please come to the office the next morning. In I went, and at once perceived that I was entering the Lion's Den! Soon and very soon, I would be able to sympathize with Daniel! Here was Gene Knudsen and Jordan Johnson, known as Jay. Rest assured, we were not long in going down to the mat! One screamed at me and said, "We heard that you said you got better scale for these low-grade logs than you do from the good logs you bring to the mill!" I said, "Yes, if you heard that, that's correct! That's what I said." "Don't you know that those d— high school scalers can't even read a tape, let alone scale logs?" the other one asked. I will not go into the tirade in any great details, for it is too lengthy, however, a lively discussion ensued! After this discussion, I finally said, "Okay, fellows, I just want you to know that I know right from wrong and you may not know it, but I, too, have scaled millions of feet of logs!" I expected to get my "walking papers", so I said what I thought was appropriate, and to my utter astonishment, they suddenly sat down! Each of them then lit a cigarette and abruptly left the room. I went back home and to work on Monday morning, logging on rock bluffs, steep terrain and poor timber! Once in awhile, we were privileged to work in some good timber, but not frequently.

I mentioned earlier that Bob Patty worked for me for over thirty-five years and during all those years, Bob was late only twice for work! He must have felt he owed me an explanation, for he told me the reason for being late was that he stopped and clubbed a possum. He motioned me towards his pickup and said he threw the possum in his pickup bed. Only problem was, that when he called me over to his pickup to show me his prized possession, he said the possum fooled him and was gone! The other time, he explained he had a flat tire and his spare tire was low on air since he had not used it for many years. At any rate, I really never did deal with the problem of rounding up my crew as so many employers now face.

Willamette called me one evening to tell me they wanted me to open up the road on the mainline and go down through Black Rock. My cat was way above Grand Ronde and I had to go up through the Long Bell holdings, which is now Stimpson. There was a stump which was guy-lined up off the road and that was as far as I could drive my pickup. I borrowed Bob Patty's snow shoes and using those, I went up that mountain and over to my cat, which was between five and six miles. Never had I worn a pair of snow shoes before, but the snow was six feet deep on the level! When I came to my cat, there was this big "bump" in the snow, it was so deep! There was about three inches of daylight between the bottom of the canopy and the snow! On the outside of my cat, I had a shovel hanging, so began digging the snow off! That morning it seemed to have warmed a bit and was about 40 degrees! As I pushed the plunger in on the cat, dug down a ways, gave it a whisper of ether, and pressed on the button, she started up! She sounded as if I had shut her off just the day before, but it had been sitting there for months! After I dug her out, I had to plow out a road in order to get my pickup in there. I needed to bring diesel in for my cat and it just wasn't feasible to carry it all the way in there. I plowed it out until I got down to the mainline, and then continued on. In some places, the snow had drifted over twelve feet high and it was quite a sight to see all that snow! You can only get a snowball rolling until it gets so high and then it'll break and come over the canopy. About seven feet high was all I could handle without having it break, then I'd side-cast it and start another one. At night, I'd shut my cat off, walk back to where my pickup was parked, drive up to the cat to diesel it up and then go home. This was a very time-consuming endeavor! In all, I plowed twelve miles of snow! It was quite a feat and anyone who has never done anything like that, can't imagine what is involved! Wimer started plowing out down at Black Rock, but they had a major breakdown. Someone hit a stump going full bore and broke the dozer assembly all to pieces. I was so fortunate to not have any mishaps!

CHANGING TIMES

About the time I started contract logging for Willamette, there was a major change occurring on the coast. The companies basically used to do all their own logging for many, many years. They had their own railroad tracks, logging donkeys, crews, and equipment. One day a smaller outfit volunteered to do some logging for a bigger company and this initiated the era of "Gypo Loggers," or Contract Loggers! It proved to be advantageous for the big companies, so many began to use these types of services. In the newspaper I read an account of a prominent meeting of the " big boys", among which were representatives from Weyerhauser, Boise Cascade, Crown Zellerbach, Georgia Pacific, and Willamette. One fellow who spoke seemed to have more than the usual amount of common sense and he told them, "Fellows, we're all wrong! I just did a survey of the Contract Loggers who logged for Crown and they have millions upon millions of their own dollars invested in equipment and tools. This leaves our money free to invest in whatever we want to. They have adequate personnel and supervision and they are performing a valuable service for the bigger companies, so we need to change our attitude!" Crown Zellerbach had a history of bankrupting any gypo logger who attempted to work for them more than two years, as did most of the other companies! This fact didn't seem to bother the "conscience" of the big companies. Matter of fact, it was almost as if they took pride in this distinction! It took some of the big companies a very LONG time to change their attitudes. Many a company grew to a huge size, and made millions of dollars, but seldom do you hear of a contract logger who was able to do the same because the bigger companies had the control and could limit the size and success of the little guys. In all honesty, I can say that picture is changing somewhat. If you're a person of substance and know what you're doing, the company will treat you in a reasonable manner. I'm happy to see that change! They do, however, still hold the club over your head and ultimately have the control.

VIEWING VASTNESS

In the wintertime of 1954, Bud Hampton called me and asked me to come into Portland to talk to him, so I went down. Bud told me, "I just came back from British Columbia and I bought 6,000 acres SL-1-61 out of Rossland. Pacific Highway goes through this piece and it is a vast acreage. In addition, I took an option on some other property, but I didn't have time to look at it. Would you go up and look at the other piece for me?" and I told him I would. I called my cousin, Ralph Emmert, of Sweet Home, to see if he'd like to go with me and we went up, in the dead of winter. The property was thirteen miles south of Trail, bounded on one side by the Pend Oreille River and the property line for quite a distance was, in fact, the International Border! The property size was 3,400 acres, and since we had no means of getting around to cruise it, we hired Don Appleton, a professional hockey player, who agreed to take us back in the bush! Don had an old Willys Jeep and he took us along the one side of the timber, but after some distance, we were forced to turn back, due to the snow being so deep. We then went to the Southerly exposure, close to the river where we could see more of the property and get a pretty good view of it! I asked Don, "What do you do in the summertime?" He said, "I'm a Duk Man." "What does that mean?" I asked him. He said, "Well, I sawmill and I hire Dukhabors." I asked, "Dukhabors?" He said, "Yes, I find the Dukhabors to be fine people even though you hear lots of different things about them. They're known to have pretty bad tempers, their women parade around in the nude, and you hear some pretty weird stuff about them, but they're good workers." He continued to drive along and I asked, "What do you call those people?" He said, "Dukhabors," and he seemed a little irritated. I asked, "Do you know what we call them in the States?" to which he said, "No," so I explained, "We call them movie stars from Hollywood, and they're the highest paid people in America!" That really made him laugh! We completed our tour of the timber with Don, after which Ralph and I returned to Portland.

Our little venture into Canada reminded me of a Bible story as I thought about the two spies in the Bible who went over to look at the Promised Land and came back with a good report! I told Bud, "I think it looks pretty good, Bud!" "Well, Kenny, I thought so, too, and my option will soon run out, so I want you boys to buy it! Each year I appropriate so much to buy timber, now I've spent my quota, and I'm fresh out of money," he told me. I said, "We're not fresh out, Bud, we don't have any!" "Well," he said, "the fellow who has the property for sale will sell it to you on a contract. Just go back up and talk to him," so I told Bud we'd go just as soon as we could arrange to get away!

MAKE IT OR BREAK IT!

When Willamette started their plywood operation, something happened that I now think is funny. At the time it happened, it wasn't about to be funny, however! Jay Johnson came up to the landing one day to cue me in. He took a cigarette out, tapped it four or five times against his thumbnail, lit up, and said, "Kenny, we are going to peel low-grade logs and will give you a gross net scale." I asked, "What's a gross net scale?" He says, "Well, if a bucker slabs a log, we will scale it the narrow and all, but it will basically be a gross net." There were three, big trees close by that showed defect. "There," says Jay, pointing to the three trees, "those trees qualify as special culls, but you'll get gross scale for them. We are going to cut your rate of pay $8 per thousand, but you can live with it!" Then he said something like this: "Say, Kenny, do you know who Gordon Olsen works for (Gordon Olsen was the Head Scaler)? He works for the Bureau! I can't even talk to him. Did you know that?" I said, "Yes, I know that!" Jay continued, "No, you don't! I can't even talk to him!" Very well, this is what happened next. We cut those three, big firs which Jay had used for illustration. They were within two inches of all being the same length, which was twenty-six feet. We put each butt log on Uel Lambert's truck, using a bed of smaller logs. These butt logs had 2,700 board feet and on those three butt logs, I got 900 feet each. This obviously was a cheap price and the cut most generous! No gross scale here, and that's the way it was most of the time I logged for them. One friend of Jay and Aaron's, who belonged to the same lodge they did, warned me, "Remember, they'll break you! No one has ever logged for Willamette for more than two years without going bankrupt!" I was logging on one side of the road for Willamette and Wimer was logging on the other when Wimer "threw up their red flag" and were taken over by Willamette. So I consider myself very fortunate that through the years I did not go bankrupt!

After learning of the scale on the three big logs, I had to take action. I am not a hothead, but after the proper amount of stimulation, I can generate considerable anger! I went into Dallas to the logging office at 6:00 o'clock that evening and just sat there - no one was in sight! Before long, a big panel truck drives up with Morris Bergman driving, and with him were a bunch of cruisers and brush cutters. He came over to me and asked, "Do you want to see Johnson?" I said, "I sure do! You have him at my landing at 8:00 o'clock tomorrow morning!" "Okay, I'll tell him," Mo promised.

Next morning at 8:00 A.M., here is Jay. By now I was getting to know Jay quite well and he had a little ceremony with his cigarette! He'd take one out of the case and deliberately tap it against his thumbnail. Soon I learned to count the number of times he'd tap that cancer stick and could thereby judge what sort of humor he was in! As he got out of his truck, he took out a cigarette, tapped it FIVE times on his thumb nail and then lit it. Jay's opening statement was, "Kenny, I'll admit it was a h— of a cut and I'll admit, you can't stand it! I'll talk to Gordon for you!" I ran right into Jay's face and said, "You can't talk to Gordon, he works for the Bureau!" He repeated, "I SAID I'll talk to Gordon for you," and again I told him he could not talk to Gordon! The third time, Jay backed up and said, "Kenny, you d— fool, I said I WILL talk to Gordon for you!" "Jay, you'd better talk to Gordon or I am all done," I promised. He did talk to Gordon and for a full month the scale was better. Then Gordon fell back into his old ways and I continued to struggle.

The big Willamette fire from previous years had gone through a lot timber there and had burned a big skidder down on Shumway. One day Willamette told me they wanted these snags cut in Section 19 and the south half of Section 18, and they would give the volume to anyone who wanted to do it. A really nice fellow named Ed Stevenson had logged up Mill Creek and I had gotten acquainted with him, so I contacted Ed. I told him what Willamette wanted and asked him if he wanted to take on this project on with me, and his response was, "Sure, let's do it!" The two of us we went over to talk with Willamette, but they wouldn't honor Ed's signature as they didn't know him, so I had to sign all the papers for the job. Gene said to me, "I want to make one thing perfectly clear to you! Don't bring one foot of wood in here, Kenny! Do you understand that?" I said, "I understand English, Gene!" He said, "Atta boy! Go to 'er!"

STEVENSON AND SHENK AND

STEEPNESS

Ed and I had to build two bridges and we knew that the Bureau of Land Management had some big snags fell up Shumway a little ways. He and I went over to Salem to talk to a Bill Cowan from the BLM. I said to him, "I'd like to get three snags up Shumway to build the Taylor bridge." He asked, "What do you mean?" so I said, "Well, I'd like to get three snags for stringers." "Are you willing to pay for them?" he wanted to know. "I have other ideas," I told him, and he asked, "Like what? "Well, we'll leave that bridge in place so you can drive across it to check on your property, others can do the same, and it will serve well for fire fighting, and a variety of things," I explained. Bill thought a moment and said, "Well, that sounds like a good idea and I'll be happy to give you the stringers if you'll promise to tear 'em out when you're finished! I'll be d—— if I'll give Willamette Industries anything!" (They had now changed their name from Willamette Valley to Willamette Industries.) "Well, okay, we can take the bridge out," I agreed.

Ed had a TD-18 cat and a dump truck and I had an HD-6 Allis Chalmers cat and we were "in business"! Here is this chasm which we need to build a bridge across, and it's about twenty-five feet straight down into the creek. The first stringer Ed yarded down for our bridge was five feet on the butt, and about eighty-five feet long! The others were about four and a half feet on the butt and nearly as long! We had quite a time getting that first stringer in place. Ed would pull up with his cat, and I would pull down on top with mine, until finally, we got them in place and built a bridge. We also had to build a bridge at Cedar Creek. There was a nice flow of gravel close to my first landing, and a friend, Tobe Yoder, used to work for me in the woods. Tobe told me that physically he wasn't as strong as he used to be and around noon, he was about finished as far as logging, but he could drive the gravel truck in the afternoons. We agreed to this arrangement, and he did a great job of putting gravel on!

On Saturday I went over to Willamette's office and asked Bergman and Mercer, "Is it all right if we start hauling logs on Monday morning? I have a brand made, it's registered, and we're ready to roll!" Bergman laughed and asked, "What you gonna do, Kenny, float them down the creek?" I said, "No, we're going to haul them down!" "You can't do that," Mo said. "I don't know why!" I answered him. They suddenly got "my drift," and come Monday morning, here they were to look the bridges over! Bergman asked, "When did you build those bridges?" "Well," I answered, "we got it done!" What do you call that first bridge," they asked, and I said, "This is the Ford Bridge at Cedar Creek and the other one is called the Taylor Bridge." "Where did you buy the plank?" one of them inquired. I said, "Never mind, they're paid for!" Bergman asked, "Well, where did you buy those plank?" I said, "From Andy Lalack at West Dallas." "How much did you pay for them?" We're going to give you a check for the plank and the nails and then those bridges belong to us and are not yours!" I said, "No, those bridges are OURS!" Then I told them we had to pull the Taylor Bridge out when we were finished. Bergman said, "No you don't, we own that bridge and I said, "No, I gave our word to the BLM man." We used to torment Bergman about that bridge!

Ed and I started logging and the timber in the burn area was fairly sound, except where the logs touched on the ground when the fire went through. On those which had some damage, we'd have to buck them back a ways. Bob Patty and Howard Parker cut for us and we generated quite a few number two peelers. We sold the low-grade logs to Shaddon Lumber Company at Carlton. One day the phone rang and Jay said, "Would you please come to the office Saturday morning?" Mo was in Jay's office when I went in, and Jay greeted me and said, "Please, sit down!" He got his cigarette going as I sat down, and asked, "Are you generating any merch?" His question meant were we getting timber which was good merchandise, and for which we could get a decent price. I said, "Some," and Mo asked, "Some? Like what?" So I told them, "I'm selling the low-grade logs to Shaddon Lumber Company and the other logs go where I can get the best price." "Are you getting any peelers?" Jay asked. I said, "Some!" My answer made him mad and he said, "Like what? Who are you selling them to?" "Well, we sell some to Georgia-Pacific and some to U.S. Ply," I answered. "Well, did it ever occur to you that those companies are Willamette Industries' competitors?" he asked. "Oh, I see you fellows have a bad taste in your mouth! You guys told me not to bring any logs in here and now you're mad about it," I said. Jay stood up and said, "Oh, to h— with it," so I assumed our meeting was over and left. Neither Jay nor Mo ever brought the subject up again!

Ed and I logged up there for quite awhile, even though it was a brutal site! It was so terribly steep! Aaron Mercer had been showing me a map and told me, "You won't be able to go above these falls on this property here." I asked, "You mean the company won't allow it?" He said, "No, you will find out when you get there why I'm saying that!" Here was a bluff about eighty-five to ninety feet high and just solid rock! We had to get a cat up there, because otherwise I'd never be able to build a road around the one side. Uel Lambert, Bob Patty, and one of my boys helped me as we winched my HD-11 cat! For an entire afternoon, we winched that cat up over that bluff! There was literally nothing to tail-hold it to, and I had to go ahead on the tracks and the drum at the same time. The last tail-hold we had, was a big tree which had blown over and the roots had burned off. This tree was laying on the ground, was about five feet through on the butt, and it was laying on top of this rock bluff. After we hooked onto it, that tree rolled over one turn. Uel saw it roll and screamed, "Get out of there! That thing is coming down on you!" He was frantic! I cannot explain yet how that tree stopped! It was full-length, laying on those rocks, but suddenly stopped rolling and let me assure you, it was a good thing it stopped! I'm quite sure there was a divine intervention that day! It took me an hour and a half to go thirty feet because it was so steep and rocky. Once I got the cat leveled off, I could begin to build a road! That's how steep it was up there! Once the road was in, we were in business!

Up the hill a ways, Bob got up on a stump and told us when he got up there and looked down the hillside, over the edge of this bluff, he never felt so tall in all his life! He reported to us, "I may be the Marlboro Man!" Of course, that became "Marlboro Mountain" to all of us! Mo came up one day and asked me, "How much more do you have here? We want you to start logging green timber!" I said, "Do you see that stump up there?" He said, "Yes!" "That's Marlboro Mountain up there!" I informed him. "What do you mean?" Mo wanted to know, so I said, "Well, that's what Bob named it! That means I can put a line to every log up here!" We had many a struggle there at that logging show, with many challenges!

Another problem logging here was that some of the logs didn't have any bark on them and they would "run" like crazy when they were fell. So many of them kept shooting into this one canyon as they fell. It's hard to describe the speed at which those trees could shoot down a mountain. There was a waterfall in the creek there with a twenty-five foot drop, straight off! Somehow I had to get in that canyon to get those big logs out! As we wrestled with this problem, Bob said, "Tell you what! There are two, big logs up above there, so we'll pull a line up there and then you hook onto them. You can pull them down, and maybe we can make a "ladder" there and you can climb it with your cat!" That's exactly what we did! We took axes and sloped the logs off a bit. The logs were just slightly rotten, so the tracks of the cat would grab hold and I went up to that canyon to begin taking these big logs out! I went back a ways and Howard Parker said, "You can't go any further, Kenny, 'cause you can't turn your cat around!" Through sheer ingenuity and determination, I actually turned that cat around on a five-foot log by running the track on the rocks, going back and forth, until I eventually got turned around!

When we went to work one Monday morning, I discovered that evidently there had been a cloud burst over the week-end, because I had a five-gallon bucket at the landing with a couple of railroad spikes in it and this bucket was running over with water. The water had gushed down and where I had anchored these logs in some nice rock, I could not get that cat up those logs again, so I had to build another skid road down at an angle to finish getting all the logs out. Ed had brought a yarder up and he logged Section 19 and I logged the South half of Section 18. That snag patch was something else! No wonder Willamette said they'd give it to whoever wanted to do it! Poor fools! Yet, all in all, it worked out okay!

NORTHERN "LIGHTS"

I had promised Bud Hampton that I would go back up to Canada and look at the property which Ralph and I had looked at earlier. So once again, Ralph and I decided to take another trip to Trail, British Columbia. I looked forward to the trip, as I had always had a fascination with Canadian Country. I had contacted a Mr. E.C. Whitelock, of Trail, to engage in some serious discussion regarding property known as the Pend Oreille lands. We arranged to meet him at the Crown Point Hotel in Trail where we had booked a room. Ralph and I were seated in the hotel lobby the next morning, making small talk, and waiting to meet Mr. Whitelock. I looked down the hallway, and said, "Ralph, here comes Mr. Whitelock!" "How do you know? You've never met him," Ralph reacted, a little amused. I responded with, "I know he's our man!" This fellow entered and immediately I noted he had the most confident look on

Bob and Ken in woods - log was 26 1/2 ft. long, 7 1/2 ft. on stump and bark 5' thick. My little HD5 Allis Chalmers cat was up to the task!

his face! He was of medium height and build, and at once, he figured out who we were! As he greeted us warmly, we proceeded to get our talks underway!

Edgar Charles Whitelock, known as Terry, was truly a great individual to meet! He was of Nobility, was a commissioned officer, held dual citizenship, had a degree in professional engineering, had done aerial photo interpretation, was a registered forester, and had traveled all over the world in the service of his country! What a list of accomplishments! Terry was, of course, from Great Britain. He told us his own family fortunes, as well as those of his wife, Margaret's family, had been wiped out in one bombing raid on Britain during World War II. His stories were most fascinating and he told us many things about his parents and his life. There was nothing dull or boring about Terry!

Here Ralph and I had gone to Trail again in winter weather, and a heavy snow lay on the ground. Terry drove us on the North side of the great Pend Oreille River, and we were able to get a good view of part of the 3,400 acres which we were interested in. One of the strange, but very distinctive, things I recall about that day we spent with Terry, was the tone of our conversations. Not all were orchestrated by Terry, but our talk seemingly always gravitated to more somber subjects, and especially pertaining to the afterlife! One dialogue he shared which I never forgot and still think of many, many times, was this: "I have seen thousands of men die in battle and wallow in their own blood. When I was stationed in India, I used to watch many people tread on beds of red-hot coals and I saw them lay on beds of sharpened steel with their bare backs! When they were lifted off, some would bleed profusely, and some would not. I knew what they were doing! When the Almighty made every person, he reserved a special place in their bosom for Himself to occupy; thus to bring peace and contentment. After so many having been denied this privilege of knowing God as their Maker, that He would then

cast them into the pit; that is not God! God is a God of Justice! I believe those heathen people were somehow trying to answer, or satisfy this longing in their hearts, by the torture of their bodies - to know the Almighty!" Terry insisted he was not deeply religious, but it was obvious he had done much thinking about God, and eternal life. Also, he was a man of complete honesty and later he told us he regarded most Americans with contempt, because Ralph, George, myself, and the Hampton's were the only honest Americans he had ever had business dealings with!

Terry wasn't the best driver in the world and he high-centered his new car on a rock. I thought the transmission was going to come up through the floorboard, as I was sitting with one foot over the transmission. He said, "You know, fellows, when you're in the Army, you learn a few things. You don't go around anything, you merely go through them!" This, then became his mode for driving! After

1959 - Old Growth timber, logged with my HD6 Allis Chalmers cat. Uel's new Ford truck. He hauled for me for 15 years.

Ralph and I were able to get our questions answered, went back to Oregon and reported to George on the property, and so the three of us proceeded to purchase those beautiful Pend Oreille lands from E.C. Whitelock.

There was a Dukhabor fellow operating on the property who had never paid any stumpage or anything, and wasn't exactly a friendly fellow! He and his partner had quite a large mill and a pond and milled millions of feet of timber. They just shot the slabs and sawdust over a bluff, down toward the Pend Oreille River and every year, this would cause a big fire to break out! Cominco, the big Consolidated Mining and Smelting Company, of Trail, had to fight the fire every summer. The Dukhabor fellow obviously made a lot of money. Finally, one of the owners died and so Whitelock got the

Mounties to go up with him and they padlocked the gate so the property could be taken over.

The first time Ralph and I went up to go onto the property, after we finalized the purchase, the gate was padlocked, so we got a key from Terry to get in. The property had a road system which ran for nine miles and our property was interspersed with timber belonging to the Crown and also to Cominco. When we drove back onto the property, there was a Dukhabor fellow back there, so we told him who we were. It was obvious, he was still operating back there, as we observed he had about a hundred thousand board feet of logs fell, bucked, and decked along a nice road. Some of them he had helped himself to were cut off Crown's timber. Our property lay in between the Crown and some of Cominco's. Previously George, Ralph and I had made plans to hire a couple brothers from Oregon to go up and sawmill the timber for us, Harold and Clayton Bender. The Bender's had decided to reside in Northport, Washington, and cross over into Canada to work. After much hassling with customs officials, at last, they moved a small sawmill up to the property and began to cut lumber and really enjoyed the operation.

Mr. Whitelock told me, "You should go down and talk to the leading Barristers, Clegg and Clegg, Inc., here in Trail." Promptly I scheduled an appointment for Ralph and I to go in. Here sat a fellow about sixty-five with the most beautiful head of hair you could ever see and he was justifiably proud of it! He said, "Please sit down, fellows. How may I help you?" We said that we were thinking of incorporating, to which he asked, "Do you have limits?" (I knew by then that in Canada, they referred to property as limits.) We said, "Yes." "Well, do you have a road system and timber?" he asked. We answered in the affirmative, so he said, "Well, you have the perfect setup! You incorporate for $300,000, then go to work and make a whole bunch of money! Mind you, you can't make more than $295,000 and then you disband. You then draw up papers for a new company, start in again, make another $295,000, again disband and start over!" I leaned across the desk, snapped my fingers and said, "Just a minute, sir! You don't understand!" He looked at me with the most incredulous look and asked, "I don't understand?" I said, "No. What we want to know, is all this legitimate and legal? Is the Queen aware of this practice?" He leaned back in his chair and gave this statement: "If the Queen isn't aware of it by now, she's d—— awful, bloody dumb!" That's the way they did business there and for the first three years, the government doesn't bother you! Bud Hampton was just delving into business interests in the Boston Bar area, in Canada about this time, so I informed Bud of what the barrister had told us. Bud looked into it and told me, "Kenny, that's amazing, but that's absolutely the way they do business!" Cominco even told us they operated in this fashion on a big mine they had. We learned a lot about the way business is done, but never used that method, as we didn't see any future in it!

Whitelock was a man with considerable influence in his community. One time when we went up to see Terry, he told us a wealthy attorney from Vancouver had financed the purchase of Knight Lumber Company over by the Crow's Nest Pass. Things were not going well, so he hired Terry to go up there to investigate for him. Terry discovered that these fellows had a high-powered, modern, portable sawmill back in the bush, roads built ahead, all graveled and yet, on the books, they showed no profit! Whitelock was able to expose the fraud and after this happened, the fellows there burned the office down and the bookkeeper committed suicide.

Whitelock was also a great historian and another time when I went to visit him, he said, "Here, Kenny, read this!" The letter he had was from General Van Fleet, of the United States Armed Forces, and he was asking Terry what the proper attire for soldiers' was during Napoleon's reign. Whitelock had all this research material and could come up with such facts. Terry also loved to paint and he did a beautiful painting for me. It is of a horse and to me, is priceless!

RAMBLIN' 'BOUT ROLLIE AND RUSSELL

As anyone who knew Russ will verify, he loved to have a good time and developed a great friendship with Rollie! In general, he'd just give Rollie a bad time and Rollie loved it! The nickname Rollie tagged on Russ was "Coos Bay," as Rollie had a story about being from Coos Bay! Russ took extra measures to see that Rollie had "entertainment", transportation, and groceries, as we all did! One day Russ took him over to Salem to see an attorney as Rollie had been in the service and had received an honorable discharge. This was basically due to the fact that, as a child he had developed double pneumonia and his lungs never completely developed. While marching and carrying a heavy load one day in the service, he collapsed and was discharged permanently. Someone had told Rollie he was also eligible for a pension, so Russ took him to Salem to inquire. The attorney asked him, "Mr. Phillips, were you ever married?" Rollie said, "Yes, once." "And what was your wife's name?" the attorney asked. Rollie thought for a long time and finally he said, "Rolena." The attorney asked, "How do you spell it?" "Don't ask me, I don't know," Rollie admitted! The attorney had a short cigar in his mouth and Russ related that the attorney began to laugh and laughed so hard, he nearly swallowed his cigar! Bear in mind, Rollie had never been privileged to get an education and as far as we could determine, he really couldn't read. Not much changed for Rollie after this visit to the attorney.

Rollie was well past sixty-five years of age and had never drawn any Social Security! Russ tried to encourage him to collect what was his, but Rollie insisted, "No, the government needs it worse than I do!" The truth was, Rollie really needed the money and barely had enough to make ends meet with his meager wages as Gate Watchman. I was determined to try and help Rollie once again to receive from the government what was rightfully due him! This fall I was in the market to purchase a bull, so I put the side racks on my big truck, then went over to Rollie's cabin and said to him, "Put your traveling clothes on this morning, Rollie! I'm going to buy a bull and you're going to sign up for Social Security!" Rollie's wardrobe was extremely limited, but he had a fine, big cowboy hat and some fairly nice clothes, so he changed, reappeared shortly thereafter, and climbed in the truck with me. I had the Salem newspaper, The Capital Press and we drove all over to look at the various livestock specimens advertised! We drove out to Scio, back to Independence, and here and there! At last I located a really fine bull over by Independence and bought him.

While I was in the Salem area that day, we went into the Social Security office and this nice lady asked, "May I help you?" I said, "Yes, Mr. Phillips wants to sign up for Social Security." "Very well, have a seat and I'll have a gentleman help you," she instructed. I had noticed earlier in the truck that Rollie had a brown, paper bag, but I had no idea what was in it! Rollie said to her, "No, I don't want to sit down, it feels so good to stand up. You don't have any idea of where I've been today." With this, he proceeded to give a dialogue of where all we had been to look at bulls! Before long, a fellow came out and we followed him to his office. "Mr. Phillips wants to sign up for Social Security," I told him. He asked Rollie, "How do you write your name?" By this stage in his life, Rollie had Parkinson's disease quite badly and began to shake! He had hold of his paper bag and it shook uncontrollably as he opened it, producing an old family Bible! He floundered around there, got the Bible open and showed the fellow his name. "Oh, your name is John Rollin Phillips!" Rollie said, "Yeah? I kinda figured maybe Mother put it that way!" After some time, the fellow said, "Mr. Phillips, you have quite a large sum of money coming." Rollie asked, "I do?" and he said, "Yes! We're going to go back to the day you became eligible and pay you through the present!" We went back to the truck, drove over to pick up the bull and head home. Rollie seemed so excited and I felt very happy for him! At last, we were able to get his Social Security for him!

The next morning I was working out in my shop and here came Rollie! He poked his finger in my face and said, "See there! Yesterday was our Lucky Day! You got a bull and I got signed up on Social Security and it was our Lucky Day! There are days you might just as well stay in bed!" For about a month, that's all the old boy wanted to talk about, he was so tickled! If I hadn't just ordered him to go with me, I doubt there would have been any other way to get him to go in and sign up.

Generally when I was out working in my shop on Saturday mornings was when Rollie was at his "conversational best!" We were pouring babbitt in the shop one morning for the drum line and chokers. Rollie was just chatting away and the subject of marriage came up. I knew that Rollie had been married for a short time and worked at a big mill. I said to him, "Rollie, I never did ask you much about your wife. Why did you break up, Rollie?" He looked very serious for awhile and then answered, "Well, I'll tell you! She got to thinking other men were just as good as I was!" I said, "Well, then it was just no use, was it!" He said, "No, No! We just broke up! We just parted blankets!" I continued, "While we're on this subject, Rollie, I want to ask you, was she a good housekeeper?" "Well, she could have been if she'd have set her mind to it," he responded. I got a big chuckle out of that! If you can be more diplomatic than that without actually condemning someone, I'd like to hear it, because I thought that was mighty good choice of words for a man who never went to school!

In 1959, Bob Patty was bucking a big tree which had a terrible side-bind in it. I helped him wedge it over and it went down through some alders. That morning I had given him a brand new saw and as he made the first cut, it went side-ways and threw him off, but he hung onto that saw! He fell straight down, landed on his left arm, and the impact pulled the muscle loose from his shoulder. He came walking out of there holding his shoulder and was just white as a sheet! I took one look at him and got him into my pickup! Into Dallas we went to see Dr. Charles. Doc said, "Mr. Patty, you have a dislocated shoulder." The doctor told him to lay down, gave him some gas, and began examining his shoulder. Bob was sort of drowsy and Doc Charles said to me, "He's the most muscular human being I've ever seen!" I said, "You're not just kidding! He's got more steam than guys a lot younger than he!" Doc said, "I'm no slouch myself, but this guy is one fine specimen of manhood!" The doctor just gave Bob's arm a big yank and asked Bob, "Doesn't that feel better?" Bob said, "No it doesn't! It hurts like the devil!" The outcome was that surgery was required to put pins in to attach the muscle to the bones once again. Bob was laid up for an entire year due to this accident, so in the meantime, I hired Bob Parker to cut in Patty's place. Patty never did fully regain complete use of his left arm and was granted a thirty-three per cent disability. In time, though, he came back to work for me and worked until he retired at age sixty-five!

LOSS OF A LOVED ONE

It seems that 1959 was a year which impacted my life in so many ways, but the biggest tragedy was that my first cousin, Ralph, was killed instantly while loading a large crane! This news was one of the most shattering events of my life! Immediately I thought of his wonderful wife, Mary, and their children and my heart ached for them at the loss of their husband and Dad! It was difficult for me to express the loss I felt, for I was very close to Ralph, and also to George. Ralph was truly one of the finest friends a man could wish for! Margaret Whitelock told me she thought Ralph was the most gentle man she ever met, and so he was! It was so difficult to understand why he would be taken at such a young age and no one would ever replace him! It took a lot of time to heal the pain caused by his death.

George, also, had so many fine qualities that stood him in good stead! He never finished the eighth grade, but went to work! Before long, he began working in the timber industry, tackling many formidable jobs which required skill and tenacity! Both George and Ralph were totally honest and would take advantage of no one! I was fortunate to have as partners and very dear friends, the two of them. Now George and I would continue our business ventures and wonderful friendship.

TRIALS WITH TANGO

Our next trip to Canada in 1973, I booked in advance for our hunt with an outfitter below Fernie, named Orland John Coroelli, and his nickname was "Tango"! Bob and I drove up to Fernie, bought our licenses, and started out to find Tango's camp. On the way, right on a bad corner, we met two old-timers with a pickup load of wood. They stopped the same time we did and asked us, "Where you boys going (having noticed our Oregon license plate)?" I said, "Oh, we're going hunting with Coroelli." They said, "You know about Coroelli, do you?" We said, "No, we don't know anything about him!" "Oh, he just got in big trouble! He got involved with some hunters from Minnesota and you need to watch him, he's very crooked!" We didn't think too much about their comments and went on to the camp. Tango's cabin was right on Ram's Creek, just below the Crow's Nest Industries big logging camp there, known as C & I. Tango peddled moonshine and was a hopeless alcoholic. He would take other pensioners into town to get groceries, booze, and supplies. Tango's camp cook was Roy Bench, and he was very pleasant, neat and clean. Unfortunately, he was dying with "black lung" disease, having worked in the mines there for most of his life. Also, he was a heavy smoker and loved to drink. Tango would give him three bottles of beer a day, so Roy was happy to live there, cook, and do the housework!

Next morning Tango took us out to the horse's corral, and he did have some fine horses, plus he took very good care of them. As we got on the horses and began to ride, soon we started up a bluff and riding along, Tango never offered any information about the trouble he had gotten into with the fellows from Minnesota. That bluff was so steep, never had I at that time, nor since, ever ridden a horse UP such a steep pitch! Tango then said, "Fellows, we have a bad one here to go through! Don't try to walk up there! Stay on your horse, lean forward, grab hold of his mane, and lay right down alongside the horses' neck! They'll take you up through there!" There was loose, shale rock and it was so steep, I couldn't believe we or the horses would ever make it! Tango went up first, then I went up, but Bob said, "It's too steep for me!" He got off his horse and somehow finally got up to where we were. We got past this steep hill, and were close to the top when Tango stopped. Then he said, "I want you to go ahead. When you get round that bend, Kenny, get ready to shoot because you're gonna see game!"

Just as I went around a corner, a bear ran up the hill and there lay a horse all bloated, feet up in the air, with the horse shoes just shining! "Hey, what's going on here, anyway?" I asked and Tango said, "Well, I'll tell you a little story, fellows. I had two hippies from Minnesota hunting up here. One was twice as big as George Forman and twice as mean! (At that time, George Forman was heavyweight champ of the world!) It began to rain and never let up and these fellows went into Fernie, secured two women of easy virtue, brought them out to camp, along with a case of Canadian Club, and they began to make merry while it rained! The rain continued for seven days and seven nights! (There were visible signs to substantiate his story, for there were grooves, ridges, and gravel washed out.) On the seventh evening the rain let up a little bit and I said, 'Let's go do a little road hunting, fellows!' 'Don't mind if we do,' they answered. They drove up to C & I Logging Camp, turned around, and were coming back down the hill very slowly, when a doe stepped out. I said, 'How about some camp meat, fellows?' One said, 'Don't mind at all!' One of them shot this doe right in the middle of the road, and were just loading it in the back of the pickup, when here came a Game Warden. He promptly wrote these boys a 'prescription' and they didn't like it! They slapped quite a fine on these two fellows and they said they never would have shot it if I hadn't suggested it."

Tango continued telling us about the episode with the hippies. "They all came back to camp and decided to go out hunting again, so rode up the same hill where the dead horse lay. One of the hippies shot a nice, five-point, bull elk and the meat was hanging in front of the dead horse. Next day they went hunting again and one of them said, 'By the way, Tango, you'd better get some game for us or I'm gonna get a horse!' Tango said he just laughed and never thought anything about it." Most guides don't hunt with their clients and Tango tied his horses to a big tree and waited while his "customers" hunted. Always he'd have an axe, hunk of rope and pair of binoculars with him. Tango said, "That evening we met at this big tree where I tied the horses, they got on and started to ride down a trail when the one hippie said, 'By the way, Tango, I happen to be a man of my word,' and he just up and shot the horse I was riding on! He shot my horse right behind the ear and that horse went down so hard, it felt like every bone in my body was broken. My horse was standing across a small windfall about ten inches in diameter and about a foot off the ground and that's where my horse landed'!" After Tango finished, I said, "Well, there's one thing I want you to do and that's to pull those shoes off that horse! I never want to ride up here and catch those grizzlies a pitchin' a game of horseshoes!" He didn't think that was funny at all! Tango said, "If I'd have had a gun, I would have shot that hippie and the other hippie would have shot me and that would have been the end of it!"

This hunt with Tango turned out to be very tragic for us in the overall picture! Two days later, right in the heart of the Canadian Rockies, we were on an old Indian trail in the mountains. That trail was blazed with old cuts, which looked as if they were a hundred years old. There were a lot of strange formations there with different colored rock, and it was very interesting. Tango warned us not to drink any water out of the creeks as there was some kind of oil oozing into it and we could get terribly ill from it. We went up on top of a bluff and saw three grizzlies that day. There were lots of grizzlies in the area and during our hunt there, I saw more than I've ever seen in my life! Tango stayed on top of the bluff with the horses while Bob and I started down this canyon. Just as we started down, we saw a great, big brown grizzly come down through the timber. Bob and I came to a long, rocky draw that ran clear up to a spire and was about seventy feet wide. There was shale rock, a little creek running down there, and then a patch of timber. In this flat opening, there were sometimes up to a hundred elk feeding in there, and sign was all over the place that they had been there, although we didn't see any elk on the entire trip!

Just as we got to the draw, here was a bull moose bedded down right by the water and Bob had just told me about a hundred feet earlier, "If you see any game, don't stop for me, shoot it!" The gun I had brought was my 7 X 57 Model 98 Mauser, so I put a bullet in that bull's back and broke it with the first shot. We were quite elated and started dressing him out. It was the first moose in which Bob had ever been in on the kill and was the third one I had gotten in my moose hunts! Finally we heard a whoop and a holler and here comes Tango! While still off a ways, he asked, "Just what do you think you fellows are doing down there anyway?" Bob said, "Well, just what do you think we're doing?" Tango said, "Cut the horns off and come up! You can't get that moose out of there!" Bob said, "Like fun we can't! See those two packboards we brought along?" He said, "Yes, but I can't get my horses down there!" Bob said, "You don't have to! We'll pack it out of here!" "No, I don't want you to," Tango said, as he came down there and was rather angry. By this time we had the bull all quartered and butchered and started back up. Bob asked, "By the way, Tango, do you have a power saw and some gas?" "Matter of fact, I do!" "Well, you hunt elk down here and we'll build a good road for you," Bob stated. Tango finally agreed to it, as the thought of a road appealed to him, so we went back up the next day with the horses, power saw, and some gas. We got right at it, going through dozens of windfalls laying across the trail, some ten to fifteen inches in diameter. The road went clear to the bluff, but there was no way to go further because of a huge, rock ledge there. I was afraid a horse would break its' leg if it went off that rock ledge. By now Tango seemed very happy and said, "We can get our horses on down there somehow, don't worry!"

Bob and I got Big Jack, the big pack horse, down there and Tango loaded practically all of the moose on him, which was a very foolish thing to do! We got back up to the ledge, but Big Jack did not want to go! Tango got his saddle horse up there, ran a rope down to Jack's neck, and told us to get a stick to encourage Big Jack, while Tango tugged on the rope. Lo and behold, it worked and we got Big Jack to the top with the moose meat and headed to camp.

Back in camp, we asked Roy to fry some liver for us, but he said, "Oh, no! No way, it wouldn't be fit to eat!" We assured him that it was fine and had kept it very clean. Even Tango piped up and said he had never eaten moose liver and maybe he'd try it. Roy decided to fry some and both of them consumed it with delight! They said they didn't know it was so delicious!

Next day we went to a different area, to where there were sheep, and I had a sheep tag. We weren't aware of it, but Tango had a salt lick out in this area and he said, "You go ahead and when you get around the corner, you ought to see sheep." Sure enough, I rode around the curve and there were about twenty sheep there at this salt lick, but a quick observation told me nothing was legal to shoot. Just then Bob and Tango rode up and at the same time, a bear paid us a visit! Bob jumped off his horse, shot this black bear, and we took it into camp.

Tango told us the next morning he had a camp, Spike Camp, clear back in the mountains and it was quite difficult to get to. However, there were sheep there, he informed us, so we packed up some grub and off we went. Upon arriving at his camp, we found quite a scene! The tent had been torn all to pieces by grizzlies and they had ransacked the little cache of grub Tango kept there for the horses. Everything had been virtually destroyed, so we tried to get things a bit organized, after which we began to ride. It had snowed some and one place we went across, there was some dead, tall grass bent down by the snow and it was as slick as grease. Tango got off to lead his horse, so I got off my horse and did the same, but Bob rode his horse through there. At this point, we were beginning to climb up a very steep pitch! Once we got up this very steep terrain, we came to a bench and you could see for miles around! What a view! We tied our horses and began to glass for game.

After some time, Tango began to lead his horse down the hill, so I followed and when we got down, Tango asked, "Where's Bob?" and I said, "I don't know, maybe he's glassing yet!" Tango said, "Well, I wish he'd come, it's going to get dark!" Here Bob got on his horse, after he refused to ride up that steep bluff the first day out, and came down that hill on this dandy little animal! The poor, little horse slipped while going down a steep ledge and Bob went flying up in the air! When he came down, he landed on the saddle horn and the impact split his pelvis! While we were wondering where he was, Bob came riding up, with tears streaming down his face, and ghostly white! He looked awful and I asked, "What happened, Bob?" "Oh, I think I ran a limb in my groin," he said. "A limb in your groin, I don't see a limb," I observed. Bob supported his weight with his hands and we got him on down to camp. Once at camp, we helped him out of the saddle, laid him down in the tent and got a nice, big fire going. Tango asked him, "Do you want something to eat?" Bob said, "I sure don't!" Poor fellow lay there and suffered something terrible all night long. I couldn't sleep and I knew Bob wasn't sleeping, so around 2:00 A.M. Bob asked me for a drink of water. As I got some water for him, he said, "I just felt my sacroiliac muscle go back into place." I kinda smiled to myself and asked, "You did?" "Yes, I did," he answered emphatically.

It was at least seven miles to go out of there, over the most rugged trail you could ever imagine, to get down to the original camp. Tango and I put Bob on Big Jack, and Bob tried to support his weight with his hand on the saddle horn. Tango went ahead to try and pick the best spot to ride along on, and he would call out, "Over here, Bob, bring your horse over here!" Bob said, "I can't turn him anyplace, I'm just gonna let him go!" That horse went his own way and picked out a far better trail than Tango did! Later Bob raved about how smart that horse was! He said the horse sensed that he was hurting and hurting darn bad, so Big Jack took care of him.

We finally got Bob into the Fernie Hospital and this was truly one of the saddest experiences I ever had! Right away a nurse came out and said, "Let me give you a shot." Bob said to her, "Get away with that needle! I don't have any drugs in my body! I don't smoke, drink booze, or coffee, and I don't want that needle!" "Oh, you're one of those tough guys, are you?" she asked. He answered, "Yes, I AM!" They soon found out that, indeed, he was! As Bob was taken to a room, Tango said he'd go into the office to take care of financial arrangements and that Bob shouldn't worry about anything. Tango told the administrators, "I belong to the Canadian Guide and Outfitters Association and have insurance to take care of this man!"

The doctor came in, examined Bob and said, "Your sacroiliac muscle has been out of place." Bob said, "Yeah, I know that! I felt it go back in place!" The doctor had just confirmed what Bob had told me during the night when I was getting him a drink. Bob was told he'd be in the hospital four or five days, so I knew I'd better stay in town with him. Tango had to go see a lawyer to file a lawsuit against the hippies for shooting his horse, and had other business he had to attend to, so he took off.

One day when I was seeing Bob, Tango came in and asked me, "Do you want to go hunting in the morning?" I asked, "Where?" Tango said, "You go out of town about two miles, walk across a railroad trestle and there's a trail which takes off to the right. Go back there a ways and there's a big mineral lick where you might be able to kill a deer, moose, or an elk!" Believe it or not, I went out there in the dark, waited for it to get daylight and then walked across the trestle. Soon I found the trail and had gone about three quarters of a mile, when I heard a terrible commotion. The air was filled with crows and ravens who were at war, just screaming and diving at one another! At first I couldn't figure out what was going on, but after going a little ways further, here was the gut pile of a huge, bull elk and these critters were fighting over these remains! I hunted a good portion of the day without seeing any game, so headed back.

During my daily visits to check on Bob, the staff told me what I already knew – that Bob was one of the toughest humans they ever saw, even though he suffered horribly! His pelvic region filled up with blood and turned black. The doctor didn't drain it, for he said that in twenty-nine days, it would be absorbed by his body, which it was. One of the nurses was a fellow, named Jerry Bockterkoff, who told us he had at one time, fell timber and used to hunt right where we had been with Tango.

Bob said to me, "I want to go home! The doc said I couldn't leave, but I told him I'm going to!" Just then the doctor came in and Bob said, "I want to go home!" The doc asked, "Do you have a place to lie down while traveling?" Bob said, "Oh, sure! We have a canopy on Ken's truck and can fix a bed back there." So the doctor said he'd release him. When we got to the pickup, Bob said to me, "I don't want to ride back there! Let me sit up in front with you!" As we left, Jerry Bockterkoff asked us to be sure and let him know how Bob got along after we got him home.

Going South, we went through King's Crossing, down by Sandpoint and Coeur d' Alene way and stopped at the border. The young, American Border Guard who came out to greet us was a real Smart Alec! He asked, "What kind of rifle do you have?" I had a brand new 7M Remington Mag and my 7 X 57 Mauser, which I love to hunt with, but never took the Magnum out of its' case on this trip. I told him, "I have a 7 X 57 Mauser." "You have a Mauser?" he asked, and I said, "Yes!" The guy stepped away from my truck and Bob said to me, "You fool! Why'd you tell him that? They'll think you're invading America!" Sure enough, that's what that knot-head thought! We were told, "Report at once to the office!" He saw then that Bob was injured, so told him he could stay in the truck. I went into the office and met an old gentleman who seemed to be very nice. He said, "How's hunting, Boy?" I said, "Not very good, my partner was seriously injured!" The young fellow kept asking, "How much did the moose weigh?" I said, "We didn't weigh it!" Again he screamed at least three times, "How much did it weigh? I have to put something down here!" "Put down 400 pounds," I finally told him. After his little tirade, we told him about the bear Bob had shot, and again, he wanted us to state how much he weighed. Seemingly, he enjoyed giving us a bad time and continued to do so! After much questioning, we were finally allowed to go on our way.

By the time I got Bob home and was ready to deliver him up to his wife, Rosena, I was very sick. We had called her in the meantime and told her Bob had gotten hurt. He did recover from that accident and was once again, a tough old man! That, however, was so sad for me to see him get injured and endure all that pain!

BULL IN BUNCH GRASS

A couple years after this Canadian hunt, Bob and I went back over to Shamrock Springs to hunt on the Umatilla. When we arrived, there was a group of fellows from a surveyor's office in Salem. Dave Baskum owned this business and at one time, he had surveyed the lines on our place up Mill Creek. A group of fellows were with Dave and their tent ropes crossed my tent rope stakes. In their camp, they had a nice generator going and more booze than I've ever seen out in the woods! Any "nationality" of booze you wanted, they had it! They'd drink and play cards until all hours of the night! Bob and I had gone over there to hunt, not to party with these guys!

One evening Bob said, "Let's get up real early, go down that ridge and see if we can't kill a bull," and I agreed. Next morning, we took flashlights, walked down a couple miles, and Bob said, "I'm going down this side, you go down the other." I went down about three quarters of a mile and saw a long opening, with some bunch grass growing there, and I figured if there was a good place where I might find a bull elk, it would be here! Sure enough, down at the lower end was a nice, big animal with his head down. I took the safety off my old Mauser and knew I was in clover! When he put his head up, I let him have it and hit him right through the heart. He made a jump and sort of stopped, as I put another bullet close by, and down he went! I dressed the bull out and hung the quarters in a tree.

Carrying the head, horns, heart and liver, I headed back to camp. Now this is no small feat when you don't have a packboard. I arrived back in camp about 10:00 o'clock, got the blood washed off my hands and went to our tent. We had a little piece of plywood which was about two feet wide and four feet long. We nailed this on top of stakes and that was our table! Underneath the plywood, I put this bull head and horns, so when you sat at our table, your feet were nearly touching it. Bob came in just then, so I asked, "See anything, Bob?" He said, "No, I never saw a thing! There's just too much man scent around here. Those bulls just aren't coming out!" "Well, I only saw one elk, too, Bob, that's all I saw," I told him. He made himself a big sandwich and began to eat it and when he was nearly finished with it, I said, "I'll tell you, Bob, I only saw ONE elk, but it happened to be a bull and I shot him! What do you think about it? Look down at your feet!" He looked down there and let out a scream, saying very loudly, "Will my luck ever change? I've been pulling on a hind tit for three years - will my luck EVER change?" The "neighbor" fellows had a card game going again this morning and came dashing over. Suddenly our tent was filled with those fellows and they asked, "Did you kill a bull this morning?" "Matter of fact, I did," I admitted. Then they wanted to know where I killed it. I said, "Fellows, I'll tell you the truth! I didn't kill it in the tent!" They began to plead, "Well, we want to go with you!" Bob lost no time in piping up, saying, "No, you bet not! You're not going with us, we don't need any help!"

Bob and I took our packboards, his little meat saw, and down that ridge we went to where I had left the bull. Bob said, "I'm gonna try these old bones out and see if they're any good!" This was the first time he had tried to pack since he broke his pelvis in Canada on that hunt with Tango! We made two trips up the bluff that day carrying the meat and got it all packed into camp! So it just goes to prove that Bob was one tough nut! The next day, Bob was fortunate to kill an elk, so that was a fun trip for both of us!

BIG HUNT AT BIG ATLIN LAKE

My next big hunt in British Columbia was with an Outfitter named Walter Erhorn, out of Atlin, in 1975. Two fellows from McMinnville, Ralph Schoof and Barney McPhillips, had also booked a hunt and were ahead of me. Frances and I traveled to Atlin and would wait there until Walter came in for me. Ralph and Barney were already out in the bush hunting with Walter.

The campground at Atlin is beyond description! Impressive Lewellen Glacier feeds it, generating a constant flow of ice and snow coming into Atlin Lake. This lake is a fabulous body of water about eighty-five miles long and so deep, I'm not sure anyone has ever been able to find the bottom! We realized that we'd be in Atlin for at least five days, perhaps longer, waiting for Walter, so we decided to go fishing. Our fishing trip was on a charter with a fellow named Ron Odion. Ron had gone out about three miles from shore when he said, "Get your line out of there, Kenny, your wife has a big fish on! Reel fast, Frances, reel fast!" Frances started reeling and working like everything. Pretty soon she gets the fish up close to the boat and sure enough, she had a fine, big lake trout on. We caught quite a few fish and they tasted great! Ron lived with his Mother and he asked us to visit them, as he was anxious to show off his nice trophies. We learned that originally they had lived at 100 Mile House. Here in the Atlin area, Ron guided for the Goodwin Brothers and when he

Frances hoilding a couple of fish we caugfht in Atlin Lake while on a charter with Ron Odion. She caught the large one, and I caught the small one!

first moved there and went hunting, he had his choice of fifty bull moose and said there were plenty of moose! The last time he went hunting there, it was several days before he found ONE moose to shoot!

Waiting there in Atlin, we basically had time on our hands and were at the mercy of Walter. For entertainment, we met many of the "natives" and discovered some interesting characters. One old gentleman we met told us he had carried mail with a dog sled from Atlin, clear through to Telegraph Creek! He was a very interesting, ninety year old man, and we were to learn later that not long after we were there, he died. His stories would have filled a book, for he had lots of fascinating tales about timber wolves and all kinds of wild animals!

Some of the natives told us about a hot springs, quite a ways out, at the end of the lake, so we decided to go up there one day to check it out. As we arrived at the hot springs, there were two couples there who appeared to be in their mid forties. They

were out there refreshing themselves, but had forgotten to keep their clothes on! When the ladies saw us drive up, they did the proper amount of screaming, while one of the fellows rounded up a blanket so they could take cover and get their clothes on! They didn't think this too funny, but it was very comical, we thought! There was a rock canyon there where a river comes springing right out of the rock, so Frances took a picture of me back there. Some beautiful water cress was growing along this river, so we picked a bunch, which Frances cooked, and the flavor was very good!

1975 - Walter Erhorn, Guide with caribou I took out of Atlin, British Columbia.

We had also been informed that not far away from Atlin was the famous, old Discovery Mine. One day we decided that going out to the mine would be a fun side trip. When we got there, a fellow was working all alone with a D8 Cat. Well, he was all alone, except for a big police dog. Many of the buildings from the original mining operation were still there, somewhat intact. We sat and watched him and because I had run a cat for twenty-four years, I always observed the slack in the tracks on a machine and can usually tell what kind of operator the fellow is. I suppose he got tired of me looking at him and after some time, he got off and came over to greet us. However, he did so with a scowl on his face. "Hello, Sir," I greeted him, "I've been watching your work and I noticed the tracks on your cat." "Oh, what do you see?" he asked. "You've got them adjusted perfectly. When you back up they don't pop or slap or anything and I believe you have them adjusted in a perfect manner," I told him. His chest just sort of swelled up and he said, "Well, I'm not a mechanic, but I try to take good care of my equipment!" At that moment we became good friends and he just up and asked me to help him move a big pump, which I did. He was reworking some of the tailings from the old mine and had dug a tunnel thirteen hundred feet long! Over the course of a number of years, he had shored the tunnel up. Walter had previously told me all about this fellow out here and his work at the mine and that his name was Carl Sager. Carl became convinced the vein was deeper than the Discovery Mine fellows had pursued and he worked there for years. On his cat, he had a ripping tooth with which he'd dig down, rip the soil and put it in a sluice box, eighty-five feet long. In his search, he discovered the ore was deeper than had originally been discovered. A big rubber-tired, front-end loader was used to scoop the gravel away and out there all alone, he worked day after day, year after year!

While we were there, he had this mine site up for sale, but I didn't know it at the time. Two American fellows came in to see Carl and asked him what he had in his recovery box. Carl said, "Let's take a look!" and the story was that when it was opened up, he had two hundred fifty ounces of gold in his box. The B.C. Mining Commission published a report stating that Carl Sager had the finest recovery system of any operation in all of Canada. I asked him how much ground he had staked and his reply was, "Well, I have enough staked right now to run me for fifty-two years, every day, including Sundays, so I have plenty!" He lived all alone there because his wife worked for the school system in White Horse, so she lived there during the school year and spent summers with Carl. While we were visiting Carl, a grizzly came up, went around the cabins and walked right up to the cat. He said, "I don't like that bear and if he comes back tomorrow, I'm going to give him the bullet!" I had never heard that expression before, but I sort of liked it! Once I broke the ice when first we met, Carl was very friendly and enjoyable to be around.

1975 - Here I'm posing with my caribou which I shot near Gladys Lake, British Columbia.

Walter arrived at Atlin and spent a couple days more in town while we waited for the pilot, Herman Peterson, who was to fly us out to the hunting area. Herman was one of the pioneer airplane pilots in all of British Columbia. He and another fellow named Pat Collison were considered two of the genuine pilots. One morning Walter said, "I've changed my mind, Kenny, I think you can drive us back there since you have a good looking rig there, good traction tires and I believe you can make it!" "Is there a road back there?" I asked. He said, "Well, yeah, well, no, well, somewhat of a road!" I should have deducted from his answer what was ahead! Although I had some misgivings about undertaking this trip in my pickup, we started out one morning and the first forty miles weren't too bad. The rest of the miles - well, that's another story! I put the hubs in and most of the time, I had it in super low, as the Indians say. There were dead trees across the road, hardly any visible track to drive in, and in one place, the left, front wheel went down in a hole, as well as the back wheel and there we were - high centered on rocks, or the transfer case, and transmission! We pried and pried as the bumper was on the ground and it's very difficult to get a jack under something when you can't get under it!

At last we were able to get out of there and Walter would run ahead of me every once in awhile to lift dead trees out. Finally I got upset, because occasionally the paint was being scraped off my pickup, and my canopy was also being scraped and gouged. My pickup still has marks on it from those miserable dead pine trees! So I told Walter,

"That's enough of that! I'm going to do something about it!" He had a power saw in the back and I had a good, sharp saddle axe, so we began cutting and managed to cut quite a few out of our way. As we continued, we came to quite a broad river and I asked, "Where's the road, Walter?" He said, "I'll be darned if I know, just kinda head her out there!" There were two big moose right out in the center of this river, and as soon as they saw us, they began to move, making it impossible to see their horns because of the spray they created as they ran! That spray must have been ten to eleven feet high! So I figured if the moose could get out, I could surely get a pickup out! Carefully, I headed out into the stream, and sure enough, water came running into the cab! I did get through without hitting any big rocks and felt very fortunate!

Our adventure continued and Walter reassured me we weren't more than a half mile from where we were to stop, when we came to a washout eight feet wide and four or five feet deep. Walter asked, "What do you think? Do you think if you put her in super low you can make it?" I said, "No, I don't think anything like that at all!" "Well, what you gonna do?" Walter asked. "I'm gonna build a bridge," I answered. "Oh, we can't do that," he said. "Well, we aren't going to cross it then," I informed him. We got out, got the saw going, cut some poles and built it up. I got in, and was able to get through. At last we were at the end of the "road", absolutely unable to go any further in the pickup, and I stopped.

I gathered my rifle, spotting scope, and we took off through the brush. "Walter, is it very far?" I asked. "Well, yeah, well, not too bad," he said. We walked about five miles and here was a lake and river – which we had to ford! After getting soaked, we finally arrived at camp and here was Harry Carlick, the Indian guide, who worked for Walter. Harry was a local man, who guided Barney and Walter guided Ralph. Walter's area lay East of Atlin, over the hill from Gladys Lake, with his camp set up on a lake called Lincoln Lake. He had rented this area from an Indian named George Edzerza and they had camped and hunted there for years. The only item which resembled a camp was a little shanigan they had built to keep meat up in the air, away from grizzly bear. Beside this little lake with beautiful blue, ice-cold water, there was a nice, little, sandy beach there and the lake was full of grayling! Sadly lacking was a wood supply, but we grubbed roots out and used them to get a fire going.

Walter's crew, Ralph and Barney were very successful and in three days time they had each killed a Mountain Stone Sheep and a nice caribou. Ralph also got a beautiful, bull moose, and when they went into camp, Walter just took the hams and tenderloin. He left the rest of the animal out in the bush. By this time, I was more than anxious to begin my hunt, but the next morning, instead of taking me hunting, Walter says, "We gotta pack those hams out for my wife!" We started down the hill with this pack outfit. Walter had plenty of gear there, but he didn't have any bracing on this pack saddle and those hams were terribly heavy! We hooked one on the El Forkas and it just ran around the horses' belly! Then we decided to cut a jill poke and got one ham back up there, propped it, then put the other one on. Buckskin was a very fine horse, but he just groaned when the second ham was placed on him.

We were just starting down a steep incline when Harry hollered out, "Hold it, Walter! Buckskin's got his head nailed to the ground!" I would love to have had a picture of that, for the poor creature could not lift his head! So Walter began to cuss profusely and in due time, we got the hams back up and loaded. That happened twice on the way down to my pickup. Harry planned to stay in my camper while someone came in from Atlin to pick him up. The fellow from Atlin who was coming to pick up Harry, was driving a big Ford pickup and when he came to the river which he had to ford, he opened it up and hit a big rock! This broke his tie rod and there he sat! Would you believe it, here came a couple government biologists and they rescued this guy. Harry and the hams went back out to Atlin – Walter's mission was accomplished!

At last, Walter and I arrived at camp and we got ready to begin hunting. He had great horses, with plenty of good food for them and as we started out, it began to storm. We had to go through a terrible muskeg area and so each day we left camp, we'd try to pick a new place. Walter would start off first on his horse and I'd hold my horse back. She'd watch Walter's horse and if the first horse had a bad moment, my horse would inevitably choose a different path and it always proved to be better! Walter had told me when he gave me the horse, "Well, you MIGHT be able to ride this horse, but be careful and watch her, she bites!" As I was beginning to saddle up one morning, she laid her ears back and bit at me! I told her in plain English that she couldn't do that! Walter planned to take me to the area where Ralph had killed his nice ram, so we began to hunt!

The first day out, we went in some very rough country and I noticed Walter was wearing the seat of his pants out more than the soles of his shoes! He was constantly falling down and would curse a streak or two, get up, and on we'd go! The first day, he had on a pair of cowboy boots which had been worn out about the day Noah landed the Ark. They were split open, with his feet getting soaking wet, and there was absolutely no sign of tread on the soles of his boots! They were as bald as his head! We never saw any sheep the first day, so back to camp we went in the evening, empty-handed!

Walter had kept the tenderloin off the animal Ralph had killed and the meat was just delicious! He had an aversion to water and I never saw him wash his hands on that entire trip. He'd cut a steak about an inch to an inch and a quarter thick, which looked more like a small roast, and he would try and fit this steak into a skillet. Any portion which wouldn't lay down flat in the skillet, he'd trim off and put into a big black kettle which he had simmering at the back of the fire. I'd fix my own steak and fry it in another skillet as Walter would always let his steak catch on fire and I didn't like mine fixed that way. One evening all I ate was steak and it was just perfect, and was great meat! It was bitterly cold and the wind came up, practically blowing the tent away. It was also raining like crazy, but Walter was just peacefully snoring away! I got up and found some rocks to anchor the tent down so it wouldn't be blown away! Each morning I'd scrounge around for some roots to get a fire going and Walter would start looking for the horses! I begged him to hobble a couple of them, but he just wouldn't do it! He'd put a bell on them, turn them loose and off they'd go! When they'd hear him coming the next morning, they would hold absolutely still, so as to not ring their bells! Talk about smart!

It was nearly twelve-thirty when we were ready to leave camp one day, and already Walter had been walking steady since quarter after seven that morning! He was looking for the horses! I made the remark that we may as well go back to bed, and with my remark, he screamed at me how he'd been walking all morning! I said, "I know, but you're not getting anywhere! You ought to tie the horses up at night, feed them and they'll be okay!" He just wouldn't do that! We rode up on a big flat and it looked like REAL caribou country. No sooner had I thought that, than I noticed off to the left, there were caribou! I said, "Walter, here's thirty-six head of caribou!" He asked, "Where?" I pointed them out and he said, "Oh yes!" Although he was only forty-four years old, part of the time it seemed as if his eyes were not good at all! At the time, I I was not quite sixty-three, but I noted that I generally saw the game first! We didn't get anything that day and went back to camp in the evening.

The next morning we went in a different direction and rode way up above timber line, where there were no trees whatsoever! Once there, I spotted eleven caribou! We put the stalk on them and an hour and fifteen minutes later, we got to the top. There were seven bulls in the band (evidently four of them had made other arrangements) and they were in the velvet, with huge horns! Of course, when they're in the velvet, they look exceptionally big! We went down into a canyon, then up a game trail, crossed a flat, and when we got up there, they had vanished! We never could figure out how they got out of there without us seeing them leave! Walter cussed and screamed and no doubt the game could hear him for five miles as he raged! I looked down the canyon where we had just come up and here came two, fine bulls up the trail. They ran out in front of us, then both turned to look at us. I said, "Walter, I've been here for five days and haven't even blown the rust out of my gun. I'm going to shoot that bull!" He asked, "You are?" "Yes, I am," I said, as I knelt down and touched off a shot with my 7 X 57! Down the bull went! He was out quite a distance from me and we took off to get to him. Just as we got up to him, he raised up on his front feet and I put another shot through him. Rather than congratulating me, as most guides would do, Walter took a generous amount of Copenhagen, shook his head and said rather softly, "He sure is one h— of a big bull!"

We dressed him out along a little creek, with some red rocks protruding there and ice partially formed on part of the water. Everything was clean and as we laid the meat out, I heard a raven overhead. I said to Walter, "Oh, oh, I'll bet that raven is going to go and tell his five brothers there's going to be a meal!" Walter said, "You wait until morning! You won't believe it!" The next morning, I said to Walter, "Let me fix your pack saddle so you won't have a problem like you did when we packed those bull moose hams out!" He said, "No, I gotta do that this winter!" I said, "Walter, we need to do it now because we have an animal to pack out NOW!" He would not let me fix it for him! When we got up to the meat, there were thirty-five ravens that we could count before they began flying around, making it impossible to get a totally accurate count! We inspected the meat and those ravens had just started working on one shoulder of the bull. We shooed them off, packed the meat on the horses and started down the hill!

Sure enough, it happened! Walter's pack saddle just didn't do the job and we would have to stop and re-pack it and did so a number of times! This was completely ridiculous and could have been avoided if Walter would not have been so bull-headed! He made a remark that really stuck with me, he said, "I wish some of those sob sisters

from the South could come up here in the Spring when the caribou are in here calving."
He was referring to some of the gruesome things which happen to young animals out in
the wild! The bull I killed was an Osborn, or Barren Ground Caribou and they come
out of the Yukon. Walter told me that as they travel South, the ravens follow along and
whenever they find a caribou calf, they pick the eyes out, the calf dies and they have a
string of meat over five hundred miles long to feed on. I was able to verify what he told
me, for later on, this very thing happened to an Angus heifer which belonged to my
neighbor.

It's quite an ordeal to cape out an animal and if you've never done it, there is much
to learn. One has to carefully skin around the eyes, lips, and everything. As we were
working on the bull, I sawed right close to the brain area, but hadn't touched the mem-
brane which held the brains. Suddenly I was seized with the thought, "I'm going to
take the brain out, fry them up with cracker crumbs, and I'm gonna have a feed!" So I
built a fire, got a skillet, and asked, "Walter, do you want some brains to eat?" He
screamed and cussed, "I don't eat crap like that!" I said, "Well, I never did either,
Walter, but I'm about to!" So I went ahead and ate them.

That evening in camp we had a tremendous meal. We discussed the fact that Walter
still planned to try and get me a ram, plus possibly a moose, which was our agreement.
The next morning we started out towards the sheep country again and I saw the finest
ram I've ever seen. He was following four ewes and I said to Walter, "Look up here!
Look at that big ram! I'm going to kill him!" "Oh, no, please don't! I can't see his
other horn," he said. "I don't need to see his other horn, he looks good enough to me,"
I informed him, but he would not let me shoot! He said, "What's he doing with those
ewes? He's a month early!" I said, "Well, he takes his job more seriously than some of
the other rams!" "Let him go," Walter said, "he'll go over and bed down on the cliff
and we'll pick him off over there!" It was already snowing then and I thought, "Here's
a chance to kill a fine ram about one hundred twenty-five yards from me," but Walter
wouldn't let me shoot! We tied the horses at timberline, then went over the top of the
mountain to the craigs, and the fury came! It began to sleet and blow so fiercely,
almost immediately our eyelashes, eyebrows and clothing became white! We had to
shield our faces as we could hardly see, so Walter said, "We gotta get out of here!" For
two hours we hunted for our horses and must have walked within fifty feet of them
several times. They were, however, completely white with snow and I thought surely
Walter would have melted the snow for at least two miles the way he was screaming
and cussing! Finally, by fate, we stumbled onto the horses! Those poor creatures were
so cold they could hardly stand there. We tried to ride them, but it was so slick, we got
off and walked, leading them back to camp. It was 8:00 P.M. when we got into camp
and just immediately crawled into bed, dead tired!

The next day I tried to get Walter to hunt for moose, but he insisted there was no
use as they were rubbing the velvet. This was now about September 20 and is the
approximate, usual period during which they are rubbing the velvet off. For the duration of this natural occurrence, the moose are very secretive and hide in the thickets. At
last, he agreed to take me out and we went to a hillside, on a Southerly slope. Before
long, we saw a big, cow moose with her calf. I said, "Walter, I am not quite that

ignorant, I know where the bulls are!" He just turned a deaf ear and would not agree to hunt moose. We decided to break camp, and as we were doing so, I "woke up!" Walter had a two-day journey taking his horses back down to his headquarters where we first came in to go hunting with him. He helped me pack the caribou down to my pickup and then he put four pack boxes, three extra saddles, all of his cooking gear, tent, a couple big tarps, and all the rigging he had up there, into my pickup! I also had Ralph and Barney's caribou horns, big sheep horns, and a set of caribou horns! I'll never know how I got that door shut and now here I was, going back to Atlin all alone, through all those fallen trees, debris, and brush which Walter did not take out of the road when I was going in. The Good Lord was with me and finally I made it! It took Walter two days to go over the mountains with those horses!

Back at Walter's headquarters, we discussed hunting for sheep in another area. A young fellow, Lance Fuller, came in that evening and of course, he had a bottle of booze with him. Lance and Walter lost no time and began drinking, although Walter wasn't a big drinking man. Lance was getting to a stage where he felt no pain and as he looked at me, asked, "So you think you're going sheep hunting, eh?" I said, "Yeah!" "How old are you?" he wanted to know. I told him and he laughed and said again, "So you're going sheep hunting, eh? Well, you'll never make it!"

"I know of a good place above Porter Lake where we can hunt sheep," Walter told me, so we drove there. He took a side road, went back in the mountains a ways, in this really, rough country and it was still storming some. We got out and started hiking, crossed a long beaver pond, and started up the mountain, which was literally straight up and down! I had my rifle, shells, binoculars, hunting axe and saw, camera, and various gear and Walter had my spotting scope! We got up a ways and found a little rock cave, so we went inside to get out of the storm for a bit. Inside there were sheep droppings, as well as moose droppings. Walter said, "I never knew moose ever came this high!" "Well, I didn't either," I admitted. I went to the opening of the cave and looked up to the highest point there and here was a nice ram looking right down at us! I said, "Look here, Walter!" He asked, "What?" I said, "See that ram there! He's going to warn his five brothers, isn't he!" Walter said, "He'll warn everybody! I know how to get up there without him seeing us." We started around the back side, up a steep bluff and off to the left, I saw thirteen sheep running! "Look over here, Walter," I said. He asked, "Where?" "There goes thirteen sheep over there," I told him as I pointed them out to him, and he began to curse and scream, "There goes our sheep!" We took off, once again climbing a terribly steep mountain. We went up four mountains that day and three of them were simply brutal!

Going towards camp, there was a huge bear eating moss berries in front of us. We were within fifty feet of him and he was just scooping those berries up as fast as he could. Walter didn't see him, so I remarked, "Walter, see that bear?" Just then he took off and Walter said, "Oh, there goes thirty gallons of the finest lard you ever saw and I don't have a bear tag!" "We got down to my pickup and Walter turned to me and said, You know something?" I said, "What?" He said, "You're one d— good hiker!" He got into my little camper, laid down and immediately began to snore. I got behind the wheel and sat there all night long with no food, no nothing, while Walter "sawed away"!

He was completely exhausted from our hike and I got a chuckle out of that, especially since young Lance had informed me I'd never make it!

While in camp, Walter informed me the hunt was over and we started back to Atlin from Porter Lake. Going into Porter Lake, I had driven over a couple windfalls with some sharp knots sticking up, and I told Walter I thought they might puncture my tires. He assured me they would not, but he was wrong and a tire was ruptured! It was raining hard as I tried to jack that pickup up, but with all the weight in there, it just kept sliding sideways and ended up in the ditch. After a lot of hard work, I managed to get the tire changed and drove out to Atlin Lake where Frances was waiting for me. We headed for the main road to travel home and as soon as we were on our way, it was obvious the road crew had put some sort of solution on this highway. The plan was to come through and grade it, but that hadn't been done yet. This highway was a mess and every time I met another vehicle, mud and gunk would coat the headlights, making it impossible to see. I stopped to clean off my windshield and lights and when I tried to go again, the pickup just began sliding sideways, so I put the hubs in, but still the truck slid. It went down over a bluff, but fortunately, never turned over. The highway department had just taken a small cat down there to clean out a culvert, so I was able to get going and pull out of there. We got to a sizable service station and sitting there was a big semi truck, which had been wrecked. Amazingly, the cab had just been wiped off, right to the top of the engine. About ten 10:00 o'clock that night, we pulled into Watson Lake, inquired about getting a room and were told there wasn't an empty bed in town! As we checked at the hotel, they informed us they were booked! With all the meat, horns, camping gear and supplies, we could not sleep in our camper! Finally a lady at the hotel said, "Well, I'll tell you, there is a room down here truckers sometimes use. There is a single bed there, so one of you might have to sleep on the floor!" We said, "No problem! We have sleeping bags!" Once we got to this room, waiting for us was a nice bed, shower, and all the comforts of home! We were so grateful, for with the storm going on, we didn't want to travel anymore that night!

A side note on the caribou I shot while hunting with Walter is that when we weighed him in, he was a whopping 320 pounds, with lots of white fat, and a great piece of meat! When I checked him out at Atlin, the Game Warden, Jamie Stevens, said that caribou was the finest caribou trophy that had gone through Atlin that year! I was happy, indeed, with this bull! We traveled on to Oregon and went directly to Ralph's place, as we had his rack of horns, as well as Barney's. The first question he bombarded me with was, "Say, I want to know what Walter was wearing when you got there to hunt with him!" I said, "I'll tell you, Ralph, he had an old pair of cowboy boots that were slit along the insoles for three or four inches, they were completely bare of tread and he would dry them out one day by the fire and then wear gum boots the next day, which were worse yet! Ralph said, "Well, that tight b———! I gave him fifty dollars when I left and told him to go buy a pair of shoes!" I knew Walter had been in town three or four days and never bought shoes! I even remarked to Walter, "You need to replace your footwear!" Ralph and Barney insisted on reimbursing us for our stay in the hotel since we were unable to use our camper to sleep in. That was our experience hunting with Walter while we were still living in Oregon.

Years later, while living in Clinton, I was out in the barnyard and had just shod one of my three horses. I looked up and saw a fellow walking towards me. He had a nice cowboy outfit on and a heavy mustache. He said, "Hello," and I answered, "Hello!" He said, "You don't know me, do you? You and I had a big hunt one time!" "Are you Walter Erhorn?" I asked and he said, "I am!" We invited him in for lunch and had a nice visit. He had left Atlin and moved to the Lillooet area where he bought an eighty acre farm, right beside the Yalakom River. We had passed by his place on our way to visit Pat Garrard, but were unaware of the fact he lived there. He had a beautiful alfalfa field close to the river and every evening, upwards to two hundred deer would be feeding in his field. He said he killed a buck and then a hippie came over and they got into a pretty bad fight, with the hippie getting the worst end of the deal! Soon after he got home, visitors arrived and said, "We don't want you here!" Walter said, "That's obvious! Buy me out," and they quickly said, "Name your price!" Even though he jacked the price up, that did not deter them and they paid him in cash. Shortly thereafter, he discovered these hippies had a big marijuana outfit and they didn't want Walter living in that area, so he moved up by Williams Lake. The last time I saw him was around 1992 and he was still living there, but in the summer of 1997, we received his obituary notice, so he died at a fairly young age!

ANTELOPE ANTICS

When Ed Phillips lived in Salem, one of his friend's was neighbor to a fellow who worked for the State Printing Department. Ed's friend called me one night and asked, "Kenny, do you want some antelope tags?" I said, "No, I didn't put in for the drawing!" He said, "That isn't what I asked you! Do you NEED some antelope tags?" I said, "I don't understand what you're talking about!" "Listen, my neighbor was just here and told me they always print up a couple hundred extra tags to give out to their friends. He can get all the tags you want for nothing," he informed me. Seven of us were just getting ready to go to the Steens Mountains and Ed was the only one who had an antelope tag. I told him, "I'm going to pass this time!"

We left on our hunting trip, drove past this little post office, called Follyfarm, south of Burns, and then traveled East towards Piute Lake Desert. There was an old, abandoned house with a spring close by and a little dam. There were antelope, wild horses, coyotes, fox, and jack rabbits and they all used this little dam for drinking! We decided to stay in this old house and just at dusk, some hunters came in driving a Willys Jeep. Their main objective was just to have a good time and they had gotten an early start by "tipping the bottle"! One of them said, "You've got company, boys!" We invited them in and one of them asked, "You boys all antelope hunters?" We said, "No, only Ed has a tag." "Well, do you want tags? I'm President of the Ontario Rod and Gun Club and I have all the tags you boys need!" We thanked them, but did not accept the tags. The next morning the Game Warden drove in and got very angry because we were all there and only Ed had an antelope tag! I asked him if he would like to "dog" for Ed and he didn't appreciate it! I didn't feel like I should tell him about all the free antelope tags we had just turned down! Little by little, we got an education in how the system works and it certainly isn't like it appears on the surface! Ed did kill a nice antelope on that trip and we had a good time!

Another time, when Ed and I were hunting up at the Carson Mines in Eastern Oregon, it was snowing very, very hard! Matter of fact, we could hardly see anything at all! The Carson Mines had been a big outfit during its' prime and the old hotel was still standing. There was room to feed at least forty miners at a time, the old blacksmith shop was still intact and things were in very good shape. While operating this mine, a great water canal had been dug, as they used a hydraulic mining operation. Ed and I walked along in the canal, which was now dry. As we walked, we jumped a big, five-point bull about thirty feet from us. My gun was in the sling across my shoulder and Ed was about four feet behind me. As soon as I saw the bull, I jerked back to get my gun off, and nearly hit Ed in the face. In the meantime, that bull jumped over the bank and was gone before I even had time to get a shot at him! Ed said to me, "What was it?" "It was a big, bull elk!" I told him, and pointed to the tracks. Ed said, "Listen, let me go down here and I'll make a big circle below and you stay on his track." Just as we were about to part, we looked down on the bench and saw a nice, big buck! We were allowed to shoot deer or elk that year, so Ed shot, and that buck went down! I slapped him on the back and congratulated him on such a fine shot. Ed said, "I don't believe I hit him good, Kenny, I think he's going to get up!" I said, "I never saw a deer get up when he went down that quick!" Ed said, "Well, I have!" Just about that quick, that buck got up and was gone! "I was sure I saw part of his horn go off," Ed said.

We knew we'd better take off and trail that buck, so away we went. Ed had been gone about a half hour when he walked onto a big elk and shot it! I heard the shot, but I figured he was finishing off that deer, so I didn't go down. That elk was Ed's first one and I was so happy for him! This was especially true, because we NEVER did find the deer he shot at. We had some tremendous hunts, which included deer, elk, moose and antelope! I certainly miss the old-timers I used to spend a lot of time with and they played a big part in my life. They didn't blow a big trumpet, but they were men of action and great people.

ERRORS AND OMISSIONS

OF THE COMMISSION

Years ago, during the deer season in Oregon, Ed said to me, "Say, Kenny, I have a friend who wants to come hunting with me in the morning. Let's take him hunting." I said, "That's okay with me, Ed." The next morning we took off and as we were having lunch, I discovered that Ed's friend had previously been with the Game Commission, but had left. Just a day or two earlier, I had read in the Oregonian a very short article which said: "Charles H. Lockwood, Head of the Oregon State Game Commission, resigned as of yesterday. Mr. Lockwood gave reasons of ill health...." I mentioned this to Ed's friend and he laughed, saying, "Would you like to know what REALLY happened?" "I surely would," I answered. "Well, they were flying hunters out of Portland to the Rez Horse Ranch in the Wallowa's and would guarantee them meat; buck, doe, bull or cow elk, and so on. They were landing them at Rez Horse Ranch and hunting out of there when some Federal Agents raided them and they got caught! The irony of it is that Lockwood was just about ready to retire with a nice, hefty pension awaiting him and now this episode happens!"

That fall we were hunting elk in Eastern Oregon, just below Anthony Lakes. Here were four Game Wardens up there, but only one was in his official uniform, a Sergeant. The others were patrolling around the area. A fellow from Lebanon had killed a cow on the wrong side of the road. On the side towards Baker, you could kill bulls only, and on the Grand Ronde River side, one could shoot either sex. This hunter had killed a cow elk on the Baker side, so the Wardens were looking for the gut pile, but they told us they were trailing a wounded elk. We weren't completely ignorant and it soon became evident to us, they were doing no such thing! I got to talking to the Sergeant and said, "It sure was too bad about Charlie Lockwood, wasn't it!" Trying to act casual, he asked, "Oh, what's too bad about Charlie Lockwood?" I said, "Well, his stomach blowing up in his face when he had this big, lifetime pension. That's a major tragedy." He pulled out a cigarette, lit it, took a drag, looked at me and asked, "How did you find out about that?" "Never mind! I found out about it!" I told him. He waited a moment and then said, "Well, it sure as the devil doesn't make my job any easier!" I often thought about that and what big shots won't do to cover up their tracks! Many years prior to this, the Secretary of State, Earl Sell, and some others were shooting geese over a baited pond down in Southern Oregon. They had bad luck and their plane crashed. So the Good Lord doesn't have payday EVERY Saturday night, but He always has payday!

OLD GLORY STORY

John Breeden asked me to go elk hunting with he and Floyd Barrenger one fall, and he wanted me to take my twin boys along. Soon we planned a trip up Dry Beaver Canyon, pretty well up towards the head, to a place called Jordan Cow Camp, in Eastern Oregon. My boys had never killed any elk, so they were very excited about this trip. John asked me, "If I put your boys on a stand, will they stay there?" "What do you mean?" I wanted to know. He said, "I just want to know if they would stay on a stand." "You bet they will!" I said. "They'll stay on a stand until I, or someone gets there!" John told us he knew where to jump the elk, so he put each of the boys on a different stand and assured us the elk would go right through those stands. Sure enough, he ran twenty-one elk through, but there wasn't a horn in the bunch! I told the boys, "Remember, your shells are paid for and if you knock an elk down, run up and put another bullet behind the ear!" I had outfitted each of them with a little axe, a knife, and 30-30 Savage Rifles.

Next morning, John said, "Let's hunt up towards Old Glory! Now this spot was up on a big hill where someone used to hoist a very large, American flag and it was really neat to see that out there! It was kind of a mahogany ridge and was a great place to hunt elk! It was several miles up to Old Glory, and Myron went off to the right quite a ways. We were unaware of the fact that the LaGrande City Watershed had a reservoir there, and in the course of his morning hunt, he got down to the grounds of the reservoir. A security guard was patrolling there and took Myron into tow and, in fact, wanted to arrest this kid! Up on the ridge, above where Myron had been, Byron was also hiking and they were about a half mile apart. About 11:00 o'clock, it was snowing very hard, and when I got up to the top of the mountain, here came John. He asked, "See anything?" I said, "You're the first object I've seen this morning!" "Did you hear anything," he wanted to know. "Yes, I heard two shots over to my right, about 10:00 o'clock this morning," I said. "Let's go look!" John suggested. We walked about a thousand feet, found a little blaze on a tree and followed that blaze to a nice elk all dressed out! John made the remark, "By George, whoever made these blazes, I'd like to hire that fellow to swamp for my D-7!"

I realized that one of the boys had shot this elk, so John and I started to pack it off the mountain. In the meantime, Byron discovered Myron was being "held hostage" and came to find John and me. When he saw us, he said, "That fellow down there wants to have Myron arrested!" Floyd had joined us by now and all of us went down to find Myron. John told this guard, "Oh, no, you're not going to arrest this innocent kid! I'll fight you all the way to the United States Supreme Court! This lad was unaware of this area, he was not hunting on your property, and he simply wandered down too far! You don't even have the perimeter properly marked, anyway!" The guard knew John meant business, so agreed to forget the entire matter!

Next day out hunting, Byron went with Floyd and they ran into a herd of elk. Floyd shot first and then immediately afterwards, Byron shot. Floyd said Byron turned to him and congratulated him on his nice elk! That night after we ate supper, I went outside the tent and Floyd came outside also. He whispered low and said to me, "I didn't kill that elk! That boy there did (he couldn't tell the twins apart and neither could John)," and he motioned towards Byron. I mentioned this to Byron, and he said, "Well, I knew that I killed it, but I didn't want to take anything from Floyd. He's such a nice guy!" All in all, we did pretty well on this hunt and it was very enjoyable!

The following year we went back, and Davie went along. The hunting was rather grim, with not many bull elk per cow ratio in that area. We hunted a little and then John said, "Let's drive out that ridge!" John had a Jeep with a factory-made canopy, which was quite heavy. That ridge was so steep, John would drive slowly along and a bunch of us would stand alongside that Jeep with our hands on the canopy, in order to keep it from tipping over! John drove way down this point on Dry Beaver Creek and as we went, I heard some elk bugle! We stopped and it was so foggy we could hardly see a thing. I said to John, "Do you hear those bull elk?" He said, "Those aren't bull elk!" "Oh, yes, they are," I said! "No, Kenny, those are coyote, I'm sure," John insisted. I was positive they were bull elk, as I could hear the more coarse tones of the older bulls, and the more mellow ones coming from the spikes. John was in command and said, "Floyd, you take Byron and Davie and go down this ridge about two miles, drop into that canyon, and we'll drop into this canyon here! With all of us, we'll make a drive those elk will be unable to escape! There is no way they can get away from us!"

Floyd started out with Dave and Byron. John, Myron, and I were left there and it was just starting to get light. To our amazement, we saw dozens of elk, perhaps fifty or sixty elk, just going down the hill! John said, "Look at those elk go!" In a flash, here was a great, big five-point running down below, but he was way out of range! John looked at us and said, "Are your shells paid for, boys?" We said, "Yes!" and he said, "Let's spend them here!" We laid down on the ground; John shot, then Myron, and then me, and we just kept taking turns! John's gun was a 300 Savage, Myron had a 30-30 Savage, and my gun was a 30-06 rifle, with a scope. One of my shots was a lucky one and it knocked this five-point bull down! John confirmed that I had him down and no sooner had he said that, when he saw a man running down the hill! He said, "There goes Floyd! What's he doing down there?" He cupped his hands to his mouth and shouted out, "Hey, Floyd!" John Breeden had the most powerful and resonant voice I believe I have ever heard on anybody. This man stopped and shouted back, "Yeah," but he couldn't determine where John's voice had come from and began running again. John shouted, "Go to your left!" The man stopped and suddenly started running over to his left. Once again John shouted, "Go to your left," and then the guy saw the elk down there. He ran up to it and fired a shot at it, even though it was already laying on the ground! Down the hill we went towards the elk and all the way, John kept fussing, "I wonder what that Floyd is doing down here!"

This terrain was very steep and it took us a little while to get there, and as we came to the bull, here was an Indian fellow and a white man just starting to skin out this bull! John came unglued! He told them, "Get away from that bull if you want to live a long life!" One of them responded with equal force, "Well, if you want to live, you'd better keep a civil tongue in your mouth!" Words flew back and forth and I was trying to find out who these fellows were. The white man was Bill, from Sweet Home, and after things calmed down, we found out he really was a nice guy! He told me he was cutting timber for Bill Hessman, Archie's brother. John then asked, "What kind of gun do you have?" He said, "Oh, I've got a 30-06." "Did you shoot him?" John asked. "Oh, yes, I shot at him," Bill said. "Where at?" John insisted. Bill said, "Well, I was way over there when I shot!" John asked, "Did you hit him?" "Oh, sure," Bill said. John then reasoned, "Well, don't you think he'd lose some blood if you shot him over there and he ran this far?" They walked over towards where Bill said he had shot at the bull and began to look for blood. The Indian fellow was still there at the bull and was just starting to make an incision to take the guts out when he backed off a ways to light a cigarette. That was our moment and Myron and I actually dived right into that bull and began dressing him out. The Indian fellow just sat there and shook, he was so angry! In a way, I didn't blame him, but we knew we had shot that bull first! Bill and John came back from looking for blood and Bill said, "That's not my elk!" This Indian said, "Well, I'm telling you, I shot a five-point elk and I didn't miss!" It was obvious he was still upset. They walked around the hill a little ways and in about fifteen minutes, I heard one of them say, "Here he is, over here!" They had gotten a nice bull, too, and here John had inadvertently directed a total stranger to our bull elk and we nearly had to fight for it! We had a big laugh out of it afterwards and agreed it was a good recipe for murder! I know a lot of fellows who would not have backed off and given it to the rightful owner, so we lucked out on this one and didn't get in trouble!

The net result of that hunt was that John hired Myron and Byron to work on his rigging crew and that cemented an already wonderful friendship. My boys always loved John, as did I, and our friendship continued until John passed away. They worked for John down on the coast, on the high lead and sometimes behind the cat. John had a Brother, Ellis, working for him and he was running a cat, picking up logs in a canyon. The twins had been out of high school a couple years at this time and one day they decided they wanted to go to college. They gave John notification, and then as the last day on the job arrived, one of them said, "Ellis, this is our last day in the woods for awhile, we're going to go to college." Ellis was a giant of a man and very powerful and it seemed he literally didn't know his own strength. He got off the cat, put his arms around those twins and said, "Boys, I want you to make me a promise!" "Okay, what do you want, Ellis?" they asked. He said, "The world is full of educated, d— fools. Promise me you won't come out that way!" They gave Ellis their solemn promise and I'm happy to say, they didn't come out of college that way!

BREEDEN, BABE AND BARBER

John Breeden and I had some wonderful hunts together and decided to hunt up Shumway one fall. John invited two neighbors, Babe Lewis and Ray Barber, to go along. I took Davie and the twin boys along. We had gone our separate ways when a shot was heard. John called out, "Was that you, Sonny?" He couldn't tell the twins apart, so they both were "Sonny"! Myron called back, "It wasn't me," followed by Byron saying, "It wasn't me, either!" "Oh, oh, no meat," John said. He called out again, "Babe, did you shoot?" "Yes," Babe answered, and John asked, "What did you shoot at?" Babe said, "Well, I just shot to turn a deer around!" John asked, "What do you mean, turn around? When I shoot at 'em, I try to turn them OVER!"

We all continued hunting and soon I saw a big buck just laying in his bed, which he had "hand-picked" in an old, reddish colored log! This log had long ago been cut by the Sheridan Timber Company and was quite badly decayed. The deer's coat was still very red, also, as it was the first part of deer season and the way I first spotted him was that he moved his head as he lay there. He never even had time to get up, as I nailed him. John heard my shot and called out, "Who shot?" I said, "John, keep quiet! I just shot an Old Doe!" He said, "You did? Well, how did that happen?" "Well, those things just happen sometimes, John," I said. Making his way to where I was, he was quite disturbed and nervous! As he walked up to my deer and rolled it over, he said, "By George, Kenny! If that's a doe, it sure has a funny looking anatomy on it!" By now, the rack of horns were highly visible and John got a good chuckle out of it! John was a good packer, so the two of us saddled it up, the boys joined us, and down the mountain we went with our game.

Going down the mountain, we decided to go through Pine Creek. All of a sudden, we heard a noise in the timber and a doe ran right through the bunch of us. Her eyes were turned up in her head and she was so terrified and spooked, we figured a cougar had been on her tail! We never did see a cougar and didn't find out for certain what scared her, but she acted as if she hardly saw us and just ran for her life!

We had so much fun with John and he really enjoyed my sons, so he invited us to go to Eastern Oregon to hunt with him. We traveled over to Dry Beaver area once again and camped at Jordan Cow Camp. On this particular trip, John brought his grandson, Scott Breeden, who was a young lad at that time. Scott had also invited his friend, Mike Wagler, son of Paul and Carmen Wagler, friends of ours! Those boys were very good on the trip, had a lot of fun, and we had a lot of fun with them! John had so many expressions that he used over and over and one of them was, "Well, I think I'll hunt South of camp." So I asked him, "John, what do you mean, 'South of camp'?" His answer was a question, "You didn't hear that story?" "No," I told him, so he said, "Well, I'll tell you! A couple of fellows from Willamina were hunting with me and some of my friends, and these two fellows took a lot of booze along. There was one fifth left and I knew this one guy wasn't going to leave camp until the booze was all gone. 'I believe I'll hunt South of camp, fellows,' this guy said, as the others headed out. They said, 'All right.' At noon they came into camp, and sure enough, this fellow was 'South of camp'! He had only made it out in front of the tent about fifty feet and lay there in a drunken stupor!" That was his story and we always got a big kick out of him! He was such an enjoyable person and his humor was genuine and pleasant!

John came to see me one day, saying "I want you to come up to my old place and go hunting in the morning!" I agreed and when I arrived the next morning before daylight, here was Mike Wagler, just thirteen years old! John said, "You take this lad, put him up there on a stump someplace, and I'll go back down here towards that mill. I know where those big bucks lay and I'll try and jump a couple!" Just before he left, John said to Mike, "Don't you go shooting some great, big old buck that has his neck swelled up! All we want is a little jerky meat!" Mike and I started up a hill and John went the other way. Soon I heard some fellows talking and I didn't know what to do! There was a big stump there, about two springboards high, that had been fell by hand, so I told him, "Mike, get up on that stump and just watch! I don't know what to do because there are guys up here, right behind me!" I went on about three hundred feet past him, and since it was still dark, I didn't realize I was right next to a road. These guys were in a pickup and were just driving by, so they weren't up in the woods with us at all!

Before long, I looked up towards Mike and saw that he was pointing his gun straight down! Then, he moved it over to the left, and I saw that a big buck had come right up to the base of his stump! Two times he could nearly have touched the deer with his gun! Then that buck started galloping up the hill toward me, so I shot him! Mike came up to me and said, "Mr. Shenk, Mr. Breeden said not to shoot a big, old buck! That buck stood there at the base of my stump and I could have shot him twice, but I didn't!" I said, "Oh, well, I don't think John really meant that!" Just then, John appeared and he said, "Holy Mackinaw! What a nice, big buck that is!" Mike said, "Mr. Breeden, I thought you didn't want me to shoot a big buck." John just reached out, grabbed Mike, hugged him and said, "I'm sorry, Sonny!" He started to cry a little bit as he felt so badly. That was so funny to think Mike took John so seriously, when John was only kidding.

OLD LADY AND THE LANTERN

Shamrock Springs was another favorite hunting spot in Eastern Oregon and several of us were there on a hunt. Bob Patty, Russell, one of the twin boys, Dave and myself were in the group. We got several bulls, and then the boys had to go back home for jobs and school, so Bob and I stayed on. We had a nice tent, good supply of wood, and adequate food. It was bitterly cold, and began to snow. The snow got so deep, I couldn't open the doors on my pick-up and we had to travel uphill to get out of this camp site! We just needed one more bull to use up all our tags, so we'd hunt in the forenoon and work on the road in the afternoon. There were some guys coming down the hill towards our camp with a big, old Dodge Command Car, sort of a power wagon, and a Ford pickup and they were fighting their way through this deep snow to get to our camp. Bob was getting rather hard to live with and the arrival of these fellows brightened his spirits! There were four fellows and they all seemed to be nice guys. One was around sixty years of age, and the rest were probably around forty. Bob said, "Come in and spend your time in our tent! It's nice and warm, we have plenty of room!" They said, "Oh, no, we'll be all right!" They built a "boy scout" type fire, which consisted of a pint of gasoline and a quart of diesel. This just flares up quickly, burns out, and the fire dies! One kept remarking how terribly cold it was, but the older fellow and one of the others actually slept in the bed of that pickup overnight! It was so cold outside, I don't know how they stood it and never did figure out how they managed to keep from freezing, but they did!

The other two decided to stay in our tent, so this was Bob's opportunity to regale and impress these strangers! Bob had very prominent ears and was bald-headed. He looked a lot like Senator Morse, a politician, who served in Oregon many years ago, whom I always considered one of Oregon's renegade senators! These fellows had no sooner come in the tent than one of them made a remark about how nice and cozy it was! Bob jumped up, grabbed his big, fancy jar full of candy, and said, "Have some candy, boys!" Each of them helped themselves and thanked him! They munched away and one said, "Man, that's good fudge!" Bob quickly got up, grabbed the jar again, and said, "Have some more," and each of them took another piece. Just then Bob said, "I used to make white fudge, but I quit that, I only make brown fudge now. That way I don't have to ever wash my hands!" This one fellow had just started to take a bite of that candy, but his hand slowly went down to his side and he got rid of that candy, somehow!

One of the fellows remarked again about how cold it was outside! Bob said, "Oh, you think it's cold, do you?" "Oh, yes, it's brutally cold," the fellow responded. Bob said, "I'll never forget the night I almost froze to death." He asked, "How's that?" Bob said, "Well, I was holding the lantern while the Old Lady was splitting wood and my hands got so cold holding onto that lantern, I thought I'd die!" Suddenly, one of the fellows started laughing and then both of them laughed! They were onto Patty! Well, he just kept on, telling story after story! The next morning one of them told me he hadn't laughed so hard for a long time! It seemed Bob was never at a loss to entertain people and that he did all the years we were friends!

The next morning, we all decided it was time to pull out and head home. The entire group of us fought our way out in that deep snow, with our vehicles! We shoveled, pulled, pushed; whatever it took, we did it until we got going. We were about halfway out, when here came an Indian fellow in a Ford pickup. Down the hill he came, without any chains, and seemingly without any regard for the treacherous conditions! With him were his wife and Mother-in-law! He zoomed around in the snow and got ahead of us. Then we had to push him and get him back up the hill to the main road! What a job! We finally made it out and headed home! I don't know what that guy would have done, had we not been there to help him out!

HOLD YER FIRE!

My cousin, Cliff Wolfer, came to see me late in the elk season one fall and told me he'd like to go elk hunting with us. Neither Bob nor I had killed an elk yet, so we gladly agreed to go over to Shamrock Springs to hunt. Cliff had been quite ill and said, "I believe I'll just follow you around today if you don't mind." I said, "No problem!" I had a cow tag and Bob had a bull tag. We went down in the canyon and I saw an elk going around the hill, so I put a bullet through her shoulder and Cliff said, "I see you got that elk, Ken! I saw her left leg fly from her side!" Just then Bob showed up and we dressed the elk out and packed her to camp.

The next day Bob and Cliff went down the same ridge and I went across the canyon towards the head. I knew there was a place there where the elk used to cross through the timber, to an opening. Bob went down towards Johnson Creek and came across a whole herd of elk! Cliff saw the entire show from his vantage point on the other side of Johnson Creek! He saw Bob shoot a bull and knock him down. After Bob shot, he then ran up to the bull, laid down his gun and binoculars and took off running for about half a mile on this straight trail. It was a game trail, and rather flat, due to the fact that the elk ran through there! Cliff said Bob just ran like crazy to come and find me. The elk were going towards me and at first, Cliff thought Bob had lost his marbles! He couldn't figure out why Bob was running like that! I had just raised my gun up to shoot a beautiful bull standing right below me, when I heard Bob give his three "whoops," or the tight-line signal, three and two! When I heard Bob, I took the slack out of the trigger and lowered my gun! That's the closest I ever came to killing a bull I wasn't supposed to! Bob had come running to tell me HE had killed a bull, so I shouldn't. Cliff got quite a "bang" (no pun intended) out of it because he had never hunted elk over there with us before.

BARELY ESCAPING BEAR

Russell was able to go with several of us hunting one fall and on this particular day, he was sitting under a tree making plans for his next move! There were lots of hunters in the area at this time and he wanted to cross Johnson Creek. As he sat there, he suddenly saw an elk clear across Johnson and shot it! I was above him on a rock bluff we called Grantham Stand and Russ called to me to come down. I said, "Well, you don't need help to dress out ONE bull elk, do you, Russ?" He said, "Yes, I do!" So I made my way down to him and he said, "Dad, I was backed up against that tree, and a bear practically came down on top of me! There were two cubs up this tree and the old bear came by. I shot one of the cubs and the other two took off!" Russ had no more than said that, when we saw a bear coming right at us! I grabbed my gun and shot her! She rolled down to the creek. A couple fellows across the hillside saw this happen and one called out, "Hey, fellows, here's your bear!" I said, "Yes!"

Marvin Fast and Russell with game in Eastern Oregon.

Soon he called out again, "Fellows, here's your bear! Do you want your bear?" I said, "No, you can have it," and we gave them the bear. Were they ever tickled!

Another time, Russ was hunting down on Johnson and he killed a big, five-point bull elk. That elk rolled down off a ledge and hung up on a bunch of what we called, "mountain maples." That elk hung there by his horns and they broke, but held together just enough to support the body weight of that elk! We dressed it out, right there, hanging upright by the horns in those branches! It was just as if we had hung him in a slaughter house to attend to! Wish we could have had a picture of that! Russ and Davie also killed a lot of elk over there and we had so many great times together! At one point in time, Davie had killed fourteen elk for fourteen years; one each year, and during this time, had gotten married! We were planning our annual trek and Mariellen, his wife said, "This fall when Dave gets his bull, I'm going to make mincemeat and some sausage." I said, "Hold it, Mari! He hasn't gotten the elk yet!" She said, "Are you trying to tell me that after fourteen years straight that he's going to miss this year?" I said, "Well, there's always a strong possibility!" Lo and behold, Davie never got an elk that year and I really think Mari thought I was the cause of his not getting one!

TURN THE OTHER CHEEK

On another one of our hunting forays, there were quite a few of us: Bob Patty, Marvin Fast, John Breeden, Russ, Myron, Byron, and myself. We were in Eastern

Oregon at the head of the Umatilla River, down on Johnson a ways, when a band of elk came over a ridge. At once, we saw a nice bull in the bunch and then they started up the hillside. There were some fellows up on the high, bald mountain we always called Cabbage Hill. Myron went down in the canyon to follow these elk, when all of a sudden these guys yelled out, "Get the h— out of there! We've got a bull coming up here!" Myron couldn't see the bull and he answered, "Oh, I'm sorry! I'll go the other way!" The outcome of it was that Myron did go the other way, just as he promised! He went clear down, across the Umatilla River, way up on a place called Woodard and there he killed a nice elk! These other guys never fired a shot, so it was sort of a fitting tribute to a bunch of hotheads to think they hollered at him to get out of there! The sounds carry a long ways and they were probably a thousand to fifteen hundred feet away from Myron! Af-

Left to Right: Ken, Marv Fast, Bob Patty, John Breeden and Davie.

ter speaking to him in such a disrespectful manner and not displaying very good sportsmanship, he just goes down the hill and was able to kill a nice bull! We all thought that was JUST GREAT!

We had set up my tent in our usual space on another Eastern Oregon trip. Mind you, we did not rent this spot, nor was it sacred, but it was OUR spot and we lost no time in taking possession! Generally, some of the tent stakes from our previous visit were still in the ground! We had retired for the night and around 3:00 o'clock in the morning, John Breeden got up and stoked the stove. This woke Marvin up, and soon he began laughing. "What's so funny, Marvin?" John asked. "John, why do you get up so early?" Marv wanted to know, and John replied like this: "I just read where 85% of people who die, do so in bed and I just decided I'd spend just as little time as I possibly could in bed." What John could have told Marvin was that for years when he was hauling logs, he got up at 3:00 A.M. to get ready to go to work, and for sure, he never had a lazy bone in his body. He loved to hunt with us because he knew we were going to get up and HUNT! We never took any booze along, either, and John told me he'd had many a previous hunting trip ruined because of liquor. As well as being a good hunter, John was a great, camp cook and we loved to spend time with him!

Bob, Marvin Fast and I went over on another trip and were quite a ways out on Nine Mile, when I killed a bull down in a canyon. We each had a portion of elk on our packboards and just as we got to the top of the ridge, here came two fellows on horseback. They appeared to be about sixty-five years of age. Just as we met them, I looked across Buck Creek and saw a bull bedded down by a big tree! Bob saw this bull at precisely the same time and said, "I see an elk!" This one fellow said, "Whoa," and he stopped, asking, "What did you say, Sir?" Bob said, "I see an elk!" "You see an elk? Where do you see an elk?" "Right across Buck Creek over there," Bob replied. The fellow got off his horse, took out his binoculars, looked and declared, "I don't see any elk!" Bob said, "Oh, I'm old, I'm blind, I can hardly see! I'm just looking for a motorized wheel chair, but I do see an elk and they said it's a bull!" I had seen it, too, and knew it was a bull, but I kept quiet. They didn't quite know whether to believe Bob or not, and kept looking. Both of them were from Portland, and the one, Emmet Shields, said he had the contract to paint the Associated Oil Company's fixtures in the state of Oregon. Suddenly, one of them picked out this elk, saw the horns, and ran up to Bob. "Oh, Sir, you have wonderful eyesight! You're not blind!" Bob said, "No, no, no! Thirty years ago I had good eyesight and I could see, but my eyes are gone now and I can't see anymore!" They argued with him, telling him what wonderful eyesight he had. After they left, we laid on the ground and laughed so hard at the way Bob tried to convince them his eyesight was poor! They couldn't believe Bob could see an elk that far off, however!

Camped out at Shamrock Springs for another hunt, was Marvin, Bob, Davie and I. About dusk one evening, Marv, Davie and I came into camp. I said, "Bob's either killed a bull or he's broke a hind leg!" Marv said, "No, no, he'll be in!" We sat there awhile and it began to get dark. I said, "Bob's in trouble!" Marvin thought he was fine and would be in soon. We waited a little while longer and finally one of us put a rifle up in the air and fired a shot. Pretty soon we heard an answering shot. Marvin said, "Hey, that was up the river, wasn't it?" Davie and I both thought it was down the river, so we shot again. Again, we heard an answering shot! We got the gas lantern, a flashlight, some knives, one packboard, and started out. We walked and walked until we got down on Zubic Ridge, looked across the canyon and saw a fire. We went towards the fire and here was Bob! He was so tired and acted like he had sort of come unglued! Soon I realized this was exactly the same area where Bob, Marvin and I had packed the elk out when we met those two fellows on horseback! We started talking to Bob and then he showed us where he had been standing, when he looked up the hill and saw an elk. He said he shot at it and was pretty sure he hit it, but when he looked for it, it was gone. So he went up the hill a little further and there was an elk, so he shot it and it went down! He went up to it, dressed it out, and got to thinking that the horns didn't look like the first rack of horns he'd seen. When he walked down the hill a ways, there lay the first elk! When he shot the second time, he thought it was the same elk, but now had gotten two!

Each of us took as much of that meat as we could carry and headed back for camp, getting back there around eleven thirty at night! Next morning we went back to pack out the rest and had quite an ordeal, but eventually got the two elk packed out. It was hard work, but we were all up to the task and had the "machinery" to pack it with! I might add that we also enjoyed it!

We set off to Eastern Oregon on another adventure and were right close to where Bob killed the two elk on the previous trip. Down in a canyon, a long ways from where we had made camp, we jumped a herd of elk. I just up and shot a nice one, dressed it out, and we started packing it out. Soon we came across a fellow from Oak Ridge, Oregon. He said he was Office Manager of the Pope and Talbot Sawmill and he had another young fellow with him. They killed a big, five-point elk right next to the ridge! They dressed it out, hung it up, and then we came along! "Hey, fellas, how much would you charge us to pack this elk in?" they asked us. Bob said, "We didn't come over here to hire out to pack elk! We're just hunting and having fun!" They tried to convince us to do this for them! Bob said, "I don't see anything wrong with your legs!" One fellow looked to be about forty-five years old; at least he was younger than we were! The other guy was about twenty-five and yet they told us they would not consider packing out this elk by themselves! Those two guys went to town, went on a big drunk and when they returned three days later, there was literally nothing left of that animal! The magpies, Camp Robbers, and so forth had worked it over until there was nearly nothing left! Those jokers had a man come in there with a saddle horse and a pack mule to pack out the remains, which were basically the horns and a few shreds of a once-fine, animal! We thought it was pretty poor sportsmanship to waste that meat! If you can't pack something out, don't hunt!

PACKING IT IN WITH PATTY

Another time, George Emmert went over to hunt with Bob and I. We went in to the head of the Umatilla River! Since the altitude there is so high, it was snowing and in those conditions, it's very easy to get snowed in. More than once we got snowed in on various hunting trips. The country in Eastern Oregon is very rough! One Game Warden told us that where we camped was the roughest country in Umatilla County. George and I started out the next morning and went down a ridge. After we had been out awhile, I said to George, "I don't know why, but I have a feeling Bob killed an elk this morning!" George said, "Aw, no, I don't think so!" I looked and saw an elk way up on a hill, just bedding down! It was too far for me to shoot at him, so we went on up to camp. After a quick look around, I said to George, "I see Bob killed a bull!" "How do you know that?" George asked and I said, "Cause his packboard is gone!"

About an hour later, Bob came into camp, terribly excited about something! He said, "Fellows, come quick and help me get that elk out! It's way down in a canyon and I just want to sail right down there and get that thing out!" George said, "Well, I don't think I can "sail" right down there!" Bob said, "Well, I can!" We went down, got the elk and brought it back to camp, packed up, and headed for home! The timing was terrific, for we knew heavy snow was on the way for that entire area! Had we stayed any longer, we most likely would have gotten snowed in! That would happen occasionally and on one hunting trip, we saw a van along the bluff where someone had diverted a little from the road to try and get around a hillside in order to get out. They were stuck, however, and that van sat there for months until better weather came along! We had many great elk hunts over in Eastern Oregon and in this one area, within a radius of about a mile, over the years, I killed a total of seven elks!

THE DAILY LOG

One time we moved up South Branch to log some scattered timber and rigged up our landing. Here is a rock wall at least fourteen or fifteen feet high! How am I going to cut a road up there? I finally found a big, old log and put it next to the bluff. I then went back, drifted rock around this log and began to get enough of a base to start up the bluff with my cat, finally making it! It was SO steep, a long-armed man could have reached down and touched the ground in front of him. Gene Knudsen asked me one day, "Kenny, do you operate on the principal that the shortest distance between two points is a straight line?" I told him, "I do," and he said, "That is most evident!"

I had never met Bill Swindell, but one day I was at Willamette's office talking to Aaron Mercer when a fellow walked in, and I was pretty sure it must be Bill. Aaron said, "Good morning, Bill," and Bill responded. Aaron asked, "Did you ever meet Kenny Shenk?" Bill said, "No, I never met him, but I sure as h— have heard a lot about him!" One of the officials told me after I had logged the snag patch and taken out over 3,000,000 feet net scale, that one day Bill called the fellows together. He said to that group, "Fellows, I just want to tell you, it will be a cold day in hell before any official of this company ever gives volume away on a deal like that again!" He was very angry that Willamette had done that! They had thought there wasn't a decent piece of wood up there fit to sell. Before I took the contract, I went up there with my big saw and fell a snag. My investigation revealed that it was sound as a dollar, so I figured I could get some good wood up there. Nevertheless, it was still a tremendous risk and undertaking and I am glad I don't have to go through anything like that again! In retrospect, now that I'm still here to tell about it, it was really not worth it, because on that particular site, we had many close calls!

My faithful and hard worker, Bob Patty, proved to be an individual who had unique abilities. One of them was that he could pick out a road through the most adverse-looking show and somehow, I always made it! One evening the phone rang and Gene Knudsen called saying, "Kenny, you will have to bring your cat down, plus cutting tools, and build some bridges!" Gene then said something that bothered me greatly. He said, "You will be working with Stuart Dory. He is an ex-railroad builder and is hard to get along with." I did as Gene instructed and went to the site, which was Gorge Canyon. When I arrived with my cat, tools and crew, Stuart and a hooker from Snow Peak, Pete Petersen, were also there. Stuart said, "Okay, Kenny, bring your cat across the old bridge." Pete said, "I wouldn't do that, she doesn't look good to me!" "Oh, I think she's okay," Stuart said, so I started across, quite slowly. All of a sudden, a terrible crashing sound rings out! Here I was, in the center of the span, which was at least forty feet long and at least thirty feet down to bedrock! I stopped the cat. What do you do now - go ahead or go home? Stuart said, "Try to back up." I did, and made it! We pulled the old stringers out and proceeded to build the bridge. Up on the hillside, Bob cut down five big trees and I skidded them down. We then peeled and ripped them with Bob's big Mercury Disston saw. Stuart chalk-lined them and when we had them ready for use, they looked as if they had been sawed on a head rig! We felt very proud of this accomplishment!

About the second day, I asked Stuart for a file. "What do you want a file for?" he asked. I said, "I want to sharpen this axe." Stuart said, "Kenny, I am not used to having fellows ask me for a file. I spend half of my time sharpening tools for other fellows!" For the South Branch bridge, Stuart picked out some fine stringers. They were cut eighty-five feet long and five feet on the stump. Now these logs are way up Boulder Creek and Stuart told me the Willamette official said, "We don't know how to load them. We could rent Sport Laughlin's big shovel and load them that way." Stuart told the official, "Well, okay, but first let me ask Kenny if he thinks he could load them onto Lambert's truck." After Stuart and I discussed this, we went up Boulder Creek and found a big, old brow log where Engle and Werth had loaded a yarder. "We're in clover," I told him. "What do you mean?" he asked, to which I said, "Oh, I'll just push them on Lambert's truck, one end at a time." His next question was, "And how is Lambert going to get up here and unload his trailer?" I said "I'll have one of the twin boys hook on Lambert and pull him up the hill with my dump truck." We put one half load of rock in the truck for weight, and in one day, the stringers were down where Stuart wanted them. Stu was one happy and pleased fellow! He proved to be a no-nonsense fellow to work with, and also a delight! We learned a lot from him.

While working up South Branch one day, Bob wanted me to pull a big fir tree down a ways so he could buck it. It was headed straight down, but had a huge limb driven into the ground, and I told Bob I couldn't pull it. He said, "Try it!" I had a new 7/8 steel core drum line on and a big choker, so up we go! I was twenty-five feet up a bluff and here comes Gene and Jay to observe the operation. They left after a little while, but that night, Gene called me up and said, "Please don't ever do that again!" He said he could not sleep that night. I never moved that big fir, either! Frances told me one time that if the situations in the woods were so extreme and dangerous that it would cause her worry, she would rather not have me describe to her the treacherous conditions. If she asked to come up to visit in the woods, I would let her know if it was appropriate for her to come. Sometimes what one doesn't know doesn't hurt them!

A funny thing happened one day while we were still working up South Branch! There was a huge tree, seven feet, six inches on the stump and I had to get a falling saw to help Bob cut it down because the bar on the power saw wasn't long enough! I was running my little HD5 Allis Chalmers cat then. That tree was full of pitch and the bark was about eight inches thick, which made it look about nine feet high! It probably was eight feet high the way it laid! I would go to the end of the drum line, dig a hole and winch that log ahead. While we were working away, here came a Caterpillar salesman! Just as I was getting that huge log close to the landing, this salesman saw what I was doing with my little cat and he threw his hat on the ground! He began carrying on, then came up to me and said, "Sir, you know that log is big enough for a D8 cat!" I said, "I know it!" "That's a shame for you to pull your little cat like that," he said and I responded with, "I know it, but I don't have anything else!" "Well, let me sell you a D8 Caterpillar," he suggested. I said, "You know, I'd be happy to buy one!" "Would you?" he asked, and I said, "Sure!" He dashed for his pickup and got his pad out, so I said,

"All you have to do is get my quota from Willamette increased to 10,000,000 a year and I'll buy it." "Oh, I can't do that," the salesman said. "Well, I can't buy your cat!" I told him. That fellow just couldn't believe I could move that log with my little HD5!

PRIDE IN PERFORMANCE

While working for Bill Harris many years earlier, with a team of horses, I learned how to take advantage of some things. For example, when you put two chokers together, it's called a bridle. When you put them down below the center of a log and then winch, it lifts the log up and makes it pull easier. One time I had an amusing experience. We were back East and visiting at the home of a professor, along with quite a large group of other people. He turned to me and asked, "What do you do for a living?" I said, "Oh, I fall timber!" He gave me a very compassionate look and said, "Well, I'll tell you, I always thought it'd be nice to do something where you could take a little pride and develop skill in your work!" I was so tickled and told him, "Sir, if you think you can fall timber on ground straight up and down for a month and live through it, you're not entirely devoid of brains!" Falling timber or bucking logs isn't just an act of brute strength, there's an element of skill involved and this often determines whether one lives or dies! Back in the days when two guys ran a saw, you develop a rhythm to sawing together, or it won't work! It's just like guys working together on a basketball team, if you don't develop a team attitude, it's going to be difficult to get anything accomplished! There were certain standards which were very important working in the woods, as well, and in my early days, never did we hear of drugs being used by fellows out there in the timber industry. The two prevailing sins were the use of tobacco and of course, the demon, rum! I worked with many alcoholics, but I know none of them would have killed a man to get money for booze. Many allowed booze to gain mastery over them because they indulged to excess. I believe that a good motto for Mothers Against Drunk Drivers would be: "If you think you can drink and drive, you may all ready be drunk!" Today many crimes committed, even the most heinous in nature, are often casually passed off by saying, "I need money for a fix!" I also came to realize that many who take up the use of drugs have no goals. Working in the timber industry nowadays, the methods are quite different and there's basically no skill involved in falling timber. If you can make a power saw run, you're a good man and they just make stumps! Things have really changed down through the years. Unless something isn't done to stop the environmentalists, I can see the day when the big companies are going to be shut down and not allowed to cut their own timber! Just because some mistakes were made in the past, doesn't mean that the cutting of timber should be brought to a halt! Oregon has billions of board feet of beetle-kill timber, wind-falls and diseased trees which need to be cut to keep the forests healthy! This also enables forest fire hazards to be kept to a minimum by cleaning up these types of trees. When the government won't even let the states harvest timber like that, then you've got to know they're way off course!

For several years we worked up South Branch and even though it was often very steep, it also yielded some nice timber. At this time, I was just loading trucks with an A-frame and end hooks, so I always kept everything in tip-top shape. We never pulled out of the top of the A-frame, it was always guy-lined and I pulled right straight down. The A-frame generally was raised by a stump, or else I'd put a big log there, anchor it down and pull it that way. Now and then the twin boys would show up when they weren't in school, and their help was always appreciated! Uel, my trucker was very good at end hooks and could help out wherever he was needed. Davie and Uel would put a load of logs on in generally a matter of six or seven minutes! Uel hauled a pile of logs for me over the years!

One summer we had such nice logs, I needed another truck, so I hired Sport Laughlin's one truck, driven by Pat Pfifer. We loaded him up one day and after finishing, began eating lunch. Rather than taking off immediately, Pat came over and said, "Fellas, I gotta tell you something funny! I've been loading up at Laughlin's and their timber isn't quite this big, but pretty close. It takes twenty-five to thirty minutes to get a load! I've been keeping track here and you've been averaging loading me in less than ten minutes on every load!" Our methods may have seemed antiquated to others, but I never saw a log we couldn't load! If we couldn't pick it straight up, we'd just do one end at a time and it worked out really great! Wimer had a truck shop at the bottom of the big, Black Rock Hill and one of the mechanics said, "Lambert goes through here every morning at the same time. I can set my watch by his trip and it wouldn't be more than two minutes variance!" We had a rhythm to our work and everybody hit her, and we hit her hard!

STORM OF ALL STORMS

Never will I forget the infamous Columbus Day storm one year, for my Mother came out from Sheridan to visit. My Dad had already passed away, and as we talked, suddenly it got very dark outside! Shortly thereafter, the lights went out, so I went outside to check things out! We had two, great big fir trees standing not far from our house and the top blew out of the one! Blowing about in the air were limbs, chunks of moss and debris, and the wind was literally howling all around, and even up on the glades. My Mother said, "I've got to get home!" I asked, "What for? To feed your chickens?" (She didn't have any, of course!) She said, "Well, no, but I've got to go home!" I said, "No, you're not going home tonight, Mother," so she stayed with us. That was one of the worst storms on the Oregon Coast and it extended up into Washington, as well. Some of the damage resulting included over 5,000,000,000 board feet of timber which was blown down! Up in the woods where I had started logging in the Rosemary District, there were five species of timber, and all the understory. A lot of this timber was three feet on the stump and during this storm, much of it blew down, falling criss-cross, and every which way! There were some big peelers scattered throughout, and they blew down on top of everything else! Big George LaFever had the Willamina Saw Shop, so he knew many, many cutters. He told me of the cutters he knew, a total of twenty-eight were killed, stretching out to as far as Astoria and back to

Willamina. Some of these cutter, I also knew personally, and Harold Kalligan was one of them.

After this storm, Walt Hill was bucking for me one time, but as we worked, I couldn't even see him and became concerned. I had begun to look for him, when from down underneath a pile of roots, he came out and hollered, "Hey, bring your cat over here, please! I can't get my saw out!" Walt was bucking on a butt log which had a horrible bind and didn't realize it! What a time we had getting his saw freed without breaking it! This timber was just terrible and was an awfully grim situation to work in. I believe we worked in this blown-down timber for over three years! Mother Nature did a devastating job during that storm and is something you can't fool with!

MIDNIGHT MARAUDER

Around midnight one time, Frances woke me up and said, "Wake up, Ken, somebody's breaking in the house! It sounds like someone is in the house!" I jumped up, snapped the light on in the dining room, which led to the front porch, and saw something out on the porch! I turned on the porch light and here was a black bear! When the light came on, he tried to go down off the porch by going right through the railing, but he couldn't make it! As usual, my rifle was handy and I shot him in the head. By this time, all the family was up to find out what the commotion was. I took him out in the front yard and discovered he was quite a big bear!

Next morning, a neighbor, Otto Debrick, was fishing on the creek and walked up the road past our house. Fishing season had just opened and there was quite a bit of traffic. Otto said, "Hey, Kenny, know what? I was sitting on Bridge Two yesterday when that bear came up and attacked me and I beat him off with my fishing pole!" We noticed this bear had collar marks around his neck and found out some people at Grand Ronde had him for a pet. He broke loose and traveled from there, over several mountains, to Mill Creek! He was hungry and MEAN and he left his muddy paw prints all over our window and window pane! I thought what a strange feeling it would have been to go out in the dining room and be confronted by a black bear! While we lived in Mill Creek, I didn't kill many bear, but we had a bear trap which the boys set out one time. They caught a black bear, and Tony, our little dog, decided he was going to kill that bear, but he got an education in a hurry! We have a picture of the kids alongside our John Deer tractor and little trailer, with the bear in the trailer, plus the dog! I think the kids, at that stage, were a little too reckless and were like that little dog: They weren't afraid of anything!

RE-GROUPING

ON THE PEND OREILLE

Back in Pend Oreille country, the Bender boys had commenced cutting lumber on our property and Harold had trucked a load of lumber to a job in Northport. Later in the day, Clayton, was driving home and a lady driving a Cadillac crowded him off the road, right where there was a sharp bluff going down to the river. The Jeep Clayton was driving, went over this bluff and ended up in the Columbia River. They found his body laying on the railroad tracks below, so he obviously was thrown out of the Jeep. This woman turned around, went into Northport to the police station and told them, "I fear I have caused a terrible tragedy!" Sure enough, she had. The funeral and subsequent events were almost more than we could bear, especially after losing Ralph! Here George had just lost his brother, and now this tragedy! Ironically, Clayton had written me a letter on Monday evening, on Tuesday he was killed, and on Wednesday, I received his letter! That was a sad experience!

Owning the property north of the border was becoming more and more time consuming. After losing Ralph, George and I went through a very trying ordeal with the property, as the people in Canada believe that every American is a millionaire. We had to have it evaluated again in order to close Ralph's estate and work with the First National Bank, executor of Ralph's will. William Schamberg, a banker with First National, called to ask that I go into his office in Salem. After I arrived, he said, "Well, we're partners now! We own one third of that property on the Pend Oreille and we don't know what we've got, so we're going to find out!" I said, "Certainly!" He never asked me for a map or anything, so I left. The next time I heard from him, it was a little different tune! He had been transferred to Portland and the first fellow they sent North to cruise the property couldn't even find it! The second man went up there, found the property, but never found the corner stakes, so he was not successful in his mission! At this point, Mr. Schamberg called and asked that both George and I meet with him. George and I arranged to meet him at the First National Bank in Portland, where Mr. Schamberg was waiting for us, along with another fellow. He said, "Fellows, we've reached an impasse!" "What's wrong?" I asked, and he said, "Well, we can't do anything with the property!" George spoke up and told him, "Well, I'll tell you one thing, I'd be happy to sell out for what I have into it!" The banker asked, "You would?" and George said, "Yes!" Mr. Schamberg asked, "How about you, Mr. Shenk?" I said, "Yes." The banker then said, "We have something to work from now, we'd be willing to sell it for what we have into it!" George and I then offered the banker $1,000 more than what he asked for and ended up with the share, which was Ralph's. Things were cleared up now and we could continue working with the property.

George and I carried on our endeavors with the Pend Oreille property and decided to approach John Hampton about buying out Ralph's interest. John had taken over much of his Dad's business, as Bud was involved in California, putting a deal together in redwood country. Bud was so busy and had been grooming John to be active in his company. John gladly agreed to join George and I, so we formed a company, The Interior Development Company, Ltd. The Hampton's knew a fellow named Clifford Crandall and suggested we contact him. He had a nice sawmill and planer at Northport, Washington, just fourteen miles from our property. The border crossing was at Waneta and there was a big dam there. When they built the dam there, the existing road was flooded, including the road into our property. It was necessary to go into Washington to get to our Pend Oreille property! The Mounties worked with us and agreed to take Cliff's word for the number of loads taken out.

To illustrate how the Canadians felt, in general, about Americans, I went into Whitelock's office one morning. There was a rather large Canadian fellow in there, raw-boned and rugged looking, named Axel Erickson. He glanced out and saw my license plates which had "Dallas" somewhere on them. Evidently he was thinking it was Dallas, Texas, and asked, "Who's the d— Yankee from Dallas out there?" I spoke up and said, "I am!" He just glared at me! We also noted that one of the forestry officials, a Mr. Johnson, formerly an American, apparently had sold his soul to the Crown because he was not cooperative with us! He would not send us any notices of timber sales and obviously was not interested in assisting us in any way. I had one good friend among the Canadian foresters, Art Walde, and he remained my friend to the end of my dealings in timber.

The first mill Cliff put in there was Sullivan Great Timber Company, and John Seitzsoft was the operator. He was a hopeless alcoholic, but he did have a dedicated crew of fellows, most of whom were Dukhabors. They did a good job of logging and sawmilling for us. A nice little camp was built, with various cabins and they cut 3,350,000 feet on a little creek, Bear Skin Creek. As far as I know, those cabins are still there. Later on a bunch of hippies moved in there and lived off the land. The story was told to us that two fellows and a gal were living in there and had killed a beef from across the river. While transporting the meat back to their cabin by fording the stream, one of them drowned and they never recovered the body.

Others were beginning development in the Pend Oreille country, and soon there were three sawmills in there, with quite a bit of timber being taken out. John had told us when he agreed to come into the company with George and I that he would take care of all the books and notify us of future timber sales. The only problem was that John only had twenty-four hours in a day! He called me on a Thursday night and said, "Kenny, you have to be up at the Canadian Border on Saturday morning! Cominco has a man who wants to talk to us!" I said, "John, I can't go, you have to go!" He said, "No, I can't go!" John won, so I did go and meet with the fellow, but it was evident that the three of us were getting far too busy to handle the Canadian property. At the time, Hampton Lumber Company was tackling the task of building a huge sawmill at Boston Bar, British Columbia. They conquered some formidable obstacles with the terrain and used to skyline those logs across the Fraser River. The Hampton's got actively involved in the Canadian lumber business, which was to our advantage, for John knew a lot of people and had many contacts. I was a busy man running a logging operation at home and trying to keep a handle on the activities of the Pend Oreille! Many a trip I made, driving all night long, to and from, in order to manage everything. Owning that fine piece of property was a great learning experience in the business world, which I might not have had access to, had I not gotten involved. No doubt, this involvement North of the border only added to my interest in Canada.

FACING THE GRIM REAPER

One of the benefits we derived from hunting wild game was having lunch meat made by Lawrence Ellis, local grocery store owner in Sheridan. He cut and wrapped meat and did some custom orders for people. After I had returned from an elk hunt one fall and had the lunch meat made, I went into Portland and gave John some. This lunch meat was just simply delicious! John belonged to an investor's club in Portland and this month, the meeting was in his home. He said he put this meat on a platter on the living room coffee table, went back into the kitchen to get something, and when he came back, it was all gone! John said, "My, but that lunch meat is unbeatable!"

My next visit with John was a very different one! I found him very somber and tentative. He said, "Kenny, I just had the most traumatic week of my life! On Wednesday I was pallbearer for my good friend, Mr. Gunderson, and on Thursday I was pallbearer for E.C. Sammons, Jr., another dear friend, and it's nearly more than I can bear!" Then he told me that shortly after the investor's club met at his home, these two fellows flew down to San Francisco and something went wrong with the plane. It went down in water and these fellows drowned.

One time when John and I had driven up to the Pend Oreille, we were sort of "marooned" in Spokane and he said, "I've got to be at a meeting in Vancouver tomorrow morning at 10:00 o'clock! That evening a plane from McChord Air Force Base in Washington had crashed and there was much news coverage regarding the incident, which only made John more squeamish about flying. Another time we flew to British Columbia, but on the return trip, weather conditions worsened and we were unable to fly into Portland, due to fog. Our plane was diverted to Seattle and we were put on a bus to drive to Portland. If you think that didn't upset John's plans, you're mistaken! As we were going along, someone reported to the driver a passenger was smoking marijuana, so the driver stopped. What a trial! Often when we did drive to Canada, we drove over very icy roads and experienced many unfavorable weather conditions!

On one of our trips to the Pend Oreille, while at the Customs Office in Waneta, we met a fellow named Warren Crow. He was a fantastic character and as time went on, we became very good friends. This fellow was utterly brilliant in so many ways and I'll illustrate just one. On the hill above the Waneta Customs office, a man named Kelly Lutz had a sawmill and a crew of workers. Kelly was quite a character, but he had a problem with booze and fell into the head rig on the sawmill. One leg was severed in this accident, but that didn't stop him. His brother, Albert, had shot his own son in a drunken brawl and was spending the remainder of his life in the penitentiary. Warren got upset at Cominco about something, so he called Kelly. Warren was Canadian and Kelly was an American, so they got their heads together to make some money.

The dam, which I mentioned earlier, was just in the process of being built, so Kelly took an old TD18 cat down there and dug a couple test holes, put up a sign advertising his trade, and they were in business! He filed a lawsuit against Cominco and stopped the building of the dam for about a year because they were flooding out his gold mining claim. The net result was that he was awarded $250,000 cash settlement, plus the right to supply all the lumber for the big dam. That is just one example of Warren's capabilities. He was respected by mining industry officials, as well as many other leaders. One time I was talking to Clayton Stewart, Head of the Legal Department of Cominco, and I asked him, "I saw something in the paper about Mr. Crow making a fabulous gold strike. Is it true?" He looked at me and said, "Of course, it's true! We had staked all the ground in that area that we thought was of any value and Warren Crow comes along and stakes something which supersedes everything that we had! He's a very capable man!"

When Ralph was still living and involved in the Canadian property, he was in his home town of Sweet Home, just after we had been up North. Dr. Langmack called across the street to greet Ralph and asked, "Where have you been? What's going on?" Doc crossed the street to meet him and Ralph told him, "I just came back from British Columbia." Doc asked, "What's going on up there?" "Oh," Ralph said, "quite a lot!" He mentioned that Mr. Whitelock told us he had a property for sale across the Kootenay Bay and if either of us could sell it, he'd give us a $5,000 commission, so Ralph began to tell Doc about the other property. "Well, I just bought a new Beechcraft, let's fly up there," Doc told him. They flew to B.C. without filing a flight plan and landed at the airport in Trail. When they landed, the Mounties descended on them, implying they were being invaded by Americans. Ralph said, "Well, I'm a friend of Warren Crow!" One of the Mounties said, "I'm going to go get Warren Crow and God help you if Warren doesn't know you!" Warren came down with the Mountie, greeted Ralph and laughed! He said to the Mounties, "Fellows, you're not being invaded, this man is my friend and I'll vouch for him!" The outcome of that trip was that Doc Langmack bought a property across the bay and we also bought another adjacent property. Terry later put a big property deal together for the construction of a retirement home there and it is quite a large operation. In this transaction, Doc Langmack and we sold our property for this development, so we did a number of interesting things! All of this was becoming time-consuming and it was time I didn't have! I read years ago that "hypocrisy is the standard juice which fuels all politicians." I might also add that it fuels a lot of company officials. Soon we were to come to grips with various forestry officials, as well as others and verified the truth of that statement!

Warren had told us that anytime we were in town to please call him so we could meet with him. He would always come to our hotel to visit and we got to know him very well. He had a mine going out of Rossland with several fellows working for him and showed us a pure, gold brick, which was very valuable. One day Terry told us that when he was out of town evaluating the troublesome Knight mill, Warren Crow called his home every night and would ask Margaret, "Is Terry home?" Warren kept calling and at last reached Terry, so they got together. Warren said, "I want to buy the Pend Oreille property." This occurred just as George, Ralph, and I were buying it. Terry asked, "Why do you want to buy it? You're not a timber man, are you?" Warren said, "I don't want to buy it for the timber, I want it for the minerals." "I just sold it to some fellows from Oregon," Terry informed him, and Warren was very disappointed.

We continued our friendship with Warren and he always had many interesting things to share with us. George was a great "rock hound" and gave Warren some of the rocks he had sliced. He could actually identify the locale and tell George where those rocks had come from! In the winter, he and his wife would go South and had done a lot of rock hunting in many areas, including Arizona and the Southern states. Many rocks were immediately recognizable to him as being native to a certain area. One rock which George showed him, Warren unhesitatingly stated that it had come from Eastern Oregon and he pinpointed the area. George was utterly amazed that this fellow from British Columbia could so accurately tell him where that rock had come from and confirmed that he was within a fifty mile radius! One day we asked Warren, "Why did you want to buy the Pend Oreille property so badly?" He said, "There is a limestone deposit which starts on Fish Creek and runs clear across that property past the International Border to the Washington side!" Sure enough, later on, a company opened up a limestone deposit and mined on the Washington side, then trucked it to Cominco. They used 400 tons of lime in their smelting operation daily and the deposit was a very lucrative thing. They built the second dam above the Waneta Dam, with the footings right on the property we had owned. There was a road across the dam in order for the limestone to be trucked across, so it was a potential fortune for someone! Another interesting thing we found out on the Pend Oreille was that the entire area had claims staked all over the footage and it ran to the edge of the Reeve McDonald Mine. This was another mine which had been a big mining operation for many years. There was a tunnel underneath the Pend Oreille River and mining was being done underground on our property and there wasn't a thing we could do about it! It, too, for quite a few years, was a very viable operation.

There was also a bridge across the Pend Oreille on our property. It was sort of a cable suspension bridge, used for many years, then later condemned by the Crown. The river is wild, and sprawling, and very dangerous due to so many undercurrents! Some of them are so subtle, they're hard to detect. Anyone brave enough to cross this cable bridge could go down into Spokane without going through customs! We were told that often Dukhabors would actually go across this bridge to go to Spokane. When I heard this, I thought this to be nearly an impossibility! However, one night as I was traveling up to our property, I stopped at Patterson at the customs house and I noticed that right in front of me was a big van, full of Dukhabors. I overheard the customs official bark at the driver, "Pull over here and park. You're subject to search, seizure, and arrest!" The van pulled over in front of me and the fellow parked. It was my turn to pull up and the Customs official asked, "Where are you going?" I said, "I'm going home," and he wanted to know why. "The way you talk to those people kinda frightens me! I WAS going up to visit my friend, Warren Crow, but I believe I'll just turn around and go home!" I told him. He was a total stranger, of course, but he leaned in my car and said, "They're a bunch of bloody Duk's and we're breathing down their necks. They're full of contraband!" Before I left the customs house, they had that van completely searched and found thousands of dollars worth of hardware, tools, and goods which the Duk's were trying to sneak across the border without paying duty. The solution for the Mounties was that they went up and blew that bridge out so it couldn't be used. Anybody using that cable suspension bridge had to have steel nerves to risk going across it in order to avoid paying a few dollars! It's just unthinkable! You couldn't hire anyone with any common sense to do that, but they did!

Terry Whitelock was involved with a number of ventures, such as land development, lumbering, real estate, and gold mining. When he was around sixty-seven, he suffered a stroke. He recovered quite well from that one, but later suffered another one. The last time I visited him, he was in the hospital in Trail and could scarcely whisper out of one corner of his mouth. I bent down close to him to hear what he had to say, and he said, "Please, Kenny, get me some cyanide pills so I may take my life! I do not wish to live, for I have lost control of my bodily functions and am a burden to my good wife, Margaret!" I remonstrated with, "Terry, I could not live with myself if I should do such a thing!" Shortly after my visit, Terry passed away. My life was enriched for having known him and he was a dear friend. As of this writing, May 1997, Margaret still resides in Penticton, British Columbia, although we have not seen her for a number of years.

INVENTOR AND FRIEND

I got acquainted with a fine fellow who was a wonderful mechanic, engineer, and inventor. In our logging show, I was pulling extra tag lines up bluffs and pulling down a lot of Old Growth trees, full length. Charles Joseph Baker, or Charlie, of Dallas, built a winch for me with five hundred feet of airplane cable. He took the cable, made a fair lead, and then plumbed it into the hydraulic system. Every time the engine ran, I had this auxiliary winch and used it extensively. It was so helpful and I'd pull Dave up rock walls after he had hung the pass line block, threaded the little winch line, and hooked onto the bull hook on the drum line. Away we'd go - and Dave, too! Charlie was Chief Engineer at Peerless Royal Trailer Company, and he also worked for Skookum. One day Charlie decided he was going to make a change and had been looking around. His phone rang one day and the caller said, "Hello, Mr. Baker, this is Ernest Swiggert of Hyster Company, and I would like very much to talk with you." So they set up an appointment and Charlie went in. Mr. Swiggert starts telling Charlie what Hyster is prepared to pay him for salary, all the benefits and perks, and offered him a position. Charlie is a very modest and honest fellow, so he said, "Mr. Swiggert, I must tell you this before we resume our conversation." "What's that?" Swiggert asked, and Charlie said, "Well, just this - I don't have a college degree!" Mr. Swiggert literally exploded, saying, "Mr. Baker, I don't give a darn about your degree! I can see you have talent and I want people who have ability, as well as education!" Charlie had plenty of everything it took to be an inventor and good businessman! He secured a number of patents and was a tremendous man in industry. Later on, he owned and operated Oregon Steel Craft and built specialty items for big industry, including a device for Cape Canaveral.

He and his wife, Jenny, were great friends to Frances and I and later, they moved into Portland.

AARON MERCER-CHIEF ENGINEER

Shortly after I started to log for Willamette, I got acquainted with their Chief Engineer, Aaron Mercer. I learned to like Aaron very much and found him to be very capable, and a man of his word. I remember about the first time or so I met him, he made and gave me a very fine map, embracing a vast portion of Polk County. This is one remark he made: "Kenny, I don't know how much you have been around, but you will find out that mostly the intelligent people work for private industry and the d— fools work for the government!" I found that, in a general sense, this was true, and I could relate many incidents which substantiate what Aaron said.

One setting we logged for Willamette in South Branch, had cruised at 350,000 board feet. We logged net scale at 750,000! They asked me where we got that much timber. I told Morris Bergman that we had cut some on the government property, which bothered him greatly. Of course, we did not do so, but what we did, was cut every windfall, and I told Gene Knudsen, "This is one thing I learned from Hitler!" He asked, "Hitler?" I said, "Yes, Hitler told his general to not go around anything, just go straight through it!" This is what we did! We conquered every foot of ground! Howard Parker, who was a cutter for me, had been a Marine and was a veteran of World War II and worked for me for some time. Another cutter I hired was Clarence Bowman, and he had also been in World War II, in the Sea Bees. Clarence and Howard rode with me and if Clarence would begin to recall and relate some of the things which had happened during the war, Howard would get terribly upset! My heart used to ache for Howard, as it was obvious he certainly knew first-hand that war was hell!

BEAR CREEK BATTLES

Another logging setting which I recall clearly was up Bear Creek and we soon learned that it was rightly named! One day Mo Bergman drove up to the landing just as we were having our lunch and Bob made the remark, "I see nine, bear-killed trees from where I am sitting!" Mo asked, "You do what?" Mo had not worked for Willamette too long and he said he was unaware that when bears would come out of hibernation in the spring, they would climb a tree (usually a Second Growth tree). Once up the tree, they'd girdle the tops, get that inner sap juice, and this would get their system organized for the summer. As Bob explained this to Mo, we could see that Mo doubted his word. About a week later, Mo drove up and said, "We just found out the bears are doing a lot of damage to many, many of our trees. Who can we hire to trap bear for us?" We didn't offer any names off-hand, so they found someone to do it for them. I was told that the fellow they hired caught forty-two bear on Willamette's property and on Boise Cascade during the first year of trapping. At the price of stumpage, it didn't take long to run into hundreds of thousands of dollars worth of timber those forty-two bear would damage. Potentially, they would kill a vast amount of timber in a year's time. Bergman ordered $1,500 worth of New House Bear traps, which I saw in their supply room.

The Associated Contract Loggers Association was formed and I became a member. One year the annual meeting was held in Eugene at one of the nice hotels. Two prominent fellows sent there to impress us, representing the government, addressed various subjects and gave their points of view. One was from the Department of the Interior and one from the Bureau of Land Management. Mr. Wilbur Heath, an Oregonian, was Chairman and a fellow from the Roseburg area, Mr. Mays, were seated on the platform with the "dignitaries". The fellow from the Department of the Interior just drove everyone crazy! He had nothing of substance to say and repeatedly reiterated how they were going to monitor road building, soil erosion, and on and on! He said if a logger was building a road and caused a stream's water to discolor and a fellow was fishing downstream, the logger would be stopped! On and on he expounded and raved! Mr. Mays obviously represented the lowly, working class, as did most of us in attendance. He asked the Department of Interior man if he could tell him how he could stay in business, pay his employees, and make a profit. This seemed to be a reasonable question, since all of us there were striving for the same goal. This big man from Washington D.C., gave him the old, "Ho, Ho. That, Sir, doesn't happen to be my problem! That is YOUR problem!"

After some time of listening, they called for a ten minute recess, after which the VIP (very important politician) from Washington, D.C., would continue to speak. I went up to Paul Danielson, who was President of the A.O.L. and I said, "Paul, I just got a message." This is what I told him: "There was a contract logger who was out in a deep stream and he was drowning. He went down under the water, came up, and called for help. He is now thirty feet from shore and there is a BLM man on the shore. The BLM man heard this logger call for help and he looked around, spied a piece of rope twenty feet long, and he threw this out toward the poor contract logger and said, May I remind you, Sir, we are meeting you more than half way!" Danielson just roared with laughter, and then ran up on the platform to talk to Mr. Heath. Soon the meeting is once again called to order by Mr. Heath, and he announced, "We just received a very important message!" He then repeated the story I had just related to Paul Danielson. The audience just roared, outrageously applauding and cheering! The very important government man had gone to the microphone to resume his speech, but it took a long time to restore order! This poor guy from D.C. was all through! That just wiped out his credibility! I felt good about it, because the contract loggers were at the mercy of every agency from OSHA to all the other governmental agencies, plus unscrupulous tactics from many sources! How's the common man supposed to make a living?

PURSUIT = PRESSURE = PENALTY

(ULCERS)

About this time, Mo Bergman came up to the landing and says, "Kenny, you better buy a big cat and a big shovel, as we have a lot of moving on the agenda for you!" So I bought a new HD16 Power Shift cat from Timber Tractor in Springfield, Oregon, and I've never done business with a finer firm. Along with the equipment acquisition, I developed a bad case of ulcers, which caused me a great deal of suffering! One day a Willamette "Knot Clipper" (this is the woods' lingo for a company official fresh out of college) said, "There is a real good doctor in Salem who's tops in dealing with ulcers. I'll give you his name and phone number!" So I got the name, phoned for an appointment, and when the day of reckoning came, I went into his office. There were enough papers to be filled out for being admitted to any secret society, or to a penitentiary, for that matter! Finally, a precocious blonde led me down a very long hall and put me in a room. I waited at least forty-five minutes, during which time I had ample opportunity to reflect on a misspent life! I did note that the room had a number of diplomas and many other documents on the wall, indicating that here is a man who has met life head on!

Finally the door opened, ever so gently, and here stood the doctor. He never shook hands, but merely stated his name. I stated mine. He said, "I don't know anything about you." I said, "By the same token, I don't know anything about you, but I see you have been to a number of schools, and I am also a member of the human race. Surely we can find some common ground somewhere!" I thought for a professional man, this was tops! After my visit, I felt he was a very honest man in that he didn't know anything about me and I had serious doubts that he knew much of anything about anyone else. However, I recovered from my ulcers in spite of some foolish advice!

When I decided to buy a shovel and also a logging truck, I had some very interesting experiences. I went several places to look for a shovel and had gone down to Eugene to a big dealer there, Ross Murray. There was one shovel there which seemed to be what I thought would work out okay. They said to me, "We'll go over it with a fine-tooth comb for you and it'll be just like new! I was also told it would pick up a three thousand board foot log and that it would heel a forty-two foot log and load it. They gave me a ninety day warranty and said they'd deliver it.

They delivered it up on the mountain and there was a twenty-six foot butt log that had fairly heavy bark on it. That log had 2,650 feet in it! They tied onto this log, but the shovel wouldn't pick it up! The salesman said, "My gosh, Kenny, that's a big log!" I said, "No, it has 2,650 board feet in it!" "No," he said, "that's a big log!" but again I said, "No, it has 2,650 board feet!" The salesman agreed to build a boom for the shovel, as I let him know the present boom wasn't satisfactory to me at all! Right off the bat, however, we got snowed out by a very heavy snowfall.

The salesman from Ross Murray called me up and said, "If you go up to the woods and count the spine (the teeth on that one gear), I'll have George Mermo make a reduction gear for you that will gear down and load those logs! I used snow shoes to go up there in the dead of winter, which was about seven miles! Inside that cab, there was a great big cover over the drive chain! I took off forty-four bolts in that bitterly cold temperature! At last I managed to get that cover off, counted the teeth on the gear and measured the shaft. The fellow at Eugene had that made for me. When I was able to use it, it actually did what he said it would do. They had not gone over the shovel with a very fine-tooth comb, however. The first time Davie moved it, there were no brakes on it. It had straight air brakes and everything, but they weren't working, as the treadle valve was shot. He backed into a stump and if it hadn't been there, there wouldn't have been a shovel – or Davie, for just beyond the stump, there was about a thousand foot vertical drop, right down into Boulder Creek! I was so grateful that stump was there. I had to continually have Don Boman and different fellows work on the shovel on Saturdays and we finally got it working in a respectable manner. After those bugs were worked out, it did a good job for me.

I had gone down to Eugene with the measurements of the gear and asked, "Is the salesman around here?" The fellow behind the desk said, "Don't talk too loud, the boss is in there!" I said, "Well, that's fine! That's a good place for him, maybe!" Again he leaned over and said, "Don't talk too loud, I don't know what you're talking about!" I said, "Well, you'll know, 'cause I have the measurements of the gear!" He was living in fear that the owner was going to come out. Well, he did come out and sort of smarted off, so I just told him what the deal was and he flew into a rage! I've seen quite a few angry guys in my life in the woods, so I just let him rave! After some discussions, the salesman finally did make part of our agreement good.

That salesman came up to my house one day and kept begging and begging, as I still owed $5,000 on the shovel. He said, "You don't know, Kenny, how it would help me in my job if I could just get that money from you!" I said, "Well, hey, look! We're snowed out, can't work the shovel, and I don't know if everything is in working order!" I tried to reasonably put him off, since I really hadn't been able to fully test the equipment. In the end, I foolishly gave him the money because he kept begging. I called down one evening to talk to him and a lady answered the phone. I asked, "Is Jack there?" She said, "Who's calling, please?" "Kenny Shenk," I explained, to which she said, "He's at the Camelback Inn in Phoenix, Arizona!" The next time I called, it sounded as if he was on a life boat someplace out in the middle of the ocean! I never talked to him once after he called me and told me to go get the measurements on that gear. It just goes to show you not all companies are honest!

The Timber Tractor Company there at Springfield had on staff the finest fellows I have ever dealt with in my life! I had hardly any breakdowns with my cats and on the new 16 I bought, the only thing that went haywire on it was the spring broke on the winch brake. I phoned down there and they said, "Where you working?" I said, "At the Valsetz Summit, first turn to the left, on top of the hill." "What time do you go to work?" "Seven o'clock," I said. "Don't worry! When you get there, the spring will be replaced," this fellow told me. Sure enough, when I got up there, Herb Buller was just leaving and he had put the new spring on. That's the way they treated me and I was so pleased! It was refreshing to know there were people who tried to back their word up and I really think the world of those people. My memories of that company are nothing but good!

The first Mac truck I bought had quite a history, none of which was known to me beforehand! The guy who had it before me, evidently opened up the fuel pump and turned up the RPM's. Anyway, different fellows I knew had hauled logs with this guy. This truck was in a shop called Northwest Acceptance Corporation when I found it. I told the salesman, "I'll buy your truck," and he said, "It's just ready to go!" I asked, "Have you seen it?" "Oh, no, I never saw it," he said. "Well, you're just a little bit off, Sir. The windows are broken out, part of the tires are flat and the battery was stolen out of it. There are several things on it which have to be attended to," I told him, trying to enlighten him! "Is that right?" he asked. He had it taken into a repair shop to a fellow named Chuck Allwad and they went to work on it. I bought the truck through the salesman from Ross Murray and went over there to talk to the mechanic. He had the engine running, took the radiator cap off and there were just little spurts of air coming up! "There's something wrong down there! Either the block is broken or the head gasket is shot," he told me. I went back to the salesman and said, "Hey, I'm not going to take that truck out of there like that!" So he called the fellow in Portland that I talked to at Northwest Acceptance Corporation and the guy screamed at him, "Do you know how many thousand dollars I've spent on that truck all ready?" This salesman from Ross Murray said, "Well, I don't know how much you've spent on it, but all I can do is tell you, this fellow isn't going to take it if you don't repair it!" At last they did repair it! The head gasket was blown. Davie went down to drive it home and they had over-hauled the steering mechanism on it. The only thing they forgot was to put a key in it and let it turn the corner. It wouldn't turn, but just took off across the street! I don't recall what Davie hit, but he did get it stopped! He wasn't more than two blocks from the shop, so we took it right back! After that, it did pretty good. It didn't have a Jake brake on it, but a Williams Air reduction brake. My niece, Beatrice, was married to Paul Nisly, who was working in a parts house in McMinnville, so I went down and asked him if he wanted to drive my logging truck. He said he would, and began driving for me. Paul had never driven log truck before and had a lot of learning to do! I'm proud to say he learned real well, did a good job, was always dependable, and I enjoyed working with him. Later I traded that truck off and got a Peterbilt, which was a good truck. Paul hauled a lot of logs for me and I'm sure it made a major impact on his life!

There were so many trying experiences while working for Willamette, believe me! We moved our logging show down on Carter Creek, out of Valsetz, up the Siletz River, to a landing there. Bob Patty and Floyd Zetterburg were cutting for me out there ahead of Davie and myself. Bob Berends was another one of my Willamette bosses, so he called me one evening and asked, "Have you moved to Carter Creek yet, Kenny?" I said, "No!" Then he stopped and said, "My gosh, I wonder how you're going to get up there!" I asked, "Why?" He said, "Oh, it's awful!" Twice he called me regarding the show and it bothered me, so I called Bob and asked, "How am I going to get up there, Patty?" He said, "When you move over there, unload your cat off that low-boy, then the first thing you do is hunt me up! I'll tell you how to get up there!" Wimer had taken some windfalls out of there before. There was one skid road there which had great gullies upwards to five feet deep, created from the water rushing through, and it did look formidable!

Sure enough, the day we moved out there, old Bob had a road picked out for me! I unloaded the cat, walked up, found Patty, and he got on the cat with me. He'd instruct me, "Go here, go there," and so on, until I got through the timber where we needed to go, to make a new landing. It was about one-thirty in the afternoon when I unloaded the cat, then I made five turns that afternoon and had a big supply of logs at the landing when we quit! I just kept blading as I went down on this very steep terrain and it just worked out beautifully! I called Bob Berends and reported to him how well it went. He was so pleased! We had some huge timber there! A number of the trees were eight feet on the stump, with lots of six and seven footers also.

Prior to moving the shovel to Carter Creek, we were working on a fork of Boulder Creek. Clarence Bowman fell a tree which had a big sucker on it and a huge limb stuck out. The result was that the tree didn't fall exactly where he had it "gunned" and it rolled over, hitting the shovel. Davie was just out putting tickets on the end of some logs and was very fortunate to not be in it! The cab was completely torn off and demolished! Matter of fact, the shovel was shaken so hard, that the hook rollers were broken off and there was quite a bit of other damage! Of course, Clarence felt so badly about it and we all did, but I had insurance. I contacted Leroy Davis at Fall City regarding my claim, so he immediately came out, looked at the shovel and said, "Oh, I'll fix that up for you - right here in the woods!" I went and bought a bunch of bolts to put in the hook rollers and we got that shovel working again. Leroy would come up, take measurements, go home, and work on it! He built a nicer cab for it than was originally on it, and everything worked out just fine!

Arriving at work one morning, there was a sign on my shovel which said, "Sorry 'bout that, fellows, but I had to have it!" Here some jug head had cut a hose off the motor and taken it! At least he had the decency (?) to leave a note. Don't know if anything about this thief was decent, but he left a note that he had done something to it and I discovered the hose was missing. Many times I'd discover that gasoline and other items had been stolen, but unfortunately, that's the kind of world we live in. Ironically, I just heard that all the crime rates have dropped so much, a lot of the policemen were in danger of losing their jobs, but I don't see that happening around here! It seems to be getting worse, but back in Washington where the "powers that be" live, they're on easy street there, I guess, although there are more murders there than any city in the United States. Clinton, however, insists that he's virtually wiped out crime!

A number of fellows set chokers for me throughout the years. One lad was a star football player and he looked pretty skookum, was well-muscled, and always had short shirt sleeves. Now anybody who has ever worked in the woods understands that for safety reasons, you don't want short sleeve shirts! I was flying four chokers, so I'd get off the cat, set three chokers and he'd set one! He would pull on this one choker as if he planned to break it, so I said to him one day, "Please don't break that choker!" He looked at me and just sort of smiled. One day he told me he had three girlfriends, so perhaps he was successful in that department, but simply was useless as a man could be out there in the woods. He got up on a stump one day, let out a scream and said, "Over here!" I motioned, "No, you come over HERE!" "No, I've got a log picked out over here!" I said, "You get on the cat!" This young man didn't realize I needed another peeler log to make a load. Davie had so many logs and he'd tell me, "Bring in two peelers," or whatever, and that's the way we worked it and it was just fine.

One day I told this fellow, "Young man, you owe it to your future posterity (if you ever have any), to go to a doctor and see what's wrong with you! You're just not 'cutting the mustard'!" "Well, when do you think I should go?" he asked, so I suggested, "Tonight!" I was very fortunate for I found out later he had been in a horrible car wreck and had he made up his mind to, he probably would have brought some lawsuit against me. With all the hungry lawyers, undoubtedly, they would have tried to nail me! Since the O.J. Simpson case, anything can happen!

Another time when we were logging, we had five different species of trees: noble fir, hemlock, old growth, cedar and larch and for awhile, we had to sort all of them separately. Davie told me when I went into the landing, "Get me two more cedars of fair size and I'll have two loads of cedar. Then get me two more peelers and I'll have three loads of peelers." When the trucks were hauling down to Huntington Shingle Mill in the Springfield area, it was one hundred and ten miles from the landing to the mill. My trucks had to leave our landing by two o'clock in order to get down there, get unloaded and scaled before closing time. Everybody wanted to haul cedar, as I guess that was more lucrative! I went back out to the woods and always carried an extra supply of chokers on the cat. The fellow who was setting chokers said, "Over here!" I said, "No, over here!" He said, "Bring your cat over here!" and he was very angry. As I got off my cat, I noted immediately that he was quite angry and he said, "Look here, fellow, I've worked in the woods a long time and I've never seen anybody log the way you log!" I said, "Well, that's okay!" "Well, why don't we log her clean?" "I'd have to rent forty acres of land from the BLM to do that," I told him and informed him Davie had already told me what he needed. "That's the way we do it," I explained. He seemed very upset, but he got over it! This fellow was one of those who had horns on his head and called the shots, so I decided I wasn't going to let him get away with it since it wasn't working out!

In all the years of logging, I never had trouble getting trucks. My policy was to always treat them right and when they came up there, they got a load of logs! The Superintendent of the Huntington Shingle Mill, Russell Rose, called me several times in the evenings and would say, "Kenny, I just can't tell you how much our truckers enjoy going up to your logging show! The drivers are so pleased to go up there. There's nobody there screaming and cussing, they get a load immediately, and they just love it!" (I just read in the paper about two weeks ago that he died.) For a long time, his truckers hauled all the cedar down to the shingle mill. Duke Limbaugh hauled for me for years and also Uel Lambert hauled for about sixteen years. Paul Nisly also hauled for me for quite a long time. I always appreciated the fact that I never had to beg for truckers. We were always careful to check for height so they wouldn't get ticketed for being over and took as many precautions as we could.

One time after I bought a truck of my own, I applied for a PUC permit and was required to show cause as to why I wanted this truck, why I wanted a permit, and all sorts of information! So I went over to Salem to hire an attorney to help me in obtaining it. The attorney told me, "I know one thing, if you don't get a permit, you'll have a lease permit you can work under." That morning, Lloyd Lewis from Willamina Lumber Company, Mo Bergman from Willamette Industries, and Russell Rose drove from clear down at Springfield to come up in a terrible snowstorm for this hearing! I was utterly amazed that Russell came that distance in that kind of weather! The Salmon River Log Truckers notified me that I wasn't about to get a permit! They had plenty of trucks that wanted to haul logs up there and they weren't going to allow it! There was a big, Cuban fellow who was going to do the interrogating, so he called the meeting to order and said, "Now ve ready for da Salmon River boys to speak." This fellow had a real accent. Nobody got up, so this fellow said, "I da-clare a fifteen minute recess!" They fooled around a while and he brought the meeting to order to continue, but no one from Salmon River Truckers showed up. Thus, the hearing was over, and I was subsequently granted a permit. Soon after this, one of the Salmon River truckers drove up to our house one day and talked to Frances. He was so very courteous and wanted to know if there was any chance he could get a job hauling logs up there for me.

The scaling system was so corrupt when we were hauling the pulp logs, it was unbelievable! To illustrate this point, when we were cutting in the defective hemlock which went to Publisher Paper at Newberg, the truckers would go down through Long Bell (which was Crown Zellerbach side), and come out at New Grande Ronde. Just past the restaurant at Fort Hill, there was a scaling shack. The truckers used to stop just off the highway by the restaurant, look and watch to see which scaler was on duty. One scaler was Jim Hardy and the other one was Buford Shoff, and depending on which one you got, there could be a difference of 1,000 to 1,800 board feet! If the truckers got cut too badly, I'd just have to pay them a flat rate! They would stop there and watch so they could get scaled by Jim Hardy.

Another instance I knew of involved the Coos Bay Logging Company. Ed Adams was Superintendent there and they had big timber. One time, three of their trucks drove onto a scaling ramp, the scaler came out and culled every log on the load! They didn't know what to do, so they called Ed and he went down there. He said to the truckers, "I want all of you to follow me!" They drove about twenty-five miles to another Scaling Bureau Post and the scaler greeted them. He docked three logs out of the three loads! Just goes to show that the bureau of scalers are human and sometimes lack a long way of being perfect!

It is with rather fond memories that I recall some interesting experiences with Stuart Dory, of Willamette Industries! One time they called me up and said, "You have to build a new bridge at Cedar Creek before you get to the old camp!" So I got my cat, hauled it up a ways, and then walked it up to where we were supposed to start in. Stuart was there at the site, along with my crew that summer, which was Bob Patty and Russ. Stuart said, "They're buying some stumpage up here from the government. We want to go up, look it over carefully, and you'll have to build a series of switch-back's to get up there!" We all had begun doing various tasks and I pulled some logs in, which Stuart wanted to lay the stringers for the bridge on. It was getting just about noon by this time and Bob was off about eight hundred feet and at the bow of a hill. He called out and said, "Bring your cat up here, PLEASE!" Stuart said to me, "Don't take your cat up there!" Russ hollered, "Up the hill! Bring your cat up, Dad!" I didn't know what to do, so I said to Stuart, "Well, just let me go up, I'll brush the road out a little bit and then I'll come back down!"

At that time, I had a little Allis Chalmers, HD-5 cat on which I had Charlie Baker put seventy injectors! Also, it had a very heavy blade with a lot of power and could really climb a hill! Ironically, I believe the blade was called a Baker Blade. I walked my cat up the hill where Russ had already swamped out a "path" for me, and Willamette had marked the trees they wanted Bob to cut. Bob said, "It isn't any steeper up here, Kenny, than where we've been working! There's no problem at all!" For some reason, Bob didn't have his power saw up there, although it was all sharpened and ready to go. So they got on the cat with me, we went back down and ate our lunch.

Stuart looked around, looked at me and asked, "What do you propose to do now?" "Well, Stu, Bob said he's going to fall a couple trees for me, so I'll go up and bring them down!" He said, "Well, you darn fools! Are you actually going to do that?" I said, "Yes!" He said, "Okay, then, I'll get on and ride up with you!" Stuart sat on the rest over the battery, Bob sat on the other side and Russ stood on the back with his power saw as we went up the hill! Bob fell the stringers and by afternoon we had quite a lot of wood down. I hadn't known what Willamette had projected regarding costs on this show. The next day, here came Knutsen, Johnson, and Mercer. Gene said, "Well, I can see where the d— fool comes down, but where does he go UP?" Stuart said, "That's where he goes up" (pointing to the steep hill). "You gotta be lying," Gene said. Stu said, "NO! I'm not!" Of course, I didn't hear this conversation, but Stuart told me about it later. I brought logs down that hill, and put them up on these big logs and Stuart chalk-lined them. We barked them and with Bob's big, Mercury Disston power saw, sawed those stringers, and once again, they looked just like they'd been cut on a head rig. (We did this for several other bridges, as well!) It worked out really well and was a job to be proud of!

We raised a Spar Tree there and had it all guy-lined to put these big stringers in place. Stuart had holes bored and great, big steel bolts sticking up out of the concrete piers. As we picked up this one big stringer, he stood by the piers and asked, "Boys, is she gonna fit? Anybody wanna bet?" Nobody wanted to bet! He said, "Let 'er down, Kenny!" I let her down as he pushed on it and engineered one end, and one of the other fellows got the other end. She went down and Stuart walked over there, grabbed a big old bolt, reached in the little man-hole he had cut there, and screwed it down! He began rubbing his belly and said, "Just right, boys! She fits JUST RIGHT!" Everyone of them just fit absolutely perfect. That man was a perfectionist and when he did something, it was done right and it worked! We had a lot of hard work and a great time working with Stuart. He was a fine fellow to work with!

Stuart built the trestle work for Willamette's railroad in one canyon which was 135 feet high! He built a double S curve in this canyon and part of it is still standing today because it can't fall down! This double S curve means that he crossed a canyon, went down a ways on the one side, then crossed on the other side, and then crossed back over. That's what they call a double S curve! That railroad hauled hundreds of millions of feet of logs to the big mill in Dallas! Stuart was one of the men who helped put it in! Some of the things they accomplished back in those days without benefit of a bulldozer is just beyond description. They did it out of necessity and made it work!

FURIOUS FIRE FOR

HUDSON CALLAHAN

When we were logging above Black Rock, on top of the Coast Range Mountains, we could see a column of smoke that did not seem to be terribly far away. Sure enough, word came soon that the Hudson Callahan Logging Company had a fire on the North Fork of the Siletz River. Gene Knudsen called and asked me to bring my entire crew and cutting tools at once. This fire was spreading rapidly and was quickly becoming a MAJOR FIRE! The state of Oregon had lots of personnel present, as did Willamette Industries and Wimer Logging Company. There were many other companies who supplied people to fight fire. I gathered my crew and away we went!

Once on the scene, my crew needed to ascertain the best way to proceed. There was a nice, flat bench on top, but the fire was down the hill and in the tops of defective and diseased hemlock timber. The smoke which was pouring forth was horrendous and the fire was extremely hot! Immediately, we built a fire trail down a canyon to the river. Large pieces of rotten logs which had caught on fire, would roll down and into the draw. I put a line, or trail, across the draw so nothing could roll up hill and cross it. One company official asked me to stay right in the draw with the fire trail. Well, I wasn't quite that naive and shortly thereafter, I heard a state official say, "Whoever laid that fire trail out surely knew what he was doing!" There was no general organization and it was very difficult to know what they wanted us to do!

One day I saw a big hemlock burning about sixty feet up and heard the peculiar noise they make before they do their swan song. Just then I saw a state official start down the hill. I hollered real loud and said, "Come back out of there, you are going to get killed!" Just as I said that, down went that tree! That guy barely made it out of there! He looked at me and said, "Say, Man, that was close! Someone is liable to get killed around here!" The officials from Willamette who were there were Gene Knudsen, Aaron Mercer, and Mo Bergman and they knew this fire was cause for great concern, so they were on deck to help and direct to the best advantage.

I mentioned that the state brought personnel, and they also brought about fifty convicts from the State Penitentiary in Salem, to help fight fire. That was a real disaster because, to them, this was worse than being locked up and they never did one lick of work! One day on this fire, Bob Patty put on a show which we will never forget. I shall relate exactly what took place! One morning it was just getting light and we had to go over, and down this big log. Bob says, "Fellows, I am sure having a h— of a time with my Old Lady." Someone asked, "What's wrong, Bob?" Bob said, "All these years she has been so faithful in spending my money that I never worried about it! Now she has this stubborn spell and won't go to town, or leave home and the money is piling up like you can't believe! Here I worked one week logging and now have money from working on this fire and I don't know what to do!" All the Willamette officials, plus probably about fifty or sixty other fellows, heard Bob say this and they just didn't know how to take it! They didn't know if Bob was griping, or what was going on.

Coming up out of a canyon one evening, I was right behind Bob and we were nearly to the top. Here was a nice, flat rock with moss on it and a fellow sitting there picking his teeth. We were both black as Koly's Hat and this fellow was neat and clean, with not a drop of sweat in sight! Bob had a shovel in his hand as he stopped and looked at this fellow. "What did you ever do to get a job like you got? You ain't sweaty or dirty. You don't look like you've been putting out any labor, how do you rate?" Bob asked him. This fellow looked at Bob, never cracked a smile and replied, "Ah killed a man to git my job." Bob then asked, "You got $5 in your pocket?" The fellow says, "I reckon ah ain't got that!" Bob said, "If you had five bucks, I would knock you in the head and bury you right here!" The fellow responded, "A seein' how rocky it is, I guess that would be fair enough!" We went seventy-five feet more and here were two trucks which had, "Oregon State Penitentiary" written on the doors! This changed the picture somewhat! This was the first day the state had brought convicts up and of course, they had not been there in the morning when we went to work. When Bob was talking to the fellow who was sitting out in the woods, we didn't know it at the time, but he had killed a man and was one of the guys from the penitentiary! Bob worked hard all day, but he could really have fun goofing off and entertaining the rest of the crew!

Aaron Mercer said to me one morning, "Kenny, there are six to eight trees on fire, will you please have the boys cut them." The fire in these trees was up about sixty feet up, burning under the first limb, which usually was a rotten limb. As we fell them and they left the stump, they'd sail down the hill and burst into even greater flames! It was quite a sight to behold - just a big ball of fire! I went over a ways where the trees were a thicker stand and I called out for the cutters to bring their saws over there! I instructed, "Fall this one!" Away she'd go - the fire just boiling! I found about ten trees like this and at first the Willamette Company officials thought I was getting cutting happy. However, when they saw those trees burst into a flaming fire, they knew that I knew what I was doing! Mercer asked me, "Kenny, how did you know those trees were on fire?" What I did was to walk clear around each tree and get the background just right and I would look for a heat wave, as there was no smoke from the trees, which was incredible! That way, I knew that with the heat being generated, it wouldn't be long before they'd begin to burn! Aaron was really impressed with that bit of information!

When we finished up, Willamette asked me how much each of my crew should be paid, including Uel Lambert, my trucker and I was reimbursed very fairly for all our work. I then received a letter from Gene Knudsen, in which he praised our efforts and he said, "Shenk Logging fellows put forth, by far, the best effort, and said that if I were ever in the unfortunate circumstances of having a fire, they would put forth their best efforts to help me suppress it." I was very pleased with the company's attitude and fairness on this fire.

THE WHITE HOUSE - LOTS OF SLEEPOVERS;

NO FUNDRAISING HERE!

The years were swiftly going by and Wilbert went off to college when he was just sixteen and from that point on, he lived away from home and eventually ended up living in the East. It seemed as if the wings were sprouting and an exodus had begun. Russ had decided he wanted to become a school teacher and attended Hesston, Linfield, and Oregon College of Education. Donna left to attend college and after the twin boys had been out of high school and worked a couple of years, they also decided to further their education. When the boys would come home from college for the summer, they all worked with me in the woods, except for Wilbert! My only regret and I don't know of any way around it, is that I enjoyed being around the kids so much and all too soon they were grown! With the exception of Wilbert, all the boys loved hunting! His interests just seemed to lie in a different direction. Bob Patty always said not to spoil a good story by sticking to the truth, but I am trying to stick to the truth in my stories, because the truth is hard to come by you know!

The kids were close in age and sadly for Frances and I, they all seemed to leave at about the same time. Wilbert was married in 1957 to a college classmate. He had taken an assignment in Jakarta, Indonesia, and so they were married there. In the fall of 1961, Donna married, Russell married the following March, in Germany, as he was stationed there in the Army, Byron was married in June, and David married in July of 1962. If you do the calculations, there were four marriages within one year! Myron spent some time after college working and living in Mexico and was married in 1967.

As the saying goes, first comes love, then comes marriage, then comes the baby carriage! Frances and I ended up with seventeen grandchildren and we were never without kids coming home to visit, or we were off to visit them! I must confess I enjoyed the grandkids most after they were old enough to talk and I could test their reasoning abilities! That way, I could also test their endurance skills.

Davie started going to the woods with me when he was about thirteen years old. We were logging

Bear Russ killed before he took off for college one fall.

up at the Foster Logging for Willamina Lumber and he used to set choker, unhook them, and whatever there was to do, he did it! After Davie got out of high school, he worked for me in the woods running the shovel and was a very capable woodsman. He could fall timber as good as any man you've ever seen, or he could run shovel and set chokers. He was dependable and we worked so well together! That made my job easier and more enjoyable, as Davie seemed to know what I was going to do with that cat and I seemed to know where he was going to be and we did many things together! One time we took out a huge log jam in Mill Creek which had pushed a new Cedar Creek bridge off its' foundation! Willamette's engineers told me the jam was seven hundred feet long and of course, the water was high! They asked me to yard this junk out of the creek, pile it up, and burn it! Bob and Davie worked with me to accomplish this. We had stacked quite a bit and Bob had just started to try and get a fire going when Bergman came up the creek to see us. He watched Bob and started laughing, "You can't burn that wet stuff!" Bob said, "Watch me!" It wasn't long before he had a fire going and it was so hot I could hardly get the cat close enough to stack more debris!

Donna holding up some fine trout we caught on one of our trips to East Lake.

We were working on this log jam one day and I called out to Davie, but he didn't answer! Some of these chunks of log were bobbing up and down in the water. This water was very still, because it was jammed. Suddenly, I felt panicked because I feared Davie had fallen in and was down under some of that debris. I lost no time in looking for him and after what seemed like a very long time, I saw him and he was fine! I was one happy man, I can tell you that!

After I bought the shovel, then the problem was — who was going to operate it? Myron was up there for a few days and in no time, he became proficient in loading a truck and maneuvering it. Davie said one day, "Hey, do it this way!" Myron said, "Well, I'm busy! You get up there and run it!" So Davie did just that! A couple of weeks had gone by and it was obvious he was good at it and it wasn't long before he was very good at it! One of the things Davie had going for him was that he could have been a Bureau Scaler! He knew whether a log was good enough to go to the mill, or if it was a pulp log and could also estimate the weight of a log extremely accurately. The truckers would hold up four fingers, indicating they wanted four hundred pounds on the trailer, and Davie knew just what to put on for them and got along real well with the truckers! For many years, he worked with me in the woods and after I quit logging, he started cutting timber. He was the only one of the kids who didn't go to college, but I can't emphasize how valuable he was to me in the woods! After Russ quit teaching and being principal, he and Davie cut timber together. As time went on, Davie started having trouble with his hands and feet and was diagnosed with arthritis, and after some time, he was granted total disability for this condition.

WHATCHAMACALLIT STEW

I had heard about an Outfitter named Manford Eisle in the Eagle Cap Wilderness Area, in Eastern Oregon, an area where the country is extremely rugged, and close to the Imnaha River. We booked a hunt for Bob and Rosena Patty and Frances and I. We drove over, met Manford at the appointed time, and was introduced to Bud Reineirson, the packer working for him. Manford had agreed to pack us back to a place called Bench Camp, but Frances said, "Well, I'm not going to ride up there!" Bud said, "Lady, we haven't lost a client yet! I'll lead you by the hand, or I'll hold your horse and lead him across, or whatever it takes, I'll do it," and he just kept begging her, making all kinds of promises! I didn't know what to think, because I figured it wasn't as bad as

Those boys have been busy bagging bucks! L to R: Byron, David, Myron

she imagined. At last she agreed to go! The funny thing was, when we went through the "bad spot", she forgot about it and it wasn't all that treacherous! Matter of fact, coming back out, she took a picture of a deer crossing the trail, and this was one of the worst places on that trail. That picture is a good one, for you could see the horses' ears sticking up with excitement, from seeing the deer. Bob and I started hunting up on the hill to-

wards Joseph, and Bob was able to kill a nice, four-point buck! We packed that in and things were looking up!

The next morning, we started up the mountain in partial darkness and fog. When it was just beginning to get light, we were pretty well to the top of the mountain. Bob stopped and said, "I see a deer!" "You do," I asked. "Yes," he said, "and it's a buck!" I had a big scope with a range-finder and after I turned it up, could also see the deer. I shot the buck and we went back to camp to let the packer pack us out.

Upon arrival back at camp, we learned that another couple, from Sherwood, had arrived, as well as another packer. Bud wasn't there that day and this new packer began beating up on this poor horse! He cursed, screamed, and invoked all manner of diverse circumstances on this poor creature! Well, he did that until this lady from Sherwood really became upset! She went out there and told him, "You get away from that horse!" She went up to the horse, put her arms around it, told him what a nice critter he was and what a nice person she was, and just loved him! She put the bridle on that horse and got him ready to go! He was a perfect gentleman for her, but he certainly didn't respect that fellow! I couldn't believe how well she handled him, but this illustrates that a little kindness is generally the best way to go!

Eisle, our Outfitter, had a number of different camps in various places and had a main headquarters. When we arrived, they had just packed in a group of Portland Firemen. They were a right jolly bunch of guys, full of stories, and fun to be around. One of them said, "I almost lost my life! We got a woman out of a burning house when she started screaming, 'My baby, my baby, my baby'! So I fought my way back in that burning house and finally in the bathroom, I found this little poodle crouched down on the floor! I got that little rascal out, but I was so mad at that woman to think I nearly lost my life for that poodle. Sure enough, though, I guess it WAS her baby!"

Davie at one of our log landings looking over a load of logs. He is getting ready to brand them.

There at the Eagle Cap Wilderness Headquarters, was an elderly lady, Ethel Thomas, who did the cooking. She had a big mulligan fixed and as all of us were eating, one fireman said, "Lady, just what do you have in this mulligan?" She said, "Why? What's wrong with it?" "Wrong with it? Why, it's the most delicious thing I've ever tasted! What have you got in it?" "Well, I thought everybody knew how to make one of those! That's a Whatchamacallit Stew!" Ethel laughed and then said, "Well, I'll tell you! The first thing you start with is a three-point buck!" I don't think she ever really disclosed everything she had in it, but it was simply delicious!

One other time, I had a mulligan which would have been equal to it, or perhaps even a bit superior to Ethel's, and that was when I was hunting with Walter Erhorn! When he'd prepare the steaks for supper and trim the meat, he would throw all the little pieces of meat into a big, black, iron kettle. During the day, he kept a lid on it and for hours, it slowly simmered. One evening when we came into camp late, Walter said, "Well, we're going to have stew tonight!" I thought, "Oh no!" He heated up the meat, added vegetables, and seasonings, and whatever he did, it was one of the finest stews I'd ever eaten! Just goes to show you, you never know what's going to come out of the fire!" He certainly had a good one! I don't know if he did it on purpose or not. If cleanliness had anything to do with it, I don't think this would have any bearing on it, for that wasn't his strong suit, but we had a wonderful mulligan!

STOPPING THEM IN THE PASS

By this time, John Breeden was getting up in years and I invited him to go over to Shamrock Springs with Russ, Bob Patty, Marvin Fast, and myself to go elk hunting. Working in the woods had it's hazards and John didn't escape. He fell out of a Spar Tree one time and broke his ankle and was also was quite crippled with arthritis, thus finding it increasingly difficult to get around. We got over there a day before season opened, so I told him, "John, let me show you the country." About two o'clock in the afternoon, as we started down a mountain, we looked across the canyon and there were two, big five-point bulls standing there with their heads down and eyes closed, asleep! John said, "You know, Kenny, I haven't killed many elk! I spent most of my time dogging for those Missourian relatives of my wife! You know where I'm go-

Twin boys with cougar who was hanging out at our barn. Our little dog bayed him across creek.

ing to be tomorrow morning?" I asked, "Where?" "Right below that tree," he answered and pointed to where those bulls were standing.

Next morning, by daylight, that old man got down that canyon somehow! There were rock bluffs which were nearly impossible to cross. In some places, it was so rocky, you had to carefully pick your trail! He waited and those two bulls came down a little ways, but then something spooked them so they never came out to where John could get a shot! I just could hardly stand it that he didn't get to shoot one of them! Russ "lowered the boom" on an elk down below the canyon and got one, plus we got two others that day!

John announced that on this trip he wanted to do the cooking! We had a total of four burners on which to cook and since Bob didn't eat onions, John fried two separate skillets of elk liver and did a superb job! That was the finest elk liver I've ever tasted and it was delicious eating! Just as I was savoring the liver and thinking it was the best, Marvin spoke up and declared that it was the best liver he'd ever eaten! John said, "It certainly is good and I'm going to put on another skillet full!" He had three skillets of liver cooking at the same time and we really got a bang out of that! This trip was memorable, indeed, and full of great FUN!

Sitting around camp, we were discussing various subjects and it was the days of the Elvis Presley craze. The comments were all different and unique; one guy liked him and his singing; another one didn't and as the comments continued, they were varied and colorful. During the discussion, John was quiet while the others commented. At last, he spoke up and said, "Well, boys, I'll tell you one thing, he has a distinct honor! There have been more hound pups named Elvis in America this last year than any other name!" I thought that was pretty fitting and we all got a good laugh out of John's observation!

Not long after this elk hunting trip, I went into Sheridan to see John. He had a number of logging trucks which he owned and drivers he hired to haul for him. It had been at least six weeks since I had seen him and he said to me, "Know where I'd rather be right now, Kenny?" I said, "No, I don't!" "I'd like to be over there at Shamrock in your old tent! I can't take the rat race, by George, there's just too much grief around here to suit me!" I could well understand why!

BIG BUCK BOAST

One time John called me up and said, "Let's go do a little hunting this afternoon, Kenny. I'd like to go up above my old home place. How about it?" I said, "Suits me, John!" So I drove up there, even though I don't like to go hunting in new country in the afternoon! I generally had most of my hunting luck in the morning. John instructed me, "Just go down this ridge and fool around and we'll meet back up here in a couple hours! The next time I see you, I want to see some horns on the ground!" That year, I foolishly had signed up for the Big Buck Contest with the Four Corner's Rod and Gun Club in Salem.

Down the canyon I started and John went off on his mission. It wasn't long before I literally stumbled onto a big buck and he jumped up, snorted and stopped. I "answered" him in the best fashion I could and it worked! He turned and walked into an opening where I could see him, so I easily put him on the ground! John heard me shoot and came back to where I was. This buck was a big five-point and was the second, biggest five-point I have ever killed! (I have only killed two, five-point Black-Tails.) John said, "Holy Mackinaw, Kenny, what a fine, big buck you've got!" "Yes, he's a dandy, all right," I agreed. "Well, you said you wanted horns on the ground, John!" He just smiled and said, "I surely did!"

Since I had entered that contest in Salem, I went over when they had the trophy meet. A couple kids had killed a spindly, Mule Deer in the cinder area, close to Sisters, Oregon, and had entered it in the contest. This area in Sisters is where the Mule Deer and Black-Tail sort of meet. These kids entered their deer as being a Black-Tail, but I knew it wasn't and told the judges that it was not a Black-Tail, but a Mule Deer. The first prize was a brand new Ruger and I told the biologist, "You know very well that deer is not a Black-Tail." "Well, the other fellows kinda thought it was, so we'll let it go that way!" was his comment. That really wasn't fair as my horns were far superior of all the Black-Tails, so I was cheated out of that! It wasn't that I wanted to beat the kids out of a prize, but when rules and guidelines are published and then they don't follow proper guidelines, what values are being taught?

OLD DOE IN LONG BELL

One week-end, John Breeden went hunting with Myron and Russell up in the Long Bell country. John, being a great cut-up, never wasted an opportunity to have some fun and we loved his antics! There were two old men sitting on a big rock right at the top of the mountain when the fellows got up there. John and the boys acknowledged them and just then, off to the left, a forked-horn buck showed up, so Russ shot it. Russ went up to get the deer and shouted out, "Old Doe, John!" He grabbed that deer and headed down through the brush and those two, old men got off that rock and tore after Russ! The old men never caught Russ, but John, Myron, and Russ laughed themselves silly because we had a habit of saying, "Old Doe," even if it was the biggest buck we'd ever killed! These other fellows thought they'd catch the guys and turn them in!

Jack Shaw had been John's partner for awhile and one time he, my brother, Ron, and one of my boys were hunting up Mill Creek with me. There were a couple of fellows we didn't know up there hunting and they could see down where we were. There was a big rock outcropping about a half mile away and one of our group said, "Let's shoot at those rocks and see how our guns carry up!" Ronnie had a 30-30 rifle and had made a stock out of yew wood on the forearm. He had done a beautiful job! He said, "Well, I'll probably have to hold down about ten feet with this new stock because my gun will probably shoot about fifteen feet too high!" Each one of us fired our rifle and those fellows jumped! John just shouted, "Down below you!" They called out, "What?" "Down below you," John answered, and those guys took off! It was really funny because John never said there was a deer, or anything, just shouted, "Down below you!" What a character! He was a lot of fun and we killed a lot of meat together!

INTRODUCING AND INITIATING

FRANCES IN NORTH COUNTRY

Frances and I had decided to take a trip to Vanderhoof, British Columbia, to visit my Brother, Ron and his wife, Barb. They had moved to Canada in 1959 and we wanted to go visit them and also go back to the Injenika country. We arrived at Vanderhoof and soon learned that Barb was unable to go with us to Injenika, but Ron would go. We drove our Dodge pickup to Germanson Lake and decided to fish and spend the night there. The fish weren't biting very well, but Frances caught one. Then we went into Injenika and was able to see country we had heard quite a bit about. After spending some time there, we went back to Vanderhoof to Ron's. We stayed a couple days longer to do some visiting, and then headed south again.

My friend, Ralph Schoof, had hunted out of Clinton with some Indian guides named

---

Grinders. He knew we were going North, so asked if we'd stop at Clinton and talk to Isadore and Phillip Grinder. We drove out to where the Grinders' lived, which is right at the foot of the Marble Range, and is very beautiful country. About two and a half miles before we got to Grinders, I noticed a sign on a gate which said, "For Sale." There was a log house, some outbuildings and a fellow out in the garden with his family. We stopped and I introduced myself and he told us his name was Jerry Salmon and he confirmed that his place was for sale. Somehow I could not get this little place out of my mind and just kept thinking about it! (Matter of fact, we did end up purchasing this place and this is where we lived for fourteen years!)

In about 1962, John Rogers, Uel Lambert, Bill Brandt and I went elk hunting in Eastern Oregon. Bill was one of the fellows I worked for when I was a kid, so I basically had known him all my life. His parents were originally from Germany and when I'd walk to school in Sheridan, I always passed their place and knew their family quite well. So here's Bill, later in life, and he's going with us elk hunting. It had been many, many years since I'd been around him, most likely at least twenty-five years! He got to telling yarns and said, "You know, when I went to school, my folks spoke German at home and of course, I spoke broken English. I'd go to school and the kids would call me 'Heinicker.' I volunteered in the U.S. Armed Forces when I was a kid and the first duty assigned me was in Germany, guarding German prisoners! Everyday I would walk by these boys and understood every word they said, as they spoke the same German dialect my folks did. One day I heard one of the German boys say to his buddies, 'You know that American fellow doesn't look like he's such a vicious monster, he looks like a nice, friendly fellow'. I heard them discussing this subject at length and am willing to admit I violated Army regulations by speaking to them in German! By this time, I was thinking that some of these boys might be my cousins and so I asked, 'What town are you boys from?' Some of them were from the same town my folks came from! They knew my uncles, aunts, and cousins, but none of them were actually my cousins! I asked them, 'What did they tell you boys?' The German fellows said their superiors told them that the Americans and Frenchmen were invading their country, violating the women, cutting people open, severing tongues, and all manner of evil acts. The stories told to the Germans were basically the same ones which the American government told their soldiers!" Bill looked at me and said, "You know, Kenny, it darn near took all the fight out of me!" I said, "Yes, Bill, the wars just don't make any sense!"

DOG PADDLING

One evening I had just returned from British Columbia and hadn't even gotten my clothes changed yet. Russ was teaching school in Sheridan and he used to do a lot of fishing. One of his favorite fishing holes was just above the end of our property line up Mill Creek, close to where Red's cabin used to be. Russ was fly fishing, had his hip boots on and was out in the water about three feet deep. Our little dog, Tony, went with him and waited patiently on the bank! Russ heard him growl, then he kept on, and Tony suddenly swam out to Russ! Russ looked around and here was a cougar also wading out to meet Russ! He hit at the cougar with his fishing pole and chased him back. That cougar went up a tree and the little dog was just barking for all he was worth! Russ tied his sweatshirt around the tree and quickly went down to the house with his hip boots flapping in the breeze like you wouldn't believe! He came into the house and said, "Come quick, Dad! I've got a big cougar up the tree!" I said, "Hey, this is no time to be fooling!" "Well, I'm not fooling!" he assured me, so we each grabbed a gun and went to find the cougar.

Tony was no longer barking treed and we could not find that cougar, even though we looked and looked! We went back to the house, called Bob Patty, and asked him if he could bring his Red Bone hounds to hunt the cougar. Bob arrived with the hounds and as we all walked, our little dog was once again barking treed! Russ and I spotted the creature, both took aim and killed that cougar. He came hurdling out of the tree, as we had both hit him in the left shoulder. He was a beautiful creature, a great big Tom. Down to the house we went with our trophy and hung him in a walnut tree out behind our house.

1963 - Russ was teaching school in Sheridan, and came out one afternoon to fish. He heard our dog growling and he swam out to Russ. When Russ looked, he saw this cougar, also wading out to meet him. He chased him out of the water, then the dog treed him. We eventually called Bob Patty to come with his hounds to trail the cougar. This cat had killed a baby calf and chewed through the hamstrings on our fine Hereford cows.

The next morning a Game Warden drove up, and also a neighbor, John Rogers. They asked, "Where did you get the cougar?" Russ said, "Up the creek about a mile from the house here." They laughed and said they wanted to go up and see where it all happened. John went up with Russell and unbeknownst to us, about fifteen feet from where he stood the evening before, one of our big Hereford's had been in labor giving birth to her third calf and this cougar had acted like the midwife, according to John. The cougar had pulled the calf out, and in doing so, cut the tendon in the cow's hind leg, ate part of the calf, and then partially covered the calf with some leaves. There were lots of scrub oaks, some fir windfalls, and Oregon Grape root, which helped to hide that cow quite well. She must have been so frightened, she did not raise up. Unfortunately, when we found her, we had to shoot her! I was sad to have to dispose of such a nice Hereford!

The twin boys hadn't been around home for a long time, as they had gone off to college, but were home for a brief stay. They heard our little dog baying out at the barn, so each grabbed a rifle and went out to investigate. This little dog had found an old cougar, which bolted across the creek, with our dog following in hot pursuit! Of course, the cougar ran up a tree! Back at the house, I was out on the front porch and since sound carries so well, I thought I heard Myron say, "Hey, it's a coon!" Just then I heard a volley of shots! Myron was standing on a little rock ledge and was so close to the animal, he could almost have tied a knot in the cougar's tail! The boys came running through the creek bearing this trophy, as excited as could be! I said, "I heard Myron say you had a coon over there!" Byron said, "Does this look like a coon to you?" We all had a good laugh out of that! The "Last Supper" for that cougar had been a skunk and he didn't smell all that wonderful! The important thing to note is that the cougar was right out at our barn - that's how brave he was!

In 1972, we were working in some real big timber and up above the shovel, there was a huge tree with the initials, L.P. carved in the bark. Rex Pemberton and some of the Willamette officials came up to the woods one day and I told them, "There's an enormous tree up there!" They said, "Leave it stand!" I said, "No, it isn't going to stand; it'll be down by spring." So they said for me to go ahead and cut it. Clarence Bowman, Bob Patty and Floyd Zetterberg were cutting for me at the time. Clarence started to fall this big tree and immediately it seized his saw as he was cutting the face in. He went down to get one of my bigger saws to cut his saw out and Floyd went over to help him. This tree was rotten on the stump and had quite a drag, so I made a nice bed for it. Finally, they got an undercut in it, and down it went! That tree was twelve feet on the stump. We had to "long-butt" it because of the rot. Out of that tree, we were able to get three, number one peelers and a big sawmill log! That's a lot of timber out of one tree. In that area, we were fortunate to have quite a bit of big timber and it was so nice to work in it!

Clarence went to fall a tree one day, and when he looked up, a big, dead limb was coming right towards him! He jumped to one side, just as the limb landed right where he had been standing. When he jumped, he broke a blood vessel in his leg and went in to have surgery. A couple fellows from the state came out to investigate so Clarence would be covered by State Industrial Accident Insurance. One of them was rather arrogant and smarted off, saying, "God help you, Kenny, if we ever catch one of your cutters working without those ear plugs in his ears!" I said, "Listen, Jack, Clarence told me if he'd had ear plugs in his ears, he'd be a dead man! What do you think about that?" He didn't answer me because he knew what I said was true! Clarence just happened to hear the crack of that limb as it came hurtling towards him! Had he been wearing ear plugs, he'd never been able to hear the limb because he heard it BEFORE he saw it coming! Of course, they always have the last word because they have the best ideas, you know! Generally speaking, as they sit in an office, they don't get an accurate concept of what goes on in the real world!

FLOAT PLANES AND FEAR

In 1974, I booked a hunt with Clarence Simmons in British Columbia. He had acquired an area up by Jarvis Lakes, up the McGregor River Canyon, where two lakes were connected together. I met Clarence in Prince George, we went to the Game Department there and I bought a bunch of tags. "Are there sheep up there?" I asked Clarence. "Oh, yes, there's sheep up there," he assured me. "Have you seen them?" I asked, and his answer was, "Well, no, but I heard rocks fall," so I bought a goat tag, a sheep tag, and the works! We flew up the river canyon with two other hunters, father and son, Clair and Paul Morton, from Yakima, Washington. Clair had done extensive hunting all over the world, including Africa and North America. Paul had been in the U.S. Air Force and they were really nice guys. We flew in on a big Beaver plane, with a big stash of groceries and various supplies. This pilot was purportedly one of the best in British Columbia, and I believe he was. He flew East, towards Alberta, for this lake was in the heart of the Rockies, right close to the Alberta border. As he turned to land on the lake, we were facing right into the sun, which was a huge ball of fire! He made a beautiful landing in the water and continued to taxi, when all of a sudden, the plane tipped up and nearly tipped over in the water. He hadn't been in there for several weeks and in the meantime, the lake had gone down and there was a large rock outcropping which ran along the top of the water. With the sun shining brightly in his eyes, this rocky ledge was hardly visible, and that's what he hit. It shook all of us up something tremendous!

Everything came to a grinding halt and the one outrigger was stuck on the rocks. We all got out and stood on the other side of the plane, getting some oars and other things to pry with, to try and get the plane loose. No dice; it just wouldn't come loose. There were some guides on the shore, so they came out in rowboats and took some supplies off the plane. Soon they came back again and took us in. That pilot stayed right there and kept trying and when nothing else worked, he got in that plane, "flapped his wings", did everything except sprout wings himself, and finally got the plane loose! That was quite a feat and we all were very happy that he succeeded!

Next morning we began hunting and the lad assigned to guide me was Bob Hopkins, from Rossland. He was a six-footer, slender and he sported a very fancy mustache, for a kid! He had never hunted anything in his life, except for a place to try and get away from work! Bob told me he hadn't hunted wild women, they just seemed to gravitate around him! No doubt, that was because of his mustache. There was another lad from Alberta, of Indian descent, with a rather strange name, who also served as a guide.

At the camp, was a fellow named Herb Barnes, along with his wife, Karen, who had trailed horses in from Alberta because they could not get horses up the McGregor River Canyon. There were some nice buildings there, except the fellow who built it forgot to reinforce the main auditorium and it had caved in, due to a big snowfall. Some of the supplies were in tins and many were broken open, rusty, and deteriorating, with jam, and various items oozing out, having been exposed to the elements. The tent assigned to me for sleeping had been torn all to pieces by a big grizzly. For opening description of a camp, not much was looking very positive at this point! Prior to my arrival, when this grizzly went into the tent which was going to be my sleeping quarters, Clarence's son, Ted, and a hunter had been sleeping in it! Ted fired a 300 Winchester Mag up through the tent a time or two and scared the bear off.

Hopkins and I rowed across the lake the next morning and then started up a steep hillside to begin our hunt. We went a little ways and soon he said, "Hold it! It's time for a smoke!" This ritual continued throughout the day and whenever he got tired, it was time for a smoke. We didn't see any game the first day!

The following day we went right into the goat craigs and saw tracks where a big, old Billy had come down across a rocky ledge, and then evidently crossed the lake. That was fortunate for Paul Morton because he killed this big, old goat on the other side and also got a small caribou. The third day out, we went into a big basin. To my left, I could see Mt. Alexander, which is on the map, and to my right, Mt. Ida, which is also on the map. Mt. Ida is 10,400 feet high and a beautiful mountain. A picture I took shows the reflection of the mountain in the lake, and it is nearly impossible to tell which side of that picture is top or bottom! It is an incredible picture and the reflection is so perfectly captured in that picture! In this huge amphitheater was a small herd of caribou. As I observed them with my binoculars, I saw a small, bull caribou, two cows, and two calves and I told Hopkins, "I see some game." Before I knew what was happening, he jerked at my binoculars until he nearly broke my neck trying to get a look at them!

There was a long "sliver" of snow, about a thousand feet long and looking through the binoculars, it is hard to describe the wonder and grandeur of this country! It is so huge! The caribou were probably at least one-half to three quarters of a mile off and we were on a little vantage point above them. I told Bob, "You go up around those caribou, spook them, and they'll come back through here, because it is impossible for them to get out without going through this 'saddle' where we are." Just before he started out, the caribou suddenly ran right towards us, just as hard as they could go and planked themselves down in the snowy area. At the time, I didn't know what they were doing and neither did Hopkins, but learned later on. There is a certain fly which gets up into their noses, lays eggs and as they hatch out, can eventually drive the caribou to commit suicide. Hunters have seen them go over bluffs because of the agony from these flies. When they lay down in the snow, the flies would leave. Hopkins started out and luck was with me, as the caribou started to come right towards me. I killed the bull and after he was laying on the ground, Bob went up to it and shot at it. I asked him, "What are you doing?" "Oh, just sort of trying my gun out," he said. Lucky he didn't hit it!

Herb was quite a yarner and he knew there was virtually no game in the area, just wolves and bear, mainly. Karen said that one day she and Herb were in the camp when Frank Pruckel, an Outfitter from around Chetwynd Country, rode in and said, "There's no game left. I have four or five of the best Indian guides in the country out hunting with my hunters. There are just small bands of caribou, they're just really fractured and I don't know what to think about it!" Right in that vicinity was the dividing line between Clarence Simmons and Frank Pruckel's hunting areas. Herb was a chronic smoker and every night he'd start rolling his brown paper cigarettes, coughing, and telling his big yarns! The next morning I got ready to go pack my bull in and took my good packboard along. Hopkins and Herb wanted to go along, although Herb had nothing to pack with. He did, however, have a huge cowboy hat and a mouth to match it! His favorite subject was about fighting and he bragged that he feared no man! If they were bigger than he was, he'd just get a bicycle chain, or something, and just cut them down to size! We started out across this tundra, going uphill at a considerable pitch, with me in the lead. He yelled out, "Hey, you crazy old so and so up there, stop! It's time for a smoke!" That suited Hopkins just fine. I don't know how many times we stopped going up there (with nothing heavy to carry), but finally we made it to where my bull was. The caribou was a good-sized animal, despite the fact that his horns weren't all that big. Hopkins and I divided the meat up, putting it on our pack boards and we gave Herb the hide. We started back by the lake, but every once in awhile, Herb would scream and cuss at us to stop and let him have a smoke. This happened so frequently, I didn't think we'd ever get back to camp that day! Much, much later we got the meat and hide to camp.

At night, Herb would begin telling his tales and Karen would admonish him to keep his blankety-blank, big mouth shut, but he rarely paid any attention to her! One evening, Karen asked, "Who's for a game of cards tonight? How about you, Kenny?" I said, "No, I never learned to play cards!" She made the rounds and finally, said to Clair Morton, "How about you, Mr. Morton?" He said, "Tomorrow night!" Karen wasn't very happy, but she had to wait! "Tomorrow night" arrived and they began playing cards, but before long, Karen got upset and asked, "Did you ever lose?" Clair said, "No!" That's all he said in response. Many years later, when we were living up in Caribou land, a fellow drove into our yard, greeted me and told me he was from Yakima, Washington. "Is there an old Indian fellow named Isadore Grinder still living up in this area?" he asked. "Yes, do you know him?" I asked. "Twenty some years ago, I hunted with him," the fellow informed me. I thought I'd have some fun, so I remarked, "Since you're from Yakima, I need to let you know I'm quite well acquainted with Yakima! I know two people!" "Oh, who do you know?" he questioned. "Clair and Paul Morton are the fellows I know." "Oh, so you know the Big Gambler, do you?" he asked. I said, "I don't know!" "You don't," he asked with more than a little astonishment! "He's a World Champion card player! He can't gamble in Reno, they won't allow him to," he explained. Later on I found out this was absolutely true! No wonder Karen got upset - he just cleaned her clock every time!

The day we were to depart, it began to storm and we were socked in for two days. On the night of the second day of waiting, we finished eating supper and the usual bull session was beginning, with Herb, the great spinner of yarns! Paul said, "Hold it! I think I hear the motor of an airplane!" We all jumped up to look and sure enough, here came a plane in the midst of these terribly stormy conditions. The wind was blowing, it was dark, but the plane taxied in, and as it did so, Paul and Clair grabbed their duffel bags, with belongings and meat all packed and ready to go! As they went to the plane, the pilot said to them, "Tell that other guy there's another plane coming," and as suddenly as it came, the plane took off again, with two passengers aboard!

In about ten minutes, here came another little "gypo" plane and the pilot alone was enough to give me chill blains! He has a strange style mustache and a straight-up forehead! It looked as if there wasn't a recess left for an honorable amount of brains! To add to this strange appearance, he had a crew cut and was truly an odd-looking character! I put my caribou in and then got in with more than a modest amount of hesitation, and off we went! We were flying West, into the wind, towards Prince George. As we lifted off the lake, it seemed that the plane would surely hit trees, but finally we were above the trees and on our way. He immediately put a light on over my head to illuminate a little map he had. That McGregor River Canyon is so narrow, yet he constantly looked at this map and it made me very nervous. Generally speaking, after the first of October, no plane would even venture into this area because of the narrow canyon and dangerous conditions! We nearly ran into a rock bluff before he jerked the controls and finally maneuvered the plane to the other side. I was ready to tell him to let me fly the plane so he could look at the map! Eventually we made it and landed at the Sea Plane Landing Base on the East side of Prince George. That was my memorable hunt with Clarence Simmons.

As I got myself and belongings out of the plane, I immediately saw Paul and Clair there, so asked Paul, "Say, was that a rough ride out of that camp?" "You better believe it! They don't get any rougher than that," he replied. That made me feel a little better because by the time we got to Prince George, I was kinda of a Nervous Nellie, I'll admit! They helped me put my gear in my pickup and as I tried to open the door, I remembered I had locked my pickup and put the key underneath on the channel iron. The people there had told me that theft was a big problem in this area and to hide my key really well. I looked and looked for that key and could not find it! Of course, I knew that inside the truck, I had a spare key. Paul said, "Look, if we can get a coat hanger, I believe we can get that door open for you!" We did get a coat hanger and that fellow actually managed to get the door open for me without breaking a window! My pickup was a brand new 1974 Dodge and I had just bought it! I was so grateful to Paul for getting it open, because I didn't want to break a window and have to drive all the way to Oregon with cold wind whistling through!

Back home, at the shop one Saturday, I was telling Davie about that key. He said, "Where do you think you put it?" "I know exactly where I put it," I said rather indignantly! Bear in mind, Paul, Clair and myself had all checked in the spot where I knew I had put it! Davie said, "Well, I'll go look!" He got down under the pickup and looked and here that miserable key was - exactly where I put it! How that key stayed on that channel iron for over a thousand miles from Prince George to Oregon, and then back up into the woods logging, I will never understand! Those experiences logged into my memory bank and accounted for my fourth hunting trip into British Columbia. I just never realized the world was so big until I began going North. The love of the country got into my blood and I could not restrain myself from hunting up there!

GARRARD FROM GOLD BRIDGE

In 1976, I booked a Canadian hunt with Pat Garrard, of Gold Bridge, B.C. After I had done this, I discovered that a friend of mine, Bill Dugger, of McMinnville, had also booked a hunt with him, so Bill and I drove up at the same time. Bill had a travel trailer, and took his wife, Dolly, and son, Bill, along. Pat had two Indian fellows from Shalalth Village working for him. At this village, a huge tunnel goes through the mountains and carries water out of Carpenter Lake, through the pipeline in the mountains, and into generators to produce electricity. Upon arrival, we were introduced to the two Indian fellows, Freddie Shields and Albert Joseph, who were to be our guides. We found these fellows easy to get along with, and nice to be around. We saddled up and packed into Spruce Lake, which was about thirty miles from Pat's place, riding over some very rough terrain. During this journey, we crossed several mountain ranges and along the way, we met two hippies! One was a tall, wild-eyed fellow who looked as if he'd never had anything to eat in his life. This lad had hair and whiskers so long we figured he never could get anything in his mouth to eat! The girl-friend looked somewhat the same, and along with them, they had a big, German Police dog. We talked to them a bit and they told us they had been staying in the cabin for two or three weeks. They went on their way and we continued until finally, we arrived at the cabin, which was owned by Empire Valley Cattle Company. As we entered this cabin, the mice just ran everywhere! Pat was an old English fellow and he said to me, "Will you please take care of the coffee pot?" I went over to the stove and there sat a huge, granite coffee pot which was large enough to hold at least fourteen cups of coffee. Upon removing the lid, I saw that the grounds on the inside were <u>within</u> <u>an</u> <u>inch</u> from the top! The topper to all this was a gray scum, which covered all the contents! I took it outside, emptied out the mountain of grounds, thoroughly scrubbed and cleaned it out and decided to boil it with clear water to get all the microbes out! No doubt that thing had never been cleaned so thoroughly, prior to my arrival, nor since!

We got supper and afterwards, Pat began whittling on some pieces of wood there, so after watching him a bit, Bill asked him, "What are you doing, Pat?" His response was a question, "You don't know? I'm making a Wilderness Mouse Trap!" "What's that?" Bill asked. "You'll see," Pat answered, as he fashioned a little square, drove two little nails into the end of the wood and added a piece so it would trip. This contraption fitted on the side of a pail and the pail was then filled with soapy water. Honey and another substance was applied to the wood piece to entice the mice to get onto this platform and little treadle. What an ingenious device! The little creatures ventured up on that platform, onto the treadle, and down they went into the water! Next morning, that bucket had around forty mice in it! The water was one gray mass and it was impossible for anything not to commit suicide in it because they'd never hit the water, just other gray bodies! That was our first experience with a Wilderness Mouse Trap!

Pat then took us on back to Tyax Creek where he had his main camp. The mainstay of this camp was a crude, but strong building, designed to be able to withstand grizzlies from breaking in. He kept salt, horse shoes, horse supplies, and other items there for his animals. Basically there was not a corral for the horses, so he just hobbled them and let them run at night. We pitched our tents there and were "in business"! Next morning we started hunting in this huge country and Pat said to Albert, "Why don't you take Kenny and go up the mountain about three miles. Then you turn to the right, take the trail there and that goes up over that bluff! Go and see what you can find!"

Albert and I started up on that mountain, which was very rugged and the trail was basically non-existent! Once in awhile we would see a blaze on a tree, but generally it was barely visible and nearly healed over. We went up to the top and decided to have our lunch. It was snowing as we built up a dinner fire. We had seen some sheep tracks and decided some must be watching us. After eating, we broke on over to the West, and went down through a slide area where the trees were leaning at such an odd manner, they were just barely anchored in soil. We rode through an area, much like a muskeg, and as we walked, the water made sort of a popping sound. I have never heard anything like it and it was a nightmare to go through! We saw where someone had just driven a Hereford bull down ahead of us and when we got down, here was a very big corral, all fenced, with horses tied up and saddled, and a little cabin in the center. Albert said, "Oh, oh! Gang Ranch cowboys! Probably all-Indian like I am; then I go talk to them." I said, "Don't bother them, Albert! It's a shame - they're eating T-Bone steaks an inch thick!" He said, "No, maybe a little, old doe, maybe rice and beans, I betcha!"

This camp was called Graveyard Valley, I was told, and was sort of an outpost of the Gang Ranch. From there to the Gang Ranch, it was about seventy-five miles, with nothing but saddle horse trails to travel on. Albert went on past and didn't stop, so we continued up a little hill, still headed West, and suddenly, the water was running toward the ocean. By this time, it was after 3:00 in the afternoon and during this trek, Mother Nature had been spitting out very fine snow, so I asked, "Albert, where are you going?" He said, "I don't know! I thought Pat said there was a saddle here, and we could go back through that to get to camp, but I don't see a saddle! We have to go back the way we came!" I said, "Oh, no, we'll never make it!" We started back up the mountain, reached the Gang Ranch outpost and suddenly, it cut loose! The wind rose to a fury, pelting down sleet in the horses' ears and eyes, so that they could not go at a certain angle! I couldn't even see the saddle horn on my saddle and by now it is close to 4:30 in the afternoon. Those faithful horses kept at it! They'd head into the storm, cut back, and go back and forth, forging ahead. They were so smart, they went to the spot where we had made our dinner fire! As we went along, Albert would call out, "Where are you?" I would answer, "I'm over here, where are you?" Finally, it had gotten so bad, that Albert's horse refused to go and he said, "I don't know what to do," and I said, "I don't either!" My horse acted as if it wanted to go, so I spoke to him, and he took the lead, so he's the one who led us to where we had our lunch. We went on past, kept going and finally got into camp at 10:30 P.M. Pat was sick with worry, as were the rest of them! They figured we'd either killed the entire mountain off, or something terrible had happened to us. When I got out of that saddle, I fell over, felt very strange, and could not stand up! I said, "Pat, I'm falling!" He said, "I know what's wrong with you!

You have upset your equilibrium just like pilots do sometimes when they fly their plane upside down!" It took me about a month to completely get over that feeling. I had strained so hard to see that saddle horn, or the horses' head, and yet I could see nothing, but it really affected my balance! That was a gruesome journey!

We went out again the next day and Pat was with me, up above Lorna Lake. Pat asked, "Do you see those tracks down there?" and I said that I did, for they were still quite evident. He said, "Well, a pilot flew in here one day and didn't make it! He went down and was killed, so I helped some fellows from the Gang Ranch bring a cat in and get the plane out." Just then we spotted three rams across the canyon, along a little creek which ran out of Lorna Lake. Pat had a good spotting scope, so we lay there for a very long time, just watching them. "Now we can make our move because the rams have separated," he commented. In fact, they were about a thousand feet apart, bedded down, looking into the wind! So we crossed over, tied the horses way back out of sight, and walked for about a mile. Pat leaned up against a big rock there, as if to rest for a moment, when instantly, we saw these three rams! They had come together, and were just preparing to head into the storm, so I took aim and killed one of the rams! Later, when I got down to the Game Warden to check out, he asked, "Who told you to shoot that ram?" I said, "Pat did!" The Warden, Clarence McIver, said, "You aren't kidding, are you?" "No, I'm not," I reassured him! Then Clarence told me he had just spent two weeks with Pat looking the country over. They took a pack train, went back in the mountains and camped out. He told me, "The only thing we saw was one, scrawny, little forked-horn deer, but there just wasn't any game there!" Well Pat and I didn't see much more than that, however, just the three rams, one of which I had gotten. He told me that my ram really wasn't legal and he didn't know what to do about it! I said to him, "You call Pat up and talk to him and he'll tell you that he told me to shoot it!" Finally, he gave in and let me go!

A day after I killed my first ram, Pat was getting ready to cape him out and had a knife made out of a planer bit. He made a pass or two and I asked, "Would you like to have a sharp knife, Pat?" "Yes, I would," he said. So I handed him my case knife, which was made in the days before stainless steel had been invented. He made a couple passes with my very sharp knife and asked, "Will you please sharpen my knife?" I said, "I'm sorry, Pat, I can't!" So everyone there wanted me to work on their knives!

Pat had told me he had permission to kill a buck for camp meat and we spotted two bucks, way off in the distance. They were so far away, in fact, that even with the spotting scope, we couldn't tell exactly what size they were! Albert, Pat, and I went up after them, while Freddie and Bill were hunting elsewhere. Once up there, we discovered two bucks, evidently twins; one a three-point and the other a four-point, bedded down among the rocks! I killed both deer and we packed them to camp! Freddie and I went hunting a couple days later, and he had begun calling me "Chief", for some reason. After hunting awhile, we headed back to camp and were fairly close, when Freddie said, "Hey, Chief, I wish you'd take that overcoat off that three-point buck (the one we had gotten a couple days earlier) and I'll put on a good steak feed tonight!" So I did that, knowing Freddie was a good cook. Shortly afterwards, Pat rode in with Albert and Bill. They were still a good ways off when Pat called out, "Who's the devil with the sharp knife?" They rode on in and Pat asked me, "What did you skin that deer for?" "Well, I had orders from the Head Cook, and nobody defies the Head Cook, so I skinned it," I explained. He said, "Well, you just ruined a fine piece of meat," and I could tell he was very angry about it! I don't know what the problem was, but we did NOT have a steak dinner that night!

One evening the "grub" wasn't all that good - there was plenty of it, but just not much variety. The potatoes were nearly always cold and Pat would make the rounds, offering the lone potato to everyone. Then after everyone turned it down, he'd always say, "Albert, you'll have to eat it!" Albert always replied in the same, monotone voice, "Might as well" and he would eat the potato! One evening I told a crazy little story I had heard about a stockbroker from Chicago who grew tired of the fast life, so he decided to quit, go out in the country, buy a little homestead and let the world go by. This sophisticated fellow drove down into the Ozarks, finally found a "For Sale" sign, went up to this old shack and knocked on the door. An old gentleman came to the door and the stockbroker asked, "Is your place for sale?" "Yes, I reckon it is," he answered. "Do you raise good cabbage, carrots, corn, and potatoes?" "Yes," the old man answered. "Oh, and do you also raise good onions," the Chicagoian asked. The old man didn't hesitate, but answered, "No!" So the stockbroker thought that the old man didn't hear him correctly, and he asked him the second time, "Do you raise good onions?" The old man again answered, "No!" "Well, I don't want to buy a place where you can't raise onions, because I really like onions. Thank you very much," the city guy said and he left. The story goes that after this stockbroker left, the old man turned to his wife and said, "Ma, do you reckon he might have meant 'eng-erns'?" That was the hillbilly term there for onions! Albert just cracked up after I told this story! He thought that was the funniest joke he had ever heard and every night thereafter, he'd bring up the subject of the eng-erns and he'd ask, "How you say him?" and I would tell him, "eng-erns!"

Albert and I were up on the mountain another day, with howling wind, and just terrible weather, so we decided to build a dinner fire. As we worked at this task, Albert said, "I feel something looking at me!" I sort of smiled to myself and asked, "You do?" He answered, "Yes, I do! I feel something looking at me!" We turned to look down the canyon, and here was a huge buck down there with strange horns; very big and tall, but not branched out very much. He said, "Better I shoot that for the Woman and the kids." He hesitated and said, "Well, maybe Pat won't like it!" We went back to our campfire and once again he asked, "How you say him?" I'd always tell him, "eng-erns", and he would get so amused!

Over a nice fire and lunch the next day, Albert said, "I come to work for Pat in July. Pat is good man to work for. I got all my money coming (and it is now September), so I have plenty of money to buy clothes for my Woman and kids, and grub to feed them for winter." I said, "Well, that's great, Albert. That's very good!" Next day I was out with Pat and I said, "Pat, you have two fine Indian helpers here!" He said, "Yes, they sure are, but it's too bad about Albert." "Oh, what's too bad about Albert?" I asked. "You don't know?" Pat asked. "Well, I'll tell you! About a month ago he went to Lillooet to the Reynolds Hotel, rented a fine room, and next morning the store keeper called me. He said Albert Joseph was there and wanted $50 from him. He asked me if he should give it to him and I told him to go ahead, as Albert had wages coming from me for guiding. This went along for quite a few days, although I never kept very good track. A few days later, again the phone rings and the hotel manager asked, but I told him, "No, you'd better just give him $35 until I catch up on my bookkeeping. In the background, I heard Albert's voice saying, 'No, it has to be $50'!" So Pat had given me the REAL story and yet, poor Albert was telling me how much money he had coming to him. Obviously, he wasn't aware he didn't have any money coming, except perhaps for a couple weeks' worth of guiding. So many people up North just don't know how to manage their money and don't handle booze any better! It made me feel very badly for Albert, nevertheless!

Our hunt came to an end soon after this and we headed home, having had a fairly good trip in spite of the fact there wasn't much game there! Bill did see a nice band of big rams and the following year, he went back there to hunt. The year before, when we hunted in that area, there were hardly any big bucks around at all. Pat felt sure they had been killed off while wintering down around the Lillooet area, and this upset him a great deal! Interestingly enough, the following year, Bill would see a trophy animal, but he had not bought a deer tag. By the term, "trophy", he meant that the horns were at least thirty inches wide and with some good height to it! So strange things can happen when you're dealing with big game and you can never be assured you will have success!

That was in 1976 and later when we moved to Canada, we bought a 1987 Ford Thunderbird at Dearborn Ford in Kamloops. We took the car in for servicing one day and a tall Indian lad dressed in very fine cowboy gear was there, accompanied by a woman. I began visiting with him, and asked him, "Are you one of the Charlie boys from the Red Stone Reserve?" He said, "No, I'm a Big Game Guide and my name is Albert." I had heard that Albert "changed women" and just then, I pounded him on the shoulder and asked, "Are you Albert Joseph?" He screamed out, "I can say eng-erns!" I said, "Albert, you can't be lying!" "No, I can say eng-erns," he told me with delight! All the time we hunted when I first met him, he couldn't remember exactly how to say it and now over ten years later, he could say it! His lady friend looked at him as if she thought he had gone nuts!

INCRIMINATING CRIMINALS

Meanwhile, back in Mill Creek, after all the cattle had been sold, I was out cleaning the barn, accompanied by Rollie. It was during fire season and we always started to work early in the woods. It was about 5:30 in the evening, no logging was being done in Mill Creek at the time and it was quiet. There really wasn't supposed to be anyone up the creek, but Rollie and I heard a vehicle. We looked out and saw an old, Nash Rambler, sort of a station wagon, with curtains inside. These curtains went up right behind the driver, but I noticed a couple fellows in the car. I said to Rollie, "There goes the most evil man I've ever seen in my life, I believe!" I didn't know quite why I said that, but he was just such a fierce looking fellow! We finished our work and I went back to the house to have supper. For some reason, I couldn't quit thinking about these guys, so after supper, I got a rifle, and drove clear up to Cedar Creek to look around. I didn't see anybody, so decided to take a run up Tillison Creek. I started up Tillison, but decided to take off on a fork in the road, went around the bend, and here sits a nice Pontiac with the wheels off, the hood was open, and the transmission was out. There were cigarette butts laying all over the ground and since it was fire season, it's a wonder they hadn't started a forest fire! I could see this car was being worked over, so I went back home and called the Polk County Sheriff.

The sheriff came out, stopped by the house to get me, and we went up the creek so I could direct him to where I had seen this car. After we got up there, the sheriff got right on his phone, saying, "We've got a hot car up here," and gave a description of the Pontiac. Shortly thereafter, the word came back that it had been stolen in Salem on Sunday evening. They told him they'd send out some backup units and soon there were five cops on the scene! Some of them were smoking and throwing the butts on the ground! Back in those days, everybody wanted to be a Marlboro Man (before they discovered smoking was bad for you), so I said to them, "Fellows, where I work, we don't do that! You don't throw cigarettes on the ground!" They sort of looked at me as if that was a novel idea! They decided to put a stake out to see if they could catch these guys, but I said, "No, fellows, go on home! These renegades will come back to get the rest of it!" They said, "Oh, no, we'll put a stake out!"

About 4:30 the next morning, I headed off to work and here was a cop going down the road right in front of me! Those dummies phoned a wrecking outfit in Salem, had wheels brought out and towed that car back into Salem. That evening, at exactly the same time as the evening before, here goes an old Buick Special sedan with that same evil-looking man driving it, traveling up the road! Of course, the sheriff had the car removed and I was convinced they didn't want to catch that guy! That just about took the cake in trying to apprehend criminals!

MILL CREEK MEMORIES

Some time back, I asked the kids what their recollection of their home life was, and they thought it was really tops! They always had plenty to eat, if they didn't want to go hunting, they didn't have to, but if they wanted to go, that was fine, too! That was always a sport we enjoyed and living there at the end of the Mill Creek Road, there was plenty of opportunity. Also, we had a lot of things happen while living there, some were pleasant and some were not! People would get stuck, or have car trouble and would come to our house at all hours of the day or night to ask for help! Only once did anyone ever offer to pay! If they'd just say, "Thank You", that would have been good enough, however, some weren't even that considerate! As I came home from the woods one day, two motorcycles came roaring into our yard and one of the fellows said, "Come, quick! Our buddy is dying!" I had never seen these guys before and I guessed their ages to be around thirty-five years old. I said, "Well, what do you want me to do -

watch him die?" Again, they said, "Come, quick! He's up at the South Branch Bridge and he's dying!" So I drove up there in my pickup and a big, husky fellow lay on the ground, obviously in pain!" He was practically covered completely with tattoos, but I could tell that underneath them, he was hurting pretty badly, so we put him in my pickup. These guys had gone up Rickerall to the big rock pit, left their vehicle there, and started over the mountain with their motorcycles. Of course, they got to goofing off, and this guy came hurtling down on the handle bars! I asked him, "Where do you want to go?" He said, "Take me up to the rock pit!" He decided that if I'd drive him back to their vehicle at the gravel pit, his friends would meet us there and then drive their buddy into the doctor. I kid you not, when I drove into that rock pit, the other two guys had ridden over the mountain, and we met there at practically the same minute, as if by just mutual accord! There wasn't one minute difference in all of us arriving at that rock pit! They took their buddy off to Salem to the doctor.

About a year later, my wife and I were in a restaurant in Salem eating dinner and a guy came walking down the aisle. I recognized him and said, "Hold it, fellow! I need to talk to you!" He just sort of snarled at me and said, "I don't need to talk to you!" I said, "Oh, yes, you do! Aren't you the fellow I hauled up to the rock pit in Rickerall one time when you injured yourself in a motorcycle accident?" "Oh, yeah," he said. "Well, tell me what happened," I said. "Well, I ran a handle bar right close to the big muscle next to my heart and I almost died! I spent twenty-one days in the hospital!" He told me his name was Bud Barton and he worked for Salem Wheel. Just goes to show you what sometimes takes place out in the country and had I not driven him to their vehicles, who knows, he may not have made it! We had so many different things happen!

The sheriff drove up one night, walked up beside our house, outside our bedroom window and called out, "I am Tony Neufeld, the Sheriff out here, and we're expecting a lost hunter to come in, as he's supposed to be coming down South Branch." I got up and went out to talk to him. The lost hunter happened to be a fellow, Cloyce Grant, from the Ford Garage in Dallas. I asked the Sheriff, "What's he driving - a two-wheel or four-wheel drive vehicle?" They said, "A two-wheel drive vehicle." I said, "Well, he's not coming down South Branch because I happen to know that Cloyce isn't stupid!" "Oh, yes, he's coming down that way!" I said, "Oh, no, he isn't!" Sure enough, next morning they found him over on the Rickerall side. He just built a fire in the middle of the road so he could be easily spotted and his son found him there, so everything turned out just fine for him. Sometimes logic escapes the "experts" when it comes to the mountains!

A bunch of deputy sheriff's came up Mill Creek another time and set up a big antenna, loudspeaker, and all sorts of paraphernalia underneath our big fir trees. When I inquired as to what was going on, they told me a hunter was lost up at the head of Rowell Creek. I said, "Well, there isn't a doubt in my mind but what he will follow the creek down the hill and come out at Valley Junction! They said, "Oh, no, we have evidence to believe that he's coming down Mill Creek." They sat there all night long and nobody showed up! Come to find out, this fellow showed up at Valley Junction! Now I'm not implying that I'm always right, but sometimes if you follow common sense reasoning, it is pretty reliable!

Years later, when the logging companies were not actively working up Mill Creek and the gate was torn down, this made the area accessible to nearly anyone. Since it was now "open territory", many people from Salem began coming out there. There were all sorts of characters, with drug rings going and it's a sad commentary on what happens in society nowadays. Of course, the authorities can't be every place at one time and the judges turn them loose when these hoodlums are caught anyway, so it's a no-win situation!

FRIEND, HUNTING PARTNER,

AND EMPLOYEE

In 1908, on January 12, George and Anna Patty, of Amity, Oregon, welcomed a son, Robert, and what a fine son he truly was! He joined an older brother, Glen, and also a sister, Florence. Very early in life, Bob learned to do everything on the farm and he was admonished to do it just a little faster than anyone else! Talk about a competitive spirit, nobody, but nobody, had more spirit than Bob! Bill, Bob's first cousin, told me that Bob's Dad made it a point to always haul more gain per wagon than anyone else. If the wagons hauling grain into Amity generally carried eighty sacks of grain, Bob's Dad would instruct his sons, "Put on one hundred!" Thus it went! Bob tabled hay into his Dad's hay baler all alone, twelve hours every day. They averaged forty-five tons per day, including the mowing! When they farmed, they opened up the governor on their tractors to increase the speed. When plowing, if the ground was just right, Bob would plow all night and Glen would plow all day!

Bob told me that one time the county did not have money to gravel the county roads and someone had gondolas of river gravel, side-tracked in Amity. The farmers came, loaded the gravel onto their wagons and put it on the roads themselves. Bob took a contract to unload these gondolas and unloaded them with a big grain scoop for $3 per gondola. He knew exactly how many scoops to a gondola and had his system down to a science!

Another project in which Bob was very active, was helping lay the new water pipes at Depoe Bay, out at the Oregon coast, and he worked there throughout the entire project. The joints of pipe weighed three hundred pounds, and most husky fellows would quit around 10:00 A.M. because very few could endure the hardship for the entire day. Every man had to weigh at least 165 pounds and not a single one, except Bob, stayed with it! The pipe were picked up and carried for three miles until the final destination was reached. The entire three miles was up steep hill all the way, but this is where Bob was at his maximum. I was the first partner Bob fell timber with in really big timber. He was a superb axeman and when we would start to saw, I nearly always let him saw his side up first. He would let out a shout every time and say, "That's corner!" If another set of fallers were within sight, he would just put every ounce of energy he had within him, in order to assure we would be finished first and nearly always, we would be first, too!

Back in his high school days, he'd run to Amity High School every morning, a distance of three miles. After he graduated, he went to Linfield College, in nearby McMinnville, for three terms. He played baseball and football for coach, Byron Wolfe. Wolfe and his teams had an impressive record at Linfield and being an outstanding coach, Wolfe later went to Colorado State, I believe. One bit of wisdom Coach Wolfe imparted to his athletes was that he believed bacon and onions would cut down an athlete's wind, so all of his life, Bob never ate bacon or onions. Over the years, we ate hundreds of meals together; whether hunting, working, or just relaxing, and I never saw him eat those two things. He certainly didn't want anything to interfere with his performance, so little things like bacon and onions just weren't a temptation to him.

While Deb Glass and I were falling timber for Bill Harris on Salmon River, about 1932, when we went to work one Monday morning, there were three new workers. They were new to us, anyway. One fellow was Al Cook, the Head Filer of Polk Operating Log Company, which was the big Railroad Log Company out of Grande Ronde, and it had just shut down. The other two fellows were brothers, Jack and Owen Doran. As we were eating lunch the first day, Jack said, "I'm supposed to fight a wild Irishman of Amity, named Bob Patty, and I think I'm gonna be sick!" That was my first introduction to Bob Patty. Bob did a lot of boxing in the area and generally he was the winner! He was always in good shape and didn't eat bacon or onions! There were other items from which he abstained, including tobacco, drinking (not even beer), coffee or tea. He could, however, go farther and do more work on sugar than was believable! This was especially true of his brown fudge! Always on hunting trips, he would take a good stash of his famous fudge.

While elk hunting late one fall on the Umatilla River near the top end, and as we left to go down, the terrain sloped off very severely and you had no choice, but to descend very rapidly! On this particular morning, the four of us in our hunting party, got up long before the crack of dawn and our Commander-In-Chief, Bob, laid out the hunt for the day. He said, "Davie and I will go down Zubic Ridge and hunt along the breaks of the river. Kenny, you and Marvin go down Nine Mile Ridge and we will stir them bulls up a little!" We all proceeded to do just that! The four of us walked about two miles together, then Bob and Dave broke off to the left and hunted down towards the river; while Marvin and I went about one mile further down the main ridge. This big ridge just jutted out, so to speak, and on both sides of it, there was a fine canyon. Marvin suggested I go on past him to the next ridge, get on a stand, and he would drive through towards me. I agreed with him that was the thing to do, so I hurried on down the ridge and got on my stand. I could see Marvin way back there and waved for him to come my way. Just then I heard three shots down towards the river and could tell they were a long ways away. Shortly I heard Bob give the tight-line signal, which was 3 and 2. In logging lingo, this was a shout of "Whoop," "Whoop," "Whoop," short pause and followed by "Whoop," "Whoop." I heard Dave return the signal with two, "Ho-Ho's". Always this was our standard practice while hunting and we never shouted out, "I got one down, I got one down!" If you shouted, you never knew who might show up to claim your animal, so Bob came up with this clever idea for signaling.

Upon hearing "our signal", I knew that meant an elk was down.

Marvin is now in the canyon and hadn't gone seven or eight hundred feet when a bull just got up and was standing in his bed! Marv didn't hesitate to shoot him, and excitedly called out, "Hey, Kenny, I got one down!" Two times he called out to me, but I did not answer, as I heard sounds of approaching game. Suddenly, here came a nice, spike bull right at me! He paused just as he got out of the timber and I placed a bullet in his heart. In less than thirty minutes, we had three bulls down and it was a long ways back to camp. For three days we back-packed those three bulls to bring them into camp. Bob said, "Fellas, we almost got into trouble. We almost overshot our knives!" By way of explanation, he said that meant you had more animals than you could skin! Bob was the neatest butcher I ever saw - no hair on his meat! I recall he once said, "I always like to pick and clean my own geese; that way I never feel *down* at the mouth!"

After Bob retired and quit working in the woods, he began extensive trapping. No one can imagine the miles which that man walked, day after day! He became very proficient and was called upon many times to catch the wiley coyotes, for often they made their den close by a band of turkeys or sheep. Frequently, their toll on the animals was very great before Bob was called upon to take care of the problem. Nobody did a more masterful job of skinning and handling furs than Bob and he was awarded distinctive honors on more than one occasion. While still cutting timber, he also began acquiring Red Bone hounds and at one time, owned seventeen. He informed me that the more hounds one has, the bigger lie he is entitled to tell. Once his dear wife, Rosena, told us she had kept track of the pans of cornbread with pork cracklings, she had baked and it was enough dog food to fatten two hundred hogs! This was before the Perrydale Hotdog Feed became so popular!

Bob was such a great story teller and one time, a group of fellows were eating lunch in the woods. Bob began telling a story and one of the guys laughed until he nearly choked! They were talking about different occupations and one of them said he always wanted to be a doctor, another said what he had wanted to be, and then Bob spoke up, "Boy, I come so close to being a minister, you wouldn't believe how close I came to being a preacher!" Someone asked, "How's that, Bob?" "Well," he said, "that old Reverend used to drive in our yard and Mother always gave him a big chicken feed. Those chickens got so educated, that whenever he'd drive in, the roosters would squawk. My parents raised about fifty Rhode Island red roosters and when they were full-grown, they'd fly into the oak trees. Mother would say, 'All right, Bob, you know what you have to do; get with it!' I'd try and try to shoot those roosters down with a 22, but I didn't want to shoot them in the body. Finally, I'd get some down and I saw so many roosters enter the ministry, I thought I'd sure love to be a preacher! All I ever got to eat was wings, but I sure love chicken!" A more colorful character never existed! Many of the phrases, lingo and titles my family and I adopted were the results of Bob's never-ending, imaginative mind! He was not without his faults, but he was fair and great company. Regretfully, Bob passed away July 29, 1996 and we miss him dearly!

THE CALL OF CARIBOU COUNTRY

Please rest assured that moving to the Caribou Country was not without some very trying moments and also mixed with a certain amount of peril. It had long been a dream of mine to retire in the land of plenty, with fishing, hunting and vast country to explore. I had visited Canada on several different ventures and began to dream about living there. First off, I purchased the property which we were to call home for thirteen and a half years. To be eligible to purchase property, we had to secure papers to become landed immigrants. The rules stated that if you desired to become citizens of Canada, this was possible once residency had been established and we were in compliance with certain rules. For years I was belabored about almost constantly by the question of why did I move to Canada, and whatever possessed me to do so, and on and on.

While being interviewed by customs officials prior to entry into Canada, we were asked many, many questions by this official who could hardly speak English, believe it or not! After all, English is the primary language of Canada, with the exception of Quebec. This official was of uncertain lineage to me, which was of no concern to me, if only he could speak plainly so we could answer the questions in a forthright manner! The requirements seemed endless! You have to pass your physical, must prove you can support yourself and not go on government welfare, and in my case, I had to promise I would not enter the labor force for five years.

We made our first trip with household belongings in February of 1977, while it was still winter in Caribou land! The area we moved to is called the Chilcotin Caribou and we lived in the Caribou District, nineteen miles out from town. Clinton is about halfway between Vancouver and Prince George, along the beautiful Fraser River, which runs through a large portion of British Columbia. Many things took on different meaning for us in the North and undoubtedly, some of the modern conveniences and comforts of Oregon were sacrificed by living up there. So how did we cope? The water system was plumbed from a lake into the house. Mann Creek flowed into this lake and the beavers had done a wonderful job of making a dam! The overflow was used to irrigate our alfalfa field. The house was made out of logs, was very comfortable and easy to heat, and a two-cylinder, Lister Diesel Generator supplied electricity. We had a large propane tank which supplied lights for the house and bought a propane stove. The house had a fine wood cook stove in it when we bought it. In back of the stove were coils which were connected to a hot water tank, so when the stove was lit, it heated the water. The house had a nice indoor toilet, bathtub, and also a fine furnace in the basement. The day we arrived, however, the water wasn't coming into the house and I knew there was some work for me to do. We got some water in town and hauled it out to the house as it was very cold, 28 degrees below zero and snow everywhere. Later on, I put in two solar panels which kept up the batteries for our phone and television. Cutting wood was not a problem, since trees were plentiful and once we got the water system going, there was an adequate supply of that as well. There was always meat, too, although not U.S. Government inspected, it was tops!

In the meantime, back in the States, Russ had expressed a desire to quit teaching and work outdoors once again. He said he was tired of fighting the school system, kids, and parents, and he missed being outdoors! So he and Lavina moved into our home on Mill Creek and we were very pleased to have them living in our house and not have it vacant. Dave and Russ had decided to begin cutting timber together.

COMMUNICATION STATION

The radio stations in Canada were certainly "down home" and totally lacking in sophistication, but served the needs of the people in that vicinity. On this score, we used to get a big bang out of the radio phone and if the parties did nor ask for privacy, one could hear both parties conversing with each other. If the party who placed the call asked for privacy, you could still hear that party talk. There was a certain logger, every Monday morning on the radio trying to get his crew up and out of bed so they'd show up for work. This logging company official would mince no words and his language was not vague in any way! He would start out asking how come this individual isn't on deck - are you sleeping on his shirt tail, and so on. Most days it was like listening to a soap opera!

This reminds me of an incident which took place in Springfield, Oregon, when the timber industry was booming and the environmentalists were non-existent! The story is on this wise: A logger was standing on a street corner with his caulk shoes, lunch bucket, and tin hat and four different crummies came by. Each driver would see him, stop and urge him to get in, and then finally his company's crummy came by and he got in! Here is a man on Monday morning, evidently sober and awake, standing upright on his two feet, so get him in the vehicle and get him quick! This story makes one very much aware of some of the problems faced by anyone trying to carry on a business, pay Uncle Sam and make a profit! I realized that the country here in Canada has a much different climate and that thirty degrees below zero is just another day. I also knew that anti-freeze is used to combat freezing weather, and that it takes lots of alcohol to keep the inhabitants happy and prevent many of them from freezing up!

I was never noted for my ability as a mechanic, so I worked on a different principal! For example, prior to moving, we bought a new 1977 Dodge Aspen car. I told the dealer where I bought it that I wanted to trade batteries with them and they wanted to know what for. I said, "I want the largest battery that will fit in that case!" So once we were in Canada, sure enough, here came the neighbors, "Say, Kenny, will you come and jump-start my vehicle?" This was standard form! They knew Kenny's vehicle would start, so here they came, asking me to get theirs started! I knew that battery would come in handy!

Bill Nelson had a Esso Service Station in Clinton, so I went in one time and had him pack the wheel bearings on my 4 X 4. When you tear them down, you always have to put in new seals and bearings. Billy tightened them up, loaded up the bearings, greased them and I stayed there and watched him do all this work. When he finished,

I went home and put my little camper on the pickup and started back into town. As I drove, I thought I heard something sort of squalling and soon the noise became even more pronounced. Bill had left for a couple days, so I drove on down to see Jim Walt. Jim pulled the bearings off and here Bill had loaded them a little too heavy and with the extra weight of the camper, it put pressure on them. They actually began to turn blue, so Jim re-worked both of them for me and I paid him for his services. Later I went into Bill's service station, since I always bought gas there (lots of gas) and said, "Bill, I had some bad luck!" "You did? What happened?" he asked, so I told him and thought he might just literally kick the stars out of heaven. Instead, he looked at me and said, "Kenny, you don't know how badly I feel about that! If it had to happen, I'm glad that you weren't up on a mountain where you would be left high and dry and have to walk a long ways!" I had just paid him for some gas, and he opened the cash register, peeled out the amount I had paid him, and handed it back to me! I really respected Billy for that because I didn't know if he was that kind of a man or not! That is the measure of a man, you know, if you make a mistake and are willing to acknowledge it, that says a lot about a person!

We soon got acquainted with Isadore and Phillip Grinder. Isadore was born in 1900, so he was 77 and Phillip was about 32 years old. At once Phillip came down and helped me and was my "Sergeant At Arms." About the fifth day, he asked me, "Can I get $3,000 cash from you?" I said, "No, you can't." He said, "I can't?" I said, "No." "Well, would you take us to Ashcroft," he wanted to know. Ashcroft was fifty-five miles from the house, and I agreed to do that, so we took off. After arriving there, Phillip and Isadore went into the Yale Credit Union and borrowed $3,000 against their property, giving the Credit Union first mortgage on the place.

Later that day, while we were talking, Phillip informed me that he knew where the pipeline from our house went into the lake. I had taken to Canada, a couple big power saws which I had used in the woods in Oregon, so with the ice being a total of twenty-eight inches thick on the lake at the time, I proceeded to cut a channel sixteen feet long and cut a V shape in the ice. My plan was to lift those ice wedges out of the lake in order to get to the pipeline. This was an impossible task, however, so all that work was in vain. Next plan was to take wood and start fires to try and melt the ice, in hopes of getting to the pipeline. That did not work, either and still we did not find the pipeline. Ed and Teresa Martin were neighbors of ours and one day Ed asked me, "Have you found your pipeline yet?" I told him, "No," and he said, "I know exactly where it is! Tomorrow night I'll show you!" We went up together the next night and thankfully, Ed showed me right where the line was! Phillip got some dynamite, blew the end of the pipe off and after about a month, I was able to get cold water going through to the house. One problem was now solved, and so I continued to work on the hot water system. One night about midnight we had all the faucets open in the house and suddenly Frances heard water running - at last we had water and our problems solved!

Soon I discovered that my education was a long ways from being complete! I found out that our neighbors were very superstitious. For example, there was a tall, beetle-kill fir off the road about a hundred yards which had been struck by lightning. Isadore said, "Kenny, that's a fine looking tree, but you can't cut them!" "Why?" I asked. "Oh, the old Indians told me you should never cut a tree struck by lightning. Something bad will happen!" So I let it go at that. The two big chain saws I had taken to Canada, were a new item to my neighbors! They had never seen any chain saws that big before. Most of them in Canada have a blade about twenty to twenty-two inches long, at the most! One morning I went to Isadore's with one of my big saws and I said, "Isadore, today is the day I cut the lightning tree!" "You're going to cut it?" he asked. "Yes," I answered, as I got in my pickup and he got in with me. We went down to the tree and I lost no time in cutting it down! Immediately I discovered it was a shake tree and split easier than I ever thought it would! I cut a great, big load of wood and hauled it up to his cabin. Then I went back and cut a load for us. Three days later I saw Phillip and said, "Phillip, you know what happened when I put some of that wood in the stove?" He asked, "What?" "A bolt of lightning-like fire went right up out of that stove and up the stove pipe," I fabricated, while his eyes grew wide and he asked, "It did?" I said, "Yes." I waited a bit and then I said, "No, Phillip, the stove got HOT!" The first explanation I gave him was what he expected would happen! At least I broke the jinx on that theory!

Isadore had permission from the Crown to cut a shake tree. Back in the woods about a mile, there was a tree which his Dad had picked out. I went back, looked at it, and noted it had all the marks of a fine shake tree; big limb hanging straight down and pretty good creases in the bark, so I fell it! That tree was so twisted, it was more crooked than some politicians are in their hey days! You could hardly split a two-foot length with a maul and a wedge, so we didn't luck out on that one!

The first time I visited the Grinders, I noticed they had very little wood cut to use in their cook stove. Having a soft heart, I began cutting wood for them, and did so faithfully for three years, until one day, I saw the light! They never froze before they met Kenny Shenk and the thought came to me, "They're not going to freeze to death now," so I quit cutting their wood. As time went on, I helped them haul hay and do lots of other jobs.

We were all settled now and still the questions persisted from friends and family, "Why did you move to Canada?" It is hard to explain, but I think that in many people, there exists a certain pioneering spirit that sometimes needs to be reckoned with! I was amazed at the pleasure that I received to just saddle up a horse, ride off into the unknown, new country and see so many things! One morning I rode to the East of our one hundred-sixty acres and took an old game trail. Upon following that, I found an old corral, way back in a canyon. Now what is this? I asked Isadore about it later when I had returned and he told me, "Oh, that corral back in that canyon was built for when we used to catch wild horses." Many of the trails we used to find were used by wild horses. As I kept venturing further and further away, I would run onto many things of interest. I found what appeared to be an old road, so again asked, "What gives here, Isadore?" "Oh," he explained, "That's the old wagon road that goes into Clinton." Feeling the challenge, I took an axe and cross-cut saw and opened up this road to 57 Mile Creek, which the neighbors promptly started to also use on their hunting ventures!

NOTEWORTHY NEIGHBORS AND

FRIENDS

One of the things which bugged me was that you always hear that people are so friendly in Oregon, but not up in Canada. When we moved up to the Caribou, we knew no one and didn't have any friends there. One day we happened to meet John and Betty Spence and they became very wonderful friends, and still are! Then another day we were told about Tom and Connie Hook, who had moved from the Denver area up to

Our good friends, John and Betty Spence of Clinton - taken in their front yard.

Empire Valley. It wasn't long before we found out we had lots of friends and those people are still our friends! The Good Book says if a man will have friends, he must show himself friendly, and we found that to be utterly true! John and Betty used to come out to visit us about once a month and sometimes Betty would bring her Mother along, or other people, and we always had a very enjoyable time. Others we became acquainted with were three brothers, Cliff, Fred, and Gordon Titford. Roy and Doty Klopp were neighbors who were nearby and we enjoyed knowing them, and Paul and Ann Blackwell became good friends.

Little by little, we started to make acquaintance with many fine people. We met Reg Robinson and his wife, Tot. Reg had a meat cutting business just on the outskirts of Clinton. Here was a man who had been tempered in the fires of adversity! He told me his Dad served in the Canadian Armed Forces and when he came home from the war, he did not wish to live with his wife. Reg was only a small lad at the time and had a number of siblings, so Reg was adopted out. When he was twelve years old, he worked as a hired man and made his own way. At one time, he was a Game Warden and owned a hardware store and a butcher shop. Later on he also owned a restaurant. His first wife left him and he then married Tot, whose name was Amelia.

When we came to know Reg, he was cutting meat and it was a source of amusement to go and visit him in his place of business. He had three freezers, one of which was called, "The Game Warden Freezer." The wardens would catch some poor soul with a deer or moose, all butchered out, ready to take home and eat, and the warden would say, "I'll take that off your hands" and he would write them a stiff "prescription!" He'd just load it in his vehicle, take it to Reg and he would carefully clean, cut

Go Ahead On 'er!

and wrap this meat and place it in the "Game Warden Freezer." Well, this meat was supposed to go to various places, such as a home for children with physical disabilities, and various old people's homes. Suffice it to say, some of it did, most of it did NOT, and that's a story in itself, perhaps better left untold!

Reg came down with a very strange illness, which the doctors in Kamloops were unable to diagnose. Tot told Reg that she didn't want to live out where they had their home and where Reg had his meat business. So Reg comes home, a very sick man, and all alone, for his wife moved into Clinton. We used to visit them and now here is Reg, and he needs help! We stopped one day to see how he was doing. He was sitting at his breakfast table and behind him on the wall was a sign that said, "You can be sure of Hell!" I cannot express the feelings that went through me as I viewed this sign. Reg simply did not deserve the treatment life was meting out to him! His wife told Frances one day that she was concerned about Reg, but her concern for poor Reg just reminded me of the government taking their pound of flesh! It's like I once heard a fellow say after he had just had an argument with another fellow, "Oh, sure, I don't wish you any bad luck, but I hope the devil goes down your throat with an armful of open razors!"

At one time, Reg had a meat cutting business and butcher shop in Clinton, but finally had to close it as too many people took advantage of his generosity and would not pay their bills. When he had the hardware store in Merritt, British Columbia, a fire broke out and the store was a complete disaster. He said that the native people opened up their hearts, homes, and pocket books and helped him in this trying situation. It reminded me of a sign I once saw in a place of business which read, "It is very difficult to remember that the initial object is to drain the swamp while the crocodiles are taking vicious chunks off your fanny."

Betty Spence's mother is Indian, so Betty had a very real understanding of living off the land and roughing it and both John and Betty loved to hunt. I had learned the rudiments of hand loading rifle shells, casting lead bullets, and reloading my shells, so John became interested. I gladly passed along my information to him, and he became very proficient in his own venture into this interesting, bad habit! I once heard that a lady said, "My husband has the best hand-loading equipment that money can buy, but we don't have enough chairs for the kids to sit on!"

John and Betty helped us out in so many ways and here is just one little example: I used to do my long-distance phoning from their house and then reimburse them. The phone at our house was more like a mobile phone and was fine for receiving and making local calls, but not ideal for long-distance calls. John and Betty lived right in Clinton and since we did not run the diesel plant steadily, we purchased a freezer and they allowed us to put it in their basement. We would go into Clinton to pick up our mail and then go get things from the freezer. John worked for Ainsworth Lumber Company, swing shift and different hours, so many times, he was home when we went into town during the day. We spent many an enjoyable hour, pondering on the evils and problems of the world and government!

One day I felt it was necessary to see John Hampton. John had taken over Bud's companies after Bud passed away. I phoned the Portland office and was told that Mr. Hampton had left for a fishing trip to the interior of British Columbia. I knew John's brother, Chuck, lived in Chilliwack, so I phoned there and the information I received was that John, Chuck, and Lloyd Lewis had just left there an hour and a half earlier! I knew they'd be coming right through Clinton, as that is the main road through British Columbia, and I had no time to lose to try and intercept him! John Spence said, "Kenny, I have a 4 X 8 foot sheet of plywood and some blue paint." Presto! A sign was made and it simply said in big lettering, "JOHN HAMPTON, STOP HERE!" I quickly drove down to Cache Creek, the next town going South from Clinton, and parked my pickup beside the highway at an angle, with the sign displayed in the most prominent manner. This spot was just out of Cache Creek and there is a large area beside the road where truckers stop to put on chains, eat at the restaurant there, and check their loads. I didn't have long to wait! I had no idea what kind of vehicles Chuck, John, and Lloyd were driving.

First to pass by was Chuck, driving a Chevy Blazer. Lloyd Lewis was with him, but they did not see me, nor my "neon" sign. They had a canoe tied on top of the Blazer. Close behind, here comes John driving a Ford Bronco! Lo and behold, he saw my sign immediately, wheeled in, got out and said, "Kenny, God only made one John Hampton, and that's me!" Then Chuck and Lloyd Lewis noticed John had stopped, so they turned around, came back, and we had a great visit! I was so grateful John Spence had that plywood and paint for me to use! He was just "Johnny, On The Spot!"

POIGNANT PORTRAITS

OF THE PAST!

Years ago, as people began to venture further north, they were met with some tremendous difficulties, one of which was the Fraser River Canyon! A party set out from Vancouver one time, led by Colonel Waddington, to try and find a route to the inland. He took a route closer to the coast and encountered much opposition from natives. In fact, in some of these encounters, they had pitched battles and a number of his party were killed. Eventually, his endeavor ended up in a Chilcotin War. A man named Simon Fraser, pioneered a passageway up through the treacherous canyons of the Fraser River! This road was basically built by Chinese laborers who were brought in. One of the results of these laborers being brought in is that even in the small town of Clinton, there were always two Chinese restaurants! These establishments are operated by the kids of these old-time miners! This is true throughout most of British Columbia. In the town of Trail, some of the finest restaurants in town are ones owned by Orientals.

As the workers hewed out roads, they were, of course, traveling on horses and mules, so the roads originally were very grim and narrow. Many of the mules would panic and just vault off into space, plunging to their death, as well as some of the pack horses! Eventually, through some fabulous feats of engineering, they were able to get roads up the Fraser Canyon. The roads which Colonel Waddington had mapped out had too much water to cross and didn't prove satisfactory, so his plan was abandoned. The hardships these workers suffered was tremendous! The main export shipping point way back then was from Ashcroft. People wonder about some of the unusual names in Canada, and generally there are fairly logical explanations. For example, Clinton used to be called, 47 Mile. They had a 16 Mile, 22 Mile, 100 Mile, and of course, the roads just went over the mountains and they didn't have a distinct route chosen, nor any roads graded up. It was all going uphill from Ashcroft and many of those mountains were extremely steep! A team of horses could travel sometimes eight miles, sometimes sixteen miles and so forth, so that's how they would name these places! They were a "stop-over" place for people and their horses and that's how it went, from 57 Mile, 83 Mile, then over the hill to 100 Mile House. There's one at 150 Mile and a turn-off point to go to Horse Fly, and that is some history on how names originated. Some fellows even made a living by having a "Snap Team." By definition, this was a team who could help pull others out if they got stuck! If you'd ride a wagon loaded down with provisions and goods and couldn't pull it, there'd be a man there at some of these difficult points who would hitch onto your wagon tongue and give you a pull! Certainly in those days, people lived a very rigorous and hard life and learned how to help one another!

A very famous packer of the North was Cataline, of Spanish descent, and in the new lodge in Clinton, there is a picture of this fellow. He was a powerful packer and one of the fastest men that ever packed a pack train. He packed clear up in the North country and was well-known. Every morning he took a shot of brandy and said, "A little on the inside and a little on the outside!" He had a fabulous head of hair and would rub the brandy on his head also. Reportedly, he lived to a ripe old age and was a tough, old man! A beautiful, young woman lived with him and one of the guys working for him got to fooling around with her. The first time Cataline found out, he warned him to cease at once! The second time Cataline caught him, he didn't warn him, but just beat him half to death! This guy found out first-hand this old man could take him completely apart! Cataline carved out for himself, a great place of distinction and honor in the annals of Canadian history.

I had the privilege of meeting two of the pioneers in the aviation industry of Canada. One fellow was Herman Peterson, whom I met at Atlin, and the other was Pat Collison. Together, the two of them started their aviation business. Those two were the renown aviation pioneers responsible for developing the Canadian industry and they later sold their first company to Ward Air, of Canada. It was my privilege to meet both of them! They were great fellows with many interesting stories of their "mercy runs" to hospitals for injuries, illnesses, accidents, and they performed a very valuable service! To my knowledge, they are both still living, but obviously, are getting up there in years.

Just before we moved to Clinton, a group of Hell's Angels motorcycle gang members rode into town! They went into a bar where a few local fellows were nursing their drinks. Well, one of the gang members just brazenly walked down the bar and kicked all the drinks off, right onto the floor, and everywhere! A fight ensued, and a scuffle, followed by shouting and cussing! The gang members left and went up on the hill, going back towards Cache Creek. There is an airport up there and these gang members formed a big circle and hunkered down for the night. Word spread throughout the area and the locals gathered and made plans to call on their visitors! They went calling with their big 303 British rifles and 30-30's, and upon arrival, immediately began shooting! They wounded one of the gang members, and as the locals were leaving, one of the Hell's Angels shouted, "We'll pay you back! We'll be back to wipe Clinton out!"

Believe it or not, one day Frances and I were traveling down to the States and we met a big band of Hell's Angels, just above the small village of Yale. Before they got to Boston Bar, the Mounties met them and said, "You're going no further! If you go to Clinton, you'll have no protection and the locals are going to wipe you out!" The locals at Clinton were ready for them, believe me! That's one community which stood up to the Hell's Angels and won! When the gang members found out they'd have no protection, they turned around and went back to where they came from. When we saw these motorcycles and burly guys, there were at least eighteen in the group, headed North. Luckily, the Mounties intercepted them and sent them back!

FISH STORY

THE ONES THAT DIDN'T GET AWAY!

One evening John Spence called me asking, "Say, Kenny, would you and Frances like to go on a big, Wild Safari tomorrow? We're going to fish, pick wild raspberries, and just have a good time!" I checked with Frances and then told him, "We sure would!" I got my boat and motor loaded and put some gear together and we drove into Clinton to meet them. Al and Emily Harvey, another nice couple, were also going along. We drove out past Canum Lake a little ways and took a little road through the tulles and here was a lake. There really wasn't a good access road, you just followed tracks! Due to lack of a real road, people would drag their boats down the hill to get to the lake and there was evidence that many before us had done just that. As we prepared to launch my boat, the women elected to pick berries. John volunteered to run the motor, and we fellows took off on the lake. After we were out a ways, I suddenly hooked a big fish! It was a nice one, so I kept on fishing and caught John's limit, as well as mine! These fish were big ones, nineteen to twenty-one inches long, and did they ever fight! What a fantastic day of fishing!

Along toward evening, Emily came down by the shore of the lake, so John said to her, "Emily, get in this boat, you're going fishing!" She said, "No, I'm not!" He said, "Oh, yes, you are!" She reluctantly got into my boat and went out with John. Emily caught a four pound fish, and was just flabberghasted, although very pleased and happy! We ended our lovely day there and on the way out, we saw a grizzly sitting on a log right above the road. We then realized the women were lucky they weren't confronted by that bear while they were picking wild raspberries! That was one of the greatest fishing days I've ever had in my life! Everything went according to Hoyle and that doesn't happen very often!

PARTING WITH THE

PEND OREILLE PROPERTY

On one of our trips to Oregon to visit our kids over the holidays, we stopped at Russell and Lavina's home. We hadn't been there long when the phone rang and Russ said, "Here, Dad, it's for you!" To my surprise, the caller was a real estate agent from Sweet Home, named Bill Mersnick, who said, "I would like for you to come to my office tomorrow because I want you to go with me to look at the Pend Oreille property." I said, "Look, I just came down from Canada to celebrate Christmas, so I can't do that!" We talked briefly and then I said, "I'll tell you what I'll do since it is not possible for me to go with you to Canada just now. I'll bring all my maps over and give you some advice and information." We agreed to meet in Salem the next day, and I gave him maps and information regarding our property, as I promised. He then flew to Spokane and rented a helicopter to fly over the property. The client he planned to show the property to was from West Germany and had brought quite an entourage with him. Accompanying the German fellow were a couple engineers, a surveyor, and a photographer! They cruised the entire area, took photos, surveyed, and did their own footwork. Matter of fact, they did a very credible job and the result was that they wanted to purchase it.

Concurrently with the potential buyer for the Pend Oreille, the government condemned a large redwood forest in California belonging to Louisiana Pacific Corporation, a large timber company. This timber was infested with beetles, so they placed it in reserve. John Hampton was downtown having lunch with some of his colleagues from Louisiana Pacific, and they told him of their problem with the redwood timber. They had just been awarded $27,000,000 by the government for that timber being placed in reserve and they needed to reinvest those funds quickly. John told them, "I know of a place where you can do that!" The outcome was that the Pend Oreille was sold to Louisiana Pacific Corporation. Owning this Canadian property was truly a fantastic learning experience and we met some wonderful people.

DIFFERENT STROKES

FOR DIFFERENT FOLKS

Ed and Teresa Martin told me that one morning they drove up to Grinders and out in the front yard, close to the creek, here was Phillip in a bathtub, about 10:00 A.M., taking a bath. The bathtub was on legs and he had sticks on fire underneath it. That way, Phillip could conveniently reach out the side of the tub and move the fire around if it got too hot in a certain place. Ed asked him, "What's going on here, anyway? How come you're out here in public, completely naked, taking a bath?" Phillip replied, "I ain't really naked, I got my cowboy hat on, don't I?" Ed said, "Yes, I suppose so!"

One evening Phillip came down to tell me he had killed a bull moose and asked me if I would help him get it out the next morning, as it was quite a long ways up in the mountains. I agreed, and went to their place early the next morning, in cold, snowy weather! He had an old Willys 4 X 4 Jeep and we drove up to the upper helicopter landing, and then walked up to where the moose was. Suddenly, Phillip decided to have some fun and said, "Say, Kenny, if I chop this moose in half and ride it down, will you ride the other half down?" I said, "Well, Phillip, you go first and I will follow!" We squared this moose away and started down the hill! There were a bunch of wind-falls, small trees five and six inches thick, laying criss-cross all over the place and I knew what was going to happen and sure enough it did! He started out and all of a sudden, lost his ride! He went end over tea kettle; Phillip going one way, and the carcass sailing another! I had a good laugh and meandered down and helped him. Gravity is always a working when she is real steep and slick and you can just count on it every time! We finally succeeded in getting that moose to Grinder's house!

Just before dark one evening, here comes Phillip asking, "Could you give me a hand? I shot a big black bear just before dark and I need help." I filled a gas lantern, got some knives and a sharpening stone, drove down the road and walked back into the woods to where this bear lay. While I took off this bear's overcoat, Phillip regaled me with stories and before too long, we were ready to go back to the pickup. Just as we got to the truck, Phillip said, "Oh no, I have a problem! How was the brisket on that bear laying?" I said, "I don't know. What's the deal, anyway?" He asked, "You don't know?" "No, I don't," I told him. "Well, we have to go back," he informed me. So back we trudged, and found that the carcass was laying with the cavity up and open. Phillip tenderly rolled it to one side, and told me, "If an Indian leaves a bear carcass open like that, it will rain and never stop until some Indian rolls it on its' side." I said, "I never knew that!" I certainly did now, for we had trudged back through the woods to check this carcass! On the way back, he asked, "Is it true they hire rainmakers in the states?" I said, "Yes, old governor Tom McCall hired some rainmakers and they seeded clouds in Eastern Oregon, but it rained in Idaho and that made some people very up-set!" "Well, I can sure make it rain, but the trouble is, I don't how to stop it," he said.

Once it was really storming and I said, "Phillip, is this normal for it to storm like this?" "It sure is," he answered. "Do you know why its' stormin' like this? Mr. Reynolds passed away and it will storm until they get his body in the ground." Sure enough, after the funeral, the storm quit! What Phillip didn't realize is that as a general rule, there are usually one or two bodies in the local morgue awaiting burial!

Visiting Isadore and Phillip in their cabin one day, Isadore told me this story: He said, "You know, Kenny, when a woman is pregnant and going to have the baby soon (he then motioned with his hands over his belly way out, as if she'd be ten or eleven months pregnant), do you know what will happen to her if she sees a bear?" and I said, "No, what will happen to her?" "You don't know?" he asked incredulously, "Well, I will tell you! She will have a bear baby, with black hair all over its' body and he will have club, or curved feet." "Well, Isadore, I didn't know that!" "Oh, yes, that will happen," he said. There were so many things they believed with all their hearts! I'm sure they thought that I was the dumbest white man they had ever met! Could have been, you know!

Isadore told me his Mother had passed away not long before we moved to Canada. She was 104 and had remained very active up until the end of her life. One time she became ill, so Phillip took her into the white doctor in Clinton, but he couldn't help her. She went back home and still didn't feel well, so asked Phillip to take her to the Medicine Doctor at Bonaparte, which is a small reserve towards Cache Creek. After she had talked to the Medicine Man, also called Shaman, he said, "I know what's bothering you. It's that fellow down there at the Pavilion. Do you want me to kill him?" Isadore's Mother said, "I don't care whether you kill him or not, I just want to get well!" The Medicine Man said, "I'll take care of that," and three days later, this man was dead. I heard a number of stories similar to that and their last ace in the hole was their own Indian doctor! They had an undying belief that once the white man failed, they must resort to their old, native traditions. Their own culture runs very deep and they think in a completely different vein than we do. They felt that the white man lied to them, took their choice lands, and left the Canoe Creek tribe with little to live on. The Indians at Alkalie Lake had a much better settlement with some timber land, a sawmill, beautiful grazing land, lots of water and game and were in good shape. Many of the Indian bands, however, were shamefully treated, and were nearly destitute! Down deep, the Canoe Creek people band had little use for white people.

I told Isadore and Phillip a story one day which tickled them so much that when they went down to the big Clinton bar and restaurant, it was repeated to every Indian and half-breed they met. The story goes like this: An Indian chief in Oklahoma went to see a banker one spring and he said, "I need to borrow $10,000." The banker laughed and said, "Chief, that's a lot of money! What do you want $10,000 for?" The chief said, "I need it, and that's all I can tell you!" So the banker said, "Well, I just can't loan it to you because it wouldn't be good business and that's that!" The chief bowed and was silent, then began to walk out. Suddenly, the banker called him to come back. He said, "I don't know, Chief, but I feel somewhat obligated to loan the money to you. What do you have for security, or collateral?" The old Chief bowed his head and thought a little while. "Well," he said, "I have fifty ponies and fifty blankets!" The banker laughed and said, "Okay, I'll loan you the money," and the deal was closed.

That summer a big, oil-drilling outfit hit oil on the reservation and come fall, the old Chief went back into the bank with a huge wad of green backs! He paid the banker off, along with the interest, and thanked him. After that, he stuffed the rest of the big stash of cash into his pocket, and started to leave. The banker's mind began to work overtime and he said, "Hey, Chief, come back here! What are you going to do with the rest of that money? Why don't you put it in my bank, let it work for you and make interest?" The old Chief turned, looked the banker in the face and asked, "How many ponies and blankets you got?"

We made friends with a fine couple who owned the Empire Valley Ranch, Tom and Connie Hook. They hired quite a few Indians to work for them and experienced first-hand, some trying moments with the trust level which can occur between whites and Indians. This was a vast acreage which they owned; Tom and Connie needed help, and they trusted these people. Many of the Indians lived in small cabins with their families there on the Ranch. One night, however, some of them came in late, had indulged in lots of booze, and the picture changed drastically. They awakened Tom and Connie, cursed them, told them white people didn't belong there, and to get out! It was a very unpleasant scene for the Hook's and came as a total shock. They told the Hook's they were going to take over their ranch and it was very difficult to sort things out after such an upsetting experience.

CLINTON STAMPEDE

One of the biggest annual events for miles around is the Clinton Stampede. In 1996, the Stampede was at least one hundred and thirty-one years old and had been held consecutively every year since its' inception. They'd have a May Day Ball and first rodeo of the season, with a great attendance! We were sitting there at this celebration, when an Indian fellow, Theodore Dick began visiting. On one of his eyes, he had a big cataract, which was completely white and nearly covered the entire eye. I asked him, "Do you know of anyone who has any ponies for sale?" He said, "Sure! My friend. He has ponies." "Do you think he'd sell them?" I asked. He said, "I go see," and with that, he left. Before long, he returned and said, "My friend, he will sell you ponies!" I said, "Good!" Then he said, "I could use a be-er." I didn't understand him at first and asked, "I beg your pardon, what did you say?" Again he said, I could use a be-er!" I said, "Oh, I left my billfold in my pickup back up there and I don't have a dime on me!" He jumped up, ran back a ways and then came back saying, "My friend said he won't sell you any ponies!" So I suppose he went up and told his friend, Percy Rosette, I didn't give him money for booze. It turned out fine for me, as later I found another place to buy ponies. That always tickled me so, because it didn't take him five minutes to change his story!

Spring arrived and I had decided it would be great to have some horses which we could ride. I inquired of my neighbors and was told to go to the Big Bar Ranch to see Adrian Amil, as he had horses. I made a visit to him and he agreed to sell me a couple horses. Phillip had some horses which he had never bothered to break and he wanted to trade his five horses for a stallion Adrian owned. This horse was a classy, Tennessee Walking stallion and Phillip really wanted him. I bought a gelding named Caesar, a speckled horse, sort of like a palomino and Adrian told me he had a nice mare, three years old, which he'd break and train for me. Frances and I decided to name her Cindy and we were to go back in a week to get her.

Phillip and I rode over to get Cindy. When we left to take her home, I rode Caesar and led Cindy home. On the way, we stopped at the edge of the lake in front of Peg Marriott's house. At one time, Peg's husband had a big ranch and raised cattle. He had a slaughter house and would butcher the cattle and sell meat to the Bralorne Mine up above Lillooet. Besides raising cattle, he also used to take out trail riders, so all in all, they had a great business and Peggy taught school. Peg's husband had passed away and she now lived with a fellow named Ed Loring. As we rode by, Peg was sitting on the porch and she called out, "Hello, Phillip." Ed was standing on the porch and we had heard he'd just had open heart surgery. Phillip and I didn't stop, but went on with the horses. The very next day we heard that Ed Loring had died; he committed suicide. The mounties spent about five hours at Peg's house the next day, trying to piece together what really happened. Most everyone around had an inkling of what had taken place because another lady was living there, who had been there before. Ed got to taking a shine to her and undoubtedly Peg told him she would not be a part of a triangle. No further information ever came out about the situation! End of that story! When we left Canada, Peg was still living there.

The Big Bar Lake Ranch which Peg and her husband, Harry, built up, was very famous and historic. One day a young fellow from England, Eric Collier, came to visit his Uncle, Harry Marriott. Eric's father was a very famous lawyer and wanted Eric to follow in his footsteps, but he seemed to have a different bent in his makeup and decided to visit in Canada. He would ride over through the woods, play cards with Isadore, and they became good friends. Later, Eric went up out of Williams Lake, to a place called Meldrun Creek and married an Indian lady named Ellie, and they had one son. A book was written about Eric's venture, Three Against The Wilderness, and is one of the most interesting books to read! I believe it was featured as a serial-style story at one time in the "Outdoor Life magazine." Frances and I drove up to Meldrun Creek one time and looked at the various buildings and the last we knew, Ellie and Veasey, their son, were still living in that area.

The Outdoor Life also featured another book called, The Silence Of The North. When my brother, Ron, moved to Vanderhoof and bought a ranch up on the Nechako River, he made acquaintance with Olive Frederickson, about whom the book was written. It detailed many of the problems she faced in her life and is a very interesting book about life in the North. Her first husband fell through the ice and drowned, so she later married John Frederickson. Her life was a real example of how the human spirit survives under pressure. Another interesting author was Richmond P. Hobson, whose father was an Admiral in the Confederate Navy. Rich met Floyd Phillips, who was called "Pan" Phillips, as they said he always was panhandling tobacco from someone. Together, Rich and Pan traveled to the North country, stopped at Clinton briefly, and finally ended up with one of the longest cattle drives on the North American continent. They formed a great cattle company in the mountains behind Anahim Lake, called the Frontier Cattle Company. Rich Hobson wrote three books: Grass Beyond The Mountains, the second book is, Nothing Too Good For A Cowboy, and the third is entitled, The Rancher Takes A Wife. Ron met Rich's wife and their daughter. A number of outfitters I hunted with, had worked for Phillips, one of them being Mack Squinas. One day I asked him, "Did you ever work for Phillips and Hobson?" He said, "Sure, one time! I don't know about those people. They put me on a horse and I ask, 'Is he a good horse?' and they say, 'Yes.' He bucked me so high and they all laughed! I don't know about them!"

Walter Erhorn also worked for them for many years and is mentioned in one of the books, as are a number of other people I met. Those books certainly have some resolute characters! Lester Dorsey, whom I mentioned, rode thirty-six hours one time, without stopping because a young lad had gotten his leg mangled when a team of horses ran away with a mowing machine. They wanted to locate a doctor and an airplane to get help for the young man. Some of the stories are of very courageous and giving people who extended themselves to help others. Occasionally on the message broadcast, I'd hear an announcement for Pan Phillips, as he had a fish camp up around Tahtsa Lake. Pan's wife, Betty, and his son are still living, as far as we know. That country is replete with history. I visited a site called Townsend, which reportedly is the place of the last battle fought between the settlers and the Indians, and it is very interesting country!

An old fellow used to come up every fall from Vancouver to hunt up on Ryan Ridge, south of Clinton. He always stopped at Billy Nelson's to buy gas and visit a bit, then he'd go up on the ridge, set up his tent, and do some deer hunting. The fellow had arrived, been to see Billy, and then left to go hunting. Billy got to thinking about him one day and realized he had not seen this fellow come back down. Some people went up to look for him, found his tent all right, and then encountered a most horrifying scene! A big, black bear had entered his tent, pulled the man out, severed his head, opened him up and it looked as if a butcher had performed the job. A trap was set to catch this bear, and when they got him, discovered he was a very large one! I've heard that wolves never attack humans and have talked to old-timers who do not agree with this! I'd never be willing to put my life on the line for a wolf, or any other wild animal, that's for sure, and they are a force to be reckoned with! Any big game hunters I've ever been out with show a lot of respect for any and all wild animals!

One time I was riding with Mack Squinas on the old Frontier Cattle Trail, when we came to a bend in the trail and here was a billy can where the cowboys had stopped to boil a pot of coffee or tea. The can didn't look old at all. Suddenly Mack fell off his horse on the right side, grabbed the horse reins and shouted, "Get gun, quick, here come grizzly!" I bailed off, grabbed my gun and here came a big silver-tip grizzly, not more than seventy-five feet from us, right in the middle of the trail. Then he stopped, looked us over and while this was happening, the horses just stood there and trembled! The bear sauntered away and Mack said one of the funniest things I've ever heard! He held his hands up and in broken English said, "Bear, you go 'way, you go NOW, now you go," and the bear turned and walked up on a hillside. After that bear had gone about thirty-five feet, he sat down, just like a dog. So Mack quickly got on his horse, and so did I. Sometimes we would ride half a day without Mack saying more than just a few words. He made a big circle off to the left, then stopped, looked back at me and said, "Kenny, long time ago when I was little boy, my Grandad tell me that grizzly bear like Indian lot better than white man!" I said, "Oh? My Grandad never told me that! Why is that?" He said, "White man use too much salt!" The Indians are very interesting people and I met some very fine ones, including Indian guides!

A story I heard one time was that an old chief and a young brave were riding up a canyon one sunny morning. Before long, they came upon a fine buck, so the young brave looked at the old chief and said, "Ugh!" The old man smiled and said, "Ugh!"

They rode a ways further and jumped a fine, bull elk. The young brave looked at the old chief and said, "Ugh!" The old man smiled and said, "Ugh." Pretty soon they found a couple buffalo and the young brave said, "Ugh, ugh." The old chief said, "What do you have to go and change the subject for?" Evidently he was on the right wave length, at least for awhile!

One of the privileges I had through the years was to meet a Dr. Turner, from New Zealand. He specialized in studying the religious heritage and culture of the Native Indians of Washington, Oregon, Montana, and all over the world. I asked him, "What do you think about their concept of the hereafter?" "Well, I am one of the few white men who have been admitted to some of their most sacred gatherings. Stop and think about it, in the old days, the Indians used to hold their sacred rites on a high hill. They'd gather together, usually build a fire, watch the smoke swirl heaven-ward, and have their ceremonies. The white man would build a huge cathedral or church, erect a high steeple, and this, too, is symbolic of man's attempt to reach God. I pondered on this thought many times. As many of the Indians shared their feelings and beliefs with me, it made me realize that God has placed in every human being the desire to know Him. The question remains as to why so many have been denied that privilege." I concluded his words to me were food for thought!

So many of the native people cannot handle liquor and of course, many of the white people aren't doing too well, either! One of the most tragic things which happened while we lived in Canada was that a van carrying six Indians going from Williams Lake to Anahim Lake was traveling in some terribly steep country. Just past Alexis Creek, they went over a bluff and somehow, one fellow survived and managed to crawl up the embankment to the main road for help. He was severely injured, but fortunately, someone came along and took him into the hospital. They cared for him and in a few days, his memory of the accident returned and then he told the hospital staff that there were other people in the accident with him. The authorities went out there and discovered the other five who had died in the van. Evidence showed they had survived for some time, but were pinned under the vehicle and could not get out. That was very sad those people perished in such a manner, but alcohol was involved. Quite a large number of Indians live at Alkalie Lake and for years it has been referred to as Alcohol Lake! A young chief came in there, however, and wanted to change things, so he made it pretty tough for anyone to come in there with any kind of booze. He turned that tribe around and is one shining example of what can happen if someone puts their foot down!

Noting the many tragic stories we heard resulting from the evils of booze, I wrote this little "jingle":

LIFE IN THE CARIBOU
She left with the kids about midnight,
His blood was all over the floor,
He now is utterly sober, but Lordy, he'd beat her before,
She told him that she couldn't take it,

This beating must come to a stop.
Oh, yes, he promised to shape up,
That he never would touch one more drop!

Now the old house is so empty,
And loudly his conscience did smite!
Oh, God, if he only had heeded,
This place might be heaven tonight!

She told him, You wicked, old Demon,
You never will beat me again,
She knew that booze was his Master,
And that he never would change!

I'll find me a man who is worthy of me,
You can live with your filth and your shame,
And though he had fathered her children,
She swallowed her pride with some blame,
These kids are part of my body,
I never will leave them again!

THE HIGHLAND FLING

Phillip came to our house one morning and asked, "Could I get you to drive my pickup down to 100 Mile House?" I said, "No you couldn't!" "You won't?" he asked, but quickly I said, "No, I won't drive your pickup, but I'll take you to 100 Mile in mine!" He said, "Please take me, 'cause I have to get some wisdom teeth pulled!" So off we go to 100 Mile House and I asked him if he had an appointment. He said, "Do I have a what?" Then he asked me if he could borrow $100 from me, and I told him I could arrange that. Leaving a little early that morning, after we arrived at 100 Mile House, Phillip went into a men's clothing store first and bought a beautiful Stetson Hat, which cost him $60! After all, all cowboys have to have a good hat, you know! Then he wanted to go to Safeway, and I drove him there. Once inside, he grabbed a cart and began shopping. I had gotten a cart of my own and was behind him, going down the aisles. He picked up a case of Coca Cola, a huge Hubbard squash and a few other items. As we got to the checkout counter, he looked at the clerk and started laughing, saying, "I didn't even know I bought anything much," as he gave her the rest of the money which I had just loaned him! After we finished there, off to the dentist's office we went and Phillip asked at the counter, "Is the dentist in?" "Yes, he is," said the young receptionist, "but he is booked up." Phillip said, "Well, you said the Doc is in and I want my teeth pulled!" To my astonishment, she said, "You come back in one hour!"

In an hour, we were back at the dentist. Phillip's teeth were really imbedded, so the Doc split them in two sections in order to extract them, then had to do quite a bit of stitching in his gums. This procedure was not just a little ordeal, but finally he finished, we started for home and about twenty miles out of town, Phillip said, "Man, oh man, I feel better all ready! I can really feel the poison coming out!" I knew that the novocain was beginning to wear off, but I didn't tell him that! When I got him to his cabin, I said, "About twelve o'clock tonight, Phillip, you will feel entirely different and will do the Highland fling!" He looked at me rather quizzically and asked, "I will?" Phillip took nine aspirin tablets and went to bed.

It's around June first, and about a week after the trip to the dentist, Phillip came down to visit. He asked, "Kenny, how long will it take that poison to drain out of my body?" I asked, "How long had your teeth been infected?" "About two years," he said. "Well, Phillip, you are a big man, but it will probably take most of the summer," I told him, and he went on home. About ten days later, I was at their place, and here is Phillip with two walking sticks, somewhat bent over and just barely moving! Isadore said, "Phillip is really in bad shape from those teeth, but that poison is coming out!" Phillip never did one lick of work all summer long and it wasn't until his moose hunter came in the fall for him to guide that he immediately was well! In the meantime, Isadore fixed fences, rustled some firewood and did all the chores. Oh my, the power of suggestion! I probably should have had my britches dusted off, but little did I realize Phillip would "milk" that one for all he could!

NEIGHBORLY NOTES

Isadore started bugging me to go sheep hunting with him. They had a cabin about seven miles from their house, back in the woods, right next to sheep country. I agreed to go with him and began riding Cindy to get her ready. Caesar was a constant problem and I just couldn't keep him home, as he'd jump the fences. Some friends we met, Pete and Joyce Coldwell, knew of Caesar, so he had quite a reputation! Pete laughed and said, "Oh, that horse came up here from Circle H Ranch! They couldn't keep him home, either, as he seemed to like it better where we lived, so he stayed at our place!" Another problem I was having with Caesar was that he shied something terrible and riding him one day, there was a big rock laying along the road, and for some reason, it frightened him! He jumped sideways so hard, it really cracked my neck, so that for at least a month, my neck literally burned from that jolt. I told Adrian I was having trouble with him, and he said he'd give me another horse, a mare, named Tiny. Tiny proved to be a good riding horse, but she was afraid of blood. We kept her for awhile, but later got rid of her.

Pete and Joyce Caldwell also became good friends, and we used to visit from time to time. Pete is now gone, but his good wife, Joyce, is still active. Charlie Coldwell lives on the home place and takes care of the Ranch. Pete and Joyce used to have a country store and post office, at Jesmond, B.C. Pete was a great fellow and had a Big Game Guiding Area. During his hunting years, he took over one hundred fine mountain sheep, rams, and over one hundred cougar, plus many trophy mule deer, as well as moose.

It was now time for me to accompany Isadore on a sheep hunt, so we took Cindy as a pack mare, I rode Caesar and Isadore rode his old horse, Smokey. I had bought a new Spacemaster Spotting Scope and the day before opening day, we rode up a little draw. Just up ahead in the rocks, I saw a ram, and then two more! I said, "Isadore, get off that horse quick! Bring your horse back here!" I set up my spotting scope to look them over and Isadore said, "Them are fine rams! Oh, I'm glad you stopped me - fifty feet more and there'd be no more sheep!" We went back home and got up at 3:00 A.M. the next morning, just tingling with excitement to get back up there and get a couple sheep. At that time, I didn't know that Isadore had never killed one! I had killed one while hunting with Pat Garrard. Isadore and I took a circuitous route, taking Cindy along, because out in the woods, if the air is just right, you can hear people talking as far away as two miles and we didn't want her back there getting excited and making a commotion! During the night, it had snowed about two inches and Isadore was having a terrible time keeping his balance across the terribly slick rocks, but at last we got up to the top!

I kept watching the same spot where I had seen the rams the day before and sure enough, it wasn't long before just one horn was in view, and then the entire ram stepped into view; the second one followed suit, and then the third one! Those sheep came out right where they did the day before! I always let Isadore go ahead of me to set the pace he was most comfortable with and I called out to him, "Lay down quick, Isadore!" He asked, "Why?" I said, "Because I see sheep!" There was a rocky ledge in front of us and it looked like an ideal place to shoot from, even though the distance was quite great - at least 200 yards, and the wind was blowing in our faces, making our eyes water. We crawled and struggled our way up to this ledge and once there, Isadore said, "I'm gonna shoot the lower one, you shoot the middle one!" I told him, "When we shoot, they're going to run right back to us!" He said, "No, they'll run the other way!" "Isadore, trust me, the wind is blowing our way, they'll run our way," I assured him! I had a 270 with a scope on it and he had an old Enfield 30-0-6, U.S. Army issue and his sling consisted of baling twine! He said he didn't want to ruin the cape of the ram, so he put a bullet right in the center of that ram's stomach and it went down. I shot my ram in the shoulder and the bullet went through, then hit a rock. Isadore saw the smoke "boil" and he said, "You missed your ram, Kenny!" I said, "No, I didn't!" True to my prediction, the ram I shot at, ran on a little trail above us and just as I was ready to shoot again, he stood up on his hind feet and toppled down the hill. Isadore's ram got up, he shot it again, and both the rams rolled down the canyon. Let me tell you, that old man was thrilled! He was so tickled and I was very happy for him! "Would you mind going and bringing my ram right down where yours is?" Isadore asked me, and I said, "Isadore, I can't think of anything right now that I would rather do!" So I went down, brought them together, dressed them out, and just as soon as we did that, here came the ravens, circling around and around. We knew we'd have to cover these rams completely with rock (and there were plenty of them around) and we did so, but even at that, when we returned later, there was one little area uncovered and those ravens picked at the meat a little bit!

We got the horses over there, loaded up the rams, and started for camp. At that time, I didn't have a very good saddle and was using one I had taken to Canada from Oregon. Isadore had the hams from his ram with him on his saddle. On my saddle horn, I also had two hams. I was leading Cindy with the remainder of the meat from Isadore's ram on her. Cindy reached over to get a mouthful of grass and the rope got tight. I had just taken a turn on my saddle horn, which one should never do, and it pulled the saddle over! The stirrups were so narrow on that saddle, I could hardly get my feet out! As I went crashing to the ground, with the hams right on top of me, Caesar stopped and never moved! Isadore got off Smokey to help me and lost no time in giving me a lecture I never forgot! He said, "Don't you EVER, EVER ride with that saddle again......", and I never did! That day I learned a real lesson and went to buy a new saddle as soon as I could! We went on down off that mountain, each with a fine ram; mine with a full curl set of horns and Isadore's ram was nearly a full curl. Isadore did not "cape" his sheep out, but I did as I planned to have it mounted. My ram was a beautiful, California Big Horn.

DYNAMITE COWBOY

When we were still living in Oregon, I had contacted an outfitter, Sherwood Henry, of Williams Lake, British Columbia, and inquired as to a hunt. He had responded and even mailed me a brochure, but the dates he had set simply were in conflict with my schedule and there was no way it would work out. So I had to contact him again and say it was not possible for me to hunt with him. After we had been living in Canada, Frances and I had gone into Clinton and were having coffee in the Lodge one morning. As we were sitting there, I heard someone say, "Hey, Sherwood!" I inquired and found out the person being addressed was, indeed, Sherwood Henry! I walked up to him and introduced myself, saying I had written to him from Oregon regarding a hunt. He asked, "Well, did I bother to answer you?" I assured him he had, and he replied, "Well, that's strange," and he laughed! In one of the books I have, he was listed as one of the great ten cowboys of Canada, was a superb horseman and a great character! He had a guiding area in the Keicheka Mountains and took out many, many hunters. His Dad, Cecil, raised a lot of horses. I saw Sherwood ride in a rodeo one time and there was no doubt that he was a good cowboy!

Sherwood loved to party and a bunch of them were making merry one night when someone lit a stick of dynamite on a fuse, passing it around as it was burning. When the dynamite came to Sherwood, he threw it, but he didn't throw it quite fast enough and it blew his right arm off, disfigured his face, and I believe he lost the sight in one eye. He told a friend of mine, "I guess I'll be a little short-handed from here on out," but it didn't stop him, for he still guides and hunts.

MEANDERING MOOSE

After the sheep season opened, that was followed by moose season. Two brothers from Oregon, Ray and Paul Wagler, good friends of ours, were on their way North to

Vanderhoof to visit family, so they stopped in to spend the night with us. I went out towards evening to start up the Lister plant and as I came back in, Paul was looking out the window, towards our hay field. His excitement was mounting as he said, "Look at that big bull, Kenny!" I grabbed my 30-0-6 off the wall and just before he went into a thicket, I put a bullet through his hump and down he went! I went on out to the moose with my 22 and that bull was looking around. He was trying to make his front feet move, but seemed to be paralyzed, and tried to get up, but was unable to do so! I went back to the house to get my 32-20 to finish the job I had started. We hung him up in a tree, skinned him, and it was obvious that moose hadn't had a big meal for a long time. Isadore told me that the moose can go up to two weeks without eating very much. The meat was very good and we certainly didn't have to work very hard for that one!

He was a big one!

This hayfield where the moose was meandering through had been an old beaver dam which Isadore and his Dad had fashioned so that the overflow from the lake could irrigate this sixteen acre field. The soil was black and rich, so I planted alfalfa. In the spring when the snow left, I looked out where I was irrigating and saw a big, black bear walking in water, about six inches deep. Now he was walking in precisely the same path the moose had used. This bear was going across the field on the way to a timbered area on the other side, so I grabbed my 06 and shot at him. He reared up in the air, let go with a death call, and that was it! I went over to him, skinned him out, and pulled him in. His fur was beautiful and I sold it, even though I was not a member of the Trappers Club. When I sold the hide in Kamloops, the fellow said, "That's not a black bear, Sir, they don't get this big! This is a grizzly!" I found out later that the hide was worth at least $250, but I didn't know it at the time. I gave our neighbors, Al and Margaret, a ham, and one to John and Betty Spence and we kept the tenderloin. For some reason, Frances has an aversion to bear meat!

Shortly after I had killed this bear, our oldest son, Wilbert and his family came from Indiana to visit us. The first evening when we were eating supper, Thomas said, "Grandma, are we going to have bear steak for supper?" Frances said, "No, not tonight!" He said, "Oh," in a disappointed tone. The next evening she fried up some tenderloin off that bear and everyone ate some, except Frances, and nobody left any on their plates!

Another bear came along and carried off the carcass of the first bear from where it had hung in a tree, although there was not a sign of the tall grass being crushed! The strange part was I never could detect a sign of where that bear had walked! I knew bear were cannibals, but never found any bones or remains of that bear! The first year we lived there, I killed three bear and never went hunting for them! Black bear were in abundance and Grinder's had told me to be sure and shoot every black bear I could because they eat so many moose calves. The Game Commission may not have known that, but the people who live out in the bush do, and Phillip used to get a minimum of five bear a year. There were also lots of cougar and when we first moved to Canada, there was an ample supply of moose around the area, as well. Often when we were going into town, we'd see a moose along the road. Later on, however, they were much more scarce, as additional development took place, bringing people into the area.

Al and Margaret Crowhurst, were mighty fine, English people, and they bought the ranch where Paul and Kathy Hudon had lived. They drove into our yard one evening about 9:00 and we knew that something out of the ordinary must have happened for them to come calling that late in the evening. They had quite a band of sheep and throughout the day, Margaret faithfully kept an eye on them, for she was the most faith-

1978 - This bear was crossing out in the field almost in the exact spot where the moose had crossed!

ful shepherd you could find. That night, with flashlight in hand, she was going around checking the sheep, and as she shined it around the corral, there were a couple, orange-colored eyes looking at her! She said, "Al, is that you playing a trick on me?" She called out again and there was no response. Suddenly, she realized Al was out in his shop working, so she went to get him. He hurried into the house, got his 303 British, and they went back out! At once, they realized their visitor was a large cougar, so Al shot him. They didn't have a telephone then, so came over to use ours to call a trapper who lived fairly close by. They knew the trapper had a license and gave the cougar to him.

Another time when Al was building a zigzag fence, he came over, rather upset. He fell a tree about a foot on the stump, took his saw to knock the limbs off, and when he looked up, there was a cougar standing right at the end of the tree, just looking at him. Al said, "Well, if you plan to kill me, you're gonna have to fight me!" He ran at the cougar with his power saw and he went off into the brush. Al came over to ask me if our friend, Paul Blackwell, was home, which he wasn't. When Paul did return from Vancouver, I called him and he came out with his dog, Ranger, to try and trail the cougar, but they were unsuccessful in finding him.

I decided to hunt one day and went back towards Big Bar Lake, close to the Crowhurst's place, going through poplar timber. I got through the timber, came to an opening and I thought, "What a beautiful place to see a moose!" Would you believe, here came a moose walking below me, crossing in front of me with his head back a ways. He was a young bull and they're referred to as a "three-spike", so I kept watching and saw that he had horns! I had my 7 X 57 Mauser which I had fallen in love with, so I raised it and shot him! He didn't go down immediately in his tracks, but went a little ways further, so I fired two more shots and down he went! That morning as I dressed him out, the weather was beginning to turn warm, so I pushed him over with some jack pines and covered him up to keep the flies away until I could get back to pack him out.

THE BULLS FIGHT

Just as I finished "hiding" my moose, I looked up and here stood Al Crowhurst about a hundred yards away, with his arms folded. I had the heart and liver in my little duffel bag, so I waved to acknowledge him, as he started walking towards me. It was soon evident that he was upset and he asked, "What did you catch?" That's a term they use there and it's always amused me, so I answered, "I didn't catch anything because I didn't turn anything loose! I did kill a moose - do you want to see him?" "I sure do," he responded, so we walked up and I uncovered the moose. Al said, "Oh, that's the bull that had the big fight in our barnyard day before yesterday!" "Oh, is that right?" I asked. "Yes, two bulls had quite a battle in our barnyard, and that's one of them!" He looked and said, "Huh! Well, you DIDN'T kill him on my property, anyway!"

We were standing right in the middle of an old, log fence and I asked him, "By the way, where is your property line?" "This log fence represents the west end of our property and on the other side, it's government property for about twenty feet," Al replied. The funny thing was that I had shot the moose on Crowhurst's property, but he died on government property! Inwardly, I was really chuckling, but didn't dare let on to Al how amused I was. "By the way, Al," I continued, "if you see a moose or buck going across the road to our property, you don't need to come down to our house and ask permission to hunt it. If you want to kill him, go after it!" "Oh, thank you very much! I really appreciate that," Al replied enthusiastically. "Well, I would appreciate it if I had reciprocal rights on your property," I told him. He hesitated and said, "Well, no. Well, only if I knew WHO was hunting there!" I figured right away his hesi-

1988 - Canadian Thanksgiving Day. Isadore's moose - pretty great for a hunter 88 years young! Picture taken outside his cabin.

tation was based mostly on Phillip, as Al and Phillip didn't get along very well. Phillip got quite angry because Al had pushed out a fence row, and the brush pile was across one of Phillip's saddle trails, and he took a rather dim view of that! It seemed they had constant trouble the entire time Crowhurst's lived there, over one thing and another! This bull was the third one I had killed at Clinton.

On a Monday morning, Frances and I decided to go out hunting and went back in the same general area where I had hunted near Crowhurst's. We went back further, however, and on this particular day, there was a light skiff of snow. As it was nearing daylight, we could hear the coyotes screaming and howling as if they were about to feast on our carcasses. They were wailing and carrying on back and forth, so I took out my "Dying Rabbit" call and blew it! Immediately all noise ceased and it grew so quiet, it seemed as if you could have heard a pin drop! I told Frances, "You stay here and I'm going to go down the hill." Being the good wife that she is, she stayed there and I took off. Just before I was out of her sight, I beckoned for her to come on down. As she came towards me, she said, "Listen, I think I heard a stick break over here!" (My hearing had gotten bad from running cat for so many years in the woods.) I said, "I wish I could hear a stick break!" She listened and said, "It sounds like an animal is going in front of us!" Pretty soon, she grabbed me by the shoulder and pointed to where I had stood in the snow

Good photo of moose horns which John Spence mounted on nice plaque for Isadore. Here Ken is holding them for the photo.

and used the call. The sight that is glorious to any and all hunters, is a wild animal and here was a nice, big buck! As she said that, I grabbed my 7 X 57 rifle and put a bullet right behind his ear, while she put her fingers in her ears to cushion the sound. I dressed this fellow out and he was a large, fine piece of meat! We went down to Crowhurst's to get permission to drive through part of their property, so we could get closer with the pickup and not have to carry the buck out too far!

The next Saturday, moose season opened, so I took Isadore and we went up on the mountain, and back to a place we called "Helicopter Landing." He went out to his favorite saddle and I made a great, big drive around the rock bluff, coming back along the edges. Walking along, there would be flat benches and then steep draws, and before long, I came to quite a bunch of poplar trees. It was obvious that animals had been rubbing their horns against the trunks and we referred to this as the trees being "horned". I could see a mineral lick where the moose had pawed out an area, which was about twenty-five feet long and from two to four feet deep! By now it was about eleven forty-five, so I went down a little ways further and saw fresh moose tracks. As I observed all of this, the thought came to me, "My goodness, what a nice place to kill a bull!" I went on past this little mineral lick and sat down on a little tuft of grass and not even two minutes went by, when here came a bull crossing down below me! He stopped just before he went into the timber, giving me a chance to aim, so I shot him in the neck, right behind his ear. He fell in kind of an oval, scooped out place, and I had the hardest time getting that bull dressed out! I tied all my nylon cords together, got one of his legs guy-lined and dressed that bull out, quartered and hung. I don't really know how I did it, but I did!

Going back to Isadore, he asked, "Did you shoot once this morning?" I said, "Yes, Isadore, I killed a bull! While I was up on the bluff, I looked and saw a huge, black, bull moose all by himself in an opening, close to where I killed the first one." Isadore said, "Well, I've got an old trail that goes right back to that opening!" I was able to convince Phillip to go pack the bull in. He went back to where the moose was, spent the night out in the woods in a sleeping bag and packed it in the next morning. He had told me, "I'll have your moose packed to the landing tomorrow morning at daylight!" At ten o'clock the next morning, I arrived at the landing, but he hadn't shown up. I needed to remind myself that he would be on "Indian time", of course!

Later on, Frances, Isadore and I went back up to this area and I said to Isadore, "Why don't you go back to your stand and I'll make a drive toward you." Sure enough, he had piled up a bunch of logs and made a real nice "blind" there, so I went around like I did before when I killed the other bull. Isadore used a call he had brought along and soon, a bull came running to him! Isadore shot and cut his jugular vein off - completely off! That bull whirled and ran right towards the sun. It was just coming up over the hills, shining on the snow-covered ground, and was just absolutely brilliant! Isadore shot several times more, but didn't hit him again. I heard the shooting and came down to where he was. Was he ever excited and said, "Oh, I shot at a big, black monster," and he cussed a bit and added, "By the way, do you have shells in your gun?" I said, "Yes, I do and they're even paid for, Isadore!" "Well, I want you to go first," he said, "and remember, you watch where you're going!" I assured him I would, so he got into step behind me. After about fifty feet, the ground was just painted blood-red and about one hundred fifty feet from where Isadore had shot him, this big bull lay, right next to the limbs of a great, big tree!

In the meantime, Frances was up on the hillside, so she came down, found us and informed us a cow moose and calf had gone by her. She had some nylon cord, so I "guy-lined" that bull up and dressed it out while Isadore sat there on the ground! He was so excited he said, "I wanted that bull and I wanted him DARN bad! It's been five years since I killed one!" As I wrestled that moose around, I said, "Isadore, I'm not really a gambling man, but I'd be willing to bet $50 that nobody 88 years old killed a bigger bull moose than you did today!"

When we got back down to his cabin, we took his picture, holding the horns. As soon as the picture was developed, Frances and I took it into the office of the local Clinton newspaper and asked them to publish it, but we didn't tell him about it. Every so often, I'd take him literature, so when the paper with his picture in it arrived, I went to his cabin and said, "Isadore, here's a paper for you." "Oh, thank you very much," was his response. "By the way, there's a picture here of an old-timer holding a nice set of moose horns," I told him. "Oh, yeah?" he commented as he picked up the paper. Watching Isadore looking at the paper with an old pair of glasses someone had given him was interesting to observe! One bow was broken off those glasses and he could barely hold them on his nose, but just then he saw the picture! He started to cry and asked softly, "Kenny, did you do that?" I said, "Yes!" "Oh, thank you so much! How much do I owe you?" I said, "You don't owe me a red cent, Isadore!" He just couldn't quit thanking me and was so proud of that!

Shortly thereafter, I took the rack of horns from Isadore's moose and had John Spence put them on a nice piece of wood. John took the photo of Isadore, put a glass-like substance over it, and mounted it on this plaque with the horns. It was really beautiful and Isadore hung this in his cabin and was so proud and grateful for that!

After Isadore and I had our sheep hunt, I noticed that he was literally barefoot and falling down all the time! I had a brand-new pair of Red Wing hunting boots, vibram-soled, waterproof and just in perfect condition, but they were just a bit too small for me. I decided to give them to Isadore and one morning, went over to see him. "Isadore, what size shoe do you wear?" I asked, and he said, "Seven, eight, nine, ten. What size you got?" So, I gave him those shoes. He had rather small feet, so he just merely cut a couple layers of cardboard, put them in the shoes and presto, he had a brand new pair of shoes! I really liked his response then and still get amused at his reply, and thought it was very "fitting"!

About two miles from the house, I had opened up an old Indian trail which went back towards Clinton. Hunting season had been open about a week and I was out riding Cindy. She was such a wonderful horse to "wind" game and always had her eyes open. Just as we came around a bend, she suddenly came to a stop and just looked straight ahead! I looked, too, and saw just the flash of a set of horns on a buck! Often I'd dab some scent on my hat and I always whispered to Cindy (and I'm sure she understood every word I said), but she never did respond so I could understand what she had to say. I said, "Cindy, let's go a little further," and she went on! Again, she stopped and I saw this buck staring at us and noted he was a nice, big buck! I thought, "I wonder what this horse is going to do when I shoot this close to her head." I got off, got my rifle out of the scabbard, and tied one loop of her rope around a little jack fir, without even making a knot in the rope. I was about eight feet from her head, as I fired, and put a bullet through that buck's heart! The buck jumped, took off and went about one hundred fifty feet before he collapsed. I led Cindy a little ways and there he lay. I always carried some cubes for horses made out of alfalfa and grain, and flavored with molasses, which horses just love! Cindy kept pointing her head back towards those cubes, so I gave her some, and while she ate her lunch, I ate mine! Then I dressed the buck out and as I did so, I thought, "Man, I'm a long way from home! I wonder what she would do if I'd put that buck on her!" I had a double-cinch saddle, which I cinched down good and tight. Taking one of the hams, I hung it on a horn on one side and put the other ham on the other side. As I continued putting the entire bunch of meat onto her, she stood there very patiently, and then I led her home. I think she was as proud as I was! Cindy and I had many great hunts together and she was a terrific horse!

Crowhurst's had cleaned out our driveway one time while we were in Oregon visiting, as the snow was very deep. When we arrived back home, here was a pile of snow by my gas tank. That tank was at least ten to twelve feet high! It had really snowed! I had some traps set out up on the hill, so went out to check them after arriving home. Here was a beautiful lynx caught in one of them! Going back to the barn, I first rode Tony up there because she was a little taller and the snow was so deep! Tony beat the trail down and I returned to the barn with her, and then took Cindy out! The snow was nearly up to her brisket as we rode up there. About a thousand feet away from that lynx, with not a bit of wind stirring, Cindy stopped, laid her ears forward, and looked intently. I asked her what she saw and what's the problem, but she didn't respond! We rode on then for another quarter of a mile and here was this lynx in the trap. He wasn't struggling, just laying there thinking about the world, I guess. I took my gun and shot him, then tied him on Cindy, right behind the saddle and she wasn't the least bit alarmed by having that lynx put on her!

We rode down to the barnyard and just as we get down by the pile of snow at the gas tank, John and Betty Spence drove into our yard. They thought that was about the nicest sight they'd seen for a long time and had to take pictures! Cindy carried this off as if she innately knew what needed to be done. A number of times she'd spot game for me! One time when I was riding along on the upper trail above Grinder's old cabin, she stopped so suddenly, I said to her, "What's wrong here?" I looked around and just then a great, big doe stepped onto the trail. I saw that doe, but what I didn't reckon with, was there was a huge buck right behind her, and before I knew it, he got away from me! Had I been more alert, I'd probably gotten that buck right there on the trail!

Paul Blackwell drove into my yard one day and said, "Come go with me, Kenny, to the Robinson's, because one of their young horses was killed last night!" So we went off in the snow, and soon discovered the remains of a nice looking, young colt which a cougar had killed. Quite a few people had walked out there and the Robinson's wanted Paul to turn his dog loose, but he knew there was no future in running coyotes with an ordinary cougar hound. There were a lot of cougar around and they killed many of the young deer as well as colts, and other farm animals.

When I rode up to Isadore's one day, he said, "I'm going to show you something," so we both rode out in the woods, and after a little ways, he pointed, "Look there!" He had found a huge, four-point buck and a cougar laying on the ground, about fifty feet apart. It was easy to see that the cougar had jumped the buck, but obviously the horns of the deer had punctured the rib cage of the cougar, causing him to bleed to death. Isadore had put the cougar carcass up in the fork of a tree, but someone found it and took it down. Another time, when Isadore and I were out riding across a meadow, at a game crossing, I tied Cindy up so we could make a drive. She started nickering and carrying on, and I knew something had been there and she didn't like it. She never did that again, but on that particular day she let me know that she didn't want me to tie her up!

Isadore told me one day when we were visiting, "Kenny, I know where there's a big, deer crossing up on the mountain. My folks used to camp up there with Harry and Peg Marriott. I know the way and I'd like to go up there. We can build a little shelter and we'll have a place to kill those big bucks!" So I went to town and bought some plastic, nails, and other supplies. The next day I gathered my saw, axe, and all the supplies I'd bought, and went up to Isadore's. He said, "I'd like to go, but I don't have a horse to ride!" I said, "You can ride my Cindy mare." "No, I can't ride your horse. I don't know anything about her!" "Well, Isadore, she's just a standard shift! In fact, she's automatic! You won't have any trouble with her," I told him. "No, I don't want to ride your horse," he insisted. Finally I said, "Well, Isadore, you're an old-time cowboy and little kids rode her over at the dude ranch, so if you can't ride her, there's something wrong!" That hurt his pride a little bit, so he said, "All right, bring her up!" I saddled up the other horse and led Cindy up to his cabin early one morning and we took off!

It was a long ways up there and very steep, but around eleven o'clock we got up to timberline, and Isadore proudly announced, "This is the place," so we tied the horses up. Just above us was a great, long barren stretch of ground, rather sandy. We began looking around and Isadore said, "Look what I found!" It was an old, granite kettle, with the bottom broken through, and as he examined it, he said, "The spring used to be up here!" In that sandy bank, he began to dig a hole and in half an hour's time, that hole was filled clear to the top with beautiful, ice-cold water! We scrounged around and found some silverware that wasn't even tarnished or rusted, yet it had been probably around thirty years since his folks had been up there! We even found some of the tent poles and used them to erect a shelter for ourselves! I had a lot of fine hunts with Isadore and enjoyed him very much!

SOCIALIZING AT THE STAMPEDE

Anahim Lake was a wonderful place to go fishing and we had some great luck there, catching some fine fish. In the afternoon, we'd go to the Stampede, which was an all-Indian Rodeo. Needless to say, some very famous characters were there and they'd come from all over, and so long as nobody indulged in shooting each other, it was rather orderly! We saw little kids ride horses over drunken Indian ladies laying on the ground in the main path going to the ladies restroom! One year a couple young lads had herded about twenty-five wild horses for thirty miles to get to the corral there at the Stampede. You could certainly tell they were WILD horses as the cowboys tried to ride them out of the corrals. The Stampede was a very enjoyable event!

As usual, at this particular one, there were some very colorful characters present. A fellow, Clayton Mack, was there from Bella Coola and Dave Wilson told me Clayton had killed more grizzly bear than other human on the North American continent. At this time, I didn't know much about Clayton, but later I verified that information as I read it in a book written about him. Also, there was a fellow there named Tommy Holt, who was featured quite extensively in the book, Grass Beyond The Mountain. Another fellow in attendance was Albert Bryant. It was impossible not to notice still another man who had part of the side of his head torn off. We were told he was Connie King, one of the all-time, great hockey players of Canada. He married an Indian lady and they lived out behind Klappan Lake. The story which unfolded was that Connie went five rounds with a grizzly and seemingly was losing, as he fought for his life! During the battle, Connie figured the grizzly was going to eat him, but he was going to make him work for his meal and he fought that grizzly with his fist and clubs. He did survive, although the bear managed to tear the side of his scalp off and he lost one eye. Even so, he was very lucky to make it!

After we had been at Clinton a while, I had our place logged and met Dave King, who ran the skidder. I went up to where they were logging one day and as Dave and I talked, he said, "Hey, Connie King is my Dad!" As far as I know, Connie is still living around Klappan Lake and that grizzly is still around there as well! Dave told me he was riding home one time, came to a wild cranberry patch and there were five grizzlies eating berries. He knew one was a mother bear and two cubs and was smart enough to know better than to try and go through the area, so he waited for three hours until the bears left, and then he rode on home.

ROCK AND ROLL

Wanting to do some fishing, we made a trip to Anahim Lake Resort and caught some very fine fish. Close to where we fished was a very strong log building, with two grizzly bear cubs inside. Their Mother had been shot, so they were being raised by Jack Magnusson. Each weighed about ninety to one hundred pounds apiece and they would stand up inside this building, fight, growl, and really carry on! They provided great entertainment for anyone to watch! Magnusson's operated the Anahim Lake Resort and many of the customers are from Washington State, which we noted on the license plates of at least five vehicles, mostly motorhomes or fifth wheelers. About two o'clock in the morning, a fellow woke up and his motor home was rocking and rolling! The motion felt so fierce, he couldn't figure out what was going on! Something or someone, was really banging away at it and he was so alarmed, he didn't know what to do! Then things settled down, but he said they never slept anymore that night! He was frightened enough that if he'd had a gun, he would have shot right through the motorhome! Woody Woodard had eleven, native horses wandering around there and they meandered into that yard. This one horse decided that motorhome would be a good place to rub himself, and that's what happened1 That poor fellow and his wife inside were so shook up! We all got quite a chuckle out of that!

COMING TO GRIPS WITH GRIZZLIES

We had been hearing about Klappan Lake, about twenty-five miles south of Anahim Lake and supposedly there was good fishing there. Frances and I wanted to go and try our luck, so we headed out. Traveling in there was a challenge! There wasn't really a road, and you'd never want to try and drive a car on it, but we managed to get back in there with our pickup. After this ordeal, we arrived at a Forest Service Campground, of sorts, and there sat a brand-new, Ford Bronco, with "Hood River, Oregon", on the license plates. Three fellows were there, so I asked, "Are you fellows Royal Americans?" They said, "Well, yes, we are!" "We're from Oregon, too," I said, shaking hands with them. They said, "By the way, folks, there are two of the meanest bears you've ever seen around here, and they're not afraid of anybody!" One of the guys said, "Here comes one now!" There was a garbage barrel and this big, black bear laid down and started going through the garbage. I said, "Fellows, you may not believe this, but I have a 7MM rifle and shells, all paid for! I also have a bear tag and a hunting license!" "You do?" they asked! "Please shoot that bear!" I said, "No, I don't want to skin him, but I'll tell you what I will do, I'll put a bullet over his ear and maybe then he'll get the message!" So I shot over that bear's back and without a doubt, it wasn't more than three inches above it, but he never even raised up, and just kept on with his work!

Everyone was getting ready to go out fishing and our new-found friends put their grub up on a picnic table. We all went out on the lake and in visiting with these fellows, we discovered they were the Lure Jensen people from Hood River, Oregon. They were designing lures, trying them out and experimenting with various bait and methods of fishing. Those guys caught fish like you wouldn't believe. Frances caught seven, nice fish, while I ran the motor. In the evening, they cleaned their fish, putting the innards right into the lake, so I mentioned to them that it was a "no-no" to clean the fish in the lake, and they said they knew it, but were afraid to put anymore in the garbage can, because of the grizzlies. When they went to their grub box, they discovered the bears had gotten up on the table and pretty much ruined the rest of their stash.

The next morning I woke up about 5:00 o'clock, looked out the window of our camper and here was a bear, not five feet from our door, then he went right down the walkway to the water. Into the water he waded, about sixteen inches deep, and began eating the fish heads and innards which were deposited the evening before. I went outside and walked fairly close to him, so I decided to have a conversation with him! "Get out of here, you Black Rascal," I told him and tossed a rock at him. Well, he was so BUSY, he sort of grunted and jumped a little bit, so I just kept talking to him persuasively, trying to chase him off. When he was ready, he got out of the water and went up a small tree which was too small for him to hang onto. Down he quickly came, so I ran him up another tree and pretty soon he started frothing at the mouth and moaning! I knew what that meant, so I left him alone. In the meantime, Frances was up and she began admonishing me to leave him alone before he ate me up! While this was going on, the other bear had arrived on the scene, so I told the Game Warden about them and his advice was: "Well, you should have shot them because when they get that bold, they're nothing but trouble!" He also said that often if they will come that close to humans, then they are more likely to attack. That was an unforgettable encounter with the bears!

ANAHIM LAKE ACTION

Because we wanted to do some fishing first, we went to Anahim Lake a week early, prior to opening day of the Stampede. Driving out to Doug's, just as we arrived, he had finished skinning and salting down a huge grizzly! The picture of Doug and his Uncle John standing in front of the hide illustrates how huge he was, for he squared nine feet! He told me this story: A rancher from over by Kleena Kleene called Doug and said, "I wish you'd come over here and try to get this grizzly because he's killing one of my beef, every two days!" Doug got a friend, his dogs and went over there. Upon arrival, he asked the Rancher, "Where do you think he's grazing?" The Rancher made a big sweep with his arms which "covered" at least thirty miles, and replied, "He's out there somewhere, I don't know!" Doug and his buddy walked down a little path at the edge of the timber, and then started through it, coming out to an opening on the other side. Practically simultaneously, here came this grizzly walking out, so both Doug and his friend shot at him. Doug's favorite place to shoot a grizzly is in the shoulder, and he uses a large, heavy rifle, a 348 Winchester, with 250 grain bullets, as this breaks the animal down so he can't run. The bear went down and Doug turned his dogs loose. Both of them began barking treed, running in opposite directions, so he thought perhaps the dogs had "running fits". This is an old term I heard when I was a kid and supposedly happens when raw meat is fed to an animal and they get worms from it. Often this would cause them to run endlessly, affecting their behavior, and they called it "running fits"! Doug went to investigate and found four black bear had been following this old grizzly around, so when he'd pull a beef down, get his stomach full and go lay down, they'd take over and help themselves to the meat supply! Doug later sold that grizzly hide, a silver-tip and was paid $1,460 for it! The claws on that grizzly were huge, nearly four inches long!

This is the Silver Tip Grizzly which squared nine feet and taken by Doug Schuk on a ranch near Kleena Kleen. His Uncle John Schuk on left.

We had a neighbor lady who was so proud of her fingernails and I always wished she could have seen what that grizzly was wearing, as she'd no doubt been jealous! Once the grizzlies get started killing domestic animals, they'll never stop - you have to stop the grizzly! They eat all they can to lay up fat for the winter and their appetites are voracious!

Just last fall, a neighbor of the Schuk's, named Sader, was riding a horse and rounding up cattle in Northern Canada when a black bear grabbed at him. As a result, his horse bolted, he fell out of the saddle, and the bear killed him. Doug's son, Edward, was the one who discovered this fellow's body. The bears are losing their fear of humans and the same thing is true of cougars as they're being crowded out of their living territory. People need to realize how terribly dangerous these animals are.

Family get-together in 1983. The first time we had all been together for several years. Back row: Wilbert, Ken, Frances, Russell. Front row: David, Donna, Myron and Byron.

After we visited at Doug's and attended the Stampede, it was time to head home. Darkness had fallen, and as we went along, it was terribly foggy and difficult to see to drive. We soon encountered a car stopped along the road, obviously with car trouble, so I stopped to ask if I could help. I got our flashlight to walk back and when I approached the car, saw an older fellow with a bottle of beer. His daughter, about thirty-five years old, got out of the car and said they couldn't get the car started. I told them I wasn't much of a mechanic, but I would try to help. They had the hood open on their Buick and the daughter wrestled some cables around under the hood, gave it a royal cussing, got back in and behold, it started! Just then, two pickups with good lights for driving in fog, came down the road and each was pulling a trailer, which also provided some light. That was my cue! I jumped in my pickup, waited for them to go by, and then trailed those guys for about thirty miles until we got out of the fog, and eventually made it on home.

"MARISH" NIGHTMARE"

Out of Chicago, there was a Jewish horse buyer, who always made his rounds through the community with his horse and buggy. One old German farmer had such a beautiful, orderly place and he raised very fine horses! Every year the old German farmer had several horses to sell and the Jewish buyer was always prompt with his money, so they did a great deal of business. The farmer had a gorgeous mare and every fall the horse buyer would try to buy the mare and always he'd ask, "Is she for sale this year?" "No, she's not for sale," the German farmer would say. The Jewish man took pictures of the mare in various poses and always told the farmer, "If you ever change your mind, just call me collect and I'll immediately put $500 in the mail for you!" As the Jewish buyer made the rounds one year, he asked the same question and the farmer said, "No." Three days later this horse was found dead in the stall and the farmer wondered if the buyer's word was good. He got his neighbor to help him load up the horse, took her to town and loaded her in a boxcar. As soon as she was sent on the way, the farmer called the Jewish buyer, told him he had changed his mind, and was shipping the mare to him. The Jewish man was very pleased and immediately sent the money for her. The next year the Jewish buyer showed up, greeted the farmer warmly and shook hands. He asked, "Well, do you have any horses for sale?" "Well, no, not really this year, the farmer answered." "Well, remember, I'm still in business, my word is good, so be sure to call me," the buyer informed him. As he started to drive away the old farmer couldn't stand it and he asked, "By the way, how did you make out with that mare I shipped you?" "Oh, just fine! I posted her picture, sold 5,000 tickets in a raffle at $5 apiece and of course, the guy who had the winning ticket got mad, so I had to give his $5 back, but I did real well!" The guys up North got a real bang out of this story because of all the horses up there, a good saddle horse always commanded a decent price. If the horse was a good rodeo and roping horse, it was amazing what they are worth!

Another story goes like this: One time a couple fellows were down at Palm Springs and as the one casually look around, he spotted another vacationer who was leisurely sun-burning himself and smoking an expensive cigar. The first fellow noticed the second guy had expensive clothing on, so he nodded to him and asked, "How did you make your money?" "Oh, I have a business, and then I have a fire." The first fellow said, "Oh yes, yes," and they both continued to puff away. The second fellow then asked the first one, "And how did you make your money?" "Well, I, too, have a business. I have a flood!" "Oh, yes," he responded. After some time, the next question was, "Say, how do you start a flood?"

LURE OF LESSARD LAKE

While at the Stampede, I bumped into Mack Squinas and talked to him about going hunting. He told me he'd take me out, but that I'd need to furnish my own food, bedding, and gear. I agreed, booked a hunt, and on the appointed day, Frances and I started out of town towards Lessard Lake, to where they lived. It is nearly impossible to call where we traveled a road, or if you did, you'd have some sort of fearful imagination! There were stumps, rocks, logs, and debris which we had to negotiate. The Lessard River had an old, rickety bridge which we crossed and as we did so, could see that someone had been working on it. At last we arrived at this lake, where there was a big, old house with a bunch of kids running around outside. Before long, Mack showed up and we met the rest of his help. As always, I was anxious to get started on our hunt, but there was nothing to do but play their waiting game, as they were not in a hurry and had a number of things to accomplish before we could leave! I filed a bunch of hand saws for Mack and before long, he noticed my fine, little guide saw which I cut wood with around camp. He wanted my saw so badly, but I wanted it, too, so I kept it! They thought I worked some kind of magic and wanted all their saws and knives sharpened!

Two other fellows would hunt with us; Aubrey Cahoose who was about twenty-three, and twenty-one-year old Hobson Baptise, Mack's son-in-law. Frances would stay in our camper, spend some time with the other wives, and do some fishing while I made my hunt.

The next day, as we made our way through the woods to where his camp was located, Aubrey was up ahead and around a bend. I heard him call out, "There go bull moose, there go bull moose!" We hurried to catch up and all I saw was a splash of water in the lake. I never did see the moose, but Aubrey said two bull moose had been in the lake, then went running when they heard us coming. Aubrey and Hobson then took a different route than Mack and I, and headed out across the Dean River. We made a hunt for those two bull moose, and Mack did his best, but he couldn't get them out, so we continued on to where we would make camp. I was quite certain that after seeing those moose, there'd be some "repercussions" and sure enough, later on, my assessment proved to be correct! After I returned, Frances told me one of the Indian wives said, "Too bad about the old man losing the bull moose!"

We set about making up our camp and the little tent I had wasn't in the best condition, although Mack's tent wasn't any better! During the night it snowed and I didn't stay completely dry! I had taken a little grill along and the first evening when the fellows saw it, they thought it was great and promptly latched onto it! The deal was I had to furnish my own food, so I had come prepared, but I noted their cooking utensils consisted of one black teakettle and another black kettle. They had a handful of tea, not more than two handfuls of caribou jerky, about a quarter of a pound of coffee, but no salt, sugar, or bread. My stash consisted of two loaves of bread, six tins of sardines, package of fig bars, a dozen eggs, about four pounds of bacon and some potatoes, plus salt, pepper, and sugar! I gave Mack a loaf of bread and he asked for salt, so I gave him half my salt, as well as the sugar. The next day I gave them my fig bars, and so it went. I don't know yet what those fellows existed on because they hardly had anything to eat!

Just after Mack and I had everything set up for camp, here came Aubrey and Hobson, very excited! Aubrey said, "Today, for you, I kill big, fat bull moose!" "Where is it?" I asked him. "Across the river, but I want to borrow your saw, your knife and axe," he said, so he and Hobson went across the river. The next morning, I never saw any meat and had presumed when they had left with my saw, knife, and axe, that they'd bring meat back into camp. This left me more than a little puzzled and no explanation was ever offered!

We hunted quite extensively and rode up several steep mountains. There were lots of other hunters out there, so we had competition and it seemed the game wasn't all that thick in the area. At last, we saw a young, beautiful bull caribou running up a hillside and when he came to the skyline at full speed, Mack said, "Look, if you shoot little bull, maybe you'll get big bull! If you kill little bull, we have something to eat!" I called to him and that bull stopped, so I took aim with my 270. It was a lucky shot, as I shot off-hand and "anchored him", breaking his neck. I quartered him, and dressed him out. Then the Indian fellows started laughing, "We got no rope!" I said, "Well, I have a hunk of nylon cord about fifty feet long and it's pretty strong," so we tied the meat onto the pack horse and down to camp we went! Now there was meat to eat on, so we hunted for another three days, but never did see another caribou bull!

I had mentally noted that both Mack and Aubrey had terribly poor footwear! In fact, Mack's shoes looked like a pair of house slippers and they were all split apart! As we were walking along a little game trail with snow on the ground, I said, "Mack, not this year, not next year, but sometime, you're gonna have wet feet," and he just laughed! I had a pair of shoes shaped like cowboy boots, but the soles were of vibram, and they were a beautiful pair of shoes! They were a little tight when I bought them and I had hoped they'd stretch a little bit, but they never did, so I later gave them to Aubrey! He was so proud of them and rightly so, for they were worth at least $100 on the Canadian market!

Since we hadn't seen any game, we started down, as we had traveled a long ways to hunt. Aubrey and Hobson decided to make another foray off to the south below us and we made camp to spend another night. While the horses we had were feeding in a nearby meadow, and Mack and I were in camp, we heard a strange cry! The horses looked intently in the direction where this noise came from, and Mack said, "All my life, I don't hear anything like that!" When I was at the zoo in Portland, about ten feet from a cougar, he "screamed" and I knew how they sounded and I've heard other wild animals, but I had never heard a noise like we heard that day. A couple years later, I asked Mack if he ever figured out what that strange scream was and whether he thought it might have been a bear. He said he was almost positive it wasn't a bear, but never did know for sure!

I knew that before long, Aubrey and Hobson were going to go to Rainbow Lake, which was over a thirty mile trek. At Rainbow Lake, they had a little shack and some American hunters were flying up to hunt with them! The horses' feet had grown over their shoes something terrible, the harnesses were shot and the old buggy was in bad shape! I said, "Mack, if I don't get that meat in, it's going to spoil!" He said, "No, we fix, we fix!" They did go to Rainbow Lake and that meat hung there and spoiled and I always felt very badly about it!

The second hunt I booked with Mack, Frances and I arrived and were waiting for Aubrey to come. Hobson was there with his wife, as well as a couple of their kids, and some other kids visiting from Tahtsa Lake. These kids had pushed Mack's hay rake off the bridge, into the water and although they couldn't swim, they weren't afraid of the water. Part of the time, they'd catch grasshoppers and go fishing, as the fishing was just simply fantastic. We went fishing, too, and I caught several, each weighing about two pounds. They were so very tasty, as we had them for our evening meal! These kids would fish, then play in the water, and kept pushing Mack's hay rake into the water further and further. I said, "Look, kids, your Granddad doesn't want you to do that!" They just scowled at me and didn't pay any attention. From what we observed, the Indians don't correct their kids, punish them in any way, but just let them go and I guess they figure when they get older, if they've got common sense, they'll survive. There was all sorts of "equipment" scattered around that place, not being cared for. In the road, we saw a rifle scope, all kinds of clothing, one of which was an expensive down jacket, and various items, but everyone just drove over it! The mood and mode seemed to be "happy-go-lucky!"

We waited there with Hobson, but Aubrey never showed up, so we rode up the mountain that morning, going way up on top! As we came to a large rock ledge, there was some timber growing on top and the horses acted sort of strange. They didn't bolt, so we continued riding and as soon as we rode a little further, here was a big, wolf den! There were wolf droppings of every size all around, indicating baby wolves to adult, and we saw a big entrance underneath the rock. I can well imagine there could have been ten to fifteen wolves living in there because they killed a lot of game. Hobson spoke and said, "Wolves really bad. Last winter Game Warden bring poison to help us kill wolves! Not much game anymore, not much moose!" I said, "Hardly any caribou anymore!" He said, "No!" I decided to just give up hunting there because the game was non-existent, so that was my last hunt with Mack's outfit. I learned that Mack's wife was blind and that later on, he suffered a stroke which left him quite crippled. It seemed as if he had to endure some difficult things, but he was a very fine man and I was glad to know him!

WILEY WILSON

Several people had told me about a colorful character, Dave Wilson, who lived in the area, and after I met him and booked a hunt with him, he proved the description to be very accurate! I had heard of several of his previous accomplishments. Dave lived on Sucker Creek and I drove in there a day ahead of time. This creek ran through his yard and there was a beautiful meadow with lots of game, and I believe it was the best moose hunting I ever enjoyed! I told Dave, "I brought my saw-filing tools along, would you have a saw you need filed?" He came unglued! "Do I have a saw?" he asked and immediately rounded up a bunch of old, rusty saws. I went to work on them, which as it turned out later, was a rather foolish thing to do! I had some emery cloth and oil, so began the task of hammering, scouring, jointing and filing them! He then asked, "Could you file a meat saw?" "Do you have an old carpenters' square," I asked. He went and got it, so I clamped the blade of the meat saw on this square, filed his meat saw, and we visited. Slowly I began to learn about Dave's background. He came to the Tatla Lake area when he was thirteen years old and hired out to a big ranch. Soon he became proficient in breaking horses, but was nearly broken himself! He had a pin in each hip, two fused discs and his back was very arched from the rough life he lived. Dave wasn't afraid of anything and whatever he wanted to do, he somehow got it done! The horses which we rode on this hunting venture had been wild horses Dave had caught and broke, and they were as gentle as could be!

Dave came to my camper and said we'd start out at 9:00 A.M. the next morning and sure enough, we were in the saddles by that time the next day, starting up the mountain. We had ridden about half a mile when I asked him, "Dave, do you call moose?" He said, "No," and asked me, "Do you?" I said, "No, I just imitate Isadore," but I do have a moose call in the pickup." He said, "Please go get it!" So I went back to get it and rejoined him as we continued our ride up the mountain. At noon we came to a beautiful, long, drawn out lake, surrounded by a lush meadow, poplar and some willow trees, and decided it was a perfect spot to enjoy lunch. Dave boiled a couple handfuls of black tea in a belly pot, but I just couldn't drink it. He was sitting there drinking tea when he asked, "Say, Kenny, where's that moose call?" The horses had gotten out in the water, about a foot deep, and I answered, "It's out there on my saddle horn!" He asked me if I would go get it, so I waded out in my boots and got it. Of course, he was just dying for me to use it, so I called rather softly the first time, and he said, "that sounds good to me!" After about five minutes, he got up, turned around and looked, let out a blast and said, "Get that big, brown rascal! Go get him, Kenny!" There was an old pack trail along this lake and I ran for about half a mile along the lake and then cut up on the hill, circling back to where Dave and I had been, but I never found the bull! When I got back to Dave, he said something that really tickled me, "You know, if I would have waited a few minutes and not bellowed out, that moose would have been down here drinking tea out of my belly can!" I wanted to tell Dave that the moose wasn't quite that stupid, because nothing on earth could drink that tea! We decided to head back to our camp.

Dave told me the next morning we would go North and he was sure we'd get a bull right off the bat. He went so far as to say he wasn't going to take much grub along, so he took just a little macaroni and cheese, some coffee, and about two cups hotcake flour. We went a long ways, covering very rough terrain, through muskegs, over some rock bluffs, and finally got back to a clearing. I thought I saw something shiny off to the right, and said, "Hold 'er Dave! I see something over here!" "Yeah, I know you do! There's a house there," and he began to tell me the story about a famous cook in Alaska. This fellow came here to spend winters and Dave had packed in on his horse everything in that house – the doors, lumber, windows, everything! All alone that fellow would spend winters there, skiing all over, but not hunting or fishing, he just loved being alone.

We got there in the evening and had a little supper before we turned in for the night. The next morning we started hunting and hunted all day, but didn't get anything, so when we got back to camp very late, I was past being hungry. Usually about 6:00 o'clock in the evening, my hunger pangs are quite vocal and I want to eat! After that, they'll subside, and this evening, I really was not hungry since it was so late. Dave didn't have a lantern, was ill-prepared for the night, and he wanted to eat, so he decided to fix the macaroni and cheese. Neither of us ate more than a cupful of it, after which we retired. The next morning Dave asked, "What can we have for breakfast?" but without hesitation, he answered his own question, saying, "Oh, I know, we'll have a hotcake apiece!" I observed him emptying the remainder of the hotcake flour on top of the macaroni and cheese, added some water and tried to stir it up! Needless to say, he didn't have very good luck and it certainly wasn't appealing to me!

As Dave was preparing his breakfast, he asked, "Do you know Lester Dorsey?" and I said, "No, I've just heard a lot about him!" "You know, he's really filthy," Dave commented. "He is?" I asked, to which Dave said, "Yes." Now I wish I could have had a picture of Dave as he was telling me this about Lester, for you just wouldn't believe it! The snoose was running off both sides of Dave's mouth and his nose had a perpetual drip! It wasn't always clear as to where these drips were landing, but I had a sneaky feeling they may have been fairly close to that hotcake! He told me that Lester would be able to fertilize a half acre of ground if he'd just clean out his fingernails! One time Lester took two doctors from New York out hunting. They tried to impress him by telling him they might be city-slickers, but they were TOUGH, and Lester told them he was SO glad they were tough! He never took any cooking utensils and when they arrived at the camp, he said to the doctors, "Well, fellas, unless you want to eat with your fingers, you might want to whittle a knife, fork and spoon for yourselves," which they attempted to do! Lester also chewed snoose and had false teeth, so he took a cup, put his teeth in it, poured in some water, and just stirred the water around with his finger. He then put his teeth back in his mouth and rinsed the cup out! As he did that, the coffee pot was boiling, so he asked the doctors if they'd like a cup of coffee. They said, "Sure," and Lester poured two cups of coffee and then he went down to the lake to get a pail of water. The one doctor started drinking coffee and immediately was gagging! His partner asked, "What's the matter?" He said, "Oh, I got Lester's blankety-blank cup!"

That day I killed a moose and we came in very late in the evening. Dave and I fixed some steaks off that moose and he looked at me with a smile on his face and said, "Kenny, this is really high living, you know!" I said, "Yes!" We talked at length and he said he wanted to tell me a story about what happened one winter. He had a couple saddle horses he had been feeding well, so they were in fine shape. It had snowed and there was a deep crust on the top, and as he observed the wild horses, he saw that they were getting thin and decided he wanted to catch a bunch of them. Dave rode out on one of his horses, rounded up about thirty-five wild horses, and was heading towards his corrals, when suddenly they split, and about twenty went to the left, so he also went to the left. These horses went out on an open, barren hillside and then the tracks just disappeared! He said, "Now I don't tell this story to very many people because they laugh at me! They can't fly - I know that and you know that. Whatever happened to those horses, I will never know!" Some strange things happen sometimes and people smile at it, but I've thought about that horse incident many times and Dave said he had pondered over it for years.

The next day we packed the moose into camp and I was glad to be able to get one. Dave was a good guide and also had a trail riding service. He had a little shack up by Perkins Peak and could take his charges there to spend the night. He told me he had taken individuals from Switzerland and all over the world on his trail rides, and I knew this was true! The ones from Switzerland he took out told him that nothing in the Alps compared or rivaled the beauty there in British Columbia. Sometimes the view and splendor of the mountains and craigs just takes your breath away and the scenery is magnificent! Dave also had another cabin at Dalton Lake, up on Dalton Mountain and the Indians used to go from Quesnel to Anahim Lake for the Stampede. They followed a trail through the mountains, knew of Dave's cabin and always stayed there, which was fine with him. There was a natural spring by Dalton Lake and he rode up there one day and breathlessly observed around two hundred caribou feeding in a lush meadow. He asked me, "Would you like to go hunting for caribou with me?" "I sure would," I responded, and he said, "Well, I'll keep you in mind!"

Two days after we came in from our hunt, Dave's wife, Roma, drove into the yard in her old, beat-up Datsun pickup. This truck had a steel bed, but no plywood on the floor and I noted that every saw I had filed and cleaned up for Dave was on the back of that truck, except for the meat saw. On top of those saws was a log chain, a jack, lug wrench and various tools bouncing around back there and no doubt none of them would have cut through hot butter after that treatment! How foolish I was to have worked so hard to sharpen and clean them up!

About the first of July the following summer, I took Frances into Clinton so she could catch a bus to Seattle where our daughter, Donna, lives, and then Frances was going on down to Oregon to visit other family and friends. While I was in town that day, Dave drove into our place with his wife, Roma, and left a note on my door saying, "If you still want to go hunting with me, I'll be at the Slumber Lake Lodge in Williams Lake. Please give me a call!" When I got home and found the note, I immediately turned around to go back into Clinton to call Dave. He answered the phone, and I told him I definitely wanted to go hunting with him, so he booked me. At that time, radio messages were broadcast at 12:00 P.M. and again at 6:00 P.M., and by now, about five days had passed since I had called Dave. Everyone around there for a couple hundred miles broadcast the same message out of Williams Lake and Quesnel, and it was received as far away as Bella Coola. That way the Indians and the white people could keep track of where their friends and family were. As I listened to the broadcast, I heard, "Dave Wilson, late of Tatla Lake, funeral Saturday at Tatla Lake Community Hall," and I could hardly believe my ears. On Saturday I went to the funeral and learned what happened. Dave had some trail riders out by Dusty Lake and every horse was saddled and packed up, except one. He went back to get another cup of coffee and just fell over a pack box and was dead. It was some time before they could get the body out, so there was not a public viewing. Dave was buried with his harmonica, two fresh cans of Copenhagen, a pint bottle of whiskey, two tickets to the Anahim Lake Stampede, and his buck hunting knife. He was a friend to everybody, a man of his word and the natives came all the way from Bella Coola for the service. Many people of note came to pay their respects to Dave Wilson who died in the land that he loved.

Some of the outfitters and packers I went out hunting with were men of notable stature. For example, Herb Leake, had Jim Bond working with him, and I had met Jim in McMinnville, Oregon, one time when he was showing pictures and talking about the Yukon. One of the projects he had done in Canada, was to conduct a Game Survey for the Game Commission. Herb told me Jim was out in the mountains for six weeks duration, with a pack train. They observed game and recorded information right in an area where we hunted. Herb thought a lot of Jim and spoke highly of him. When we first got to Herb's place, there was a huge elk carcass laying off to one side. He said, "I suppose you wonder about that carcass, do you?" as he noticed me looking at it. "Yes, I do," I said. "Well, I just had Mr. Eaton, of the Eaton Stores Chain, out hunting and I got a Royal Elk for him, a seven-pointer, but he only wanted the horns! He shook hands with me and said the rest is all yours!" Herb said there was so much elk steak in his locker he didn't know what to do with it, but for our hunt, he took at least fifty pounds of that meat, so every evening there was as much delicious steak as you could eat! Herb was a great provider, had a wonderful camp and had packed out many well-known people! One of them was Elmer Keith, author and well-known woodsman from Montana, and another was Jack O'Conner. Always I learned something interesting from my guides about these other characters.

GARLIC, GIZZARDS AND BRAINS

We enjoyed another "social outing" which included John and Betty, as well as another young couple from Clinton, Gregg and Sylvia Faddigan. Gregg was Principal of the Clinton High School. At this point in time, Frances and I didn't know Gregg and Sylvia very well, but all of us went back to McKindley Lake, which is twelve miles long, and a long ways back in the mountains, in very wild country! The ladies decided that they'd each take a turn making the evening meal. Betty would cook the first evening, Frances the second, and Sylvia would do it the third evening. Even though Betty really wasn't feeling very well that first evening, she prepared a mulligan. Some fellows were camped close by and told us they were going into the closest store and asked if we wanted them to pick anything up for us. Betty whispered to John, "Ask that fellow to buy me a big bulb of garlic!" John asked the fellow and he said, "Okay!"

In the meantime, we began eating Betty's mulligan and Sylvia asked, "What are these dark objects here in this mulligan?" Betty said, "Well, to tell you the truth, they're chicken gizzards!" Sylvia jumped up and said, "Oh, my! Mother never fixed any of the organ meats at our place," and she disappeared. The rest of us were fairly silent during our meal and before long, Sylvia came back.

The fellow camper returned from his trip to the store and handed the garlic to John. He peeled off a clove, handed it to Betty, and asked me if I wanted one, so I took one, as did John. Gregg and I decided to go back out in my boat before it got dark. He looked at me and said, "Mr. Shenk, we're regular folks, but....., well, my wife puts garlic powder on food, but to eat the pure clove of garlic, oh gee whiz, no! No way!" One thing led to another as we visited, and I soon realized Gregg was a great fellow and they were, no doubt, just regular folks! I began thinking about the time I was hunting with Walter Erhorn and how I fixed those brains and now on this trip, Betty had used these gizzards and we had consumed this garlic. So I began thinking that perhaps I should help educate Gregg and Sylvia! He and I came in from fishing and I noticed a piece of cardboard there in camp. I took the cardboard and wrote this little "jingle" on it: "If people ate gizzards and garlic and brains, it would banish their trouble and alleviate pain"! Everybody laughed.

About a month later, John asked me, "Did you ever finish that jingle?" I said, "Yes, I did!" He said, "No, you didn't," but I assured him I had. One night I had been awake around midnight and a whole bunch of nonsense came to me, but John didn't know this yet. I didn't know how Sylvia would react to my poem, so hadn't "broadcast" the fact I had finished it. Shortly after our little trip together, she had broken her leg and so that fact is addressed in the jingle, too. In the meantime, I had taken it into John and he made a copy.

We went down to a Christmas Party one evening at the little church in Ashcroft and John said to me, "I'm going to read your poem this evening," but I said, "Please don't, John, we'd just as well be friends here!" Of course, later in the evening, he did read it and Sylvia just laughed and laughed! She wanted a copy, also, and we remained friends! Don't ask me why the words for this poem came to me just like that, when something else worthwhile could just as easily have "enlightened" me! It goes like this:

ODE TO SYLVIA

If people ate gizzards and garlic and brains,
It would alleviate suffering and banish all pains,
But people are stubborn and learn very slow
They suffer in silence and eventually go.

To the disperser of pills and doctors of shame,
They write on their stones, of the families they came.
And now, here comes Sylvia, a right comely lass,
She loved to go sledding, and go very fast.

While going down a hill, all lickey-split,
She thrust out her leg, to slow down a bit,
Alas, and for shame, she saw her mistake,
For truly and surely, she had a bad break.

The Doctor said, Lady, you'll pay for your sin,
For she didn't know the bad shape she was in!
They put on a cast, but she wouldn't heal,
They gave her some shots, along with the deal!

And then in the end, as she couldn't mend,
The doctor said, Lady, do you have a Friend?
Or someone to nurse you and pamper no end?
And Sylvia said, Yes, there is a lady I know,
She taketh the garlic, and her breath she does blow,
My leg, she's a hurtin' and hurtin' like sin,
I'll take of the garlic and heal up within!

So Sylvia did eat of the fruit of the ground,
And like Mother Eve, word soon got around.
One evening her husband came in through the door,
She rose up to greet him, just like before.

He suddenly stopped, and started to scream,
Don't tell, Dear Sylvia, you're into this scene!
For Sylvia, I tell you, your breath is quite bad,

It smelleth of garlic and maketh me mad!
Why don't you renounce these fables of herbs,
You're not in some tent, but in the suburbs.
For people will pass you, and shun you as well,
I tell you, forget it, be rid of this smell!

Now Sylvia said, No, I can't part with this vice,
It may smell quite high, but it sure is so nice!
It healed up my bones and made me like new,
I think I'll entice you, and put some in my stew!

But Gregg was insistent her nonsense to stop,
For truly and surely, their marriage would flop!
I'll roll up my loot and go miles away,
And you can eat garlic, yes, eat garlic all day!

So Sylvia was faced by a problem quite vast,
She thought of her future, she thought on the past,
She thought of her children, she thought of her friends,
And then in the finale, Gregg won in the end!

If people ate gizzards and garlic and brains,
It might NOT relieve quite all of their pains!

One of the things that always struck me was the measuring stick that so many people have as related to others and to their social standing, status, and how they measure up. Every community has its' colorful characters and I can tell you that the area around Clinton was not sold short! One neighbor told me, "Ya know, I only went to school for three months, but the funny thing was, the teacher didn't show up the first two months, so I guess I got a limited education. Could be, you know!

When Hampton's built their big mill at Boston Bar, Chuck moved to British Columbia and made his home in Chilliwack. Hampton's became very involved and active in the Canadian Lumber Mills Association. I was visiting with John one day, as I tried to do occasionally, when I was in Oregon, and he said, "Kenny, I want you to get acquainted with Mr. Dave Ainsworth." I said, "John, I don't know Mr. Ainsworth and have nothing in common with him, so why should I meet him?" John said, "Well, you have something in common! Dave is my friend, and so are you! You have that much in common!" Every now and then John would ask, "Have you met Dave yet?" One day I was in a barber shop in 100 Mile House, with four fellows ahead of me, and their conversation was normal for a group of guys. Suddenly, I was just struck with the thought, "That fellow over there in the chair is Dave Ainsworth!" He had his turn in the barber chair, paid for his haircut, and went outside. I beat it outside and said, "Excuse me, Sir, would you happen to be Mr. Ainsworth?" He said, "No, I'm just Dave, one of the boys!" So I introduced myself and told him of my association with the

Hampton's. He warmly greeted me and said, "Well, I'll tell you something, I sure wouldn't sell those Hampton boys short!"

Dave began visiting and said, "You may know that I accompanied the Hampton boys to Europe and also to New Zealand." He stated that they had plans to build a big pulp plant so they began looking at existing plants to get some ideas. They were in Tokyo one evening in a large restaurant, and after being properly wined and dined, John asked the waiter for a guitar. A guitar was brought to John and Dave told me that John began to play that guitar and sing for all he was worth, and soon there was quite a large audience. Many of the songs he sang and played were old cowboy ballads and various folk songs. For about an hour, John continued, and when he quit, his audience warmly and enthusiastically applauded. Dave said a waiter went up to John, tapped him on the shoulder and said, "You come back, I hire you!"

The next time I saw John Hampton, the lumber market was quite soft and he made a remark pertaining to this. I said, "Oh, John, don't let it worry you. You can always go back to your first love and entertain people!" You should have seen the look on John's face! He then knew I had met Dave Ainsworth!

A funny thing happened when I hunted with Clarence Simmons out of Jarvis Lakes. Earlier I mentioned Herb and Karen Barnes, whom I met hunting there, and Karen was the cook. One evening she said, "Kenny, you said you are a lumberman. Did you ever hear of the Hampton boys, John and Chuck?" I said, "Karen, you are crazy! I know those boys very well! Are you sure it's the same Hampton boys I know?" She said, "Oh yes, they are from Boston Bar Mill!" I knew then that we both knew the same fellows! Karen told me she was a secretary for a large mill at Williams Lake and at a big Christmas Party one year, she danced with Chuck. The next time I saw him, I said, "Chuck, I ran onto one of your old girlfriends the other day." Chuck laughed and asked, "Which one?" I said, "Karen Barnes." He said, "Get off my trap line, will you!" We both laughed and then he asked where I had met the Barnes. I told him the circumstances in which I met Herb and Karen, but it just points out once again, we live in a small world!

BEAR OR DEER?

WE'LL TAKE BOTH

When we moved to the Big Bar country, there was a large ranch which was known by different names. Led Schmidt and his partner bought it, but when we moved there, Bob and Elva Newberry lived on the place. We heard about them and their boys, but hadn't met them. In the meantime, they traded places and moved down on the Jackson Ranch, below Clinton. They had hundreds of head of cattle and this winter was a cold one with lots of deep snow, so they had to pull all their cattle out. Going into town one day, we saw three head of cattle at the barn where the Newberry's had previously lived. We thought the neighborly thing to do was to notify them, so we drove on down to where they lived to tell them. Let me assure you, they were overjoyed because those cows were worth around a $1,000 apiece as the price was up then. Norm went up and was able to retrieve a couple of them, although one got away. We became very good friends with these nice people!

There was a road up through Newberry's property, which went to a big logging site back on one side of Scotty Creek. One hunting season, towards evening, Frances and I drove up this road until we got to an old logging landing where we camped for the night in our camper. That way, we could get an early start the next morning. At daylight, we began to drive. I was going along quite slowly when Frances looked down the hill and said, "Ken, there's a black bear down there tearing the bark off that log!" I stopped, took aim, and shot him. He just laid down on the log for his final resting place. We then continued to drive and came to another landing, where we immediately saw lots of deer! I picked out a nice, three-point and shot him. It was only a little ways from where he laid to where the pickup was parked, so I pulled him down there and dressed him out. We then drove back to where the bear was, skinned him out and headed home.

We had met the taxidermist at 100 Mile House and he had said to me, "Look, I'll give you $50 for any bear hide and $35 for a deer cape." We went into 100 Mile and he was glad to buy both the cape and the bear hide. If a person wanted to eat bear, that looked like one good piece of meat, but I've never been able to convince Frances that it's good for her! We discovered the area back of the Newberry's was a good place to hunt and did so more than once!

DETERMINED DEMPSEY

Another fellow we became acquainted with was Dempsey Callison, who had been born at Telegraph Creek. His Dad's name was Fred Callison, a white man, and he and his wife had nine kids. When Fred and his wife were around sixty-five years of age, they got into a big argument and split up. Then he married a young, Indian girl whose maiden name was Quock, a resident there at Telegraph Creek. Fred and his new bride had four more children; Sam, Jerry, Dempsey, and Ann, and we became acquainted with Jerry, Dempsey and Ann. Dempsey was a very interesting person and was married to a very fine, white woman named Ruth, and we used to visit back and forth quite a bit. One day, Dempsey said, "I'm going to take out two hunters from Switzerland and I want you folks to go along with us. We are going to the Ruth Redfern Wilderness area, behind Canum Lake. Would you go with us?" We said we'd be happy to go!

Frances and I met up with Dempsey and party on the scheduled date. Among the group were the two, Swiss hunters, one of whom had saved money his entire lifetime to come on this trip. The one fellow was named Heinz and he was a giant of a man. Believe it or not, he had brought along a fishing pole and some worms from Switzerland and those worms were still alive and in good shape! His fishing pole was a neat one; collapsible, and about nine or ten feet long, which was very "fitting" for a man of his size! One was a baker and the other one, an electrician. Cory, Ruth's son from her first marriage, was also along.

Dempsey didn't know the trail very well, but we made it back to where we would camp in this Wilderness area. The rivers and lakes were very high, as they'd had a lot of rain, and this meant the lake wasn't good fishing. We couldn't really get in good fishing without a boat, so we didn't stay too long. Coming back out, we had to ford a pretty swift river, close to one hundred feet wide. After we had gone along for awhile, Dempsey decided to take a snooze! I tied up my saddle horse, but he tied the other horses, head to feet and let them graze! One of the Swiss fellows called to Dempsey, "The horses are going!" "Oh, yeah, they won't go far," he responded. He had his little snooze and was just waking up and said, "Come on, Kenny, grab that bridle, let's go!" We started running down that trail and had gone about a half mile down the river when he said, "You go back and get that saddle horse, quick!" I hurried back to get my saddle horse and he took off on the run. I could hear him screaming like everything and he got to the river just before the horses were ready to enter the water! I rode my horse at great speed to get back there! It's a good thing he got there before those horses got into the water because they all would have drowned. The rope was so short between their heads and front feet, their movements would have been vastly impaired and they never would have made it through that swift water! These horses belonged to the Block Brothers Riding Stables. That was a very close call to having a major tragedy on our hands! Cory was riding a mule named Harvey, and what an ornery little rascal he turned out to be! Fortunately, Cory rode him through that river, even though he didn't want to go! That was our first venture with Dempsey, but not the last!

Many years earlier when Dempsey was just a kid, his father had a fabulous hunting area on the Keicheka River, adjacent to Skook Davidson's territory. Skook was the famous horseman of the Interior of British Columbia, with quite a notorious history. Fred also had quite a reputation as a packer and at one time, packed for the government. The plan at one time was to put a telegraph line across the ocean and it was supposed to start from Telegraph Creek; hence the name, Telegraph Creek! Fred was a great horseman and one of his sons, Lynch, from his first marriage, used to ride with him. Usually they'd have a couple Indian lads and would pack over seven hundred miles through the wilderness area, sometimes in the dead of winter, with fifty-five head of horses! The hardships they suffered would fill a book and were absolutely incredible!

Dempsey once again called Frances and I and said he was taking some hunters from Austria out of the Dease Lake area and wanted us to go. He said, "My half-brother, Lynch, has a service station and restaurant at a place called Forty Mile Flat Service Station," and he wanted to stop there. Forty Mile Flat was forty miles from Dease Lake. We told them we'd go with them.

We met to go on this trip and the group included Eddie Morris, Larry Novakowski, Ruth, Frances and myself and four more hunters were to join us. Larry was a very fine taxidermist and had his business in 100 Mile House. In a couple days, two more of the four expected, joined us and we learned their names were Paul and Jerry Hunt, brothers, from Coeur d'Alene. Paul was quite a big time operator and had flown over the area with Dempsey to look things over. They had contacted an Indian guide, Thomas Dennis, of that area and he agreed to have horses there for us, all shod and ready to go back into this wilderness area to hunt moose and caribou.

Eddie had a big, Ford van and I took our pickup and camper. Dempsey rented a big Ford pickup to pull the horse trailer. We took seven horses from the Block Brother Stables as Dempsey was managing the riding stable at that time. All of them were really nice horses and fairly big, except for the one Frances would ride, called Patches. This old trailer which Dempsey latched onto had come up to Canada from Texas, many years before! Someone had hauled a piano and other household articles in this trailer. It had a dual axle, but the tires were so old, they were rotten, as this trailer had sat out in the weather, only the Lord knows how long! One hub cap was off, the bearings were rusted, exposed to the dirt and grime and it wasn't a pretty sight! This trailer had a good husky tongue on it, but the frame had broken loose and Dempsey asked me to get some wire, saying, "I can work wonders with wire!" I said, "Well, you're not going to work wonders with wire on that, you need to get a welder and weld it properly! Dempsey put the horses in there, plus a stash of food for them, oats and hay, saddles and other gear. Well, by the time he put everything in, the tires were virtually flat before he ever left and I said, "Dempsey, those tires are flat!" He said, "Yeah, they're kinda low, Brother, aren't they?" "They certainly are!" I said emphatically, but he said, "Well, we've only got ten miles to the service station. I'll blow them up there!" I never dreamed he'd get that far, but he did! He blew them up and said, "You go ahead to that big wrecking yard close to Williams Lake, and get some hub caps." I went up there and they asked, "What kind of trailer is it?" I said, "I don't know!" We waited for Dempsey to arrive and when he got there, it was obvious he had a terribly big load behind that pickup. I looked down into the ditch and saw an empty Miller High Life beer can, so I picked it up and kicked that crazy thing on that axle! As far as I could see, there was no grease or anything in the bearings; yet that crummy thing went clear up to Dease Lake, which was hundreds of miles from there! That trailer was something else because the springs were so overloaded and weak, it would sway from side to side and make the smoke boil off those old tires.

At last we arrived at Lynch's domain! Lynch was a big man and had been in a horrible wreck in 1945 and this was about 1980. While we were there, Lynch's cook was on a big drunk and wasn't of use to anyone, so Lynch asked Frances if she'd cook, but she graciously declined! Also, the gas man hadn't delivered gasoline, so he was out! It seems that our "oasis" in the wilderness wasn't performing too well!

The two other hunters had sent word there that they wouldn't arrive for another four or five days, so Dempsey said, "Let's pack up, go back to Ice Mountain and do some sheep hunting!" We got the horses and the one Demsey gave me was a big, husky quarter horse, called Cheko. Lynch instructed Dempsey where to go, as he had never been on a side venture out there where we would go to hunt sheep. Lynch said, "You go down to a long opening and watch real close, towards the end of this opening, you'll see some blazes, and take off there!" As we started out on a trail, Dempsey said, "My ancestors traveled here for centuries!" We rode along as Lynch had instructed and found the blazes he told us about, then we came to a long muskeg, about fifteen hundred feet long, which didn't look all that grim. Continuing on, we saw the trail Dempsey described, so Dempsey turned there and I followed. About five hundred feet in, the top of my stirrups touched the top of the muskeg and I bailed off Cheko into a clump of willows, which weren't very big! Before I knew what was happening, this horse jumped on me! Larry called out to Dempsey and without looking back, Dempsey called out, "Give him his head, Kenny, give him his head!" I said, "Dempsey, that's the sad part! This horse doesn't have a head - he's crazy!" Dempsey laughed and said, "I rode him the other day down at the riding stable and I seen he wasn't no mountain horse, that's why I gave him to you! I didn't want nothing to do with him," and he just laughed! I was pretty sure right off the bat that was the reason Dempsey had told me that Cheko would be my horse! At last we got through that muskeg and Dempsey said, "I'll tell you one thing, fellas, we're not going back through there!" We proceeded on up the mountain and finally came to an old Indian campground and it was a very nice place to camp. We tethered the horses, fed them, and set up a little camp, which didn't amount to very much!

Next morning as we prepared to go out, Larry commented that he'd never seen a wild sheep, but I had killed two. We decided to split up; Dempsey and Larry went together and I went out on my own. The country was very steep and I went about a mile when I looked up to the top of this hill and saw a ewe! She was just staring intently at me, her eyes fixed on me, so I just laid down and watched her with my binoculars. Immediately I wondered if she was alone and almost as if my thoughts had been read, three rams appeared off to the left, looking down the hill in my direction. They'd look over at the ewe, then they'd look towards where I was, and I felt that I knew what was going through their heads! They wondered what that crazy, old ewe was looking at! They kept staring at her, then they'd stare down the hill, but they never saw me! It was so humorous to watch! They were barely legal, but I just decided I wasn't going to kill one, so I never even shot at them. Instead, I went on up the hill a ways and ran into another band and once again they didn't have a really good ram among them, so I didn't fire a shot!

Back at camp that night, when the other fellows came in, Larry said, "You know, if I could just SEE one, Kenny, if only I could just SEE one wild sheep, I'd feel good!" Larry, being a taxidermist, had mounted animals from all over Alaska and the Northwest Territories. He was a very fine taxidermist, and had won many prizes, but never had he seen a wild sheep! All of a sudden, he said, "Hey, Kenny, I see a SHEEP!" I said, "You what?" Very excitedly, he said, "I SEE a SHEEP, right up here!" There was a ewe about two hundred feet from camp, just looking down at us, and so at last, Larry got to see a wild sheep. In a little while, Dempsey decided we were going to pull out of there. This area belonged to Bruce Creyke, who's still in business there and some fabulous heads come out of this territory. We rolled up our "ball of twine", got out of there, got down to the muskeg and Dempsey said, "You fellows stay right here and don't attempt to follow me! I'm going to pick out a new path!" He rode in a different area and those horses sunk right down! He spoke to the horse and said, "Get up," and the poor horse just started lunging and putting forth all his effort, and was just barely able to get out of there! Dempsey was leading a big pack horse and said to us, "Don't come in here!" The upshot of it was that we had to cross in exactly the same place we had the first time and it seemed as if the mud settled in, and it was a mess! I was the last one to come through on Cheko and he just floundered and struggled until I didn't know if we were going to get out of there with that horse alive or not! Undoubtedly, that was the most horrible muskeg I've ever experienced in my life! So back to Lynch's we went!

A lady stopped there with her son, who was about twenty-five, and they came into Lynch's station. They asked him, "Are you Mr. Callison?" He said, "Yes, I am!" "I have a present for you," she said. "Oh, what's that?" Lynch asked. "Well, my son loves to scuba dive and was in a lake and he found something which might interest you," she explained. While this young man was in the lake, he saw something shiny and brought up one half of a propeller. An aluminum prop had been broken off of the plane that Lynch had crashed in and obviously had gone into this lake. Lynch laid in the wilderness area for five days and five nights before they got him out! His right shoulder was broken and all of his ribs caved in on one side, which permanently crippled him for the remainder of his life. This young man had found part of the propeller and presented it to him. Lynch felt very proud to receive this as a souvenir!

While we were staying there waiting for the other hunters, there just wasn't much in the way of groceries available in Lynch's station. Frances and I had our good supply of groceries along, so we fed Dempsey and the entire gang out of our camper for a couple days until the other hunters came. As we visited with Lynch and became better acquainted, we discovered he was a very famous man in the North country. During the next few years, we became quite well acquainted with him. One fall he came down to Clinton in a big, three quarter ton Ford pickup with a big camper on it and pulled a small travel trailer part of the time. Usually, on top of the trailer, he had a canoe. His daughter, Cheryl, lived in Clinton and Lynch would come down to spend the winter sometimes. On this particular trip, he came to Cheryl's daughter's wedding. Before the wedding, Lynch's grandson, the bride's brother, was killed, so Lynch attended a funeral before he went to a wedding and this was a very sad time for his family.

Lynch knew all the old time fellows, such as Simon Gunnanoot. Simon is the man the Mounties couldn't catch for thirteen years! He was accused of a murder, which he maintained he never committed and was eventually exonerated. He knew Cataline, the great packer who packed from Cache Creek up to the North Country and a number of various people I had not met, but had read about. At one time, Lynch had a store in the wilds up North and had just stocked $16,000 worth of supplies. His wife left the store one evening to go visit some neighbors and while she was gone, the store burned completely, as well as three of their children! It seemed that Lynch's life was touched by so many tragic things. He and his wife subsequently split up, he was in the airplane wreck, and while we were living up there, his son, Coyne, was killed in an airplane crash, plus he lost a grandson. Coyne was famous in his own right and very well known and well liked! Although Lynch suffered through a lot of problems, he had an indomitable spirit and was afraid of nothing!

In earlier years, Lynch packed for the government and laid out a large section of the Alaskan Highway for the United States Army. There was quite a large contingent of American troops up there working on this project. One fellow in the troops was a famous boxer and the locals told him, "You'll be the champion until you run unto Lige

Callison!" This boxer asked, "Who's he?" They said, "Oh, he's a local fellow around here and he's Lynch's brother! When Lige sees you, he'll whip your butt off!" The boxer said, "I want to find him!" Lynch said that fellow would go around to all the saloons and taverns and call out, "Is Lige Callison in here?" One time they were in Fort St. John and this guy went to the tavern, called out his usual question, and Lige answered, "Over here!" The boxer said, "Come on out, I want to fight you!" "I don't want to fight you," Lige insisted, but the confident boxer said, "I WANT to fight you!" Lige asked, "Does it have to be done?" "Yes," the fellow said, and with that they went outside where a large group quickly gathered to witness the show. Reportedly, the U.S. champ never touched Lige with one blow and Lige just beat him to a pulp!

Even when I was hunting with Herb Leake, he was telling me about Lige and said, "That man is so fast on his feet, it's unbelievable! In the saloon one time, he had some old Canadian Mukluk's on and a fellow said, "I'll bet you can't jump up here and touch the ceiling!" Lige said, "Well, I think if I wanted to, I could take a run and put my feet up there!" At this time, he was at least fifty-five years old, but he jumped up and put his muddy Mukluk's on that ceiling! The bartender was so impressed that he never took the mud off the ceiling! Herb said, "I can tell you one thing, Kenny, no ordinary, husky man would have any business picking a fight with Lige Collision, 'cause he'd whip his pants off so quick the guy would hardly know what hit him!" Lige never looked for trouble, but never ran away from it! Dempsey told me Lige once went five rounds with a grizzly, lost every round, but he never lost his courage!

Some time later, back in Clinton, Frances and I had been gone a couple days and when we returned home, here was Lynch Callison in our yard, with his pickup bogged clear down to the rear-end housing! Unfortunately, he had gotten into a terribly bad, soft spot out there and was stuck and had been there most of the day, so we invited him to eat with us. He asked, "Kenny, how are we going to get my pickup out of there?" I said, "Well, it won't be easy, but we can do it. We're going to jack it up, build a platform underneath and get you out," which is what I did and he was very grateful. He told us, "I'm going to go to Salt Spring Island and retire down there." He did go down there and discovered everything was so expensive, it made him angry, so he went back to Dease Lake. However, we heard that he moved into the Elk's home in Fort St. John later, where he lived until he passed away in 1992. We saw a picture of him in a book entitled, The Peacemakers Of The Peace River. In this picture, he has a big, wolf parka on and hardly looks like a human. In fact, he looks more like a huge grizzly bear, for Lynch was a big man! In that book we learned he had a dog team of about twenty dogs, bought firs for the Hudson Bay Company and was quite a fellow. We certainly felt enriched for having met him for he was very interesting and a great character of the North!

While waiting for the other Austrian hunters, Dempsey went to see Thomas Dennis, from whom we were supposed to get pack horses. A group of hunters had just left and everyone there was on a big drunk, so guess what? No horses, even though he had promised he'd have some for us! Dempsey had another friend there, Willie Williams, so he borrowed a couple horses from him. Thus, we started on our journey into the back country and I've never seen a hillside like the one we were traveling on. It didn't look bad at all - looked kind of rocky and yet there was no bottom to it! The horses would sink down, lunge, struggle, and the poor creatures labored so hard JUST to keep moving! Dennis told Dempsey that nobody had been back there, but where we started out, we found a bunch of fresh caribou hides. When they cut logs out, they'd cut them down half way, chop them off, and leave it just about as high as a horses' belly, and the horses would have to jump over these windfalls, which isn't a good way to keep a pack on!

We finally got back to camp and the second pair of hunters from Austria had arrived, as had the grizzlies. They had made an appearance, dug up all the cans, ransacked things in general, and left so many grizzly droppings around there, it was unbelievable! Some piles were so high, the two tall Swedes could hardly shake hands over it, but we hurriedly cleared things off and set up camp. Two days later, another fellow, Elmer Dennis, arrived to help Dempsey guide and without a doubt, he was the greatest snorer I've ever heard! His timing on the intake and exhaust valve was perfect! He slept in the cook tent and wouldn't get out of the way in the mornings so Frances could do the cooking! Dempsey told Ruth, "Now you watch that lady start that stove and all this, 'cause I want you to learn!" She said, "Dempsey, you know I don't know how!" "I know you don't, but you're going to learn," he'd inform her. She said, "No, I'm not going to learn!" "Oh, yes, you are," he insisted, and so they argued, back and forth! At the onset of our trip, I had told Dempsey that I had to be in Clinton on September 21st. He always said, "No problem, Brother, no problem!"

In this great wilderness area, we made a big hunt, but there was just no game; just grizzlies and wolves! We saw a cow and calf moose and one day I saw a band of ewes running, but not a ram in the bunch! We also saw one small band of caribou. The one fellow from Austria got a shot, but did not kill a caribou. One morning I told Dempsey that I had to go back to Clinton the next day, to which he replied, "No problem!" The next morning, Ruth came over and she heard the air going out of my air mattress. I had a tent, tarp, cooking stove, lantern, extra gas, ropes, and a lot of supplies needed for this area. She asked, "What are you doing, Kenny?" and I answered with a question, "What does it sound like to you?" "You're not leaving, are you?" she asked. I said, "Yes." "Are you going, Frances?" "Sure am," Frances said. Ruth said, "Well, I'm not going to stay here alone in this camp with all the grizzlies around here," and she began to cry. Dempsey heard her, came over, and asked, "What are you doing, Brother?" "Dempsey, what does it look like to you? I told you I had to be in Clinton by the 21st!" "Well, you can't get out of here! How are you going to get out of here?" he asked. "Well, there's nothing wrong with my legs! I'll leave all the necessary articles with you, but we're going out," I told him. When he saw that I was rather determined, it made him half mad. I said, "By the way, Dempsey, here's one hundred dollars, but he said, "One hundred dollars? I owe you folks a couple hundred dollars!" I said, "Well, I have a feeling you should take it," which he did.

As we started down off the mountain, I had about seventy-five pounds on my packboard and Frances had about twenty-five to thirty pounds in the packsack. There was one ford to make and it was really a bad one! Frances walked on a little log and I waded into the river and held Frances' hand and we made it across safely. Around

10:00 o'clock in the morning, back in camp, Dempsey said to the group, "Let's get out of here! We gotta help them poor, old people get down to their pickup!" They pulled camp and started out. When they arrived where our pickup had been parked, however, we "old people" were probably seventy-five miles on down the road!

As Frances and I drove down the highway, there was a young, Indian fellow right out in the middle of the road, waving his arms like crazy! We stopped and he immediately said, "I want a ride; I have to go to Prince George! My name is Gordon Abu and I've been guiding in Cold Fish Lake, but I hear my Mother die. I want to go to the funeral. I have nothing to eat and I have no money! I was driving my pickup and ran out of gas, so I just run it off in the brush. Please give me ride." So I said to him, "We'll give you ride and I'll have Frances cook something for you," which she did.

We continued and were not far from Forty Mile Flat Service Station, so I told Gordon I had to stop and give Lynch Callison a message from Dempsey. He looked at me and said, "I know that man. One time I cut wood for him and he don't pay me!" I said, "Well, you just stay in the camper, it'll just take a minute while I run in and give Lynch a message." To my utter astonishment, when I stopped, that rascal beat me into Lynch's little restaurant and Gordon said, "Hello, you remember me?" Lynch said, "No, I don't know you!" "I cut wood for you one time," Gordon said, and Lynch responded, "Oh, I remember you now! You're that little devil I paid off and you got on that big drunk! Yes, I remember you!" The color came up in Gordon's face, but Lynch continued, "Well, I'll say one thing for you, you did a nice, neat job! I wouldn't mind hiring you again sometime!" Gordon brightened up and said, "I cut wood for you again!" So, this completely changed the picture from what he told us before about not getting paid. He had gone on this big drunk and didn't remember that he had gotten his money!

Gordon was full of a lot of stories and when we first picked him up, he told us, "I get in bad trouble! You know, I'm the champion Kick-Boxer of British Columbia and I'm not supposed to fight anybody! I guide for Ray Callingswood and his brother, at Cold Fish Lake. I kicked one of them in the neck and Adams Apple and almost killed him, but he made me mad, so I knocked him down!" I wondered what the complete story was, but that's what he told us! His stories went on and on as he told us about some of the big fish he caught. He then asked, "Where do you live?" and as soon as we told him, he lost no time in adding, "Do you have horses?" "Yes, I have horses," I told him, "I'm just breaking a horse," he said, "I'll go home with you and break your horse! I'm a champion rodeo rider!" It seemed that this fellow wasn't too responsible and had I taken him to Clinton, he'd probably tried to run off with my horses, robbed us, or something!

About sixty miles further down the road, we came to a little Indian village, Iskut. Gordon piped up and said, "You stop here. My woman come from here one time, so I want to stop. You give me some money." I decided to give him $20, as we dropped him off, but I said, "Look, I'm going right through Prince George and I'll take you right to the mortuary!" "No, I want to stop here," and that was it. Later on, Lynch went into Prince George and learned the entire story and this is how it goes: Gordon went into Prince George about a week after the funeral was over, broke into a store, was caught, and put into the brig! He served thirty days and when he got out, somebody killed him, so that's the story on Gordon Abu! The amazing thing is that he came from Fort Ware and my brother, Ron and his wife, used to care for Indian kids who came from broken homes and some who were in dire circumstances. Gordon knew Ron, had been to his home, and knew Ron's kids! It was really something the number of people Gordon knew and that we happened to pick up a total stranger, who knew my brother, Dempsey, Lynch, and others that we also knew!

As Dempsey started out with that trailer to return to 100 Mile House, we heard through the grapevine that the bearings went out on it and he had some flown in from Prince George. Whoever told us this also said that a plane flew over the highway and just dropped those parts right out of the plane for Dempsey! He never did get back to 100 Mile with the horses. Some were dropped off at Smithers, but we never knew what he did with the others. So, the $100 I gave him turned out to be a blessing in disguise, because he certainly lost a pile of money on that trip! This trip was rather traumatic, as I'd get so nervous driving behind that old trailer, seeing that smoke curl up, that I just could hardly stand it, but Eddie Morris told me it also made him nervous, so we finally took turns! All in all, that trip was full of lots of different experiences, to say the least!

HART AND HART

Neighbors to the south, right below our place, were Herb and Judy Hart, who had originally come from Holland. They had a bit of a Dutch brogue, which amused me to no end, and they were delightful people! During moose season, Herb drove over one evening, terribly agitated and he lost no time in saying, "Folks, I need help! Somewhere, back there, over that S curve (that is the term up there for a ridge), my Judy is lost!" We said, "Why, sure, Herb, we'll help you look for Judy," and immediately jumped in our pickup to drive back to his place with him. When we arrived at their house, Herb got out of his truck to come back to talk with us, and Frances said, "Listen, Herb, maybe Judy came in while you were gone. Perhaps you should check in the house!" He was reluctant to do that, but we walked to the house with him, and here's Judy! She said, "Herb, what is wrong with you? When I "yoo-hoo", you don't answer!" Herb said, "Judy, what is wrong with you? When I "yoo-hoo", you don't answer!" She said, "But I call and you don't answer"....back and forth it went! Anyway, it had a happy ending, as they figured out what happened! Herb was just fixing to shoot a big bull and Judy was going to shoot a rabbit with her gun and they were separated by a little distance! Judy then saw our fence, got her bearings, and went back to their house. It was so funny and I'm sure they spent a happy evening together that night!

Herb and Judy had a CPS office in Clinton and did tax preparation, were both well-educated and capable people. Another time Herb came over on a Saturday morning and I noticed a little smear of blood on his hands. He asked, "What's your program today? What do you have scheduled?" I said, "Herb, I don't have an agenda, nor an itinerary, what's your problem?" He said, "I need help and I need help bad 'cause I've got a moose down." "Okay," I said, "I will help you!" He described to me the area where he had the moose down and lo and behold, his description was good! I went up on the hill, caught Cindy and saddled her up, along with my meat bags, knives, saw and essential tools and over the hill I went! Shortly I found Herb and the big cow he had down, and also quickly discovered he had only cut her throat before he rode off to my house. So when I arrived on the scene, that moose was so filled up with gas, the sun could hardly shine over her and there were some delicate moments there getting that paunch open without rupturing anything! I packed that moose in for Herb and they were highly elated, for it was the first moose Herb had killed there! Two people couldn't have been happier for this moose, and we were pleased for them, too.

Before this, on another occasion, Frances and I had a compass and were trying to run the back line on our property. This was still wild country and Frances said, "You know, we're really foolish out here! So what would happen if we ran onto a bear?" I said, "Oh, forget it, Frances! You have an active imagination - we're not going to see a bear!" Do you know, we didn't go more than a thousand feet, or even less, and here's a bear! He wasn't in any hurry to leave and just fooled around! We went back to the house, I grabbed a rifle, and we went back out! That bear was still in his leisurely mode, so I shot him! Perhaps the moral of the story is to listen to the little wife's advice once in awhile!

Herb was thinking about doing some fencing, so he said, "You come over tonight and I'll show you where the fence line is." Hart's had a dog, Arthur, a big, black Labrador and rest assured, Arthur was part of their family and I'm sure he was related to both of them! I hadn't had a chance to dress that bear out yet and he had actually died just over the line on Hart's property! Herb and I met out there, were about seventy-five feet away from the bear, and any moment now, I expected that Arthur would announce that we were approaching something, so I said to Herb, "I have something to tell you." "Sure," he said, as he stopped and looked at me rather quizzically. I continued, "I shot a bear up here a little while ago and he's right in front of us!" Herb asked, "He is? You shot a bear?" "Yes, and he's right down there," I said. Arthur had come to it by this time and was busy looking it over, when Herb said, "Well, now I'll tell you something, I don't know if Judy would like that or not. Please don't you tell her and I won't tell her." "I have no problem with that," I told him. We agreed and he never told Judy and I didn't either, although I never did know what the deal was, but I was amused by this. There were lots of bears around there and they could be a real nuisance! The old saying, "Hungry as a bear," is a true term for a bear is always hungry from the time he comes out of hibernation in the spring until he goes to bed in the fall, he's trying to put on fat to go through the next winter and they work at it constantly! They will kill calves of beef, moose, or anything they can get their claws on!

During the period Hart's were our neighbors, Bill Vanderzam was elected Premier of British Columbia. Mr. Vanderzam was also from Holland and had made a fortune selling dahlias, I believe. I wrote a little jingle about the New Democrats, as in Canada, they had the New Democrats, Liberals and the Conservative Parties. Since Herb and Judy were also from Holland, I gave Herb a copy of this one and he was so tickled he said he was going to mail a copy of it down to Bill Vanderzam, which he did! This is how it goes:

THE DEMOCRAT

Dear Father, must I go to work?
Why, no, you lucky Brat!
We're livin' now on Easy Street,
We're Plain NEW DEMOCRAT!

But Father, if the well runs dry,
And I might have to work,
What would I do if comes that day,
For I have always shirked!

I want no other questions,
You nosy, little Brat,
You do far too much reasoning,
To be a Democrat!

But Father, if my girlfriend's Dad,
Should run me out of town,
And if, perchance, you're in your grave,
How would I get around?

Well, Son, he said, I got no plan,
It's mostly up to Fate,
It might be well if she'd get a job,
And keep you up to date.

But please, don't bother me no more,
You nosy little Brat!
You worry and you fret too much,
To be a Democrat!

THE DEEP FREEZE

One winter we had repeated warnings from Isadore of a cold winter, as he kept saying it was going to get so cold we wouldn't believe it! I asked him how he knew and he said he'd been watching the squirrels. Their dens were full and they had mounds on the ground, and had dug holes and filled them up, he had observed. Lo and behold, it went down to 59 degrees below zero! Reg Robinson, heard a banging on his door at 2:00 in the morning and here was a truck driver in horrible condition, so Reg let in him, made coffee, and got him warm. This fellow was working for McGavin Bread Company and his truck had stopped, so Reg called a mechanic for him. They found out this fellow was driving a brand new, diesel truck, but the heater wasn't working properly, or at least not good enough for the extreme cold. With the speed he was going, they figured the chill factor was about ninety below zero. Not only did the diesel freeze solid in the tank, but the fuel pump injector, and in fact, everything was frozen solid! Jim Walsh took two Tiger torches out and got everything thawed out and going again. That fellow was extremely fortunate to survive! Some of our nearest neighbors out on Big Bar Lake Road when we first moved to Clinton were Paul and Kathy Hudon. Paul asked, "Are you familiar with cold," and I answered, "No, I'm not!" "Well," he advised, "let me tell you a little definition for cold. Just remember, it penetrates, and if there is a hole, it will find it!" I found his statement to be utterly true!

Paul had injured himself working at a local mill, and being close neighbors, I wanted to help them out, so I cut wood, plowed a field, did numerous chores and tried to be Good Man Friday. He had twenty-eight head of really fat Angus and his heifers had trouble calving, so I went over one morning and Kathy said to me, "I know what's going on out there, Kenny, I've been hearing them all night long." So I went out in the corral, discovered one of the heifers had been in labor all night long and this calf was partially born. Those vicious ravens had picked the eyes out of this poor creature, and we finally pulled it on out, knowing it hadn't survived. You can begin to understand how hated those ravens are and one Game Warden told me the ravens had been protected so long they had become a very real nuisance. He also said he'd like to look the other way, call them a crow, and not worry about their survival, because at that time, crows weren't protected, nor were the eagles. Eagles were also very destructive to calves and on the Gang Ranch would kill Hereford calves and even claw out the eyes of yearlings! These environmentalists are great on bed bugs and microbes, but they don't always know what happens out in the wilds and possibly they never will know!

KK - KARL KRAMER

Our good neighbors, Herb and Judy, decided to move to Clinton to be nearer their work, so they sold their place to Karl Kramer. Karl hired a local cowboy, Billy Spoonamore, to work for him part of the time. Karl was quite a remarkable fellow; very energetic and capable in that he could build a saddle, corral, house, in fact, he could do most anything! He told us he was an engineer by profession, and had built a big fiberglass boat which he sailed to the Hawaiian Islands. I always had trouble getting my boat across Big Bar Lake, let alone all the way to Hawaii! When he moved to the Hart place, he went into

Karl on crutches with a buck he shot. I helped him dress this one out.

the riding business, taking out trail riders. People from all over the world booked with him, and he took me along on a number of occasions. He built a very good outfit, with a beautiful barn, riding stable, high corral to train horses in, and everything was in A-1 condition!

Some people from Vancouver had a very mean horse which they gave to Karl because it had either crippled someone for life, or killed someone. At any rate, they wanted to get rid of it, so Karl took it and was out in the corral training this horse. After some time, he got on it and as he started to ride, that horse reared over backwards with him, fell on him and broke his

Karl Kramer with a bear he shot near his house.

leg! Karl was six feet tall, weighed two hundred pounds and was about forty years old when this happened, but there he was, all alone and he couldn't get out of the corral! His leg was laying at an awkward angle and he knew it was broken. Karl dug a hole with his hands, crawled underneath the logs and began to work his way to his house, which was about two hundred fifty feet away. There were some high steps leading into the house and in order to get to the phone, he had to crawl up those stairs. He'd crawl a ways, pass out, come to, and crawl some more. No one knows how many times he repeated this procedure and it was hard to estimate how much time passed before he actually got to the phone and called for help. Someone came to take him to the hospital and once there, the doctor operated and put a big sleeve in there. The doctor told him that sleeve would have to be in there for a year and then they'd take it out, but that he'd get along just fine. It bothered him terribly for a long time and he suffered a lot of pain.

Karl had a 375 H & H rifle on a Ruger single shot axon, had done his own hand loading and when he loaded

Photo taken on top of Marble Range Mountain, close to good sheep hunting. Karl Kramer, our neighbor, asked us to pose for photo to insert in his Big Game Guide brochure. Pictured L to R: Ken on our lovely horse, Tony, Claudia, a young lady from West Germany, and Billy Spoonamore, great cowboy, who was Karl's hired hand.

a cartridge up, it was loaded for bear, believe me! It wasn't for chipmunks! He had a beautiful target set up at one hundred yards and he could put three shots out of that Ruger and a quarter would cover them! So here comes the opening day of season and Karl is on crutches, but as he looked out the window of his house, there stood two nice bucks, right by his target! He gets his 375, takes the rest where he always did and shot the first buck right in the center of the gut! Talk about convenience!

Billy Spoonamore, the cowboy Karl hired to work for him, was a wonderful horseman and I thought a lot of him. He did professional horse shoeing every spring and summer, as well as corrective shoeing. Somewhere I read a story about Bill and another local fellow named Robby Grinder, up in the Yukon, guiding a West German hunter. They held the distinction for guiding to and getting the largest set of moose horns recorded in the world. As I recall, they were seventy-eight inches! Bill used to come over, eat supper with us, and he brought over a bunch of his pictures to show us, which were incredible! This set of horns was later superseded by a set which a trapper found on a skull out in the wilds. Those horns, still intact, were eighty-one inches! The moose Bill and Robby found for the West German man didn't have a terribly big body, but rather, it looked as if it took most of his strength to carry those horns around! Those horns were certainly enormous, that's for sure! Bill told some fascinating stories and more than once, he had stayed by himself out in the wilds throughout entire winters. At one time, he lived across a river in a very remote area and fed a bunch of cattle for a rancher. Remember, Canada has long winters! Billy certainly was a fine person to be around!

WALTER'S WANDERINGS

Of all the people we met up North, Walter Erhorn was one of the greatest, and he loved to hunt! Walter had also guided some very well-known people during his guiding career, and was a real bush man! When he first took me out, he was forty-four years old and he told me he had cooked more over an open fire than he ever did over a stove! His Headquarter Camp was out about twelve miles from Atlin, close to the old Discovery Mine. We were out on a hunting trip and I asked him, "Walter, you must have had some close calls in your life out in the bush, tell me about your closest call with the undertaker?" Walter said, "Well, just before Ralph Schoof and Barney McPhillips came this fall, I was swimming my horse across a lake, when she had a heart attack and went down. I had my rifle, spotting scope, binoculars, and gear, and all of it goes down! I can't swim a stroke, but this time I used my head. The water was about eight feet deep and I would go to the bottom, give a big jump, and as I came up, I would head for shore! I kept this up until I could touch bottom and wade into shore!" Walter later retrieved his gear as the horse's body bloated, came up to the surface, and floated close enough to shore for Walter to get a rope on the horse and pull her in. All of it was water logged, but he was able to salvage most of it. On this trip, however, he did use my spotting scope.

Walter continued, "I had another close call, which was also one of my closest! A few years back, I was running my trap line on a stormy, windy day and 35 degrees below zero temperature. I wanted to take a short cut across this lake and I guess I just quit thinking! Quite close to shore was a spot that had a warm spring in it and steam used to come up. I had my snow shoes on and wasn't too far from shore when I broke through the ice and down I went, but I kept clutching at the ice. It just kept breaking until I was totally submerged in the icy water. By some stroke of luck, I got one snow shoe off, laid it on the ice and slowly worked my way towards shore and onto stronger ice. Finally I got on ice which was strong enough to hold me and as I did, I knew I had ten minutes to live!" As he was talking, he reached in his pocket and pulled out a Marbles Match Safe, just like the one I had in my pocket. He said, "I knew what to use as kindling and got a fire started and by this time, my clothes were a solid sheet of ice! I managed to get them off and danced around the fire while my clothes dried out." There was no one to cheer his dancing, either! He said, "That was close enough!"

Another time, Walter was going into Atlin from his cabin on Gladys Lake, at ten o'clock at night, it was forty below zero and he was on his Ski Doo. Thirty miles from Atlin, that machine broke down, so he had to walk into Atlin, just barely making it, in the extreme temperature and snow! What many people do not realize is that freezing to death is rather painless, because after you get so cold, you just want to lie down and rest, and then it happens. Douglas Schuk's grandfather was found sitting upright on a stump, frozen to death. I have a book on the Eskimos and in it there is an interesting story: One time in a small village, times were hard and their food nearly gone. The Eskimos held a meeting and knew they had to decide who should live and who should die. The older people and the men who could not hunt or see too well, would then volunteer to vacate their lot in life! Usually a man and his wife would walk out a short distance from their igloos, stand there and in thirty or forty minutes, it was all over! They were frozen stiff.

ACRES AND ACRES -

ONE ACREAGE

Some of the largest ranches in the world are up in Caribou Country and many years earlier, one of my first big game ventures into the great North country, was to the world famous, Gang Ranch. The total acreage of that ranch is so vast that it's hard to comprehend. The acreage which is owned is 60,000 acres, and another 30,000 acres is leased. In addition, the Crown grants them grazing rights to endless territory, making the total available grazing area over a million acres! It would be quite a challenge to keep an eye on all that, to say the least! This ranch is located approximately fifty-five miles from where we lived in Clinton. One time on the Gang Ranch, many years ago, it got down to seventy-five below zero. They kept their big, breeding bulls in a separate pasture, but when it was so cold, these bulls came together in a shallow, depression-like area and crowded together in a tight circle to stay warm. The cowboys found them later, frozen stiff, still standing upright, and over fifty bulls perished on that ranch during the cold spell. Unfortunately, many animals in the North country perish this way.

On the subject of survival and facing life in real adversity, Isadore is a good candidate! Here is one man who never went through a depression - he just never had good times. He never griped about it and had a good disposition, as well as a lot of fortitude! He had trapped over eight hundred fifty squirrels when he was eighty-five years old! Once in 1978, I took a bundle of furs up to Prince George for him, when furs were still valuable. He used to trap them and receive twenty cents apiece, but he topped that fur sale when I took those to Prince George for him and got $3.17 per squirrel hide! He told me that when he was fourteen years old, he used his Dad's old, single shot rifle and he had to kill ten rabbits a day. Some Indian ladies gave him ten cents per carcass and he got ten cents a hide, which gave him $2 per day. Top wages back then were $1.50 per day for a ranch hand, sawmill worker, or whatever. Some days he'd have to hunt until afternoon and some days he had ten rabbits by ten o'clock in the morning and he told me, "I used to get so tired, I could hardly go, but I wanted to help my folks out!" As I've said before, life back in those days wasn't always kind or easy!

One night I spent the night in Isadore's cabin as we were going to hunt early the next morning! I had a pair of wool socks and a pair of sock holders, and as I was slipping them on the next morning, Isadore said, "What have you got there?" I said, "Oh, they're a gismo to hold my socks up!" "Well, what is it?" he wanted to know, so I took one and showed him the piece of elastic with a little clip on it. He said, "Well, I never saw one of them in my life!" He paused a bit and then said, "Well, I had something like that one time to hold up my shirt sleeves!" I said, "Well, it's the same principal, these are made to hold socks up." When Frances and I were in Kamloops one day, I tried to buy another pair so I could give them to Isadore, and could not find a store in town who sold them! I tried several cities in British Columbia, and all to no avail! They'd give me a strange look as if I were from the dark ages, so I just gave up on the idea, knowing if I wanted to buy a pair of sock holders, I'd have to buy them at Les Newman's in Salem, Oregon!

CHRIS KIND (CACTUS) -

ONE OF A KIND

I'm sure every small town has their colorful characters, but of all the towns I've been around, I don't think any could hold a candle to Clinton! Some are renown, some are feared and some are loved! One morning Frances and I went into Clinton to pick up our mail and get a few items, and while in the Clinton Lodge getting coffee, we were introduced to Cheryl Phillips. We started visiting and she made the remark that there was a guide sitting two booths away who guided for Howard Paish and he had just come in from guiding at Cold Fish Lake. I told her I would like to meet him, so she motioned for me to follow her, and then introduced me to Chris Kind, or "Cactus", as he was called. We visited briefly and I found him to be a very friendly fellow.

The next day Isadore said, "Kenny, let's go buck hunting," and I told him I'd love to. We saddled up, took one pack horse, and off we went to the Marble Range. Since snow was on the ground, the tracks of deer were most evident and we could tell that the deer were moving! Most of them were going in a Northerly direction and I have never seen so many deer tracks in one place! Very shortly, a terrible wind began to blow so hard the air was full of branches, and it was so extremely cold - just like a step-Mother's embrace. Isadore said, "Kenny, this isn't good. We must get off the mountain," and we quickly headed out, towards home. That night, here comes Chris Kind to our house, and he asked, "Say, Kenny, do you want to go and get a really big buck? I know where they are!" "Sure do," I said, to which Chris responded, "You get your gear together and I'll come in the morning to pick you up in my Land Rover, and we'll get some big bucks!"

Chris and I went the next morning up through the Gang Ranch, and proceeded up into Churn Creek, which was noted for game. Reportedly, there were a good number of California Big Horn Sheep in this area, as well. Upon arrival, we set up a nice camp, made a great supper and began to visit, although it wasn't long before problems appeared, as the wind began to blow and continued to increase. We went up the mountain the next morning and while up there, the wind blew a big fir over the road, so we had to make a new road around it. That evening, Chris began to tell me of some of the details of his life. His Dad was a Captain, or Naval Commander in the British Navy and was stationed off the isle of Malta and he often played polo with some of the famous Play Boys of Europe. Chris certainly was "one of a kind", for he had been a professional rodeo contestant, traveling all over doing that, and had also been a guide for many of the big outfitters. He played the guitar, sang, and loved to entertain people! "Say, Kenny, do you know who the Jesusites are?" he asked, and I said, "Yes, I do, they are the strongest group in the Catholic Church." Chris replied, "You're right! I went to their school for six years and studies for the priesthood." "Why did you give it up," I asked, and he said, "I got so fed up with all the d— paraphernalia, I just told them to shove it!" We visited for a long time and then called it quits for the night.

After we went out the next morning, I found the complete skeleton of a three quarters, curl ram. It was an amazing thing, for every bone was in place and moss was growing and covering part of it. Still the wind continued to blow with gale force and Chris said, "We can't kill any game with this wind! Let's break camp and go home." Heading back to Clinton, as we were going along, right on the drivers' side of the 4 X 4, stood a really, big doe! Upon seeing it, Chris clamped on his brakes and said, "Give me your gun, the season's still open, isn't it!" "Here's my gun, but I honestly don't know if season's still open or not," I informed him. Again he asked, "Well, it is, isn't it?" I said, "I don't know, Cactus!" Just then, the doe decided that she had business elsewhere and took off, so we went on down the hill, through the Gang Ranch, and to the big bridge across the Fraser River. Oh, now we have a problem! Here is a blockade, with a sign, "All Vehicles Stop for Inspection!" There were two Game Wardens there and one of them was at least six feet, five inches tall and weighing at least 295 - 310 pounds. Soon the Warden recognized Cactus, and to my surprise, Chris said, "It sure feels good to not be accused of something you're not doing!" The Warden said, "Oh, you are not guiding an out of province hunter?" Chris quickly replied, "No, you d— right, I'm not," and then for some reason, Chris said, "Kenny found some sheep horns." "Get them out," the Warden demanded. Now these horns were clear on the bottom, under the tent and all our gear was piled on top of them. The Warden said to me, "You need to report to Williams, the Warden in Clinton, as they keep a record of every ram that's found." Guess what! The season had closed the day we made camp and had Cactus shot that doe, we would have gotten a stiff fine. The reason the Warden asked Cactus if he was guiding an out of province hunter needs explanation. It goes like this: Chris told me, " Only a week or so ago, I took two American friends fishing, so we're out on a big lake, had a nice camp made, and here comes a Game Warden by airplane. They searched through all our gear and found my firearms, so they seized my gun and fined me." Later, I went to Clinton, went in the Warden's office to have a ram checked by the young Warden, Heins Luenberger, and Chris was in Clarence Williams' inner office, but the door was open. Williams said, "I suppose you want your gun back, don't you?" I heard Chris snarl, "Well, I sure as h— ain't a gonna let you fellas have it!" It was truly some rifle, a 308 Norma Magnum, jeweled bolt, fancy engraving, and it had a great scope. I had asked Chris where he got that rifle and he answered with a question, "Did you ever hear of Aaron Jones, the lumber man from Eugene, Oregon?" I said, "I sure have! He owns the Seneca Lumber Company Sawmill Plywood Plant and raises race horses." He said, "You got that right! I guided him on a hunt and we got some fine trophies, so Jones gave me his gun."

Chris was a great horseman and a good hunter. One time he was guiding for Ross Peck and Sons and was about four miles out from camp, riding one horse and trailing another one behind. Along the trail, he met a very, pretty young lady, and could see immediately that she had been weeping. She saw Cactus and said, "Oh, Sir, I am lost, I am lost! Can you tell me where I am?" Cactus said, "I am lost also! When I started out, I had three pack horses, but I ate one of them, as I have been unable to find any game and I am about to shoot this one, my last pack horse." Cactus said that young gal sat down and cried as if the end of the world had come and she wasn't ready! Cactus said, "Well, young lady, you're really lucky! Get on and ride my saddle horse and I'll take you to Peck's Headquarter Camp," and he said he had never seen anyone light up like she did. Chris experienced many narrow escapes, and one happened when he was guiding out of Hudson Hope. He was in the lead, had a number of horses tied head to tail, and a young, husky hunter came behind Cactus. His instructions to this kid were, "Now this river is deep and she is swift! Whatever you do, don't take a rap on Dolly on your saddle horn, in case your pack horses shy, or rear up!" Cactus then urged his horses into the stream, fought them across, and just as he got to shore, he looked back. To his horror, this fellow had taken several raps on his saddle horn, the pack animals jerked, lunged, and pulled his saddle horse under water. Cactus said all the horses finally came up, but sadly for all, they never found the body of the young hunter.

Early one morning when the lake was frozen solid up in Fish Lake country, Chris watched a huge, bull moose go out on the lake. Five wolves took out after this moose and pulled him down, so he took a tarp and some ice pins and ran out to the moose. He put the tarp over the moose, went back to the house where he was staying, and for several days, he watched. Those wolves laid around that moose for several days, and Chris went back out on the ice, took the tarp off the moose, and went back to the house. Without hesitation, those wolves fell on that moose, which was frozen as solid as could be, and they literally devoured it in short order!

One of the things Chris had told me was that if he ever found a lady good enough to bed down with, he would marry her, and he said, "None of that 'shackin' up for me, Kenny!" Sad to say, that's one thing he did not do! He had two help-meets, or help-eats while we were in the Clinton area, but had not married. One of the first things we learned in the Clinton area is that marriages are the major cause of divorce; hence, many were not married. My young Indian neighbor said, "It's lot easier to part a couple blankets than it is to get a divorce."

GREAT MAN OF THE NORTH -

CURSE OR BLESSING?

Before we had moved to Canada, my friend, Ralph Schoof called and said, "Kenny, bring your wife and come over to our place on Wednesday evening 'cause we're going to meet a great man from the North!" I had no idea who he was talking about, but we agreed to be present. When we got there, we met Barney McPhillips and several other people and the great man from the North (as Ralph described him), Howard Paish! He had some beautiful pictures to show, lots of brochures, and he's telling about the wonders of Cold Fish Lake. Howard put his best foot forward and booked four hunts that night! Unbeknownst to me as to what was going on, Ralph made the remark, "This character is moving up to Clinton!" Howard looked at my wife and me and said, "Is that right? Well, there's an Indian up there who's been guiding for me and he's a wonderful guide. His name is Bert Grinder."

After we moved up to Clinton, at Isadore's cabin one evening, I made the remark about meeting Howard Paish and Isadore said, "He's in trouble and in jail, isn't he?" I said, "No, not as far as I know," and I told him how I met him. "Well," Isadore said, "he was charged and found guilty on eighty-five counts so he's all out of business!" "Oh, no, he's booking hunters again and I have literature to prove it," I told him. Phillip came over later, got quite excited when I showed him the brochures from Howard, and went down to Clinton to see Clarence Williams, the Warden. He informed Clarence that we had just moved up there and had literature from Howard Paish and that less than a month earlier, Howard was booking hunters! Clarence said, "You tell that man to come to town to see me, or I'm coming out!" Phillip relayed the message and we went into town to see Clarence. I took the literature in and he was utterly dumb-founded, asking me, "Where did you get that?" I said, "Off of Ralph and Gwen Schoof's coffee table!" "You're kidding!" Clarence said, but I assured him, "No, I'm not kidding!" "Why, that man swore on the witness stand in the big trial they just had, that he was all done guiding, he'd never book another hunter, he had no horses left, and was all done!" Clarence phoned a judge in Kamloops and really raised cain, so all this proved to be a rather intriguing story! Isadore had clippings out of the Vancouver Province relating to this story and now here I meet Chris, and he had just been guiding up there! Clarence told me that Chris was on the witness stand for two days and he thought Chris told the truth because he said it's awfully hard to get a man mixed up when he tells the truth. When I was out with Chris, I asked him, "What was your problem with Howard?" He said, "He tried to beat me out of some money, and anytime anyone tries to beat Cactus out of money, he's in bad trouble!"

SHOOTING WITH SCHOOF

Ralph booked a hunt with Phillip, so he and Gwen came up to visit us, parking their trailer close to our house. It was so convenient for them, as I'd just start up the old Lister plant and plug them in! We'd visit, shoot the breeze, and had a most enjoyable time and during the day, Ralph would go out with Phillip. As Ralph came in one evening, he asked me, "Did you kill a bull today?" I said, "Yes, I did, Ralph, I killed a fine, bull moose! You tell Phillip in the morning I know where some moose are and he can hunt them!" Gwen spoke up and said to me, "Well, I'd like to go with you when you pack it in and see where a bull lived and died!" I said, "Well, you ladies are more than welcome to go along!"

Next morning, I warmed up the pickup for Frances and Gwen, put my pack gear on Cindy, and up we went several miles from the house, going back in the woods on a side road. I don't know what possessed me, but for some reason, I never took any matches along. We drove as far as we could and then Frances and Gwen walked back with me. I told them it wasn't too far, and of course, they thought it was the biggest lie they'd ever heard, but at last, we got back to where this bull lay. I had just dressed it out and hadn't quartered it before, so I proceeded to quarter it, loaded it on Cindy, and took the first load to the house. Those gals decided to stay there and practically froze to death, although I never figured out why they didn't go to the pickup and get warm! I returned, loaded up the rest of the meat, and we all went back to the house.

While we were out packing in my bull that morning, as a fellow went up to Grinder's, he saw a bull standing by their gate, so Phillip and Ralph followed the tracks into the timber a ways and here were five bulls bedded down! Ralph shot a fine, young, fat bull and they said it was great meat. Their first hunt with Phillip ended on a successful note, and Ralph was one happy hunter!

Ralph and Gwen came back for a second hunt and Ralph asked, "Why don't you come go along?" I said, "No, I don't want to do that! Phillip is sore at me." "What for?" Ralph asked. "Well, I have no idea," I said, so Ralph went up and worked Phillip over in good fashion! Phillip said to Ralph, "Tell Kenny to come on up," so I took some grub and rode over to Grinder's on Cindy. All of us rode up on the mountain a ways, to a place called Big Little Camp. It was unbelievably cold and we didn't have any luck that day, but we did have a nice hunt and a good time!

The first time Bob Patty booked a hunt with Phillip, my brother, Ron, and his son, Glen, were also hunting sheep there, so we all went up and camped at Grinder's upper cabin. Bob's guide was Larry McDonald, Phillip's nephew. I hunted on my own and killed a huge buck. He was so big, I could not hang him up by myself, so Ron and Glen went with me to hang him up. That evening in camp, Larry had a terrible backache and laid down, right on the ground. As he laid there, smoking a cigarette, he announced, "When this package is gone, I'm all done smoking!" Bob jumped up, grabbed his pack of cigarettes and said, "I'll fix that for you right now," and he motioned, as if to throw them in! Larry screamed, "Don't do that, don't do that!" Bob asked, "Why?" "Well, because," he said. Ron and Glen each got a sheep on this trip and Bob killed his first moose! Bob was so elated over his good luck that he sort of got hooked on moose hunting!

The following year, Bob came back to hunt with Phillip again, and also, Don and Mary Strunk from Oregon, came up. They arrived on a Wednesday, although their hunt didn't begin until the following Monday, so they stayed with us at the house. While the four of us were still sitting at the breakfast table enjoying a leisurely meal, someone came barging through our door, unannounced! There was no knock or anything, and here came Patty into the room! He said, "Get up from that table, Don! You can always eat! I want you to come see where a bull just died," and of course, we got up and went with Bob. As we were walking back there, that rascal was so excited, it looked as if he never put his heels on the ground and it seemed he was going about ten feet between each step! Don began laughing and was tickled silly watching Bob go! We had gone about three quarters of a mile from our house, and then came to a muskeg, which is where Bob had shot a nice, big bull! When that moose fell, he went down on his horns, making it impossible for Bob to get him rolled over to dress him out, so we helped Bob dress him out. It was so much fun watching Patty, as he was so excited and pleased!

The third trip Bob came back to Clinton to hunt moose, he brought Dave DeWeiss with him, but they didn't have any luck. That was so interesting, because I found out the Indians never say, die and never say, no! They always have an alibi. I heard Phillip tell Isadore one day, "The reason they never had any luck is that DeWeiss's feet were too big!" Isadore said, "Oh! That won't work! His feet too big, oh yes, too big! You can't hunt that way!" (He implied he made too much noise!) I noticed on other hunts that if they see game a mile off and you don't kill it, you're a poor shot or poor hunter and they indicate you should shoot game as far away as it's seen. Of course, that's not the way to hunt, but they always have a way out!

RUNAWAY RAM

On the first trip my brother Ron made down from Vanderhoof to visit us at Clinton, when he saw this country, was quite impressed with it and asked me how I ever found it! I took him up to Grinder's to meet them and he booked a sheep hunt with Phillip. When the time came, they rode up on the mountain and camped on kind of a "bald rock," fairly close to sheep country. Phillip said, "I'm going to go on down and see what the Old Man is doing with his hunters at the cabin." Ron told me he was up there for two days and two nights all by himself and he was more than just a little mad, and I don't blame him! The evening of the second day, he saw a beautiful, big ram and shot at it. He knew he made a good hit, but as darkness fell and Ron looked all over, he was unable to find it. The next morning Phillip came up and asked, "What's going on?" Ron said, "Well, I crippled a big ram." Phillip said, "No problem, we'll go down and find it," but they both looked and never did find it.

About two weeks later, Tippy Robertson, from Clinton was hunting up in that area and noticed a bunch of ravens circling around and then they'd go right down to the ground. Tippy was a good hunter and he knew what was going on, so he went down and here lay this big ram Ron had shot. He had a very nice set of horns, so Tippy took them off, but of course, the cape wasn't any good by this time. When he got into town, he took those horns into the Game Warden and told him about it. Grinders came down to tell me, "Tippy found your brothers' ram! He'll sell the horns to Ron!" Immediately, I called Ron and asked him if he wanted to buy the horns from his ram. He asked, "Are you kidding?" I told him what had happened, so he came down and bought the horns. The Game Warden said that was the finest ram that had been killed in the Marble Range for many years. His hunt was successful in one respect, but tragic in another.

One time in December, the season closed the 15th and around the 12th, Isadore came down to see me, saying, "Kenny, we have no meat down and I want you to come with me. We're going to go up to the cabin and try to kill a big buck." We started out for the cabin, arrived there and found some wood for a fire. I went over to the little water hole and got a five gallon bucket of ice, cold water. After this was done, we fed the horses in the corral and hunkered down for the night! During the night it turned bitterly cold. We found out later, that further down in the valley, it was 20 below zero, so no doubt, it was even colder back here in the mountains! Although we had no way of knowing exactly how cold it was up there in the woods, it literally froze that creek solid, so that's cold! As we set out to hunt the next morning, I made a big drive for Isadore up in Box Canyon, and as we generally did, he built up a fire to keep warm while I made a terrific circle through there. At last the sun came out and I thought, "Maybe the deer have gone to the South hillside to get warm!" I went around there, got down behind a jack fir, and blew a deer call I had brought along. To my amazement, about a quarter of a mile away, I saw three deer get up and they came running around the hill on an even keel, through this canyon. They never took on any altitude nor lost any, and three does came right up to me! They stomped the ground, snorted, and carried on, giving quite a performance, but I didn't shoot any! I went back to tell Isadore what happened and he asked, "You didn't kill one?" I said, "No," and he was very upset about it!

As we went back to camp, I asked Isadore, "Where do you think those bucks are?" "Oh," he said, "they're around!" The next morning we went up into the sheep country and he asked me to make a drive clear underneath Mount Kerr. Once again he built up a big fire down below on a nice saddle where he could watch. I went up within five hundred feet of where we both had killed the rams, got down behind a tree and blew the deer call. Right up where the rams had come out, a nice buck makes his appearance and just went barreling down the hill! About a hundred yards from me, he stopped, put his

Go Ahead On 'er!

head up and looked around. What a perfect opportunity for me, so I put a bullet in his brisket and down he went! After dressing him out, I pulled him down to the trail, and headed back to Isadore. I decided I might as well go around Mount Kerr on my way, but couldn't jump anything. By now it was about quarter 'til eleven when I got back down to Isadore. "Did you shoot this morning about 9:00 o'clock?" he asked, and I said, "As a matter of fact, I did!" "What'd you shoot at?" he wanted to know. "I killed a nice buck," I told him, which made him very happy! One time Isadore had been thrown off his horse and his shoulder bothered him so that he could hardly raise his left arm. I asked, "Shall we go down to camp, get the pack horse and pack it in?" He said, "No, let's just go up there and we'll cut that deer down, load it on my horse, and I'll

walk and lead him." "No, you can ride my horse, Isadore," I said. At this stage in her life, I was just breaking Tony, but he said, "I don't want to ride your horse! And I'll tell you something - when that horse of yours gets up there, you know what's going to happen?" "No, what?" I asked him. "Frankly, all hell's going to break loose!" I thought he was probably right because Tony's Mother would get terribly upset around blood!

1988 - the largest deer I have ever seen!

We rode up there and amazingly, Tony saw that deer, but she kept pulling on the bridle rein and I let her go up there. She put her nose right on the buck, took a big sniff and then started eating on some brush nearby. We got the deer, loaded it up and started going for camp and Tony kept insisting that she wanted to be right next to that deer! Isadore was riding Caesar and she would practically step on him, trying to get close to the buck. We were nearly to camp when Isadore stopped and said, "Kenny, you've got a mighty fine horse there!" With a smile, I said, "I believe it, Isadore!" This buck had not gone through a rut. Usually in December, they're very strong in flavor and not always the best of eating. This meat, however, was marbled through with fat and Isadore told me he never had eaten a better piece of meat in his life! What a fine hunt we had up there and provided them with meat to eat!

The following summer Isadore and I rode out to their cabin out in the woods, and what a sight we saw! The big window was broken out and everything was in disarray! They always put the dishes and everything on the table, right below the windows. When Isadore saw the silverware and utensils strewn all over the floor, he started cussing and screaming and said, "Oh, I know who did this! I'll get even with that guy yet! You just wait and see!" As we set about to repair the damage, I said, "Isadore, look here!" There was bear hair in what was left of the window pane, and hair all over the floor! I had taken up about twenty dollars worth of grub, as well as forty pounds of crushed oats in a saddle box for the horses. Everything had been taken out; Danish bacon, pork and beans, peaches, and assorted items. I was finally able to convince Isadore that a bear had done the damage! That bear had gone back and forth through that window, carried everything out and ruined every bit of it!

Isadore had two cross-cut saws there, so I positioned and nailed them so that when the bear was going to put his paw through the window, he'd have something to reckon with! The cabin was in pretty bad shape and I had to chop the door off as it was dragging, due to this old cabin settling over time. Still, this place of refuge served the needs of the wilderness and we had some great old times there!

LOOKING FOR MOOSE

WITH CAHOOSE

In July it was once again time for our annual pilgrimage to Anahim Lake. The annual Rodeo is traditionally held the second week-end in July, after the Williams Lake Stampede closes. We went fishing first and then attended the Stampede. I knew of Andy Cahoose and began visiting with him. I said, "Andy, I would like to go hunting with you!" He said, "Sure, I take you out! I charge $900, you feed yourself and I pack out anything you kill!" I said, "Andy, I'm not really a horn hunter, I like to kill a good set of horns, but what I kill, we plan to eat, and I want you to pack out everything I kill!" He responded, "Sure, no problem!"

Later in the fall, we drove to Anahim Lake, arriving a day ahead of our scheduled hunt with Andy. He has a fabulous place there in the mountains, with his pasture skirting the Dean River. We went fishing and caught about twenty fine fish and Andy had a brand new place in which to smoke them . After cleaning the fish, we prepared them for smoking. When I would go out with the guides, Frances usually stayed at the camp in our camper, so I cut a supply of wood for her for when we were out in the bush. There were other people there in the camp and four big dogs. About a hundred and twenty yards from the house, they had a sheet of 4 X 8 plywood nailed to a stump and Dennis said to me, "You shoot at plywood." I asked, "What do you mean? What for?" He asked, "Can you hit the plywood?" "Of course, I can," I reassured him. "Why?" "Well," he said, "lots of hunters with big Magnums can't hit the plywood!" "Well, I'm not quite that bad," I told him and was quite amused.

We started out the next morning with Andy, his wife, Annie, his twenty-three year old son, Dennis, eighteen year old Freddie, and two fellows from Washington. Their names were Dale Hefley, a high school teacher for many years and a rancher around Ritzville country and Brian Talbot, who at the time, was Superintendent of Schools for the State of Washington, I believe. Brian had his forty-fourth birthday back in the mountains during our trip. We packed the entire day, going as hard as we could and finally decided to make camp on a very steep hillside. It was so steep, we nearly had to tie ourselves in to keep from falling off that bluff! Andy had decided to take a shortcut which took us through timber and over windfalls and all sorts of debris with those horses - you just wouldn't believe it unless you saw the conditions.

After Andy and our gang left, Frances decided she'd smoke the fish a little longer that day, so went out, but discovered the fish were gone! Those dogs had dug a hole, gotten in there and devoured those great fish! Frances took a rather dim view of those dogs, but that's life in the wilds!

The next day we got back to a place called Pan Creek which went into Pan Meadows. This is named after the noted legend of British Columbia, Pan Phillips, whom the author, Rich Hobson, immortalized in the great book, Grass Beyond The Mountains. Dale and Brian had a couple fancy rifles. Brian's was a brand new 338 Winchester Mag, Model 70, and they sighted down to the creek, which was quite a long ways off. One of them said, "That'd be too far to shoot game," but the other one said, "Oh, I think I could," and they kept discussing this between them. Just as we were getting ready to unpack our horses, two bull moose appeared from the brush along the creek and Andy said, "Quick, quick, come with me," (and he pointed to the fellows from Washington), so away they went on the horses through the timber to get ahead of the moose!

The rest of us continued to unpack the horses and in about a half hour, Annie said, "We go now!" She led the way and we followed Andy's tracks for about a half mile when we came to an opening in a meadow. Just as we got to that opening, a big bull came out. I begged her to stop so I could shoot him, but she said, "Oh, no, I think too far!" I said, "No, it isn't too far!" "No, no, you can't shoot bull," Annie insisted, and just then he went back in the thicket. In my mind I had already figured out what was going on and found out soon that I was right. We went about a quarter of a mile and here's another big opening and over next to a bluff stood Andy and the two hunters. The bulls never went their way. Dennis galloped over to Andy and continued on up the draw. I glanced ahead about a quarter of a mile and saw a bull following two cows. We rode on up to where Andy was and he said, "Shoot bull, don't shoot cows!" I laid down on a rock, shot that bull and everybody saw him turn end over teakettle, as he landed on a bench. He had fallen down a very steep mountain and it was quite a long ways down there. I said to Freddie, "Help me go down, get a pole, and we'll pry that moose loose and roll him clear to the bottom of the draw!" Freddie said, "Oh, no, that will make the meat all blood-shot." I said, "No, after the heart stops, the meat won't get blood shot!" Freddie and I went on down there, pried the moose free and rolled him clear to the bottom, just as I had suggested! How I wish I could have had a picture of that bull falling down the mountain! Once down there on the bluff, I dressed him out and when we finished, went back to camp. The other fellows had continued over the hill when they left us and Brian shot a young caribou bull for camp meat.

The next morning Dennis and I took the pack horses and saddle horses to ride up to get the bull I killed. We took it back into camp and put up a meat pole. Just as we got back to camp, I looked down at the same place where the fellows had been sighting their guns the day before and here came a fine, big caribou bull! I said, "Dennis, look what's coming here!" "What?" he asked, and I answered, "Nice caribou bull in the thicket right there!" He got all excited and asked, "Where'd he go?" "He's in the brush, he'll come out," I told him. This kid was so excited and said, "Come with me, run, quick," and he started running. I asked, "Where are you going?" Just then I knew he'd gotten a glimpse of the bull and I said, "I'm not going to run up there!" I walked over to a tree, rested my 270 across a limb and I downed that bull! We went down there and Dennis just had a fit of joy! I got a picture of him sitting on that bull, holding the head up. Looking at me and smiling, he asked, "You always lucky, Old Man?" "No, lots of times I'm not lucky! Sometimes I pull on a hind tit," I told him, but he insisted, "Oh, you lucky Old Man!"

That evening the other hunters came in empty-handed and suddenly I felt rather unpopular! Andy was quite upset and came to me, pulled me off to one side and said, "I can't do that!" I asked, "Can't do what?" He said, "You kill two fine, big animals; I gotta have more money! I can't do that!" "Andy, you told me you would," I reminded him, but again, he repeated, "I can't do that," and demanded $700 additional monies. I very firmly said, "Look, I'm not going to give you $700 more!"

Out hunting the next day, Brian killed a bull as big as the one I killed, although the horns on his animal weren't developed as nicely as the ones on mine. Andy decided it was time to pull out of this area, so we all saddled up, and rode to where Brian's bull had been dressed out to take it back to camp. Dale Hefley, who was a big man, weighing around 275, had a new meat saw with a fine aluminum handle and I think he was so proud of it that he slept with it, although I'm not sure. Around camp he had his big hunting knife on one side and the saw on the other. We got up to this caribou that morning, but my tools were all packed in my duffel bag, and other gear was piled on top. So Dale said he was going to saw this meat up, and he started in. The blade was hardly buried when he started puffing, so Brian said, "Here, let me give you a hand," and he grabbed the saw and went at it with a vengeance! He got in about two inches and that's all she wrote! There was no set in that saw, it was brand new and had never been filed, so he asked, "Where's your saw, Kenny?" "It's in the bottom of that duffel bag," I answered. All of a sudden, Andy stands up there with a double-bited axe and he said, "You stand back now. We lose enough time," and he started in. They threw a nice diamond hitch, but they weren't very tidy with things and left ends of rope dragging. Everybody started out with that one rope, which was at least ten feet long, just dragging on the ground! This made me very uneasy, as I was positive something was going to happen. Sure enough, we had gone about a mile through some bad thickets and in places, the trail hadn't been swamped out at all. True to what I had been thinking, that dangling rope caught on something. This caused the bull to shoot ahead, putting a half-hitch around a tree hanging over the trail, jerking the pack off to one side, and nearly causing the horse to go down! I was in back and saw it all happen, so I called out, "Hold 'er, fellows! This pack horse is getting rid of his pack!" They came back, spoke a few words in the native tongue and a few in English, and then repacked the load. That happened three times going back to camp!

About a mile further, we came to a bluff, the trail was extremely steep, and the pack slipped again on this beautiful pack horse. The fellows said that horse could pack three or four hundred pounds, and I know he could. Once again I called out, "That pack horse is going down, fellows!" Andy hollered, "Not here, no good to pack here," and about twenty feet further, the poor horse stumbled and down the hill he went! He rolled sideways, then landed by a big rock, with his feet up in the air! I thought for sure he was dead and Brian and Dale thought so, too. It broke the saddle all to pieces, as the horse rolled on his side and we all rushed down there! I really felt sorry for this creature, for this could have been avoided, but they started talking to that horse, and stroking him. After they convincingly told him what a great guy he was, they helped get that horse up on his feet in about ten minutes. So their rope was broken and they wondered what they'd do now! Well, my trusty little box came through again! I have a little cigar box which a druggist in Sheridan gave me when I was sixteen years old and on every hunting trip I've ever made away from home, I've carried it with me! In that, I have a pair of pliers, stove wire, cord, needles to sew buttons on, and all sorts of supplies. With the loot I had, we managed to put that saddle together in a manner so that it held. They repacked the major part of that bull moose on the pack horse and we got back to camp. Brian and Dale hung their caribou in a woodshed and the next morning this fine piece of meat was laying on the ground in the dirt. I don't know if the dogs got to that meat, or if the rope broke, but those two were mighty angry hunters to see their meat treated in that fashion and I certainly felt the same way!

This hunt with Andy had been booked through a white lady from Nimpo Lake, Mary Ratzloff, and I had nothing in writing between myself and Andy. When I was ready to leave, I wrote Andy a check for $500, and as I handed it to him, I said, "Andy, if you cash this check, you're in big, bad trouble!" He didn't answer me and I left. When I checked the caribou out at Williams Lake, three Game Commission people came out, asking questions about our hunt. Since statistics were being kept on the various hunts, they took a tooth out of the caribou's jaw, a chunk of meat, and snapped pictures of him from all angles. One of the guys asked me, "Did you have a good hunt?" "In some ways I did," I told him, "but I almost overshot my knife!" "What's that?" he asked. "Well, that's when you get down more than you can skin!" They laughed and then I did tell them what happened. The one said, "Well, I'm sure glad you told us because these poor fools up here have been robbing the American hunters blind!" (Of course, I was now living in B.C.) "They don't realize they're cutting off their means of livelihood," he continued. We drove into Mary's place on the way home and she wasn't there, so when I got to Clinton the next day, I called her up to tell her about Andy. She said, "I can't believe what you're telling me, Andy never did that before," and I informed her, "Well, he'll never take advantage of me again, I'll tell you that!" She said, "I'm going up to talk to him," so she drove over a hundred miles round trip, over some very rough road, to see Andy. About a week later I received a Canadian money order for $200. The sad thing that happened was that Annie had an aneurysm which left her completely helpless, and I don't know whether she's still living or not, but we felt very badly for the family. The next year I went to the Stampede and I saw Andy, but he didn't want to talk to me at all. I know he felt condemned over what he had done to me, although Dennis willingly talked to me. Unfortunately, when one gets treated like that, it leaves a sour taste in one's mouth!

LUCK WITH LEAKE

Another couple we got acquainted with were Herb and Judy Leake and Herb guided, so I booked a hunt with him. They lived out of town quite a long ways and we started out to find them. About twelve miles before we got to the Beaver Indian Reserve, we turned off to the left, then went quite a ways and came across a sign which read, "Warning: Steep Hill. Do Not Attempt Without Four Wheel Drive Vehicle!" We went down a hill and came to a very, wide river, at least one hundred twenty-five feet wide, flowing quite swiftly! I lucked out in fording that river as Herb had dozed some rock out with his cat and I was fortunate enough to drive in just the right places. We got across in great condition and finally arrived at Herb's. There was a cabin for us to stay in, so we unloaded our gear. Frances would stay here while Herb and I went back on the mountain. Bill Harris was the name of Herb's cook. He had his own pack horses and gear, and also there were two fellows from Fort St. John, Keith Derkaps and his son, Larry, going on this hunt. Herb's helper, Danny Chips, an Indian lad, would accompany us as well. The day before we left, I helped Herb check over all the gear. Herb had wonderful horses and every pack horse was muzzled, but he never shod any of his horses because of riding in the snow. The horse shoes used then didn't adapt very well to snow, but nowadays they have designed them so the snow will not stick to them! They are much more expensive, but well worth it!

The next day we rode over nine miles on this big plateau, and then came across Herb's horses grazing out in the wild. He had five different stallions and more mares and colts than I've ever seen in my life! As we rode through, they never bothered the pack train and seemed to be very well behaved. We had to ford the Procter River a number of times and came to quite a large camp ground, where motorcycle tracks were quite visible, debris littered all around and the bones of some animal lay there. Herb explained, "This is where some hippies from Fort St. John have been camping, and I ought to swamp the trail out, but if I did, they'd move in here and take over!"

Herb and I continued back into the woods, going through some very brushy alders, terrible undergrowth and foliage! In fact, there was so much foliage, it was very difficult to get our horses through there! The horse I was riding, named Husky, was thirty-two years old, Herb informed me, and he weighed about fourteen hundred pounds! Husky was a great horse, but the biggest problem with him was his girth! Herb rode a gelding weighing about nine hundred fifty pounds, and Danny's horse weighed about the same. Both of their horses were young, black Persian geldings. Herb had placed my scabbard with the butt of the rifle in the air, sort of pointing towards Husky's ear. As we rode, we came to a place where we had to make a turn, and suddenly, the rifle stock of my gun came against a tree and pushed the saddle back! I could hardly believe it didn't break the stock of my gun because it was shoved so hard! I never carry my guns that way and immediately made different arrangements!

At last we got back to quite a large cabin, with a nice corral there. Herb put the animals in for the night, fed them, and we got ourselves settled down also. Bill prepared a wonderful supper for us, after which we just visited. Around 8:30 in the evening, someone said, "I hear a horse bell," and no sooner had we heard that sound, when here came a bunch of fellows! They didn't have a light, but barged right in, and one asked, "What are you doing in here?" One of them recognized Herb just then and said, "Hello, Herb!" They told us they were on their way back to their main camp and had planned to stay in this cabin overnight. Herb asked, "Have you fellows had supper?" "No," they told him, so Herb said, "Look, I'll have Bill get supper for you," so Bill had to cook another meal! One fellow started talking and had quite an accent, so I asked him, "Are you from Texas?" "No, I'm from Florida," he said and informed me that three of his group had bought shares in this hunting outfit and they were up to make a big hunt!

In the morning we left to go on back to Herb's main camp. He had a brand new cook tent and cook stove in his camp there and it was quite nice. Danny was assigned to be my guide and so we started out on our hunt, riding up some long draws, looking for moose. The first day, however, we didn't see any game, but quite a few tracks.

Danny said, "Well, we'll go down the river in the morning and go up a steep mountain back there! When I had another client out earlier, I saw a big bull and I swamped out a good trail going up there."

1986 - only goat I ever shot - taken in the Homathko Wilderness area, out of Tatla Lake, B.C. Rifle I used was 7 x 57 Mauser with iron sights and shells I had re-loaded myself. I was about 300 yards away when I took aim. The horns were 9 1/4" long. I was 74 years of age and walked a total of 24 miles that day. Taken on hunt with good friend, Doug Schuk.

Next day I discovered that kid had cut a jack pine off about three feet high, just at the height to pull the innards out of a horse! I don't know how he ever expected a horse to get through there, but we finally made it and got up on this bench, right at the timberline. It was very cold, with snow falling and the wind blowing. Every day on this trip, I wore my rain gear because the brush was so wet, you'd just get soaked. That day we worked hard trying to get a lunch fire going and just had a terrible time! We chopped some stumps completely in two trying to find some pitch to help start a fire! At last, we were able to get sort of a "smudge" fire going and tried to toast our sandwiches, but they weren't fit to eat! We got there at 9:30 A.M. and sat there until 2:00 P.M., but the fog came rolling in and it was nearly impossible to see, so all we could do was wait and visit! After waiting all this time, in the end, we had no choice but to go on back to camp.

Herb said to me one morning, "Kenny, there's a big cranberry patch up the mountain and I want you to ride up with Keith and me. I'm going to put you on a stand and you've got a good chance to kill a bear. We rode up the mountain a ways and he said, "Just build yourself a good fire and watch right here! Keith and I will ride over the mountain and be gone about four hours!" I tied my horse up and began preparing to build a fire. Keith looked up on the hill just as they were ready to ride off, and said, "There's a cow moose!" They rode off and I began watching, and sure enough, I could see a big cow, and as I watched her, there soon was another moose. I looked up above those two and saw another moose, one of the biggest I've ever seen! He was bedded down with two or three cows up there, so I kept glassing and watching. Suddenly, off to my left, I spotted two rams bedded down. Boy, this was interesting and exciting - passing time, watching the rams, watching the moose, and everything was so very quiet out there, as they were not moving. Just then, here came a small band of caribou, and they ran between the moose and the rams! Here I was with three different species of big game, all at the same time and that's quite a phenomena! It's like the saying, "Go ahead, make my day," and I felt so privileged to witness all this! Keith and Herb returned, and weren't successful. I never saw any bear, but I touted that as being a very fine day because I got to see those beautiful creatures right where they live!

Danny told me he had guided for a number of big outfitters and he said, "This is the last white man I'm going to work for (meaning Herb)." He said he was going to work on his own, and told me about his Mother. Every morning she'd go down to the river and would catch four fish, two for herself and two for her dogs. One time while she was fishing, she got jumped by a bear and was nearly killed! Danny said, "I want to go home, go across the river and kill four cow elk for my Mother. We don't eat moose meat anymore, we just eat elk meat." Besides his mother, his thoughts constantly gravitated to women! He said for several years he had such a lovely gal with him and she was a wonderful worker. They'd parted and he'd gotten a new woman but then she had gone to Alberta. He'd received a letter from her and now she wanted to come back to him, so he had all sorts of women troubles!

While Danny and I were out the next day, once again it was foggy and as we visited, he rambled on for a long time and finally said, "Well, we have to go home now! There's no use fooling around here anymore." I agreed with him and just then a strong wind came up, lifted the fog up the canyon and the weather looked halfway decent. Looking towards the top of the canyon, about a half mile away, we saw three dark objects, and behind them were big, high, rock bluffs. Danny looked at me and said, "Them sheep!" I smiled at him, "Yes, I see them," to which he said, "They see us!" I said, "No, they smelled our smoke, but they can't see us!" He said, "Oh, you wouldn't know!" I said, "No, I'm sure I wouldn't!" Danny was of the opinion that no white man knew anything about the woods and hunting! At last he said to me, "Do you want to go after them," and I lost no time in informing him, "I sure do!"

We started up the mountain, went a ways, and just before solid rock started, there was a bunch of tall grass. That grass was bent down with snow and it was the slickest thing I've ever tried to go on! Finally we dropped into a draw, began climbing up and just kept going. We decided to take our rain gear off to make the going easier, knowing we were going to get wet! At last we got up fairly close to where the rams were, so stopped to assess the situation. The middle ram seemed to be the largest and was facing into the wind, away from us! The upper ram also faced into the wind and was right next to the edge of this high, rock bluff, which was about two hundred feet high! The third ram was positioned down below the middle ram, could see both ways, and we were visible to him. He was just chewing his cud and wasn't too excited! Danny said, "We're going to go closer," but I said, "No, please, Danny, this is close enough! I don't have a claw hammer, I have a 36-0 rifle here!" "Well, maybe he'll get up," Danny whispered to me. It was as if the old ram heard what Danny said, as immediately he got up on his front knees and began to get up. Just before he got to full stature, about all I could see was his hind end and his horns, but I put a bullet in his left hip! That ram came cart-wheeling down the hill and Danny ran up there as if he'd been shot out of a boot jack. As Danny did this, the other two rams came running right to Danny! I walked up to the ram I had shot and Danny said, "Boy, you've got a good one!" He immediately got his jack knife out and I said, "Hold it, Danny! Let's take this ram down to the horses." "No way," he said. "We're not going to do that, we're going to take his cape off right now!" He did a good job of taking the cape off and went back to do a good shoulder mount. Then he cut off a chunk of meat and said we were going to leave the rest of it. I just couldn't understand it, but we went on down to the horses and back to camp.

Trophy Ram I took with Herb Leake on the Prophet River. Shot with my 30/06 Springfield, 180 grain bullet. He scored 186 and I could have entered him in Records Book, but was afraid I might get a swelled head!

No more had we gotten into camp when Herb started in, "Danny, you poor fool, why did you do that? Don't you know we have to go back up and get that ram?" The next morning Herb and Danny went back up and the other two rams were bedded up against the ham of the dead ram. They never even offered to run away as Herb and Danny approached, but just walked away about thirty feet and stared at them! Herb and Danny returned and I'm sure Herb had lectured Danny on the extra work he had created by leaving the ram out there overnight! Herb got out a piece of paper, pencil, and his tape measure and shortly he asked, "You know what you've got here, Kenny?" I said, "Yes, I have a nice ram!" He said, "You know that's a $16,000 ram, don't you?" I said, "No!" He said, "That's what Lynn Ross gets for them!" (Remember, this was in 1986!) Herb scored it and said, "Your ram scored 176! It's a 38 - 1/2 inch length horn, 14 - 1/2 around the bases, and he's nine and a half years old!" When I later checked it out at Fort St. John, the Game Commission scored it exactly the same as Herb had, and when the taxidermist mounted it in 100 Mile House, he said, "Kenny, your ram is good enough to go in the record book, let me put it in!" I regret it now that I didn't tell him to go ahead and do it! The taxidermist did a beautiful mounting job and my Stone Sheep is quite a sight to behold. This was the first ram I had ever killed. Back to camp that night, the hunting tradition called for a big drunk in camp the first night that anyone got a ram! There wasn't any booze in camp, however, so that was unusual!

The day we arrived at Herb's, there had just been an airplane accident and Coyne Callison had been killed. The Callison's and Leake's were very close and Herb and Judy really grieved because they thought so much of Coyne and his wife. The two couples had a lot in common, one of them was that Coyne had just taken over a big guiding area and was a successful hunter. I sort of wondered if maybe Herb had put a stop to having liquor in the camp because of the increased chances of accidents. At any rate, Herb never allowed liquor in his camps and I really appreciated hunting with him as I've had more than one trip ruined on account of liquor! We heard of so many tragedies up in the North country and often people don't realize what an awesome foe the weather is and when one loses respect for nature, you're taking your life into your own hands! Too frequently, when liquor is in the "mix," it's like double jeopardy! I've witnessed many brutal fights because of liquor and Herb's camps were so enjoyable without it and it was great to be on a hunt with him!

The next day we went down the Procter River quite a ways, fording it five times and making a bunch of lazy S's in the valley. On this day, there was a little fog and it was just barely sleeting, but visibility was so much better than it had been the day before! I looked up the river and here stood a bull elk, standing in the middle of the river. Danny said to me, "Look there, bull elk!" I said, "Yes, I see him!" There were two really high, rock walls which looked like white, chalk cliffs, probably eight hundred to a thousand feet high on either side and simply a spectacular sight to behold! Between us and the elk was a little point of timber, so we forded the river and went up on this little point. Quickly, Danny jumped off his horse and threw the bridle reins down. If it had been me, I would have tied my horse up, but not Danny! He instructed me, "Come over here!" We walked about fifty feet to one side and the elk suddenly noticed us and came running right up to us! About thirty feet short of us, he stopped. Judy had bought Danny a new camera and it had sixty exposures on it! Danny didn't even know how to operate it and pressed on the wrong button and sixty exposures went by almost instantly! That elk heard the noise from that camera and jumped right back out into the water, and it really was funny! Danny looked at me and said, "You know, that is nice bull. Why don't you shoot him?" I walked off to one side, rested my rifle on a limb in a tree, and shot that elk. Again, rather than taking care of tying up the horses, Danny started running up towards the elk whose horn caught under a rock and he was sort of bobbing in the water. Danny said to me, "No problem, I'll go back, get my horse and a rope and we'll lasso his horns and bring him in!" He got back about a hundred feet from the horses and I knew what was going to happen! Just like that, Danny started swearing, as he had to take his britches off, wade through the river, and just then those horses took off! They went clear back to camp, which was over five miles and he had to ford that river five times to get to camp!

Here I was with that elk and it is still bobbing out in the water. I didn't want him to bloat up and float away, so I started figuring out what I had to do to get him out! There was a ledge of rock about eight inches thick and I discovered I could break it off in chunks. So I thought perhaps I could build a bridge out to where he was and immediately began my project! I carried rock, placed them down solidly, and began building them up above the water! This took me over two hours, but I worked and finally had rock clear up to the elk, and could touch him. Once I was able to get to him, I gutted that elk in the water, which was a nearly formidable operation! I wouldn't recommend to anybody that they try this method and it's a chore I wouldn't want to repeat! Out there all alone, I didn't even have my camera or anyone to witness this old man gutting that animal out! At 3:00 in the afternoon I heard a commotion and here came Danny, Bill, and two pack horses. Of course they walked out on my wonderful "bridge," put a rope around the horns, and pulled him in!

Once ashore, Danny asked, "Do you want the cape?" "I sure do," I said, and Danny took it off. He then grabbed an axe and chopped the elk right ahead of the tenderloin. I knew he planned to take the tenderloin and ham, so I said, "Hey, fella, I want that brisket and the rest of the meat!" It wasn't shot up, and was a fine looking piece of meat, but he said, "No, we don't want that!" "Well, I do," I insisted and again he said, "No, you don't!" He would not let me take that meat in, so back to camp we went with the heart and liver. Bill began frying the liver for supper just as Herb came into camp with the other two hunters and when Herb was still about five hundred feet away, he began hollering and cussing! Even before he got into that tent, he yelled, "Get that liver out of the tent right now!" Bill asked, "What's wrong?" "Don't fry that liver in that tent, it'll kill you. It isn't fit to eat," Herb insisted. Since he had already fried some for us and it looked so good, the fellows from Fort St. John went right ahead and began to eat it. I ate a little bit and it didn't bother me, however, the other fellows did get dysentery. Herb said that after a certain day, the elk liver wasn't good.

Visiting at the dinner table one evening, I asked Danny, "Is your Dad still living?" He got an awful look on his face and retorted, "If I ever see that s.o.b. and he's a white man, I'm going to kill him! The first time I ever see him, I'm going to kill him!" I reached across the table, got hold of his wrist and I said, "Put 'er there, Kid, you're not Indian! You're a white man! You haven't got a drop of Indian blood in your veins," and instantly, that kid was livid with rage and nearly came unglued! It was very strange, as he looked like a full-blooded Indian, and I was just trying to have some fun with him.

I had some strange experiences on that trip and went out one evening to sit by an open fire. The Derkaps came out and we began visiting when Keith asked, "Did you ever hear about the big computer in Brussels, Belgium?" I said, "Yes, Keith, I have." He asked, "You know what they're doing with it?" I said, "Yes, they're putting the name of every human who has a name, their social security number and other pertinent information in that machine." "You're right, and you know what they call it?" Keith continued. I said, "No, not really." "They call it 'The Beast'." Herb came out and even though he is a white man, he grew up on the Cruscucina Reservation and I don't know how much education he had, but he was a very intelligent fellow. He joined in and said he'd never heard anything about this and knew nothing about the Bible or the end times. Keith and I explained that the Bible talks about taking the Mark of the Beast, in the end times, and we had a very interesting discussion! Keith had a very good knowledge of the Bible and made many comments, so I learned some things from him and he said he learned things from me! In the end, we just called a truce!

We hunted another day, as I had scheduled a ten-day hunt with Herb, then we left and later Herb told me Keith had more than one chance to kill a big bull moose, but he never got himself in gear. He and his son both had fine, brand new 300 Winchester Seiko rifles, and he'd take aim, then back off, arguing with himself, "Well, I want the horns, but I don't want the meat, I don't know what to do," and so on. He fooled around so long, the bull made different arrangements and walked off! Keith and his son also had the most beautiful, genuine cowhide leather, waterproof scabbards for their rifles. Eventually, Keith did get a ram and a five-point elk, so I was happy for him. The elk I got and the one Keith bagged were the only elk seen on that trip. We saw some deer; both white tail and Mule deer, but they were not in abundance.

Herb finally agreed that Danny could leave camp with me since he had "guided" me, and because we were going out, Keith asked a favor of us. "I own a Coachman Inn in Fort St. John and I want you to stop and tell my wife that we're okay. Tell her we haven't killed anything, and we're going to stay a little longer." Herb said to Danny, "I have a cabin down there and you know where it is! Don't you dare go home tonight, you stay in my cabin. Do you understand that," and Danny replied, "Shore!"

Just before we took off, Danny tied a knot in the end of a three-quarter inch, raw lead rope and started whacking that gelding constantly in the ribs to make him trot, and he just kept pouring it on. As Danny and I rode down the trail, we could tell that a grizzly and timber wolf were going down the trail ahead of us, and that both animals then turned off about a mile from Herb's cabin. Along the way, Danny and I found two pack boxes and later discovered that an outfitter from up the river quite a few miles, had a horse go down in the river and he was swept away. Those pack boxes had drifted down the river, so we took one out and laid it by the trail. That country is rough and rugged and if you make a serious mistake, it can be fatal! We got down to that cabin about two o'clock and Danny said, "We're going to put our feet under Judy's table tonight," but I said, "No, Danny, we're going to stop here!" "No, we're not," and he just kept going, riding down the river! Husky's feet got hot and began to crack, so I took a short cut. Even so, that poor horse's feet were just ruined and Judy told us later they'd never let Danny guide again for them because he ruined that horse. We got in that evening and sure enough, had dinner with Judy. Immediately after we ate, Danny took off to see his girl friend! Later when I checked out a caribou, the information was given me that Herb and Judy had purchased this area and it was known as the Big Nine, or the Procter River Outfitters. We did have several close calls on that trip, but fortunately came out unscathed!

We had heard that Danny ran a sixty-mile long trap line, back in Herb's area. Judy told us about an experience and Danny had also told me about it around a campfire one evening and it goes like this: The girlfriend living with him was such a wonderful skinner and took care of all the furs from the game they took. One day he was going out on his Ski Doo, so she said, "Danny, I want to go with you!" They traveled over forty miles; then the machine broke down. The snow was deep and they had no snow shoes, but they started walking. They walked a little more than twenty miles and she just couldn't go any further! She was a little, slender gal weighing about 110 pounds, so Danny carried her on his back, at least ten miles, to save her life, so it was a very harrowing experience, and they barely survived this ordeal!

Most people don't know this fact, but the reason I mentioned about Danny not having any Indian blood in him, is because the blood line is carried from the Father, and not the Mother. Danny became so angry because he didn't know that, and he certainly didn't want to hear it, since he hated his father so much! He also told me that if I'd go back the following year, he'd guarantee me a huge bull moose and a six-point elk in three days! I said, "Danny, don't lie to me! I'm not quite that stupid! Any fool knows there's no game within forty miles of an Indian Reservation!" I just loved to give him a bad time and after awhile, I think he began to appreciate me and my humor! He said, "No, Kenny, that's not true, because the Government just put in a big, diesel generator and they have television, electric lights and a big recreation room at the reservation, so the people are in there watching TV twenty-four hours a day!" So he threw some humor back at me, which I enjoyed! He did tell me that only he, his brother, and one other fellow hunt, as most of the residents are older people. As time went on, I did find out Danny's statements were true and Herb told me there was lots of game over there. I also noticed in the 1995 Game Laws that Danny had an advertisement in there and takes out hunters and photographers, but is limited to British Columbia residents only. Danny is capable, but not the most dependable fellow in the world!

When I checked the ram and elk out with the British Columbia Game Commission at Fort St. John, they took a drill and drilled into the ram's horn to insert a slug. This slug has a self-locking device, and as it is tapped in, locks in place, and is impossible to remove without ruining the horns. This is a procedure which the Game Commission initiated to prevent theft, since all game is registered and with this device, is traceable! In the past, theft of trophies has been a very lucrative business and they are trying to pass a law prohibiting selling mounted game heads. Earlier I wrote about Ralph Schoof, my friend. He had a cabin with many fine trophies, but someone broke in and stole a lot of them. A few of them were cached in a little wooded area and when he found them, the hair had come off the capes and they were ruined. Trophies from all over the world are considered valuable and I read that at one time, a golden eagle would easily fetch $5,000, just for the feathers. Bear claws, also, have been in huge demand up North, as the Chinese buy them and they are considered very valuable. While I was hunting with Lionel Collins, one time, I killed a caribou which still had the velvet on his horns and wasn't marred in any manner. My neighbor, Karl Kramer, told me he could take those horns to Vancouver and sell them for at least $1,000 to the Orientals, as they grind them up and make some type of high-powered medicine out of them. It seems as if nearly everything is salable if you know where the market is!

BROWNING FROM BLAINE

Way back in 1936, I had a brief acquaintance with Rollin Browning, who lived up above Blaine, out towards the Oregon Coast. This was the time during which I worked on the Hayden Road when I was filing saws and cutting for Elmer Weaver, when I first met Rollin. Many years later, our paths crossed again as his place was right close to where my brother, Lloyd, lived out at Blaine. Rollin told me he and his brother-in-law,

Jack McDonald, had been doing some hunting up North during the last four or five years, out of Nimpo Lake, with an Indian fellow named Willie Sullin. He told me about several of his hunts and basically had very good luck. One time they went up and found Willie in a store and he said, "Yes, I'll take you hunting! Just give me $30!" Rollin asked, "What for?" to which Willie said, "Oh, I just need $30!" The storekeeper there at Nimpo Lake heard Willie ask for the money and he said, "Look Willie, you've got hunters now, you don't want to start drinking!" "Oh, no, I just need $30," so Rollin and Jack finally gave him the money, after which Willie told them, "I'll be ready to go at 4:00 in the morning!" The next morning, at the appointed hour, Willie was nowhere to be found! They went out on their own as they had hunted there before and knew the area. They didn't have any luck and came back in the evening and here was Willie! He asked, "Where were you? I hunted all over for you, but I could not find you!" They said, "Well, we hunted all over for you and we couldn't find you!"

Frances and I drove up to Nimpo Lake one time and there was a husky looking Indian gal sitting on a big horse by the entrance of the big store. Across this wide thoroughfare, an Indian fellow was sitting high up in the air on a little spring wagon. He had a fine pair of Morgans hooked up to this wagon and they were beautiful horses! Soon it was apparent this couple was going back and forth, across the street, arguing to beat the band! In fact, they sounded as if they wanted to kill each other! We couldn't understand their language, but they were going at it! I walked over to the fellow and he just grunted at me, as I said, "Hello, I have a friend in Oregon who has hunted up here with an Indian guide and my friend's name is Rollin Browning." This fellow grunted, "Yeah." I continued, "His partner's name is Jack McDonald," and again he said, "Yeah." "He's hunted up here for a number of years," and each time I made a comment, his response was the same - same tone - same monotone - sort of expressionless! "Was he here last year?" I asked, and again he said, "Yeah." I asked, "Are you Willie Sullin," to which his answer was, "Yeah!" There was a string of five or six "Yeah's" out of him, and that was the extent of his hospitality!

Rollin told me Willie had a nephew helping him guide, and this nephew was one of the finest specimens of manhood he had ever seen! The nephew's name was John, who was six feet tall, weighing about one hundred ninety pounds and just stout as a bull, according to Rollin! One year when Rollin went back, John was all crippled up and was a horrible looking mess! He found out John was drunk, riding a horse, and he fell over backwards in the saddle. The horse bolted, John's foot hung up in the stirrup, and that horse ran for miles through the timber, with him hanging there, just one foot caught in the stirrup. That episode nearly beat him to death and he was lucky to even survive.

TRAILING BIG GAME?

Isadore and I got together one time and he said, "Why don't we make a hunt back there by "Ladder Stand". Do you know how to find that?" I said that I did and we agreed that the next day, we'd meet there. I had a couple miles to walk in this great hunting country, so made my way back there and soon Isadore arrived. He had heard a Kilroy joke and would always take a little piece of paper and write on it, "Kilroy was here" and he'd put the date on it! It was so comical, as he had these little "signs" all over the mountain up there and we'd see them from time to time. He put his little sign up and we conversed a little bit, then he said, "Well, I'm going to hunt back over there," motioning behind him, "and hit the trail which goes back to my cabin." I said, "All right, I'm going to hunt over towards Big Bar Lake." We separated and I went about a quarter of a mile when I heard Isadore call on his moose horn, or so I thought. Soon I heard the call again as I continued on and when I saw him later, I remarked, "Isadore, I heard you call on your moose horn!" He said, "No, I didn't call." I said, "Well, I was sure I heard you very plainly." "No, I didn't even blow it," he said. Then I realized that there was a bull moose between Isadore and myself, and had I gone over to investigate, I'm confident I would have found him, for at this time the bulls were "in the rut". Lots of times they're easier to come upon when they have other ideas on their mind, rather than saving their hides!

Another time Isadore and I rode up on the mountain and he said, "Follow me!" After we had ridden up quite a steep hillside, we came to a very big area, which appeared to be dug out. The ground looked as if it was seeping, and was covered with a grayish substance. There were holes here and there and Isadore said, "This is a real link, or meeting area, where the deer and moose come, so if you want to check to see if there are any game around, always check here first!" I found his information to be true and later found other areas where it was obvious a number of animals had gathered in an area. In fact, there was a place on Mill Creek where our horses used to go out, paw the ground, and eat the soil. The soil appeared to be much the same substance as what I was seeing in the Caribou. The animals seem to have an innate sense of minerals and other properties which their bodies need and are more sensitive in that regard than humans.

"Kenny, I want to borrow a team of horses from my friend, Julia," Isadore told me, "Her Dad, Louie, is my friend. I borrowed them once before. It's time for me to mow my hay, so would you drive me over to their place?" The two of us drove to Indian Meadows, inquired if Julia and Louie lived there, and were told to go to Dog Creek. After heading over there, we saw an Indian fellow on a pony, and he started to ride towards my pickup. Isadore said, "Don't talk to him, I want to go down and talk to the Indian Chief at Dog Creek." The fellow shouted out, "Hello, Isadore! I want you to come to my house for lunch!" Isadore said, "Well, that's Crazy Johnny!" I'd heard about Johnny Grinder for a long time and had never met him. He and his brother had volunteered in the war and even though they had no training, they ended up in front lines. Johnny's brother was shot and unfortunately, Johnny was the one who had turned his body over to identify him and discovered it was his brother! That incident was very devastating for such a young fellow! Johnny wanted us to go to his house for lunch and was sure we had driven down to go salmon fishing. We went to his home and met his lady, Big Ida, who did his cooking for him. He had caught eight or nine salmon the evening before and Ida fixed the most delicious salmon feed for us! Johnny said several times, "I'll take you out, but I'll have to be careful!" Isadore said, "No, we don't want to go fishing, I came here to find Julia." Johnny didn't know of her whereabouts, so after lunch, I drove Isadore up to see the Indian Chief. They talked awhile and then the Chief directed us to drive over towards the Gang Ranch and possibly we'd find Julia there. Their method of communication, however, is that you stop and talk to everyone you meet and inquire of everyone to find out whether they have the information you're looking for. We met a couple of other people and they told us they thought Julia was on the Old Pigeon Ranch.

Away we went, to the Old Pigeon Ranch, with Isadore directing me, over rough, dusty roads, and upon arrival, there was an old house with the windows all broken out. Several Indian ladies, all about forty-five years of age, were there with several little kids running around. Sitting out front was an old coffee can, and I quickly observed that these kids ranged all the way from a toddler in diapers, to kids about eight years of age. All of them were chewing snoose and would lean out the window to spit in that coffee can! In a way, it was so sad, and yet it was comical to see those little tikes trying to spit in that can! They were laughing, happy-go-lucky and without a care in the world! I didn't see any wood around there for the old, wood stove and they were trying to get supper. They did tell us they had scrounged around trying to get wood. Julia was there and she said, "Isadore, you're too late, I loaned the ponies to another fellow!" One look at him told me he was sorely disappointed, so Isadore and I headed out to go home. After I delivered Isadore home, I checked my mileage and had driven one hundred thirty-six miles and he hadn't found a pair of ponies to borrow! He wanted Julia's horses, for they were Morgan, very gentle and easy to ride. The Morgan horses were very valuable in the Caribou as they're so sensible and easy to train.

DIGGING UP

THE FAMILY TREE ROOTS

Our daughter, Donna, came up to visit us in Clinton and since it was time for the annual Clinton Stampede, we decided to take it in. We drove into town and Frances went into a store while Donna and I waited in the pickup. As we were sitting there, a young lady dressed in very nice Western-style, clothing tapped on the window, so Donna rolled it down. "Are you going up to the rodeo," she asked. Donna said, "Yes, we are." "Well, my name is Amy Johnson and I need a ride up there as I'm a contestant," she said. Donna told her, "Well, I'm just riding with my folks, but I'm sure it's okay if you ride along." Frances returned and we started for the rodeo, with all four of us crowding into the cab of the pickup. Soon the young lady asked, "Do you know Guy Lombade?" I replied that I'd heard of him and she said, "He's my Uncle." Amy continued to talk, asking about one person after another. "Well, do you know Ralph Grinder? He's my Old Man now, I'm living with him," she volunteered. "He's got all my money!" I told her I'd heard of Ralph Grinder and that we were neighbors to Isadore and Phillip. By this time, we arrived at the rodeo and went to the gate to buy tickets. Amy said to the lady, "I'm a contestant," so they let her in. We all looked down into the arena and Amy pointed to a horse, saying, "That horse there, is my horse!" Amy smelled so strong of liquor, there was quite a stench in my pickup, and her breath so strong with liquor she could have chinned herself on it! Later on we became quite well acquainted with Amy, but undoubtedly she'd never remember riding to that rodeo with us!

Soon after we pulled into the parking lot, I noticed a fellow with a knapsack on his back and sort of a Mexican style sombrero, and he immediately approached my pickup and tapped on the window. I rolled the window down and he said, "Hello there, Old Timer! Where've you been?" I said, "Oh, I've been around!" Then he leaned in the pickup and said, "Hello, Little One!" We weren't sure whether he was speaking to Donna or Amy! Then he said to me, "I see you have Indian blood in you, too, don't you!" I said, "Yes, I'm part Cree!" (I'm really not, but decided to have some fun!) He said, "Oh, yes! When are you coming down to visit me?" I said, "Well, I don't know, what do you call home now?" He answered, "Well, I'm from Alberta, but I'm down at Salt Springs Island. I have two hundred gallons of home brew to start in on!" "Well, that's sounds like quite a little beverage to get away with," I remarked. He said, "Well, sure," and he just kept talking. John and Betty Spence came down to the rodeo that day and John happened to sit down beside this same fellow, and on the other side of John was a Mountie. This fellow was absolutely loony! He didn't know whether he was coming or going, and nobody ever knew anything about him, or where he went! It was so funny that he thought I was part Indian and that's the first and last time I've ever been tagged in that manner! Donna remarked that her trip North to visit us gave her quite a bit of new information regarding family history!

Floyd Grinder was quite prominent in Clinton and was a handsome, husky fellow who was a top rodeo rider and I believe that at one time, he held the Canadian record for bulldogging. If Floyd made a good catch and the steer had good handles, Floyd promptly turned him over, and that was that! When we lived in Canada, he was still doing some rodeo, as well as logging, and also had a guiding area over towards the Bonaparte area. Once the Ainsworth Logging Company began building logging roads, they wiped out his hunting area. Ralph Grinder, Floyd's brother, also cut a wide swath and was a top ranch hand, in his day. Floyd and Ralph were sons of Henry Grinder, Isadore's brother. There was another Indian fellow in Clinton and Isadore always called him, "Jimmy Corn." His real name was Jimmy Semour and usually Jimmy was drunk! If he could get his hands on liquor, then he was drunk and you'd swear with every step, he would fall down! Catcus told me one time that Jimmy had an unusual ability which wasn't apparent to everybody! Catcus said Jimmy knew where the game was and Isadore told me the same thing. If someone went hunting and Jimmy was there, he'd go into some kind of trance, or concentration, and then he'd tell them where the game was, and he never failed! I never hunted with him as he seemed like a tough, old man, but I'd see him in town every now and then.

Another fellow named Sam Burchell lived in the North country and he shoed horses. Evidently while working, a nail went into his wrist and blood began spurting out, but he was miles and miles from help. When he finally made it into a doctor, he was nearly dead from the loss of blood. Another Indian fellow named Henry Ferguson, was a strong fellow, but he had problems with the bottle. A bunch of them were standing up in the back end of a pickup going up the hill toward Jesmond one evening. One of them had a tube of super glue and they told Henry, "If you put some of this on your fingers and press them together, you can't pull your fingers apart!" He laughed at them and said, "That little glue there can't keep me from pulling my fingers apart!" So they smeared it on and sure enough, he couldn't pull them apart! When they cut them apart, a big bunch of raw flesh came off with the glue, so he learned the hard way! It seemed that we heard so many tragic stories about people up North.

One year the Game Commission had some checkers at Cache Creek and if you lived in the area, they were supposed to put a sticker in your windshield. The government agent at Clinton told me that I didn't have to stop there - that it was totally illegal! To have some fun, I put a B-B gun on my gun carrier in my pickup and drove on through town. We were in Mr. Mike's Restaurant having lunch and here came a checker down there, ready to tear the place down, he was so rabid! He wanted to know the name of the government agent who told me I didn't have to have a sticker and was very angry! Of course, I didn't divulge any names and when I went back to Clinton, I stopped and told the agent what happened! I told him, "I'm sorry, I hope I didn't get you in a jam!" He told me not to worry, he'd take care of it! They had some strange ideas and you never knew what was next, but of course, the same thing is true in the States!

Up at Isadore's one day, there was a big, husky Indian fellow named Wilfred Haller, with lots of booze, which he was gladly sharing with everyone. Amy Johnson, the rodeo contestant we had given a ride to, was living with him at the time and she was there also. The booze wasn't setting too well with Isadore and was getting to him! Amy had a bottle of whiskey and came over to me, asking, "Do you drink?" I said, "No, I don't!" "Well," she said, "I drink to beat h—!" I said, "Well, that's your problem, not mine!" All of a sudden, Amy started for Wilfred's nice, Chevy pickup and said to him, "Come on, let's go!" Wilfred said, "Well, you're going to drive!" She said, "I don't drive a stick shift, I just drive automatic!" "Well, you're going to drive that one," he yelled at her! I said to Phillip, "Don't let those people drive, they're going to have a wreck!" He just laughed at me and I drove on home. Soon after I was home, they passed our place and about a half mile further, they hit a big fir tree head on! They hit it so hard, the drive line was broken out and laying on the ground. Amy was thrown into the dash of the pickup and the impact caved her rib cage in. I'm sure it would have killed a white man because that Chevy had some steel in the middle of it! They came to our place, opened our gate, then decided they didn't know us well enough to come asking for help. They went on down the road about a mile and slept under a tree, then went to Isadore and Phillip's the next day and stayed quite a while. Isadore said to me, "Wilfred is working for one of the Rosette's at the Gang Ranch and he needs to get home!" I said, "Yes, he does!" Isadore kept saying that to me and I knew he was hinting that I should drive them the hundred and twenty-five miles to take them home! Wilfred had a bunch of booze which he had bought in town and he told Phillip he hid it, so a lot of people looked and looked for that booze, but never did find it! The Chevy truck sat up there for years and served as a reminder of what whiskey does! It did quite a number on the truck, as well as on both Amy and Wilfred.

Later Amy started living with Ralph Grinder, a relative of Isadore. She was a hard worker when she wasn't drinking! I had been told she helped build a beautiful, Russell-style fence over a mile long, down by High Bar. The last we heard of her, she had gone to Alberta to live. The strange thing about the Clinton country was if you happened to end up without a woman, all you had to do was to go down to the big tavern and wait a couple days and you could find one if you weren't too particular! That's the way they operated!

BIG BAR LAKE ROAD

One year after the moose season closed, I was hunting deer through the thicket, back quite a ways, quite close to the Big Bar Lake Road. I had never hunted in this area and came across a trail which was quite straight for a ways and when I looked up, here came some black legs! I got off to one side and suddenly Isadore rode up on a big, strong, jet-black horse! He looked at me and asked, "What are you doing back here?" "I'm lost," I said! There was snow on the ground and he said, "Just follow my horse tracks and you'll come to my house after about three and a half miles!" Then I confessed, "I'm kidding you, Isadore, I'm not lost, I'm hunting deer." He said, "Well, we don't have any meat, I'm looking for some meat," and he rode on past me. About a half mile after he went on, he came across two cow moose bedded down. When they saw him, they got up, so he shot the one close to the heart, and it went right down. He dressed it out and took it home to hang up. The way to do it in cold weather is that you don't skin them, and by leaving the hide on, the meat stays clean, it freezes solid and the supply of meat is kept very nicely! Isadore told me what a fine horse he had been riding that day, but said he just couldn't ride him in hunting season for fear somebody would shoot him, thinking it was a moose since it was so black. I agreed with him because those things do happen!

About two weeks later, I went to Isadore's one morning and here he had the brisket cut off that cow and was skinning it. It was so fat, every tin can, every container he could find, was filled with this moose tallow which he had rendered off. It was a nice, white color and it reminded me of the widow in the good book where her vessels were running over with oil. Isadore said to me, "I don't know what I'm going to do, I have so much oil, but I want to give you some fine meat!" I told him we didn't really need meat, but he insisted and he gave me a chunk weighing about twelve pounds, right out of that backstrap and I took it home. We had some friends come from Oregon to visit us, so Frances prepared for them, some of the finest moose steaks ever eaten, and they were just simply impressed! One of their kids ran to the window to look out and see if there was another moose crossing the meadow, as I guess he thought we'd get more moose meat for them to eat!

When Isadore and Phillip were out hunting together one day, they each went different directions. Both of them were great at calling moose. One of them called, the other one answered, and as this went on, they were getting close to each other; each one thinking they were stalking a moose. They'd tell me this story and then stop short of telling me if one fired at the other, but they were now very cautious about what they were shooting at! Another time when I was riding Cindy down along the beaver ponds, Phillip had a hunter from Tacoma, Washington, out hunting. I came up through some timber and brush and when I got to the opening, this fellow had his gun all drawn, ready to shoot. When Phillip saw me, he got a funny look on his face and said, "Boy, I told my hunter, "Here comes a bull moose! He dang near shot you!" I said, "Well, my word! Cindy doesn't have horns!" "Well, it just sounded like a moose coming," he said. Obviously, one can't be too careful, that's for sure!

Phillip came over to our house one evening and said, "Why don't you come up in the morning. I want to go up above the Helicopter Landing and make a big hunt." I asked, "Shall I come on fast time, or standard?" "Oh, no, come on fast time!" I did my chores and went up to Grinder's, arriving there about 5:30 A.M. the next morning. I noticed Isadore had a light on in his cabin, but Phillip's was all dark. I went to Isadore's cabin and visited and finally about 7:00, saw a light on in Phillip's cabin. Phillip had a young lady living with him then and she was laying in bed reading a bunch of romance magazines. About a week or so earlier, he had killed a bull and laying there on the counter, was a tenderloin steak from this moose. It was about a foot long and four inches thick, so he got a fire going and put a big skillet on. Into the skillet, he put about half an inch of grease, cut the steak in one-inch cubes, and filled the skillet completely full of moose meat! It began to cook and he said, "You'd better have some breakfast!" I said, "No, I've already had breakfast. He sat down and began to eat the meat right out of the skillet! He also had a teakettle there and said, "Well, you at least have to have some tea with me!" I said, "No, I've had two cups of coffee and I don't want to drink tea now, it won't set too well with me!" He drank at least six cups of tea, putting about three heaping teaspoons of sugar in each cup!

After waiting a long time for him to get ready, and finally going up the canyon, I thought I'd better give him a working over for this and I said, "You know, Phillip, the birds are nearly finished singing in the trees, the moose are deep in sleep and here we are, just going up the mountain! I should have stayed in bed two hours longer!" He asked, "You should have?" I said, "Yes," and he answered, "Well, I was sleepy this morning, so I just slept until I wasn't sleepy anymore!" In other words, "What's your problem?" He didn't have any, I was the one with the problem!

OFFICIAL (?) MESSAGE BROADCAST -

TRUE OR FALSE?

Earlier I mentioned the communication system in Caribou Country, which was the Message Broadcast and at this time, it was aired twice a day. Everybody listened to the messages and as it aired one day, we heard this message: "To Alex Rosette at the Gang

Ranch. Your brother, Raymond is dead. More information will follow." Twice we heard this message, and then three days later, the message said: "To Alex Rosette at the Gang Ranch: Your brother, Raymond, is alive and well!" Before long, we learned the real facts and this is the story: Raymond and a friend of his were in Williams Lake on a big drunk, when Raymond keeled over in the gutter. As he lay there, his wallet was half out of his pocket, so a fellow came along and lifted it. Even though it's hard to believe, that fellow walked a block or so, and fell over dead with a heart attack! The Mounties picked him up, took him to the morgue, they picked Raymond up and took him to the slammer! When they went through the personal belongings of the fellow at the morgue, of course Raymond's wallet and I.D. was found and that information used for the news release regarding this heart attack victim. I talked to Raymond myself and he said he had been in the slammer forty-seven times for being drunk! Finally, he was able to overcome his alcoholism and would go around to the bars and dances, giving his friends a real lecture on the evils of drinking! One day I saw his brother, Mike, who was in very bad shape, and looked like a skeleton! At one time Mike had been a fine cowboy, so strong and such a friendly guy. Raymond said to me, "Look at my brother! That's what booze and drugs do to my brother!" I'm sure as of this writing that Mike is no longer living, but Raymond is still living up in the area of the Gang Ranch. At fifty-four years of age, he went into school at Dog Creek to learn to read and write as he wanted to be able to study the Bible! With God's help, he changed his life around and was doing good the last I heard!

Former neighbors from Oregon, Don and Mary Strunk, came up to Clinton to visit us. Don was one of the fellows I had logged with during some of my timber days. When they visited, I was really just beginning to handle and train our horse, Tony, as she was just approaching her third birthday and was a nice size. I tied her up in the corral, put a saddle on her, cinched it up, and Don said to me, "You know, that's the way to break a horse. Just get over there and ease yourself into the saddle and see what she does!" So I did and she just seemed to tense her muscles a bit and was just fine. Feeling really encouraged, I rode her around in the driveway and everything seemed okay. One morning I rode her up to Grinder's. To ride a horse out of a corral with two other horses calling after her is quite a task! I had a little trouble getting her organized and tugged on her neck rein to teach her, and at last, she seemed to get the message. When I got over there, Isadore and Phillip weren't home, so I turned her around and we started the three miles back. On the way, we met Phillip and Isadore. Phillip drove his pickup off the road and out into the timber and he shouted at me, "You can't do that! You're going to spoil that horse!" I said, "Well, cheer up, Phillip, she's paid for and I don't think this is going to spoil her!" "Oh, yes, it will," he shouted and really carried on!

Around four months after this incident, a young woman, Lynn, was living with Phillip and they paid us a visit. The horses were close by there in the pasture and they always came up to the gate when anyone came in the driveway, so Lynn asked, "How much do you want for your horse, Kenny?" "She isn't for sale!" I answered. "Yes, but how much would you take for her?" Lynn insisted. I said, "Well, I just don't know because she isn't for sale!" Still she persisted, "But how much would you take for her?" Politely, I just answered once again, "She ISN'T for sale," hoping she'd understand English! This is the same horse, mind you, that Phillip told me I was spoiling and now his girlfriend wanted desperately to buy her!

Around Caribou Country, there was a fellow named Mike Liskey from Hungary who was a great entertainer and spent a great deal of time around 100 Mile House. He and Dempsey used to chum around a lot. One time Dempsey came to our place, looked up at Marble Range and said, "Let's go hunting tomorrow, Brother," but I said, "No, I can't do that, Dempsey!" He asked, "Why not? You've got horses here, what's your problem?" I said, "My problem is I don't want to infringe on Phillip's hunting territory." "Oh, come on!" he insisted, but again I said, "No, I won't do it!" Dempsey was quite upset with me and what did he do, but the next day he drove up 57 Mile Creek, to the end of the road, got Mike and the two of them took off for the top of the mountain! They went clear to the top, into the sheep country and saw three moose. About a week later, I saw Dempsey and he said, "I almost got a shot up there!" "Well, the season has been closed for three weeks," I told him. He wanted to argue with me and insisted it wasn't closed, so I got the game laws out to prove it to him. I thought what a risky thing it was for him to do that, but that was Dempsey. The following year, Mike got into it! As he was going out by Lone Butte, he saw a big cow moose standing alongside the road, so he stopped and shot her, a mere fifty feet from the road. He butchered her out and the entire time he was doing this, a neighbor saw the whole show and called the Mounties. Just as he finished his task, the Mounties were there to "assist" him! They took the meat, his guns, fined him $1,000 and gave him a good lecture! Just goes to show you some days you'd be better off staying in bed! One day I was talking to the Game Warden and he admitted the laws up North are somewhat like they are in the States and the legal description of a piece of property read something like this: "Thence East to height of land," and I asked the Game Warden, "What's the height of land there?" The Warden said, "I'll be darned if I know!"

The incident I just described was not uncommon at all, however, and often things happened in good faith, but in the end, it sometimes takes a Philadelphia Lawyer to determine the laws. For example, when I checked my big caribou out at Atlin, Game Warden, Jamie Stevens, had a set of caribou antlers about a foot high. Guide, Arnold Edzerza, came in with some sheep and goat horns. Upon seeing the antlers Jamie had, Arnold said, "I like your horns there!" "Would you believe it, I took those away from a Canadian hunter and had to fine him," Jamie told him. Arnold replied, "You're kidding!" "No, but if some American hunter had shot him, I wouldn't have thought so much about it, but this fool Canadian shot that caribou for a bull. He didn't know that the gals have horns," Jamie joked. Anyway, I got a real bang out of that and so did Arnold!

Earlier I told about a hunt with Walter Erhorn in the Atlin Lake area and Ron Odion, who took Frances and I fishing on his charter boat. Now we were living in the Caribou Country and one day, while I was in the Hudson Bay Store at 100 Mile House, I saw a fellow and thought, "Man, he looks like Ron Odion." This fellow sort of glanced at me, so I walked up to him and said, "Let's get this over with! Are you Ron

Odion?" "Yes, I am," he said, "Why, hello, Kenny, what in the world are you doing up here?" When I told him we had moved up there, he could hardly believe it, so we renewed our friendship with him and used to see his brother and sister-in-law downtown. Shortly thereafter, we heard the news that Ron was getting married, but just before the great day arrived, his bride-to-be called the wedding off. Sadly, Ron, who was forty-seven, went out and shot himself. Frances and I were so saddened to hear this, for Ron's word was as good as gold and he was one of the nicest fellows we ever knew! It truly is difficult to understand the depths of despair so many demonstrate!

TRIAL OF SURVIVAL

It may come as a surprise to you, but I can assure you, the conservation officers in British Columbia were not the best friends some of the native people had! One time two Indian fellows were fishing and the Game Warden drove up. The one guy grabbed his pole and ran as hard as he could, so the Game Warden took off after him. After quite a chase, the fisherman finally stopped. "Let me see your fishing license," the Game Warden demanded! The guy pulls out his fishing license and the Warden noted everything was in order. Being puzzled, the Warden said, "Why, you fool! Why did you run like that from me?" The fisherman said, "Because my partner didn't have a license!"

It seems that some of the Indian people, such as Isadore and his cousin, Eddie Grinder, had such a knowledge of things which keep people healthy. There was a little area down below our house where a bush grew and many of the Indians picked the leaves and made Labrador Tea, or Indian Tea. It makes a great, little brew and every fall Isadore would gather these tea leaves for some Indian ladies in Kamloops. He'd pick a 20-pound flour sack full and those ladies would drive to Isadore's to get them from him. One day when I was visiting him, he said he had a letter he wanted me to read. The writer informed him she was out of a certain kind of bark which he also gathered and needed some more. She stated she was getting along pretty well but needed more. After I read it, Isadore asked, "You know that tree I showed you up on the mountain below the cabin?" I said, "No, you never showed me." "Well, we have to go up and get some bark, and I'll show you," he said. This lady had cancer for a number of years, but she'd boil this bark and make a tea out of the brew and lived to be a very, old lady. They knew all sorts of things like that the white people just don't know about. When I was in Clinton one day for medical treatment, Dr. Campbell's nurse said to me, "Kenny, I wish you'd go up and talk to Rosa Semour there at Canoe Creek and just try and write down the things that woman knows. When she's gone, we're going to lose a century of folklore that will never be recaptured. We never did get to know Rosa, but I hope someone who lived there recorded some of the knowledge which Rosa had.

Isadore had a brother, Bill, in Kamloops who had been a Section Foreman on the railroad most of his life. Occasionally Isadore would go to Kamloops and stay with him, as Bill would hire Isadore to do some odd jobs. About a week was all he would stay, as he said he couldn't stand to be there any longer. Frances and I made many trips to Kamloops during the years we lived in Clinton, and we never noticed that the water there was terribly obnoxious in that town. Isadore, on the other hand, claimed it had this rat poison in it to keep people's teeth healthy, so whenever he'd go over there to visit, by the time he was home, he'd always have dysentery and be sick.

Eddie Grinder, Isadore's cousin, had a very bad drinking problem, but he loved to play cards with Isadore. Now old Isadore never had a drinking problem, so long as nobody bothered him, but if someone insisted he drink with them, he'd eventually end up drunk. About once a month, Eddie would go by our place about 2:00 o'clock in the morning, having already imbibed in the sauce! As he went by, he'd lay on the horn, wake us up, and go on to Isadore's. He'd promptly get Isadore out of bed, then they'd play cards and drink until morning. I'd always get a report from Isadore and he'd tell me that the next day his head would ache, but his stomach felt okay. Interestingly enough, for some reason, his stomach did not tolerate the chlorinated water, however! The last time I visited Isadore in Clinton, in 1995, he was in the Senior Citizens home there and he had a large, glass jug. He asked me, "You know what's in that jug, don't you, Kenny?" I said, "I kinda think so." To this he replied, "You'd better believe it! It's water out of good, old Mann Creek. I can't take this city water!"

SAVORING THE SAMPLES

Phillip used to come down to our place quite a lot and every time Frances would make something like a fruit cake or other dessert, he always wanted the recipe, as he really had a sweet tooth! Of course, whatever she made always tasted SO GOOD! Anybody who's ever put their feet underneath France's table will attest to the fact that she is one of the best cooks ever! I never could figure out where Frances learned to do the many things she could do. One example is, she made wonderful homemade soap. Very few of the ladies up there knew how to do this, but Frances could, and the same thing was true of sausage making. One time when Frances was with me, I saw a big buck, so I shot it. We walked about fifty feet away from that deer, she stopped and said, "I've always wanted to do this and I believe now would be a good time!" I wasn't quite sure just what she was referring to, so I watched

Frances looked as if she knew just what she was going to do, and she did! Fine buck we bagged about two miles from our house in Clinton.

her! She went back, got hold of the end of that deer's gut and started walking back. I thought she went about fifty feet before it broke, but she claims it wasn't that far! She knew how to turn them inside out, boil them to sterilize them, and then stuff them with sausage. We made some of the most delicious sausage that anybody ever ate, and wherever we have lived, I always have a smokehouse, which was put to good use. Another specialty which we made was lunch meat, well seasoned and sort of our special recipe! One day when I went up to see Grinder's, I took a chunk of this delicacy about fourteen inches long, and two and a half inches in diameter. When I arrived at Phillip's, a lady with a couple kids was also there. I handed the lunch meat to him and said, "Here you go, Phillip." "Is it ready to eat?" he asked. "Matter of fact, it is," I answered, so he reached up and got his hunting knife out. Without hesitation, he cut a slab off about a half inch thick and ate some. His pronouncement was, "Oh, man that's good," and cut off some more, devouring that; and then some more! By this time, the woman held her hand out and then here came those kids! While I was still there, those people ate that entire hunk of lunch meat! Obviously, they had a good appetite!

It's a sad thing that so many people there in the Caribou don't know how to take care of meat. Years ago I bought a book, Campfires In The Canadian Rockies, and it is the account of Colonel William T. Hornaday. He was sent up North by the American government to secure specimens for the Carneige Museum. In that book is a recipe for curing meat, with just simple things which can be bought in most any frontier store. Very few of the people we met have the knowledge of how to do this! When the meat is fresh, they have plenty to eat, but they don't seem to know how preserve it, which is a shame. Meat used to be such a major part of their diet, and to not know how to properly care for it, is indeed a detriment to their livelihood. Flies and bees don't generally go higher than fifteen feet, so if you pull a deer up in a tree and leave it hang in the sun, it will get a glaze over it. Then if the prescribed ingredients are rubbed over the meat and it's left to cure, it will keep for a long time.

Some of the natives in Canada who live out in the wilds have developed some phenomenal survival skills, which often is a matter of life or death. One of the things they can do is follow tracks. Out hunting with some fellows one day, one of them said, "Listen, I think I hear something!" The other one said, "Yes, I do too!" Suddenly a big deer got up across the canyon and I said, "Man, you guys sure have good hearing!" This one fellow said, "No, I can't hear like I used to hear." "You can't?" I asked. He said, "No, I used to be able to hear rust forming on steel!" When I was a young fellow, I always had good hearing, but I never was quite that good!

Early one afternoon Phillip came riding his horse into our yard and it was soon obvious that he was terribly excited. On the television news broadcast, we had heard that a helicopter had gone down and four people were missing. Of course, there was the pilot, and the other three passengers were Game Wardens. Phillip had been riding his horse up on the mountain when he heard a terrific boom, and his horse just stopped immediately. He came right down to our house and said, "Kenny, I heard the plane go down and I know approximately where it is! I know I heard a plane go down," and he was visibly shaken. I drove into Clinton to tell the Mounties about it and they sent the word out. The next day a big Buffalo plane landed out between our place and Herb

Hart's to begin their investigation. They flew over the area repeatedly, but seemingly could find no trace of anything. Later it was determined that a jet had broken the sound barrier and this is what Phillip heard. In the spring when the snow had melted, the helicopter was located across the Fraser, above the Big Bar Ferry. Upon inspection of the wreckage, they found the four bodies and also making himself at home, was a big raven inside that plane!

Phillip was full of a lot of antics and stories when he was feeling good and here is a sampling of one of his stories: One day he told me that he thought a 308 Winchester rifle was absolutely worthless, so I asked why that was true. "Well," he said, "I had an American hunter up here last year and I saw a big, bull moose standing off about a hundred yards. So I told the hunter, to bust him right through the lungs and when he shot him, the bull dropped his head and coughed real loud. To make a long story short, that hunter put five bullets through that moose's lungs in about a five-inch circle. Every time he hit him, the bull would drop his head down and cough, and then suddenly ran off. We went over to where he was standing and here he had coughed up these five bullets and they were laying on the ground! That's why I have no use for a 308 rifle!"

As I mentioned earlier, the sanctity of marriage was viewed rather casually and a constant source of amazement to Frances and I while living in Canada was the way men traded women! One day I was riding along with Eddie Murdock and he was talking about a friend of his who was head honcho down at O.K. Cattle Company. He said he hired a certain fellow and when he named him, I asked, "Didn't your head honcho friend have his wife stolen by the guy whom he hired? Why didn't he shoot him?" Eddie said, "No, no, they're the best of friends!" "Well, in America, if someone stole another guy's wife, that's grounds for murder and they usually shoot 'em," I explained. "Oh, no, we don't do that here," he was quick to reply. I recall reading of an incident in the Eastern United States that on a certain tombstone, the man's name was written, his date of birth, and date of death. Underneath that was engraved this statement: "He lived with his wife for fifty years and died in the confident hope of a better life!" I can tell you not many people in the Caribou ever have this achievement that they could have this put on their tombstone because most relationships and marriages don't last that long!

DAY OF CONFUSION

Living there in Clinton, it seemed as if we were constantly learning new things and it was getting very close to Father's Day. One of the natives made the remark, "It really IS Father's Day here in Clinton, but we just call it the Day of Great Confusion! That's because very few people here actually know who their Dad is." Unfortunately, the longer we lived there, we discovered that to be the truth! For example, Isadore's Father had two wives at the same time and when we were having a discussion one time, he said, "Please don't go into that!" (He didn't know the term for genealogy.) "Mary so and so is supposed to be my sister, but I don't know if she is or not," he told me. Another Indian fellow told me he knew Isadore's Father and it was a fact that he had fathered twenty-three kids, for sure, and four or five "suspects"! Obviously, Isadore's Father was active and prominent in the various "affairs" of the community, to say the least! So, as you can see, it became rather complicated! We knew a fellow who had two women and twenty-two known children, with emphasis on the word, "known"! This triggered a poem in which I tried to point out, delinquent parents generate delinquent minors!

HAPPY FATHER'S DAY
Since Father's Day will come at dawn, I now must talk to you,
For you don't know the plight I'm in, I know not what to do.
My girlfriend will a Mother be, and that's not far away,
So Father, you must hear me out, perhaps you'll make my day!

I need some dough, I need it bad, and that so very soon,
So do not scream or turn away, for that would spell your doom.
You see, one night not long ago, I wandered into town,
And so I thought, Oh, what the heck, I'll take a look around!

I went into a smoke-filled room, I heard some voices plain,
And would you know, that in that crowd, I did not look in vain.
I saw you with a pretty gal, and she was not your mate,
So Father dear, I'll tell you now, that I control your fate!

If you don't give me plenty dough, and do it right away,
I truly will your spouse inform, and she'll put you away!
His Father turned so ghastly pale, his Son almost took fright,
He said, Now listen here, dear Boy, I think she'll be all right.

I'll pay your bills, I'll hold your kid, I'll do just all I can,
If you will cover up for me and help me be a man!

THE BURIAL
An old man just passed from his toil and his strife,
Word quickly was passed through the village that night.
On the day that was set, the crowd gathered to pay
Their respect, and to duly lay their comrade away.

The Reverend then entered the Community Hall,
Where the departed had danced at many a ball.
The Reverend then said, "Let all stand and sing,
So don't be afraid to let your voices now ring."

The Old Rugged Cross was the song that was chose,
And a more motley crew, you could hardly suppose.
The Reverend then spoke of the deeds of the dead,
He told of his kindness and giving of bread.

When the service was over, one spoke of his friend,
Does anyone know, is this really the end?
The Reverend said, Well, I suppose he's at rest,
I don't really know if he was one of the best.

Then came an old lady, all withered and bent,
And said to the Reverend, I'm not really content,
Of the things that you said, as you laid him away,
I can hardly conceive of him being that way.

He was mean and lazy, and not worth his salt!
And now you're a saying, he had not a fault?
The Reverend turned pale and he started to cry,
Well, my poor, dear old lady, I gave it a try!

If he was so bad, as you're a saying he were,
How come you had such a worthless old cur?
The old lady said, Well, I'm speaking real plain,
If I did it all over, I'd have him again!   (January 21, 1990)

CLASSIC COMMUNITY CELEBRATIONS

To my knowledge, the Williams Lake Stampede is the third largest in Canada. They celebrate with much activity and aplomb. Among the attractions is they set up a regular Indian village, with an authentic teepee and everything which would replicate the real thing! Visitors drive over a thousand miles from all over Canada and the states to go up and see the sights! The Mounties really don't "ride herd" during these celebrations, as they expect people to get drunk and party, so as long as someone doesn't get scalped or murdered, they pay very little attention to all the extra-curricular activities! They have a classic community spirit there and the May Day Ball and Parade are some of the most colorful and interesting sights to see anywhere! The Mounties show up with their beautiful, black horses, with all the "trappings", the Indians will come in with their wagons, horses, and mules and they have a gala time! It is quite an experience because this is where people live!

SHELLS AND SHRIMP

It was winter when Phillip came over one day and said, "Next time you go to town, buy a bunch of shrimp and have Frances save all your egg shells. Then we'll go fishing over at Beaver Dam sometime soon." The time came for us to go fishing and one cold, Tuesday morning we decided to go over to Beaver Dam. In most places, the ice was over two feet thick on the dam that morning! On the previous Sunday, they'd had a Fishing Derby and the Game Warden said there were at least two hundred holes bored through that ice, which I can believe, for the evidence was there. When Phillip and I arrived, there was a nice, warm fire going and two Indian couples were there, just goofing off and having a good time in general. The lake was rather shallow in this one area and the fish were feeding in water about six to eight feet deep, so these people had some poles set out. Phillip and I decided to go down a little distance from where the others were and only had to break through about four inches of ice. Besides our gear, each of us had also taken along a five-gallon bucket. As soon as we broke through the ice and set up our poles, we were in business! This one woman came out to talk to us and Phillip soon realized that he was related to her, as was one of the fellows. Phillip proceeded to take some of the egg shells and crush them up, and as he did this, she asked him, "What are you doing, Phillip?" He said, "Well, we caught some huge fish here last week and these are the eggs we took out!" She said, "Oh, Phillip, you must be lying!" "I don't tell lies," he retorted. He shredded those egg shells up, tossed them into the water, and they went right down! It's simply amazing how those shells lighted up the bottom of the lake, so we could see real well. Sure enough, before long, here came these big, lake trout and we started catching fish! These other people said they had been there for two days fishing and hadn't even had a bite. I had let the shrimp sit out for a couple of days before we went fishing so they had a little bit of an odor to them and it worked like magic! They said, "Phillip, you better quit, you have such a pile of fish," so we went into shore, where we started cleaning fish. They had foil along and some potatoes, so over their fire, we baked potatoes, fish, and Indian fry bread. They also had a bottle of whiskey along, but it was interesting that the men weren't drinking; just the women. After we had this delicious meal, the women got to wrestling around and one tried to push the other one into this big bed of coals. I thought to myself, what a dumb thing to do because that's how tragedies usually start and I was ready to get out of there. The fishing there was fantastic and Phillip was a good fisherman.

Phillip also used to go down along the beaver dam below our place and catch fish. One time he got the Game Commission to bring some fingerlings out to plant and I helped him carry them for about three quarters of a mile and we released them into the water. We took two buckets full and planted them in various, isolated beaver ponds. The fish did real well and Phillip caught some fine ones!

One of the main attractions in Canada is that there is a great abundance of lakes! Phillip and I went down to Little Big Bar Lake to go fishing, and he said, "I want you to drive up here about a mile because I want to show you something." So I drove and before too long, we came to a cabin, still in fairly good condition. He said, "When I was fourteen years old, I lived here for about a year." I noticed the skeleton of a horse head up in a tree and part of the neck and I asked, "What's that?" He got a rather sheepish look on his face and said, "Well, when I was a kid I had my own pony, but I didn't know how to tie him up. There was a big, oval shaped rock about twelve feet in circumstance and I tied him up to it. The rope was too long and somehow he got all tangled and choked to death, so I just crawled up in the tree, pulled the horse head and neck up there and it is a reminder to me not to do something foolish like that again!" It was all bleached out and white as could be and did serve as quite a monument to him and was rather amusing to see.

Frances and I were hunting one time in a thicket above our place towards, the Big Bar Lake country, and that morning before we left, I had put some special lure scent on my cap. The snow had begun to fall and the wind was blowing very strong. The big bucks were beginning to rut very heavily, as it was towards the end of the season. Through a little point of timber, I spotted two bucks a long ways off, running away from us and they were really traveling! We made a big circle, heading back towards our home when I heard Frances call out. There was a little bench about thirty feet long, which dropped down fifteen to twenty feet. Here came one of those big bucks with really big horns, just running down that hill at great speed! He hit a tree head on, right behind Frances, not more than fifteen feet from her! My rifle was in a sling, over my shoulder and around my neck! You may not believe this, but that big buck got away before I could shoot him. He nearly hit Frances head on, and I've never seen an animal do that before, but that big buck was really packing the mail and was in a terribly big hurry! Just goes to show that you don't know what can happen to you when you're out in the mountains!

MY GUN'S BETTER THAN YOUR GUN!

The various guides I used to talk to in the mountains regarding rifles always gave me a big chuckle. One fellow had a 300 Winchester Mag and he asked me, "What kind of gun do you have, Kenny?" "Oh, it's a 30.06," I told him. "You know, don't you, that my gun has more than twice as much power as your gun," he informed me. He went on and on telling me about his gun, but of course, I had lots of hand loading magazines which he didn't know, and which I didn't bother to tell him. I knew how much power his gun had and what the power of a 30.06 was, so his comments to me were rather amusing! Most of them have 30-30 rifles and they feel sorry for anyone who's carrying a bigger gun. Once I asked Walter Erhorn, "Walter, of all the moose you killed and been able to weigh, what's the biggest?" He said, "I killed a moose below Kinney Dam that weighed eleven hundred fifty pounds after it hung two weeks! I shot him five times in the lungs with a 30-30 rifle. He never bolted and ran, but just looked at me and started to walk off. Then suddenly, he got weak in the knees, laid down and died." That is an enormous animal!

Walter told me that on one of his hunts he had Jim Carmichael out and that Jim had a new fang-dangled rifle. I asked him what kind of rile it was, and Walter said, "Oh, a 280 and I've never heard of 'em before!" Later, I read Jim Carmichael's story about this hunt up North and his 280 rifle. Many of the hunters who go up there have much more high-powered rifles than they need. They shut their eyes and pull the trigger because they know they're going to get kicked. They just simply can't handle those magnums. Some of the guns the Indians use nearly always had the stock broken off, with parts wired or glued on. One guide I went hunting with had baling twine for bridle reins on his horse. The truth is, he didn't really need them because his horse was very gentle, so all he had to do was nudge it, do some talking, and it went wherever he needed to go. Often when they'd go out, they wouldn't bother to take food, so sometimes would go without food two or three days. If they forgot blankets or other gear, they'd just make do without. There was no set time for doing anything; whenever they decided to do something, that was fine.

YOUNG'S LAKE YARNS

There was only about a week before moose season would be over when I suggested to Frances that we go over to the Young's Lake area and hunt. We gathered groceries, gear, and away we went in our camper, about fifty miles from our house. There was a certain road I wanted to drive back on as I had been there once before and it looked like real nice country. Somehow, I missed the road and went a mile or two further, so I turned around to go back, and when I looked up, a moose was crossing the road! He stopped in a thin patch of timber and I said, "Frances, please get me a shell out of that clip!" I always carried my shells in the old Army issue clips. She said, "Ken, you don't want a shell out of there, that's a <u>cow</u> moose!" I said, "No, get me a shell out of that clip," and as I pulled off the road, she handed me one. Quickly I put a shell in my gun and shot where I thought his heart would be, and lo and behold, down he went! I drove up closer to him, grabbed a tarp, some meat sacks, my knives, meat saw and gear. There were vehicles going by on the road and we were off about thirty to forty feet, just out of sight from the traffic. I dressed that big bull out and he was a fine piece of meat! Every time I kill an animal, I learn something. The funny thing was that the Forest Service had built a fence with five strands of barbed wire and a post every sixteen feet, just fiddle-string tight! That fence would have been no problem for that bull, but I got him before he had time to exert the energy to get over it!

BEAR AT BONAPARTE

One day in the spring I heard that the bear were coming out and feeding over on the Bonaparte. There is a huge gas line which goes way up North, out of Kamloops, into quite an isolated area. We drove over there, spent the night in the camper, and next morning about daylight, we started driving. The road was pretty good, so we drove up the hill, and once we got to the top, turned around to come back down. Just then, Frances asked, "What's that down there? Sure looks like a bear to me!" So I stopped and sure enough, it was a bear! He was busy feeding on a little clover called Japanese Clover, which comes up in the spring. Just then he raised up, so I put a bullet right in the white spot in his throat. He jumped up and ran and I foolishly took off, too. I made a big circle, close to half a mile through the timber and started back to where I had last seen him. In the meantime, he had only traveled about twenty feet from the original point. Then we put the hubs in four-wheel drive on the pickup, I backed up, put the tailgate down and loaded him in (feathers and all). Since I had a bear tag, we got that out and put it to use. We were about three miles from Ainsworth's Main Haul Road and just as we got out to this road, here came a little Toyota pickup with a big, red light! You just never know where you're going to meet your best friends! The Game Warden stopped and said, "Hello! Are you just out enjoying the scenery?" I said, "Yes." "Have you seen any game?" he asked. "Matter of fact, we did! I saw a black bear," I confessed. "Did you take the bear?" "Yes, I did," I said. "May I see the bear?" We showed him the bear and my license, had a nice little conversation, and he went on his way. It was a beautiful, mature bear, with gray whiskers and we had a lot of fun on that trip.

EMPIRE VALLEY EMPIRE

Our friends, Tom and Connie Hook, used to invite us every now and then to go hunting on their ranch, Empire Valley, and so we headed out one morning to go see them. We drove back up toward a road which leads to the Black Dome Mine site, and took a side road. The deer were just traveling into this area and we were told they come in from way back in the Taeseko Mountains. At that time, when the migration was on, it was just unbelievable the amount of deer that would come through sometimes. It was getting along toward evening and as we traveled back toward the main road, Frances said to me, "Ken, there's a doe standing up there! Here comes another deer!" Just then,

Buck I shot in alfalfa field at Tom Hook's place in Empire Valley.

here came a fine, big buck. I didn't realize Frances was going to shoot this buck and I jumped out and shot him before she had time to get the lever closed on her gun. She gave me quite a scolding for it and I felt right humble, because I should have asked her if she wanted to shoot the deer! Of course, my excuse (reason) was that I knew there wasn't much time to wait, or he'd change his agenda! We dressed him out, put a block up in a little tree and hung the meat up with some rope. It was a lovely spot there, so we decided to spend the night in our camper. We had a little water in the wash basin that night and forgot to empty it, so next morning, it was frozen solid, as was that buck! As I was getting that buck down, I began to realize how big he was and had to saw the legs off of him to get him into the camper! Even at that, we had a difficult time getting all of him in!

Another time when we headed over to Empire Valley, Tom had a nice, big alfalfa field cleared off, out towards the breaks of the Fraser River and at the edge of Grinder Creek. Frances and I went out there, camped for the night in our camper, and the next morning, here was a large band of deer feeding on the alfalfa. Tom had a water system rigged up on big wheels in the fields and as Frances began walking down along the water system, I went around the edge of the bluff. From the movement of the deer, I could tell they were watching Frances, even though I couldn't see her! Foolishly, I just up and shot a buck through the heart and he took off on a dead run (no pun intended) and went over this bluff! It was so steep there, he just went over and over, probably a hundred and fifty feet down the bluff. To show you how steep it was, I had to tie him up to dress him out. I took out my nylon cord, tied one end around him and the other end to some brush in order to anchor him. It was too steep for me to carry him up whole, so I cut him in half, making two separate trips with my packboard. The last piece, with the horns and the rest of the meat, was so heavy, it was quite a feat for me to cut that cord loose and not loose my load AND my balance! To give you an idea of what was down below, it was at least eight hundred feet down into the bottom of a very big canyon and I just didn't choose to go down that way! Two different times, I had animals run over a bluff and had a very treacherous time getting them out! If only they would have died on top, but they weren't very cooperative and life isn't always easy, especially in the Caribou, but we had some great hunts up there!

Probably the second or third time we visited with Tom and Connie, shortly after lunch, Connie asked me if I would mind going with their Ranch Foreman up to the calving barn to drive her pickup back. I told her I'd be glad to and she directed me outside where I could meet this fellow. Evidently they had told their foreman what my name was, but I had never met him before. I crawled into the pickup with this broad-shouldered fellow, wearing a big cowboy hat! As he started driving, almost immediately he asked, "By chance are you Byron Shenk's Dad?" "Well, Byron used to eat a lot of hotcakes at our place when he was a kid! Matter of fact, I am! Why? Do you know Byron Shenk?" "Yes, I do, if it's the same Byron I know," he said, "I'm Steve Oswald and I attended Goshen College, and was there when Byron was coach. Matter of fact, I was at the soccer game when Goshen beat Notre Dame!" I said, "You gotta be kidding!" "No, I'm not kidding," he said. We struck up a friendship immediately and I thought how unusual to meet someone up North up knew one of my sons! That really took the cake!

While visiting at Tom and Connie's one day, here was Alex Rosette shoeing a horse. Now remember, this is the same Alex Rosette who had helped guide on a couple hunts way back during my maiden voyages to the North country! Now he was employed by my friend, Tom Hook. About fifty feet away from Alex, was another Indian working on another horse. I asked, "Alex, who's your friend," to which he replied, "I don't know! I think maybe he's an Indian from Red Stone Reserve, but I don't know who he is." So I walked up to the other fellow, then I noticed he had a deformed hand and it looked as if a piece of shoe leather had been grafted onto the back of his hand. I greeted him and started a conversation and then asked him, "Is Willie Sullin your Dad?" "No, he's my Uncle!" I then remarked that some years earlier, my friend, Rollin Browning, had hunted with Willie and Willie's nephew had been injured so severely. He looked at me and said, "That's me!" He then related some of the trials he went through in his recovery from that accident. The doctors grafted his hand with skin from his stomach, and this procedure continued for over six months, due to the number of surgeries required. It was a gruesome ordeal to endure and here he was, working for Tom. Tom told me John was a terrific ranch hand and good cowboy. Also, he was in shape, and someone you didn't want to fool with!

About a year later, I went on a moose hunt with Don James. We took a canoe and paddled three miles across Davis Lake and then we portaged over between another big lake about a mile and a half. This canoe was a sixteen-foot fiberglass and we had all our gear in there and just carried that thing! We then went on another lake for about three miles, went ashore, and made camp. Prior to this trip, I didn't know Don all that well and in the course of our conversation, I mentioned Willie Sullin. He asked, "Do you know Willie?" I said, "Not really, just through my friend, Rollin." "Well, he cowboyed for my Dad one time down at the Circle S and I was also cowboying. We were in a cabin and there was a young lad there, so Willie told this kid to go shut the door. The kid never moved, so Willie said to him, 'Did you hear me tell you to shut that door'? The kid just looked at Willie and Willie said to him, 'I killed a man one time for less than that!' That kid jumped up and shut the door." Don said that some of those Indians surely had a "hair trigger" and you never knew when they were going to explode.

RACOUS ROSETTE

I had heard about a fellow named Arthur Rosette and some of the stories were legendary, I suppose. Arthur had worked for my friend, Tom Hook for awhile. Tom had told me Arthur was a very talented guy and could do nearly anything in connection with life on a ranch! Arthur did not, however, do as well in the legal department and had several brushes with the law. Never did he go out of his way to get involved in trouble, but he certainly didn't seem to avoid it, either! One time he was in some sort of a scrape, so a Mountie just parked his car crossways on the Gang Ranch Bridge to block the road. Arthur knew he had to get across that bridge without getting caught, and the story I heard was that they claimed he galloped his horse at a dead run and jumped over that car! Anyone who would tell the story swears this actually happened! All I can do is suppose that it DID happen.

Another story I heard about Arthur came from persons of good repute, and they said this is "the gods truth" (as my trucker, Uel, used to say). There was a fellow named Alfie Higgenbottom who could pick up a rifle (even one which didn't belong to him), and if he could see a deer, no matter how hard it was running, he could hit it! Arthur had so much experience and shooting practice that he was a great shot! Tippy Robertson told me he one time personally saw Art pick up a 25-35 rifle, which he had never seen before. About two hundred yards away, a buck was running. Arthur pointed the gun at the buck's head and put a bullet right behind that deer's ear.

Alfie Higgenbottom had a son, Doug, who was very strong. Phillip knew Doug real well and said he was one man he couldn't whip! When Phillip was younger, he'd fight anybody and supposedly they might be able to knock him down, but never could knock him out, or kill him. Phillip said he and Doug would always come out with an even stand-off, although Phillip was much bigger than Doug's one hundred seventy-five pounds. Doug always bragged that the Mounties would never take him alive and was in more than a few scrapes with the law. Once Doug grabbed a man by his shirt collar and seat of his pants and threw him right out of a tavern.

Another story regarding Doug goes like this: He got into a scrap one time and two Mounties put him in a car. Once inside, he grabbed the gun of the one Mountie and supposedly shot the one in the leg. The other Mountie shot Doug and he was killed, so they didn't take him alive. That happened shortly before we moved to Clinton.

GRUESOME GRAVEYARDS

Another gruesome tale was that not long before we moved to Canada, along the railroad track, someone found the head of an Indian. This fellow was related to Grinder's, but they would not talk about it. Others would tell me, but if I questioned Isadore or Phillip, they would not talk about it. It seems that not a lot of them died from old age. However, due to the drinking, and the shootings, the funeral directors and cemeteries were kept in business. There were a few I heard of who did live many years, and several of the Robinson fellows made it to 100 years of age. The climate up there is very healthy, weather-wise and lacked pollution and other trappings of heavily populated areas, so should promote longevity.

An American-owned, big lumber company, Weldwood, from 100 Mile House, was building road up on Big Bar Mountain, when the operator of the cat skidder came across some human bones. The Superintendent went up there and said, "Get that cat away from there at once!" It was ascertained the bones were human, the word went out about the discovery, and the road building project was shut down so that the local tribe wouldn't be upset. There was an old fellow, Amos Fowler, who had been the Superintendent of the Clinton sawmill for a number of years, and when he heard this news, he laughed and said, "Oh, I know what that is! That's the old Hangin' Tree!" They asked him what he meant and he said, "Years ago when I first came to this country, some ranchers caught a couple guys butchering out a steer and they just hung those fellows right there and then buried them! We just called that the Hangin' Tree!" That problem was solved in a hurry and work resumed on the road. More than one location had rather strange names. For instance, there was "Graveyard Valley". Albert Joseph and I were back there one time and the story told me, was that a bunch of Indians were marooned back in the mountains, about seventy-five miles past the Gang Ranch. They got a terrible "white man epidemic" and began dying like flies. Graves were dug, more died, and at last, only one man was left, so he dug a grave. The next spring some people went back there and here was this man sitting up in the grave. He had no one to cover him up!" That's how that valley got it's name, although I didn't see any graves when I was there, as the ground was snow-covered and I was busy hunting moose!

FENTON OF CLINTON

One of the characters of the North there was Charlie Fenton, who was born and raised in that area. He was a Shuswap Indian and had lived a very colorful life! He was the one who came up to our vehicle in 1953 when we had gone hunting in British Columbia and were parked in front of the government office. Charlie had never gone to school and couldn't read or write, but knew the license plates on our vehicles weren't from British Columbia. After we moved to Clinton, we visited with Charlie and his wife, Susie. They were so friendly and Charlie regaled me with hunting stories, as well as things he did when he was a kid! Isadore also knew Charlie well and could verify many of the things Charlie told me. At one time, the Gang Ranch was owned by a couple of fellows from Great Britain, who were men of considerable wealth. They imported several of the finest Arabian stallions which the world had to offer. These stallions had been turned loose and we had driven through portions of the Gang Ranch on different occasions and saw bands of these Arabian horses just running wild. The bands were sometimes as large as one hundred fifty to two hundred horses just out in the wild. Whenever anyone from the ranch wanted a saddle horse, they'd go out and run some of these wild horses into a place where they had built wing fences. They'd corral them in order to break and ride them! When Charlie was fourteen years old, he rode a little stallion that just seemed to enjoy helping catch the wild horses! Of course, Charlie was a wonderful horseman and very capable, having learned this from a very young age!

One day when Frances and I went to visit Charlie and Susie, he was very ill and in bed. When his friends came to visit, they'd always bring him a bottle of whiskey. All his life he had been a drinker and his doctor said if he were to quit then, it would kill him. Of course, he obviously wasn't going to make it anyway, so what did that doctor know? That day, there on his dresser, sat a big, square bottle of Jim Bean. Charlie was propped up in bed, and greeted me by saying, "Oh, it is so nice of you to come visit me again - I forget your name." Then he called out, "Susie, please bring the gentleman a drink!" She said, "Charlie, you're all ready legally drunk and you've had twice as much as the doctor said you should have! I'm not bringing you anymore booze!" Charlie would look at me and say "Oooh," and then he'd go right on to his story telling!

Charlie said once he was up behind the Empire Valley acreage walking along, when he met an old Indian who had two, five-gallon buckets full of gold! As he told me this, he would shake his head and frown, "It was heavy! Oh, my gash, it was heavy!" Charlie had done considerable mining throughout his life, too. Up beyond the great Chillicothe Ranch, which is above Lee's Corner, they found a vein of gold in the side of a mountain so rich with gold, it was incredible! The Indians really didn't know what to do with it, so they told some white guys. These fellows had a company, and sent one of their engineer's up there. While the engineer was up there, it thundered and lightening followed, then it hailed, snowed, and they experienced just terrible weather for about a month! I asked Charlie, "Well, what was the matter?" Charlie replied,

"What was the matter? Why, this man was a white man and the mountain wouldn't accept him!" I said, "Oh, I didn't know that!" "Why, sure," he replied! Stories like that fascinated me and were fun to listen to!

We had gone another day to visit Charlie and it was getting towards evening, so I said, "Charlie, I've got to go home!" He said, "Well, I'm not through with my story yet!" "Well, I'll have to come back," I told him. He said, "The next time you come back, I will tell you the story of the time I went from Big Bar Ferry through the mountains to Chelquote Lake with my pack horses." That was a long ways through there and I'm sure his story would have lasted all day! About a year ago, we heard that Charlie passed away, but he was a living legend and his experiences would have made very interesting reading!

Frances and I had heard about the Reynolds Ranch across the ferry, so we took off one fine morning to go over there. Across the ferry and up a very, very winding, steep hill we traveled. We got up on top, went a little ways, and suddenly descended down the other side - into a beautiful valley! There were several buildings there and this is where Tillie Reynolds and her son, Sonny, lived. Tillie was probably sixty-five years old at the time and very happy to meet us. Sonny was up on the hill hauling hay and she told me if I wanted to walk up there, I could meet him. So I walked up on the mountain and found him, along with his new bride, where they were busy pitching bales of hay. Her son was stacking the bales, Sonny was driving the tractor, and the terrain they were working on was very steep! I began to throw bales up on one side and Sonny's wife threw bales up on the other and it didn't take long before we had a pile of hay hauled in. Then it clouded over and began to rain and the hill was like grease! I had just put my highway tires on the pickup and didn't bring any chains along, so we decided we'd better leave. Frances inadvertently left her purse there, which was something she never did for it's generally never more than two feet from her side! We get back to the ferry and here is Eddie Murdock, so we told him about Frances leaving her purse and he said, "That's no problem! I'll get your purse for you!" He had a little radio, so he notified them, and they returned her purse. Eddie never missed an opportunity to tease Frances about the time she lost her purse and as recently as 1995, when he saw us, he was still giving her a bad time about it!

John Spence and I made plans to go hunting at Reynolds Ranch and went over the day before season opened. Sonny had done a lot of trapping and guiding and for years, he was a big game guide, and had an old cabin out in the bush he said we could stay in. He also had a new cabin, and there were four Game Wardens staying there for the night, waiting for the season to open the next morning. John and I knew two of them. They were celebrating and one of them came over to our cabin to visit and spent the evening. He told us a lot of things, many which I'm sure he never would have shared so freely, had he been completely sober!

The woods were very dry and though we put in a lot of effort, John and I couldn't find any game! The second day we went up to Nine Mile Ridge and still we didn't find any bucks. As we started down from the ridge, John said, "Say, would you please drive into Reynolds Ranch. I know them well and need to talk to Tillie." We drove in and there was a white man and a young Indian boy. Tillie was overjoyed to see John and she remembered me. She said, "Something's going to happen here! I don't know what's going on, but I'm scared to death! The boys are up to no good! Would you fellows stay for dinner?" We said, "Oh, no, we've got lots of grub!" She just insisted and told us she planned to have potatoes, gravy, and some braised deer ribs from a deer they got last year! I said to her, "Tillie, I hear you are a wonderful game shot with a rifle!" She smiled and said, "Well, I do pretty good." "I'd like to see your rifle. What kind of rifle do you have to do all this high powered shooting?" I asked her. She was pleased that I asked, and replied, "I'll be glad to show you," and with that she went into the bedroom. She came back carrying a long barreled 30-30, which at one time, had the stock broken off on the tang that the stock fit in, behind the hammer. It was an old 94-30-30 Winchester and someone had done a crude job of braising it where it had been broken, but she had a new stock on it and it held. After I looked at it and handed it back to her, Tillie set the gun behind her in the corner. We were about halfway through our meal when the Game Warden drove into the yard, and suddenly Tillie grabbed her gun and ran into the bedroom. John said, "Hold it, Tillie! You said these ribs were from last year!" As it turned out, the Warden just stopped to leave a message for a hunter and he took off fairly soon. John said again, "Tillie, you said these deer ribs are from last year!" She blushed like you wouldn't believe and said, "Well, I thought it was better to not have to do a lot of explaining, John!" Well, we thought so, too! It was very funny the way this all came about, however!

When John and I made this hunting trip, I didn't know John all that well and had never been out on a camping trip with him before. I had taken along some chuck steaks and Frances had cooked up a real fine kettle of beans. For some reason, I mistakenly put too much pepper in those beans and literally painted them black! John looked at me, started laughing, and asked, "Ken, do you like pepper?" I said, "It's quite evident that I do! John never let me forget, and the entire time we lived in Canada, he'd always bring that up the pepper incident! John and Betty were always fun to be around and very good company. On another occasion, John and Betty, Frances and I were in a restaurant in Kamloops having dinner. Two pieces of bread came with my meal and as I picked up the one slice, I didn't notice it was buttered on one side, so I put jam on the other side. This tickled John until he could hardly stand it! I always told John that if a man couldn't tell the difference, you'd better make allowance for him 'cause he just isn't responsible!

When Tillie Reynolds was about seventy-seven, she got to hurting so badly that she went into Kamloops to the doctor. He said, "Mrs. Reynolds, your one kidney is torn loose and we're going to have to operate on you," so they performed surgery. After she was out of the recovery room, the doctor came back to see her. He sat down and said, "Tillie, I have something to tell you. I guess you should know by now that your days of riding a saddle horse are long over with and you'll never be able to ride again!" She didn't have a lot to say to him, but after a couple days went by, she said, "Doctor, I have to get out of here!" He asked, "Why?" "Because I have a favorite saddle horse and I just know that fellow Sonny hired to work for us is riding that horse! I don't want him to ride my horse," Tillie explained. She got out of that hospital, went home, and sure enough, this character was riding her horse! So she went right back at it, being a cowboy and doing what had to be done on the ranch. She was a wonderful person and so capable! She lived to a ripe old age and when she passed away, was lovingly laid to rest on the banks of the Fraser River, close to where she spent her entire life.

BIG BAR BASH

The Big Bar School had an annual celebration, the Old-Timer's Rendezvous, and we had heard about it, so decided one day to attend. They played all kinds of games, many which we had never heard of before, had bucking contests, a rifle-shooting contest, and always a big feed in the evening. This meal was complete with baked salmon, moose meat, deer meat, and all the trimmings! It was a community get-together, well-attended, a lot of fun. Although I hadn't told anyone that I was a saw filer, I took along a bucking saw, which I had filed. After we arrived, I observed that they were lining up the competition to saw logs, so I laid my saw down on a log. An Indian fellow came

over and asked, "How much swedge you put in your saws, Kenny?" I said, "Oh, I just put in whatever a bucking saw takes, using my gauge." "Well, I don't have a gauge, but I just put it over a little piece of steel and pound her," he said. I thought that in the competition, I would be bucking against an individual, but as I laid my saw down on this log, I noticed five other saws had been placed there before mine. Almost as soon as I went to join the crowd, I looked over towards the competition, and saw two women bucking with MY saw! Just prior to this, a big Indian fellow came up to me and said, "You look to be about my age; I'm gonna buck with you, but first I want to give you a good drink of whiskey!" His name was Glen Brady and I was old enough to be his Father, but he didn't know that, I guess, and I said, "No, thanks, I don't need any of your whiskey!"

Old Timer's Rendezvous at Big Bar School - I took my saw, in which I had put real appetite - no saw dust - just shavings and wood! Glen Brady and I beat all the others - hands down! I was 76 years of age.

As we watched the two gals sawing, I recognized the one as Marge Zimmerly, and she ran a saw like a man would. Most of the women get right behind the saw, then they just bump the saw back and forth, right into their chest, and that doesn't work very well. Marge, however, knew how to run a saw properly. Soon a couple fellows bucked and then two Indian fellows took their turn. One of them was Louie Duncan, so after he finished bucking, I walked up to him and said, "Don't dissipate all your strength yet, Louie, I'll make a run with you pretty quick." He just stared at me, but before long, I grabbed my saw, and Louie and I took a turn. At this time, he was living with Marge

Zimmerly and she was easily old enough to be his Mother! Louie and I wiped the men out, while Marge and her partner won the womens' contest! Each winner received $10 apiece, so I gave my money back to the school, since they had a fund-raising endeavor to take the kids on a sight-seeing trip when school was out. The thought occurred to me that Louie and Marge had an extra $20 sort of "out of the blue" and if nothing else drives people to drink, that will! Once in awhile I'd see Louie downtown and speak to him, "Hello, do you know where I could get a bucking job?" and he would laugh.

Leaning against log is Henry Grinder, behind him in white cowboy hat is Floyd Grinder, a very fine cowboy!

Shortly after our visit to the Rendezvous, when we returned home from town one day, there were five saws standing against my garage. One of them was eight feet long! A fellow had found it in a dump at 100 Mile House, so he took an old power buffer and buffed the rust off of it. Some of the rust was pitted so deep, it looked as if you could almost see through this saw! He put it in a vice, took a crescent wrench and tried to set the teeth and unfortunately, broke them off! The fellow who did this was John Sarver, a truck driver, and he told me, "I want to come up to your place and learn to file a saw!" I decided it was pretty futile trying to begin such a project because those saws were in such horrible shape! When a saw gets rusted so badly, you can't work it, as it gets case-hardened and you can't swedge the rakers. They just break off, as if they were made of glass, and are impossible to correct! I did file a few saws for some of the neighbors, but very few, as I didn't want to get involved in something like the rusted ones, because some of those are simply hopeless!

TATLACO VALLEY COUNTRY

While hunting in the Anahim Lake country one time, we heard a little about the Tatlaco Valley, which is on the road going to Anahim, before getting to Nimpo. There is a Y in the road; the fork going up the hill leads to Tatlaco and the valley, and we wanted to go to Tatlaco, as we had heard of the Schuk's. Edward Schuk had a guiding service in there for many years and a son, Doug, who was now living there. We drove into Doug's place, introduced ourselves, and I said, "I hear you take out goat hunters." "Yes, I do," he said, "and we hunt other game also." Doug motioned out towards the Homathko River and up on the mountain and said, "You see that snow up there on that high peak?" I acknowledged where he pointed, and he continued, "Well, I don't think you want to hunt with me, but that's where my goats are. Do you think you could walk up there?" I said, "Yes, of course, I can walk up there!" "Are you sure," he asked, and I emphasized, "Yes, I'm sure!" "Well, all right, if you can walk up there and want to hunt with me, I'll take you up there! I guarantee you'll kill a goat!" "Well, I'll guarantee I can walk up there! I'll book a hunt with you!" As I said that to Doug, he smiled. At that stage of the game, I sort of think perhaps Doug wondered if this Old Man could make it up there! After Frances and I got back home, I contacted Russell to see if he'd like to go with us and he said he'd love to, so I arranged a hunt.

The great day arrived and we traveled to Atlin at the appointed time and just as we arrived, out of the blue, Doug's cousin, Randy, arrived, also! Randy was born and raised in that valley, but had moved and was employed in the construction business. Randy was a delight to have along and proved to be a wonderful hunting companion. I had a pair of insulated, vibram soled, expensive boots which I had worn before, but somehow they just never felt very comfortable! They didn't conform to my feet, were utterly impossible to feel secure in, hurt my feet, and once on my feet, they sort of felt like clubs! Here I had at least forty pounds on my back, including my spotting scope, food, rifle, camera, shells, axe, and so on, and up the mountain I go! Truthfully, I was no more physically fit to climb that mountain than a school mom would be if you took her right out of the classroom and told her to climb the bluff! Russ had been working in the woods and was in pretty good physical condition. He had a U.S. Army packboard with an even bigger load, of at least seventy pounds, carrying all kinds of gear and grub needed for our trip. Randy was a big, husky fellow and was carrying supplies for himself, as well as a chunk of meat which his Uncle Joe had given him. He had invested over $2,000 in his camera gear and had some great equipment, including a telephoto lens, and had brought all of this along. To get up to the mountain, we would go through a canyon called Hell Roaring Creek, and believe me, the name was NOT a misnomer! This creek was appropriately named and was to be respected!

Up the mountain we trudged, at least three miles. During this foray, we had gone through Devil Club's thickets with all sorts of brush, and the traveling was brutal! Before long, we saw a cabin which belonged to Doug. Randy looked over at me and said, "Hey, let me take part of your load, Kenny!" I think Randy thought I was about fifty years old, but I was much, much older! I said, "Okay!" Soon I started getting muscle cramps in my thighs and the calves of my legs, until I could hardly go. Once we were on top, I got into my shaving kit, took my toothbrush out to brush my teeth and discovered that my fingers were cramping so badly, I could scarcely hold the toothbrush.

That evening Doug and Randy fixed their food and Russ began to fry some bacon. When it was done, he went over to the fire and drained the bacon drippings into the fire. Doug said, "Oh, oh!" "What's wrong?" Russ asked, to which Doug replied, "The black bear and grizzlies can smell that grease for five miles and will come to find that scent," and he laughed. Before we retired for the night, they threw a rope over a limb and pulled all the groceries up into the tree because there were lots of grizzlies and black bear in that area.

About two weeks prior to our hunt, Doug had flown over the area with his brother-in-law's plane and had seen goats. Next morning we started hunting, but there just weren't any goats to be seen. To Doug's consternation, the goats had moved! He said, "Well, they're not here now, but I know where they are! We'll have to go over two, big high mountain ranges, up and down the Homathko Wilderness Area and this country is tremendously rugged!" My legs still ached and I was quite sure that it would be foolish for me to attempt the climb. Randy couldn't stay out any longer, and was going back, so I decided to walk back down the mountain with him.

Randy and I cut off to one side and took sort of a circuitous route to get back to camp. We walked onto a bench which was just absolutely devoid of timber, but had small clumps of brush growing there. As we went along, we soon saw four of the biggest bucks I have ever seen! They were quite a way off, but just stood there and looked at us! No doubt they had never seen humans before and seemed very curious. What a beautiful picture! There was a little stream of water meandering through the flat there and everything they needed was there, except protection from the wolves and cougars! Randy took out his camera and as he took pictures of them, it seemed they were posing for him! Two of them had the velvet rubbed off and the other two were still "in the velvet"! Randy said, "I don't know about you, Kenny, but my trip is a success!" After what seemed like quite a long time, they leisurely and gracefully trotted off into the woods.

Back to camp Randy and I went and later that evening, Doug came back in. Russ was not with him and Doug quickly explained that he had left Russ at his other cabin back in the woods. Doug said to me, "Kenny, Russ and I walked over ten miles today, and we found some goats! I'm going to ride a motorcycle back to the cabin tonight. Do you think you can walk up and find my cabin tomorrow morning? If you can, I'm sure you can kill a goat!" "Sure, I think I can," I said.

The next morning, I took off, walking! There was no sign of a trail and at times, I'd have to go over solid rock bluffs. All I had to "guide" me was what little verbal description and direction Doug had given me! Up those bluffs by myself I went, arriving at that cabin about 5:30 in the morning! A day or two earlier, Doug had remarked that an ordinary man, in good health, who smoked and was past forty-five years of age, would undoubtedly never be able to make it! It is ten miles of intensive, dangerous climbing! By now it was snowing slightly and there were still a few embers from the big fire Doug and Russ had earlier that morning. I lost no time in reviving the fire and noticed it was beginning to snow harder!

Just as the fire was really blazing nicely, I looked up to see Russ and Doug coming into camp. Out of the pack Russ had on his back, I just happened to see a little chunk of white hair sticking out! As Russ came walking up, I never looked up from the fire and just said, "Well, hello, Sonny!" He said, "Hi, Dad!" "Well, I see you got your goat," I remarked. "Goat? Where's a goat around here?" he asked. "Don't kid the Old Man," I said, and he laughed! "Yeah, I got a goat, Dad," he said with pride! We spent the night in that cabin, which was about six feet and one inch wide, with a bunk in there. It was so small in there because normally Doug stayed there by himself!

As we woke up the next morning, Doug said, "We gotta get out of here, and get out fast, or we're gonna be in here all winter!" We made our way down off the mountain as quickly as we could go because of the snowy weather. Doug was still terribly apologetic to me and bothered that I hadn't gotten to go goat hunting! Matter of fact, he didn't forget it and later said to me, "I told you that if you could climb that mountain, you could kill a goat! You climbed the mountain and didn't get one!" I said, "Well, that's the way the ball bounces!" Doug said, "No, I made the statement and I'm going to make that good to you!"

SHOOTING WITH SCHUK

The next year, Russ and his son, Alex booked a hunt with Doug. Since Frances and I were now residents of British Columbia, Doug told us to come on up and go hunting on our own, which we did! Hunting was very grim, with an East wind blowing, it was dry and it seemed everything was against them, but Russ and Alex hunted hard. Finally, one day, Doug called Alex to one side and said, "We're onto a big bull

moose!" They kept trailing him until they found him and Alex killed a nice bull! They dressed him out and went into camp for the night. The next morning, we took a power saw and axes and made a road so Russ could get his 4 X 4 pickup back fairly close to where the moose was. Those horns were one of the biggest sets I've ever seen! I believe they had a fifty-one inch spread, which is very big for that area. We took that moose down to Doug's ranch where he had a John Deere tractor with a front-end loader, so he picked that moose up with the tractor, and it looked as if it was twenty feet tall! Doug asked Alex him if he planned to have it mounted and Alex said he didn't, so Doug kept the cape, and had it tanned.

Again the next year, Russ and Alex went back to Doug's to hunt and once again, the hunting conditions were not very favorable. It seemed that the weather was to-

Nice buck taken near Tatla Lake area in 1987 - Ken shown with labor of love.

tally against them, but Alex was able to kill a fine, fat buck, which was great meat. After this trip, neither Russ nor Alex got back to that area to hunt for several years.

Hunting season had just opened for another year and Frances and I went up to Doug's. He told us to go down by Chelquote, about twenty-five miles from his place, as he thought we might have good hunting there. We drove down there and camped for the night in our camper. The next morning I told Frances I was going to go up towards a rock bluff which had some timber on it, and was about three quarters of a mile from the camper. I told her she could come up the hill a ways as there were long openings, interspersed with poplar and some scrub jack pine and I thought she might have a good chance to see a deer. I took off and walked about three eighths of a mile from the camper. Stopping to look around for a moment, I looked back and saw Frances about a quarter of a mile from the pickup. She was waving her arms, motioning for me to come back to her, so I went back! Frances said, "I just saw a big buck go around the edge of that rock bluff!" "Okay, I'll go trail him" I told her, and hurried up there. Immediately, I saw the tracks of the deer, mixed with some other tracks, but I couldn't

Fine trophy moose Russ bagged on hunt with Doug. L to R: Alex, Ken and Russ.

follow him. On and on I walked, hunting for his tracks, but couldn't find that buck! Eventually I went back, found Frances, and we decided to go back to Doug's cabin to spend the night. The next day, we headed home to Clinton and would do some hunting there.

At least two years after my first hunt with Doug, he called me up one fall and said, "I suppose you know I owe you a goat! I told you if you walked up there to that mountain, you'd get a goat and you didn't get one, so I owe you one! I want you to come over, and if you'd come a week before hunting season, you could give me a hand." I told him that suited me just fine! Frances and I went over and I helped Doug with his haying and we put a roof on his barn. He built a trailer, using motorcycle wheels, and pulled this behind his Honda. It worked out just great and he still uses that trailer. His son, Edward, was thirteen at the time and he wanted to go along with us. Edward was such a nice little kid that I really enjoyed him and he walked up the mountain with us. Doug was able to get his motorcycle up there, loaded down with our gear.

As we were walking along through the snow, we could see signs where a bear had gone through. Going up the one hill, Doug said, "A big grizzly just went ahead of us!" I said, "Is that right?" and Doug said, "Yes." As we continued, I could see more and more evidence on the ground of a bear having been there! We only went another two hundred feet up a steep hill, through a very brushy area, when Doug picked some fine, bear hair off a bush, handed it to me and just smiled. I knew this fine hair was from the undercoating of a grizzly!

A day was left before season opened and we wanted to go out and just scout around. I had bought a new spotting scope and said, "I'm going to try this spotting scope out, Doug." I set it up on the little tripod and focused it up on the hill and could hardly believe what I saw! Here were a bunch of big objects moving by and I said, "Come over here, quick, Doug! Here's six, big bucks!" He smiled and said, "Yeah, I knew they were up there, Kenny. I flew over in a plane the other day and saw them, but you told me you wanted to kill a goat!" "Well, I do," I said, "but I certainly wouldn't be adverse to shooting a big buck like that!" "We'll see once. I thought maybe I might bring Russ and Alex up here if they come up to hunt," Doug said.

The next morning season was open and we started up the mountain. This area was high altitude, very rugged, and extremely steep. We climbed for a while, then stopped to catch our breath and Doug said, "Let's try that scope out!" I set it up on a rock and way across the canyon was a Billy goat, just sitting on a little cliff, chewing his cud! I could even see his little chin whiskers waving in the breeze, and he definitely was at peace with the world! Undoubtedly his taxes were all paid up and he was quite a happy individual. Doug said, "We can kill that goat, because if we crawl across the face of that one ledge there, you can either kill him, or shoot all your shells!" So, down the mountain we go, crossing a series of three ponds, just as blue as Indigo and beautiful bodies of water, each about a quarter of a mile long! There was sort of a beaver dam in between, in a valley, and we got across this water and started up the mountain. After climbing a lot of altitude once again, Doug stopped and said, "Let's have our lunch here!" We had packboards, rain clothes, meat saw, and various gear which we un-loaded and began to eat our lunch. Doug said to Edward, "If you want, you can stay here, but if you hear Kenny shoot, you bring this gear over to us, will you?" Edward said, "Yes."

We left Edward there with the extra gear, went about seven hundred feet and when we looked down, could see quite a long valley. Just as we were preparing to get down on our bellies to crawl across the face of that cliff, we saw a goat walk out, way down at the bottom of that valley! Doug and I had crossed just below where this goat was, and he said to me, "Well, look down there, will you? You know, I believe that goat has your name written on it! We can kill that goat easier than we can get this one up on the cliff!" We crawled downhill a short ways and the goat started walking. "That goat's going to get away from us, you'll have to shoot from here," he suggested. Doug had a 270 and I had a 7 X 57, with a receiver sight on the back, but it didn't have a scope. I made a front sight out of a piece of horse shoe and was justly proud of that sight and loved to shoot it. I said, "Doug, I'd like to kill a goat with iron sights. I think that'd be quite an accomplishment for a man of my tender age!" He said, "Well, that's fine with me! I take hunters out with bow and arrows and I know that's a lot more deadly than a bow and arrow!" Doug put his 270 down and said, "Shoot over the forearm of my 270." He stuck it down on the ground, but between the two of us, we were waving about too much! I said, "Doug, that won't work! I'm going to crawl down here to this ledge and shoot from there!" He said, "Well, you can try it, but I'm sure you're going to lose that goat!"

I went down to the ledge and shot, but on my first try, I overshot and should have held (my aim) almost below him, but didn't. Once again I took aim, held below him a bit, and rolled him! As Doug and I were going down there, he estimated that I shot at least 385 yards. At last we got to the goat and discovered it was a beauty, with horns nine and seven eighths inches long, a big animal! Rather than Edward bringing our gear, as we had expected, he started down the mountain and left all the gear where we had eaten lunch! One of us had to go back up and get the gear, so Doug volunteered to do that. When he came back, we took the hide off the goat and cut off a bunch of meat. We packed up the hide, horns, and the meat and started out. I had heard Doug say that Edward had to be in school the next morning, so I said, "Listen, if Edward has to be in school, there's no use getting everything in an uproar, we'll all go down the mountain together!" "Well, Kenny, I had planned to take Edward down and then come back up here and help you get a buck. I hate for you to have to do that, but I guess we should," Doug admitted. So down the trail we all trudged, arriving in camp around 9:00 that evening. That day I walked more than twenty-four miles and carried quite a load, as well as climbing the steep mountain. All in all, I thought that was pretty good for an old Duffer! Frances picked us up at the end of the trail, so that concluded that hunt. I was very happy to have gotten a goat!

The following year, Frances and I went back up to Doug's, arriving there at 3:00 in the afternoon. Doug greeted us and said to me, "Would you feel up to a hunt yet?" "Yes, of course," I quickly answered. "Where do you want to go?" he asked. "I want to go back up where Frances saw that big deer go around the bluff!" "Well," he said, "it's been awful dry this year and I don't think there's any water there for miles. I doubt there's any use going there, but if you want to, we will!" "I want to," I said, and so we drove back there. Doug said, "I'm going to hunt down over here towards the lake. By the way, if you happen to kill something, wait five minutes, fire one shot, and I'll come to you!" We separated, and that's EXACTLY what happened! I went up on this bluff, came to a clearing, and just then I thought I saw a movement at the crest of the hill, quite a long ways up there. I looked intently and here was a great, big buck standing behind a windfall, so I took aim and fired! For an old fellow, with open sights, I made a very fine shot! I hit that buck in the shoulder, somewhat below the spine, and it knocked him down. It was so steep there, but I ran up to him and that buck was already in the throes of death! I put a nylon cord around one horn, tied him up to a limb, and dressed him out. About three quarters of an hour later, here comes Doug. He looked at me and started laughing, "Kenny, you'd hunt a long time before you'd kill a finer buck than that!" I said, "Doug, I've hunted a lifetime and this is the finest one I've EVER killed!"

Doug and I stepped back from the buck a little, looked down the hill and here was a lake, at least a half mile long! Doug said, "Well, I didn't know that lake was here! Guess they had plenty of water after all!" That lake wasn't over a quarter of a mile from where we had been. Then Doug wanted to know where I was standing when I shot the buck, so we went down and I showed him. He started laughing and said, "Kenny, you were standing right in the middle of that buck's bed!" That's precisely what happened, too. Without a doubt, he had heard me coming up the ledge, so he jumped, ran up to the crest and stood behind the windfall, and that's where I shot him. "I believe I can get my motorcycle up here pretty well," Doug said. So we dragged the buck down to the ledge, and went home to get Doug's motorcycle and trailer. Doug got it started and said, "Get on, Kenny, I'll give you a ride," so I got on. Of course, I had my axe so I could cut windfalls out of the way and Doug maneuvered his way up to the buck. After we got down off the mountain, Doug picked that buck up with his John

Deere Front-end Loader and took pictures of him. Later, I had him mounted and it is one of the biggest deer I'd ever seen and I honestly believe he weighed at least three hundred pounds! He was so thick through the girth and when others see the size of his head, they tell me he probably weighed closer to four hundred pounds! He was one beautiful deer and every time I look at that mounted head, fond memories of the Tatlaco Valley come to mind!

DIFFERENT BUCK FOR THE BANG

It was just at the last of deer season another year when Doug asked me to come up to hunt. There was a little snow on the ground, as we traveled down along the edge of Chelquote Lake. Aldo drove us down there in his Toyota rig, as well as his neighbors who were going hunting with him. He dropped Doug and I off and then they continued another three miles further down where they would hunt. We walked up along Barren Ridge and noticed a deer track, then soon found a couple more. Doug looked at the

track and said, "This looks like a real fine, big buck here, let's follow him!" We began following these deer tracks and walked for quite a long ways. After some time, the tracks went into a terrible thicket! That thicket was full of little windfalls, about three feet off the ground and short, jack pine about twelve feet high, making it next to impossible to get through there! We could see deer tracks all over the place! I don't know where all those tracks came from or what their intention was, but they were thick! Finally, Doug got this same buck lined out and we kept following his tracks, climbing uphill constantly. At last he started going to the West in a rather straight line, going through some beautiful stands of poplar trees, interspersed with pine. We trailed him for over an hour and then Doug whispered, "We're getting close now!" We went about two hundred feet further and I looked

This is a buck with huge girth - taken in Chelquote Lake area.

off to my left and saw a pretty big deer standing with his head down! I had my 7 X 57 Mauser and when he put his head up, I shot him! Doug was ahead of me about ten feet, looking the other way, but when I shot, he whirled and said, "I saw that bullet strike that deer!"

We started walking to the buck and he said, "That isn't the buck we've been following!" "It isn't?" I asked. "Oh, no," he said! When we got up to the deer, he was a nice, big three-point buck and sure enough, he wasn't the deer we'd been following! The amazing thing was, the wind had been blowing strong from us to this buck, and he was facing me. When I shot him, the bullet hit him right in the brisket. Doug said, "It'll take us another hour now to come onto the big one! Do you want to follow the big buck?" Then without waiting for me to answer, Doug continued, "My Dad really needs

Doug Schuk (on left) hoisted him up - he was a big one! Ken on right.

a big buck, Kenny; what do you think?" I said, "Oh, it's getting along in the day. This one is okay!" He had some cord, so we hitched onto him and got that deer down to the road. Doug said, "Let's walk on down to where Aldo's Jeep is!" I told him, "Well, that's a long ways down there, Doug, but I'm up to it if you are!" "Oh, sure, it's just a little ways down there," he assured me. We began walking and walked for quite a long time. Finally, I said, "By the way, would you do me a favor, Doug?" He said, "Sure, what do you want?" "I want you to look at Aldo's speedometer when we go back and see how far it is!" I said. "Okay!" he agreed. We finally found Aldo's Jeep and shortly, Aldo and his friends came in, empty-handed. So back up the road we went to pick up my buck. Doug looked at me and kinda laughed, "Well, Kenny, you're right! It was three

miles and three tenths! Well, I've been accused many times of getting lots of mileage out of a mile!" He got to figuring and said, "We pulled that deer for way over three miles, didn't we!" "We sure did," I said, as I knew we had gone quite a long ways. This deer had gone through a heavy rut and the meat had sort of a pinkish tinge to it, but it wasn't strong tasting or anything. It was good meat and he was a really nice deer!

GRIZZLY GETS GAME

While hunting with Doug another fall, the snow was really heavy, so I chained up all four wheels on my pickup. Doug and I were going up a hill and right at the crest, Doug said, "Well, well, I see where a band of wolves have run across the road!" I could basically see nothing, except that the snow had been disturbed and I was concentrating on keeping my pickup in the road! Sure enough, we got up there and here was a band of wolves running through the snow. We couldn't find any game and had started back down the hill, when he asked, "Could I get you to turn off here and drive back for about three quarters of a mile?" So I turned where he said, drove down a ways, and then Doug said, "Please stop here! Would you mind walking about half a mile? I want to show you something." I said I'd be glad to, so we began walking, went about a half mile and came to a big hemlock tree with limbs very close to the ground. There were bones scattered all around there for more than forty feet! The bones were from a huge, bull moose and a big grizzly bear. Doug then told me this story: He had a hunter from Austria out, and was able to get standing shots for him at a big mule deer, bucks, and moose. However, this guy would grab his gun, sort of squeeze it, but he never offered to shoot it! For some reason, he just would not shoot. As he and Doug were walking, with about twenty feet distance between them, they walked right onto a grizzly who had just killed this big, bull moose! Doug said he knew they had only seconds to live, so he shot the grizzly right behind the ear! As Doug and I stood there looking over the site of the fracas, Doug said, "I want to take that moose skull in," so he picked the skull up and took it to his house. That was one enormous bear! The leg bones looked as if they had come off a three-year old steer! Doug said that bear stood up just like a big Angus when he shot it!

Earlier I mentioned that Doug had asked Alex for the cape off the bull moose he had killed, and Alex gave it to him. Doug took that cape and he had a taxidermist attach it to the set of horns from the bull moose this grizzly had killed. He told me not long ago it took five years for him to get it back from the taxidermist, but when he finally did, it is really a beautiful head! Most moose heads are so big and clumsy-looking, they're difficult to hang in an ordinary house! Doug's house is built in such a manner that he can display lots of trophies on the walls.

TRAILED BY THE WARDENS

One evening, Doug, Edward and I were going back to his cousin, Calvin's place, to hunt deer. There was a big alfalfa field on the way and the deer would come out there to feed. As we were driving along on a side road, past Coachman Lake, Edward said, "I think I hear a horn!" I looked in my rear-view mirror and saw a bunch of flashing, "Christmas lights", so I stopped. Two Game Wardens got out of their vehicle, and came up to talk. One said very sarcastically, "Sir, do you ever bother to look in your rear-view mirror?" I said, "No, I don't! I try to watch ahead so I can dodge the stumps!" I doubt that he thought too highly of my attempt at humor, and he said, "Well, that's for darn sure! Do you know how long I've had those lights on you?" I said, "No, I don't!" "Well, clear back on the big Tatlaco Road before you ever turned on the Coachman Road," he informed me. "Now I don't doubt that a bit," I said, still trying to humor him a little! "Well, we're not mad about it," one of them said, "we really just need to talk to Doug!" They often called on Doug to check things over when various problems arose. Previously they had informed Doug that someone had killed a cow moose and left her unclaimed and wanted to see if he had any information regarding this. They asked Doug what he had come up with on this cow, and he told them, "Well, I know that no native around here killed it!" We visited with them for a bit, and then went on our way.

Doug had some really unique abilities! When I'd drive into his yard, even if I hadn't been there for two years, usually the first thing he'd say would be, "Well, well, I see you have a new set of tires!" He'd be right, of course, and was very observant! One time I was driving along in the snow with Doug, when we came to a pool of blood in the road, and he asked me to stop. I stopped, he got out and looked and immediately took off running across the meadow. Before long he came back with an udder off a cow moose. The season was not open for cow moose at this time, and he said, "I know who killed that!" He told me the man's name and as it just so happened, I knew this person, just casually. Sure enough, a couple days later, this fellow was bragging about the big, bull moose he had killed. We happened to know better because Doug went right to the animal, and had the udder to prove it! Of all the hunters I've been around, Doug has such a fantastic ability to trail game. Even though Doug is good, Edward is "breathing down his neck" and is also very good. Unfortunately, Edward lost the sight of his right eye, but his left eye is wonderful! This kid has been cowboying all summer long for a number of years now and is at least twenty-one years of age. He is a very fine lad and has up to this point in time, kept himself from some of the evils of that country, such as strong drink and wild wimmin'!

THEY NEVER FORGET

One of the things which we really enjoyed while living in Canada was having the horses. When we moved back to Oregon in 1990, I sold Tony to Doug Schuk and had told him I didn't know if she would pack a big buck or not. The first thing Doug showed Russ and I when we drove in his yard in the fall of 1990, was a picture of two huge bucks on Tony. It had taken three men to load this meat on her, but she packed

July 1994 - Posing with my pride and joy, Tony, now owned by Doug Schuk. She remembered us!

them into camp, and he said she acted as if it was a privilege to do so! He was so happy with her performance and it made me happy, too!

In 1994, when Frances and I went to British Columbia, we went out to visit Doug, and of course, looked forward to seeing Tony. She was born out in the corral, near our house in the Clinton area. Generally, when we lived there, I always had three horses and they used to graze in the alfalfa field, after the hay was cut. I'd call them with a shrill sound, and if they were within hearing distance, they'd never refuse to come, for I'd always reward them with a little cube made of grain and molasses. I earned their trust and confidence, and they received a little treat! Here we are, four years later, up at Doug's and Tony is out in a big pasture, with other horses. Suddenly, I thought, "Why not try calling her, like I used to do," so I did just that! As I watched,

she came running at full gallop! She ran up to me, and I kid you not, her eyes were just wide with astonishment! I spoke to her and she actually laid her head on my shoulder, as I stroked her and told her what a nice, beautiful horse she was! Frances came out of the cabin where we were staying, so Tony went up to Frances and paid her tribute, also!

The next morning, at 5:00 A.M., I got up, went to the door, and here stands Tony, waiting to see if we were still there! I must admit, this touched our hearts and brought tears to our eyes! Who can ever doubt the intelligence of some animals! We are so grateful that Doug really likes Tony and she has a good home! As I mentioned earlier, there is a wonderful feeling one experiences in saddling up a horse, riding into the mountains, and enjoying the wonders the Great God of heaven made for mankind to enjoy!

Many interesting things happened as I broke Tony to ride and taught her how to become a mountain hunting horse! Once while riding a trail, a nice, black bear decided that he, also, was going our way! Tony started to gallop after the bear and I just let her go! When the bear saw we were gaining too much, it just turned into the bush, so we went on our way! Another time when I was out riding Tony, we came upon two, cow moose and she promptly gave chase. Soon the jack pines were too thick and my knees couldn't take the beating from the brush, so I called a halt. I am so thankful, however, that I could experience so many things out in the bush and it's things such as this, which has rewards, unlike any other!

EAST-GOING EDWARD

Edward, Doug's son, told me an amazing story in 1995 when we were up there. He said, "Kenny, a friend of mine is a retired minister from England. At age sixty-five he retired and decided he was going to become a cowboy. So he hired out to a big ranch in the states, where he worked as a cowboy, proved to be a top hand, and worked at that for several years. After doing that, he felt very fulfilled, as he wanted to prove to himself that he was capable of living the rigorous life of a cowboy. Once he accomplished this, he returned to England. He wrote me a letter one fall, inviting me to go to England to visit him, and along with the invitation, he offered to pay all expenses, if I'd come. I wrote back to him and said I'd go. My friend sent the money, I went down to Williams Lake, got on a plane, and flew to England!" After Edward told me this, I asked, "Did you enjoy it?" to which he replied, "Yes, I did. It was interesting to see how people live over there, but I sure wouldn't want to live that way! The Tatlaco Valley looks good enough for me!" I thought that was pretty good. He told me, "I have no desire to have a high-powered car or anything, I want to live a simple life and I've got my horses!" Edward is a fabulous horseman! He has two wild horses he and Doug caught, broke, and trained. When Edward calls those horses, they come and knowing they used to be wild, it's hard to believe how gentle they are! He has a trap line, is a good hunter, loves to fish and there is everything there that a man needs to survive. Edward seems to be very happy in his environment!

DUMBO GUMBO

A tall, raw-boned fellow moved up to Grinders to stay awhile and brought a woman along with him. This guy, whose nickname was Gumbo, was a hopeless drug addict, however, he decided to work on one of the old cabins at Isadore's. He put in his time whenever he felt like it, but in the end, built a fairly substantial cabin to stay in with his woman. Of course, in due time, this woman "got in a family way" and gave birth to twin girls. They were premature and very tiny, so the government flew them down to Vancouver via air ambulance. They were hospitalized for a long time until one infant finally was able to return home, and the other one was transferred to a Kamloops Hospital. We were told that in the end, the cost to the government was more than a quarter of a million dollars for those twins!

I had never been out hunting with Gumbo, but one day he came down to our house and asked, "Say, would you like to go buck hunting up on Big Bar Mountain?" I told him I would, so the next day we drove up in my pickup to a place where he told me he could ALWAYS kill a buck! Well, we didn't get a buck there, so he said, "I know of a place over on another mountain; we can get a buck there!" He told me where to go, and as we went along, this was all new country to me. After driving to where he directed me, I parked the pickup and we began to walk back along this mountain. We separated, and about an hour later, I heard Gumbo shoot, so I went to find him. He had a nice, big forked-horn buck already down. "Gumbo," I said, "I can pack that buck down to the pickup!" He said, "You can what?" Again I said, "I can pack that deer to the pickup!" "Oh, no, you don't! We're going to hang him right here and I'll come back in the morning with a pack horse and get him out," he said. We were about thirty-five miles from home and I couldn't believe people were so adverse to a little labor! There was no way he wanted to get it out right away, so in fact, he did go back the next day! I just couldn't figure this one out! We were right there on the level, no hills to climb, and we only had about two miles to pack him to the pickup, but there was no way Gumbo would go for that!

The natives in Canada were not supposed to hunt out of season, at that time. In some places, however, the authorities would grant them a permit to kill an animal, with the understanding they report it to the Game Commission. Of course, the people back in the bush naturally lived off the land. The government would do nothing about the varmints, which kept increasing in greater and greater numbers and one time, a band of sixteen wolves came right close to our place. I saw their tracks and it looked like a herd of cattle had been through there. Phillip got a shot at one as they started pulling the game down, so the residents were always on the lookout for them. Some of our friends began talking about the wolves killing so much game, especially in the Keicheka Valley, an area adjacent to where Herb Leake had his big guiding area. There was much being publicized regarding the wolves, in the Vancouver Province, on television, and in smaller, local papers as well. The government had promised to do something. Specifically, they said they'd shoot the wolves from an airplane. One evening two ladies from California were on television and they said, "We are going to parachute between the government plane and the wolves, in order to save the lives of the wolves!" Those two women attempted to do that, but weren't successful, and nearly lost their lives over it. We thought what an incredibly foolish thing this was for them to do!

A fellow from Greenpeace, named Paul Davis, decided he was going to go into the woods and put a stop to the Game Commission shooting the wolves, so he hired some

Indians to guide him back into the mountains to where the wolves were. It was very cold, the snow was extremely deep, and the poor fool didn't realize the Indians in no way appreciated, nor shared his point of view. So they took him back into the mountains in a circuitous way and this fellow nearly perished. Of course, he didn't apprehend nor accost the government fellows and the paper reported that they killed at least 385 wolves, although the exact amount wasn't reported. A guide told me that at that time, it was very rare to ever see a caribou cow with a young calf, or a moose or elk with a calf, because the wolves got them! After the government killed large numbers of the wolves, within two years, they began seeing young calves again! Herb told me it really made him happy because two adult wolves can also kill an adult caribou, moose, or elk!

I was over at Paul Blackwell's visiting one time and his phone rang. After he hung up, he told me it was a Game Warden asking if he wanted to kill a big wolf. Of course, Paul said he'd love to, so the Warden told Paul to go over on the Gang Ranch Road to Mile Marker 36, go off to the right past a long meadow, and in the area back there, a timber wolf had been spotted. Paul invited me to go along, so at 9:00 o'clock the next morning, Paul and I started out towards the Gang Ranch to find this wolf. At this time, the snow was nearly knee-deep, but we found the spot, and saw some tracks leading out in the snow, and we began following them. We walked and walked and had nearly given up hopes of finding the wolf when we came upon the scene of a murder! Laying there in the snow was probably about 250 pounds of meat left on a moose, and also a dead wolf. As we went back to where the wolves jumped the moose, there was blood and hair all over! We could tell there had been six to eight wolves on this poor creature and he had carried them for about two hundred feet before they got him down, but what carnage! Whoever put a shot in this wolf, did a great job! This wolf was now frozen stiff, so we put a rope on his jaw and pulled him back to the pickup. After loading him, Paul took him home and put him in the basement. The next morning his wife, Ann, woke up and she smelled a smell! She started screaming, "Paul, get that thing out of my basement right now!" As this animal thawed out, these gases started permeating the air, as it had been shot through the stomach! I don't blame Ann for wanting it out, for it wasn't the best of smells, that's for sure! Paul never would tell me how much he got paid for that animal, but it must have been a pretty penny because it was such a beautiful, big animal! I'd guess he was paid between $750 and $1,000 for it because another neighbor, Bob Newberry, killed two wolves, had a rug made and was offered $750 in Cache Creek before he ever took it home! Ann was a taxidermist, so they had the hide tanned and she made a rug out of it!

It was very cold, with snow on the ground, when Paul Blackwell and I went up on Big Bar Mountain hunting one day, and at this particular time, any deer were legal fare. This was new country to me, but we separated and I went up on the hill a ways and before long, I heard Paul fire a couple shots! A little more time passed, and then I heard another shot, quite a ways off! Suddenly, here came a big deer up the hill towards me, so I lost no time in taking aim, getting him down, and dressing him out. As I went on down towards the pickup, soon I heard some more shooting and could tell it was rather close by. Just as I got down to my pickup, here came Paul, and he told me that he didn't get a really good shot at this buck, but did cripple him. For three hours Paul trailed that buck! As we discussed it, we figured out that undoubtedly the buck made a big circle and came back towards the pickup, and sure enough, we found him! There was a stock trail up the hill by a fence and I said, "Paul, I can pack those deer to the pickup!" "Oh, no, you don't! We're gonna go First Class!" What did he do? We went back to his home, got a Ski Doo and a sled, went back up to the deer, and yarded those deer out! It was nearly dark when we got them in and of course, it had been done the Caribou Way! Paul didn't know that I knew how to saddle a deer up and had packed some enormously big bucks in my time, if I do say so! In fact, some I had carried weighed well over 200 pounds! I grew up doing this and then taught my boys how to do it, and they also packed some huge deer. There's nothing like experience and knowing how to do something!

Phillip had a cousin, Hector, who had the reputation of being a great mechanic, although I never got to meet him. When he was a little kid, his Dad was working down at the O.K. Cattle Company, along the river below the Big Bar Ferry. This ranch was a huge one, and employed many Indians. Hector was still in diapers, out playing in the yard, when a big eagle swooped down, picked him up and carried him through the air about twenty feet. Then the eagle dropped him and all his life, Hector had the prints of eagle claws on his head. That shows how vicious eagles can be! A rancher, Gene Mooney, from Canada told me he was sitting under a tree, preparing to shoot some coyotes, and had just used his rabbit call. Before he knew what was happening, an eagle swooped down and grabbed the wool cap off his head, drawing blood, as he did so! Again, this is just another illustration that when these critters get hungry, they can be very mean!

NEVER TOO OLD TO BE A COWBOY!

When I moved to the Caribou, I decided I would try to learn to do various things. So, even though I really wasn't a cowboy, I broke three horses and learned as much as I could about them! As I went along, I observed and knew the proper way to mount a saddle horse was to watch his tail end, and not his head! I enjoyed shoeing them and decided to buy an outfit. While in Lac La Hache one day, I went into a second-hand store where I found a nice, horse-shoeing hammer, which I decided to buy. There was a name carved in the handle and it was, "Mike Rosette." This cowboy lived on the Gang Ranch, had gotten into dire straights, needed some money and so he had hocked this hammer. Besides the hammer, I also bought a few other tools I needed to shoe my horses. Isadore watched me one day and said, "Kenny, you do a fine job of shoeing your horses!" I said, "Well, I do the best that I can!" A lot of cowboys wouldn't shoe their own horses, but would hire a professional farrier, but I figured if I could go through the process of breaking a horse, I certainly had the capability of putting shoes on it!

There was a lot of work in keeping up our ranch! The grass grew so profusely, every spring the ditch had to be cleaned out, and usually, I'd have to burn it out! Then I'd check it carefully for any debris, limbs, chunks of wood and anything which would hamper the water flow in our water system. I also built over a mile of fence and cross-fenced several places. I can't tell you how many different years, the moose would go through the fence, knock it down, and I'd have to repair it again. There was always something I had to attend to and always managed to keep more than busy. Of course, I'd always keep wood cut and dry it properly before using. That poplar was wonderful wood to burn. Some fellows invented a product similar to chipboard and the poplar wood is far superior to alder for that purpose. Ainsworth Lumber Company is now producing a board similar to that with a Strand Mill. This device has a bunch of steel "fingers" which scratch out little grooves. The fine wood which is removed is impregnated with glue and rosin, making a very substantial board, superior to actual lumber. That is in operation now in 100 Mile House. Ainsworth is a very progressive company and I believe they may have a good future for this product.

It seems that for all the positive features we enjoyed while living in Canada, there were always the tragedies. A local Indian lad, Jackie Cherry and another fellow, John Phillips, were to guide up North with an outfitter and his wife. These two fellows were in a plane with this couple, headed up there, but unfortunately, they crashed. John survived and the other three were all killed. It was very sad as Jackie had a reputation for being a very fine guide. Then another plane went down with four on board. One fellow was a survival instructor out of Quesnel, and was on the way to Kamloops. For a very long time, the wreckage of this plane was not located. Jackie's wife insisted, "You don't know Jack like I do! One of these days, he'll walk in 'cause he's one, tough nut!" That didn't happen, however, and the following spring they found the plane up by High Hume Lake. It had been buried in the snow, with all four bodies still inside! While we were living there, many accidents of this nature took place. Anytime one loses their respect of nature, they are taking their life in their own hands and often pay a big price for that! I've always tried to operate under the premise that nature is something you should respect whether it's snow, a deep lake and rough water, or whatever!

Down by Vancouver, British Columbia, in big timber country, there is a very large logging camp. A story was told to me regarding a Bullbuck. This strong, husky fellow decided that if he would consider hiring anyone, he'd wrestle them first. He figured if they could put up a good struggle, they'd be good in the woods! One day he needed a bucker and a fellow showed up, seeking employment. Now this prospective employee looked to be very strong and as if he would willingly tackle anything, or anybody! The Bullbuck knew this fellow could "clean his clock," so he just said, "I'll give you a job," and the new guy went to work! A couple days later, as they were eating lunch, the new hire said, "The ground in the camp I just came from was absolutely flat, but had huge trees, five and six feet on the stump, and only three and four feet apart! The amazing thing is there were many moose there with such huge horns! Why, some of the horns were six feet tall!" This ornery Bullbuck said, "Wait a minute, how'd the moose get through these trees if their horns were that big?" The new bucker said, "They pull their horns in just like you did!" We got a bang out of that!

MURDERED IN THE VALLEY

The sun was shining brightly one morning as we left for Clinton rather early. A series of events happened that day which were quite startling and had long-term effects on that valley and its' residents! We drove into town, did our shopping, ran our errands, and returned home. When we left home that morning, we had closed our gate, as usual. Shortly after we left, Phillip came down the road and saw Roy Klopp's stallion and two mares approaching. Phillip was very angry at Roy for taking trail riders up the canyon, so he thought, "Here's a good chance to get even!" He took the fence down in the corner to let our horses out in the road with this stallion. Al Crowhurst came along, saw this situation and immediately chased our horses back inside. Being the good neighbor that he was, he also fixed the fence.

As we were coming home from town and turned off the Big Bar Road, here was Phillip's pickup in the middle of the road. He was getting a rifle out of his truck, so we stopped and I asked, "What's cooking here?" "Oh," he said, "I just saw Roy Klopp's stallion go into the brush there and I'm going to try and catch him! I'll tie him up, then I'm going to go down and get Floyd Grinder and we're going to geld him!" Frances and I drove on home, thinking this could be an unpleasant situation, and very soon the plot began to thicken! Later that afternoon we went over to see the Crowhurst's and Al said something about "the shooting". I didn't know how he had heard, or exactly what was told him, so I said, "I didn't see Phillip shoot anything, but we did see him with a gun."

The next evening Phillip came down and asked, "Say, would you want to go riding tomorrow in the mountains?" I had just shod Tony and since she was an eager, young horse and wonderful to ride, I said, "Yes, I do!" Next morning, we started up

Taken in March, 1989, L to R: Henry Grinder, Pete Coldwell, and Isadore Grinder. As of May, 1997, only Isadore is left. He was born in 1900 and resides in Clinton.

the mountain and I noticed right off the bat, Phillip began talking about Roy's horse being "on the loose" and he asked, "Did you ever see a mean stallion?" I said, "Well, I hear they get pretty mean sometimes." Phillip was getting more and more agitated, working himself up emotionally, and he said, "Oh, they're really vicious! Just suppose your wife had been riding Cindy and that stallion would have come onto you folks, why she could have killed your wife, or killed you!" "Yeah, that's right," I said, and soon I changed the tone a little bit, asking, "How many bullets did that stallion have in him, Phillip?" He said, "Well, I don't know! I don't know anything about it!" I asked, "Was he shot in the head?" "I don't know!" he said. "Well, I heard the Mounties got the bullets," I continued. He kept talking about this mean stallion and placed great emphasis on what trouble that stallion COULD cause! Just prior to this time, Phillip hired a logger, Dale Dickey, to log his place. There was lots of slash and brush laying around there, and I said, "Phillip, you know what? I'd really hate to be in your shoes right now! You're a 'sitting duck' because those Robinson boys could burn you out and man, it's terrible what could happen to you!" In short order, he got very scared! Remember, up to this point, he had admitted nothing! All he said to me was, "I know a bunch of bad things on Roy! I'm going down to the Mounties and tell 'em!"

After Phillip and I returned from our ride, sure enough, he went down to the Mounties and said, "I want to tell you some bad things about Roy Klopp." They said, "Well, isn't that nice! We were just coming out to visit you. We happen to know you shot that stallion." They began telling him all sorts of things and Phillip broke down and confessed that he did, in fact, shoot the stallion! The next day, I was outside by our little smokehouse, and two Mounties drove into our yard. "Are you Mr. Shenk?" they asked. "Yes, I am!" "Are you prepared to make a statement?" they asked, and I said, "Yes I am!

Band of Rocky Mountain Big Horn Sheep taken near Spence's Bridge, B.C. on return trip from Oregon. I'm sure they knew the season was closed!

What do you want me to say?" You have never seen two Mounties change colors like they did! "Well, what do you know about this horse shooting?" I said, "I never saw anybody shoot anything!"

Come to find out later, Tick Robinson, Roy Klopp's brother-in-law, was going down the road when a bear ran across the road in front of him. He stopped and went into the brush where the bear came out and here lay this stallion, just off the road about one hundred fifty feet! Soon there was an RCMP vehicle sitting at the road which went back to Roy and Doty Klopp's. That road was terribly rough, so Phillip took them back in his pickup and they had a meeting of the minds there. It was agreed that Phillip would pay for the stallion. This stallion was a beautiful horse and came from some great blood lines, so he could easily have been papered and been worth some money. It really was a shame this event happened and when Isadore found out about it, the poor old fellow was really upset! He said to me, "Phillip never shot that horse! Not down there! If he'd have come up here, oh yes, Phillip would have shot him, but he never shot him down there!" Of course, I knew better than that! Phillip has taken some awful blows there in the Caribou, but he isn't usually silent about it! He told me once that he was going to go set a fire and I told him, "Don't do it, Phillip! They'll nail you!" He said, "They'll never catch me!" So I said to him, "Did you ever hear of the term, 'guilt by association'?" He said, "No." "Well, that's what might happen," I told him. Different times we had lots of excitement living in the North country! Some of it was good and some of it wasn't very good! That, however, is the story of the beautiful palomino horse that got shot two and a half miles from our house!

FROM THE WILDS TO THE MALL

In late November of 1989, we journeyed to the Seattle area to spend some time with our daughter and her husband, Al, before going on down to Oregon. We went shopping with Donna to the Alderwood Mall, which is close to her house. While she and Frances did some shopping, I sat and was momentarily overwhelmed with the throngs of people and wrote the following:

THE MALL
While I was waiting in the mall,
Here came a woman, really tall.
She had a kid that trailed along,
And he was moving with the throng.

Then came a woman in a chair,
Her husband pushed her everywhere.
I watched a woman try on clothes,
It made me laugh, she didn't know!

Most people wore a somber face,
They traveled at a hectic pace.
I watched them shop, and saw them spend,
As if the world would never end!

Then came a dame on heels so high,
Her head was really in the sky.
She walked right by the bargain bin,
Her heels a clacking, worse than sin!

The old folks wore real shabby clothes,
And most were drippin' at the nose,
The young gals wore those scrubby pants,
They don't deserve a second chance,
To follow all the latest fads,
Would shame the most of current dads!

While I was waiting in the Mall,
I saw the great; I saw them all.
I'm really glad I don't have to compete,
With all the sights now in the street!

DEVASTATING DIAGNOSIS

After spending Thanksgiving with Donna and Al, Frances and I went on down to Oregon to visit other relatives before going to Indiana for Christmas. It was now December, and we went to visit with Russ and his family. We noticed that he was terribly thin, and when I expressed concern, he admitted to us that he had not been feeling well. By this time, Russ and Lavina had purchased a home in the Amity area and lived there. He had been falling a right of way out at the coast in a stand of timber. The timber was big, on very steep ground and the job was a difficult one. Then, besides this, the commute to and from work each day was a very long one! At night, when it was time to go home, he said he'd be so tired, it was hard getting back to his pickup. Having been in the Medics in the Army, he was always so concerned with anyone around him and aware of medical needs. Thus, when he had a low-grade temperature for quite some time, and felt something in his rib cage, he knew it was time for a visit to the doctor. First he saw a local doctor and he told Russ there were some tumors, and recommended that specialists be consulted. Good Samaritan Hospital in Portland was recommended and an appointment was set up for further testing. In the meantime, Frances and I got on the train and went to Indiana to spend Christmas with Wilbert and his family.

While we were in Indiana, we received a call that Russ had been diagnosed with cancer of the liver; three tumors had been discovered on his liver. The small lobe of the liver had a tumor the size of a grapefruit and the large lobe of the liver had two tumors the size of baseballs. Immediately they began the usual treatment with chemotherapy and told him that most likely he had about sixty days to live. You cannot know the shock all of us felt at this dreadful news!

While in Elkhart, I went down to the city library, checked out some health books and began reading them. I picked up a book by Dr. Virginia Livingstone Wheeler, in which she said in the treatment of cancer, that cancer cells could not live in the presence of absisic acid. She mentioned a number of things which have a great amount of absisic acid, such as avocados, carrot juice, cabbage juice, and so forth. Russ had a friend who also had been battling cancer and told Russ, "Drink raw carrot juice!" We gave him our juicer and he began a daily regimen of fresh juices.

After some of his treatments, Russ went down to see the doctor in Portland. The doctor greeted him with, "Why hello, Russ! Gosh, I didn't expect to see you again! I mean, you look like you're getting better! (He had let the first part of that sentence slip out and tried to patch it up!) What are you doing that's making you feel better?" Russ told him how he was making carrot juice each morning, sometimes adding apples, oranges, and a variety of other vegetables, as well, and that he had gained weight, looked and felt much better. His normal weight was about 165 pounds when he was cutting timber and had gone down to 122. He had put on some weight again and his energy was increasing. Amazingly the doctor told him, "I think you're overdoing it on the juices!" Russ asked, "You do?" Besides having been in the Medics after high school, while in Valsetz, he was the First Aid person and took advance training in order to serve that community. Russ had a very good knowledge of the human body! His health continued to improve and he got much stronger once again. This doctor actually told Russ that he was surprised to see him because when the first diagnosis was made, the doctor figured Russ would be fortunate to live six months!

Unless you have been through an event such as this, it is difficult to express all the emotions, the feelings of helplessness, concern, and love that one experiences. Frances and I knew that we wanted to be in Oregon in order to be available to help Russ and Lavina, in the event our help was needed. I had been under great pressure to move back anyhow! Dave found a place on Mill Creek, below where we had lived for so many years. We purchased this little place and in 1990, moved back to Oregon.

BACK ON THE OREGON TRAIL

At this time, Russ was improving and seemed to be getting along quite well. One day I went over to see him and said, "Say, Russ, I have a hunting license for British Columbia and a moose and deer tag. Why don't you go up and go hunting with me!" He said, "I'd love to do that, Dad!" So I went home and called Doug to make arrangements for a hunt.

Frances, Russell and I went to British Columbia to Doug's for this hunt. Edward, Doug, Russ and I went up Potato Mountain one morning. Russ had bought a pair of elk hunting shoes, called "Lifetime Elk Hunters", and they were as heavy as a pair of caulk shoes, but he climbed that mountain without any problem! Doug had been hunting every day and Russ hadn't been out doing much walking or working because of having been ill, but he had no trouble at all! Edward and I hunted in some timber, right close to the bottom of the mountain, while Doug and Russ went over the mountain, and through snow, which was clear up to their knees! They went to a Weather Ranger Station and while they were there, a helicopter came and landed. Their purpose in landing was to check their instruments, but all the commotion from that copter chased the game away!

The first evening of that trip, Doug came over to me and said, "Kenny, I can't believe you claim Russ was so sick and near death! I am really tired and Russ just trooped all over with me and didn't complain of being worn out! I just can't believe it!" "Well, Doug," I said, "you don't have to believe it, but he really was at death's door!" Russ killed a fine, bull moose on this trip and was just elated!

Going back down the Fraser, Russ said, "Well, the saw-bones want me to come back to Portland to take another treatment of chemo. I don't enjoy it, but I have my strength back and don't dread it as much as I used to." We stopped in the Seattle area to spend the night with Donna and Al, and Russ told them how great he felt and what fun it had been for him to get that moose! In fact, he was just feeling great! A day after we got back from hunting, he went back to the doctor for the chemo treatment. A couple days went by and then the doctor told Russ they'd like to try something experimental on him and they injected pure alcohol, 200 proof into him. They went through his rib cage in his back and got one charge of it on the small lobe of his liver. The tumor which had been there, had completely vanished and there was just scar tissue. The other portion of this absolute alcohol got into his stomach and literally burned his stomach up! He came home on Thursday and immediately began to hemorrhage, so around midnight, Lavina took him back into Portland, as he was so ill. Once there, they gave him six blood transfusions and then he returned home. Four days passed, and he had to be hospitalized again in Portland..

About 8:00 A.M. on Sunday morning, Frances and I went down to Portland and as we arrived, a doctor was leaving the room. He left three X-rays there of Russell's stomach, as well as a picture of a normal stomach. This surgeon had told him, "Russ, I go to Mayo Clinic, Sloan Kettering, Stanford University, and have a good reputation as being a dedicated surgeon. I can suture your stomach up and you can live a fairly good life. I want to help you!" Russ said, "I want you to help me! Go ahead!" The two doctors who had done the terrible deed said, "We strongly recommend against it, Russ, as it could cause you to have an aneurysm!" In the end, at least eighty-five per cent of Russ's stomach had been burned by the absolute alcohol and he literally starved to death! To any parent, this is a devastating fact and one which I have had to wrestle with. Even as the years have gone by, it still doesn't make any sense, nor will it ever be easy to accept!

Russ lived out his last days at home, putting forth a valiant effort, yet losing weight and strength. We all began to realize that the end for him was not to be avoided and on October 17, 1991, he passed away. I can tell you, that was undoubtedly the saddest day of my life! For his wife, Lavina, and children, Alex, and Sylvia, and all our family, his passing was a great loss! I know death is part of life, but it seemed that what those doctors did was uncalled for. They even told him, "Russ, we're very sorry that we made this mistake. We overdosed on the amount of the alcohol!" It's my honest conviction that Russ would be alive and well had they not burned his stomach up! That's in the past now, but the pain is still there, and I do take a dim view of the doctors in their treatment of cancer. It seems the things they practice most readily in treatment of cancer are to cut, burn, and use chemo and those methods aren't working and they know it! There are other remedies which have been proven over the years, but it seems the AMA really fights other alternatives! This is to the utter shame of human dignity and suffering, but this is what goes on! Simply put, they cut, poison, and burn - those are the three modus operandi! Russ was just a week short of celebrating his 55th birthday. During the months of his illness, he touched so many lives. The night before his funeral service, I wrote this tribute:

TO MY SON, RUSS

What is this journey here below,
That all must travel before we go,
To regions yet beyond this pale,
How many really did prevail?

Does God in heaven really care,
That men don't seek Him everywhere?
Can He not cause the blind to see?
Can He not staunch the misery?

But God would have His kingdom come,
And so we say, "His will be done."
Farewell, farewell beloved son,
We know for sure your race is run.

You suffered long, endured much pain,
And now you have achieved this gain.
We say good-bye, but not for long,
For soon we'll join the ransomed throng!

TRADITION, TRADITION

In 1994, we put in for Antlers' Cow Elk tags, as did my grandson, Alex and successfully drew the Grizzly Unit, above Prineville, Oregon. This was new country to us, so Alex took his Cherokee Jeep and we took our pickup, camper, tent, and groceries and went to Prineville. We camped next to the road and there were quite a number of fellows camped in behind us. Some loggers were working up above this area and the truckers would chain up right next to our camper and tent, so we'd visit with them from time to time. There was a lot of snow on the hills above where we wanted to hunt and we decided to drive Alex's Jeep out. One day we found some elk, at the end of the road, but were unable to get back in there as the snow was just too deep. Alex took off on foot and I went down the draw, but we never did find any that day. A couple days later, we drove up to a big Y in the road and Alex decided to park there. I'd always heard that if you come to a fork in the road, you should take one! This day the wind was blowing quite hard and as we got out, Alex asked, "Did you hear those elk, Grandad?" I said, "No," and he said, "Well, I did!"

Alex began running back down the road to where a ridge took off to the right, and

I went down a draw. When Alex went up on this ridge, he followed the elk a ways. Meantime, down in the draw, I passed a beautiful cabin, with a root cellar and a little spring, in a very idyllic setting. I heard someone shoot a couple shots and eventually, Alex and I came together. He said, "Well, I got an elk down, Grandad!" We walked to where the elk was, began skinning it out, and then Alex said, "I might have hit another one. I need to go down and check it out!" He went to look, but didn't find anything, so came back. After we got the packboards, we packed the elk up to camp. Things were looking up now; we had fresh heart and liver to eat!

We continued our hunt a few more days and enjoyed the wonderful country, although I didn't have any luck. On Tuesday we decided to go way up to the head of Trout Creek to hunt. Alex was driving down a hill when I looked up and saw some elk running! As Alex stopped, I got out, took aim, and shot a nice cow elk. The snow was about ten inches deep and we began trudging to where the elk had fallen. After dressing her out, we got her down to the truck, just as a logging truck came by. The trucker stopped to visit and upon seeing my elk, he seemed delighted and said, "Well, I'm sure glad you fellows got an elk!" I said, "Well, I am too!"

As we started home that afternoon, it was snowing quite heavy on the Santiam Pass and we heard on the radio that it was nearly impassable. Soon there was a sign along the roadway which said, "No vehicles beyond this point without traction devices," so I spoke on my CB to Alex and asked, "What do you want to do?" We both had good traction tires and he replied, "Just keep going, Grandad," which we did, and never had any trouble. There were vehicles everywhere as some trying to put chains on were blocking roadways. Since it was the day before Thanksgiving, traffic was extremely heavy! After much determination and careful driving, at last we arrived home from a successful and most enjoyable trip!

NO MAGIC IN MONTANA MOUNTAINS

The next year I wrote to several outfitters in Montana and Idaho and received numerous responses. They have a little quirk that if you book through an outfitter, as a non-resident, you are guaranteed a tag. If you don't, you'll probably end up with zero chance of getting a tag! A fellow named Tom Brogan, of Big Sky Outfitters, out of Wilsall, Montana, indicated in his information that he had a set fee, for which he would pack us back, and then he'd let us hunt on our own. Also, his offer was to pack out any game we bagged, so I decided to book a hunt with him.

Early in the fall, Tom wrote me a letter informing me that the State of Montana had just passed a new law that we'd have to have a guide, furnish his food and pay for him, so this changed the picture somewhat from our original deal. The appointed day arrived, and on this hunt we experienced some very strange things! From what he had written in his letter, I decided I would prepare, so I began by packing extra provisions to take along, but still wondered about this new law and other details. My son, Davie, and I drove to Montana in my pickup, finally arriving at Tom's Lodge. We began visiting and Tom told me, "I couldn't sleep at night if I packed an old fellow like you back there (in the woods); I have a 'New Deal' for you! I'll put you up here in a little camper with a propane heater, furnish your food, and you can ride horses out during the day, for so much per day!" We decided to accept the "New Deal"! Tom had a guide school, when upon completion of the course, these young fellows were given a diploma and thus they were "full-time hunters!" It was amazing the lack of experience those fellows had and I think they only had to learn how to throw a diamond hitch, complete a little book work, and then they were qualified???? Most of them were pleasant to be around, except for one lad. Unfortunately, his wisdom teeth had never come in yet and he was absolutely crazy! Most of this hunt was nothing more than an exercise of futility!

First morning, while still quite dark, we took off on the hunt, and rode down over a bluff, rather than going down the trail. Let me hasten to assure you, that ride was simply brutal! Dave had never been out hunting on a horse before and how he ever managed, I'll never know! We got down and crossed quite a big creek, rode a little further, and then we heard the bugle of a bull elk. Our guides said, "Hey, you fellows ride up to the top of the hill and you'll get an elk." They said they'd go down the center of this field and meet us down by the creek. The exception was that the one fellow said he'd pick Dave up down at the creek so he wouldn't have to climb the hill, because Dave's arthritis was really bothering him. We said that was fine, so we go up there, separated, and were about half a mile apart. An hour passed and then I heard Davie shoot once. I made my drive, came out and went down to the guides. They asked, "Where's Davie?" I said, "I don't know, but he's probably down at the creek waiting for the young lad to pick him up." That kid never showed, as he had said he would, so after quite a long time, here came Davie up the hill. It had been quite a climb, his arthritis was very bad and the trek was quite painful for him to walk that distance. I asked him, "Did you get one down, Davie?" "Yes, I did," he said. "How many points?" I eagerly asked. "It's a cougar," he said. They laughed at him and said, "You're kidding!" He said, "No, I'm not, I killed a cougar." Davie rode with them to show them where he had downed the cougar and then we all returned to camp.

When we got back to camp, Brogan was informed of Davie's kill, so early the next morning Tom takes a young guide with him and goes out to bring the cougar down to the Lodge. When they returned, Tom called the Montana Game Commission and created quite an uproar! Before we left, Davie was required to sign a Quit Claim Deed in order to leave Montana! Well, not quite, but he signed more papers than would be required in order to purchase a home! I thought they were going to put us both in jail, but evidently they didn't have enough food to go around! After we were home, the one Guide, Carl Fishon, wrote to me and told me he was nearly jumped by a cougar and that one of the other fellows was mauled by one, but was fortunate to not be severely injured in the incident. A cougar even came up on the porch of the lodge and was able to get a deer which was hanging there. Tom had a place to hang the meat until he was ready to take it down to a butcher and that cougar helped himself to some fresh meat! There were hunters there from all over the United States, but the game was sort of scarce! They would tell us in the evenings, "Well, tomorrow we'll hunt in a new area!" We rode up Hatfield Mountain, which is 9,600 feet high and proved to be a very brutal climb for the horses. This was up above Ted Turner's big ranch and we could see for a long ways up there. What a spectacular view from on top of Hatfield! We saw vehicles parked a long ways off and the guides told us Ted had hunters out and the cost for a six-point bull was $17,000!

A second day we again rode up Hatfield Mountain and I was able to kill a nice sized, four-point buck, although he had small horns. He was running at the crest of the hill with some does, quite a long ways off, so the shot was rather difficult. It was bitterly cold and I could hardly get my hands warm enough to operate my rifle, so I overshot him twice! On the third shot, however, I pulled right down to the snow line and got him!

Tom also took us over to the Crazy Mountains, to hunt deer, and we went into some wonderful country! We drove up by Grason and Davie killed a forked-horn deer there. Brogan's outfit wanted to skin the deer I killed and take it down to camp, but I said, "No way! Leave the hide on!" They did skin Davie's deer, however. I remarked to Tom when we left that I was bitterly disappointed, overall, in our hunt because the country is very much "over hunted" and there wasn't much big game there. This didn't please him too much and he reacted in anger! He told me he and his fellows had killed twelve big bulls and that was a heck of a pile of game to take out of that area! In one way, that might be true, but if you average out what had been taken, to the number of hunters, then the percentages go way down and the hunting's not all that hot! Incidentally, while preparing this manuscript, I received a letter from the Montana State Game Commission asking me to tell them of all my hunts there, so I wrote and told them about a hunt which we had there, which was very unsatisfactory!

MAMA, PAPA SPEAKETH!

One evening while we were at Tom's, I became terribly ill from something which didn't quite "fit!" I told Davie the next morning, "You go ahead and go hunting, but I'm not eating any breakfast and I'm not going hunting!" About ten o'clock, I went over to the cookhouse and figured I'd get a cup of strong coffee and maybe that would make me feel better. There was a lady about fifty years old there helping Hilda, the cook. This lady asked, "So, how are you doing?" "Well, I don't know," I said. "I could be better, could be worse! I've got something that's really bothering me, I just can't believe that people could sink so low - even women!" "Oh, how's that?" she asked. "Well, I heard a story the other day about an old couple who lived quite a ways out in the boon docks. They had one daughter, Esther, and her whole life revolved around her Father, whom she called "Papa!" One day the old man had a stroke and went into a coma. Since Papa was unable to speak, the entire family was called in to watch around the clock, hoping Papa would regain consciousness and leave some parting words of wisdom for them all. Devoted daughter, Esther, stayed upstairs at Papa's bedside! Her Father could not speak and she was so hoping to be able to talk to him again! She fanned his face, washed his brow and just attended to his every need! The old lady, who was sort of a large, boisterous woman, for some reason, suddenly took a new lease on life. She was humming away downstairs, cleaning, mopping, baking and would burst forth in song every now and then! As Esther was keeping her bedside vigil one evening, she looked down at her Father and thought she saw Papa's lip move. Esther bent down close to him and asked, "Papa, what is it? Papa, are you trying to say something?" She ran to the head of the stairs and called down, "Mama, Papa is trying to say something!" The Mother asked, "What did he say?" Esther ran back to her Papa, leaned down and said, "What is it you want, Papa? Tell me and I'll get it for you!" Very weakly, Papa asked, "Could I have a bagel, please?" Esther ran to the stairs and called out, "Mama, Papa said could he please have a bagel!" Her Mother said, "No! You tell Papa, no! The bagels are for the people AFTER the funeral!" The lady I had told the story to said, "Oh, that's awful," and she began to cry! She carried on and said again, "Oh, that's awful! That's terrible!" Then Hilda started laughing and she just roared! Taking all this in, the other lady asked, "Sir, are you putting me on?" I said, "No, I cannot vouch for the voracity of the story, I just heard it!" This story was one of Russell's favorites!

Another story I heard goes like this: An old Indian guide up on the Peace River took two Americans hunting. He stayed a little ways off from where they were camped, but he came over to visit them in the evening. He said, "Well, tomorrow we have fine day. We make hunt on the moose! Tomorrow we kill big bull moose." They went hunting the next day and the weather was fine, but they never killed anything. The second night he came over to them and said the same thing! Third night; same thing! The fourth night he never came over, so on the following morning, the American hunters said, "Why didn't you come over last night and tell us what kind of weather we were going to have?" He said, "Oh, batteries go dead on white man's radio!"

DUST BOWL DESPAIR

I read a story about the Dust Bowl days when the Okie's came out from Oklahoma to the West Coast. There was a very poor family, so poor that they had virtually no money! They had just a few sandwiches to eat and suffered incredible hardship going through Death Valley in California. They picked up a bunch of old "Life" and "The Saturday Evening Post" magazines and would put them in their old tires. The tires were full of holes so big you could stick your fists through, so they'd stuff these magazines in there, put the tire back on the rim, and pump it up by hand. Each day they'd mark down the speedometer reading and drive so far, stop and let the air out of the tires. In this manner, the tires wouldn't blow and when they were ready to drive on, they'd put in more magazines, and that's how they got there! It was one of the most amazing stories I've ever read. They learned, however, that the paper in the one magazine was much tougher and they could get fifty miles more out of that one!

FLAG TAIL UNIT FAILS US

Alex and his wife, Patty, Frances and I put in again the following year for elk tags and drew for the Flag Tail Unit, which was a portion of the old Murder's Creek Unit. Earlier I wrote about hunting deer way back in 1936 in that area and had not returned there since! With the addition of logging roads, that territory was all strange country to me. There was a good number of deer there and we saw one hundred and twenty-five deer on our trip (without counting any of them twice), and everyday saw some fine, big bucks we could have easily shot. Unfortunately, the elk were not there! When we were setting up camp, we noticed Dodge Diesels and big Ford's going by, pulling horse trailers which held four and five horses and knew there were a lot of hunters in the area.

The next day we went over a big hill, and on a big flat, along a creek there were camped many fellows who had come in driving the trucks and horse trailers we had seen earlier. In three days time, all the other hunters were gone and we never saw any elk on that trip! There were plenty of deer, but our elk hunt was fruitless! You just never know! The Game Commission in Oregon uses the method of hunters drawing for tags and so if you draw an area and the game isn't there, you're just out of luck! The lack of game can be due to weather conditions, but if you draw a certain area, then you are confined to hunt only there and you can't go where the game is! The Game Commission is attempting to control the amount of game, but Mother Nature is the one who controls that! I have never talked to one hunter who is happy with the way the Game Commission is operating, but no one is willing to try and change the situation! We need a Bill Sizemore to carry the ball and make different arrangements!

DEATH VALLEY - NOT IN CALIFORNIA

In the spring of 1996, I went down to Portland to attend the Sportsman Show and talked to different fellows, as well as acquiring lots of brochures and information. Many brochures contained addresses, so I wrote to different ones, requesting information regarding their fall hunts. At the show, I met Ed Wright, of World Class Outfitters, out of Kalispell, Montana. I visited with him and he seemed to be a fine fellow, so I booked a hunt with him. Of course, there are always a few details one forgets to ask! His area was North of Phillipsburg, called Smart Creek, and it runs up close to Henderson Mountain. Davie and I drove up to Montana, and let me tell you, the country was just beautiful! We were really ready for this hunt! Ed met us and took us to his camp. There were four fellows there from California, two from Washington, and Dave and myself from Oregon. Ed had a beautiful camp there, with very nice accommodations for us, and another fellow who assisted him. Off to one side, there were quite a few ranches and a field of alfalfa which ran for quite a distance. Up in the Smart Creek area, there were also ranches which ran for about four miles, but no hunting was allowed. Much of the country was very rugged, with sharp canyons, but the game could easily hide away in those canyons. There was considerable game in there, but it seemed to be in the areas where we weren't allowed to hunt! Joe, a doctor from Mt. Vernon, Washington, hunted with us. He was a very nice fellow and had been in the Gulf War. His partner's name was Skip and they'd been hunting in Montana in the bull season. During that hunt, Skip shot at a bull but didn't get it, so they had returned for the rifle season. We had all been assured there was an ample supply of white-tailed deer, lots of elk and there were mule deer as well, but we'd have to hunt hard to find them. Indeed, there were elk all over the place!

Ed's camp consisted of a tent-house with a good stove, a big cook tent, well outfitted, but with something sadly lacking - FOOD! The first thing he told us was that he didn't serve breakfast! He suggested we come in around eleven o'clock in the morning and we'd have a sort of lunch! Whoever heard of a bunch of hunters going out before daylight and then coming in around eleven to have breakfast! Davie told Ed that he had to have something to eat early in the morning, because of the strong medication he had to take. Most medications are not to be taken on an empty stomach, so Ed said he'd make breakfast for Davie. Then I suggested, while he was at it, I'd like a couple eggs and a piece of toast, as he just planned to offer coffee and orange juice for the hunters. This just wasn't what we were accustomed to! After hunting a couple days and not seeing any game, Ed told us that two days before season opened a plane came in, buzzed the thickets and scared the game to kingdom come! Whether this happened or not, we really don't know! There was one spike bull killed amongst eight hunters! Joe confirmed that when he and Skip were there in the bull season, the elk were there! We found only two cows and a calf in a thicket, way up on a mountain. One day we went up 7,400 feet on Henderson Mountain and met a local guide and his wife. He told us his hunters had gone home, and said, "Fellows, the game just isn't here! The coyotes have done their job and eliminated the deer!" I never saw a mule deer buck; just four does and a white-tail doe, as it was getting dusk one evening. Davie never saw a buck either. One of the fellows from California shot at a little forked-horn buck but didn't get it! Joe killed a spike bull that Davie jumped. So, out of eight hunters, only one got a bull. We were so disappointed once again, having driven miles and miles and hunting very diligently. One day we drove at least twenty-five miles, back to a beautiful area and didn't see one track of big game or deer – only coyote tracks everywhere! I named the area Death Valley, as it was simply devoid of game!

Our hunt there was totally unsatisfactory and I still feel the State of Montana should bring judgment against this outfitter and he, in turn, refund the hunters' money! That's the way the ball bounces and you never know until you go down to the mat with your man! Once again, I don't understand why the Game Commission allows this to happen. Already the coyotes are practically living on the back porches of people in town and pretty soon the pets are going to be disappearing! Then what are the environmentalists going to do? It's like the sea lions and seals wiping out the salmon! Yet the "specialists" think that more dams should be built, water taken away from farmers and residents so the sea lions and seals can be fed! It's a no-win situation if you're a member of the human race!

CROOK AT CRUICKSHANK'S

An incident happened right here in Mill Creek which goes to show you one never knows what a day may bring forth! The day prior to the incident which I am going to relate, a cop was cruising up and down Mill Creek Road, which is a county road, and found this young couple in a rock pit. When the cop found them, a young fellow and his girlfriend were smoking dope, and the officer said, "You're under arrest!" They just jumped up, ran into the brush and disappeared! Of course, that was the end of the story because the cop couldn't find them. It wasn't, however, really the end of the story! In the meantime, they made their way down along Mill Creek, which runs right past our place. Right close to our property, there is a little building, so they decided to take refuge in it. Our neighbor, Kenny Cruickshank, lived next door at the time, and had his place up for sale, so an appraiser was to come out. Kenny was logging up on the hill, not far away, and from his vantage point, could see down to his house very well. During the morning, he saw a strange car drive in his driveway, so came barreling down to his house and asked the stranger, "Are you the appraiser?" "Yes, I am," the fellow answered. "Will it be necessary for you to go in my house?" "Yes, I need to do a walk-through," the appraiser told him. Kenny said, "I'll open the house up for you," and unlocked the door to his house. As he walked through the door, he wondered what was going on! Here were a number of articles in the center of the room, among which was his VCR, television, stereo, and miscellaneous items. Suddenly, someone hit him over the head and knocked him down! Looking up, he saw a young fellow standing there, and as Kenny struggled to get up on his knees, he grabbed hold of this fellow's arm! Then he saw a gun in this kids' hand! Kenny grabbed the gun and turned it towards the guy's stomach, but just then the guy kicked Kenny really hard, and down he went again! This young punk then dragged Kenny into the first bedroom. As this was all happening, Ken's son, Bryce, drove into the yard and that morning had just taken a 243 rifle OUT of his pickup. No sooner had Bryce driven in, than another neighbor, Bill Bogus, drove up, just at the edge of the driveway. No one was aware of what was going on inside the house with Kenny. This punk kid was still in the house and shouted to Kenny, "Get out of that room and go get in the back bedroom!" After barking orders to Kenny, the punk came to the front door, opened it and fired two shots at Bryce, at close range! He never cocked the gun, just pulled it over on the trigger! Fortunately, he missed Bryce, because this crazy guy wasn't more than sixty feet from him! This appraiser took off running and came over to our garden, where we were outside working. As he ran towards our place, this intruder then took aim at this poor appraiser, shooting at him three times! The appraiser was shouting, "He shot at me, he shot at me!" We quickly took him into our house and he got on the phone! His mental state of being was not too good, and we soon well understood why! We quickly learned from this poor fellow that he was a Vietnam veteran and the poor fellow just came unglued! We felt so sorry for everyone involved and believe me, it was not pleasant for any of us! It was very frightening!

Back inside his house, Kenny didn't know what all was taking place, but he had heard the shots and figured this lunatic must have shot the appraiser, as well as Frances and I. He didn't even know Bryce nor Bill had driven in, but decided he had to do something. He made a run for one of the big windows, crashing right through it and falling five feet to the ground. Down towards the creek he went running and crossed it! On the other side was a house, with some new neighbors who had just moved up from

California, so he ran for all he was worth to their house. By now, he was completely out of breath and panting, as he knocked on their door! They let him in and he asked them to try and call our house to see if we were still alive. He told these neighbors, "I'm afraid that Mr. and Mrs. Shenk were shot!" Of course, we answered the phone and Kenny was so relieved to hear that we were okay!

After Kenny left his house, the punk jumped in his pickup and took off, going towards Dallas. He then turned left onto the Red Prairie Road and after traveling a few miles, abandoned Kenny's pickup. As this saga continued, the punk hitchhiked a ride with a passerby and this person took him home with him, where reportedly the fellow was calm and very matter-of-fact! They said he combed his hair, then said he'd go back out to hitchhike a ride into Dallas. Sure enough, again he was picked up and given a ride, clear into Dallas. The cops tracked him down the next evening in the Gailor Hotel in Dallas and told him, "You're under arrest!" Would you believe it, he got away from them! They kept watching and through one of his girlfriends, they caught him at last and put him in jail. It's kind of hard to believe those officers sit around waiting to catch him instead of getting out and cold-trailing him! There were five officers out at Kenny's house for awhile. They conferred and agreed this kid was a dangerous criminal, with a long record! I know, however, there are so many criminals out there it has to be a difficult task! I'm sure the punk is out again, and undoubtedly did very little time and is most likely back to his old antics! It makes a person wonder why Bill Clinton could say that citizens don't need guns. Why, according to Bill, the government is utterly able to protect us and yet, he has a number of secret service men around him all the time! Obviously, he doesn't have to live like the average citizen! No wonder he thinks the crime problems have diminished!

PONDERING ON THE PLIGHT

OF THE PEOPLE

Following is a letter I wrote to the editor of the Statesman Journal, a Salem, Oregon newspaper. "Reference is made to the building of the bridge to usher the United States of America into the New Age. This bridge will be a toll bridge. The fee to enter will be the surrender of life and liberty as we now know it! The first step in building any bridge is laying a foundation. This should consist of a basis of trust and confidence in leadership! It is said that this New World Order, of which the United Nations is just a step-child, has as one goal, the elimination of two billion people from the earth. This is to be done by various methods, such as war, starvation, disease and attrition. The present swearing in ceremony of placing the left hand on the Bible simply isn't getting the job done! I favor a baptism by immersion and formaldehyde being used instead of water, which would be more solemn and lasting. The current ranting about the passage of Measure 47 is ample proof that the people simply do not trust the government! They knew the raise in taxes would never stop and what about money for schools? We are told that we learn through the eyes, as well as through the ears. If a teacher can't get these long-billed caps off the kids' heads, which are down over their eyes as well as their ears, no wonder they can't read or write! How are they ever going to learn to eat with a knife, fork, and spoon? As to the restoring of the salmon run, ask any commercial fisherman and he can set you straight! Since the sport fishermen are severely limited, it follows that the sea lions and seals should also be limited! They could perhaps be monitored by these environmentalists that have lost touch with reality! I am amazed that the Arkansas Traveler has not replaced the Star Spangled Banner as the national anthem! Yours truly, Kenny Shenk"

While living in the Clinton area, I wrote a number of poems and writings and during this time period, Jim Baker fell from grace. This prompted me to write the "Ode to Tammy Faye," as well as other writings regarding events in that area, and the world in general. Following are some of my thoughts:

THE LATEST WORD

A logger sat musing and pondering his fate,
No need to hurry, for he isn't late.
The crummy don't run, since the sale is on hold,
While the Big Shots still argue and the timber grows old.
The yarder is in and some timber is cut.
And now comes the word, that the owls are in rut.

The ENVIRONMENT suddenly is all that is heard,
And mostly it's centered on one lousy bird.
So this is the medium the clever ones use.
But I tell you quite frankly, it may be the fuse,
To ignite the same people to the designs of this clan,
What goes 'round, will go 'round and come back again!

I'm sure mighty glad, I'm no government man.
So the fish can't swim up river, they've cirrhosis of the liver?
No, it's not because the river's getting low,
Let's take all of this criteria, ship the whole bunch to Siberia,
And pray these fools get lucky and will drown.

These sea lions and the seals, plus these Eco Big Shot Wheels,
Are the cause of all this misery in our towns.
Since we've sent these kids to college and they've gotten all this knowledge,
 I fail to see we're gaining any ground! (May 1991)

FAREWELL TO REASON

A wise old owl sat on his snag,
He told his clan, she's in the bag!
We got these loggers by the throat,
So it's now time for us to gloat.

Because of these here college grads,
We got more friends than we ever had.
We don't need trees from which to hoot,
But we can't lose all this to boot.
If common sense should ere come back,
We might well be on another track.

These stupid fools think we need trees,
To propagate and scratch our fleas,
These Old Growth trees are way too high,
We're gettin' old and hate to fly.

To get degrees and go through college,
And be devoid of common knowledge,
Is truly sad, but plain to see,
So I'll just use this smaller tree! (March 20, 1991)

THE DESPONDENT
Here I set my knees are shakin',
Have no meat, I'm short on bacon,
My woman took my dough and ran,
She left me for another man.

Guess I'll go back in the hills,
Build a cabin, devoid of frills.
Then I'll get a husky lady,
Even though her past is shady.

There I'll while away my time,
Never spending one more dime! (1984)

THE TAXPAYERS LAMENT

Tax the public, tax them well.
Tax them to the gates of hell,
Soak the poor, but spare the rich,
It matters not if people bitch.

Tax the gas their cars must burn,
Keep them ignorant so they won't learn.
Tax the clothes right off their back.
Let them wear a gunny sack.

Tax the food that they must eat,
Tax the shoes right off their feet.
Tax their coffins, tax their shrouds,
Tax their souls beyond the clouds.

And if your luck runs out some day,
And they, in turn, lay you away,
When you before St. Peter stand,
With nothing good in either hand,
And he then asks what you've to tell,
You then must say, they made life hell! (May 10, 1981)

THE PENTITENT PARSON/

ODE TO TAMMY FAYE

Put on your makeup, dry your tears,
The Judge just gave me forty-five years.
These bars sure do, a prison make,
And I now see my great mistake!

I lie awake, I cannot sleep,
A thinkin' how I fleeced those sheep.
They sent to me their hard-earned cash,
I blew it all on many a bash!

So now while wheels of justice grind,
I hope, Dear Tammy, you can find,
A lovely place where we can dwell,
I'm not so sure and one can't tell,

I'll cast our Gospel Net again,
And I'm quite sure we'll take them in,
We'll get their cash and salt it away,
So Tammy, you must make my day!

When Tammy Faye received this note,
Her fury up and risen,
You mean to tell me, Jim my man,
Is really now in prison?

I'll get that Judge, she up and cried!
For I can't stand this tension,
And I for one, will make real sure,
That he will lose his Pension!

He's sat upon that bench for years,
He has no heart, he can't shed tears!
How can he do this to my Jim?
I'll find a way to do him in!

Now Tammy Faye, just simmer down,
And listen now to reason,
You never will this Judge remove,
Unless you prove it's Treason!   (February 16, 1990)

TRIBUTE TO FRANCES

The span of life is very swift,
It spares not man nor maiden.
Before you stop to realize,
Your powers are 'a fading.

Slow down, slow down, Old Father Time,
How come life goes so fast?
They always say it's speed that kills,
Why can't we make life last?

These eighty years gone swiftly by,
And now the time has come,
We never know what lies ahead,
Or when our work is done.

The giver of this span, called life,
For each one has a plan.
He only asks of each of us,
To do the best we can.

Today we celebrate the life,
Of one who's done her best,
She bravely battled many odds,
And sure deserves a rest.

You truly have a Mother been,
And that is plain to see,
Our God will save a place for you,
Through all eternity!

(Written for 80th Birthday Celebration for Frances - August 18th, 1996)

LIFE CONTINUES IN THE FAR WEST

As I have written these many stories, I am continually astonished at the changes which I have witnessed throughout my life! A large number of the incidents which I related were from working in the woods and many times I looked the Death Angel in the face! How many times? I really cannot even estimate, for I had many, many close calls! I am so thankful for the many great employees who worked for me throughout the years.

In this last chapter, I will bring you up-to-date on our family and their activities, and in order to not be partial, I shall choose no particular order, so beginning with Myron, he has worked for Oregon State University for over thirty-three years. He signed up in their Overseas Agricultural Program and lived in Mexico for over a year; in Brazil for three years, Equador for two years and Costa Rica for six years. For many years, his responsibilities have taken him all over the world. He speaks Portuguese fluently, as well as Spanish, and has been giving classes to some of the immigrants from Mexico. Many of them are in Oregon, seeking employment from the farmers and ranchers and find it difficult to understand and communicate effectively. Myron has spent quite a bit of time in South America and one time, while living in Brazil, he'd drive an OSU van out to their project. Nearly every day, as he drove along, there was an old man with a great, big hoe just trudging down the road, so Myron would stop and talk to him. He'd then say, "Please get in and ride with me," but the old man always said, "No." Every morning Myron would ask him, and then, finally, one day the old man got in and even though there was no one else in the van, he went clear to the back and sat down. Myron said, "Please come up and sit by me, I want to talk with you," but he wouldn't do it and this went on for several days. At last, one morning, Myron was able to persuade the old man to sit in the front seat with him. As Myron conversed with him, the fellow broke down and cried! He said how unjust it was for him, a poor son of the soil, to ride with a white man in the front seat! That just couldn't be! Myron said he was utterly appalled at how beaten-down this poor man was. Eventually Oregon State abandoned the project in Brazil because the rich natives who were ruling, abused the system. They were shown how to raise more beans and different crops, but the rich people would not allow the poor people to have anymore food than they'd had previously! So the injustice continued and that's why the rich get richer and the poor get poorer! He has had some fabulous experiences over the years!

Riding on a local bus to go downtown to his office in Brazil one day, Myron was visiting with one of his colleagues. They would tell the driver where they wanted off, but the bus driver would never stop at the exact spot. They noted that he would continue for another three blocks! When the bus did stop, three men would also get off with Myron and his friend. It didn't take them long to discover it was these same, three fellows who would crowd, bump, and jostle them as they got off the bus. Sure enough, one morning, the one guy lifted the wallet of Myron's co-worker. It made him so mad, he told Myron he was going to get a gun and kill one of them! Myron told him, "If you know what's good for you, you're not about to do that!" Another time, a fellow had his hand into Myron's pocket to try and grab his wallet. Fortunately, Myron felt the tug, got hold of this guy's wrist and hung on! The man couldn't break his hold and they went round and round! Finally the guy let go and decided he'd better not try that! I know he had other harrowing experiences which he decided not to share with Mom and Dad! Myron is still teaching at Oregon State University, and he and his wife, Carol, live in Albany. They have four children, Dan, Alicia, and twins, Jon and Tim.

Byron was always interested in athletics and became a coach, teaching and coaching at a college in the East for eighteen years. Also, he and his family spent four years in India, where he taught at the Woodstock School. After returning again to the States and teaching quite a number of years, he decided to attend the University of Virginia to get his Doctorate in Sports Medicine. A fellow said to me, "Just what does Byron do?" I said, "Well, he goes to these ball games and if a player goes down, Byron runs out, examines that person and he can determine right then and there whether their life can be saved or whether they have to shoot them!" Well, it isn't quite that grim, but he is the Ladies' Head Soccer Coach for George Fox University in Newberg, Oregon. He enjoys his work very much, is very dedicated, and is a much-loved teacher! He and his wonderful wife, Ina, live in McMinnville. Byron has three sons, Eric, Todd, and Troy.

Lavina, who was married to Russ, lives in McMinnville as well. She keeps very busy in her church, cosmetics business, and other interests. She was such a dedicated and devoted wife to Russ and throughout all the years, we have appreciated her a great deal! Their two children, Alex and Sylvia, live close to McMinnville also.

Wilbert got on steady being a professional student and after he left home, he graduated from Goshen College, Goshen, Indiana, and then attended the University of Oregon. Quite a few years later, when he and his family were living in Elkhart, Indiana, he decided to move to Aberdeen, Scotland, to attend King's University to earn his doctorate. King's University is one of the oldest universities in the world. He lived there with his family for three years. Frances and I went to visit them in Scotland and it was a great experience, but also very traumatic!

We went downtown to purchase train tickets for the EuroTrain, and tried to talk to a young fellow! He was speaking so rapidly, and with his accent, I simply could not understand him, and neither could Wilbert. Wilbert would try to repeat what he thought the fellow said and could scarcely decipher what he meant! His parting shot to us was, "Cheerio," rather than saying, "Have a good day," as that was the common greeting there, and I rather enjoyed that! Frances and I toured through Holland, France, Germany, Austria, and Switzerland. The biggest problem was that we could only speak and understand English, which proved to be a real handicap. Also, with such a variety of currencies, it was taxing to try and figure out the monetary system!

One evening while in the foyer of a hotel of Basil, Switzerland, we noticed two fellows with U.S. Army uniforms on, visiting with two young ladies. As we walked by, we overheard them speaking English. I tapped one of them on the shoulder and said, "You're under arrest! I'm with the Gestapo!" That fellow gave me one of the most wicked looks you could ever imagine! Then he realized I was giving him a bad time and began visiting with us. The fellow I had "accosted" introduced himself, Sergeant Tonmey, of Elkhart Indiana! Would you believe he lived close to where Wilbert lived in Elkhart! He was stationed in Germany, as was his friend and the friend was planning to marry a young lady from McMinnville, Oregon! To make the story even more interesting, this bride-to-be lived on the same street in McMinnville as one of my log truck drivers! We had a delightful little visit there and it just goes to prove that the world isn't that big, after all! For quite a few years, we corresponded with Sergeant Tonmey, but eventually we lost contact with him.

While on this tour, we saw many interesting things. We also learned that when it is announced that the train will leave at 7:00, it doesn't leave five minutes before, or five minutes after, it leaves at 7:00! We were sitting in the train waiting to leave this one town, with a chatty lady seated nearby, just talking a blue streak. Suddenly we felt a little movement, and within a short time, the train was going sixty to seventy miles an hour! This lady began screaming out in broken English, "Conduc-toor! Conduc-toor!" The Conductor was not to be found! They took her all the way to Germany before they let her off! She was a resident in the little town where we had boarded and hadn't planned to stay on that train! Poor lady, got a ride she didn't want, but she should have known better! We got quite a chuckle out of it, even though she didn't!

While visiting in Aberdeen, I'd walk downtown. This little village is right on the sea coast and the raw winds which come off the ocean there are very invigorating, to say the least! Everyone looks as if he is a Seagrams Seven Crown imbiber! Even little ones being pushed in baby carriages by their Mothers had fiery red faces, due to the brisk wind. They have a very famous place called "Queens Crossing" where six streets come together and a fellow they call the "Lollipop Man" escorts people across this intersection. He just stops traffic and walks across with pedestrians, so as I waited to cross, he said something to me, which I could hardly understand. Not wanting to appear rude, in reply, I said, "I am one of those Royal Americans from America!" "Oh," he said, "and do you have Lollipop Men in America?" I didn't know then what he was referring to and I said, "Oh, sure, oh, very well!" When I found out later what the Lollipop Man was, I realized I had mislead the poor fellow! That trip was a very fine one for an old woodsman, although I wouldn't care to go over there again.

For our visit in London, Wilbert arranged for a former American to be our guide. He was an elderly fellow, but still full of both vinegar and vigor! He went to school one day a week to learn about the city of London because no one person knows everything about that city. As is the case in many places, it is expanding, with a lot of building taking place. He was a very capable guide and took us into a great cathedral, Buckingham Palace, the Tower of London, and many other places of interest. We went into where the crown jewels are kept and immediately saw three bobbies with their big "billy clubs". I was standing by the jewels and walked up to the one bobby, even though he looked as if he might hit me. I said, "Sir, tell me, what's going to happen if Liz Taylor decides she wants some of these jewels?" She was married to Richard Burton at this time. He leaned over and replied, "She bloody well better not come here!" I was very amused by his answer. Down by the sea, we saw hooks on the posts in the water where, many years earlier, slaves were brought in from the ships. Our guide said they used to cut a chunk of flesh from their shoulder blade and just hang them there! We went through a museum which showed all the early instruments of war. Truly mankind has lost his way to think that the greatest brains in the world have lent their geniuses to the art of destruction, rather than building for peace. Just think of all the hospitals, good schools, and so many great causes which could be promoted with all the money spent on destructive purposes. Man is eventually going to destroy himself if the Almighty doesn't intervene!

In March of 1992, we visited Wilbert's when he was working at Birmingham University in England. We flew to London with our daughter, Donna, and her husband, Al. We rented one of those left-handed cars (the only kind over there), and Al did a masterful job of driving! During our sight-seeing tours, we drove over seven hundred miles, visiting some old castles, historical York, and many other places and things of interest. While touring this one castle, there were ladies about every fifteen feet, serving as tour guides and they took great delight in their history! They also took their jobs rather seriously! In one place, we saw a rack which was used to pull the prisoners apart. There was sort of a chain harness into which a victim was put and then they winched him up off the floor. A trough was built right in the concrete into which the blood drained and a dungeon was right close by where prisoners would be sent. In this contraption, a person could not lay down nor sit up! By listening to the cries of his comrades, it would soften him up and make his passage easier. There was also a device with which they could squeeze the thumbnails of victims off. I said to this one lady, "Are you telling me that some enlightened Englishman developed these methods of torture?" She bristled and said, "Oh, no, Suh! They came from Germany!" Her defense tickled me! We did learn that most of those torturous methods did come from the Spanish Inquisition. There was a big, high tower, completely surrounded by a moat, so their battles could be fought. That old castle was still in a very fine state of preservation and I believe it had been built in the 17th century! That was quite a tour and we went to many wonderful places of interest! One big church we visited bore the ravages of a German bomber which had gone through, with some of the remnants still inside! They rebuilt it, but it is a very impressive thing to see. It's great cause for contemplation regarding the foolishness of man and how bent he is on destroying himself!

Presently, Wilbert and Juanita live in Pasadena, California, and he is teaching at Fuller Theological Seminary, for a three-year assignment. Their three children are, Suzanne, Maria, and Thomas.

Davie lives on Mill Creek Road, not far from us, and continues to battle health problems, although he deserves a medal for his courage, unwavering faith, and good humor! I have mentioned in earlier chapters about his work with me in the woods for so many years. I can say, without reservation, I appreciated working with him, and never had a better employee than Davie! He loves people and visits many friends, family, and acquaintances. He and Mariellen have two daughters, Simone and Sonia.

Donna, our daughter, has lived most of her adult life in Washington. In high school and college, she really took a liking to business classes, so for most of her life has worked in various offices, including a high school, and a law office. She always enjoyed secretarial work and is a detail person! Donna attended Hesston College for two years, and Oregon College of Education for a short time.

She always said that she would liked to have finished college and taught high school, but got involved in marriage and family. Her activities include church, community and boating. This January marked the beginning of her second, six-year term as Alderwood Water District Commissioner. This responsibility takes a lot of time, but she takes it seriously! Her home is North of Seattle, in Lynnwood, with husband, Al. Donna's three sons are, Derin, Kent, and Dirk.

Looking back, I know Bud Hampton had a great bearing on my life! As I became better acquainted with him, I knew Bud didn't have a good knowledge of the falling and bucking game as I did, but together, we complemented one

Lester Meridith
Hampton ("Bud")

Bud was born in the Randall, Washington, area. His first job was working in the woods with a team of horses, as they didn't have bulldozers at that time. This, of course, led him into the timber industry. Bud possessed uncommon ability, vision, courage, and a certain element so that when you conversed with him, you could readily discern that he was a man of utter integrity and character. When Bud shook hands on a deal, it was unnecessary to have an array of witnesses, for this was his bond and he was a man of his word! Indeed, I was privileged to have Bud for a friend!

another. He had wonderful principles and kept them in focus and <u>never</u> <u>let</u> <u>me</u> <u>down</u>! Bud believed in fair play and demonstrated that over and over. I know that my time as Bullbuck and filer with Willamina Lumber Company was one which was rewarding, in spite of hard work and long hours! I feel enriched and blessed from my association with Bud.

Years later, when the logging companies were not actively working up Mill Creek and the gate was torn down, this made the area accessible to nearly anyone. Since it was now "open territory", many people from Salem began coming to our lovely community. These visitors included all sorts of characters, with drug rings, illegal activities, and lots of nonsense! It is so very sad what happens in society nowadays, but of course, the authorities can't be every place at one time and the judges turn them loose when these hoodlums are caught anyway, so it's a no-win situation! To illustrate, Willamette Industries had a nice park constructed at Cedar Creek, with tables, restrooms, and other amenities. It was a beautiful spot, right along the creek and was just ideal. One day Bob Berends noticed that some people were living at the park, weren't leaving at night and just making this park their home. So he went up one day, just in time to observe a long-haired hippie sitting on top of a table with an axe, chopping up this table for wood! Bob took this fellow into town to the authorities. Willamette had a meeting subsequent to this incident and the head honcho said maybe they'd better not maintain a park up there! They were afraid that hippie might seek retribution, go back up there, and with one match, could burn the timber companies out! So, they were forced to remove all the park facilities, and other companies have had to do the same thing. Weyerhauser Company said they'll never build another park for the public because of abuse.

It seems that such emphasis is placed on the necessity of securing a good education, along with a goodly number of degrees. Preference is generally given to the one with the degree, while ability is secondary. Now, I'm all for education - most of our kids attended college, but it seems that good judgment is tantamount to book learning! I am reminded of a little slogan which is used among the clergy, "If the Greek you cannot read, you're not likely to succeed!" Well, I also recall the fable of Rip Van Winkle, as he was rousing from his long sleep, it was said, "By degrees of Awe and Apprehension, he began to slowly come back to life!" So he had at least two degrees! We have only to look at Congress and the things which are now taking place in Washington. The President is having his share of problems and many nominees he recommended have been rejected. Additionally, several of his cronies have made the "slammer" - surely, none of these have been short on degrees! Again, I've always believed the saying that God doesn't always have payday on Saturday night, but He always has payday! I have seen this come true many times.

Frances and I presently live on Mill Creek, below where we lived for at least thirty-five years and I still hunt and fish. In 1995, I enjoyed an elk hunt and killed a nice one! In October, 1997, I killed a nice buck in Eastern Oregon. I sincerely trust that all who read these pages will enjoy them and get a small glimpse of the life which I enjoyed and my gratefulness to God for his protection and everlasting care!